ART ON THE JESUIT MISSIONS
IN ASIA AND LATIN AMERICA,
1542–1773

When the Jesuit missionaries ventured from Europe to newly discovered territories in Asia and Latin America, they brought with them the rich traditions of Renaissance and Baroque art and architecture. What happened to the artistic and social practices already thriving in the communities that the missionaries encountered is the story told by art historian and Jesuit specialist Gauvin Alexander Bailey.

The Jesuits, determined to convert both spiritually and culturally, put great effort into imparting their own artistic techniques and knowledge. At the same time they were unusually tolerant of the non-European cultures, making artistic accommodations in order to communicate with each particular society. The resulting hybridization was complex: German, Italian, and Flemish as well as the dominant Spanish and Portuguese idioms mingled with multiple Asian and Amerindian traditions.

Bailey argues that this cross-pollination of early modern art became the first truly global visual currency for cultural exchange. Through a sweeping look at Japan, China, Mughul India, and Paraguay, the author focuses on four of the most flourishing artistic encounters and discovers much unrecognized or misunderstood art. He overturns the simple thesis that art was imposed on subject cultures in favour of the more difficult paradigm of exchange. This meticulously researched book has over 100 beautiful illustrations and a thorough index.

GAUVIN ALEXANDER BAILEY is Assistant Professor in Renaissance and Baroque Art at Clark University, Worcester, Massachusetts. He co-edited *The Jesuits: Cultures, Sciences, and the Arts, 1540-1773* (UTP, 1999) and recently curated the exhibition *The Jesuits and the Grand Mogul: Renaissance Art at the Imperial Court of India, 1580-1630* at the Freer and Sackler Galleries of the Smithsonian Institution in Washington, DC.

2000 Roland H. Bainton Prize Winner for Art and Music History – Winner

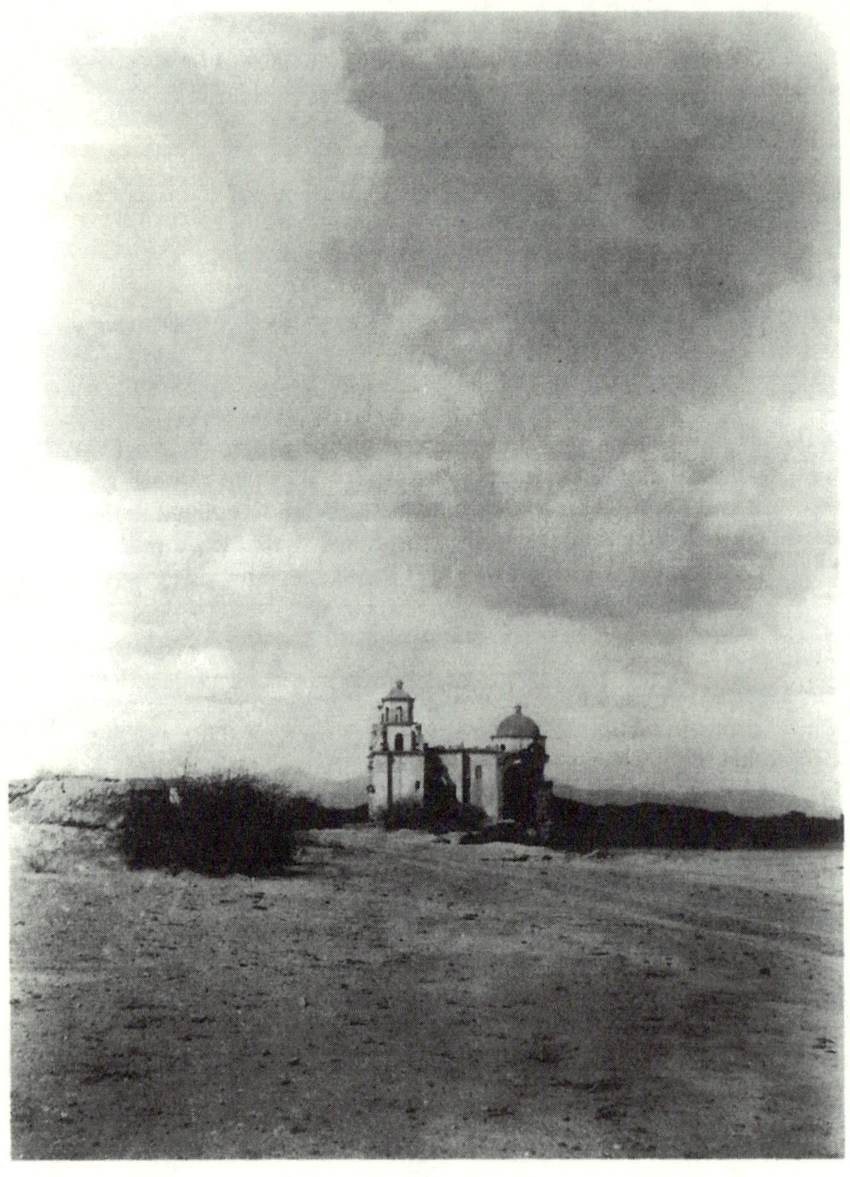

Mission church of La Purisma Concepción, Caborca (Sonora, Mexico). The 18th-century Franciscan church, which replaces an earlier Jesuit foundation in adobe, epitomizes the frontier aspect of the outer-circle missions of the Roman Catholic Church in the early modern period. From a photograph of the early 20th century. Courtesy Visual Collections, Fine Arts Library, Harvard University.

Art on the Jesuit Missions in Asia and Latin America, 1542–1773

GAUVIN ALEXANDER BAILEY

UNIVERSITY OF TORONTO PRESS
Toronto Buffalo London

Toronto Buffalo London
Printed in the U.S.A.

Reprinted in paperback 2001
Reprinted 2012, 2013

ISBN 0-8020-4688-6 (cloth)
ISBN 0-8020-8507-5 (paper)

Printed on acid-free paper

National Library of Canada Cataloguing in Publication Data

Bailey, Gauvin A.
Art on the Jesuit missions in Asia and Latin America, 1542–1773

Includes bibliographical references and index.
ISBN 0-8020-4688-6 (bound)
ISBN 0-8020-8507-5 (pbk.)

1. Jesuit art – Asia – History. 2. Jesuit art – Paraguay – History. 3. Jesuits – Missions – Asia – History. 4. Jesuits – Missions – Paraguay – History. I. Title.

N7972.B35 1999 704.9′482′0950903 C99-930991-9

Publication of this book has been aided by a grant from the Millard Meiss Publication Fund of the College Art Association

MM

University of Toronto Press acknowledges the financial assistance to its publishing program of the Canada Council for the Arts and the Ontario Arts Council.

University of Toronto Press acknowledges the financial support for its publishing activities of the Government of Canada through the Book Publishing Industry Development Program (BPIDP).

Canada

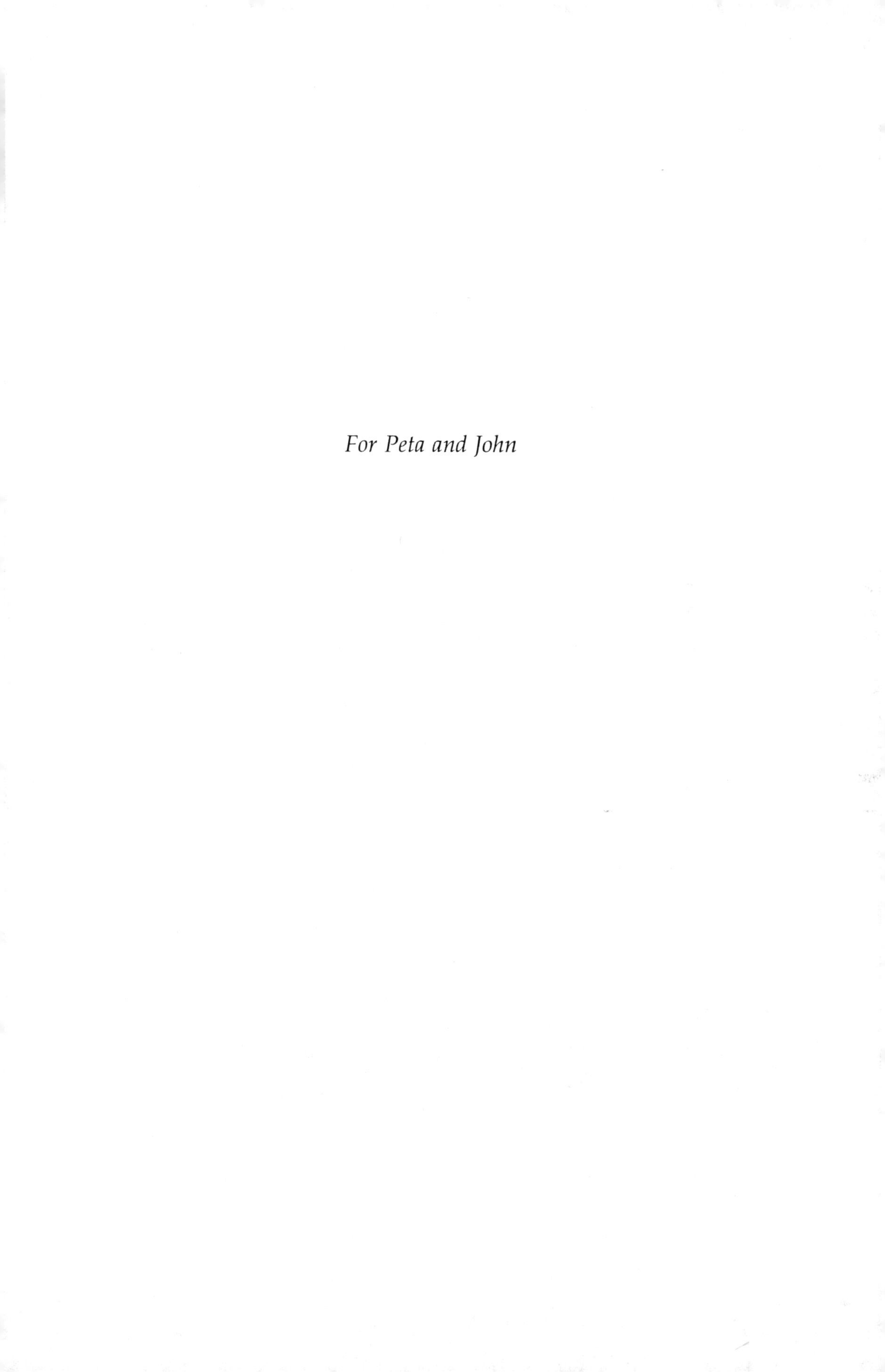

For Peta and John

Contents

Acknowledgments

This book is about a global partnership, and, appropriately, it would not have been possible without the assistance of many kind and generous individuals and institutions around the globe. I am above all deeply grateful to two people who have not only been dear friends and companions but who were quite literally inspirations. The first is my wife, Peta, whose idea it was in the first place to combine my two passions, Asia and Latin America, under one cover. Without her active encouragement, I would never have attempted this daunting task, and she provided insight and ideas throughout the writing of this book. The second is John O'Malley, S.J., who motivated me to explore a third interest since childhood, the Society of Jesus. John has opened doors, provided friendship, inspiration, assistance, and support, and has been generous both with his time and his thoughts. John also invited me to serve on the steering committee of the symposium 'The Jesuits: Culture, Learning, and the Arts, 1540–1773' at Boston College in 1997, a project which put me in touch with Jesuit scholars around the world. I dedicate this book to both of these partners.

I would never have been able to begin this book without the generous assistance of Michael J. Buckley, S.J., and the Jesuit Institute at Boston College. As Jesuit Institute Fellow during 1996–7, I was able to undertake extensive research travel in South America and spend a year on campus writing what became the essence of the present book. I benefited greatly from conversation with this Jesuit polymath, whose encyclopaedic knowledge of the field and sharp wit were a welcome resource on campus. Special thanks must also go to another dear friend, T. Frank Kennedy, S.J., the scholar of the music of the Jesuit missions in Bolivia and Paraguay, who encouraged me at a very early stage to extend my field of study into South America. I have had many memorable lunches at St Mary's with this co-conspirator in the Jesuit Conference. I would also like to acknowledge the assistance and friendship of the last of the four steering committee members, Steven J. Harris, whose command of the literature on Jesuit science is unparalleled.

I also have special gratitude and affection for Pamela Jones, who was generous with her friendship and scholarship and who provided stimulating criticism for this book at an early stage. Pam has always been available to react to ideas and is always willing to provide her own insight. Two other scholars have been especially encouraging and helpful in my preparation of the Latin American half of this book. One is Sabine MacCormack, one of the great minds of our time, who approached the early colonial art of South America from a subtly interdisciplinary perspective long before it was fashionable to do so. Her scholarship was an inspiration before I even began my research, and her personal encouragement has been much appreciated. The other is James (Barry) Kiracofe, who organized a conference on early colonial Latin America in 1995, which remains one of the finest I have ever attended. Barry encouraged my expansion of scope into the Americas and has remained a good friend and scholarly companion.

Since two-thirds of chapter 5 of this book began life as my PhD dissertation at Harvard University, I wish once more to express my gratitude to my three readers at Harvard: Miroslava Beneš, Norman Bryson, and Gülru Necipoğlu, as well as Wheeler J. Thackston and Stuart Cary Welch, friends and mentors. Mirka has been particularly supportive throughout this book's writing and earlier. I also acknowledge the assistance of my three readers at University of Toronto Press, who provided insightful comments and helped me restructure the manuscript into a better book. My editors at University of Toronto Press, especially Suzanne Rancourt, Kristen Pederson, and Ken Lewis, turned this book into something readable. I am also grateful to the students in my biannual seminar at Weston Jesuit School of Theology for their challenging criticism and insights, as well as my students at Clark University, particularly Andrea Lepage. I must also say a word of thanks to my indefatigable travel agent, Lee Shih of ATI Travel, for getting me there.

Additional funds for research travel in Asia, Peru, and Europe were provided by the Andrew W. Mellon Foundation, Sophia University in Tokyo, the Aga Khan Program for Islamic Architecture at Harvard University, the Social Sciences and Humanities Research Council of Canada, and the Higgins School of Humanities at Clark University. I am grateful to all of these institutions for their assistance. The publication of this book was greatly facilitated by the generous support of the Renaissance Society of America and the Millard Meiss Publication Fund of the College Art Association, to whom I am greatly indebted.

The research and preparation of this work owes much to the generous help and hospitality of many in Asia, Latin America, Europe, and the United States. I wish I could express exactly what I owe to each; however, limitations of space compel me simply to list them alphabetically by region.

In Japan I benefited from the assistance and hospitality of Richard Curé, S.J.; William Currie, S.J.; Robert M. Dieters, S.J.; Fernando Garcia Gutiérrez, S.J.; Yoichiro Ide, Professor at Tokyo Junshin Women's College; Yoshiaki Ishizawa, Dean of the Faculty of Foreign Studies, Sophia University; Hiromitsu Kobayashi, Professor in the Faculty of Comparative Culture, Sophia University; Shinzo Kawamura, S.J.; Hisashi Kishino, Professor at Toho Gakuen Jr College, Tokyo; Toshiaki Koso, S.J., Director of the Kirishitan Bunko Library at Sophia University; Kimitada Miwa, Professor at Sophia University; Yasujiro Ohtaka, Professor at Sophia University; Mitsuru Sakamoto, Professor at Seitoku University; Manuel Silgo, S.J.; Antoni J. Üçerler, S.J.; Keichi Uchida, Curator of the Machida City Museum of Graphic Arts; Cyril Veliath, S.J.; Midori Wakakuwa, Professor at Chiba State University; and Diego Yuuki, S.J., Director of the Twenty-Six Martyrs Museum in Nagasaki.

In Hong Kong and Macao, my stay was enriched by the help and kindness of Marciano Baptista, S.J., of Wah Yan College; Beatriz Basto da Silva; Monsignor Francesco Belfiori, S.J., of Xavier House in Kowloon; César Guillen-Nuñez of the Luis de Camões Museum in Macao; Marcel Masson, S.J., of China News Analysis; Harold Naylor, S.J.; Alvaro Ribeiro, S.J.; Luis Sequeira, S.J., Superior of the Residencia on Largo de Santo Agostinho, Macao; Nicolas Standaert, S.J.; Father Manuel Teixeira; Benjamim Videira-Pires, S.J.; and the staff at the Tak Pou Luen Kei Café in Macao.

In India I was helped and hosted by Valente G. Azavedo, S.F.X., the Rector of the Monastery of Pilar; Charles Borges, S.J., of the Xavier Historical Research Centre in Alto de Porvorim; Lourdes Bravo da Costa Rodrigues of the Rare Books Department of the Central Library in Panjim, as well as her husband, Lionel, and her mother, Mrs Madalena Fernandes e Costa; Helder Carita; John Correa-Afonso, S.J., Father Velinkar, S.J., and especially Harsha Asarpota of the Herat Institute in Bombay; His Grace Cecil D'Sa, Archbishop of Agra; Sadashiv V. Gorakshkar, Director of the Prince of Wales Museum, Bombay; David Kowal; Mrs Kishori Kunkanrenkar, Curator of the State Museum, Panjim; Father Mathew, Rector of St Lawrence Seminary in Agra; Lucio de Miranda; K.K. Muhammed, of the Archaeological Survey of India; R.C. Puri and Mr Parvaz of the National Archives in New Delhi; P.P. Shirodkar, Director-General, and M.L. Dicholkar, Archivist, of the Goa Archives in Panjim; Nalini Thakur, General Secretary of the Conservation Society, New Delhi; and S.D. Trivedi, Director, and Ashfaq Ahmad Khan, Numismatist, of the State Museum in Lucknow.

In Pakistan and Turkey, I had the invaluable assistance of Khalid Anis Ahmad of the National College of Arts, Lahore; Mrs Nusrat Ali, Keeper of Paintings at the Lahore Museum; Akbar Ali of Dharmi Ram Road in Lahore; Filiz Çağman of the Topkapi Sarayi Museum Library in Istanbul; Dr Saifur Rahman Dar, Director General of Archaeology of Pakistan; Muhammad Hajji of the Pakistan Tourist Agency; and Sayyid Ishrat Ali Shah of the State Archives of the Punjab.

In the Philippines and Malaysia, I was indebted to Pedro Galende, O.S.A., Director of the San Agustin Museum in Manila; René Javellana, S.J., of Ateneo de Manila University in Quezon City; Regalado Trota José, Project Director of the Documentation/Inventory of Philippine Church Antiquities; and the helpful staff at the Philippine National Archives in Manila and the Stadthuys Museum in Malacca.

In Argentina, Paraguay, Brazil, and Peru, I benefited from the kindness and assistance of Estella Aurea; María Bestani; Maria Inês Coutinho, formerly of the museum at São Miguel, Rio Grande do Sul; Felix Cruz of Viajes Universo, Cuzco; Susana A. Fabrici; Mauro Herlitzka of the Fundación Espigas, Buenos Aires; Leo Leise, S.J., of the Museum at San Ignacio Misiones; Norberto Levinton; Ernesto Maeder; Mario Mongi; Michael Petty, S.J.; Leo W. Hillar Puxeddu, former director of the Museo Histórico Provincial de Santa Fé and his wife, Lylita, and daughter-in-law Carmen; Marcelo Eduardo Rapela, Director of the Complejo Museografico Enrique Udaondo in Luján; Brendan Rumley, S.J.; Hugo Salaberry, S.J.; Hector Schenone of the Academia Nacional de Bellas Artes, Buenos Aires; Bozidar Darko Sustersic; Alicia Telsky de Ronchi, Director of the Museo Histórico Provincial de

Santa Fé; Salvador Veron Cardenas, S.J.; and the staff at the Archivo General de la Nación in Buenos Aires; the Museo de San Cosmé y Damian and Santa María in Misiones, Paraguay; and the Biblioteca Nacional in Lima.

In Europe, Mexico, and the United States, I am indebted in various ways to Richard Ahlborn of the National Museum of American History in Washington; James W. Allan and Andrew Topsfield of the Ashmolean Museum in Oxford; John Atteberry of the John J. Burns Library at Boston College; Clara Bargellini; Milo C. Beach, Director, and Thomas W. Lentz, Deputy Director, of the Freer Gallery of Art and Arthur M. Sackler Gallery in Washington; G. Ted Bohr, S.J.; David Block; Sheila Canby of the British Museum; John Carswell, formerly of Sotheby's New Bond Street; Jonathan Chaves; Hui-hung Chen; John Clarke of the Victoria and Albert Museum; Francis X. Clooney, S.J.; Maria da Conceição S. Borges de Souza, Técnico Superior of the Museu Nacional de Arte Antiga, Lisbon; Sylvia and Bruce Corrie; Samuel Edgerton; Claire J. Farago; Janice Farnham, R.J.M.; Jordão Felgueiras; Marc Fumaroli; Fathers Gramatowski, De Cock, and Zanardi at the Archivum Romanum Societatis Iesu; David Hogge, Librarian at the Freer Gallery of Art and Arthur M. Sackler Gallery; Mrs Patricia Kattenhorn of the India Office Library, London; Cecilia F. Klein; Jay Levenson; Douglas Lewis, Curator of Sculpture and Decorative Arts, National Gallery of Art; Stuart Lingo; José Lico; Peter Lynch; Michael W. Maher, S.J.; Aliocha Maldavsky; Martín Morales; David Morgan; Franco Mormando; Magnus Mörner; Amina Okada, of the Musée Guimet in Paris; Ursula Fischer Pace; Catherine Pagani; Mario Polia; Julian Raby, of the Oriental Institute at Oxford; Elisa Rhodes; Louise Rice; Clare Robertson; Andrew Ross; Michael Ryan, Director of the Chester Beatty Library in Dublin; William R. Sargent, Curator of Asian Export Art at the Peabody Essex Museum in Salem; Jeffrey Chipps Smith; Robert Skelton; Gretchen Starr-Lebeau; José Torres García, S.J., of the Toledo Archives of the Society of Jesus in Alcala de Henares; James T. Ulak, Curator of Japanese Art at the Freer Gallery of Art; Edmund De Unger; Nuno Vassallo e Silva, Director of the Museu de São Roque in Lisbon; Catherine Wilkinson Zerner; Mary-Ann Winkelmes; and Barbara Wisch.

Finally, I am grateful to various members of my family for different kinds of assistance during the course of my research. To my parents for their hospitality and help during the early stages of my research in England and India, my father-in-law, Guy Gillyatt, whose love of the music of his youth in Argentina helped kindle my interest there, and especially to my mother-in-law, Sherry Ballantyne, for sharing my enthusiasms for missions and Amerindians, and for agreeing to go on a mission tour with us in the American Southwest. Sherry also gave me the camera equipment without which this project would have been impoverished, not to mention my dogs. Finally, a word of gratitude to those two Jack Russell Terriers, Harriett and Bingo, for being there.

ART ON THE JESUIT MISSIONS IN ASIA AND LATIN AMERICA, 1542–1773

1
Introduction

Posterity is rarely kind to expatriated artists whose work is nurtured by two different cultures, each totally foreign to the other. Rejected as much by their own culture as by the one they have adopted, their art falls between two artistic traditions and intermingles them. Its unclassifiable character, its hybrid nature, its strangeness, in short, its exoticism disturb the viewer of such art.

Michèle Pirazzoli-t'Serstevens, 'The Emperor Qianlong's European Palaces,' 61

History is full of art that refuses to be categorized as belonging to one culture or another. A hybrid blend of two or more traditions, it is hard to reconcile with other works from either culture and winds up being neglected or even avoided by scholars, collectors, and the art-loving public alike. These objects are admittedly strange, startling – even unsettling – like the results of an experiment gone wrong. As one Edwardian-era observer commented about such hybridity: 'There is something unhealthy in it all, – it is like a hothouse plant that has been forced too much and is killed by the first current of fresh air. It reminds me of extremely sweet iced lemonade ... one finds it delicious, but one does not care for another glass of it – the first was too sweet.'[1] But even though they may take us by surprise at first, these artistic cross-breeds merit a second look. Many of them turn out to be works of astonishing creative power and innovation – more so, even, than many works of 'purer' stock – and some even deserve to take their place among the masterpieces of world art. One of the most fertile roots onto which such 'hothouse plants' were grafted was the art and architecture of Europe during the late Renaissance and Baroque periods, or the 'Age of Exploration' (sixteenth to eighteenth centuries).

The art styles of early modern Catholic Europe rank among the most immediate and approachable ever devised in the Western canon. Few ask for such complete emotional and sensual surrender, and yet few can be so inclusive and flexible. Eminently adaptable and appealing to a wide popular audience, the *arte sacra* of the Late Renaissance and Baroque was deftly capable of becoming the first truly global style in the arts. This manner of painting and sculpture possessed 'timeless,'[2] easily legible qualities of simplicity, realism, emotional empathy, and drama that allowed it to connect with the widest range of local vernacular traditions – both inside and outside Europe – yet maintain its overall integrity as the visual manifestation of the Church of Rome. The architecture of the period was also very easy to understand and accommodate, since it was neatly reducible into orders, structural components, and decorative details, and reproducible using printed Renaissance building manuals. In addition, thanks to the graphic medium in general, early modern Catholic art and architecture were also both disseminated and replicated with ease around the world in a way that had not been possible earlier, and thrived on that very multiplicity. Nevertheless, peoples' perception of the Late Renaissance and Baroque is generally limited geographically to Europe and perhaps metropolitan Latin America, so that the impression it created was that it was a purely Western phenomenon. This idea is far from the truth and ignores the rich artistic legacy of the outer reaches of the Catholic missionary enterprise in Asia and frontier Latin America, where these styles merged with indigenous traditions of the greatest conceivable variety, creating hybrids that nevertheless maintained ties with European culture.

From the jungles of Paraguay to the jungles of the Philippines; from the rivers of Venezuela to the rivers of India; from the islands of the Amazon to the island of Macao, late Renaissance and Baroque art was claimed, altered, and enriched by the people of the four corners of the earth. Today, the southern Indian state of Goa alone boasts scores of lavish churches inspired by Vignola and Serlio – many of which equal their Italian counterparts in size and splendour – parish churches in the Brazilian outback house intensely moving sculptures by forgotten contemporaries of Bernini, and in Japan hidden Christian families have preserved indigenous paintings from the sixteenth century which rank among the most delicate and moving products of the Renaissance canon to be found anywhere. The international spread of Catholic devotional art – we might call it the most successful advertising campaign in pre-modern history – was brought to its furthest extent by a group possessing exceptional energy, commitment, and learning: a missionary order called the Society of Jesus, better known to all simply as the Jesuits. These Jesuits, and the art they helped engender, are the subjects of this book. But they are not the only ones.

The traditional view of the Jesuits as the sole agents of their mission culture is flawed, at best only telling us half of the story. Since our main sources of information were written by missionaries and their supporters, historians have until recently been biased toward their European protagonists, usually depicting the indigenous communities as a kind of passive and silent backdrop to Jesuit efforts. The art inspired by the missions, however, tells a very different tale, and is a vital key for retrieving the often lost voices of indigenous peoples. Far from being a product of a single proactive Self, Jesuit mission art was a global partnership with the Other. The story is not about the triumph of Western culture but of cultural encounter. In many cases, the non-European participants even had the upper hand in shaping mission art. The encounter involved intimate contact among the widest spectrum of peoples, representing different races and religions as well as political, social, economic, and cultural traditions. The European Jesuits came from nations as varied as Italy, France, Germany, Spain, Portugal, Flanders, and

Eastern Europe; and non-Europeans – non-Jesuits and Jesuits alike – included Southeast Asians, Chinese, Japanese, Indians, and Amerindians. Moreover, even within these boundaries the two 'sides' of the encounter were much more diverse than the homogeneous nations described in history books. Within the Jesuit ranks were both humanists and reactionaries, geniuses and men of mediocre abilities, bigots and human rights advocates. The mission host cultures were further divided among merchants and nobles, shamans and warriors, literati and peasants, women and men. Socially, the dynamics of cultural convergence varied widely according to nationality, religion, and class, and their effects ranged from overt conflict and resistance to accommodation, acculturation, and syncretism – often all at once.

The remarkable new amalgam of artistic styles resulting from the Jesuit missions owed as much to the goals, preferences, and reactions of the non-European peoples whom they encountered, and was shaped by their needs, tastes, and world-views. 'Mission art' – for want of a better term – embraced indigenous art traditions ranging from the representational to the schematic, and included works that were strongly figural, landscape-oriented, or abstract. Produced by Europeans, non-Europeans, and people of mixed ancestry, the art inspired by these encounters manifested as wide a range of reactions as the encounters themselves, from warmly positive to fiercely negative. It was taken up by converts on the missions and non-Christians living in the mainstream indigenous communities alike. It was used in both religious and secular contexts, and ranged from images of devotion to those of comedy, eroticism, or derision. Sometimes its effect on the non-convert populations at large was minimal. In other cases, it caused a stylistic revolution that extended well beyond the confines of the mission. Most art and architecture on the Jesuit missions was produced with the more or less willing participation of indigenous communities, and almost all of it can be described as a hybrid. Sometimes the admixture contained more European ingredients than indigenous ones, as was generally the case in Japan and Paraguay. Elsewhere, as in eighteenth-century China or Mughal India, the indigenous element prevailed, relegating European styles or ideals to the details. In every case, however, the merging of two alien traditions inspired new solutions and ideas, often of great originality. It demonstrates the creative potential of cultural convergence, with its blending, confluence, overlap, and ambivalence – art that is considerably more than the sum of its parts.

On 6 May 1542 a warship carrying a weary Francis Xavier landed at the port of Goa, an impudent Portuguese boomtown that would soon be hailed as 'the Rome of the East.' After more than a year at sea, the indomitable first missionary of the Society of Jesus had visited a random sampling of coastal islands from Mozambique to Hormuz, administering to the spiritual and temporal needs of colonists and indigenous people alike, whether European, African, or Asian. Thus began, in the haphazard and itinerant manner typical of their earliest enterprises, the world's first Jesuit mission. Although the Society was barely two years old and Francis worked from no real predetermined strategy, three aspects of this embryonic expedition already foreshadowed Jesuit work in the centuries to come. First, it was international. Although travelling under the auspices of the Portuguese Imperial government, Francis himself was a Spaniard acting as the Papal Nuncio to the Indies, and one of his two companions whom he left behind in Mozambique, Micer Paolo, was an Italian. Second, Francis was willing to listen to what non-Europeans had to say. During a brief stopover in Malindi in present-day Kenya, for example, he engaged a Swahili noble in a conversation comparing Christian and Muslim worship, after which both parties chose politely to disagree with each other. Third – and most importantly for our purposes – Francis used art as a mission tool. Along with instruments of the eucharist, vestments, rosaries, bibles, and prayer books, Francis also brought with him engravings, paintings, and statuettes of the Virgin Mary and Jesus for assistance in preaching and catechizing, items which served him well upon his entry to Japan in 1549.

All of these aspects became trademarks of the Society over the next decades as it expanded from these humble beginnings to occupy the vanguard of global mission enterprise. By the end of the century, nearly nine thousand Jesuits served in twenty-six provinces around the world, including places as disparate as Peru, New Spain (Mexico), Brazil, Congo, Ethiopia, India, Sri Lanka, Malacca, Philippines, Japan, and China. Although several of these regions had recently been conquered by the Spanish and Portuguese empires, others such as China, Japan, and Mughal India were strong, independent nations with nothing to fear from European powers. The Jesuits had the extraordinary ability to enter these foreign realms and make themselves not only welcome but even useful to societies that remained firmly Buddhist, Confucianist, or Muslim. At times it almost seemed as if cultural exchange was as important to them as religious indoctrination.

Founded by Ignatius of Loyola in Rome in 1540, the Society of Jesus was a centrally organized company of priests and brothers whose reliable lines of communication and lean hierarchy allowed them to operate with comparative ease with a handful of members spread over long distances. Unlike other orders, they did not spend their days chanting the hours in 'choir and other ceremonies,'[3] but stressed preaching and other active ministries. Conceived primarily to function in diaspora, the Society was answerable directly to its General, who was elected for life, and ultimately to the Pope. The Jesuits were uniquely committed to mission work. They were among the first to use the word 'mission' (*missio*) in the sixteenth century, and in addition to the three vows of chastity, poverty, and obedience common to other orders, they introduced a fourth vow to do ministry anywhere in the world, 'whether they are pleased to send us among the Turks or any other infidels, even those who live in the region called the Indies.'[4]

Although the Society is often mistakenly equated with a military organization (the often cited title 'General,' for example, is only an adjectival short form for *praepositus generalis*, or 'general leader'), it had less to do with molding blindly loyal soldiers of God than it did with training personnel capable of maximum mobility and sufficiently sound judgment to make important decisions on the spot. The Jesuits also had a lot less to do with conquest than accommodation. To a greater degree than any other Catholic order, the Jesuits pursued a flexibility that would allow them to approach every branch of humanity, be it Catholic, Protestant, or non-Christian. This approach derived explicitly from the Jesuit manual, the *Spiritual Exercises* (1548). Written by Ignatius of Loyola, the *Exercises* are a flexible set of directives designed for a spiritual director to lead a spiritual retreat, the final goal for the participant being to find love for God above all things. But it was understood that a person must freely choose to follow Christ and not do so through coercion. This attitude gave many Jesuits an exceptional tolerance toward non-European societies that would characterize their missions as more of a dialogue than a harangue: 'The relationship of missionary to neophyte was, therefore, not simply an action but an *interaction* – not a "conversion," ... but a "conversation."'[5]

Often located in regions far outside European colonial control, the Jesuits were the architects of what theologians call 'inculturation,' a post–Vatican II mission term referring to the adaptation of Christian ritual to the traditions of different societies.[6] On a very practical level, inculturation was an acknowledgment of a cultural imperative: the only way to approach non-European societies without force of arms is through adapting to their ways. The main proponents of this politically radical but very expedient new methodology were Jesuit missionaries José de Acosta (1540–1600) and Alessandro Valignano (1539–1606), working in Peru and East Asia respectively.

Of course, the Jesuits were not free of many of the religious bigotries or racial biases of their era. Many showed a preference for people whom they considered 'white' over those deemed 'black.' As did many other institutions and religious orders of the period, they kept slaves on the plantations and farms that financed their missions. As well, they operated under the conviction that theirs was the only True Faith, an attitude which prevented a complete rapprochement with non-Christian cultures and meant that the Jesuits stubbornly refused to adapt elements of foreign religion. This policy put them at a disadvantage, since many non-Christian peoples were quite willing to exchange ideas on the intellectual and cultural front but would have been insulted at the idea that they were to give up their faith. Nevertheless, the Jesuits' openness to the cultural and intellectual aspects of non-European peoples was very unusual and remarkable. In a world of *conquistadores*, the Jesuits were ahead of their time.

But it was not merely a willingness to adapt and indigenize that won the Jesuits the respect and cooperation of the likes of the Ming Emperor and the Mughal court. They had to give these societies something that they would want to adapt to in the first place. It was, above all, the Jesuits' commitment to providing a high level of culture that put them in the forefront of mission enterprises worldwide, and separated them from the policies of most other orders – not to mention, the Imperial Iberian governments. The Jesuits came to enlighten the missionized about European culture, not simply to convert them. Fuelled by Renaissance humanism, the Society stressed learning, oratory, and the arts in Europe and overseas alike. Missionaries were thoroughly trained from a young age in the art of disputation, the ability to build arguments and respond to criticisms, and brought these talents to bear in debate with representatives of foreign civilizations worldwide. Great care was taken to select 'global humanists'[7] for mission work, who were not only capable of ministry in the back of beyond but who could also represent the cream of European civilization. Many of the most remarkable and active of these men – who numbered among the main intellectual players of the entire Jesuit enterprise – were Italians and Flemings, and, later on, men of Germanic background. Italians were so ubiquitous in the China mission, for example, that the official Ming history, the *Ming shi*, refers to the Jesuits simply as 'the Italians.'[8] Their particular brand of missiology, which they called *il modo soave* (the gentle manner), anticipated by nearly four hundred years methods adopted by the Vatican in the latter half of the twentieth century to deal with an increasingly global Catholic church.

Typically a jack of all trades, a Jesuit missionary could be at once an accomplished scientist, doctor, botanist, musician, sculptor, painter, and architect, all the while devoting most of his energy to attending to the spiritual needs of his community. Without doubt the most visible of this panoply of skills involved the fine arts. Taking their cue from classical rhetoric, to which all good humanists were committed, the Jesuits envisioned art as the visual equivalent to sacred oratory. Applying to art the rhetorical theories of Cicero and Quintilian, which were refracted through the writings of Saint Augustine and John of Damascus and further focused in Alberti's treatise *On Painting* (1435), the Jesuits recognized that, like preaching, art had an extraordinary ability 'to delight, to teach, and to move' (*delectare, docere, movere*). By harnessing art's mimetic realism, expressive power, and emotive capabilities (what John of Damascus called 'anagogic' and I call the 'delight factor'), missionaries could move non-Christians to abandon their faiths for Christianity – or at least to respect it – incite Protestants to return to the Catholic fold, or teach Old Christians and neophytes alike to live their lives in a more pious and Christian manner. The Jesuits also stressed an image's potential for meditation, an emphasis deriving from the *Spiritual Exercises*, which exhorted its followers to meditate by forming mental images with the senses. This intellectual exercise was as important for the spiritual formation of the Jesuits themselves as it was for their congregations. Like the Early Christians, who were faced not only with paganism but iconoclasm, the Jesuits also recognized the important role images could play in surmounting the language barrier – a vital tool for a society committed to overseas missions. Finally, images played an important mnemonic role. In communities where everyone was an acolyte learning the rudiments of a completely alien religion, pictures served to fix the ideas and events of Christianity in the mind. In accordance with mnemonic theory developed by Pliny, Quintilian, the author of *Ad Herennium*, and more recently by the popular Cypriano Suárez, whose *De Arte Rhetorica* was taught in Jesuit schools, missionaries taught adults and children alike to use images to store and retrieve information.[9]

The Society also enlisted supernatural help. The Jesuits perpetuated the early medieval devotion to the miraculous image, or *acheiropoieton* ('made without human hands'), icons whose artistic merit was enhanced by divine properties, such as the Madonna at Santa Maria Maggiore in Rome supposedly painted by Saint Luke – whose likeness, thanks to the Jesuits, probably enjoyed wider currency than any other image on earth by the turn of the seventeenth century – or the very popular Madonna del Popolo (fig. 1).[10] Similarly, the cult of the Virgin of Loreto was given priority in Jesuit missions; for example, in Paraguay, where every mission had a Loreto chapel (fig. 96), and Japan, where the Litany of Loreto was recited daily at Jesuit schools.[11] The Saint Luke and Loreto Madonnas and similar icons could cure, and they could also convert. It was these and similar justifications for imagery – shared with other Catholic orders of the period, but with a uniquely Jesuit emphasis – that made the production, distribution, and use of artworks one of the most important features of mission work in the Society of Jesus.

On the missions, the Jesuits maximized art's powers 'to find a meaning that binds and reconciles.'[12] But these very powers could equally be seen as a threat and inspire strong resistance. This other side of the coin was visible when communities expressed their hostility toward Christianity against these very images. As Carolyn Dean wrote about colonial Peru, 'paintings and sculptures could function as battlefields in these conflicts.'[13] When in 1565 the Japanese leader Katodono, 'the greatest enemy of God's law that there is in Japan,' attacked a flotilla of Portuguese ships at dock, he reserved special dishonour for an altarpiece he found there:

> Since there was a picture of Our Lady with the child in it [on a supply ship], a very fine painting that came from India, he took it with him in his house and painted the face with many indecent things and wrote lustful verses under it and hung it in his room out of contempt so that he and his people could daily insult and mock it.[14]

Judging by the tone of the Jesuit commentator, this act was deemed almost as hurtful as harming living, breathing Christians. Similarly, a few decades later in Paraguay, when the shaman Nezú and his warriors murdered the Jesuit missionary Roque González (1576–1628) at Candelaría, they took special care to deface the devotional imagery from the chapel, particularly the painting of the Virgin known as *La Conquistadora,* which González had himself endowed with militaristic symbolism by unfurling it when entering non-Christian territories.[15] Similar stories abound in mission history around the world, attesting that Christians and non-Christians alike were aware of the power of images and their ability to be manipulated.

The Jesuit missionaries provided huge numbers of artworks for their overseas missions, which naturally increased in quantity as the centuries progressed and the enterprise expanded. As we will see, many historians dismiss Jesuit missionary artistic efforts in distant localities as paltry and insignificant. Surely, they assume, missionaries were only able to bring a scant few prints and even fewer canvases with them on their adventures, and could have produced very little on site. This volume will show how wrong this assumption is. As a random illustration, let us consider the inventory of a minor Jesuit farm – not even a mission – on the island of Luzon in the Philippines at the time of the Jesuit expulsion from Spanish territory in 1767. The tiny chapel at the *hacienda* of San Juan Bautista de Calamba was furnished with a painted tabernacle, wood and ivory images of the Virgin with the Rosary and Saint Anthony, an oil painting on canvas of the Immaculate Conception, four wooden panel paintings of Saint James, Saint Paul the Apostle, Saint Francis of Assisi, and Saint Paul, a reversible portrait of Saint Ignatius, a pair of portraits of Saint Ignatius and Saint Francis Xavier, another painting of the Madonna, thirty paintings of the Passion of Christ, and several frames attesting to other paintings which no longer existed.[16] Several of these would have been imported from Europe, but others were probably made in Manila by Chinese or Filipino Christians who produced religious images for the Society.[17]

The art brought by the Jesuits from Europe was also remarkably representative of Renaissance, and later, Baroque culture. In addition to original Italian, German, and Iberian oil paintings, they transported thousands of engravings of the work of artists such as Michelangelo, Raphael, Federico Zuccaro, Rubens, Velázquez, Martin de Vos, and the Carracci, including the finest products of German and Flemish printmakers and a full range of classical, Renaissance, and Baroque books on the fine arts and architecture. The prints and printed books, in particular, by masters such as Dürer, Cort, Golzius, the Sadelers, and the Wierixes, were the finest engravings of their day and rank with the greatest works of art in other media. In Europe, the Jesuits combined a concern for economy with one for quality in the visual arts. Similarly, these engravings, often commissioned directly by the Society, provided that quality in an affordable and easily transportable medium. Neither were the Jesuits simply trying to entice the natives with pretty pictures; as always, a commitment to education was a primary concern. The Jesuits actually accumulated mission art and art book collections with the purpose of providing a teaching collection for mission academies in much the same way that European academies such as the Accademia di San Luca in Rome (founded 1577) and Federico Borromeo's Ambrosiana in Milan (founded 1607–20) assembled collections of original works and copies for the use of their members.[18]

Although the Jesuits' overseas art production was no more extensive than that of a number of other European missionary groups, its distinctive character was conditioned by the Jesuits' accommodation policy. Certainly the Spanish and Portuguese colonial church governments produced art and especially architecture on a greater scale than the Jesuits, but they were, for the most part, limited geographically to colonial possessions. Moreover, these entities used art primarily as a tool of political hegemony, spreading a comparably homogeneous Iberian veneer over the lands they entered. Consequently, despite the presence of especially Flemish and some Italian artists in colonial Latin America in the first century, their commissions are marked by a relatively monolithic stylistic unity, especially in the seventeenth and eighteenth centuries. Mendicant missionary orders – especially Franciscans, Dominicans, and Augustinians – financed artistic and architectural projects overseas on at least the same scale as the Jesuits, and in the sixteenth century operated in a spirit of cultural acculturation that would later inspire the fledgling Society of Jesus. Nevertheless, most of these efforts were abandoned by the end of the century as mendicant orders became more orthodox and doctrinaire in their methods, and their mission art and architecture came to manifest the same uniform climate of largely Iberian cultural hegemony as their secular colonial counterparts. The Jesuits, by contrast, by making accommodation a cornerstone of their approach to the arts, pursued what was perhaps the *least* unified artistic enterprise of the era. To an extent which gained them the jealousy and derision of more conservative orders, the Jesuits actively encouraged the blending of Western art with local, indigenous traditions right into the eighteenth century.

Despite much talk about a 'Jesuit style' in the arts in Europe (see chapter 2), even the European element of Jesuit mission art was far from homogeneous. The art the Jesuits brought from Europe was as diverse as the missionaries themselves. They presented foreign dignitaries with Flemish, French, German, Italian, and Byzantine images, built churches emulating Early Christian basilicas alongside ones built from High Renaissance manuals, and their commissions reflected the whole spectrum from simple and austere to triumphalist and exuberant. With this diverse blend of traditions in hand, the Jesuits penetrated deeper into the non-Christian world than any other order. They initiated a more complete hybridization of the arts in a greater number of cultures than anyone else was able or willing to attempt. At no time prior to the industrial age did any single organization have such a pervasive impact on world art.

Although the Jesuits have attracted much attention in recent years, only a few isolated studies have considered the artistic legacy of their missions – remarkably, since many of the art objects are distinguished works of high aesthetic value.[19] The years following the Columbian quincentennial in 1992 have witnessed a burgeoning of interest in cultural convergence, especially the meeting between European and non-European civilizations.[20] Scholars in fields as diverse as anthropology, postcolonial theory, mission history, and cutural studies have suggested strategies for interpreting images produced by intercultural encounters. Art historians have also considered this subject in several provocative studies, conferences, and museum exhibitions on isolated artistic exchanges between Europe and the peoples of Asia or Latin America in the early modern period. To date, however, no major study has moved beyond the confines of area studies to look at this interaction on a global scale, comparing the variety of artistic approaches by European agents with the even more varied responses by non-European host societies. This book will bridge this gap by comparing selected Asian and Latin American artistic encounters of the Society of Jesus, and their impact on the art of indigenous people, not only Christian converts, but the greater non-Christian community. While it is regrettable that space constraints have compelled me to leave out important mission regions such as North America and Africa, I have included the areas which the Jesuits themselves held in greatest esteem and to which they devoted the most attention, particularly in the realm of the fine arts.

A good example of the complex styles and traditions that coalesced in Jesuit mission art are the works produced in the Seminary of Painters in Japan, a giant art workshop staffed by Japanese and Chinese neophytes which was founded in 1583, a year after the Carracci Academy in Bologna. These paintings, sculptures, and even engravings blended European and Far Eastern styles to supply Asian missions and the palaces of the Japanese nobility. At the same time, a handful of Jesuit missionaries, none of them artists by trade, had inspired the Muslim emperors of Mughal India to overhaul their imperial court style; the result was a dynamic hybrid art enhanced by a new interest in realism and devotionalism. By the last decade of the seventeenth century, the Jesuit reductions of Paraguay housed one of the most extensive art enterprises in either of the Americas, and by the early eighteenth, Jesuits served as court artists for the Chinese Emperor, designing his pleasure gardens and porcelains, and painting his portraits.

Like any mission history, this book is founded on institutional history, and the grand majority of extant archival and published sources are Jesuit or at least European in origin. As with any study of the Society of Jesus, which kept such exacting records of its every activity in a wide range of languages, this is an extremely daunting task. This volume is founded on new archival research in institutions around the world, principally in Rome, London, India, and Buenos Aires, but also Madrid, Dublin, Lima, Manila, and elsewhere. By far the most important sources are the original letters of the Jesuit missionaries, addressed to Rome, their friends, and their families, as well as the Annual Letters written every year by the Provincial (the superior of each Jesuit province) to report on activity in his jurisdiction, which are full of valuable circumstantial detail. Other documents, including catalogues of Jesuit missionaries, ledger-books, legal documents, reports by Jesuit Visitors (officials who made periodic assessments of Jesuit missions), and especially the vast inventories of art objects written at the time of the expulsion of the Society of Jesus from Iberian territories (from Portuguese possessions in 1759; from the Spanish Empire in 1767), have been very revealing. In addition, I have had to contend with a formidably comprehensive published primary literature, some of it dating back to the time of the first missions.

Finally, I have faced the even more overwhelming task of dealing with a mountain of secondary literature on the individual missions. The four principal missions in this book have generated so much literature that at first glance they would appear to have been exhaustively studied. Serious scholarship on the Mughal mission, for example, dates back to the earliest days of the British Raj in the mid-nineteenth century, and the Paraguay reductions have been interpreted and reinterpreted since Voltaire's day. In comparison, intensive studies of the Japanese and Chinese missions began in earnest only in the 1920s, but have proliferated in recent decades. However, the quantity is deceptive. First, and most relevantly for us, very little has been written about the arts. Second, although much of this literature has been rigorously researched, it is usually flavoured by a strong confessional bias, either for or against the missionaries; and third, later research tends to rely on published sources rather than going back to archival source material, with the result that the mistakes of earlier writers are repeated time and again. There are exceptions, of course, such as the work of Magnus Mörner in Paraguay, René Javellana in the Philippines, or John Correia Afonso in India, but, on the whole, the topics need to be subjected to a more rigorous historiographical treatment. The scholarship for some areas, particularly the Mughal mission, is woefully antiquated, and the Paraguay reductions seem eternally condemned to be viewed by many people through the rose-tinted lenses of Utopianism. Most importantly, however, except for a few recent articles on isolated missions, very few studies consider the responses of the non-European players in this artistic partnership. Most of the ground-breaking work in that field has been done by Latin Americanists working on mendicant orders in sixteenth-century New Spain and Peru.

In order not to make this book yet another hagiography with Jesuit protagonists bringing civilization to the pagans, I have tried to balance Jesuit reports with non-European sources. In every case covered in this book, the Jesuits only got as far as they did because their host communities let them. Without the willing interest, cooperation, and participation of these often largely non-Christian communities, they would have foundered. And far from being impressed by the 'superiority' of European culture, these societies compelled it to submit to their own canons. Therefore, where they exist, I have made use of primary textual sources from the non-European cultures, both previously published or, in the case of most of the Indian sources, unpublished. Much more work remains to be done in this area, particularly in China and Japan, and thankfully a new generation of scholars is focusing on these very areas.[21] However, the process of extracting the indigenous reaction through texts is slow and usually unrewarding, even though it is ultimately very important. As an example, after translating a large number of often extremely dense Persian verses which accompany Christian-inspired paintings from Persia and India, I came reluctantly to the conclusion that the words had on the whole nothing to do with the images. Relevant texts of this kind are much fewer in number for the simple reason that very few non-European people wrote about European art, a phenomenon recently noted as well by a Japanese scholar.[22] I have tried in some cases to glean indigenous attitudes toward the Jesuits and their art from the mainstream literature of the period, but the results are few and far between. Fortunately for us, the most compelling non-European voice can be found in the art itself; unraveling this message is, of course, one of the purposes of this book. As Elizabeth Boone recently remarked about early colonial Mexico, images 'bypass spoken language and preserve meaning visually and within their own pictorial conventions.'[23]

My principal aim in this book is to offer the first interpretation of hybrid art to encompass the diversity of cultures that came into contact with Europe in the early modern period. The objects themselves include paintings on paper, canvas, and cloth; murals; sculptures in marble, wood, and ivory; engravings and woodblock prints; jewellery, costume, and objects of daily use; as well as architecture. Their styles range from strongly European to predominantly indigenous. Many of these artworks are unpublished, and considerable travel throughout Asia and South America was required in order to find them. My second intention is to find out what attracted non-Europeans to the Jesuits and especially to European Late Renaissance and Baroque art in the first place, and above all to explore how they reacted to it. I will look at how the Mughal and Chinese emperors and the Japanese daimyos harnessed Catholic devotional art to glorify their own reigns, and how the Guaraní of Paraguay indigenized Christianity by bringing its art closer to their own canons. Although many members of these groups actually converted to Christianity, others remained for the most part firmly non-Christian. For it was one of the ironies of the Jesuits' mission enterprise that their greatest successes were ultimately cultural, not spiritual, and that many of their most active proponents and supporters never entertained the faintest intention of converting to Catholicism. Finally, I want to try to understand the ideological underpinnings of the whole missionary enterprise. How did these men view themselves, how did they view non-European peoples and cultures, and why did they devote so much energy to purveying high culture when a more low-brow, practical approach would clearly have been a more successful way of winning converts? They may have been greeted by 'the powerful, the noble, and the beautiful,'[24] but their greatest pastoral victories were always among the ordinary and neglected, precisely the people who received the least press and attention in their day.

Chapter 2 gives an overview of the origins and nature of missionary art, in general. I also raise there the main methodological issues and interpretative problems of this vast subject. I look at myths and topoi about mission art which were contemporary with the missions and continue to influence scholarship today. I consider the problems with naming the process of acculturation and its art, and I examine the heated debate over the presence or absence of an indigenous quality in the post-contact art of Latin America, in striking contrast with scholarship about post-contact Asia, where the indigenous element has always been taken for granted. I look at the issue of copying, considering terms such as 'folk art' and 'provincial art,' and question current assumptions about marginalization and the 'periphery.' I show that the cultural blends were not always simple or uniform: they comprise syncretism, complete displacement of either indigenous or European tradition, and absolute clash.

In this book, I divide Jesuit overseas missions into two main categories according to their degree of cultural interaction: the 'inner' and 'outer' circles. The inner-circle missions were run by regular, as opposed to secular, clergy who ran parishes, and took place in regions subjugated by European (usually Iberian) force, and therefore were strongly reliant on the colonial administration; they included the core areas of Latin America (Mesoamerica, the Andean region, and the coastal areas of Brazil), as well as Goa, Macao, and metropolitan areas of the Philippines. In these inner-circle areas, colonial governments had forcibly suppressed indigenous civilizations and imposed Christianity and European culture from above. The Spanish and Portuguese crowns managed the Church, including missions, by right of an authority granted by the Pope beginning in the early sixteenth century and codified by Philip II in 1573, known as *Padroado* in Portugal and *Patronato* in Spain ('Patronate'). According to this law, the rulers of Spain and Portugal were empowered to appoint bishops, to license churchmen and control their movements, to intervene in matters of religion and spiritual jurisdiction, to collect tithes, and even to approve the construction of religious buildings, a power which the Spanish kings did not even enjoy in most of Spain until the eighteenth century.[25] Originally intended as an assurance that the spiritual needs of the conquered peoples would be taken care of, this power became so absolute that the Pope was effectively removed from command, even after the foundation of a centralized Catholic mission bureau in 1622 known as the Sacra Congregatio de Propaganda Fide (Sacred Congregation for the Propagation of the Faith), which had a limited effect on the Portuguese Empire and none on the Spanish.[26]

Although by the letter of the law the Spanish and (less so) the Portuguese crowns were tireless in their support of the rights of indigenous peoples, the reality was dictated by colonists. In Spanish territories, relations with indigenous peoples were coloured by infamous labour systems, which were intended, ironically, to ensure the spiritual well-being of the workers but which usually amounted to little more than slavery. First came the *encomienda*, by which an indigenous group was assigned for the long term to a single colonist; this system began to be replaced in the second half of the sixteenth century by the *repartimiento*, by which smaller parties were divided among different colonists for shorter times.[27] In the Portuguese Empire, exploitation of the indigenous peoples was even more arbitrary and cruel. Under pressure from such regimes, Jesuit policy in colonial regions tended to be more Eurocentric and less open to exchange. Cultural influence was always filtered through Seville or Lisbon, giving the colonized region's art a strongly Iberian flavour, and in general there was little room for indigenous dialogue after the first post-conquest generation. Jesuit enterprises in these areas concentrated mostly on the needs of the colonists, although their colleges were still very much devoted to training missionaries, for example, in indigenous languages.[28]

This situation is in strong contrast to the outer-circle, or periphery, missions, regions which have received far less scholarly attention, especially in Latin America. These areas include Momoyama Japan, Ming and Qing China, Mughal and Madurai India, Vietnam, the missions to Sonora, Moxos, Chiquitos, the Orinoco Valley, Southern Chile, and the Argentine Pampas, not to mention the famed Guaraní 'republics' of Paraguay. With a few exceptions, notably on the frontiers of New Spain where the *presidio* system of paired mission and military outpost prevailed, the outer-circle missions of the Jesuits tended not to involve soldiers or any other secular officials, and therefore they were neither subject to close colonial control nor could they rely on coercion. The outer-circle missions were based in regions where non-European civilizations flourished, either because they retained power over their territories and only invited the Jesuits in as guests, as in Japan, or, in the case of Paraguay, because they fell into a buffer zone between Portuguese and Spanish interests and maintained a comparable degree of independence and contact with unconverted tribes. Of course, what is 'peripheral' to Europeans is the opposite to the non-European target populations, for whom these missions were in the cultural heartland. Consequently, the Jesuits in these regions were able to indigenize more thoroughly. Non-European artists played a much greater role in the outer-circle missions, and their work manifests a greater freedom in interpreting European models. In addition, the European element of these missions was also more representative. More so than in the colonies, the personnel and art of these missions came from all over Europe, reflecting the international nature of the Society, and since artworks were ordered directly from Jesuit headquarters in Rome, they were more cosmopolitan as well. The outer circle allowed the most active and creative synthesis between Europe and non-European cultures, combining a more direct contact with current metropolitan European culture – especially Italian, Flemish, and Germanic – with stronger indigenous contributions. It was a potent mixture.

My discussion of the inner- and outer-circle missions will concentrate on the four outer-circle missions that involved the most flourishing and creative artistic exchanges. Chapter 3 focuses on the mission to Japan (sixteenth to seventeenth centuries), by thirty years the earliest of the four, and a true pioneer in mission art activity. Chapter 4 explores the mission to China (sixteenth to eighteenth centuries), best known for its scientific and literary contributions, but also active in artistic acculturation on the mission front, not to mention the infamous participation of Jesuit artists at court during the eighteenth century. Chapter 5 considers the mission to 'Mogor,' or Mughal India (sixteenth to eighteenth centuries), involving perhaps the most extensive artistic exchange of any Jesuit mission. Chapter 6 moves to the Americas, to look at a strikingly similar art policy implemented in the so-called reductions of Paraguay in the seventeenth and eighteenth centuries. The Japan and China missions inspired hybrid artistic trends of great originality and delicacy but left only a limited legacy in the mainstream artistic life of these nations. The Jesuits' endeavours in Mughal India and Paraguay, by contrast, made a thorough and enduring impression on the arts of two proud and very different non-European peoples. In fact, the mission to Mughal India was unique in that the greatest impact of European art was felt, not in the art produced by the mission communities, but in the non-Christian mainstream art of the Imperial court. It is in that mission perhaps that we can see hybrid art at its most untrammelled – completely free of religious or political compulsion. It was also the most intellectual and theoretical of the artistic exchanges described in this book and, consequently, the one providing the most indigenous-language textual evidence about reception.

My conclusion (chapter 7) is devoted to the partnership itself. In this chapter, I focus on reception: what did the two sides of this exchange see in each other? I consider what factors made the cultural exchange possible, given that the imposition of force was not present in any of the four missions, and also what conditions hindered it. I ask what social groups were most involved, and whether they acted out of genuine intellectual interest or religious allegiance, or simply out of pragmatism and political expediency. Finally, I explore what non-European cultures saw in European art of the time. What made the Renaissance visual tradition attractive, or at least intriguing, to people in the four corners of the globe? Why did so many different cultures react to it in such similar ways? In the end, the Jesuits are not really the subject of this book; they are merely the catalyst for a very compelling example of human cooperation.

Note

Although the history of missions is intimately connected with geography, this book does not have any maps in it. There are two reasons for this. This book covers virtually the entire world, which would have entailed such a large number of maps that there would have to have been fewer pictures. More important, however, is the fact that the missions in this book were usually very transitory. Some, like those in Japan or Paraguay, moved every couple of years or even every few months, so that a mission with one name could have existed in five or six places in its history. In some cases it is impossible to say exactly where a mission was at any given time and it is therefore difficult to map them. Nevertheless, the missions have been related to major geographical locations and larger, more permanent settlements in an effort to allow the reader to locate their general area.

2

The Origins of the Partnership

They made converts in regions which neither avarice nor curiosity had tempted any of their countrymen to enter; and preached and disputed in tongues of which no other native of the West understood a word.

Lord Macaulay on the Jesuits in Macaulay, 'Ranke's History of the Popes,' 20

Until recent years, scholars have tended to view the Christianization of the New World and Portuguese Asia as a more or less complete suppression of indigenous culture.[1] Yet even for several decades before the Jesuits began their program of accommodation, colonial and ecclesiastical foundations in these regions were already experimenting cautiously with cultural borrowing, while at the same time indigenous people were able to preserve a substantial portion of their pre-contact traditions on their own. In this chapter, I will look briefly at some of these cultural exchanges, many of which were short-lived, but which nevertheless anticipated later work by Jesuit missionaries.

The colonial authorities did made active use of indigenous social and political traditions, mostly for the very practical reason that it was easier to employ existing methods than import new ones. For example, Spanish soldiers in the sixteenth-century Paraguayan hinterlands participated in indigenous patterns of kinship alliance to maintain security with the warlike Guaraní; meanwhile, in Peru and New Spain, even the hated *encomienda* system capitalized on existing patterns of work rotation.[2] These compromises did not reflect any respect on the part of the colonists for pre-contact cultures, but served immediate needs expediently: 'Major policy decisions of Spanish authorities, including the establishment of encomiendas and ancillary parishes, were made in awareness of the nature of indigenous structures; there was no other choice.'[3] This kind of 'accommodation' was, therefore, frankly exploitative.

However, there were also borrowings of a more cultural nature, driven by a humanist, even visionary, spirit of learning and dialogue, which make the first decades after the conquests one of the most fascinating case studies for hybridization. The driving force behind such efforts was the Franciscan Order (founded 1209), the missionary group closest in spirit to the Jesuits, which laid the ideological foundations in every way for the latter's overseas mission enterprise. One of the most pronounced examples of such acculturation occurred in New Spain during the several decades after the fall of the Aztecs in 1521 until the later 1580s. During this period, the Franciscans inititated several attempts to Christianize indigenous culture, including the arts, fuelled by a Utopian euphoria in the wake of Cortes's conquests. The other major mendicant orders in this region, the Dominicans (founded 1215) and Augustinians (founded 1256), also participated in these activities. The mendicants preceded the Jesuits not only in New Spain but also in Peru (where the Mercedarian Order, founded 1218, was also a powerful presence) and in all the major colonial centres of the Iberian empires, from Paraguay to the Philippines, providing a precedent for accommodation that made the younger order's work easier. But mendicant efforts were weighed down by the Patronate's heavy hand and were ultimately doomed by the rise of secular parishes, by the mass death of Amerindians, in New Spain following the great plagues of the 1560s and '70s, and also by a more orthodox shift in their own attitudes during the last decades of the sixteenth century, which had followed on the Council of Trent (1545–63), a series of ecclesiastical meetings aimed at reforming the Catholic Church in the wake of the Protestant Reformation. This radical change in mood was also a reaction, however, to a more localized problem: the missionaries believed that their methods were simply not working. As Charles Lippy writes about Peru, 'as time went on ... and the difficulties of the missionary task became more apparent, there was a stronger tendency to rely on compulsion and constraint.'[4]

At the same time that colonial and church officials were allowing a limited hybridization of Christianity, many of the indigenous people actively resisted the new religion. On a clandestine level, indigenous religion persevered and even prospered – a fact which few contemporary European sources were willing to admit, or even dared to believe.[5] Occasionally, practitioners of non-Christian religions were not so secretive; for example, when the messianic Nahua priest Martín Ocelotl openly challenged Christianity in the 1540s.[6] The friars who began missionary work in colonial territory believed that conversions would be swift and easy. Without paying enough attention to instruction, they baptized thousands of neophytes who lacked even a basic understanding of Christian tenets, often using corporal punishment as an extra incentive.[7] Although they feverishly stamped out all traces of temple buildings – whether in New Spain or the Deccan – they often turned a blind eye to the perseverence of idolotry and other non-Christian practices, many of which were pursued in defiance of Christianity, but most of which existed on a domestic level and enjoyed a syncretic relationship with the new religion.[8] The Jesuit José de Acosta, for example, compared the 'Indian Christianity' he found in Peru in the late sixteenth century with that of the Samaritans, in which Christian tenets coexisted with pre-conquest traditions: 'They adore Christ yet follow the cult of their gods; they fear God, yet do not fear him.'[9]

The tragic result, in Latin America and Asia alike, was this conservative shift in church policy, sometimes leading to a crackdown by church officials who suddenly found themselves impotent in the face of flourishing grass-roots indigenization (even this did not stop it; indigenous religious practices were discovered in

Latin America well into the eighteenth century and indeed persist today).[10] These backlashes, or extirpations, happened at different times according to local situations, but most of them fall within the last decades of the sixteenth and first decades of the seventeenth century – precisely when the Jesuits were first moving onto the scene. In Asia especially, there was much concern over what was considered an overhasty assimilation with indigenous culture on the part of the friars. This took on an artistic aspect in Goa, where in 1588 church authorities forbade for the third time the common practice of hiring non-Christian (Hindu) artists to sculpt or paint Christian religious imagery for fear of doctrinal contamination.[11] Ironically, as we will soon see, it is in the Goan churches of the later seventeenth and eighteenth centuries – and not the earliest ones – that the strongest Hindu elements appear in the ornamentation. The Jesuits were not innocent of this backlash either. In several areas (e.g., Peru), the Jesuits took part in the suppression of indigenous religion. This behaviour should not be seen as inconsistent with Jesuit aims, for even though the Society became the strongest promoter of indigenous culture, it never showed the least sympathy with indigenous cult, and worked tirelessly to stamp it out. Fortunately, this dark period in mission history did not inure the Jesuits to further intercultural experimentation, as it seems to have done for many of the mendicants.

It is also a commonplace to insist that mission target populations never embraced Christianity consentingly. Certainly among given groups (e.g., the Muslim aristocracy in India or some of the descendants of the Yucatec Maya), this was true. But elsewhere, whether for political, social, or purely spiritual reasons, whole communities embraced Christianity – but they did so selectively. They indigenized the Christian religion, and interpreted it on their own often very idiosyncratic terms, giving it their own stamp of identity. Consequently, it was not so much a case of converting to Christianity but of converting Christianity. In central New Spain, many of the Nahua peasantry incorporated Christianity into their own pantheon, claimed its saints as symbols of civic pride, and rewrote their histories in a heroic mode and a Christian key; in China as we will see, elements of Christianity were neatly merged with Daoism and Confucianism. Nor was Christianity, as understood or practised by non-Europeans, necessarily a unified body of tenets or beliefs, as it was in the Catholic Church. It varied considerably according to time and place, and even between individuals. To many non-European peoples, 'Christian' and 'non-Christian' were not polar opposites, as they were to Europeans, and could easily coexist. As we will see in chapter 6, the early mission Guaraní were quite comfortable going back and forth between the Christian and 'pagan' realms, seeing them as two sides of the same reality.

'Christianity' – whatever that meant to them – was often merely a system non-Europeans used to operate within the new colonial world, particularly in the Americas. Christianity provided indigenous people with a key for maintaining a stable, peaceful environment within the new society, and a legitimate means for expressing ethnic identity. As James Lockhart writes about the Nahua, they 'accepted the new in order to remain the same.'[12] David Block notes the same phenomenon a century later on the Jesuit missions among the Moxos of the Upper Amazon: 'The missions ended forever the monopoly of native cultural modes ...

But they established a viable substitute for premission life-styles, one acceptable to both priests and Indians.[13] And even David Sweet, who is unsympathetic toward missionary efforts, concedes: 'The truth is, of course, that though many resisted the mission system, most of the Indians who managed to survive its epidemics and its disciplines ended up in an attitude of acquiescence to missionary rule.'[14] However, we should not depict their accommodation in such passive terms as 'acquiescence.' The non-European 'converts' actively created their own Church.

Embracing Christianity was not, after all, necessarily an acknowledgment of European superiority. We may see the encounter, somewhat romantically, as a meeting of two worlds – as if two worlds in their entirety could ever meet. However, most of the 'encountered' saw the meeting in more local terms, involving much more limited groups of people; for example, a single Nahua *altepetl* (local state) and a handful of Dominican friars, as opposed to such vast abstractions as the 'Aztec Empire' and 'Europe.' Christianity was an alien religion at first, but then virtually every indigenous group in Asia and the Americas had already come into contact with other foreign religions through immigrants, merchants, or invaders prior to contact with the Spanish or Portuguese. In China, for example, Christianity was seen merely as a less exalted successor to Buddhism, itself a foreign faith; in Korea, when certain young urban intellectuals adopted Catholicism in the eighteenth century, they thought they were embracing a Chinese school of Confucianist philosophy; and, in New Spain, despite the unquestionable disruptions to indigenous lifestyles brought about by the new religion and society, Christian saints can be interpreted as the latest wave of new deities added to an accumulative pantheon that reflected the contributions of every invading people since the arrival of the Olmecs during 1200–900 B.C. Certainly, in Asia, a heritage of earlier contact with other Old World religions such as Judaism, Islam, and Christianity itself made some cultures more capable of coming to terms with the new religion, but the New World was also far from being a homogeneous universe and had plenty of experience with religious diversity. Once Christianity was indigenized by non-Europeans, it could no longer be considered an aspect of European culture.[15]

I could cite many illustrations of active indigenous contributions to the new religion, but perhaps the most striking is the communal building of churches and erection of monumental crosses. In areas from Peru to the Philippines, communities of converts built and even financed churches and convent buildings of extraordinary size and grandeur, in some regions adorned with extensive ornament that blended European with indigenous styles. In New Spain, the immense Augustinian convent of San Nicolás in Actopán, for example, was built at the expense of the Nahua patrons Don Juan Iñica Actopán and Don Pedro Izcuicuitlapilco, and massive convents in the Lake Titicaca region of the Andes were constructed by whole villages of indigenous masons and artisans.[16] I hasten to point out that we could easily – and quite understandably – discount this activity as purely exploitative. After all, we must keep in mind that the indigenous people, at least in colonial territories, had little choice; the 1563 Ordenanza de Pobladores issued by Spain declared that a third of the means necessary for the construction of every church had to be provided by the indigenous population, a tax which was usually translated into labour since most of the people had no other means of paying it.[17] Churches were built larger than necessary because it was thought that keeping the community busy on building projects was a cure for sloth (colonists constantly believed indigenous people to be lazy, whether in America or Asia). Elsewhere, people worked on these projects to avoid paying tribute, or as a humanitarian alternative to back-breaking work in the mines, particularly in Peru.[18] Still, after having studied a wide range of mission contacts, I believe that there was more to this activity than simple pragmatism. How, for example, can we explain similar phenomena in regions beyond European control such as Japan or Paraguay?

Contemporary sources, all written by Europeans, of course, leave no doubt that many communities took to these projects with enthusiasm. But even keeping in mind the bias of the writers, there appears to be some truth to these statements. Recent scholarship on New Spain, in particular, is showing that communal Christian buildings and the new religion itself became the focus for local pride and identity, with the friars and Indians acting as 'partners in the creation of their own society, different from European society and from that of the colonists and mestizos around them.'[19] Often, indigenous people in New Spain and Peru employed pre-contact rituals of communal construction, as is also recorded later in several early Jesuit missions in Paraguay and the Philippines. These public performances enhanced the sense of celebration and connectedness with the past that characterized many of these foundations, and gave Christian liturgical ritual in these areas a genuinely indigenous identity.[20] José de Acosta recounts how the work of building the Jesuit church in Cuzco in 1579 was organized according to the customary Andean fashion as a cooperative venture and festival:

> For the foundations [the Andean people] have brought ancient cut stone in such quantities that even if the church were to be twice as large, there would be a surplus. They take these stones from old buildings ... of the time of the Incas. Organizing themselves by *ayllus* or kin groups, to carry the stone to our church and dressing as for a festival with their feather ornaments and adornments they came through the city singing in their language such things as occasion devotion, for instance 'Come brothers, let us bring stones to construct the house of the lord ... there they teach us the law of our God and redeemer' ... Even women transport stone and do their work while singing ...[21]

Another striking example is the phenomenon of the communal cross-raising in sixteenth-century Japan, which I will discuss at greater length in chapter 3.[22] History has shown us that new converts will gladly die before abandoning their faith (Japan, perhaps, is the greatest example of this fealty, as we shall soon see). By contrast, the prevalent view that various peoples were merely – sheepishly – succumbing to European pressure in expressing sympathy with Christianity and building churches and monuments would seem to deny them any choice in the matter, or an active role in their own destiny.

Indigenous people had more say about what form their church or parish would take than many realize. There is evidence, for example, that certain more isolated communities in Latin America were even able to choose which religious order to invite into their territory. Scholars have proposed that the Oaxacans from South Central Mexico selected the Dominicans, in preference over other orders, because it was politically and socially advantageous for them to do so.[23] Therefore, I believe that it is a gross oversimplification – despite the very real and compelling evidence to support such a statement – to claim that the 'very existence' of colonial architecture 'presupposes the suppression of native culture and the exploitation of native labour.'[24] Indigenous people were often active participants in these projects and through them displayed a keen sense of civic pride. Even though such acquiescence may have represented the better of two evils, these activities were often consenting and sincere.

Trying to Name It: 'Acculturation' and 'Mestizo Art'

The process I have been talking about, the encounter and merging of two cultures, is often called 'acculturation.' Beginning in the mid-1930s in the United States, a separate branch of anthropology known as 'acculturation theory' devoted itself to studying situations of continuous and prolonged contact between people of different traditions.[25] The problem with this model was that it depended upon an element of dominance; one of the two cultures had to be militarily superior. This insistance on domination and subordination not only overlooked the many cases where no such relationship existed, but it also tended to cloud over the active and creative role played by the 'recipient' culture even in the cases where it did. By the 1960s, anthropologists such as George Foster, Thomas Glick, and Oriol Pi-Sunyer were adjusting this approach by suggesting that even the 'recipient' culture retained some choice about which elements of the new culture it would accept or reject (Glick and Pi-Sunyer call it a 'boundary-maintaining mechanism'), but the basic understanding persisted of a dominant cultural donor and a passive cultural recipient.[26] Meanwhile, since the 1940s, Latin American scholars have been tipping the balance in favour of a two-way partnership, coining the more accurate term 'transculturation' to accommodate the more reciprocal nature of cultural exchange.[27] Transculturation allows influence to run in two directions, each side experiencing partial loss and partial gain as they forge a new, third culture. Scholars such as Ticio Escobar recognize that such changes should not be seen as condemnable, nor do they destroy ethnic identity – they merely reorganize it, and can have a reinvigorating effect.[28]

Postcolonial theorists Marshall Sahlins and Homi Bhabha, working primarily on Asia and the Pacific Islands, have continued to refine the issue of acculturation by focusing on reception. They have identified a wide spectrum of reactions to a received culture, ranging from misinterpretation, mimicry, and multiplication of meaning to hybridity.[29] They also challenge the concept of homogeneity within cultures, recognizing sharp divisions, such as class and sex, that exist even within a single culture. Anthropologists such as James Lockhart and Serge Gruzinski, working on early colonial New Spain, have explored issues of reception similar to those defined by Bhabha, acknowledging the 'double mistaken identity' between peoples or 'the dialectics of misunderstanding, appropriation and alienation.'[30] Lockhart shows how two civilizations with little in common will mutually misunderstand each other's symbols, iconographies, and ideologies, each maintaining that theirs is the prevailing interpretation. We will see this phenomenon at work in the Jesuit missions in Asia, for example, where the non-Christian powers appropriated Catholic art for their own ends, while the Jesuits continued to maintain (at least officially) that their iconography was not being perverted. But views such as Bhabha's about cultural 'hybridity' tend to be too exclusively negative, centring on its ability to disrupt and weaken authority (again, the dominance model). More recently, art historian Claire Farago and the other authors in her volume *Reframing the Renaissance* (1995) have used Bhabha's insights to concentrate on the more positive elements of hybridity; for example, its fertility and creative power.[31] A more positive approach is also offered by anthropologists Dennis Tedlock and Louise Burkhart, who perceive intercultural exchange as a 'dialogue' between two parties.[32] The term 'dialogue' is especially appropriate for the Jesuits, who raised it from the status of an accidental phenomenon to that of company policy. But a dialogue need not indicate that both parties had reached a consensus. As Francis Xavier himself wrote after his conversation with the Swahili nobleman in Malindi, 'After we had conversed for a long time, we still retained our own opinions.'[33]

Whether we call it 'acculturation,' 'transculturation,' the theologians' 'inculturation,' or any of the rich variety of other terms made available by anthropological and ecclesiastical theorists,[34] the aspect of intercultural exchange that interests us most here is art. Acculturation in art is one of the most hotly contested issues in early colonial art history, especially in Latin American fields (in contrast, the acculturative qualities of Ibero-Asian art have never been questioned). Although most scholars acknowledge that a certain amount of hybridization existed in early colonial art in Mesoamerica and Peru, few can agree on its extent or even what name to call it.[35] One of the most perennially popular terms, especially in Latin America, is 'mestizo,' a term developed by historians of Mexican and Peruvian art in the early twentieth century that equates artistic syncretism with the racial blending resulting from the intermarriage of Europeans and non-Europeans: 'this art like the new race was procreated by the crossbreeding of the two races.'[36] Although the idea that art is a product of race is no longer tenable, this term remains common and has the (perhaps dubious) distinction of actually having been used in the early colonial period itself.[37]

The term 'mestizo art' was first applied to highland Peru in 1925 by Angel Guido in reference to a late-seventeenth- and eighteenth-century style of architectural ornament characterized by a planimetric appearance and including native flora and fauna, as well as revived Inca symbols (fig. 2).[38] It was later taken up by scholars such as Harold Wethey, who used it interchangeably with the term 'creole' (*criollo*), another racial derivation, this time to denote art of European origin made in America; 'mestizo' continues to be used commonly in art histories, not only for architecture but for the Cuzco school of painting.[39] Some scholars, including Guido, Wethey, and more recently Damián Bayón,[40] maintain that the 'mestizo' style marked the resurgence of indigenous motifs after an initial period of suppression. Others, such as George Kubler and Graziano Gasparini,[41] discard the term because they believe the style to be merely a provincial art form born from a poor knowledge of European canons, and even Wethey concedes that the 'natural primitivism of the design and technique' is this style's most characteristic feature.[42]

In the 1940s, Alfred Neumeyer was the principal proponent of a 'mestizo art' in New Spain, again in reference to a planimetric, more symbolically abstract style, which John McAndrew (1965) and Elizabeth Wilder Weismann (1985) later credit with a 'genuine Indian quality' (fig. 3).[43] In New Spain, however, the pre-conquest civilizations had a much stronger figural arts tradition than in Peru, and early colonial art is full of such imagery. Therefore, a term was needed to denote the perseverence of iconographic motifs, and not merely style. The term, coined by José Moreno Villa in 1946 and used by scholars to this day, was *tequitqui*, a Nahuatl word meaning 'vassal,' or 'one who pays tribute.'[44] It referred again on a basic level to planimetric carving in low relief, but also more specifically to Nahua glyphs and other figural or faunal motifs that appear in early viceregal church and civic art commissions (fig. 4). One problem with the term *tequitqui* is that it clearly relies on the victor/vanquished model of acculturation studies, and in practice has tended to refer exclusively to a certain kind of sculpture, leaving out important media such as book and mural painting that demonstrate similar traits. Also it suggests that all of the art was done by pure-blooded Nahua, when in reality we know very little about who was responsible for these works, though it is likely that many of the artists were mestizos. I prefer the term *indocristiano*, used by Constantino Reyes-Valerio (1978), which, despite also being racially determined, better reflects the active role played by the 'conquered' in the indigenization of Christian art.[45] Again, as in Peru, some scholars dismiss most of this art as being little more than a provincialism and degradation of form, which Kubler calls 'folk art,' although he does admit that actual pre-conquest survivals exist.[46]

It is time to step aside and reconsider some of the conceptual models and terms taken for granted in the studies cited above. First, there is the matter of a racially or nationally based style. This notion has its origins in the nineteenth century, when scholars influenced by Hegel proposed that an individual people (*Volk*), rather than the individuals it is composed of, had its own genius or spirit (*Volksgeist*).[47] Nations such as Germany and Italy tied such ideas nicely to their nationalistic agendas, and they gained popularity in the years leading up to the Second World War. The idea of *Volksgeist* also came into play when the styles of one nation appeared outside its borders, even though such occurrences, albeit produced by citizens of the original country, were not considered as important as artworks done at home.[48] More significantly, since Italianate styles diffused outside Italy or French styles outside France could still be seen as expressions of the genius of a superior nation, scholars could belittle or ignore the role of the recipient culture, whether it be Polish or Turkish.

Scholars from nations such as those of Eastern Europe reacted to this cultural chauvinism in the first half of this century, with their own version of *Volksgeist*, to bolster the reputations of their own countries.[49] They distinguished local variants of Italian and other Western European styles as being characteristic of a *genius loci* peculiar to the region. Scholars often reduced the Italianate styles of these areas into individual motifs, which they characterized as being tempered by a uniquely

Polish, Russian, or Turkish spirit. Nevertheless, these concepts were still based on the notion that a people had a racially based artistic impulse. Thomas da Costa Kaufmann recently reviewed the attempt by the Polish scholar Jan Białostocki to tackle the problem of Italianate styles in Poland, which he sees, on the one hand, 'as the product of individual Italian artists and, on the other, an indigenous response to them.'[50] Białostocki's notion of the reciprocity of influences is sound; however, his insistence on a style based on the genius of a people is problematic. Although the romantic notion of *Volksgeist* is no longer current in art historical literature, we are still left with the problem of what to call local variants of the style of a foreign country. We cannot escape the fact that the features which make them different from the 'mainstream' are distinctive and unique, if not an expression of the genius of a race or nation.

This problem, also often posed in terms of 'centre' and 'periphery,' leads us to another problematic term: 'folk art.' I do not consider the term to be a universal attribute or even a very scientific label – quite apart from the fact that it has an obvious perjorative slant. Every group or individual has its own way of reacting to an alien style, and these reactions can be at once technically 'provincial' (i.e., less canonic than the art of metropolitan centres, whether a few miles away or overseas) and distinctly representative of culture (if not a *Volk*, then at least a certain group of individuals and set of conventions). For example, I far prefer Serge Gruzinski's understanding that the 'decided imperfection' of Nahua copies of European engravings 'is to be attributed more to an interpretation of European language than to native clumsiness,' over Martín Soria's dismissal that 'even the best Colonial [Latin American] artists, painters and sculptors, remained far below the best European standards. In comparison with Europe, a greater proportion of painting and sculpture is to be considered folk art ...'[51]

Perhaps, with Gruzinski, the best terminology to be applied to this problem is linguistic. If we say that different cultures have their own visual 'dialects' (but not in the sense of 'vernacular,' which, like 'provincial,' has low-brow connotations) of the same basic language, we can try to place these stylistic differences in a more equal, less hierarchical, relation to each other. Białostocki uses the term 'dialect' to describe a local redaction of a more general stylistic form (in this case, the Polish version of Italian Renaissance architecture), in preference over his original choice of 'vernacular,' which he had used in the sense of a *genius loci*.[52] Similarly, James Cracraft apples a linguistic term for Italianate art in Russia, noting that a hybrid culture's development of 'original ornamental forms, a distinctive symbolism, and an independent artistic conception' could potentially lead to the emergence of 'a complete and independent language.'[53] Nevertheless, I believe that it is important to link the sense of 'dialect' to that of 'dialogue' in order to get both sides of the equation; 'Moscow Baroque' is not just a redaction of Italian Baroque but also (probably more so) a redaction of Russian architecture. There is more than one language at play here.

These terminological issues bring us to the problem of style periodization. How can we use labels such as 'Renaissance,' 'Mannerist,' 'Baroque,' and 'Rococo' when discussing art inspired by those styles in places outside of Europe, Italy, or even the Florentine-Roman sphere?[54] By giving something produced outside this cultural centre the same label as something produced within it, we run the risk of making the 'peripheral' work look incorrect, or anachronistic. Anachronism is a major problem with such labels. Styles such as 'Moscow Mannerism' or 'Turkish Baroque' often occur long after Mannerism and Baroque were current in metropolitan Italy or France, and even coexist – something they would never do in Rome or Paris. When Rastrelli built his Baroque churches for Czarina Elizabeth of Russia in the mid-eighteenth century, for example, much of Western Europe was moving into the Neo-Classical period.[55] The art treated in this book works the same way. Usually European styles used on the Jesuit missions abroad occur much later than they do in Italy or Flanders and are integrated, as we shall see, with earlier styles from Europe – not to mention, indigenous ones. Elizabeth Wilder Weismann, writing about early colonial New Spain, refers to this phenomenon as a 'chronological anarchy.'[56]

Scholars working on subjects such as Italianate architecture in Eastern Europe and French-influenced architecture in the eighteenth-century Ottoman Empire have spilled much ink arguing over whether 'Mannerist,' 'Baroque,' or 'Rococo' is the better label, never arriving at an adequate solution. I also have no sure answer to this problem. I believe, however, that it is important that we not overemphasize terms such as 'Renaissance' and 'Baroque' ('Mannerism' is completely untenable) when talking about areas beyond certain metropolitan European centres. That is why I have referred to the art in this book as 'early modern Catholic,' '*arte sacra*,' or 'mission art.' In the early modern period, thanks to colonial powers and missionaries, certain styles and motifs became widespread around the globe; this diffusion is one of the subjects of this book. But whereas the different cultures that produced them can be considered to be speaking a dialect of the same international language, they are also carrying on conversations in different, and unrelated, tongues, which brings us back to the term 'dialogue.' Therefore, terms such as 'Renaissance' and 'Baroque' in a global context are partly correct, but also partly mistaken. We must always be conscious of this dichotomy and treat such terms with caution.

In order to look at these influences from the receiving end and focus on reception, let us return to the seemingly universal phenomenon of planimetricism and a tendency to focus on surface patterns. This response to the vocabulary of Italian art, which we have observed in New Spain and Peru, has been cited for Ottoman Turkey and Eastern Europe, as well. Białostocki characterizes the Polish version of 'Mannerism' as a 'lack of interest in space composition, an enthusiasm for ornament, and lack of functional thinking.'[57] Similarly, in his study of 'Turkish Baroque,' Aptullah Kuran comments:

> ... that which is baroque does not penetrate the skin, but merely scratches the surface ... Unlike its European counterpart, Turkish baroque architecture does not possess an intricate space conception or a strong sense of movement. What it does have is surface plasticity inspired by, and in the manner of, the European baroque, or better still, the French rococo.[58]

Dogan Kuban characterizes this same style as 'two dimensional.'[59] The Russian scholar B.R. Vipper described a very similar phenomenon in what he called 'Moscow Mannerism': the Italianate forms are simplified and generalized, typical qualities are emphasized, and spatial contrasts are replaced by surface rhythms.[60] The main features common to all three of these examples are that their models are made more two-dimensional and planimetric, and that they exult in ornamentation, leading one to the conclusion, with Kubler, that these and other redactions of Italian or French Renaissance architecture worldwide are 'just another example of the flat pattern and prolixity which characterize provincial or rural designs everywhere in the world.'[61] But one culture's planimetricism is not always the same as another's. Let us observe how this works in two examples from the missions.

Although any artist unfamiliar or unsympathetic with three-dimensional pictorial effects will produce adaptations of Western European art that appear planimetric, planimetric art produced by Nahua carvers in New Spain is obviously not the same thing as planimetric art by Visayans from the Philippines. The similarities are striking but deceptive. As an example, let us compare two contemporary treatments of the same image, Our Lady of the Immaculate Conception, by sculptors from Southern India or Sri Lanka (fig. 5) and Guaraní sculptors from Paraguay (fig. 6). Both statues differ from their European model – most likely an engraving – by making its naturalistic, irregular pose and features more rigid and symmetrical. The three dimensions suggested by the print are also made flatter and two-dimensional. We could argue that they did this solely because they misunderstood European canons of representation. We can also suggest, however, that both cultures did so because their own stylistic traditions favoured a more symmetrical, linear treatment of representation – in the case of the Indians, it was the strongly iconic tradition of Hindu and Buddhist sculpture, and among the Guaraní, it was non-figural geometric patterns which flourished in ceramics, basketry, and body painting.

If we look closely, we find that the treatment differs accordingly. The Indian ivory carvers arranged hair and other body parts in a more schematic way than was usual in European art of the period, but they still allowed a certain degree of naturalism to persist. This naturalism is especially apparent in the drapery, which clings to the body and reveals the forms underneath, despite the somewhat linear treatment of the individual folds, a legacy inherited ultimately from classical Greece in the days of Alexander the Great. They also continued to give their figures the wide shoulders, subtle curves, narrow waist, almond eyes, double chin, and solidity that are recognizable features of Hindu and Buddhist statuary of the period.[62] The Guaraní image has straighter and bolder lines, and is more strictly geometrical and less naturalistic, especially in the drapery, which dissolves into a riot of jagged, two-dimensional zig-zag patterns. Non-Christian Guaraní art, unlike the art of India or Sri Lanka, avoided figural representation, so that we cannot relate the facial and body features to indigenous traditions in the same way. Nevertheless, they do at the very least recall the symmetry, interest in surface patterns, and static nature of pre- and post-contact Guaraní visual arts, which were often dominated by zig-zag motifs (see chapter 6 and fig. 82). On a more obvious level, as with many Guaraní statues, the face of the figure has been adapted to Amerindian physiognomy. In conclusion, therefore, while both sculptures are, strictly speaking, 'provincial' – compared to their European models – and both cultures have interpreted their models in similar, planimetric ways, it is also possible to trace both of them to completely unrelated indigenous traditions. They are therefore both a dialect of the same language – here, Late Renaissance art – but they are simultaneously in dialogue with their own cultural traditions.

Art historians – again primarily in the field of Mexican colonial art – have developed more detailed terms to describe intercultural exchange on the level of individual images and motifs. Realizing that in any situation of acculturation it is very rare for a symbol belonging to one culture to be accepted by another without a change in meaning, scholars such as Kubler and Jeanette Favrot Peterson have labelled the transformations that inevitably occur in hybrid art.[63] These often complex models can be reduced for our purposes to three main phenomena, the first of which involves no interaction: juxtaposition, convergence, and syncretism. Juxtaposition is the rare exception when a motif from one culture, say an Aztec speech volute or toponymic glyph, turns up alongside European symbols in post-contact art (e.g., a Mexican conventual mural or colonial map) with little or no change in its original meaning. This usually happens on a 'marginal' level (e.g., in ornamental borders) where it supposedly is reduced to the level of decoration and has little bearing on the main subject of the artwork. I will add two caveats to this hypothesis. First, while the symbol's meaning may not change for the indigenous artists who painted it, it would have been different for the other half of its audience: the friars. Meaning, after all, is in the eye of the beholder, and both sides interpreted it according to their own traditions. Second, what is 'marginal' or not also depends on the viewer. In the sculpture of the Paraguay reductions, for example, or religious painting of seventeenth-century Cuzco, the 'ornamental' aspects of an image may have been as important to the indigenous audience as the image itself was to its European or *criollo* patrons.[64] Since the pre-contact Inca and Guaraní had less interest in figural imagery than, say, a Nahua, they naturally were more concerned with what a European would call 'surface decoration.'[65] It was therefore precisely in these apparently superficial aspects of a work of art that indigenous artists could encode often very complex statements of alliance, identity, and belief, which could interact closely with the main image(s).

Convergence and syncretism can involve a blending of both form and meaning. Convergence can occur when both cultures have a very similar interpretation of a single image; for example, the Islamic and Christian understanding of Jesus as a saintly man who devoted his life to charity and asceticism. Nevertheless, the meanings are rarely exactly the same – Jesus, for example, is the Son of God for Christians and merely the Breath of God for Muslims – and these subtler differences (Bhabha's 'slippages') are often more significant and difficult to detect than more obvious ones. Not only is convergence possible for individual motifs, but it can also involve entire themes; for example, the Heavenly Host, which has similar but not identical connotations for Islamic Sufism and early modern Catholicism. It is useful when one culture wants to perpetuate a comparable but nevertheless different tradition within the framework of another's.

In the case of cultures with no shared history at all, such as the Spanish and Tagalog, convergence is purely coincidental; hence, Kubler's term 'accidental convergence.'[66] Accidental convergence can also involve form as well as meaning. One example of accidental convergence in art can be found by comparing an eighteenth-century statue of Saint Michael and the devil carved on the reductions in Paraguay (fig. 7) with an eighth-century Chinese Buddhist Tomb Guardian trampling on a demon (fig. 8), both of which are of a common type and demonstrate very similar themes of the victory of Good over Evil. The martial costume, flowing scarves, bent head, and forceful gesture of the principal figures, both of whom originally held a lance in their right hands – but above all the hideous demons being crushed at their feet – make these two images look as if they belonged to the same iconography. Yet – the Jesuits in China notwithstanding – I have very strong doubts that the Guaraní sculptors, or the European artists who inspired them, would have had any knowledge of Buddhist sculpture. This coincidence should serve as a warning for us to use caution when tracing stylistic influences in hybrid works of art – the kind of caution that would have been salutary for those who sought to derive Mayan art from Asian roots, the pyramids of Teotihuacan from ancient Egypt, or the Nazca lines of Peru from UFOs.

Syncretism, which overlaps with convergence, refers to the incorporation of elements from one culture into another. This process can involve a fusion of forms and meaning that is very hard to discern. In Syncretism, the same image can have quite different meanings and resonances for two cultures – Cecilia Klein calls it 'visual bilingualism,' and Jill Leslie Furst uses the term 'parallel reading.'[67] Syncretism was a problem for the early Jesuits in China, for example, since the Catholic image of the Madonna was so close to the Bodhisattva of Mercy, Guanyin, that the two were immediately confused (fig. 46). Syncretism is another very useful tool for encoding covert alternative meanings into a work of art; for example, when the Cuzco school of painters in seventeenth-century Peru mass-produced images of the Virgin Mary, which some believe make references to a variety of pre-conquest Andean holy figures and concepts.[68] Nevertheless, very little 'purity' survives when two cultures amalgamate, and syncretism tends more often to involve the fusion of two similar images into a new one with a truly hybrid meaning, enriching it and allowing for a creative ambivalence. Hybrid art's seamlessness is precisely its strength. For example, a rural Mexican titular saint can be perceived by its community simultaneously as a symbol of local pride with pre-conquest roots and as an exotic figure from a foreign culture.[69]

We should perhaps spend less time trying to categorize motifs as European and non-European, and devote our energies instead to exploring their very hybridity. After all, we are travelling in murky waters (just think of the Guardian figure). In many cases, motifs that look distinctly indigenous can also be traced to lesser-known European sources. Take, for example, the motif of separated locks of hair radiating down the shoulders and back of a saint, which is a common feature of Indo-Portuguese ivories and Paraguayan reduction sculpture (fig. 100). Some scholars see this motif as a reflection of indigenous style, particularly among the Guaraní, where it is related to plant motifs in traditional ceramics or basketry. But these strands of hair are also a common feature of sixteenth- and seventeenth-century Iberian statues of the Virgin Mary. Certainly the strands themselves are more geometrical and tendril-like in the Guaraní version than either the Indian or European examples, but the Spanish or Portuguese source must be considered. The European source does not negate the indigenous ones, but it does show how confusing cultural amalgamation can be and how careful we must be when tracing the sources even of individual motifs.

So far we have been talking about an interaction between two cultures. But restricting dialogue to two cultures, with its echoes of *Volkgeist,* is an oversimplification. Complex divisions exist within cultures along lines of caste, class, sex, and religion. The Aztec state, for example, was a notoriously heterogeneous society, with a myriad of horizontal divisions between regional groups and a rigid vertical division between the Aztec nobility and the Nahua peasantry. The citizenry of the Mughal Empire included Sunni and Shi'a Muslims, Hindus, Jains, and Zoroastrians, and they were divided according to two alien class systems: the medieval Islamic organization into nobility, clergy, and peasantry; and the traditional Hindu caste system. The same, of course, goes for the other side. The term 'European' is no more specific than the term 'Indian,' and considering the squabbling and competition that divided settlers from governors, European-born from *criollo*, and even regular clergy (friars) from secular clergy (bishops and parish priests), there should be little wonder that they did not present a uniform audience. Even a single order, such as the Jesuits, comprised a variety of ethnic and social backgrounds – not to mention, ideological attitudes. This heterogeneity characterizes and enlivens mission art, even within a single mission. It also makes it very hard to assign dates to artworks and even to suggest lines of influence.

Keeping in mind the complexity of artistic convergence, we should look for a moment at the issue of copying, which is central to art production on the overseas missions. Every single Jesuit mission, as well as every single Franciscan, Dominican, Mercedarian, and Augustinian mission before them, produced and taught art by copying. Usually the models were European engravings – the vast majority were Flemish – but they also included paintings, sculptures, and *bozzetti* (wax or clay models). Sometimes, images were copied faithfully in their entirety, with the occasional added twist or flourish; sometimes several models were merged into new compositions; and elsewhere creative new works were produced which departed so far from their models that they were barely recognizable. Artists were taught by painting directly over the engraving like a paint-by-numbers, or by tracing them using ocular devices, pouncing, or translucent paper, until they had gained the requisite skills to produce copies freehand; they enlarged them with graph paper, provided them with brilliant colours, reversed them at will, and even gave them three dimensions in bas-relief carving or sculpture. Although life-drawing had become standard for artists in Europe by the turn of the sixteenth century, there is virtually no evidence for life-drawing on the missions. Of the two exceptions – the Jesuit mission in Mughal India and the work of the Italian painter Castiglione in China – both derived from Asian traditions, not European ones. Even buildings usually followed, to greater or lesser degree, models in printed architectural treatises, such as those by Serlio, Alberti, Vitruvius, and Vredeman de Vries, which were known from the earliest period in missions throughout Asia and the Americas.[70] It is these shared sources which gave them their remarkable unity and not, as one scholar suggests, a 'classicizing collective memory.'[71]

But if they are copies, does this make them second-rate art, as many would have it? The two categories are not necessarily interchangeable. For one thing, copying, including the copying of engravings, was standard workshop practice in Renaissance Europe, and masters from Mantegna to Annibale Carracci borrowed figures, settings, and sometimes entire compositions from earlier artists. In Spain and Portugal, the very same Flemish engravings found on the overseas missions were commonly used as models.[72] Even Velázquez and El Greco used these engravings for iconography and composition – although not for style. It was what one did with the copy that was important, since copying was always considered an interpretation.

Between the sixteenth and eighteenth centuries, Iberian artists were ranked according to their degree of independence from their engraved original models, with the lesser artists producing nothing but exact copies, the better ones making pastiches out of various engravings, and the best producing works of great originality only loosely inspired by the models.[73] These three levels of copying were codified by the Sevillian painter and art theorist Francisco Pacheco (1564–1654) in his hugely influential manual for painters entitled *Arte de la Pintura* (1649).[74] Style, on the other hand, was considered a separate entity (stylistically, for example, Velázquez was more influenced by studying original Titians than Flemish engravings),[75] so that a copy of the same image by two artists would reflect their own personalities yet still remain faithful to the subject and composition of the original. This is precisely what happens when artists from non-European cultures interpret European models. When they add to the formula their own art traditions, along with the complex potential for amalgamation hinted at in the preceding paragraphs, 'copying' in reference to mission art becomes a hopelessly inadequate term. The people of the world reacted to the challenge of Euro-Christian representation in original and creative ways deriving from a rich range of cultural traditions and personal idiosyncracies.

Myths and Topoi about Mission Art

Some of the motivations which drove mendicant foundations in the early sixteenth century, and Jesuit efforts in the later sixteenth to eighteenth centuries, engendered myths and detrimental attitudes about the nature of non-European societies that would persist throughout the early modern period in mission areas around the globe. Some of these myths, recounted by chroniclers of the time, relate directly to the visual arts – particularly those concerning the mental capacities of Amerindians and other non-European peoples – and these topoi continue to cloud our view of mission art today. I call them 'topoi' because, like topoi in the biographies of antiquity, they were not intended by their writers to recount a factual event, but were used as a rhetorical device to further an argument. Like the episodes in ancient artists' lives elicited by Vasari and other Renaissance writers to underscore the genius of their modern subjects, these 'urban myths' are remarkably consistent over time and place.[76] Some of them may even derive directly from the same Plinian sources mined by these Renaissance biographers. But first let us look at the wider ideological climate from which they derived.

The very foundations of mission work in the Indies were built on millennialist and Early Christian ideology. It is well known that the early friars, especially in New Spain and Peru, undertook the task of converting the newly discovered peoples of America in a spirit of millennialism.[77] Driven by a utopian vision that considered the Amerindians to be one of the ten lost tribes of Israel – who through their naïvety and simplicity were uniquely free of the sins of Western society – the friars understood their missionary work primarily as a preparation for the Second Coming. They also saw their spiritual conquest in terms of the Early Church. Like early Christians, they believed they were waging a courageous battle for Christ with the numerical odds stacked against them. Anxious to draw parallels with the heroism of those early days, the friars even used some of the earlier techniques, most notably the replacement of pagan rites and ritual sites with Christian ones.[78] They drew direct parallels with the Christian past, especially by linking the legends of the apostles Thomas and Bartholomew – both of whom are traditionally believed to have travelled to the Indies – with similar indigenous tales such as the Aztec story of Quetzalcóatl, the Inca myth of Viracocha, the Tupí-Guaraní tale of Zumé/Sumé, or the South Indian legend of Saint Thomas, to legitimize their activities. The same spirit of the Early Church inspired the Jesuits in China, where they saw the Middle Kingdom as equivalent to the Greco-Roman world of Saint Paul. Especially relevant for the arts was the mendicants' construction of churches on three- or five-aisled plans to emulate early Christian basilicas, a phenomenon characteristic of many of the earliest missions throughout the New World and Asia, and also relatable to a palaeochristian revival in Rome at the end of the sixteenth century (fig. 9).[79] In most cases, however, only the plan of these modest churches was worthy of the exalted term 'basilican.'

Although this expectant spirit inspired the friars to make pioneering experiments with acculturation, it also had the deleterious effect of encouraging them to think of their charges as simpletons. The perception of Amerindians as 'children barely capable of reason,'[80] and therefore *tabulae rasae* for conversion, led ecclesiastics and colonists alike to treat them in a patronizing and paternalistic manner – despite early Franciscan advances in mission education by such men as Archbishop Zumárraga and Bishop Quiroga of New Spain.[81] Although theologians had advanced beyond the 'Natural Slave Theory,' by which intellectuals had used Aristotle to justify Amerindian slavery, the image persisted that the indigenous people of the Americas were eternal neophytes and spiritual minors.[82] Of course, preserving their charges' status as neophytes also legitimized the missionaries' custody over them, a legality which I will return to shortly. One of the most devastating notions, deriving from the Europeans' poor knowledge of the languages of the New World, was that Amerindians were unable to think abstractly and incapable of creativity or imagination.[83] As a consequence, for example, Amerindians were banned from the priesthood, and early Franciscan attempts to educate them in the high humanist tradition were abandoned (the latter action often being as a response to stern denunciations and threats from colonial officials).[84]

Many Jesuits inherited this detrimental attitude toward the indigenous peoples of America, even after they had learned from their Asian missions how advanced non-European societies could be and had fought with the Patronate for the right to train indigenous priests in their missions and colleges.[85] Inheriting cultural bigotry from contemporary theologians who considered cities and written languages to be the hallmarks of civilization, they divided the peoples of the world into 'white' (Europe, China, Japan, and the great Muslim empires), and 'black' (Amerindians, Filipinos, Indonesians, Indians, Africans).[86] Typical is this remark by the Jesuit Visitor to Asia Alessandro Valignano, who wrote that since the Hindus of India are 'negroes and poorly talented people, great difficulty is experienced in fostering the faith and making good Christians of them.'[87] Even when Jesuit leaders fought for the rights of Amerindians, they did so in a paternalistic spirit, fighting for their right to live independently from colonial exploitation but under Jesuit custody.[88] However, this was only official policy. Some of the greatest Jesuit missionaries, such as Acosta and Roberto de Nobili, demonstrated the deepest reverence for the 'black' races, and as we shall see in subsequent chapters, day-today Jesuit activities in missions worldwide betray a much more tolerant attitude that went on under the guise of orthodoxy.

The main topoi relating to the visual arts of the missions will appear over and over through the course of this book. The most prevalent tells of indigenous people dazzled by the artifice of European pictorial realism. In Japan, Mughal India, China, and throughout Latin America, Jesuit missionaries eagerly related how their paintings, usually of the Madonna, caused great excitement – *tutti stupiti*[89] – and drew huge crowds when they were exhibited. Always taking care to note that this was the first time the indigenous people had ever seen the wonders of Renaissance realism, chroniclers describe the near miraculous effect these pictures had on their audience. In fact, these events are often described literally as *maraviglie*,[90] and their supernatural quality is often further enhanced by the fact that the images happened to be of an *acheiropoieton* (such as portraits of the Virgin after Saint Luke). There is almost always a chief or king who falls to his knees and asks the missionaries to lend him the image so that he can show his wife or mother, and then inevitably asks for a copy to be made by his finest court artist. Nobles and commoners alike are always moved to devotion and even conversion by a mere gaze at the holy image. Everyone makes the same remarks about how it looks like a 'mirror,' or a 'sculpture,' or that the eyes seem to move and follow the viewer as he walks around the room.

There is more than a shade of Pliny's Apelles legends here, in substance as well as name, especially those involving paintings that look so lifelike that they fool the birds or other artists into thinking they are real. Everywhere the message is the same: Alberti's perspective and Leonardo's naturalism are capable of working miracles, and their rationalism transmits Christian truth.[91] These stories also serve conveniently to underscore what many believed to be the simplistic, childlike level of understanding of non-European peoples. While in certain cases it was no doubt true that non-Europeans seeing Renaissance naturalism for the first time were intrigued and even amazed by it – this was certainly the case in Mughal India – and while sources in non-European languages show that Apelles-like metaphors were sometimes actually used (the Chinese themselves wrote about 'mirrors'), it is also suspicious that similar stories turn up everywhere. In the case of China, one scholar asks whether Jesuit chroniclers 'are not somewhat mistaken, and whether [the Jesuits] did not accept as proof of profound admiration compliments which Chinese politesse lavishes voluntarily.'[92]

Related to this myth, but far more injurious to the scholarly assessment of mission art, is the topos of the slavish copyist. Over and over again, Franciscan and Jesuit missionaries write in their personal correspondence and annual letters that the indigenous artists working on their missions are incapable of artistic creativity.[93] Whether writing about the Japanese, Chinese, Mughals, Goans, or Guaraní, chroniclers uniformly claim that indigenous artists have no capacity for imagination or originality, and confine themselves to making exacting but derivative copies of European engravings and paintings. If they are left unsupervised, or stray ever so little from their models, they fall into error. The flip side to this myth is the topos about the Rubens of the jungle. The same reports that belittle indigenous imaginations make extravagant claims about the technical skills of these artists. Jesuit and other sources recount the miraculous abilities of these natural men to ape the work of Michelangelo, Rubens, or even Apelles himself.[94] The ultimate test of indigenous aptitude, according to these writers, is to place their work against the originals of those great masters (by which they usually mean engravings), a test which they performed with remarkable regularity from the Japanese castle of Sawa to the Paraguayan mission at Yapeyú.

If these sound suspiciously like further incarnations of the '*tabula rasa*' myth, it is because they are. As I hope to show in this book, the art itself presents irrefutable evidence not only that these artists were among the most creative of their day, but that their work draws deeply upon indigenous traditions in the fine arts, and often bears very little stylistic resemblance at all to the work of Italian or Flemish masters (not to mention, ancient Greek ones). The slavish copyist myth relates to Plato, who considered the artist an 'instrument of the deity,'[95] a mere imitator of nature, mentally inferior to the poet. It also perpetuates the notion of simple natives, and does so by relating them to a stage of copying discussed by art theorists like Pacheco as only fit for beginners or persons of little skill. The Rubens-of-the-jungle story, of course, directly recalls the Apelles legends. It also relates to another common classical topos in which a young 'wild' boy, often a shepherd, is discovered to have miraculous gifts in the fine arts (Vasari, for example, uses this story about Giotto). Who could be wilder in the European imagination than a 'savage' from the New World or the Orient?

Even though they perpetuated these and similar stories, the Jesuits were almost certainly aware of what was really going on and even encouraged their artists' creative and acculturative abilities. Once again, they were saying one thing and doing another. Why the disparity? It may have been a simple case of difference between theory and practice. Nevertheless, I believe that they were also trying to placate the authorities in colonial centres and Europe. Jesuit acculturation efforts were extremely controversial and were frequently used as fodder for their enemies. The missionaries were justifiably sensitive about advertising their methods too freely in such a hostile climate. José de Acosta warned in his handbook for Jesuit missionaries: 'Above all, we must do everything we can not to appear odious to the parish priests [i.e., secular clergy], whether it be through an excessive display of zeal, or by taking on the role of impertinent reformers or critics.'[96] The Society also played two very different roles in Europe and abroad. In the courts and colleges of Europe and in colonial centres, it was a defender of orthodoxy and often worked closely with the Inquisition, while in the outer-circle missions it was on the cutting edge of accommodation.[97] Therefore, missionaries were wisely reticent even to their superiors, especially considering how widely circulated the annual letters were among Jesuits and non-Jesuits alike.

Finally, we must remember that these processes of accommodation were by no means entirely in Jesuit hands; in fact, the missionaries were merely allowing the inescapable and inevitable to happen, a piece of news which would not have sat well with their European superiors. Ultimately, the cultural partnership was on the natives' terms, and the Jesuits knew it. It is as if they constantly had to remind themselves out loud that everything was going well; as Bhabha remarks about Anglican missionaries in nineteenth-century India, 'the colonialist is an exhibitionist, because his *preoccupation* with security makes him "remind the native out loud that he is master."'[98] But here it is not the natives the Jesuits are reminding, so much as their superiors. To admit the truth would have been to admit that European culture was not inherently superior. And although many Jesuit missionaries were able to live with that fact, to their audiences in Europe it would have been nothing short of blasphemy. From their distant outposts, the missionaries of the Society of Jesus applied the same care that they used in navigating the rivers of the outback to negotiating the murky waters of dogma.

The Precursors: Outer-Circle Missions before the Jesuits

In the formative years of the Iberian empires, little distance separated the inner- and outer-circle missions.[99] With colonial towns only in their infancy, nearly all mission enterprises were by definition peripheral. Mendicant orders, beginning usually with the Franciscans, were awarded monopolies over large geographic regions, and suffered little interference from either the civil government or the few colonists who had yet appeared on the scene. In fact, the special status of these missions was supported by crown law.[100] In the Spanish and Portuguese empires, missions among the indigenous people (called *doctrinas* in Spanish and *aldeias* in Portuguese) did not fall under the jurisdiction of local bishops but were directly answerable to the Pope, so that they had a greater degree of independence from the Patronate than parish priests.[101] They were also free from parish tithes. And in practice, the farther away the missions were from the colonial centres of control, the less they had to worry about Patronate interference.

Theoretically, *doctrinas*, as opposed to parishes or inner-circle missions, were responsible only for neophytes who still required constant supervision in their faith. As early as 1503, a Spanish royal decree argued that Amerindians had to be settled into such villages, so that the civilized lifestyle (often referred to as *policía*) deemed necessary for salvation could be inculcated in them.[102] The most symbolically significant features of these settlements were the church (or, more specifically, the bell, since churches took time to build) and holy pictures. In fact, the 1512 Laws of Burgos specifically declared that even *encomenderos* had to provide their charges not only with a church with a bell but with 'images of our Lady.'[103]

Doctrinas also had the advantage, for the friars, of being more conveniently administered – or exploited – especially if they were located near colonial settlements requiring cheap labour. In the Spanish Empire, *doctrinas* were also known as *congregaciones* (congregations, common in New Spain) or *reducciones* (reductions, common in Spanish South America), a term later used explicitly in the codification of Spanish imperial law called Recopilación de los leyes de Indias (1680).[104] Many of the first reductions were founded on the shores of Lake Titicaca under Viceroy Toledo (1561–81), a leading proponent of peripheral missions (fig. 2).[105]

Although missiology before the eighteenth century had not yet been reduced to a standardized science – missionaries simply made pragmatic responses to the situation at hand – most *doctrinas* or *aldeias* were founded in a similar manner, aptly described as 'ceremonial games.'[106] In the Spanish Empire (and similarly in Portuguese territories), these games took on a standard form. First, scouts would select an existing indigenous village as the *cabecera*, or head, of the *doctrina*, which would have jurisdiction over smaller settlements called *visitas*. *Visitas* also each possessed a small chapel and a house for the priest. The missionaries would then enter the non-Christian area (a procedure known as the *entrada*), bearing trinkets, metal tools, and artworks to entice the indigenous people to join their new settlements in what Charles Polzer calls 'a kind of social seduction.'[107] Especially important were large oil paintings and statues (e.g., the ubiquitous images of the Virgin Mary as 'conquistador') which missionaries paraded about in overtly triumphant processions. They also often brought maps to show how far they had come to save their charges' souls, as did Matteo Ricci in China. Very symbolic was the erection of monumental crosses to mark the new missions; for example, in Japan and all over Latin America. In Jesuit missions to literate civilizations such as China and Mughal India, artworks were often augmented with books, which included volumes on rhetoric, European history, and even art and architecture, in addition to the expected bibles, catechisms, and sermons. After this came the *conversión* (conversion), when the non-Christians attained the status of neophytes. In Latin America, the most enthusiastic of the converts were awarded with titles such as *fiscal* (petty official) or *temastian* (catechist), often together with economic benefits as well. During the final stage, the *doctrina* proper, indigenous officials under the leadership of a *cacique* (a Caribbean term for chief) were made responsible for temporal affairs, including corporal punishment, thereby often clearing the missionaries of any direct involvement in the unpopular matter of social discipline.[108]

Since many of the first outer-circle missions in Asia and Latin America were Franciscan foundations, the first efforts at acculturation also came from that order. These hesitant attempts at cultural borrowing began with language. A furious debate raged in the early Spanish Empire about the use of indigenous languages in mission work (in contrast, the colonial Portuguese simply imposed Portuguese or pidgin-Portuguese on their charges).[109] Most missionaries believed, with Saint Augustine, that a mastery of pagan languages and even oratory was necessary to make an effective impression on mission populations.[110] Most colonists, by contrast, saw the encouragement of indigenous languages as a subversion of Spanish or Portuguese authority and legitimacy, and eventually they prevailed – at least in the areas under their direct control.[111] But during the sixteenth century, and later in outlying regions, serious language study continued. Franciscan and Dominican friars wrote grammars and dictionaries in languages such as Nahuatl, Quechua, Aymara, Tagalog, and Chinese which served as models for later missions worldwide.[112] Even more remarkable were early attempts at incorporating indigenous rhetoric, pantomime, and drama into Christian ritual, plays, and processionals. The first Franciscans in New Spain, for example, adapted elements of Aztec religious plays for their own sacred performances, featuring indigenous traditions of singing, dancing, and puppetry, and even employed native playwrights to help write them.[113] There were even attempts to harness the grandeur of indigenous prayer, as in Peru, where the Franciscan friar Luis Jerónimo Oré tried to employ invocations written by the Inca Pachacuti in Christian worship – admittedly a short-lived exercise.[114]

Artistic acculturation also originated in language. In New Spain, since Aztec glyphs were at once writing and imagery, the Franciscans relied from the beginning on indigenous art to communicate with the Nahua people.[115] Treating glyphs like a *biblia pauperum* ('poor man's bible') as defined by the Second Nicene Council (787), they created an artificial language of symbols, which they used to compose documents known as Testerian Catechisms. They devised combinations of native glyphs to spell out words like *Pater Noster* or *Amen*, for example, believing – naïvely – that Aztec glyphs were a phonetic script.[116] We have already seen these glyphs and other Aztec motifs appear in early colonial mission art. A similar method was used over a century later by Jesuit missionaries in the Upper Amazon.[117]

The friars did not just accommodate to symbols, as in these linguistic experiments, or styles, as in the conventual murals or carvings referred to as *tequitqui*. They also accommodated to indigenous media, which were sometimes profoundly meaningful to the Nahua. One example is the production of religious sculpture using a combination of corn pith, paper, and wood. These lightweight images of Christ and the saints were eminently suitable for use in processions, but the use of corn probably also referred to pre-conquest religious symbolism.[118] Another remarkable adaptation of indigenous media involves the Aztec art of featherwork. Featherwork was a highly skilled, painstaking, and expensive process, which had been greatly prized by the Aztecs.[119] Aztec royal houses even maintained special aviaries to raise the exotic birds needed to farm these feathers. Nahua featherworkers, called *amanteca*, wove or glued feathers onto a piece of *papel de amate* in a mosaic so that they overlapped like roof tiles to produce patterns. After the fall of Tenochtitlán in 1521, the aviaries and *amanteca* were shut down, but only a few years later the Franciscans hired the same workers in their own feather workshops to produce Christian liturgical costume as well as pictures. The new feather paintings, extremely detailed copies of Flemish engravings in brilliant colours and occasionally signed by the master featherworkers, had the breathtaking beauty and delicacy of their pre-conquest counterparts (fig. 10). The Franciscans' intention was also to share in the prestige enjoyed by such featherwork in its pre-conquest context.

Architectural acculturation also derived from Early Christian practices. The earliest missionaries and secular clergy frequently built their churches directly on top of temple foundations (this was common in New Spain, Peru, and elsewhere), taking their cue from Gregory the Great, who advocated building churches in or on top of pagan temples in England in 621.[120] The Franciscans and other mendicant orders may also have directly borrowed architectural elements from Aztec structures, including temples, although this remains a hotly debated issue among scholars.[121] At least the basic idea of outdoor worship, natural to the Nahua and unusual for Western Europeans, was probably encouraged by Aztec practices. Missionaries in Peru also built churches with large open-air patios on high prominences like Andean temples (fig. 11), and some of the same ideas and structures were taken up later in Paraguay and Japan by the Jesuits. It was as if, over the years, the missionaries began to formulate a composite idea of what a 'pagan' temple should look like, regardless of region. Recent work on Peru has suggested that this composite temple type, at least by the eighteenth century, may also owe something to imagery related to the Temple of Jerusalem that was very popular at the time.[122]

In the Philippines, friars and Jesuits alike adopted an architectural form related to pre-conquest religion. Their first churches took the form of the *simbahan*, the rectangular house of a village chief augmented by a temporary shed on each side during the annual *mag-aanitos* festival, thus neatly merging with the iconography of the Early Christian basilica.[123] This felicitous employment of 'accidental convergence' was also possible in Japan, where, as we shall see, the Jesuits adapted the rectangular Buddhist worship-hall, or *hondō*, with the addition of flanking reception parlours, or *zashiki* – again, conveniently recalling three-aisled basilicas.

Architectural acculturation was not always limited to the peripheral missions. It could even happen in more heavily colonized areas, as long as the artists were recruited from the hinterlands. This was the case, for example, in Goa and the other outposts of Portuguese India, where indigenous craftsmen were brought in from outlying regions (in Asia, such places were never far away). There, artists commonly incorporated designs from local Hinduism into church furniture, retables, and even façades, while Hindu communities near the border borrowed European forms and techniques to build their own temples in the seventeenth and eighteenth centuries, one of which, the Shri Manguesh Temple at Priol, is more than slightly reminiscent of the Piazza dei Miracoli in Pisa (fig. 12).[124]

Art education was also introduced into the very first mendicant missions in the New World, and involved a certain degree of hybridization at the earliest period – sometimes unconsciously, sometimes covertly, and sometimes with the tacit approval of the *maestros*. At the same time they were founding colleges to bring Erasmian humanism to the sons of Aztec nobles in Texcoco (1523) and Tlatelolco (1536), Franciscans such as Pedro de Gante and Juan de Zumárraga established modest schools for musicians, craftsmen, and artists in Mexico City (San José de los Naturales, 1526) and at the school in Tlatelolco, training a new generation of image makers.[125] The same thing happened in South America a few decades later, where colleges and ateliers were founded in Lima, Quito, and Bogotá to instruct indigenous children in Christianity, Spanish, and a trade.[126] The Colegio de San Andrés in Quito (1549), founded by Fray Jodoco Ricke, for example, gave training in carpentry and masonary, as well as in other practical trades. Although the methods used at these early art ateliers have yet to be studied (if they can be discovered at all), it is possible to deduce from extant religious art of the period that engravings and other European models formed the foundation of their training.

After the cities grew and the countryside became dominated by colonial estates, the original missions lost their peripheral status, along with their ability to act freely. Their position was often further undermined, as in New Spain, by a devastating loss of indigenous congregations to plagues, labour in mines, and other horrors imported by Europeans. A common fate for these *doctrinas* once they had been swallowed up by European settlement was to be converted into parishes, with control handed over to the bishops – and the Patronate. This process was made especially easy in the Spanish Empire by a document called Cédula general del patronazgo (1573), Philip II's codification of the power of the Patronate, which sought to make religious orders subservient to bishops and viceroys.[127] Any spirit of acculturative experimentation that had existed was usually extinguished by the orthodoxy of the secular clergy. Reorganized to meet the demands of their new colonial, urban environment, missionary orders came to resemble more closely their metropolitan counterparts in Europe.

One vital contribution of mendicant orders in the more colonial environment of the inner-circle missions was higher education. Throughout the colonial centres of Asia and Latin America, the mendicant orders founded colleges to serve colonial society. The Jesuits would come to dominate this field, devoting equal time to colonial colleges and their outer-circle mission enterprises. Jesuit foundations such as San Pablo in Lima (fig. 13), or the Colleges of São Paulo in Goa and Macao (figs. 44, 73), ranked among the greatest institutions of higher learning outside of Europe. San Pablo (1568–1767), the first Jesuit college in South America, played a central role in colonial and even mission life in the region. It served as a training ground for missionaries, held classes and published grammars in the Quechua and Aymara languages, and had one of the premier libraries in South America; as well, its pharmacy was an internationally renowned centre for pharmacological research. The college hosted a series of controversial debates defending the rights of Amerindians (although in the paternalistic sense of the day), and even enrolled Amerindian and African students before finally bowing to colonial pressure in the seventeenth century. Like many inner-circle missions, San Pablo served what we might call 'inner city' congregations; for example, the community of Angolan slaves, who lived in a suburb of Lima, even producing the first grammar and dictionary of the Angolan languages. Although this book concentrates on their peripheral missions, we must not forget this equally important branch of Jesuit overseas activity.

After the first outer-circle missions were incorporated into parishes (which occurred in many colonial centres toward the end of the sixteenth century), new peripheral foundations were established beyond the constantly advancing border of the colonial world. In the late sixteenth and early seventeenth centuries, there began a second major penetration of indigenous territory, into regions that were hundreds of miles beyond colonial settlement. By the eighteenth century in the Americas, these included California, Texas, and New Mexico, eastern Bolivia, the upper Orinoco in Venezuela, the upper Amazon, and Paraguay, and included Franciscans and now also Jesuits.[128] In Asia the process began slightly earlier, in the sixteenth century, and came to include China, Japan, Persia, Central Asia, Tibet, Madurai and Mughal India, and the Filipino Visayas. Here the Jesuits were more dominant, although the Franciscans were also active.

Appearing on the scene much later, the Jesuits had the luxury of hindsight. They took over the role of revolutionary innovators at the same time that the Franciscans lost their momentum. The Franciscans apparently never regained the Utopianism, zeal for experimentation, or high intellectualism that had marked their earliest enterprises in the New World. Partly, this change in attitude was the result of the tightening grip of the Patronate, to whom Franciscans were more directly answerable even in places like Paraguay and Japan. In Japan they even infamously served as the vanguard for a Spanish invasion plot (see chapter 3). But the mendicants also lost their taste for the humanist educational tradition of their forebears. After their arrival in New Spain in 1572, for example, the Jesuits revived the study of Nahua culture and religion, even allowing public performances of indigenous religious festivals, yet the Franciscans were now seemingly reluctant to explore such 'hybrid religious forms.'[129] And, as we shall see in this book, the Jesuits redoubled their efforts to acculturate throughout Asia and the Americas, going further than any of their predecessors had done before them.

Two randomly chosen comparisons of Jesuit and mendicant missions from the early eighteenth century show how great the division had become between the two orders' mission methods by this time. An independent report on Franciscan and Jesuit efforts in the peripheral lands of northern New Spain in 1715 illuminates the disparity between the approaches of the two orders.[130] The inspector, Don Pedro Tapís, Bishop of Durango, found the Jesuit missions better run and cleaner than those of their Franciscan neighbours, with more prosperous revenues and a stronger sense of communal spirit. Most significantly, the people on the Jesuit missions were much better educated. While the Jesuits continued to promote indigenous languages, the Franciscans lost interest in them after their initial *entrada* and resorted to Spanish or the nearest lingua franca. The same was true of the contemporary Franciscan missions in the Peruvian central *montaña*, whose personnel stayed relatively briefly among the Campa people compared to their Jesuit counterparts in the region, and were unable effectively to minister to the community.[131] On top of everything, the Jesuits did all of this with an average of only two fathers per mission in contrast to the Franciscans' fully staffed convents. While I hesitate to make a blanket statement about the inferiority of Franciscan methods after 1600 – the scholarship has not advanced far enough for me to do so – I feel it is safe to say that the Jesuits showed more aptitude for innovation and experimentation than their brethren in other orders, particularly from the 1580s onward. Nevertheless, we must not forget that the young order inherited this very experimentation from their mendicant predecessors.

Some of the methods the Jesuits brought were entirely new, and allowed them to penetrate deeper into the indigenous mind than the Franciscans ever did. One of the most fascinating examples is the Jesuit approach to the dreams and visions experienced by indigenous people. The Jesuits actually sought to acculturate even such amorphous and unpredictable phenomena, experiences which held prime religious importance for many non-European cultures and which often had a strong impact on the arts.[132] Gruzinski characterizes this approach as the 'colonization of the *imaginaire*,' and suggests that it is characteristic of a new post-Tridentine spirituality. The Jesuits were very receptive to the dreams and visions had by the Nahua, many of which they recorded with exacting detail, and they organized their preaching around them. Of course, their aim was still conversion; they provoked their audiences into reliving the dreams of their companions, but then provided standardized reactions and models of interpretation based on Catholic stereotypes, in effect making Nahua dreams into Christian dreams. But this colonization could run both ways, as it appears to have done in Paraguay, where the Jesuits had the same dreams as Guaraní shamans and took careful stock of their meaning and portent. The imagination is a far too volatile thing for even the Jesuits to believe that they could completely control it.

A New Direction in Jesuit Missiology: José de Acosta

The intensification of Jesuit mission efforts, resulting in increased acculturation and a higher standard in mission arts, began with the work of one man in Peru: José de Acosta (1540–1600).[133] Known as the 'Pliny of the New World' for his descriptions of the people and geography of the Americas, Acosta was both an active missionary and a prominent theologian at the Jesuit college in Lima. Born in Medina del Campo and trained at the Jesuit college of Alcalá de Henares, Acosta left for Peru in 1571, where he soon became known for his vigorous opposition to the oppression of indigenous peoples by colonial powers. Although he was an academic, and played a leading role in the life of the College of San Pablo in Lima, he was also the leading proponent of peripheral mission work, single-handedly changing Jesuit policy by having new recruits concentrate on the indigenous population. In his grand rhetorical prose, he asked his fellow Jesuits:

> For what have you undertaken such a grand mission, and why have you traversed this long route over land and sea, if you did not want to work for the salvation of the indians? ... If you had desired the salvation of our Spaniards, would it not have been better to stay in Spain and Europe, where there is such a far greater abundance of this merchandise, in both number and rank? ... Your compatriots who have worked such extraordinary wonders in the East Indies, in Malabar, in Malacca, in Hormuz, in the Moluccas, in Ethiopia, in Japan, and in China and further regions of the east have made the world abuzz with their heroic deeds which they refer to in their letters. Could they possibly have achieved such great renown without sweat and great danger? And if you only want to stay in the Spanish cities, if you want to make your abode in Mexico, Lima, or Cuzco, and not in the middle of the indian nations; if you avoid living among the Carangas, Collas, Sacacas, Yauyos and other barbarian provinces; all of your efforts to procure the salvation of the indians will be mere smoke and mirrors. For how do you expect to win a nation for Christ if you do not establish a base there, build a single spiritual fortress, or live there permanently?[134]

It was partly thanks to Acosta's efforts that the first Jesuit reductions were founded, beginning in 1578 with the town of Juli, where the Jesuits took over from the Dominicans in the highly populated Lake Titicaca or Chucuito region (fig. 2). This new direction in missiology was quite a contrast to most earlier efforts by the Society. Although Jesuits had settled into some non-Christian communities in Asia, they had only done so in America and Portuguese Asia on a temporary basis. Unlike the more permanent Franciscan outer-circle missions, Jesuit mission work had consisted of a pair of itinerant fathers who ventured out on temporary assignments from such colonial bases as the Jesuit colleges at Lima, Macao, Manila, and Goa. In Brazil, the only New World region to date where the Jesuits had been the first missionaries (they arrived as early as 1549), the fathers had worked more permanently with indigenous peoples, but they had made the fatal mistake of removing them from peripheral regions. Beginning in the 1550s under José de Anchieta, the so-called Apostle of Brazil, the Jesuits had settled the semi-nomadic Tupí-Guaraní into *aldeias* near colonial centres in the naïve belief that the latter would serve as effective moral exemplars.[135] Not only had this policy been coercive, but it had resulted in the provision of convenient labour pools for Portuguese settlers.

Acosta realized that such efforts were grossly insufficient. After having made several lengthy trips of his own through the Peruvian highlands in the 1570s, where he witnessed ineffective Dominican mission enterprises and the horrors of indigenous labour in the mines, Acosta was ready to overhaul the entire system. As spelled out in his enormously influential mission manual, entitled *De Procuranda Indorum Salute* (1576), Acosta advocated what Claudio Burgaleta calls the 'Theology of Adaptation,'[136] a policy with roots in humanist oratory. He called for missionaries to immerse themselves in indigenous communities, not only physically but intellectually and spiritually. Missionaries were exhorted to learn local languages, customs, and beliefs, and to explain Christianity using native terms: '... it is necessary to find another method of preaching the Gospel that accommodates to the new condition of these nations.'[137] Acosta especially stressed the importance of indigenizing Christianity; he warned that traditional rites and customs must not be obliterated, but should actually be translated into Christian rites and customs: '... regarding those aspects of their culture which do not conflict with the Faith or Justice, I do not believe that it is reasonable to change them.'[138] He backed up his arguments with Plutarch and Saint Gregory the Great. Acosta stressed that only missionaries of the highest calibre were suitable for the overseas missions, a piece of advice that was subsequently taken very seriously by his colleagues: '... no one needs to possess greater skill than those who take upon themselves the task of preaching the Word of God and winning the souls of the infidels – even more so if they are indians, since among them there is so little assistance and so many impediments.'[139] Attitudes like this inspired the Jesuits to send brilliant scientists to the Chinese court and a student of Alessandro Scarlatti to teach music to the Guaraní. It also encouraged them to maintain higher standards in the arts than any other missionary order.[140]

Acosta practised what he preached. His other great work, *Historia natural y moral de las Indias*, was the first history of the indigenous peoples of the New World to be based on empirical knowledge, an impressive statement of his commitment to understanding people who were usually considered – when they were considered at all – as savages or cheap labour.[141] The *Historia* has been called 'a more thoughtful and more thorough account of the Indian world than anything then available,' and shows such a deep understanding of the Amerindian people that it even proposes for the first time that the first tribes came from Asia in the Northwest, which is now generally accepted as the Bering Strait theory (all the more remarkable since neither the Bering Strait nor the American Northwest had even been charted at the time).[142] Although he at first shared the common view in his day that Amerindians were somehow servile by disposition – equivalent to European peasants – Acosta later revised his attitude and declared that they were capable of higher understanding.[143] Acosta also called upon missionaries to use the visual arts to ease the transition to Christian life, especially among non-literate peoples.[144]

Acosta, himself an avid scholar of Asia, had a direct impact on contemporary work in Asia at a crucial period when the entire Eastern mission enterprise was being reformed. Roberto de Nobili (1577–1656), for example, a Jesuit who donned the garb of a *samnyasin* (Hindu holy man) among the Brahmin in Madurai and wrote works in Sanskrit and Tamil, defended his policy with a book very similar in tone to Acosta's writings called *Adaptation* (1619), and the Filipino Jesuit Ignacio Alzina wrote *Historia de las islas y indios de Visayas* (1668), which resembles Acosta's history.[145] Most important, however, was Acosta's impact on another great pioneer, Alessandro Valignano, whose forceful leadership reconstructed the Asian mission field. But that story will have to wait for the next chapter.

The Jesuits and the Arts in Europe and Beyond

Considerable ink has been spilled in the past over the question of a 'Jesuit style' in the arts. Since the first half of the nineteenth century, scholars have tried to isolate a specifically Jesuit manner of painting, sculpting, and building, and have even gone so far as to credit – or blame – them for creating the Baroque.[146] The crusade continues.[147] The main problem with this hypothesis is that the Society's foundations tended to adapt to the styles and techniques of whatever region they happened to be in, so that even Neapolitan and Milanese Jesuit churches were remarkably different – never mind Amazonian or Tibetan ones. The designs of Jesuit churches were also often simply innovative – for example, in New Spain – making it difficult to relate features even to local styles.[148] The scholars who have come closest to discovering a 'Jesuit style' have done so on an extremely localized level; for example, with Jesuit architecture in France or Italy. Their conclusions are completely untenable when the focus is broadened to include the overseas missions. Howard Hibbard has eloquently shown us how little stylistic unity there was even in the Gesù (the Jesuit mother church in Rome [fig. 14]) during the Society's first century.[149]

Nevertheless, the Jesuits themselves believed that they had a style, even though it was a vague notion that does not fall within the modern art historical definition. Contemporary sources frequently use the term '*noster modus*' ('our way [of proceeding]') to refer to this perceived visual unity, but the phrase encompassed such a wide variety of styles – from severe Herreran classicism to sugar-coated Bavarian Baroque – that it is largely meaningless for us.[150] It turns out to be virtually impossible to link this term, used mostly by non-artists and having a largely pastoral and practical meaning, with the modern notion of style and stylistic development with its roots in nineteenth-century academia.

Noster modus meant no more or less than the repeated Jesuit claims that virtually every mission church they built around the globe was 'just like the Gesù' – even when the mission church in question might be a converted Japanese temple or a Filipino *simbahan* hall of logs and thatching. There is no doubt that the Gesù was an extremely influential building, especially in Italy; however, anything beyond a basic emulation of its plan is rare even in Europe. In France, for example, François de Dainville points out that 'just like the Gesù' referred more to size and commodiousness than style – precisely the qualities implied by *noster modus*.[151] When we expand our scope to include the rest of the world, we are even less likely to find miniature Gesùs with Della Porta façades and Farnese barrel-vaults. On the overseas missions, Jesuit mission churches supposedly 'just like the Gesù' were almost uniformly built with rudimentary three-aisled floor plans imitating Early Christian basilicas, a tendency they shared with mission churches of the Franciscans, Dominicans, Augustinians, and others. In their elevations, these structures often diverged even further from Roman prototypes, adapting to a wide spectrum of regional variations in technique and style, probably to a greater degree than the other orders. Those that did pay lip service to Italian architecture did so, not by copying engravings of the Gesù, but on a much more basic level by referring to the major classical and Renaissance treatises on architecture, which – as we will see – were commonly found in Jesuit libraries in Asia and the Americas.

Only at the turn of the eighteenth century did Jesuit foundations overseas begin to quote literally from Jesuit buildings in Rome, but this time they emulated newer foundations, especially Andrea Pozzo's decorations in the church of Sant' Ignazio (1693–4) and the Chapel of St Ignatius at the Gesù (1699), which, for example, was the model for the companion altar of St Francis Xavier in Goa (ca. 1700). Thanks largely to Andrea Pozzo's own *Perspectiva pictorum et architectorum* (Rome, 1693) and to engravings of the sculptural groups at the chapel of St Ignatius, churches in China, India, and Paraguay reflected Jesuit Roman models in a way that the modern mind might consider more stylistically accurate. The earlier structures 'just like the Gesù' had a different concept of the copy, one that had much more to do with semantics than style – precisely what makes *noster modus* so difficult to define.[152] Perhaps the best illustration of what the Jesuits meant by this term is found in a Peruvian annual letter from 1574, whose highest praise for the newly dedicated church in Lima has nothing to do with its style, but is that it is 'well accommodated to the use of the Society.'[153]

In their first century, the Jesuits had no idea where they wanted to go stylistically, and had not even decided whether they preferred austerity or magnificence.[154] An often-quoted rule from the First General Congregation of the Society of Jesus (1558) calling for practicality and plainness in Jesuit foundations referred only to houses, leaving the door wide open for church architecture.[155] Moreover, in those early days, the Society was also constantly strapped for cash, forcing it to abandon, prolong, or alter artistic and architectural commissions, which often ended up looking haphazard and unplanned as a result. The Jesuits' concerns were perforce more pragmatic than stylistic. Many of the first artists they hired were either cheap, such as Niccolò Circignani or Gaspare Celio, or, like Giuseppe Valeriano (1542–96) and Giovanni Battista Fiammeri (d. 1617), were Jesuits themselves.[156] Even after the Jesuits became more confident art patrons in the second half of the seventeenth century, Rudolf Wittkower's remark still held true: '... insofar as style was concerned, it was the artists who influenced the Jesuits rather than vice versa.'[157]

Although certain specifically Jesuit characteristics can be isolated – such as an emphasis on didacticism in the visual arts and accoustic buildings that were ideal for preaching – these were also shared with other orders. In general, the Jesuits were interested in the very same religious imagery as their counterparts in the regular and secular clergy, and they hired the same professional artists to produce them. Some were great, such as Domenichino and Guercino, but most were humbler. In sixteenth-century Italy and Iberia, many Jesuit designers preferred Serlian, Vitruvian, and Palladian styles of architecture, but that probably had more to do with the availability of the treatises by those architects than anything else.[158]

Some Jesuit devotional practices did promote types of imagery in the late cinquecento that, if not exclusively Jesuit, were at least more favoured by the Society than by any other order and had a powerful impact on European religious culture, on the whole.[159] The Jesuits commissioned more martyrdom cycles, whether in frescoes or books, than anyone else at the time.[160] Equally typical of the Jesuits was an emphasis on the Life of Christ and natural landscapes in their paintings, which has been seen as reflecting the 'composition of place' in the *Spiritual Exercises*. It was only in the seventeenth century that a new spirit of triumphalism and *magnificenza* gave the art of the Society a more distinctive flavour, first in Antwerp, with Rubens's 1617 paintings of the Jesuit founders and a series of lavish illustrated books in the later sixteenth and early seventeenth centuries, and then in Rome, with the patronage of Father General Giovanni Paolo Oliva (1664–81), whose favourite artist was Gianlorenzo Bernini.[161]

For the first time, Jesuit art celebrated the Society itself on a large scale. The art of this era was also of more consistently high quality. The Jesuits were more aware of their role as art patrons and of the relationship of their art commissions to those of other orders. Murals of the lives of Jesuit saints began to proliferate, beginning with Saint Ignatius and later including Francis Xavier (both canonized 1622), Stanislas Kostka, and Luigi Gonzaga (canonized 1726), embodying a uniquely Jesuit iconography. Although earlier Jesuit saints' cycles existed outside of Rome in places such as Lisbon (1619),[162] the first sizeable Roman example appeared in 1667 in the Casa Professa. The Eternal City also enthusiastically embraced the great Jesuit ceiling frescoes of Pozzo and Baciccio in the last decades of the century, which made the ceilings of the Gesù and the new Church of Sant' Ignazio seem to burst into the sky itself. But these artworks played too intimate a role in the general culture of the High Baroque to be referred to exclusively as a 'Jesuit style.'

Like other religious orders, the Jesuits tried wherever possible to use in-house artists. Most of the labour for their churches and colleges in Europe came from *fratelli coadiutori* (lay brothers) working under a *capomaestro* (foreman), who were few and far between and consequently always on the move.[163] Jesuit brothers, or temporal coadjutors, did not aspire to priesthood, and traditionally came from humbler backgrounds and were not as highly educated as ordained fathers. This is not to say that they were not a vital force in the Society, however, and they were expected to engage actively in ministry according to their capabilities. Jesuit brothers taught catechism, engaged lay people in spiritual conversations, and visited the poor and infirm, as well as providing most of the manual labour for the Society. Most importantly for us, however, Jesuit brothers often came from professional backgrounds and had a wide range of specialized skills that made them invaluable technicians. Such were the numerous masons, carpenters, painters, sculptors, and architects whom we see throughout Jesuit history. Although not all Jesuit artists or architects were brothers, most of them were. They brought a level of professionalism to the practical aspects of the Jesuit enterprise that would certainly have been lacking had the Society relied entirely on scholastics. Prominent brother artists and architects in Italy and Spain included Giovanni Tristano (active 1555–75) and Fiammeri.

Like other orders, such as the Oratorians, the Jesuits submitted architectural plans to an internal review called a *consulta*, which invited outside criticism to ensure that the plans were practically and ideologically sound. Plans of architectural projects were sent to Rome, where they were approved by the *consiliarius aedificiorum* (the Jesuits' architectural commissioner).[164] In the early period, some even more elaborate procedures of consultation were entertained. After the Third General Council (1573), for example, the Society tried to arrange for a pool of ideal church and college plans to be used worldwide; in 1580, Valeriano proposed writing a practical handbook on Jesuit architecture; and in 1616, a Jesuit architectural academy was planned. Although none of these materialized, the tradition that a copy of each Jesuit building project be deposited in the archives in Rome persisted, and a fairly comprehensive collection of them (at least for Europe) still survives.[165] In addition to Jesuit labour, the Society hired specialists in devotional painting active in Rome at the time who produced small, portable icons for use in overseas missions. Such, for example, was the Roman painter of Bavarian origin named Sigismondo Laire (1550–1639), mentioned by Baglione, who produced small paintings on copper which 'filled souls with extreme marvel' for the Jesuits to send to Spanish America and Asia (earning him, incidentally, 'a great sum of money').[166] Caravaggio himself named Laire among his friends, but – significantly – not as one of the *valentuomini*, or good painters.[167]

Even more than in Europe, the artistic direction of the Jesuit projects in Asia and the Americas depended upon Jesuit personnel, although here they were augmented by considerable indigenous talent and manpower. In Brazil alone, for example, no less than twenty-one Jesuit architects lent a hand to mission building projects.[168] Most Jesuit mission 'artists' did not have a background in the fine arts, but they would have had at least rudimentary exposure to drawing and perhaps painting. In European Jesuit colleges, scholastics and other pupils were taught to illustrate texts with pictures to help them understand them, and also to create extravagant painted emblems, or *affixiones*, often demonstrating precocious skill.[169] Missionaries were faced with daunting architectural and artistic projects. Florian Paucke, for example, described his building of a bell tower among the Mocobí of the Paraguayan Chaco (eighteenth century):

> Never in my life have I ever held in my hand ... a carpenter's chisel. Yet, all the same, I took it up and along with my indians I used it in making everything necessary for the residence: we made doors, windows, window-frames, tables, and other similar things ...[170]

Even more desperate was Father Antonio de Orellana of the Moxos missions in the Upper Amazon in present-day Peru, who wrote from the mission of San Ignacio to his superior in 1696 urging him to hasten the arrival of the brother architect José del Castillo:

> ... for the love of God don't let some greedy Rector detain the brother who knows something about carpentry and is coming to these missions, since we need him very, very much – especially my [mission], which stands without doors, without windows, bereft of a sacristy, and with no way to assemble before God ..[171]

A more famous personality is the Italian missionary Eusebio Francesco Chino (better known as Kino, 1645–1711), who himself built the original church and residence of San Xavier del Bac in present-day Arizona.[172] Many of these amateurs turned out to have hidden talents – found, as it were, their 'inner artist.' But from as early as the late sixteenth century, the Society also sent accomplished artist-missionaries to its overseas missions, showing a greater commitment to the fine arts than other Catholic missionary orders. Chosen primarily as artists or architects, many of them had professional training in places such as Rome, Naples, Paris, Germany, Prague, and Flanders.

Many were Italians, such as the painter Democrito Bernardino Bitti from Camerino, who arrived in Lima in 1574 and painted devotional images in the luminous, delicate style of the Italian late *maniera* until his death in 1610 (figs. 15, 16).[173] Bitti specialized in willowy full-length figures of the Madonna, Christ, and the saints, and also produced smaller, half-length images of the Madonna and Child or the youthful Christ. He also prepared cartoons for sculptors, such as the fellow Jesuit Pedro de Vargas (b. 1553), a job he would not have had to perform as often in Italy since Spanish colonial churches gave much greater emphasis to sculpture in their altarpieces.[174] As Vargas lamented in 1585, '[Here] it is necessary for us to be more than just painters, since we are responsible for making the whole structure and figures for them, and after all of that I have to do the gilding and tooling of the retables.'[175] Especially typical of Bitti's style is the drapery of his figures, which combines crisp folds with an electric, supernatural energy reminiscent of Lelio Orsi (1511–87). The linear drapery also suggests that Bitti worked from Flemish engravings, which, as we have seen, was common practice on the missions. Although Bitti's powers of anatomy and foreshortening sometimes leave something to be desired, such as in the sleeping figures in his *Oración en el*

Huerto (Cuzco, ca. 1595), his figures have elegance and grace, particularly in their hands, necks, and faces.[176] This aristocratic quality, combined with his preference for luminous golden hair, recalls the work of Scipione Pulzone (1550–98), one of the Jesuits' favoured painters in Rome at the time and the creator, according to Federico Zeri, of the 'timeless' quality in the *arte sacra* of the late sixteenth century.[177] Bitti and Pulzone both capture the aloof sweetness that makes their figures profoundly moving without giving in to sentimentality.

Bitti had studied painting since about the age of fifteen, and already had five or six years of training before entering the Society.[178] His contemporaries praised his 'great talent in his role as painter,' which served him and the Jesuits well in Lima, Cuzco, Arequipa, and the Chucuito area.[179] After an initial eight years in the Santiago residence in Lima, Bitti rarely spent more than a couple of years in a single place, moving great distances over the rugged terrain of the Andean highlands and between there and the coast.[180] Where he was not actually present to do work, he sent designs and *bozzetti* for other artists to finish. Bitti was so influential that his style became the favourite of Peruvian viceroys and bishops well into the seventeenth century, and he is considered the founder of the Cuzco school of painting.[181]

Italian Jesuit painters were active in Asia as well. In fact, in a request made from Manila in 1599, the Philippine Vice-Provincial asked specifically for Italians, since 'there are usually brothers [in Italy] who are skilled in the trades.'[182] In response, Father General Aquaviva sent the painter Simone de Aquila (1580–ca. 1613) to the Philippines along with the Spanish painter Luis Fernández (1580–ca. 1613), where they played a leading role in colonial art production.[183] Fernández divided his time between the mission in Bohol and the capital, where he spent most of his time. In the next century, the Roman Late Baroque style was brought to Manila by the Italian sculptor Giovanni Battista Daccio (Daxio, 1695–after 1722) and the Spaniard Manuel Rodríguez (1657–1734), who painted the lavish ceiling fresco that was once the pride of San Ignacio Church in Manila – a conscious echo of Pozzo's masterpiece in its namesake in Rome. We will see three more such ceiling paintings in China from the same period, all following Andrea Pozzo's own published guide to perspective and architectural design.

Other mission artists in Latin America and Asia were Germanic or Eastern European, especially in the eighteenth century. Bitti's role in Peru was inherited circa 1717 by the Bohemian Adalbert Marterer, who was praised as '*utilísimo*' for the Peruvian mission churches, which were 'adorned by beautiful retables, pulpits, confessionals, and other magnificent works, which he executed.'[184] The high altar and pulpit of the Church of San Ignacio in Bogotá were by the German brother Joseph Lössing.[185] The great retable-maker Georg Winterer was responsible for the high altar of the Compañía in Quito, as well as many sculptural projects in that city in the first decades of the eighteenth century.[186] By far the most Germanic of South American regions, however, was eighteenth-century Chile. The artistic life of colonial Chile was very briefly enlightened by the Tyrolian Johann Bitterich (1675–1720), a professional artist who had already served several important patrons in Europe, including Lothar Franz von Schönborn, Archbishop of Mainz (who was none too happy to lose him).[187] His skills in painting, sculpture, and architecture were constantly in demand, as he himself complained when asking for more artists to come in 1720: 'I have an excessive amount of work here throughout the Province of Chile, since our Superiors from all of the houses consistently request statues, altars, and [plans for] buildings from me, since in these regions there is neither a sculptor nor an architect who understands anything of his art.'[188] Unfortunately, the Jesuit artist died within a year of his arrival; although, owing to a misreading of the sources, scholars have traditionally believed that he was in Chile for almost ten years.[189] Other Germanic artists in Chile from the same period include Wilhelm Millet (b. 1683) from Luxembourg, who reached Chile in 1708, and not 1724 as some contend; Michael Herre (b. 1697), who reached Chile in 1720; the Bavarian Johannes Haberkorn (b. 1670), who arrived in 1724; Adam Englehard (b. 1685), who came to Chile the same year; and the architect Peter Vogl (b. 1692), later an important figure in the artistic life of South America, who set foot there in 1737.[190]

Bitterich's example was followed in 1748 by a gargantuan Jesuit art and crafts academy at the hacienda Calera de Tango near Santiago, which was founded by the German Jesuit Karl Haimbhausen (1692–1767) and staffed by a boatload of almost fifty artists and artisans, also mostly from Germany.[191] The main goal of the workshop was to provide painters, sculptors, and craftsmen to build the Collegio Máximo at Santiago de Chile, but since it was the first large-scale art workshop in Chile, it went on to exert wide and lasting influence, creating not just paintings and sculptures but bells, textiles, clocks, other metalwork, retables, and other furniture. Academy staff included the architects and masons Peter Vogl and Benedict Griner (b. 1731); the painters Johann Redle (b. 1718) from Swabia, Josef Ambrosi (b. 1732) from the Tyrol, and Giovanni Leoni (b. 1685) from central Italy; the sculptors Jacobus Kelner (b. 1720) and Georg Lanz (1720–ca. 1770) from Bavaria, and the Chilean native Ambrosio Santalices (1734–1818), of whom the latter two have left surviving works; the woodworker Franz Grueber (b. 1715); the bell-founders and metalworkers Johann Baptist Felix and Jacob Rothmayr (b. 1723) from Bavaria; the Bavarian clockmaker Peter Reutz (b. 1719); and tapestry weavers Philip Ossemayr and Thomas Semiller.[192] The Calera had little time to help Jesuit efforts since the Society was expelled from Spanish lands in 1767, but it can be seen as the last great flourishing of Jesuit mission art, a tradition which began in the late sixteenth century with the Japanese academy that is the subject of chapter 3.

Several capable Jesuit architects worked on the missions in Asia and Latin America. Some specialized in fortification architecture and found their skills in great demand abroad. Such was the Spanish nobleman Antonio Sedeño (1535–95), who built the first stone architecture in the Philippines and was hired by civil officials to design the fortifications of Manila and other towns, and Melchior de Vera (d. 1646), another Jesuit specialist in military architecture in the Philippines. Jesuits were soon known throughout Asia as experts in fortification architecture (fig. 17). Other Jesuit architects in the Philippines include Gianantonio Campioni (1592–1651), a Genoese nobleman who designed the Baroque Church of San Ignacio in Manila, whose façade was emulated as far away as the remote Visayan mission of Guiuan (ca. 1700, fig. 18); the Italian Giancamillo Riccio (1563–ca. 1613), who supervised the construction of mission chapels in the Visayas; the Sevillian Cristóbal Miralles (1629–1708), who may have introduced the first stone churches in the Visayas; Francisco Diez (1654–1716), from Burgos, who built churches and retables in several regions as well as performing the duties of a priest; and the Austrian Josef Zanzini (1616–92), who, while building churches and retables in the Visayas, also found the time to write several books of devotions.[193] Although not a professional architect, the Granadian noble father Juan de Salazar (1582–1645) constructed three important Jesuit churches in Luzon, including the church at Silang (before 1645), whose stolid classicism has recently been made even more sombre by a coat of Portland cement spread on the walls.[194]

In the Americas, Jesuit architects were no less prominent. In Peru, the Jesuit Martín de Aizpitarte designed the solemnly classical Compañía church in Lima (1624–38) (fig. 13); and the Compañía of Cuzco (1651–68), possibly by the Flemish Jesuit architect Jean Baptiste Gilles (1596–1675), inspired the first distinctive metropolitan school of architecture in the region.[195] The German Jesuit Johann Röhr had achieved enough of a reputation in the colony that he was asked to reconstruct the cathedral at Lima after the earthquake of 1746 – quite an honour given the number of first-rate architects available in the city at the time; and in New Spain, the Czech brother Simon Boruhradsky (d. 1697) was reponsible for many important architectural commissions for the Society.[196] The great Church of San Ignacio in Bogotá (begun 1610), one of the most distinguished early foundations of the Society in South America, was built by the Jesuit architect Giovanni Battista Coluccini from Lucca.[197] In present-day Colombia and Ecuador, Jesuit architects Simon Schönherr and Leonard Deubler designed several important churches, including the Compañía of Popayán and the fine Baroque façade of the Compañía in Quito (1722–6).[198] Two Italians also contributed to the Quito church: Marco Guerra, who arrived in Quito in 1636, and the Mantuan brother Venancio Gandolfi, who finished the façade in 1765.[199] The reductions among the Chiquitos in present-day Bolivia, in reality an extension of the Paraguay reductions, bear the architectural legacy of the great Swiss polymath Martin Schmid (1694–1772), who was also an accomplished musician.[200] One scholar has even made the provocative suggestion that his design for the mission churches of San Rafael, San Javier, and Concepción were constructed according to different musical keys.[201]

Italian, German, and Flemish Jesuits were largely responsible for a revolution in the religious architecture of colonial Argentina in the late seventeenth and eighteenth centuries, moving it away from the provincial Peruvian style which had predominated there before. Andrea Bianchi (1677–1740) finished Córdoba Cathedral, Argentina's greatest colonial monument, vaulting it and giving it its distinctive façade, and also built the Franciscan jewel of Buenos Aires, the Church of El Pilar (1716–32) (fig. 19). A contemporary source emphasized how vital Bianchi's skills were in the region: 'He is an incomparable and indefatigable brother. He is an architect, impresario, builder, and it is crucial that he is here, since the Spanish do not know a jot.'[202] His colleague the Milanese Giovanni Battista Primoli (1673–1747) devoted most of his attention to the Cyclopean churches of the Paraguay reductions, and he will be treated in more detail in chapter 6. The Bohemian Johann Kraus (1664–1714) and the Bavarian Anton Harls (b. 1725) designed two of the greatest Baroque treasures in South America, the Church of San Ignacio in Buenos Aires (begun 1712) and the Estancia of Santa Catalina (completed 1767) in the Sierras de Córdoba (fig. 20).[203] The Flemish woodworker Jean Conté (1665–1740), the Roman sculptor Tommaso Rosatini (b. 1680), and the Bavarian sculptor Johannes Wolf (b. 1691) also worked on Argentine foundations of the Society, including Salta (fig. 81), Córdoba, and Buenos Aires.[204] Finally, mention must be made of Brother Philippe Lemaire (1608–71), who had an archetypical early modern South American career. Born in Flanders, Lemaire began life as a naval architect and spent many years building ships in Flanders, England, Portugal, and Brazil. After joining the Society in South America, Lemair was asked to put his skills to work designing a roof for the Compañía church in Córdoba. Although it is now known that he used as a guide Philibert de l'Orme's *Nouvelles Inventions pour bien bastir et à petits frais* (1561), Lemaire's roof was nevertheless designed in much the same way as the hull of a ship, upside down.[205] Many other painters, sculptors, and architects with professional backgrounds were sent to the missions in Japan, China, India, and above all Paraguay, as we shall soon see.

Despite the importance of these zealous Jesuit technicians, our study is equally concerned with the indigenous artists, builders, and craftsmen who provided the majority of the labour and much of the creativity of Jesuit-sponsored art on the missions. In Asia, for example, the Jesuits employed more indigenous artists than any other missionary order. To train these men, the Society founded art academies all over the world – precisely the schools which would become the primary site for artistic acculturation. As was the case with the Franciscan missions before them, these schools were at first rudimentary affairs. For example, as one scholar remarks about the Jesuit missionary to the Filipino Visayas, Brother Fernández: 'These should not be interpreted as art academies, but as a zealous and young Fernández teaching the Leyteño children how to illustrate the mysteries of the faith.'[206] Art was also taught on a similar level at places such as the Amazon missions in Moxos, where neophytes were taught to paint frescoes on the façades and interiors of their massive churches by Jesuit brothers.[207] The Moxos missionary Brother Manuel Carrillo was one such instructor. Working on the mission of Loreto in the 1690s, Carrillo taught the Moxos Indians the fundamentals of carpentry and also probably painting, since he himself painted many altarpieces during his stay there. His superior described his popularity among the Moxos, and expressed his hope that art workshops would become better established on his missions: 'In a few years there will be artisans who will adorn [the mission churches] perpetually, just as the group is learning to do now with Brother Manuel, who is extremely useful and is ornamenting the church of Loreto very well.'[208] But after the Society changed its policy in the 1580s and devoted more attention to artistic production, these smaller schools began to be complemented by large-scale workshops of a kind never seen before in mission history. Founded in Japan, China, and Paraguay, these predecessors of the Calera de Tango were capable of supplying not only the needs of the mission but also a much wider art market, producing paintings, sculptures, engravings, books, and ready-made altarpieces on a grand scale, and their influence on colonial and non-Christian societies was profound. The mission academies were responsible for a sensitive and creative synthesis of styles and techniques, borrowing extensively from non-European traditions and creating a rich variety of new dialects of Late Renaissance and Baroque art.

3

'The Greatest Enterprise':[1] The Jesuit Mission to Japan, 1549–1622

Of all their worldwide enterprises, none were closer to Jesuit hearts than the Japan and China missions, the one short-lived and tragic, and the other lasting for over two hundred years yet also ending in its own distinctly tragic way. The Far Eastern missions brought Renaissance Europe face-to-face for the first time with cultures that it considered to be technological and intellectual equals. For a Europe that quite literally divided the world into black and white, and believed that the former was doomed to some form of natural servitude, the discovery of non-European peoples they judged to be 'white' and 'rational' forced missionaries to revise their attitudes toward the Other. The Japanese and Chinese were seen as natural aristocrats in an era when even the missionary church was dominated by the ruling class – people who seemed to feel more at ease with princes of foreign nations than with commoners in their own countries. Beginning with Francis Xavier himself, who wrote that the Japanese were 'the best [people] that have as yet been discovered,'[2] and later including the Visitor to the Indies Alessandro Valignano (1539–1606), who characterized them as 'the upper classes among the non-European nations,'[3] great churchmen gave Japan and China pride of place in the non-Christian world. This attitude has persisted into our own century, when scholars such as Ludwig von Pastor, the historian of the popes, praised Xavier for showing that 'the work for the conversion of Asia must be directed not only to the effeminate and visionary Hindoos and Malays, but rather to the Japanese and Chinese.'[4] It is worthwhile noting that neither the Japanese nor the Chinese returned the compliment to their European visitors.

The Cipangu and Cathay of Marco Polo became the most coveted mission fields on earth, and the focus of political aspiration, intellectual creativity, and Christian hope in a period of revitalization for the Catholic Church. The second post-Tridentine pope, Gregory XIII (1572–85), later earned the epithet 'Pope of the Missions' for his liberality toward the Jesuit mission cause in Asia, personally financing colleges in Japan and receiving with great pomp the Japanese 'embassy' in 1585. More importantly, these Far Eastern adventures generated a whole genre of mission literature, which had a tremendous impact on Catholic Europe at all levels. Best-sellers in their day, these tales of Christian heroism in exotic lands were largely responsible for an unprecedented rise in membership in the Society of Jesus. For the first time, becoming a missionary to Asia was a goal with comparable merit to battling Protestants in the North. In fact, the Jesuits' primacy in the Far East anointed them as the nobility of Catholic missionary orders, displacing the Franciscans from the position they had gained by taming the Aztecs – a nation that had ceaselessly been compared with China, but was nevertheless deemed 'black.'[5]

It should come as no surprise, therefore, that Japan and China were chosen as the site of the most ambitious mission art studio that had ever been conceived. The 'Seminary of Painters' of Giovanni Niccolò (1583), an art academy founded just five years after the Accademia di San Luca in Rome by the same Pope, became not only a centre for the diffusion of European visual culture throughout Asia, but a fertile ground for cultural adaptation and hybridization. Although it did not initially set out to adopt Japanese styles and iconography, as Jesuit artists were to do in seventeenth- and eighteenth-century China, it did address the specific culturally based iconographic needs of its Japanese and Chinese audiences. As Japanese and Chinese pupils increased in number, the Seminary quietly shifted direction as indigenous artists began to incorporate their own styles and techniques into their mission art commissions, creating a delicate balance of East and West that would anticipate later Jesuit art enterprises around the world. The Seminary also enjoyed influence outside the mission communities, as its pupils went on to execute secular art for Japanese lords and non-Christian artists flocked there to learn European painting techniques. Although the missionaries never wrote about this cultural synthesis in their letters to Rome, always being careful to say how European their art was, the pictures tell us a different story.

In the later sixteenth and early seventeenth centuries, the Japanese mission was at once the most successful enterprise of the Society of Jesus and the most tenuous. The English sailor Will Adams – by no means a friend of the Jesuits – was deeply impressed when he reached Japan on a Dutch ship in 1600 to discover a prodigious community of Japanese Christians and numerous churches in the land, primarily the fruit of Jesuit efforts.[6] His reaction was well founded. At the time of Xavier's entry into Japan, there were but a handful of missionaries of that order in all of Asia. Francis himself never learned Japanese, and several years passed before any Jesuit had sufficient proficiency in that language to express anything more than the most rudimentary catechistic litanies. And yet, thanks to the Church's enthusiasm for Japanese skin colour, the mission in Japan grew to include 85 Jesuits (20 of them Japanese), approximately 150,000 Japanese Christians, two hundred churches, ten residences, two colleges, and a novitiate in just over thirty years (1580).[7] The Japanese converts, who, to the great satisfaction of the whole Catholic world, comprised local warlords (*daimyō*, the Jesuits sometimes called them 'kings') and Buddhist monks as well as the peasantry, reached an astonishing 300,000 by 1614.[8] Valignano wrote with pride that 'Japan is the only oriental country in which the people have become Christians for the right reasons.'[9]

However, these glowing reports and optimistic numbers masked a much more unstable reality. The mission operated against a background of chaotic civil war, with rulers constantly vying for power, shifting alliances, and migrating from place to place. As a result, the Jesuit missionaries were constantly on the move, and the protection and patronage they won from one ruler could as easily be taken away by the next. Diplomacy was precarious and violence common. Very soon the Japan enterprise surrendered its image as a great Christian kingdom for the more dubious reputation of a place of martyrdom. Its miserable finish in the decades after 1614 was a cataclysmic genocide that ranks among the most systematically cruel and thorough pogroms in human history. Yet the tenaciousness of the Christian community faced with this horror also showed how deeply the Jesuits had planted the root of Christian faith.

The Japanese Context for Cultural Exchange

Ironically, the Japan mission was only possible because Japan was caught up in a state of constant war, a disjointed and disorderly political situation called *Sengoku Jidai*, literally 'The Age of the Country at War' (1467–1568). Japanese politics presented a confusing spectacle to Western observers at the time. Although in name an empire with an emperor based in Kyoto, actual political power in Japan had belonged to the *Shōgun*, or leader of the military aristocracy, since the end of the twelfth century. In a further degree of separation, even the Shogunate was reduced to a puppet office after the 1467 civil war that ushered in the *Sengoku Jidai*, when authority was divided among rival daimyos holed up in their largely independent castle towns and served by fiercely loyal samurai attendants. Secular rulers were not the only warlords either. Leaders of different sects of Buddhism also vied for land and influence, making religion a central feature of the political landscape and one which the Jesuits could harness to their advantage. Nevertheless, although they did not realize it at the time, the Jesuits had arrived toward the end of this development, and their opportunity was to be short-lived. The sixteenth century witnessed the slow but final showdown between the rival daimyos, as they reduced each other in number to about half a dozen in the 1560s and finally to a single overlord by the turn of the century. The tightening grip of absolutism, which also gradually smothered the power of the different Buddhist schools with an established Buddhist state orthodoxy, left no room for the Jesuits or Christianity. The era of the Tokugawa shoguns (1615–1868) brooked no deviations from Heaven's Mandate.

The religious situation in Japan by the mid-sixteenth century was itself highly complex. Japanese religious life was divided between the indigenous Shintoism, Confucianism from China, and various forms of Buddhism, also from China but deriving ultimately from India. Shinto, or The Way of the Gods, was originally an animist religion recognizing divinity in spirits, as well as natural formations and human figures, all of which, together with sacredness in general, are placed under the rubric *kami* ('god'). One kind of Shinto authority was based on the clan and clan leader (culminating in the Emperor, whose tutelary *kami* was the Sun Goddess Amaterasu), and another on that of the shaman, through whom the *kami* spoke. Beginning in the sixth century, Buddhism and Confucianism reached Japan from China. Although Confucianism's influence was largely restricted to aristocratic or academic circles, it did resurface under the Tokugawa as a state philosophy. On the other hand, by the Kamakura Period (1192–1333), Buddhism had penetrated every level of Japanese society and had been integrated with Shintoism.

Since its origins in the Asuka Period (552–645), orthodox Buddhism had become a state religion, with the government establishing official temples and monasteries with a strict hierarchy of clergy, monks, and nuns. In the centuries which followed, a bewildering number of schools of Buddhism were imported in rapid succession. Many of these new sects now appealed to the masses, some of them possessing a charismatic and others a contemplative character. An important development in the Early Heian Period (794–951) was Esoteric, or secret, Buddhism, divided into the Tendai and Shingon schools, whose teachings were revealed only to initiates and which focused on chanting the mantra. By the Kamakura Period, important Buddhist movements included Zen Buddhism (in Chinese, Chan), as well as Pure Land Buddhism (Jōdo), which had tremendous popular following, often in defiance of state-controlled religion. Whereas Zen was based on a direct perception of reality and sudden enlightenment, Pure Land Buddhism believed that enlightenment was achievable through faith in Amida (the Buddha of Infinite Light) and the recitation of the *nenbutsu* chant. Like other popular schools, Pure Land Buddhism was often perceived as a troublemaker by the nobility and was the victim of persecution.

With its complex iconography and architectural forms, Buddhism also played a principal role in the development of the arts in Japan, bringing with it a powerful legacy of Chinese influence. The Esoteric schools and their successors served as a conduit for intricately detailed, brightly coloured iconographies from China, which embraced a wide variety of types ranging from serene Buddhas and Bodhisattvas to lively guardians and demons with animated expressions and martial poses, such as the Divine Guardian in figure 21 from the Kamakura Period. Pure Land and Zen (especially the Rinzai sect) were particularly active patrons of the arts with their own distinct styles and forms, features which later had an impact on Jesuit mission painting in Japan. Pure Land Buddhism favoured brilliantly coloured depictions of Amida's Western Paradise, typically with elaborate palaces, lotus ponds, and bejewelled trees. The imagery of one variety, mandala (*mandara*) paintings, focused on schematized and extremely detailed images of Amida surrounded by a host of deities, architectural elements, and genre details in a highly symmetrical composition. *Raigō* painting, by contrast, depicts Amida descending to earth with his attendant bodhisattvas or seated on a mountain with Kannon and Seishi.

Art produced in the Zen tradition contrasted strongly with this elaborate empyrean, although it also had Chinese origins. Zen art was characterized by *wabi*, a concept which privileges austerity and solitude, as well as objects weathered by time. This was perceivable in the Zen contemplative gardens, as well as the artificially aged ceramic vessels for the tea ceremony (*chanoyu*), itself a fifteenth-century Zen development. The most typical form of Zen painting was black ink painting (*suibokuga*), a largely monochromatic style created by calligraphic lines of varying width and limited shading (fig. 22). These paintings were often executed rapidly to recreate a moment of sudden insight and depict Buddhist figures such as divinities, monks, and scholars (*dōshakugu*), as well as imaginary landscapes (*shigajiku*). Zen Buddhism, with its emphasis on personal mentorship, had a strong tradition of the master priest-painter, such as the great masters Kichizan Minchō (1352–1431), Kaō Ninga, and Mokuan Reien (fifteenth century), a custom that may have paved the way for the reception of Jesuit artist-teachers on the Japan mission.

Japanese paintings appeared most commonly as hanging scrolls (*kakemono*), or horizontal illustrated handscrolls (*emakimono*), which were read from right to left. Although the style of painting tended to be calligraphic, with strong outlines and a general two-dimensionality in modelling, painters had developed a limited amount of shading and a sophisticated technique for depicting spatial depth using isometric perspective. A distinctly Japanese style of painting called *yamato-e* developed in the Heian Period; it depicted dramatic narrative scenes, *monagatari-e*, usually of literary origin. Originally painted on handscrolls, these themes were transferred to large-scale decorative paintings by the Momoyama Period (1573–1615), immediately prior to the arrival of the Jesuits, usually on sliding-door panels (*fusuma*) and folding screens (*byōbu*) (fig. 23). Patronized primarily by the rising class of daimyos and samurai, who used them to decorate their castles and homes, these panels either used brilliant colours on a gold or silver background or the monochromatic ink-brush style wrought large. These monumental paintings were pioneered by the Kyoto Kanō School of Kanō Eitoku (1543–90) and his pupils, as well as independent painters Hasegawa Tōhaku (1539–1610), Kaihō Yōshū (1533–1615), and Sōtatsu (active 1600–40), and reflected the aspirations to power and culture of the feudal class. After the arrival of the first Portuguese ships in the 1540s, these paintings also began to feature European genre elements, particularly the 'southern barbarian' variety of screens (*namban byōbu*) (fig. 24), which I will discuss in more detail later in this chapter.

The Jesuit Mission before Valignano, 1549–79

The Japan mission began with Francis Xavier himself, who arrived in a Chinese junk at the southern Kyushu port of Kagoshima in 1549 with his Spanish companions Father Cosmé de Torres and Brother Juan Fernández, an Indian servant, and three Japanese Christians who had studied at the Goa college. Although they had come from Goa, and were officially answerable to the Portuguese crown, there was not a single Portuguese among them. Already, therefore, in their first major outer-circle mission, the Jesuits had moved beyond the cultural monopoly of the *Padroado*, a tradition which they would maintain over the next century as many of the important personnel of the Japan mission came from Italy, Germany, and Spain.[10] In fact, by the 1580s the mission's very ideology would be shaped by the Christian humanism of the Italian Church, whose *modo soave* substituted open dialogue and cultural accommodation for the severity and intolerance of the Portuguese Church.

Less than a decade had passed since the first Portuguese sailors set foot in the Land of the Rising Sun, and Francis consequently had very little knowledge about Japanese society or religion. Nevertheless, the Portuguese had become an important presence there. In just a few years, the annual Portuguese *Nao*, or ship, from

Macao had already become a fixture in the political landscape, as rival daimyos tried to entice it to dock in their ports and acquire its silk from China, and especially its European firearms. The Jesuits benefited tremendously from their association with this ship of riches, and within a generation were participating actively in the silk trade, a move made necessary by the prohibitive costs of financing what had so quickly become an extensive mission operation far from regular European patronage.[11] Missionary expansion began first on Kyushu, and later expanded to Honshu in the 1560s. In Honshu their activity focused on followers of daimyos who supported Oda Nobunaga (1534–82), at the time the greatest lord of the land and de facto Shogun. Nobunaga himself became a friend of the Jesuits and remained an important supporter. Conversions were few in number and bases extremely migratory. Kyushu, by contrast, was the scene of dramatic mass conversions reminiscent of those in early colonial New Spain, where typically once the daimyo accepted Christianity his people followed suit. At a very early stage, the Japanese converts played a vital role in mission life, either in Jesuit houses as *dōjuku*, a name for catechists and lay assistants taken from attendants in Buddhist monasteries, or as *kambō*, who served as lay leaders of the local Christian community.

In fact, from the very beginning the driving force behind the spread of Christianity was not so much the Jesuits themselves as indigenous Catholic lay organizations, or confraternities, based on European prototypes with origins in thirteenth-century Italy and popular with the Jesuits.[12] Confraternities in Europe and Asia alike strengthened the Christian community, administered public charities, organized festivals, and also provided social insurance for their members. The remarkable success enjoyed by Catholicism in the first missionary century in East Asia is largely attributable to such lay societies, who were uniquely capable of indigenizing and popularizing the new faith. More importantly, confraternities also served as the people's main contact with Christianity, since missionaries were few and far between. By far the most developed of these confraternities was the Misericórdia, a charitable and philanthropic organization with origins in Portugal. Confraternities were also among the most important patrons of the arts in Christian Asia. Their myriad activities required a variety of works of art, including objects of personal devotion for the members, altarpieces and images of the patron saint or symbol for the chapel, and especially banners and statues for processions.

From the very beginning, the mission was constantly on the move. After the daimyo of Satsuma, who ruled Kagoshima, lost his enthusiasm for the Jesuits, mission headquarters were transferred north to Bungo, where daimyo Ōtomo Yoshishige (Otomo Sōrin) became their most active supporter in the 1570s and 1580s. A rising star himself at the time, Otomo Yoshishige had conquered about half of the island of Kyushu and was referred to as 'a very great lord' by Francis.[13] The Jesuits were therefore ecstatic when he converted to Christianity, taking the name Don Francisco. Although he was no doubt aware that acceptance of Christianity would make his ports more attractive to the silk ship from Macao, even the unsympathetic Elison admits that 'it is tempting to judge that he converted in purest sincerity after observing for almost thirty years the efforts and the effects of Christianity in his domains.'[14] Soon the daimyos of Ōmura, Arima, and Amasuka followed suit, as well as numerous Buddhist priests, renowned scholars, and thousands of commoners. Throughout the 'Christian century' in Japan, the vast majority of the converts came from the lower classes, as many daimyos were less willing to allow their nobility to convert.[15] In 1571 the Jesuits moved to Nagasaki, which was to remain an important base for them in the decades to come – and, not coincidentally, also the favoured port of call for the Portuguese *Nao*.

The mission flourished as Oda Nobunaga grew in power. In 1580 the entire nation appeared to be on the verge of conversion when the daimyo Ōmura Sumitada (Dom Bartolomeu, 1532–87) granted the Society of Jesus legislative authority over the cities of Nagasaki and Mogi. Nagasaki was seen as a Christian capital, a new Rome. Expectations were further fuelled by glowing Annual Letters sent to the Roman Curia, describing the conversion of whole 'kingdoms' and failing accurately to portray the precarious nature of the entire enterprise.[16] But the truth was that Nobunaga himself did not have long to live, and that the tide would soon turn. Less than a decade later, Nagasaki was occupied by Toyotomi Hideyoshi (ruled 1582–98), a leader whose attitude toward the Jesuits was anything but sympathetic.[17]

Characteristics of Japanese Mission Art and Architecture: The Early Period

Fewer examples of the visual arts survive from the Japan mission than virtually any other. Although mission art and architecture were produced on a grand scale throughout the 'Christian century,' very little has survived the seventeenth-century pogroms, and often we have no choice but to rely almost entirely on textual sources. Despite the itinerant nature of the Japan mission, hundreds of churches were founded all over Kyushu and southern Honshu in its first decades.[18] Some of the earliest chapels were set up in existing Buddhist temples, such as the temple given over to the Jesuits in 1551 by Yoshitaka, the daimyo of Ōuchi, or the Saikōji Temple in Arima, given to them by the converted daimyo Dom Andrés in 1580 to serve as a seminary, while others were erected in private houses.[19] The recollection of Gregory the Great would not have been lost on these early missionaries. Even when they were built from the ground up, Jesuit mission churches tended to use materials taken from Buddhist temples or residences, were built in the Japanese style of post-and-lintel wooden architecture with a hipped-gable roof (figs. 24, 25), and employed Japanese builders.[20] They were even popularly known in Japan as *nambanji*, or 'southern barbarian temples,' after the perceived southern origin of European missionaries (Nagasaki is in the South).[21] The finest were built of cedar (e.g., Funai, Usuki, and Ikitsukishima), the most humble were of bamboo, and only one, the church at Okayama, is known to have had a tile roof.[22] Fire was a constant problem, and most of them had, in the Japanese manner, a stone outbuilding known as a *kura*, which served as a treasury for protecting church plate and art objects.

In the manner of Buddhist temples, the main nave of the church was located in the main hall of worship (*hondō*), usually a separate rectangular building in a courtyard surrounded by an open cloister (fig. 25). In place of the pagoda, which usually stood on a platform in front of the *hondō*, the Jesuits erected a monumental wooden cross (some were so tall that they served as landmarks for sea captains), reminiscent of Franciscan missions in Mexico, where crosses were erected over Aztec ritual spaces. The replacement was particularly appropriate in Japan since, like a pagoda, the cross was a largely symbolic structure embodying the sense of a reliquary, and both monuments are dominated by a vertical thrust. Japanese churches also had ablution fountains, fish ponds, and gardens in the Japanese manner. Some were quite grand. The Church of the Conception at Ōmura (1568–9) had a courtyard capable of accommodating two thousand people, and the *hondō* itself at the church at Ikitsukishima could hold six hundred.[23] Owing to the precarious nature of their mission, the Jesuits preferred to build their churches on the seacoast, so that they could flee in boats at short notice. Usually churches were positioned in the middle of isolated coastal gardens or orchards, which were surrounded by high walls and even sometimes moats. Such was the church at Hakata, rebuilt during 1570–1 on coastal land donated by Ōtomo Yoshishige, and the church compounds at Yokoseura, Ikitsukishima, Takatsuki, and Shimabara.[24] The inland churches were also built with safety in mind, generally being in the immediate environs of castles, and often even behind the ramparts (e.g., at Okayama and Sawa). One of the most important churches was the Church of the Assumption in Kyoto, built in 1576 through the generosity of Japanese Christians, since Kyoto was not only the Imperial capital but the largest city in Japan, with a population considerably larger than any European city of the period outside Paris.[25] We can obtain an idea of the appearance of these churches from the *namban byōbu*, or 'southern barbarian screens,' even though they were painted at the end of the century (fig. 24).

Clearly, although they had not yet made it official policy, the Jesuits were already accommodating wholesale to indigenous styles in architecture. Their reasons, of course, were largely pragmatic ones – it was both prudent to keep a low profile and practical to use local architects and materials – but the presence of ablution fountains shows that they were already adapting local practices of worship, as well. However, this was not the message they were sending back home. When the life of the 'Pope of the Missions,' Gregory XIII, was celebrated in a luxury illustrated volume by Marcantonio Ciappi entitled *Compendio delle heroiche et gloriose attioni et Santa Vita di Papa Gregorio XIII* (Rome, 1596), the Japanese colleges and churches built under his patronage were depicted as buildings in the Roman Late Mannerist style. While some scholars have cited this book as proof that the Society erected European-style buildings in Japan,[26] their appearance has more to do with the nationality of the printmaker than his subjects. Tellingly, a book by Alonso de Ovalle on Jesuit missions in Chile that was also printed in Rome fifty years later (1646) depicts buildings in a suspiciously similar style.[27]

The proliferation of churches, the need for attractive gifts, and the persistence of the language barrier in the early mission in Japan created a great need for devotional images. Xavier himself brought oil paintings of the Madonna and Child and the Annunciation, as well as an illustrated bible, and wrote, in a set of instructions to his confrères, about the importance of using imagery to communicate with the Japanese.[28] As did Jesuits in Rome and around the world, Francis used these pictures when he preached, and believed that they possessed miraculous properties. Francis wrote that during a homily before daimyo Shimazu Takahisa of Satsuma (1514–71), the painting made such an impression on the ruler's mother that she tried to have a copy made for her own personal devotion.[29] Francis and his successors also used images as gifts, which were well received – not only devotional pictures but battle scenes and portraits of knights.[30] At first, most of the churches were decorated only with crosses and simple paintings on paper (missionaries noted that the Japanese had a particular devotion for the cross),[31] but as the number of churches grew, so did the number of images. Each chapel had at least a retable, some of which were elaborate enough to be crowned by a baldachin, and many also had silk altar cloths and church plate.[32]

At this time, most of the artworks were likely imported from Portugal and Portuguese Asia, although Japanese daimyos also had copies of paintings or even metal retables made by their court artists for their own churches when originals could not be obtained.[33] There was even a proposal, in 1575, to send Giuseppe Valeriano, the Jesuits' finest artist and architect in Europe at the time, to Japan, although he had his hands full in Spain and Italy and would never travel beyond Lisbon.[34] Very few engravings are mentioned, but we can assume that they were as common as they were on the other Jesuit missions in Asia; a few originals have survived.[35] Most devotional images in Japan depicted the Madonna and Child, as well as other scenes of the Virgin's and Christ's life, and there were plenty of crucifixes and wooden statues of Christ.[36] A reference to an image of Saint Bartholomew suggests that the legend of the itinerant apostle may have been as important in Japan as it was in many parts of Spanish America.

What did these pictures look like? McCall proposes that these earliest paintings were in the Flemish style current in Portugal at the time, and some may even have been made in Flanders, where pictures were regularly made for the Iberian export market.[37] Flemish artists themselves worked in Portugal and her colonies; for example, the Jesuit painter and sculptor Father Markus Mach of Goa (known as Marcos Rodriguez, d. 1601), whom Francisco Cabral tried to have sent to the Japan mission in 1576.[38] The primacy of the Northern Renaissance style in Japan would not have lasted very long, however, since Portugal and Flanders itself soon adopted the Italian Mannerist style. Portuguese painters such as Francisco de Holanda and António Campelo themselves spent time in Rome in the 1540s and '50s, helping to usher the Italianate style into Portugal after 1560. Through prints and possibly original paintings, the Italianate style of the Fleming Martin de Vos (1532–1603) was almost certainly as important here as it later was in Mughal India and Latin America.[39] Sadly for us, nothing survives today that can be assigned with any assurance to the earliest phase of the mission.

The Jesuit Mission and the Arts after Valignano, 1579–1622

The 1570s and 1580s witnessed a dramatic change in the ideology of the Japanese mission, as the Jesuits began to stress higher education, the arts, and especially the learning of the Japanese language and the emulation of its culture. This new direction is attributable to a new wave of Italian influence, beginning with Organtino Gnecchi-Soldo and Francesco Pasio and culminating in the reforms of the Visitor to the Indies, Alessandro Valignano. The Italian method, steeped in Christian humanism and marked by what Valignano called *'il modo soave,'*[40] was much more open to acculturative experimentation than the more colonialist approach of the Portuguese. The latter was exemplified by Mission Superior Francisco Cabral, a former Portuguese soldier, who joined the Order in Asia and reached Japan in 1570 along with Gnecchi-Soldo. Cabral was a man of great energy and zeal, and was responsible for reinvigorating and promoting the mission in a period of unprecedented growth. He was also strict, inflexible, and intolerant.[41] One of his first and most symbolic changes was his decree that Jesuits stop wearing silk kimonos and sport black cotton cassocks as in Europe, an order given him admittedly by his superiors in Rome, who were worried that the Society was going native.[42] His goal was to bring the Society in Japan more into line with its activities in Europe, moving it away from acculturative advances that had already been made at the local level. But his gravest fault was his treatment of the Japanese *dōjuku*, lay catechists, who were responsible for the bulk of the new conversions.

Even though he was a strong proponent of Japanese recruitment, Cabral was not interested in Japanese culture, and forced indigenous lay catechists to adapt to European dress, food, and way of life, which they naturally found disgusting, given the Japanese tradition of cleanliness and avoidance at the time of meat other than seafood. Insufficient attention was paid to learning the Japanese language, and Cabral felt that higher learning was not only unnecessary for Japanese Christians – including Jesuits – but dangerous, since he believed it would make them haughty – which was ironic since he was one of the first to propose admitting Japanese into the Society, several years before Valignano's arrival.[43] He also felt that the Japanese were somehow incapable of understanding the deeper aspects of religion. In this matter, Cabral and other Jesuits in Japan, like João Rodrigues 'Tçuzzu,' were simply part of the tradition that (as we have seen in chapter 2), believed non-European peoples to be eternal neophytes with little 'talent to govern or penetrate deeply into things of religion.'[44] Cabral's policies, according to which Japanese Christians were treated like second-class citizens, allowed a rift to develop between indigenous and European Christians. Needless to say, this did not endear him to the Japanese – Christians or otherwise.

A very different approach was taken by the widely popular Gnecchi-Soldo (1533–1609), who referred to himself as Father Organtino to spare Japanese and Portuguese tongues his unpronounceable surname. The pioneer of *il modo soave* later promoted by Valignano, Organtino dressed in Japanese clothing, adapted to Japanese customs, and was 'outstandingly successful in dealing with the Japanese.'[45] He was also dedicated to higher education for indigenous people, and was later placed in charge of the first seminary, at Azuchi, by Valignano in 1580. Organtino recognized the importance of *magnificenza* for Jesuit foundations in such an aristocratic country, called for beauty and decorum in churches and colleges, and organized grand religious processions through Japanese towns on feast days. He was also concerned about the fine arts. In a letter of 1577, he asked the General to send architects, sculptors, and painters to Japan, and even asked Valignano to try to obtain paintings and other adornments from rich Portuguese sea captains.[46] Organtino's compatriot Francesco Pasio, who arrived in 1578 and became Vice-Provincial in 1600, was also a proponent of adaptation, and distinguished himself as 'the first superior of Japan not to need an interpreter.'[47]

Alessandro Valignano has been credited with introducing the policy of adaptation into Japan.[48] There is no doubt that he was the first to make it official policy and that he was that method's most important promoter in Asia, but, as we have seen, the pre-Cabral mission had already adapted to indigenous clothing, architecture, and lifestyle. Valignano's main contributions were to reverse the policies of Cabral (who resigned his post in 1581), to admit Japanese into the Society, and to stress higher education.[49] But in many ways he simply moved the mission back in the direction it had been going – if tentatively – before 1570. He codified and regularized these practices, weaving them into a new Jesuit ideology that would dominate mission policy throughout Asia. Valignano arrived as Visitor to the Indies for the first time between 1579 and 1582, and returned twice more before his death in Macao in 1606. Of aristocratic stock, he was a proud, arrogant, and impatient man with a violent past and a prison record. Nevertheless, he brought the Japan mission to a new level of gentleness and receptiveness to indigenous culture, believing that Japanese and Chinese culture both possessed frameworks on which Christianity could build.

An admirer of José de Acosta, who himself possessed a strong interest in Asia, Valignano became the most outspoken opponent of the Patronate and its *conquistador* mentality, whereby becoming a Christian meant becoming a Portuguese or Spaniard. Despite racist tendencies of his own, he was appalled by the treatment of new converts by Portuguese colonists, and was even more concerned by the menace of Spanish imperial expansion from the recently conquered Philippines. He recommended, in 1579, that no mendicants or even Jesuits from those islands be allowed to enter Japan or China, fearing (along with many Japanese) that they would represent a 'fifth column' of colonial expansion.[50] He stressed time and again that the Far East was not like Mexico or Peru, to be won and looted by Western powers. He was also shocked with what he found among the Jesuits in Japan. The mission had become so intolerant under Cabral's tenure that the Japanese community was quickly losing its patience. Valignano not only reformed the treatment of Japanese Christians, but vastly improved their education, particularly in the Japanese language, in founding institutions of higher learning. These included a novitiate at Usuki for the training of Jesuit novices; two 'seminaries,' at Arima and Azuchi, for the schooling of young Japanese boys in the humanities and other sciences, including Latin, Japanese, and etiquette; and the College of Saint Paul at Funai, which provided higher-level education in both Japanese and European studies, including Buddhist doctrine.[51] These institutions moved with great frequency – sometimes as often as every few months – but all of them were finally located in Nagasaki, near the Church of the Assumption.

Perhaps the most telling aspect of Valignano's new policy was his insistence on training an indigenous priesthood, a radical move which contrasted sharply with policies in the Americas and India, and which resulted in the first Japanese ordinations during 1601–3.[52] Struggling against hostile colonial authorities, Valignano even mounted a spectacular public relations stunt between 1582 and

1590 to solicit European support for his venture and to show off Japanese readiness for the priesthood.[53] This famous Japanese 'embassy' to Europe was little more than a fabricated spectacle created by Valignano with the somewhat distracted compliance of the daimyos Ōtomo Yoshishige, Ōmura Sumitada, and Arima Harunobu. The 'ambassadors' who purported to represent these rulers were four Japanese Jesuit novices (only two of them were really nobles). These young men visited Lisbon, Madrid, and Rome amidst great jubilation, were received by Pope Gregory XIII in audience, and – thanks to their fortune in being in Rome during the latter's death – attended with great pomp the installation of Sixtus V (1585–90). A second Japanese expedition has been made famous by novelist Shusaku Endo. This time actually sent by a Japanese potentate and therefore more worthy of the title 'embassy,' it travelled via Manila to New Spain and Europe between 1613–20, creating a similar stir in Paul V's Rome; however, the Christian enterprise was already doomed by the time they arrived.[54]

Valignano's mission policy was outlined in a handbook entitled *Advertimentos e avisos acerca dos costumes e catangues de Jappão* (1580), prepared at the instigation and with the collaboration of the daimyo Otomo Yoshishige.[55] The recommendations are aimed principally at reforming the daily behaviour of the missionaries. Jesuits are exhorted to live cleanly and politely, and to maintain a dignified and authoritative demeanour at all times. Valignano stressed adaptation to Japanese eating habits, diet, and clothing, and adherence to the Japanese code of conduct and etiquette. Like Organtino, he also expected his missionaries to maintain a degree of grandeur and *magnificenza*, a vital means of earning Japanese respect in this period. He even advocated adapting the hierarchy of the Rinzai sect of Zen Buddhism to Christianity – an idea reminiscent of De Nobili's adoption of a Hindu title in India. This innovative policy was later abandoned, however, as Buddhism fell out of favour with Oda Nobunaga's successors.[56] Valignano was not able, however, to allow missionaries to wear the silk kimono as they had before, being forced to retain the black cassock that had been decreed by Rome.[57]

An entire chapter of the *Advertimentos* (chapter 7) concerns architecture. Valignano orders that all Jesuit buildings in Japan be built in the Japanese style by Japanese architects, and that they accommodate to Japanese ceremonial, including the tea ceremony and the proper division of social classes and sexes. He wrote: 'Since their manner of construction is so different from that which we use in Europe ... we are unable to design them well ourselves.'[58] His choice was also a matter of personal taste. In another text, he demonstrated the highest regard for Japanese architecture:

> Their houses are made of wood and covered with boards or straw, and are very pretty, accommodating, and well made. They are always furnished with mats which are like mattresses, which make them appear very clean and tidy. It seems to me that they are the most neat and honourable people on earth.[59]

Sometimes we have been left with the names of these Japanese architects, who were not mere amateurs. The Japanese Christian Justino Kazariya was an accomplished architect who was invited to Nagasaki from Sakai in 1583, where he also founded the Nagasaki Misericordia confraternity.[60] He built many churches for Nagasaki Christians, and, together with his wife, he served as a religious leader in the area.

Valignano laid out ten principles of architectural design for Jesuit churches, colleges, and residences, which combine the practical with the stylistic. Although most of the recommendations focus on maintaining appropriate divisions between ranks of people, and between the Jesuits and outsiders, others concentrate on design elements, such as the use of Japanese-style reception parlours (*zashiki*) with sliding doors (*shoji*), special cabinets to house requisites for the tea and sake ceremony (*sakazuki*), and ornamental gardens. *Shoji*, which became popular during the Momoyama Period, were made of sheets of translucent white paper pasted on one side of a wooden lattice framework. They allowed in light and gave the room an open sensation. Valignano's recommendations for Jesuit residences reflect recent architectural innovations in Momoyama Japan, when a complex form of residence known as the *shoin* was developed to accommodate the highly structured and hierarchical etiquette of samurai society. Like Valignano's residence, the *shoin* focused on a central reception hall, and included special alcoves, levels, sliding doors, verandas, and shelves for displaying art objects.

In the case of churches, however, Valignano was less flexible. He ordered that the nave and choir were to extend along the length of the *hondō* in the European fashion, instead of across the width as in Japanese Buddhist temples, 'because in the construction of churches it would be improper to imitate them, since theirs are synagogues of Satan and ours are churches of God.'[61] What a striking contrast this statement makes with his comments on Japanese houses! *Zashiki* were allowed on either side of the nave to house noblemen and women, which by means of *shoji* could open onto the nave, creating a single large room. Finally, Valignano ordered that churches have a veranda in front to act as an atrium, and in front of that an ablution fountain for parishioners to wash their feet in the Japanese manner, both of which were already incorporated into Japanese church architecture before Valignano. The spacious and open hallway was ideal for preaching, and echoed Jesuit constructions in Europe and the Americas.

The single nave, two-*zashiki* plan also coincidentally evoked the three-aisled basilicas of the Early Church. This basilical reference is evoked in Valignano's description of the new church at Arima, built in 1582, in which the reader is given no clue whatsoever that it was built in the style of a Japanese temple – even though Valignano mentions that Japanese woodworkers sent by the Lord of Arima did the job: 'In Arima a very beautiful three-nave church has been built, and it is the finest, and most spacious of all the churches we have in these parts of Christendom.'[62] In another document of the same year, the *Regimento para el Superior de Japón* (1580), Valignano specifically calls for churches to be outwardly grand, recommending 'fine churches, especially in the chief centres, constructed in our style of architecture according to the plan followed at the Church of the Assumption in Nagasaki, consisting of one or three aisles depending on the number and quality of the population and the locality.'[63] It is interesting to note that in this statement Valignano explicitly refers to Japanese building traditions as 'our style of architecture' – *noster modus*, once again.

The Jesuit approach to architecture is really brought into context when compared to that of the Franciscans. The Franciscans established a permanent base in Japan in 1593, contrary to the most emphatic wishes of Valignano. Coming from New Spain, the friars built convents in places such as Miyako (Kyoto, 1594), where they conducted open public masses *en voz alta*, dressed in the European manner, rang bells, and acted very much as if they were in Mexico City or Manila. Although we have no proof that their churches were built in the Spanish colonial style, the superior Fray Pedro Bautista Blázquez y Blázquez (1542–97) wrote proudly that they did everything in the Spanish manner, and that they gained permission to build 'a convent and church and perform our holy offices just as in Spain.'[64] The Franciscans wrote with nationalistic pride that the Franciscans in Japan were showing the Japanese 'our ... manner of living,' whereas the Jesuits 'travel[ed] about very fearfully in Japanese dress.'[65] Largely in reaction to Franciscan behaviour, Hideyoshi ordered the mass crucifixion of 1597, in which twenty-three Franciscans (including Blázquez) met their demise. Shortly after that massacre, in which three Japanese Jesuit novices also perished, virtually all of the churches in Japan – Jesuit or Franciscan – were destroyed.

If Valignano's reform of mission architecture in Japan was partly a codification of existing practices, his recommendations for the visual arts were revolutionary. Art formed an important part of Valignano's mission policy from the beginning of his tenure as Visitor. He commissioned artworks himself while in Goa, and asked the General to send brothers to Japan who were trained as painters, architects, masons, and in other handicrafts.[66] As did other Jesuit missionaries at the time, he also gave away copious quantities of religious images as gifts. Upon arrival in Miyako (Kyoto) in 1581, for example, according to Josef Schütte, Valignano presented Oda Nobunaga and his nobility with 'many sets of vestments and other church requisites, small oil paintings and altar pictures of larger size, and probably also musical instruments, books and other articles.'[67] His famed 'embassy' to Europe returned in 1590 with illustrated printed books, Gobelin tapestries, and Italian oil paintings, and while they were in Italy the ambassadors sat for portraits by Tintoretto (1519–94) and another painter named Urbano Monte.[68]

However, above all, Valignano recognized the urgent need for an art academy at the Japanese mission, including a printing press, that was capable of bridging the profound gap he perceived between Japanese and European aesthetics. He wrote at length about this cultural fissure, first focusing on colours:

> So much do [the Japanese] have the opposite taste to ours in every manner, that they abhor and despise the things which we commonly think are tasty. On the other hand, we could not put in our mouths the things which they esteem greatly. The same goes for colours, and for the objects which appeal very much to our eyes. Ordinarily, they do not like them at all. And we attribute the least value to those things which are pleasing to their gaze. For example, white, which is for us a happy and festive colour, is for them the colour of mourning and sadness And black and purple make them very happy, yet for us they represent mourning.[69]

Later in the same document, Valignano discusses differences in the kinds of art valued by the Japanese and Europeans; for example, this discussion of Zen *suibokuga* (black ink painting) which demonstrates a keen awareness of the media and styles that appealed to local sensibilities:

> They are the same way with a piece of paper that has been painted with a little bird or tree in black ink. When it has been painted by the hand of some famous ancient, they will buy and sell it among themselves for three, four, or ten thousand ducats – this for something which to our eyes or opinion has no value.[70]

Valignano showed great respect for Japanese art appreciation – 'their art connoisseurs have a fine eye' – and a sensitivity to the Japanese way of looking at things, even if he was not always in agreement with them.[71] Therefore, just as indigenous lay preachers and priests were crucial for penetrating the subtleties of Japanese culture, only indigenous painters of devotional images would be capable of manufacturing images suitable for Japanese sensibilities.

Valignano's proposal for a painting and engraving school was also inspired by a more pressing problem: the dire need for religious images that could be produced cheaply on site for Japan and other Asian missions instead of shipping them from Europe. The Japan mission alone had expanded so quickly that earlier missionaries had made requests for paintings from Rome a regular litany. Luis Fróis reported in 1584 that more than fifty thousand devotional images were needed to satisfy the growing community in Japan, explaining that the Japanese Christians were particularly upset that they had no pictures to replace their household deities.[72] Three years later, he added in frustration that images were so coveted as gifts in other missions that a priest could set out for Japan with a thousand pictures and be obliged to part with all of them before he even reached the islands, later citing the example of a painting destined for the Japan mission which never made it beyond Goa.[73] Other missions were being founded at that very moment in China and India which could also benefit from a comparably local art workshop.

Valignano's dream came true in 1583, with the foundation of a Japanese Jesuit art academy, referred to in the sources as a 'school' or 'seminary' of painters, but known to scholars fancifully – and erroneously – as the 'Academy of St. Luke.'[74] The largest mission art academy ever founded in Asia, this Seminary of Painters began as a department of the seminary at Arima, which, as we have seen, Valignano had founded together with one at Azuchi in 1580.[75] Valignano chose as director the professional artist Brother Giovanni Niccolò (1563–1626), a native of Nola in the Kingdom of Naples, who entered the Society in 1577 and had apprenticed and worked in Naples and Rome before coming out to the East in 1581.[76] A capable painter, engraver, and sculptor, Niccolò was the perfect choice to lead such an extensive and multifaceted workshop. Like his contemporary Bitti in Peru, Niccolò possessed a wide range of talents, as well as a capability for hard work and innovation. A eulogy written at the time of his death praised the Italian painter as 'possessing great gentleness and probity, having a special talent for mathematics, painting, and clockmaking, instructing students in painting, and providing religious pictures for the churches.'[77] Despite ill health on his long voyage via Lisbon, Goa, Malacca, and Macao, Niccolò was already executing oil paintings for missions before he reached Japan. Niccolò was kept as busy as his Peruvian contemporary during his long stay in Japan, not just by running the art academy but by executing large-scale and smaller oil paintings for churches and Christian families in Japan, and also for the nascent mission in China.

Although no signed work by Niccolò survives today, there is at least one picture that can safely be attributed to the master. *Madonna and Child* in Osaka in oil on wood panel looks as though it is by an Italian hand and bears no traces of Japanese style (fig. 26).[78] More importantly, the work is unfinished since the artist has only applied an oil sketch in umber and has not yet added colour, which strongly suggests that it was painted in Japan and not Europe. It is unclear whether this whole painting is merely a *bozzetto* (a project for a larger altarpiece) or the preparatory drawing for the work itself, although, given the expense of artists' materials overseas, it is unlikely that they would be used on elaborate *bozzetti*. Also clearly visible, especially at the lower half of the panel, is a grid pattern drawn in black chalk, demonstrating that the image was transposed from a model, most likely an engraving, the most common method of copying on the missions. A full-length image of the seated Madonna adoring the child on her knee, the painting has the classical stability and grace of Raphael's Madonnas, and also recalls Leonardo in both its composition and rocky landscape setting. Although the drawing is fairly formulaic, it is quite capable, particularly in the lines describing the body and legs of the Christ Child, and in the drapery of the Madonna. The simplicity and conservative piety of this image is precisely what we would expect of this young brother painter and is consistent with the *arte sacra* found elsewhere on the missions.

Although the school did not really get going until 1590, Niccolò was almost certainly already training painters from the time he arrived in Japan. Three of his earliest students, who are most likely to have been working with him before 1590, are the young Japanese lay brother painters Watano Mancio (b. 1573), Mancio João (b. 1571), and Pedro João (1566–1620).[79] As was typical for all Jesuit enterprises in Japan, the Seminary of Painters was frequently on the move. In 1587 it would have transferred to Urakami, near Nagasaki, along with the seminary, and to Nagasaki itself after Hideyoshi seized Urakami in 1588, and then on to Hachirao.[80] In 1589 the seminary was transferred again, this time to Katsusa, where they were joined by the equally itinerant students and novices who were most recently at Arie. In 1591 Niccolò's workshop transferred to the college at Kawachinoura (known as the Amakusa College); five years later, it moved to the seminary at Arie. Niccolò and his academy were back in Amakusa in 1600, where the college itself had just returned following a brief period in hiding in Nagasaki; following a short stay in Arima again in 1601, the Seminary of Painters returned to Nagasaki once more (Niccolò was by now a priest), this time remaining for more than a decade in an outbuilding near the Church of the Assumption, where the college had also found a relatively permanent home; and, finally, in 1614, the whole enterprise was forced to flee to Macao after all missionaries were banned from Japan.[81] Although in some cases the entire school appears to have moved, in others, only the instructors may have travelled. Such behaviour was not unusual. Itinerant art teachers were common in the Paraguay reductions, for example, where the more skilled instructors moved from mission to mission, leaving their students behind to contribute to the art projects of their own community. Given its humble beginnings and itinerant nature, it is all the more extraordinary that by the early 1590s the Seminary of Painters was an academy in size as well as name.

Niccolò supervised ateliers of astonishing size – including Jesuit brothers, college students, and boys from the seminary – who executed oil paintings on copper, wood panel, and probably canvas, in addition to watercolour and ink paintings on paper and bronze plaquettes and sculpture, on a vast scale.[82] For models, the art students used oil paintings such as those brought back by the 'embassy' of 1590, as well as engravings, primarily of the Antwerp school. After the arrival in 1590 of Japan's first printing press – another innovation of Valignano's, responsible for a rich tradition of Japanese Christian literature – students trained in engraving pictures as well.[83] Although, unlike the later Calera de Tango in Chile, Niccolò's academy did not produce furniture or textiles, it did manufacture clocks and musical instruments, the latter being essential for the new *magnificenza* called for by Organtino and Valignano.

Jesuit chroniclers wrote glowing reports of the Seminary's progress. These enthusiastic outpourings of religious zeal are among the most detailed descriptions of Jesuit mission art enterprises ever written, and give us enormous insight into their workshop practices. Father Fróis described an already extensive operation in 1592, when he commented that since the young Japanese in the academy

> learn to paint, and engrave plates with the burin for printing images, it follows that we have much cause for admiration to see what skilful hands they have and with what facility they learn, and when Your Paternity sees some of these works and realizes that they are the work of mere boys who are only beginners, it will console you indeed.[84]

Jesuits Pedro Gómez and Francesco Pasio both left descriptions of the academy when it was in Amakusa in 1594 which demonstrate that it had already expanded dramatically in two years, possibly with more than twenty students. Gómez wrote that Niccolò had eight *dōjuku* students working on watercolours, as many more on oils, and five on engraving:

> Some of [the boys] make no less progress in painting, for example in engraving plates for printing, since eight of them were executing images in watercolours and others in oils, and five of them were engraving plates, and these and other [pupils] show such aptitude that causes us great admiration, because some of them draw most naturally paintings of the finest quality which the Japanese *fidalgos* [i.e., ambassadors] brought from Rome, with such perfection both in colour and form, that when afterwards, among our own fathers and brothers, many could not tell which were the ones they made and which had been done in Rome. And some declared that those made by the Japanese were the ones which had come from Rome. And since this may seem to be hyberbolic, the father Vice Provincial decided to send some to Your Paternity and to the Father Bishop of Japan and to the Father Visitor.[85]

In a letter written some months later, Gómez again reported that 'in the Seminary ... there is much activity in singing, playing the organ and *monarcordios*, and painting,' but repeated the old cliché that the Japanese artists were incapable of originality and were completely dependent upon their European models.[86] In a similar report of the Amakusa academy, Pasio pointed out that the *dōjuku* were busy supplying altarpieces for the churches in the region, a job which kept them active the year round.[87] Fróis also attests to the hectic pace of the artistic production at the academy when he wrote in the Annual Letter for 1595:

> Also, not a day passes in which those who are learning to paint images in oils and watercolour, and those who learn to engrave plates for printing, do not perfect their skills even more, as Your Reverence has seen by those which we sent you from here.[88]

In a later, more extensive description of the painting academy, which was by this time (1596) at Arie, Fróis described an operation so large that it took up a substantial portion of the Seminary as a whole:

> The Seminary is divided into four classes, and one school for reading and writing. In one of these they read facts about Japan to those who have already begun their study of Latin, which is a very important matter here for those who are going to preach and deal with the gentiles who know Japanese characters. The other three classes are for the purpose of other *dōjukus* who occupy themselves in painting images in oils, in watercolours, and in ink, with such exactitude and beauty ... or they are busy engraving plates with the burin, in which they draw and copy very well various prints which come from Europe.[89]

In the same year, the Jesuit Bishop Pedro Martins of Japan visited the Arie Seminary, which now had ninety-three students, in addition to other people making the *Exercises*. Like Fróis's letter, his report demonstrates that the painting academy served as an important adjunct to the seminary's humanistic studies, and probably played a role in every student's education. On his first visit to the Seminary, Bishop Martins was shown a display of student artwork in one of the humanities classrooms that was similar to exhibitions in Jesuit schools in Europe: '... for this reception, the seminarians had adorned their class with various sonnets, epigrams, paintings, and prayers written in our letters.'[90] In this very room, the Bishop attended a play in Latin and listened as three Japanese students gave orations. Later on, the Bishop returned to the Seminary, this time together with a group of Jesuit and Portuguese dignitaries. Martins first visited a humanities classroom, where a Japanese brother gave a presentation on Buddhism which was attended also by thirty students from the Latin class; next Martins visited the elementary school, where children were learning to read and write in Latin letters; and lastly, they reached the music class. Then the entourage passed on to the art academy:

> From here they went out to the office where they print books, where they started right away to print several of them, which the Bishop distributed with his own hands to his companions. In another place there were other young men who were busy engraving plates with the burin. Finally, the thing which astonished them the most was to enter a long building overflowing with boys and young men who were painters, every one of them

with his picture in his hand, painting various images in oil, which, when they were finished, the Father Vice-provincial went to hand out to the Christian gentlemen and those in the Society. At the front of this building was placed an image of Our Lady after St Luke, painted by one of these students who was nineteen years old [possibly Luís Shiozuka]. They were at great pains to believe that such a perfect and accomplished work had been produced by a mere boy.[91]

The painting hung at the front of the workshop was none other than the Virgin of Saint Luke at the Church of Santa Maria Maggiore in Rome, the miraculous image mentioned in chapter 1, and probably the most popular image of the Jesuits worldwide (fig. 1).[92] The original picture, known in Europe as *Salus Populi Romani*, was a Byzantine icon of the tenth century that later became the centrepiece of the Borghese chapel, and is also commonly known as the *Borghese Madonna*.[93] It was the favourite image of the Jesuit general Saint Francis Borgia (1565–72), who used it for preaching, and with the permission of Pope Pius V he had a copy made in 1569 by 'an excellent painter' in an updated Late Renaissance style from which other versions could be produced for the missions.[94] During 1569–70 Borgia sent copies to the mission in Brazil, to several European monarchs, and to the noviciate in Spain and Prague; by the late 1570s, versions appeared in Macao, China, Japan, and the Philippines, where they were repeatedly copied by local artists working for the Society; and by the early seventeenth century, others were sent to Abyssinia, Persia, Paraguay, Peru, and New Spain.[95]

Bishop Martins had himself possibly made efforts to advance the cause of the Seminary of Painters. He may have earlier asked another European painter to join the academy, a man known only as the 'Portuguese painter,' who had worked on the Jesuit mission to Mughal India in 1595 (see chapter 5). Since he was not a Jesuit, this man's name does not appear in any of the official records, and it is impossible to say whether he ever reached Japan. One other European artist, or at least draughtsman, who entered Japan seven years later was the Italian Jesuit Carlo Spinola (1564–1622). An aristocrat from Genoa, Father Spinola studied mathematics at the Collegio Romano under Clavius (1538–1612), drew up plans for the Jesuit church in Macao (fig. 44), and may have taught drawing in his academy of sciences, which he ran in Kyoto during 1611–12.[96] With his martyrdom, however, nothing remains but his name.

The Seminary of Painters continued to grow during the first years of the next century. The Annual Letter of 1601 described bustling production in Nagasaki and showed how the academy supplied all of the churches and Christian families of the region with images:

In this city are the students who study painting, who live in a separate house in the manner of a seminary under the apprenticeship of two of ours [i.e., Jesuits]. One of these came from Rome a few years ago, and is now a priest. He has trained such capable disciples in this art that the churches of Japan are adorned with retables of such richness and quality, that truly they are comparable to those of Europe. With these, and other images printed in great quantity and distributed among the Christians, Christian devotion and piety expand greatly. Thanks to the industry of this same father, many organs and musical instruments are made for the principal churches, and many mechanical clocks, some of them very curious, showing the movement of the sun and moon ...[97]

The other Jesuit mentioned may have been Pedro João, Niccolò's eldest pupil (see below). Two years later (1603), Diogo de Mesquita, rector of the college, wrote a similar report, which also emphasized the extraordinary volume of its activity. After remarking that the students work in oil, watercolours, and engraving, he commented: '... they supply all of the churches of Japan and all of this Christendom, since the Fathers give them to Christians as presents. They also use them to supply their foundations in China.'[98] Bishop Cerqueira added in the same account that he found these churches 'well adorned with oil painting and watercolours which they execute very well, since some of them are very fine painters. And the Fathers distribute a great number of pictures, painted and printed, which the Christians treat with great devotion.'[99]

As these reports attest, the Seminary of Painters was capable of producing art on a grand scale beyond anything else available in Asia (even in Goa, the Flemish Jesuit painter Machs was told to spend less time on art and more on proselytization, and the colony as a whole had very meagre artistic resources before the seventeenth century), and it consequently became a model for missions everywhere. As we shall see missionaries doing later in Mughal India and Paraguay, the Jesuits in Japan proudly sent examples of the Seminary's work to Rome to impress the authorities; for example, in 1592 and 1595.[100] The academy's output was substantial enough to supply the churches and confraternities of Japan, and the missions of China and India, as well as providing temporary art for processions and festivities such as the lavish festival of the Holy Sacrament held in Nagasaki in 1606.[101] The Seminary of Painters apparently also produced significant numbers of images for the export market, since *namban* wares were extremely popular in Europe. It is a testament to the mission's magnitude that we have as many paintings as we do after more than three centuries and one of the most thorough persecutions in early modern history.

Niccolò's pupils, primarily Japanese Jesuit brothers and *dōjuku* lay assistants, went on to direct and disseminate Japanese Christian art in Japan, China, the Philippines, and possibly even Peru.[102] Many of their names – although not their paintings – are known to us. Brother Pedro João (b. 1566), perhaps a painting instructor at the Seminary of Painters, also served as a choir master (*mestre da capela*) in the city of Nagasaki;[103] Brother Leonardo Kimura (1574–1619), also based in Nagasaki, was both an accomplished painter and engraver;[104] Brother Luís Shiozuka (1577–1615), who entered the Arima college in 1588 and joined the Society in 1607, worked in Nagasaki as a painter, organist, and choir master;[105] Brother Mancio Taichiku (1574–1615) became a very eminent painter and was credited with decorating most of the church interiors in Japan;[106] Brother Thaddeus (1568–1620) was listed as a painter in Nagasaki in 1603 and in Miyako in 1613, but fled in 1616 to the Philippines, where he lived in a house devoted to Japanese Jesuit refugees, and finally to Macao in 1619.[107] Of Brothers Watano Mancio (Amakubo) and Mancio João, Niccolò's original pupils in Amakusa, Mancio João accompanied his former master to Macao in 1614, but we hear nothing more of Watano Mancio after 1596.[108] The Seminary of Painters also taught Chinese pupils who went on to direct mission art projects in their own country. Such were the famous Brother Emanuel Pereira (Yu Wenhui, 1572–1630), the painter of Matteo Ricci's only portrait (fig. 27), and possibly the half-Chinese, half-Japanese Brother Jacobo Niwa (1579–1635), about whom more in chapter 4. Finally, and most significantly for the history of Japanese art, Niccolò's academy trained a large number of non-Jesuits, and probably also non-Christian Japanese artists, including members of the celebrated Kanō school. We will look at some of their work below.

We also know something about the printers and engravers who worked for Niccolò's academy. The master printer was the Italian brother Giovanni Battista Pesce, who managed to supervise the huge production of the Jesuit press at the same time as the infirmary, and died in Macao in 1607.[109] The first book printed by the press was *Sanctos no Gosagueo no Uchi Nuquigaqi*, or the Acts of the Saints, published in Katsusa in 1591, including an engraving featuring elongated, late *maniera* figures on the title page (fig. 39). The Japanese brother Shiko Miguel not only assisted at the press with Latin letters but created type in Japanese characters, since his Italian supervisor knew 'little of the language.'[110] Another Japanese printer, known only as Brother Pedro, also worked with Japanese type.[111] As we shall also see happening later in Paraguay, a native author used the Japanese press to publish a series of his original sermons, showing that even within the arguably limited parameters of Christian oratory a Japanese Christian could demonstrate that there was such a thing as indigenous creativity. His name was Brother Romão Nishi.[112] The Japanese press was sent on to the Philippines in 1611, a destination that had already been suggested for it as early as 1594.[113]

Characteristics of Japanese Christian Art

Although none of them can be assigned to any particular artist, a surprising number of paintings, engravings, and sculptures survive that can be attributed to Niccolò's academy (figs. 28–39). Some of these works were preserved by hidden Christian families and appeared only in this century. Others only survived because they were in Europe or Latin America at the time of the Japanese persecutions; they have come to light only in the past twenty years. The images include medium-sized oil paintings on canvas, copper plate, wooden panel, and Japanese paper (*washi*); watercolours on paper; engravings; bronze plaquettes; and sculptures. The paintings primarily depict the Madonna or Madonna and Child, including the Madonna of Saint Luke,[114] scenes from the life of Christ, and pictures of saints. They are delicately drawn, with soft and nuanced modelling and rich, vibrant colours. Most of them are based on Italian or Flemish engravings, and they possess the classicism and sentimental piety of Roman *arte sacra* of the 1580s and '90s – the very style we have observed in Niccolò's own work. Many scholars and collectors maintain that the majority of these paintings, especially the ones that adhere most closely to European canons, were mass-produced in Goa and Europe and are not the products of the Japanese academy.[115] Although this is likely true for some of them, it is very doubtful that the majority came from outside Japan. First, we can discard Goa right away since there was very little painting in Goa in the period and it was extremely crude in comparison (fig. 63).[116] Second, the media of these paintings (oil and watercolour on copper, wood, paper, and possibly canvas) were all commonly practised by Niccolò's workshop, and, given the incredible volume of the school's output, there is no reason to suspect that they would not have been made there. Scholars often refer to the European style of these images as proof of European provenance, conceding only that the least canonic ones might come from Japan. Yet the historical sources fall over each other praising the skills of the Japanese painters in copying. In addition, the sources tend to report assiduously any European painting that reached Japan, and it is clear that they were few and far between. In any case, even the most 'European' of these pictures either demonstrate a slight lack of understanding of European conventions of shading and foreshortening, or subtly recall in some way traditional Japanese painting. Finally, several of these paintings copy the same source or appear to have been painted by the same artist, further evidence that they were produced in the same workshop. If, as many contend, the lacquer shrines were shipped empty to Europe to be fitted with paintings, why do they not all conform to a standard size? The shrines come in a variety of different sizes, suggesting strongly that they were made for specific paintings – in Japan. I shall make further remarks on these features below.

Several of these images are contained in traditional Japanese black lacquer (*urushi*) travelling shrines adorned with gold and silver dust (*maki-e*) and inlaid mother-of-pearl (*raden*) patterns in a style which flourished in the Momoyama Period (figs. 28, 31, 32, 33, 34).[117] Although in technique and colour these *namban* lacquers resemble mainstream Japanese lacquerware (they were made by the same craftsmen), they differ from them greatly in style. The making of traditional lacquerware is an extremely painstaking process which can take from a few months to years to complete, from the making of the wooden base to the final polishing stage. The designs on Momoyama lacquers are made by sprinkling metal powders or flakes over the drawing before the lacquer hardens so that they adhere to the lines of the pattern. In more traditional lacquerware (e.g., *kōdaiji* wares), the patterns are loosely painted, naturalistic foliate patterns, often of tall grasses and flowers, and they tend not to use mother-of-pearl. *Namban* lacquers, by contrast, make extensive use of pearl inlay and feature symmetrical, tightly woven arabesques of vines, trees, and birds, as well as purely geometrical patterns, all of which recall Islamic art. The artisans may have chosen this kind of ornament for *namban* lacquers because they believed that Europeans were culturally very similar to the traders from the Middle East and Central Asia with whom Japanese merchants had been in contact for centuries. Most *namban* lacquers show signs of having been made more hastily than *kōdaiji* ware, suggesting that they were made for the open market, either for Japanese Christians or for export to Christian Asia and Europe. Some of these patterns may make symbolic statements about the paintings they enclose, as we will soon see.

The Japanese Christian paintings demonstrate a wide range of reactions to European art. Most of them are primarily European in style, yet they show a slight unfamiliarity with Western conventions, or a hint of Japanese convention.

Others are a striking blend of European realism with Japanese draughtsmanship and colour, occasionally allowing the Japanese elements to prevail. It is tempting to construct a chronology with the most European pictures at the beginning and the most indigenous at the end, but such a schema tends to be meaningless in the world of mission art, where a multitude of styles coexisted simultaneously according to the experience and taste of the artists.

Among the European-style paintings is a delicate *Dolorosa* in oils on canvas which was preserved in secret by a Christian family from Echizen, but which is unfortunately badly worn and creased from constant folding (fig. 29).[118] Although canvas is not specifically mentioned as a medium produced by Niccolò's atelier, there is no reason to doubt that it was used. A deeply introspective work, the soft and delicate face is contrasted sharply with the starched white drapery of the veil, which is arranged in deep folds. These shadows, together with the dark background of the picture, give the whole a ghostly *tenebroso* effect, so that the face seems to be only barely emerging from the darkness. Although the image is a close copy of a *Madonna* by the Roman engraver of French extraction Antonio Lafreri (active 1544–77), the distinguished use of modelling and colour betrays the hand of a master, and the resulting picture is considerably more moving than the original. The arched eyebrow, narrow eye, and long nose offer the slightest hint of Japanese painting convention (see fig. 23) and suggest that the artist was not a European.

The only dated Japanese Christian painting is a striking *Salvator Mundi* from 1597 in oil on copper panel, which is inspired by a Theodor Galle/Martin de Vos print of that subject and is signed on the reverse in Latin letters: 'Sacam Iacobus' (fig. 30).[119] Some scholars have suggested that this is the signature of Jacobo Niwa, a pupil of Niccolò's who would later distinguish himself in China. As we shall see in chapter 4, Niwa's art was highly regarded by his contemporaries; the fine quality of this image, therefore, would tend to corroborate such an attribution. The subject of the Salvator Mundi was a favourite of Niccolò's, as we have already seen. Thanks to its medium and to the vivid colours dominated by bright reds, the image has a fiery brilliance. The draughtsmanship is expert, despite some awkwardness with foreshortening in the execution of the hands, and the face and head in particular show the careful attention to detail and tiny brushstrokes which are typical of Japanese Christian work. It is precisely the sort of work that some scholars would dismiss as European or Goan if it did not have the inscription indicating a Japanese origin. The face itself has few traces of Japanese style, although the brilliant gold borders on Christ's robe recall a similar convention used in some portraits of samurai to highlight their armour. A hint of the warrior would be quite appropriate in this almost apocalyptic image of Christ on Judgment Day, rising, as he seems to be, from the flames.

Another painting in a more European style is a lively and colourful *Holy Family with St John the Baptist* in the most exquisitely ornate of all the lacquer travelling shrines, which is based on a Wierix original and is also in oil on copper panel (fig. 31).[120] The brushwork is again extremely precise and delicate, the inscriptions are carefully and legibly inscribed, and like the 1597 *Salvator Mundi* it makes prominent use of gold highlights. The lavish use of gold on the drapery of the Madonna and the bedclothes of the child reflects the equally lavish floral arabesques in gold lacquer on the frame and doors of the shrine. As in the *Dolorosa*, the facial features of the Virgin, particularly her 'bee-stung' lips, recall more traditional Japanese painting. In fact, the face of the Virgin closely resembles faces on a series of Japanese screens in the Western style from the late Momoyama Period associated with an artist who signed his name 'Nobukata,' one of which is at the MOA Art Museum in Shizuoka (see also fig. 40).[121] In addition, this *Holy Family* was done by the same artist who painted the works in figures 32 and 33, a similarity immediately apparent in the tilt of the head of the Virgin, the treatment of the eyebrows and ears, and the slight awkwardness in the foreshortening. These two works are also *urushi* paintings, this time of the Madonna and Child with Christ reaching for his mother's breast, based possibly on an engraving by the Italian engraver Luca Bertelli (active 1550–80).[122] Here, the artist has flattened the foreshortening, particularly in Christ's face. The Virgin's face and hands are quite delicately drawn, and her high forehead, arched eyebrows, and 'bee-stung' lips again betray a Japanese hand. This quiet scene of motherhood is set amidst a riot of tree-and-bird ornament in gold and mother-of-pearl on the side panels.

In general, the lacquers seem to bear no relationship whatever to the painting inside. After all, they were made in two separate workshops. Lacquer workers were a very specialized and tight-knit group, since lacquer is not only extremely difficult to work but causes allergic reactions in most people. Operating in small groups and in isolation, lacquer workers would not have even occupied the same workshop as the painters of the images. Nevertheless, given that the designs were often supplied by the client, there are occasional examples where the lacquer ornament seems to comment on the painting inside. A painting of the Holy Trinity in oil on wooden panel, for example, has a pattern of meandering grapevines in gold and silver on the side panels, which is often found in *namban* wares and may be a reference to the Eucharist.[123]

Most of the images we have looked at so far are primarily European in style, suggesting only the merest hints of a Japanese hand. However, the finest of the Japanese Christian paintings show much more of an even synthesis between the two cultural traditions, offering the most compelling evidence of cultural partnership. One of these more hybrid images is the *Madonna of the Snows* in the Museum of the Martyrs in Nagasaki, to my mind one of the finest paintings to survive from any of the Jesuit missions anywhere (fig. 35).[124] A delicate watercolour on Japanese paper, it was hidden for centuries in the family of a crypto-Christian in Nagasaki and discovered only in the 1960s by Diego Yuuki. The image itself resembles closely the oil sketch of the Madonna and Child by Giovanni Niccolò (fig. 26), although it is hard to tell in its damaged state whether or not the child was originally included. It also bears very close resemblance to a print of The Virgin Adoring the Child from *Cruz no Monogatari* (The Story of the Cross), published by the Japanese press in 1591, even going so far as to include the mole on the Virgin's left cheek, as Diego Yuuki has recently pointed out.[125] Despite its clear adherence to a European model, however, the artist transforms every element of his image into equivalent Japanese style and technique. The brilliant colours on a gold background reflect current trends in mainstream Momoyama painting, as do the high, arched eyebrows, the narrow eyes, the double chin, and the 'bee-stung' lips which we have noted elsewhere (fig. 23).

The Virgin demonstrates Japanese concepts of beauty; as in typical Japanese portrayals of women in the period, her head is accented by sensuous wisps of hair, and her cheeks and forehead shine with an ivory-like brilliance. The most overtly Japanese element of all is its manner of framing, the *kakemono* or hanging scroll. Traditional *kakemono* include a painting or piece of calligraphy which has been mounted on a larger paper backing capable of being rolled up for storage. The artwork is framed by textiles such as figured silk or brocade, and attached to a wooden dowel at the bottom. Although the framing materials of *Madonna of the Snows* are in very poor condition, they are are clearly a more humble version of this same technique.

Another painting likely to be of the Salvator Mundi, in oil on copper plate, could not be more different from the 1597 version (fig. 36)[126] – in fact, it is so different that some believe it to be a secular subject. For reasons which I will discuss below, I believe it dates from several decades later, perhaps the 1630s. It comes from property seized by the Nagasaki Magistrate's Office. Not only is this image of the head of Christ strongly Japanese in style, but it fits into a Buddhist tradition of holy portraiture. The facial features have been flattened and the lines thickened to give it a cruder appearance. The nose, in particular, looks broken, and the lines of the face and around the large, staring eyes give the figure an ominous, even frightening aspect. We could discount these changes as merely the work of a hand unaccustomed to European perspective; however, there is compelling evidence that it was done on purpose.

A tradition of Japanese Zen ink painting, known as *zenga* (Zen painting), flourished in the early seventeenth century as peace returned to Japan. Painted primarily by Zen masters and monks as a form of meditation or mnemonic aid, these works were meant to be hung in the house or other private setting. Among the most popular subjects of such paintings were images of Buddhist hermits or especially the Indian missionary Daruma (Bodhidharma), who was said to have founded Zen (fig. 22).[127] In keeping with the Zen appreciation for rusticity and roughness embodied in *wabi*, these pictures often show a gnarled, elderly man with the exaggerated features – large nose and big eyes – of a foreigner. Like this *Salvator Mundi*, they often only show the head and shoulders of the figure. Furthermore, beginning in the first half of the seventeenth century, a whole series of coloured paintings of Daruma, and Zen hermits and eccentrics, was painted using European techniques of shading possibly by some of the artists trained in Niccolò's academy, including 'Nobukata,' who will be discussed below.[128]

Therefore, the artist of the *Salvator Mundi* roughens and exaggerates the features of his model, not because he lacks the requisite skills, but because he is trying to fit his image of a Christian holy man into a tradition of depicting Buddhist holy men, many of whom, like Christ, were foreigners. This connection with a seventeenth-century genre, together with the eyelashes, which link it to a painting datable to the 1620s or '30s (see below), inclines me to place it in the 1630s. A Christian picture of such a late date in Japan would have to be cryptic; therefore, if this image is of Jesus, it makes perfect sense that the artist would try to hide it safely within a Buddhist tradition of iconography. The *Salvator Mundi* would have been made for a private setting of meditation, just like the Zen images, demonstrating the syncretic nature of Christianity in early modern Japan.

Other Christian images are transformed by Japanese hands by adding indigenous decorative elements, costumes, or props, often giving them a festive flavour. One of the most striking is a large painting of Saint Michael slaying the dragon (oil on wood panel) in the Seminario de São José in Macao (fig. 37). This altarpiece was probably painted in Macao for the new Jesuit college church after 1614 by a Japanese member of the Seminary of Painters (either Luís Shiozuka, Mancio João, Leonardo Kimura, or Mancio Taichiku).[129] Inspired by Jerome Wierix's print *Quis Sicut Deus?*, this image of the archangel trades in the angel's lance for a samurai sword and transforms the edges of his helmet and sleeves into variations on the Chinese-inspired *lingzhi* fungus motif. As we have already seen with the 1597 *Salvator Mundi*, the borders of the costume are outlined in bright gold, another hint of the figure's warrior status. The stance is also very warrior-like, in a Japanese, as opposed to European, way (see fig. 21). The figure is standing with his knees facing outward in a confrontational pose which, together with the windswept look of the drapery and the bright colours, recalls traditional images of Buddhist guardian kings, an iconography whose 'accidental convergence' with that of Saint Michael has already been discussed in chapter 2 (figs. 8, 21). The São José picture shows how convenient this kind of convergence sometimes was to Christian missionaries.

Another example of 'accidental convergence' may actually have been accidental. It appears on a pair of images framed by smaller images arranged into square panels like a comic strip (fig. 38; watercolour on paper). Depicting Ignatius of Loyola and Francis Xavier honouring the Host and the Madonna and Child, the larger images are framed by scenes of the mysteries of the Holy Rosary in fifteen panels, and may have been made for a confraternity.[130] These pictures have been given widely different dates and provenances (from 1596 to the 1640s, and either Japan or Macao), but there is a general consensus now that they are from after the 1622 canonization of Ignatius and Francis, and were executed by Japanese artists in indigenous watercolours on Japanese paper. The Francis portrait has been traced to the frontispiece in Orazio Torsellino's 1589 biography of Saint Francis. The prominent eyelashes suggest that they were done by the same artist, or at least around the same time, as the later *Salvator Mundi* (fig. 36).

The motif of a border of panel paintings around a central image, as we have for these two pictures, was common in Europe, and a European model was certainly used by these painters. But the same motif is a standard feature of the Taima Mandara, the principal icon of Jōdo Pure Land Buddhism, which developed from the thirteenth century in Japan.[131] In the Taima Mandara, the border of iconic and narrative images depicts the basic ideas of the sutra in much the same manner as these rosary cycles, although in the Buddhist versions the strips run along the sides and bottom and in the Christian ones, along the sides and top. It would be tempting to propose that the mandala was evoked by these Christian painters – especially since both are devotional images and mandalas were so familiar to a Japanese audience. However, it is unlikely that the Christian artists meant to make that connection.

The printing press of the Seminary of Painters published a substantial amount of Catholic literature in Japanese, as well as dictionaries and anthologies of Western writing, attesting to the humanistic goals of the mission. As we read in the excerpts from Jesuit annual letters above, the academy also manufactured a comparable number of figural engravings. Many of these engravings survive, both in books and individual sheets, and some of them demonstrate a level of workmanship that equals anything produced in the colonial centres of either Iberian empire (fig. 39).[132] Several of these prints bear dates from the 1590s, including a signed print from Niccolò's school which survives in a Chinese copy with the signature and date: 'in[venit?] Sem[inari]o Jap[ã]o 1597.'[133] Unlike the paintings we have considered, however, these engravings tend not to deviate much from their European models. Perhaps the painstaking and mechanical nature of copper engraving allowed less room for innovation. Japan did not have an indigenous printing press at the time, and the technique would have been so alien to Japanese artists that it would not have been as easy for them to introduce traditional styles from other media. These engravings provide a striking contrast with the products of the Jesuit press in China during the same period, whose woodblock prints were often entirely Chinese in style (see chapter 4, figs. 52–4). China, unlike Japan, had a native printing tradition, and the artists working for the Jesuits there were not obliged to learn a new technique.

One final surviving medium represented by the Seminary of Painters was metalwork. A sizeable number of bronze plaquettes, as well as a painted bas-relief zinc panel, have survived, which suggests that the academy at least made aftercasts of Italian originals.[134] These small bronzes depict the Madonna, the Madonna and Child, Christ, the Crucifixion, or the Pietà. Douglas Lewis of the National Gallery has recently traced two of these to their prototypes.[135] The *Pietà*, three examples of which were made in Japan, is based on a Roman original inspired by an oil sketch of El Greco after Michelangelo. Another plaquette, *The Madonna of Victory, with Dominican Saints and Sovereigns of the Holy League: Thanksgiving for the Battle of Lepanto,* although a specifically Dominican iconography, enjoyed wide popularity as a symbol of Christian victory over pagan forces (here, the Ottoman Empire) and recalls the unfurling of *conquistadora* Madonnas to celebrate Christian conquest in the New World. Three Japanese aftercasts survive of this Central Italian image from ca. 1571–2, which reproduces the composition of an altarpiece in Lucca by Francesco del Brina (ca. 1530s–1586). After the Japanese persecution of Christians began in earnest in 1614, as we shall see below, the plaquettes made in Niccolò's academy were used in the 'foot-treading' ceremony of apostasy. After these were 'worn out,' as Lewis puts it, a new series of much cruder examples were made by Japanese foundrymen on the orders of the local government purely for the purpose of continuing the persecutions.

Some Japanese Christian painters produced more secular works in a subtly hybrid European style on *byōbu* screens and *kakemono* scrolls which were made to adorn the castles of Christian daimyos and the homes of their nobility, as well as for the export market (fig. 40).[136] They are bold, brilliantly coloured compositions, featuring figures in European dress either against a golden background or in a rich, verdant landscape and include knights, kings, peoples of the world, and cityscapes. Their colours, technique, and interest in genre details show that their authors were strongly influenced by the Kanō school, yet their adeptness at European modelling and draughtsmanship betray their training at the Seminary of Painters, which would have been the only place at the time where they could have learned such techniques. The screens were probably collective efforts, involving artists specializing in different areas such as figure painting and landscape.[137] For some of them, oil paints have been used for the figures, and Japanese colours for the background. For others, indigenous water-soluble pigments have been used, but thickened with a white body and glue binder to simulate the opacity of oil painting. The facial features, linear drawing, burnished modelling, and poses (many of them with the cocked head of contemporary Kanō painting; and see also figs. 31–3) point toward mainstream Japanese painting, but the models are Flemish engravings of figures, landscapes, townscapes, and maps.[138] Some of them depict pastoral scenes with Christian references to the Good Shepherd. A common theme is a European figure reading a book, a motif which was also popular in Europeanate paintings of the Mughal school in India (see chapter 5).

Several of these screens, known as *namban byōbu* (southern barbarian screens), were produced before 1591, when they formed part of the wedding dowry of the young sister of the Christian Gamō Ujisato, a senior bodyguard of Hideyoshi, and others decorated the dwellings of daimyos and samurai. They have been assigned to the Japanese Christian artists 'Nobukata' (active ca. 1591–1608) and Yamada Emonsaku (or Emosaku, ca. 1570–1650s), both of whom were almost certainly alumni of the Seminary of Painters. Nevertheless, many of the attributions are still being debated. Emonsaku eventually entered the service of Matsukara Shigemasa (1574–1634), the Christian daimyo of Shimabara castle, where he was retained on a salary to paint European-style *byōbu* paintings to adorn the castle. After the castle was taken in 1638, Emonsaku was spared by the Shogun's forces because of his skill as a painter, and remained active into the 1650s or '60s.

The Niccolò Seminary of Painters – or, at least, the Jesuit missions themselves – also influenced mainstream Japanese painting for several decades to come. The Kanō school of Kyoto produced a series of monumental genre screens between 1590 and 1686 depicting European figures, ships, and buildings, including Jesuits and their churches and colleges (fig. 24). Also known as *namban byōbu*, these colourful and lively panels were produced to decorate wealthy merchants' homes. Very few of the approximately sixty known screens are signed, but one bears the signature of Kanō Naizen and another Kanō Sōshū.[139] They depict European subjects in a Japanese style, usually showing the arrival of Westerners in black Portuguese ships, and tend to follow a set pattern. The left-hand side shows the foreigners embarking, the central section shows them landing in Japan and encountering missionaries, often in procession, and the right section depicts Jesuit churches and foundations, often with a priest celebrating mass before a thoroughly Japanese image of the Salvator Mundi or the Madonna and Child. Boxer has suggested that these zones could be read as secular, secular/religious, and religious. Many have tried to show that these paintings represent specific historic events, some suggesting that they were at least inspired by Valignano's triumphal entry into Japan in 1590,[140] but they are entirely idealized. Recently, Mitsuru

Sakamoto and Yūjirō Ōchi have shown that the painters had a very generic sense of foreignness, throwing in exotic details from Chinese, Mongolian, and Southeast Asian art, as well as European models.[141] The Freer screen (fig. 24), for example, depicts Chinese ladies in the entourage, since the Japanese would never have seen European ladies and could not have known what they looked like. It is worth noting, incidentally, that none of the people in any of the missions covered in this book would have ever met a European woman, except in the most unusual circumstances. For most non-Europeans outside the colonial centres of Spain and Portugal, the only 'European' woman they would have met was the Virgin Mary and the occasional female saint seen through pictures. Their view of Europe was in many ways heavily filtered indeed. In an era when lords and traders alike devoted their energies to controlling the annual Portuguese silk ship, these panels are an appropriate reflection of the obsession of the day. Like 'peep shows,' the later ones satisfied the tastes of a xenophobic society at once fascinated and horrified by foreigners.[142]

These fragments are all that remain of the rich and extensive artistic enterprise of the Japan mission of the Society of Jesus. Unlike the mission in China, where the Jesuits would remain active artistically into the eighteenth century, the products of Niccolò's atelier remained predominantly European in style, only making tentative moves toward indigenization, as we have seen with the *Madonna of the Snows* (fig. 35). What would have happened had they been allowed to stay after 1615, and third and fourth generations of Japanese artists continued to paint Christian images? The answer may lie in a series of fascinating paintings kept by crypto- (or 'hidden') Christians (*kakure-kirishitan*) as deities in the storage rooms of their homes in the islands west of Nagasaki.[143] Never published, and soon to be put on public display at the Kakure-Kirishitan Nandogami Museum, these hanging scrolls in watercolours on Japanese paper depict Saint Ignatius of Loyola and Saint Francis Xavier praying below the Madonna and Child, in much the same way as the *Mysteries of the Rosary* in figure 38, or the Immaculate Conception and Salvator Mundi. Their style, however, has been completely indigenized. The figures are very linear, without a trace of shading, the facial features are purely Japanese, and the two Jesuit saints are dressed in samurai costumes. These paintings date back to the seventeenth and eighteenth centuries, although they have been repainted many times. It is intriguing to think that the Christian art we have been looking at in this chapter represents only the beginning of a development toward indigenization that was bluntly cut off in the early seventeenth century but which would have gained momentum in centuries to come, resulting in images like the *nandogami* pictures – Christian in iconography, yet Japanese in style.

Just as the Seminary of Painters was at its height and its pupils were disseminating Christian devotional art throughout Japan and Asia, the Jesuits' general political situation collapsed. Their decline in rank from the stewards of Nagasaki to the victims of persecution occurred in several stages. After Oda Nobunaga's death, the nation was unified for the first time under his general Toyotomi Hideyoshi (1583–98), who quickly showed himself to be no friend of Christianity. Suddenly, in 1587, Hideyoshi issued a decree expelling Jesuits from Japan. Although his edict was never carried out, it cast a pall over the entire mission and was a harbinger of things to come. With a few exceptions – most notably, the crucifixion of twenty-six Christian martyrs, inspired largely by the Franciscans – full-scale persecution of Christians did not begin until 1614, when Hideyoshi's successor, the shogun Tokugawa Ieyasu (1600–16), prohibited the entry of Catholic Europeans into Japanese territory. The second Tokugawa shogun, Hidetada (1616–30), and his successors expelled and hunted down Catholic Europeans or Japanese Christians, staging massacres like the 'great martyrdom' of 1622, and elaborate torture procedures aimed at apostasy (immortalized in Shusaku Endo's haunting novel *Silence*). Despite a few pathetic Jesuit attempts to enter Japan in the early 1640s, the mission would now be Japanese in name alone, as it was based at Macao and administered mostly to Southeast Asia and Tibet.[144]

In an ironic tribute to the Seminary of Painters, the images produced by the Jesuit missions themselves became the symbolic focus of the persecutions of the Tokugawa Bafuku government. In the famous 'foot-treading ceremony' (*fumi-e*), begun in 1633, the government of Nagasaki forced its citizens to affirm their abjuration from Christianity each January by walking on paintings and plaquettes of Christian devotional images.[145] The *fumi-e* images – those 'weary, haggard, worn and sunken face[s] of Christ' evoked by Endo[146] – were originally the products of Niccolò's school which had at one time belonged to Christian families. Although this ceremony began when the Christian community was still very large – and an astonishing number of people preferred death to symbolic abjuration – the procedure took on the milder character of a census as the Christian population dwindled, lasting for two more centuries. Like the Byzantine iconoclasts or Cromwell's puritans in England, this act of the Nagasaki police was, in a macabre way, an acknowledgment of the power of Christian devotional imagery. This same power inspired several groups of crypto-Christians in the islands west of Kyushu to preserve such images and secretly worship them against all odds for two-and-a-half centuries, until the Japanese relaxed their attitude toward Christianity following the Meiji Restoration in 1868.

4

'With Much Gallantry and Ornamentation':[1] The Jesuit Mission to China, 1561–1773

Artistically, the China mission was heir to the Japan mission as it assumed the latter's role as the centre of Asian mission art and pursued Valignano's policies of cultural accommodation into the eighteenth century. New generations of Jesuit artists came to China and Macao, beginning with Niccolò's Seminary of Painters in 1614, and culminating with the most eminent European artist ever to work in the East, Giuseppe Castiglione (1688–1768), pupil of Andrea Pozzo (1642–1709) and court artist to the Qing emperors, who collaborated with the largest circle of Jesuit artists ever assembled on one mission – an extraordinary group of men from Italy, Germany, and France. The quality of art instruction and artistic influence from Europe had never been higher, and the degree of Jesuit artistic acculturation had seldom been so strong and so creative.

These efforts, however, were not sufficient in the face of profound cultural barriers. Unlike the Japanese, the Chinese literati had little use for European styles or techniques in the visual arts, and outside of court circles and the world of commercial and export art, their influence was never more than a ripple. Largely unimpressed with the tricks of pictorial realism, one-point perspective, and shading – the visual currency of conversion worldwide – Chinese scholar-artists commented bemusedly: 'Students of painting may well take over one or two points from [Europeans] to make their own paintings more attractive to the eye. But these painters have no brush-manner whatsoever; although they have skill, they are simply artisans and cannot consequently be classified as painters.'[2]

Despite Herculean efforts and the finest personnel, it was, in the end, the Jesuits' inability to appreciate the importance of the brush-stroke and calligraphy that limited their artistic venture in China.[3] Naturalistic art, in general, was considered mechanical and trivial, and was something the proudly amateur literati attributed to mere 'professionals.' Another fatal mistake on the part of the Jesuits was their insistence on associating themselves with the art of the Imperial court, which by the time of the Ming was widely reviled by scholar-painters as a dry academic tradition marked by stagnation and superficiality – as being, that is, at the very heart of the much decried world of 'professional painting.'

The Chinese Context for Cultural Exchange

Unlike Japan, China was administered in a manner more familiar to Europeans, with centralized rule under a single emperor in Beijing. At the time, the Ming

Dynasty (1368–1644) appeared to be at the height of its stability and prosperity. Perceived by the Chinese as a glorious return to native rule after the Mongol Yuan regime (1271–1368), the Ming revived the cultural traditions of earlier great native dynasties, the Han (206 BC – AD 220), Tang (618–907), and Song (960–1279). In contrast, the Yuan had thrived on its foreign trade and embassies, reflecting the foreignness of the regime itself, and its culture was cosmopolitan and open to outside influences. By the time of the third Ming emperor, however, the state showed much less interest in foreign trade or culture, and an attitude of superiority prevailed, with disdain for 'barbarian' societies. Ming China, the largest contiguous empire on earth, with 120 million subjects, was larger than all of Europe.[4] Self-consciously a nation of ancient tradition, China's massive bureaucracy, divided between Beijing and the various provinces, each ruled by a governor, was without parallel anywhere. The Beijing administration was organized into a complex hierarchy around the Emperor, with a bureaucracy divided into six ministries; an advisory board of senior scholars and academicians, who supervised the education, ritual, and chronicling of the Imperial family; and finally the community of court women, eunuchs, and other palace staff, who looked after the immediate person of the Emperor. These groups, particularly the last two, were often at odds. The third ministry, the Ministry of Rites, included the Board of Astronomy, a staff of mathematicians who each year prepared the Imperial calendar – a vital element of Imperial ideology which was later to become a Jesuit preserve.

Chinese society valued highly the attainment of literacy and education, a stringent and rigorous process which culminated in the three levels of state civil service examination, which, in turn, provided access to a career in the bureaucracy and social prestige. The Chinese canon was based on a group of great books (the 'Four Books' and 'Five Classics'), known collectively as the Confucian classics. These books defined a humanistic moral and social code of behaviour according to status, which formed the foundation of Chinese society. A central theme to the classics was filial piety and the formal veneration of ancestors, an important trait in a society whose families were divided into complex clans. The wealthier and more influential clans built ancestral halls resembling temples, where family members offered sacrifices to their dead.

Although the Confucian code was more a philosophy than a religion – it is concerned more with this world than with the next – it is considered one of the three Chinese sects, the so-called Three Teachings (*sanjiao*), together with Daoism (Taoism) and Buddhism. Like all three of the sects, Confucianism came in different varieties, ranging from the narrow Buddhist-inspired Neo-Confucianism of the state to the local academies of literati (*wenren*) with whom the Jesuits would first interact. Daoism, popular among commoners and literati alike and providing a foil for Confucianism, was a naturalistic cosmology encompassing animism, magic, alchemy, mysticism, and popular lore. Based on the *Dao* or 'Way,' Daoism focused on the inner life as opposed to the social life of Confucianism. Its emphasis on the dynamic forms and ageless laws of nature was also instrumental in the development of monumental landscape painting in the Northern Song (960–1127). Buddhism arrived in China much earlier than in Japan, in the first century A.D., and, as in Japan, it had a tremendous impact on the arts. Among its main legacies were colour and shading in painting, and an enhanced plasticity in sculpture. As it became indigenized, Chinese Buddhism exchanged ideas with Daoism, and a degree of synthesis developed between the two.

The peace and prosperity of the Ming allowed art connoisseurship and patronage to flourish, particularly in the larger commercial towns, where the literati and wealthy landowners defined artistic taste. Placing great value on ancient tradition, painters returned to prototypes from periods such as the Northern Song (960–1127), and evoked antique styles (*fang gu*). Chinese painting includes figural and landscape traditions, the former with origins in the Tang Dynasty and earlier, and the latter experiencing its first flowering in the Song. Figural painting took the form of court scenes and portraiture, but was predominantly the realm of religious art, with a rich and varied iconography of Buddhist and Daoist deities (figs. 41, 56). Traditional landscape painting is characterized by landscapes of real or ideal locations meant to evoke inner truth, enlightenment, or, in later periods, the artist's temperament (figs. 42, 50). Often ideal composites of different scenes, landscape paintings are rendered in an even tone, with no single light source, and often include multiple viewpoints. They are more concerned with metaphysical realities than with realism in the European Renaissance sense. Traditionally the landscape is conceived in the mind of the artist before it is produced, and painted with varying degrees of intensity, without the possibility of correcting mistakes.

The dominant formats for Chinese painting were the hanging scroll, the handscroll, and the album, all on silk or paper. Since painting derived from calligraphy, it focuses above all on the line, whose subtle variations in thickness describe form and movement, accented by shorter brush-strokes and colour washes. When Chinese paintings use shading, they only do so very sparingly, and colour, when it exists at all, is merely an accessory. Painting did not simply operate on its own as it did in Europe, but was one of the 'Three Perfections' (*sanjue*) of painting, poetry, and calligraphy, whose synthesis was the true goal of the gentleman scholar. The three arts interacted in the same painting to evoke different levels of meaning. Even the critical apparatus of art appreciation in China derived from calligraphy. Perhaps no painting tradition in the world was subject to a more rigorous and discriminating criticism – dating back to a third-century A.D. treatise on the arts by the painter Gu Kaizhi (ca. 345–ca. 406) – which focused on the brush-stroke. In China not only the artist himself but the viewer was classified in a typically Chinese hierarchy of taste. An example of ranking of artists according to talent is the system attributed to Jing Hao (fl. 900–60), from the 'divine' and 'sublime' to the 'marvellous' and merely 'skilful,' the latter meaning 'an artist [who] cuts out and pieces together fragments of beauty and welds them into the pretence of a masterpiece. His style is forced, and the spirit and form are highly exaggerated. This is owing to the poverty of inner reality and to the excess of outward form.'[5] Jesuit mission art, with its emphasis on visual realism, drama, and outward form, could only too easily fall into this category of empty artifice.

Chinese painting had made great advances in pictorial realism as early as the Northern Song, when atmospheric perspective was as sophisticated as Leonardo's and the characteristic Chinese isometric projection gave architectural settings a convincing form of linear depth. Such feats of illusion are particularly evident in works such as *Lady Wenji's Return to China* (second quarter of the twelfth century) (fig. 43). However, Yuan and Ming painters also explored much more sparse and sketchy styles, which had greater spontaneity and freedom and were a greater showcase for brushwork. The Ming in particular was a period of great variety. Some artists showed a renewed interest in naturalism, using detailed brush-strokes called *cun* to build up a play of light and shade in rocks and trees. Some scholars have suggested that realist trends in Ming and early Qing landscape painting (figs. 42, 50) were influenced by the Jesuits' art activities in China, and I will examine them in greater detail below. At the other extreme, a continued development of the painterly, spontaneous brush-strokes, with distortions in drawing, gave some of the best Ming works an abstract quality; for example, the work of Liu Jue (1410–72).

The Jesuit Mission and the Arts under Ricci, 1583–1610

Owing to the xenophobic foreign policy of the Ming, and thanks to the constant threat of piracy in the Pearl River Delta, China was nearly impenetrable by the late sixteenth century. A few hardy European merchants had been able to sell their wares at Canton (Guangzhou), the Pearl River's largest city, and even to establish a rudimentary European base there, but they were always at the mercy of the local authorities, who could expel or imprison them at will. A handful of missionaries had also reached Canton, including Spanish mendicants from the Philippines, but their ignorance of Chinese and association with Spanish colonial expansion did not endear them to Chinese officials. From as early as 1557, however, the Portuguese had managed to lease the tiny peninsula of Macao, near present-day Hong Kong, and also not far from Sancian Island, where Francis Xavier died in 1552 during his own vain attempt to enter the Middle Kingdom. Macao grew to become an energetic, if small, Portuguese colony, with foundations from all of the major mendicant orders, and a cathedral after 1576, built for a Jesuit first bishop, who arrived in 1569. There was virtually no artistic activity in Macao prior to the arrival of Niccolò's academy in exile, but in the seventeenth century, painting, sculpture, and architecture thrived. The Jesuits arrived as early as 1565, where they maintained an urban base dedicated primarily, like most *Padroado* or inner-circle foundations, to the welfare of the Portuguese colonists and their Macanese subjects.

At the beginning of the seventeenth century, the Jesuits also built the most imposing monuments in the city. One was the Fortaleza de São Paulo do Monte, which demonstrated that the Jesuits here, as in the Philippines, possessed an expertise in fortification architecture. The Church of Nossa Senhora da Assunção (better known as Madre de Deus or São Paulo, 1601–40) was the Jesuits' other main contribution, its granite façade surviving today as Macao's most famous landmark (fig. 44).[6] Nossa Senhora da Assunção, designed by the Italian Carlo Spinola and no doubt supervised by the exiled Niccolò himself, contrasts with other churches in the city by its Italianate style, and by its borrowing of symbols and styles from Chinese art. The church is predominantly Serlian, with bold freestanding columns alternating with statues in niches, and is very similar to the equally Roman Bom Jesus Church in Goa (which, nevertheless, only uses columns on the ground floor) (fig. 45). Contemporary writers made explicit comparisons with another Goan church; for example, the Annual Letter from 1602, the year the first foundation stone was laid, observed: 'It is a church with three naves, three chapels, and two altars at the crossing like S. Paulo in Goa' (fig. 73).[7] Such classical façades, with their Roman emphasis on verticality and on the centre, separate Jesuit foundations from those of their mendicant or secular contemporaries, although later churches by other orders in Macao were influenced by their Jesuit precursor, particularly in the use of columns. David Kowal has demonstrated the same phenomenon in Goa.[8]

The rich sculptural decorations of Nossa Senhora da Assunção – in both stone and bronze – are a retable wrought large, with images and symbols of the Holy Spirit, Christ, the Virgin, the instruments of the Passion, and allegories of temptation, damnation, and salvation. The upper storeys represent the Church Triumphant, while the lower ones portray the church on earth. It also possesses one of the earliest series of Jesuit saints, on the second storey, cast locally in bronze by Chinese or Japanese artists in a subtly hybrid style. Together with these figures and motifs are explanatory texts in Chinese characters – the first in any Christian building – and other Chinese features, such as the temple lions supporting the obelisks at the corners, which are executed in a purely Chinese manner. Even the Christian figures betray their hybridity, with a typically Chinese bevelled line, windswept drapery reminiscent of scroll painting, and miscellaneous decorative details such as the Chinese cloud patterns under the angels' skirts. The angels are reminiscent of Buddhist *apsaras* or bodhisattvas (compare their drapery even to the attendants in the Japanese painting in figure 21). Some of these features, such as the stylized treatment of the waves, the Chinese carp, and the treatment of the dragon's feet, are clear echoes of patterns found on Chinese ceramics and in other decorative arts. The façade's location, in front of a square on the summit of a grand staircase, was perfectly sited for outdoor worship, and echoes mendicant structures in early post-conquest America and the Philippines.

However, this façade was the product of a later age, more responsive to Chinese culture. Alessandro Valignano was not at all pleased when he reached Macao in 1579 to find the Jesuit community there behaving more like parish priests than missionaries. Like the other *Padroado* foundations in the city, the Jesuits were compelling their Macanese converts to adopt a European lifestyle and Portuguese clothing, and had all but given up working in China itself after an early reconnaissance mission to Canton. Valignano acted swiftly by appointing two Italians to take over the Chinese part of the mission and learn the Chinese language. The first was Michele Ruggieri, who learned Chinese and made several short visits to Canton in the face of ridicule from his Portuguese co-religionists. Unlike his Iberian precursors, Ruggieri impressed the Chinese authorities with his sensitivity toward Chinese politesse, especially when he performed the kowtow before senior officials. His actions show that he was already implementing Valignano's principles for Japan in a Chinese context, and was having success. He was allowed to say mass in the foreign quarter of Canton, and by 1582, together with Francesco Pasio, he set up the first European mission on Chinese soil in a former Buddhist temple in Zhaoqing. After a brief interregnum, the Zhaoqing mission was re-established in 1583, this time under the leadership of an even more remarkable Italian, Matteo Ricci (1552–1610), known in Chinese as Li Madou (fig. 27).

Few Jesuit missionaries anywhere are better known than this polyglot from Macerata, who perhaps more than any other tried to integrate European Renaissance culture into Chinese civilization. Ricci was a student and friend of both Clavius and Valignano, and his mission reflects the mathematical acumen of the former and the acculturative policies and *modo soave* of the latter. His literary, moralist, mathematical, and scientific contributions, as well as his astonishing memory and linguistic ability, are famous, and more has been written about his 'scientific apostolate' and its legacy than any other aspect of Jesuit mission activity in Asia.[9] In Zhaoqing, Shaozhou (1589–95), Nanjing and Nanchang (1595–8), and finally Beijing itself (1601–10), Ricci dazzled the Chinese with his knowledge of their language, learned the Confucian classics by heart, and made the Four Books the foundation of his ministry. Ricci also notably made great use of maps of the world and clocks, part of the 'ceremonial games' that were typical of missions worldwide, but here playing a more central role in the Jesuits' self-representation and being fairly widely disseminated in Chinese publications.[10] He quickly gained influential friends among the literati and forsook the garb of a Buddhist for the more respected clothing of a Confucian scholar – only after earning that title through his knowledge of the classics.

However, all did not go as smoothly as many scholars in the past would have us believe. Ricci's accommodation could only go so far. He realized that a marginal religion such as Christianity could never hope to be accepted in China at an elite level unless it conformed to Confucianism, which represented that which is *zheng* or 'orthodox.' Anything that did not operate within the Confucianist matrix could be labelled *xie* ('heterodox') and therefore potentially subversive – and, indeed, this happened to Christianity after Ricci's death.[11] Although much has been said about Ricci's amazing abilities to accommodate to Chinese cultural traditions, we must keep in mind that Confucianism remained largely irreconcilable with Christianity. Even Ricci was unable to cross this theological barrier, which included such fundamental differences as Confucianism's lack of a precise idea of the afterlife, as many scholars are now realizing and as I discuss at greater length in chapter 7. Also, whereas Ricci was remarkably flexible in his adaptation to areas such as Chinese language and medicine, he was much less tolerant about the central theses and topics of Confucianism. Again we have the Jesuit dichotomy between culture and cult. Ricci moved slowly and carefully.

Accordingly, Ricci did not aim at mass conversions such as those in Kyushu, since he saw himself as laying the foundations for later ministries. His missionary work was not overtly religious, since he realized that Christianity had to be presented as a complete philosophy in its fullest context before the Chinese would take it seriously. For Ricci that context was found primarily in the sciences, in geography, and in his literary works on morality. A prolific writer, his most famous works are his catechism *A True Account of the Master of Heaven* (*Tianzhu shiyi*, 1584), written together with Ruggieri; and his *A Treatise on Friendship*

(*Jiaoyou lun*, 1595), which was the first book he wrote directly in Chinese and the one that established his reputation as a great scholar. In contrast to other mission territories, the Chinese had a thriving indigenous press, using the woodblock technique, which gave Ricci a headstart in disseminating his ideas. Ricci's cartographic and astrological knowledge led to an invitation to help revise the Imperial calendar, an honour which the Jesuits would hold later in the seventeenth and eighteenth centuries. In Beijing he was at the centre of a lively intellectual circle which included many converts from the literati, including Xu Guangqi (1562–1633), Li Zhizao (1565–1632), Yang Tingyun (1557–1627), and Wang Zheng (1571–1644).[12]

Although Ricci's coterie in Beijing included prominent court painters, as well, such as Zhang Ruitu and Li Rihua (1565–1635), his activities in the arts were not nearly as successful, nor as sophisticated, as his scientific and literary apostolates. Perhaps aware that he and his colleagues were not equal to the task of satisfying Chinese aesthetic standards, Ricci appears not to have promoted the artistic acculturation that became the trademark of the mission in the later seventeenth and eighteenth centuries, although some scholars maintain that he did.[13] I say 'appears' because virtually no works of art survive from this period, but written records, including Ricci's own remarks, corroborate my suspicion.

In fact, when it came to the arts, Ricci was a chauvinist. As the following statement demonstrates, he believed that Chinese art was innately deficient:

> The Chinese, although great enthusiasts of painting, nevertheless cannot approach our [artists], and they fall very much behind them in the manufacture of statuary and the art of foundry or casting, even though they make great use of all of these, as much for many kinds of arches, and statues they make of men and animals in stone and bronze, as for their idols and images in the temples, for the clocks, the large braziers which they put in front of their idols, and other works of art. It seems to me that what prevents them from becoming skilled in these arts is the rarity or the absence of communication with other nations who would have been able to come to their assistance; since they are as capable as any people for their manual dexterity and natural gifts. They do not know how to paint in oils, nor can they depict shadows [*dar l'ombra alle cose*] in the things they paint, and therefore their paintings are dead and lifeless [*smorte e senza nessuna vivezza*]. In their statuary they are completely unfortunate, and I do not suppose that they possess any more rules for proportion and symmetry than the eye, which, in objects of large size, is deceived easily, and they make immense figures both in stone and bronze.[14]

These remarks come as something of a surprise, considering Ricci's subtle appreciation for the Confucian classics. We must keep in mind that in some areas of culture (drama and theatre are two other examples, as well as calligraphy), the Jesuits were unable or unwilling to accommodate at this stage.[15] Perhaps they were too difficult to master (although an appreciation for Chinese landscape painting should be easier than learning the Confucian classics), or they were considered simply too alien to European tradition. We must keep in mind, as well, that even in his more famous 'accommodations' to Confucianist philosophy, Ricci and his successors still believed in the universal validity of Western scholastic learning over Eastern traditions.

Nevertheless, Ricci was sensitive to specific Chinese iconographic needs; for example, he replaced some images of the Madonna with images of the Salvator Mundi because the Chinese confused the former with the Buddhist Bodhisattva of Mercy, Guanyin, as well as the Chinese goddess protector of sailors, A-Ma. Both of these substitutions were very appropriate, however, since bodhisattvas play a similar intercessory role in Buddhism to that played by saints in Catholicism, and the Virgin Mary as *stella maris* (Star of the Sea) was also a protector of sailors in Western tradition. The convergence between these two figures became even closer than this. Among the most popular images made for Buddhist devotion in the home in sixteenth- and seventeenth-century China was the figure known as *songzi Guanyin*, or 'Guanyin the sender of sons,' in which the deity assumes a female form and is shown holding a small male child (fig. 46). In fact, to make things even more complicated, her ubiquity in that period has been linked with the Jesuits' very introduction of Madonna imagery.[16] The same thing happened in Japan, incidentally, where the Hidden Christians worshipped household statues of Guanyin (Kannon, in Japanese), who also held a baby boy in her arms; this figure was known as Maria-Kannon. Therefore, given these two figures' affinity, it is not surprising that Ricci eventually changed his mind, and he and his successors went on to capitalize upon the Madonna/Guanyin phenomenon, which is why the Madonna became such a common image in Macao and China. But other convergences were not as felicitous. Ricci also famously avoided the Crucifixion and scenes of the Passion in certain contexts because people found them repulsive; some even believed that crucifixes were evil charms meant to kill the Emperor.[17] Ricci was all too aware of the dangers of openly worshipping a figure who was scoffed at, in the words of one contemporary anti-Christian writer, as 'a Barbarian executed in a humiliating fashion during the Han Dynasty.'[18]

This is not to say that Ricci was no friend of Western art. He was a tireless promoter of European painting, sculpture, and architecture, and made extensive use of imagery in his preaching, remarking that 'these images are necessary to allow us to console and help the new Christians.'[19] Like missionaries in Japan and the Americas, Ricci believed firmly in the miraculous power of holy pictures, and their ability to cause conversions.[20] He was only too eager to point out how amazed the Chinese were with European one-point perspective, *chiaroscuro*, and the other effects of pictorial realism. His attitude toward European paintings is apparent in an interesting account (1618) by a Chinese acquaintance who recorded one of Ricci's lectures. Ricci comments:

> Chinese painting only paints the light (*yang*), it does not paint the shadow (*yin*). Thus to look at, people's faces are completely flat, with no concave or convex physiognomy. My country's painting combines the *yin* with the *yang* in drawing, so that faces have higher and lower parts, and arms are round. When anyone's face is towards the light (*yang*), then it is entirely bright and white, but if it is turned then the side which is towards the light will be white and that which is not towards the light, the eye, ear, nose, mouth, and concave

places will have a dark appearance. The portrait painters of my country understand this principle, and by using it are able to ensure that the painted effigy is no different from the living person.[21]

This speech shows not only how much Ricci believes in the inherent difference and superiority of Western art, but it also implies that he placed great confidence in Renaissance pictorial conventions for 'enlightening' non-Europeans.

Supposedly, as Ricci tries to show elsewere, Chinese observers of Western paintings even felt that they had come face to face with God Himself, as if these pictures struck them with a thunderbolt of Christian grace. The most famous reaction was that of the Wanli Emperor (1575–1616) – whom, incidentally, Ricci never even met in person since the monarch had long given up receiving foreigners. Upon regarding a Roman oil painting of the Salvator Mundi in 1601, the Emperor supposedly exclaimed, 'This is a living Pagoda [*pagode vivo*].' Ricci explained that what the Emperor was saying was 'this is a living God,' and therefore a superior one to the 'dead' gods worshipped by the Chinese.[22] Jacques Gernet has shown that Wanli instead probably said, 'This is a living Buddha' [*huofo*], since it conjured up for him an image of the Buddha, and far from demonstrating an acquiescence to Christianity, it showed that 'assimilation with Buddhist traditions was both total and immediate.'[23] It was Guanyin all over again. No doubt the Emperor appreciated its lifelike qualities (it may have reminded him of Tang painting), but there were no thunderbolts here. Like most Chinese of the ruling and educated classes, he only considered Western art to be a curiosity. Likewise, we cannot take seriously Ricci's claim that this and other images frightened the Emperor and his mother so much that they ordered their servants to lock them away in their treasury for fear that they would cause them harm.[24] Falling into the 'children barely capable of reason' category of missiological myths, the tale is reminiscent of Spanish reports of the Nahua citizens of Mexico City, who supposedly fled in terror when the scaffolding was removed from the vaulted stone roof of the Church of San Francisco in 1525, never before having witnessed the technical feats of European architecture.[25]

The same image seen by the Wanli Emperor elicited a suspiciously similar reply from the Governor of Nanjing: 'You don't have to explain [whom this image represents],' he supposedly said, 'because this image demonstrates on its own that it is not the portrait of a mere mortal';[26] and visitors to the Jesuit residence in Beijing in 1605 were, according to Ricci, 'amazed by the books of images which made them think they were sculpted [*scolpite*; i.e., three-dimensional], and they could not believe that they were pictures.'[27] There is also the usual reference to a potentate showing an image to the women of his household, who invariably want a copy made, as we saw in Japan; here the ruler was the Governor of Jining, Shandong Province.[28] Ricci's colleague Niccolò Longobardi (1565–1655) directly credited European technique with such miracles when he wrote in 1598 that 'people here find such works very artistic and subtle, because they have shading, which does not exist in Chinese painting.'[29] These reports of Chinese reactions have some basis in truth, since as we will soon see seventeenth-century Chinese sources make similar remarks about European paintings, but they almost certainly also considerably exaggerate the degree of Chinese astonishment. Pelliot suspected the same thing when he wrote the comment I have already quoted in chapter 1 (pp. 33–4).

Although not much European art reached the China mission during Ricci's lifetime, the art that did arrive was apparently of surprisingly high quality.[30] In fact, there are few missions where the issue of quality was so frequently and insistently raised. Recognizing the important position held by painting in the Chinese scholarly tradition – and the formidable fastidiousness of Chinese artistic taste – Ricci, Ruggieri, and others wrote to Rome stressing that they needed the best images available. They believed, naïvely, that the best European art would be sufficient to impress their hosts, not realizing that the very nature of European art made it incapable of satisfying Chinese scholarly audiences. Ruggieri asked for many different kinds of pictures in the 1580s, including 'a book of images of the mysteries of the life of Christ Our Lord and of some Old Testament stories, with descriptions of Christian lands,' 'scenes from the Old and New Testament,' and 'several illustrated volumes,' and also urged that Rome provide the mission with oil paintings.[31] In 1584 he asked for something to satisfy the growing Chinese curiosity for pictorial realism, including 'some well-painted images on copper [*immagini di rame ben pintate*] of Our Lady and the Saviour, which these Chinese gentlemen want very much, and some images on paper [*de carta*] with the mysteries of our Faith, to demonstrate [it] to them more easily, since they are very interested in pictures'[32] Ricci himself wrote somewhat desperately from the gates of Beijing in 1599 for something of sufficient quality – or even size – to impress his literati friends and the Emperor, including 'some painter, the best whom you can find,' and 'some oil paintings, especially masterpieces [*capolavori*], as large as possible, to offer to the Emperor.'[33] The same year, Emanuel Diaz, rector in Macao, also stressed that only the best pictures would have any chance with Chinese connoisseurship: 'some oil paintings, truly fine, with good colours ... because the Chinese will not be satisfied with anything else.'[34]

Most of the handful of paintings that reached Ricci and his companions were painted in Italy, although there were also some from Spain, perhaps New Spain, and of course Niccolò's Seminary of Painters in Japan. Italian pictures, perhaps by Sigismondo Laire and his circle, included a small Borghese Madonna *molto ben pinta in Roma* which impressed visitors to the residence at Zhaoqing with the *maraviglie* and *artificio* of its realism, until the Jesuits realized that the Chinese thought they were looking at a portrait of Guanyin and they quickly replaced it with a *Salvator Mundi* by Niccolò.[35] Another, much larger Saint Luke Madonna, supposedly also 'very well painted,' reached the mission in 1599,[36] and thirteen years earlier the mission was enhanced by a framed Italian oil painting of the Salvator Mundi behind glass 'made by an excellent painter.'[37] Spanish paintings included two large altarpieces, one of Nuestra Señora de la Antigua of Seville, which broke into three panels during the journey to China but was apparently valued all the more by the Chinese for seeming older,[38] and a brightly coloured painting of the Madonna and Child with Saint John '*di raro artificio per la vivezza de' colori e figure*,' which, according to different reports, came from Spain or New Spain via the Philippines.[39] The enthusiasm of these descriptions betrays how few images of any kind were available to the China mission at the time.

Niccolò sent two of his paintings of the Salvator Mundi to the China mission, one of which Ricci described as *molto bella*, as well as an image of Saint Lawrence in oil on copper.[40] There were probably more Japanese Christian paintings in China, as well, since it would have been the main market for the Seminary of Painters after Japan. A Chinese inventory of the Nanjing mission from 1616 does mention several shrines which sound as though they could be Japanese *urushi* with gold and silver *maki-e* ornament (figs. 28, 31–4).[41] Three of Ricci's European paintings, the Sevillian Madonna, the Christ behind glass, and the large Borghese Madonna, were presented to the Wanli Emperor in 1601, and we know from Chinese sources that Wanli received at that time ten other European (and possibly Japanese) paintings of unspecified nationality.[42] There was even less sculpture at the mission in Ricci's day. Sculpture was restricted to small statues of the Madonna and crucifixes, one of which sounded decidedly Iberian in its gory realism: 'a very beautiful crucifix sculpted in wood and painted with blood, which looked alive.'[43] The 1616 inventory lists other statues, including some in amber, bronze, and ivory.

In the request letters by Ruggieri and Diaz cited above, there are also orders for Mexican feather paintings – not, perhaps, what we would expect Catholic missionaries to be using in China. But, in fact, these remnants of the thriving Aztec technique of feather art, which had also impressed the Habsburgs and Medici, were apparently quite well received in China – perhaps even more so than European paintings (fig. 10). The first recorded Mexican feather painting in China was an image of the Magdalene that the Franciscans had brought via the Philippines in 1578 'rendered so well that [it] appeared to be painted by hand' and which pleased the local Chinese very much.[44] We only know the subjects of four of the feather paintings brought by the Jesuits; four images of the Four Seasons were apparently presented to the Wanli Emperor and were inventoried by Chinese authorities in 1616.[45] Mexican feather painting must have struck a common chord in China through its affinities to indigenous featherwork in jewellery and costume, which had been traditional in both China and Japan since the eighth century. The emperors were constantly trying to obtain rare and exotic feathers from abroad, and – coincidentally – they charged the Jesuits with helping them do so.[46] Ricci even included references to feather production in Latin American countries in the world map he produced for the Chinese literati, the *Mappamundi*. There is also evidence that Mexican feather paintings reached Japan in this period. One example, showing a martyr being stoned, is enclosed in a Japanese *urushi* lacquer shrine which was sold at auction at Christie's in 1982, and another featherwork painting from Japan depicting Saint Francis of Assisi is mentioned by Philip Hainhofer, an art dealer, in an inventory of 1612.[47]

Ricci also had a few Flemish prints and printed books, although not enough to go around. One image, probably by Wierix, showing the Pope, Holy Roman Emperor, and other potentates kneeling before the monogram 'IHS' interested the Wanli Emperor enough that he had a large copy painted in full colour by his own artists, probably more out of an interest in Western diplomacy than Christian faith or Late Renaissance art. By a remarkable coincidence – and probably for the same pragmatic reasons – the same image, within a decade, was enlarged in colour by court artists on the walls of the palace of the Mughal emperor Jahangir (see chapter 5).[48]

Both Ricci and Longobardi wrote frequently to Rome asking for a copy of Nadal's illustrated gospel *Evangelicae Historicae Imagines* (1593).[49] This lavish work featured 153 images (figs. 55, 57) engraved by the Wierix brothers and others, and may represent the Jesuits' greatest and most successful artistic achievement of the sixteenth century: 'the earliest such series of the whole of the New Testament of any size or importance ever produced.'[50] Well before the engravings were published in 1593, the preparatory drawings were circulated in Rome, and their subjects may even have been selected by Ignatius himself, who originally commissioned the work.[51] The earliest sketches, by Livio Agresti da Forlì, were already available in the late 1550s or early 1560s, but these were later substantially reworked into their present form (ca. 1579–82) by Giovanni Battista Fiammeri, and redrawn by Bernardino Passeri after 1587; in addition, eight were further altered – in detail only – by Martin de Vos before going to press.[52] Nadal's gospel would have a profound impact on the missions in Asia – particularly, China and Mughal India – as well as Latin America. When asking the Father General for a second copy, Ricci praised the work's usefulness in the mission field: 'this book is more useful itself than the Bible [i.e., the Antwerp Polyglot Bible (1568–72)]; since with it we can explain by placing an image before the eyes that which we could not perhaps explain with words.'[53] Although Ricci finally got a copy in 1605, he had to give it up for the benefit of the Nanchang mission.

The China mission also had an impressive library of architectural and picture books, although several of these would have come after Ricci's death. By the eighteenth century, these works included the great architectural treatises of Vitruvius (in Latin, Italian, and French), Vignola, Scamozzi, Palladio, and Andrea Pozzo; Giovanni Rusconi's *Della Architectura* (1590); architectural works by André Félibien (1619–95) and Jacques Androuet du Cerceau (1520–85); books on fountain architecture by Carlo Fontana (1638–1714) and Giovanni Battista Barattieri; Theodore de Bry's *Topographia Urbis Romae* (1597), a three-volume work on the monuments of Rome, and his *Antiquités romaines* (1600); and Abraham Ortelius's *Teatrum Orbis Terrarum* (1579).[54]

With such an army of books at their command, it is little wonder that the China missionaries built architecture in the style of Palladio and Vignola. Although, as in Japan, the earliest mission compounds were set up in existing Chinese buildings,[55] and the earliest mission at Zhaoqing even tried openly to emulate a Buddhist temple with its wooden post-and-lintel construction, pitched roof, and a door plaque with the name 'Temple of the Flower of the Saints,' Ricci's church in Beijing was a conscious statement of the Roman Renaissance. A remarkable feat of determination, this miniature Gesù built under the direction of the Italian father Sebastiano de Ursis *'con tutte le regole dell'architettura delle altre nostre chiese'*[56] was fifty feet long by twenty-five, and boasted a façade equipped with arches, lintels, and cornices. It took only twenty days to finish. Trigault wrote the following:

Our chapel in the residence is so small and narrow that the Christians are obliged to remain in the atrium to assist at the Mass, both in the hot season and the cold season ... To remedy this, the Fathers have decided to construct a very spacious room, in the Chinese manner [*all'usanza cinese*], because our poverty does not allow us to spend any more. But later, so that our church would not resemble temples of idols, they decided it would be preferable to build one in the European style [*all'usanza di Europa*], even though it would not be very large; it would serve as a model for the Chinese, for even though it was small it was also cause for everyone's admiration, except for ours, since we still remember the buildings of Europe.[57]

Father de Ursis described the little chapel:

It was built seventy palms in length by thirty-five in width. It was built in observance of all of the rules of architecture possible, with Chinese workers who understood nothing about it. It had a façade [*frontespicio*], arches, cornices [*cornichões*] and lintels, all in the European manner [*ao modo europeo*]. The principal chapel [*capella mór*, or sacristy] was raised by three degrees in relation to the body of the church. This building impressed the Chinese far more than we had anticipated, and many came to see it; by doing so they began to know our Holy Law.[58]

The church was still standing in 1635, when the Chinese authors of *The Guide to the Imperial Capital (Dijing Jingwu lüe)*, Liu Tung and Yu Yizheng, described it as 'narrow and long; the ceiling resembles a net [a reference to coffering?], while on the walls hang marvellous pictures and magnificent decorations, according to the custom of Ricci's country.'[59]

This final, extravagant expression of nationalist pride was the last project ever undertaken by this extraordinary Italian priest, who stubbornly refused to accommodate in the arts as he had done so famously in literature, philosophy, behaviour, and personal appearance. Ricci died in 1610, the very year the chapel was finished.[60] At the time of his death, the mission did not possess a cemetery, and since Chinese law did not allow burial inside city walls, Ricci's colleagues had to find a place outside the city. With the assistance of his scholar friends and local and Imperial officials, the mission procured an Imperial grant of land just outside the city, on a property known now as Zhalan.[61] On 22 April 1611, Ricci was given a state burial in a confiscated Buddhist temple, which had been converted into a chapel dedicated to the Saint Luke Madonna, with a traditional Chinese stele, table, and stone urn.[62] Niccolò Longobardi, Ricci's successor in the mission, constructed a hexagonal tomb chapel in the cemetery for future Jesuit burials, a structure which sounds very similar to one built in the same year for the same purpose in Agra for the Mughal mission. Liu and Yu wrote:

Behind the grave is a hexagonal structure, on the top of which is a cross. The back wall is decorated with floral designs. The design on the ridge resembles a dragon with a split tail, while the design on the transoms looks like a pair of butterfly's beautiful antennae. And the design on its sides looks like an elephant curling its trunk.[63]

The cemetery fulfilled its promise as the burial place of the Beijing Jesuits through the centuries, and the exquisite Chinese-style gravestones that can be seen today are a testament to the acculturative destiny of the China mission.

The Chinese Reception of Jesuit Mission Art of the Ricci Period

Although the Chinese may not have been quite as excited about Western art as Ricci and others would have us believe, their reaction to European pictorial realism did elicit comments remarkably consistent with those made by other non-European peoples. An often-cited group of Chinese commentators found the pictures to be like mirrors, statues, or real people, and others remarked that it looked as if the paintings were moving. Ricci's acquaintance Gu Qiyuan (1565–1628) wrote in 1618 about a painting he was shown by Ricci in bright colours on copper (perhaps a product of Niccolò's atelier?):

> This Lord of Heaven [Jesus] is painted as a small boy, held by a woman called the 'Heavenly Mother.' He is painted on a copper panel, with the five colours spread on top. The face is as if living, the body, arms and hands seem to protrude from the panel, the concave and convex parts of the face are no different from those of a living person to look at.[64]

The seventeenth century author Zhao Yi, in his *Miscellaneous Notes from Under the Exposed Cave* (*Yenbao zaji*), remarks that the image of Christ in the mission church at Nanjing 'was painted on the wall but ... looks like a round body, protruding from the wall;'[65] and Yu and Liu (1635) described the altarpiece in Ricci's church as if it were alive:

> One picture of Jesus is placed over the [altar]. When one looks at it, it looks like a statue ... and his mouth gives the impression that it has just said a word; of all these things Chinese art is not capable.[66]

The scholar Jiang Shaoshu described Ricci's copy of the Saint Luke Madonna in this passage from his *History of Silent Poetry* (*Wusheng shishi*; ca. 1640):

> Li Madou brought from the Western Regions an image of the Lord of Heaven, being a woman holding a small boy. The eyebrow and eyes, and the lines of the clothing are like reflections in a mirror, about to make a slight movement. Their dignity and elegance are such that a Chinese artisan painter could not set their hand to it.[67]

Elsewhere he wrote about human figures in Western painting that 'their eyes seem to move and follow you like the eyes of living people.'[68]

Despite some genuine interest in the effects of Western perspective, colour, and shading, Chinese literati painting of the Late Ming and Early Qing reflects little of this exotic new style. Virtually no direct copies of Western images are known from this period, except for those made by Chinese Christians – almost all of which are known exclusively from texts. Two Chinese Jesuit brother artists worked at the mission during Ricci's tenure, and they were kept very busy supplying devotional pictures, not only for the chapels and residences, but also as gifts for catechumens and local authorities. Emanuel Pereira (Yu Wenhui, 1575–1633) and Jacobo Niwa (Ni Yicheng, 1579–after 1630s) were both pupils of Niccolò's Seminary of Painters; however, they did not have comparable abilities.[69]

The Macanese Pereira worked at the Nanjing mission with Ricci until the latter lost patience with his 'mediocre' abilities and asked Valignano to send him Niwa.[70] In contrast, the half-Japanese, half-Chinese Niwa impressed everyone with his skill, and was in constant demand to paint works in oil both for the mission in China and the Jesuits' church in Macao. His reputation would seem to be well founded if the 1597 *Salvator Mundi* is in fact his work (fig. 30). Niwa also manufactured coloured devotional woodblock prints on paper of the Salvator Mundi and the name of Jesus (IHS) to substitute for the images of Chinese door gods that people put on their homes.[71] Many praised his work. The Rector of Macao, Valentin Carvalho, wrote in 1602 that 'without a doubt he has a skilful hand, and is a capable boy in his craft, his pictures are so beautiful and accomplished that they bring pleasure to the Chinese.'[72] Ricci himself frequently praised the work of this 'excellent painter,' particularly an altarpiece of the Saint Luke Madonna which was displayed in Christmas of 1605:

> Last year, for the festival at Christmas, we placed on the altar in lieu of the image of the Saviour which is always there a new image of the Virgin of Saint Luke, with the Child in her arms, very well painted [*pinto molto bene*] by a young man who is in our house and who had been a pupil of Father Giovanni Niccolò, and everyone was marvellously pleased with this [image] ...[73]

Emanuel Diaz's opinion, expressed in 1602, that Niwa 'knew very well this art [of painting],' was apparently also shared by some of the Imperial authorities in Beijing, which made it necessary for him to go into hiding and work in secret to avoid being pressed into service for the Emperor.[74] Only descriptions survive of Niwa's work in China, and they tell us nothing about his style, showing us only that his subjects were the standard kind of image derived from prints. For example, a French viewer described an altarpiece made by Niwa for Ricci's tomb chapel: 'In it one sees Jesus Christ our Saviour and Redeemer seated on a magnificent throne, the angels on high, the apostles below seeming to listen to him on all sides, as if he were teaching to them.'[75] The reports about Niwa painting replacement door gods, however, hint that the artist also worked in a more indigenizing mode.

Ironically, the only one of these artists to have a surviving work today is the 'mediocre' Pereira. In 1610, while at Beijing, Pereira painted the sole surviving portrait of Ricci, a wooden and awkward likeness known through even poorer reproductions, which has been hanging at the Jesuit Casa Professa in Rome since 1614 (fig. 27). The image merits some interest since it does show some hybrid features. The sweeping, linear curve of the nose and eyebrows recalls Chinese painting convention, and the figure's three-quarters pose before a blank background is typical of traditional Chinese portraiture. In fact, the picture's very stiffness and lack of character bring it close to traditional Chinese portraiture, which Cahill has characterized as a 'staid, functional, relatively unexciting art.'[76]

A few other Chinese convert artists are recorded in Jesuit letters, here and there making copies of altarpieces for use in their own homes.[77] Although none of their names survive, they are likely responsible for two very interesting adaptations of European devotional prints which are datable to the Ricci era. Formerly attributed to Matteo Ricci himself, the first depicts a semi-nude man relaxing in an apparently intoxicated state under the shade of a tree with his pet lion or tiger (fig. 47).[78] The pose and subject are strongly reminiscent of traditional Chinese portraits of the Buddhist Seventh Lohan Bhadra (Batuoluo); for example, one in the Museum of Fine Arts, Boston, by the Southern Song painter Lu Xinzhong (active late twelfth to early thirteenth centuries) (fig. 41).[79] Like this anonymous work, Lu's Lohan portrait shows Bhadra sitting at the base of a tree in a landscape, attended by a tiger who has responded to his call. Both images show the main figure seated sideways, with bare shoulder(s) and sandals. The landscape, lion, sandals, wine flask, and flowerpot of the anonymous painting are rendered in a typically Chinese manner, although line is suppressed in favour of shading. The delineation of the features of the man's body, however, is entirely by shading, and this together with the interest in nude anatomy – also unusual in Chinese painting – point toward a foreign model.

This curious picture, in fact, is an adaptation in reverse of *Saint Jerome* (1564), by the Italian printmaker Mario Cartaro, which itself was an adaptation of Michelangelo's *Noah* from the Sistine Chapel ceiling.[80] The positions of the tree and lion are identical, and the skull, Bible, and crucifix have been replaced by more neutral decorative items. Most importantly, the nude upper body is a showcase for the artist's take on Michelangelo's musculature. The Chinese artist has cropped the frame and consequently drawn the main figure's legs toward his body. There is little reason to suppose that it was intended as a religious picture – even a Buddhist one – and most likely is little more than a genre study with an exotic twist. Nevertheless, its smooth convergence with Buddhist iconography, reminiscent of that of Guanyin, supports Gerson's statement about the rapid assimilation of Christian imagery to Buddhist traditions in China. Coincidentally, the same Cartaro print inspired two paintings by the Mughal court artist Kesu Das (active ca. 1570–90s) (fig. 65), whom we will consider in chapter 5.

The other Chinese adaptation of a European print is more overtly religious. It is also one of the most exquisite hybrids in the history of Jesuit mission art. An image of the Madonna of Saint Luke, taken from one of the many altarpieces of that subject in the possession of Ricci's mission, this large silk scroll is painted entirely in a flowing, calligraphic, Chinese style in indigenous watercolours (compare figs. 1, 48).[81] The Chinese artist has lengthened the figure from a bust portrait into a full-length image, and although the drapery follows its model exactly in the upper part, he has resolved it at the bottom in a typically Chinese manner. Ending in an extremely elegant and dramatic circular sweep, the outer garment encloses the windswept inner robe, above the figure's delicate bare feet. The long Byzantine lines of the original face have been subtly sinicized without adding or subtracting a line. The Christ child, here without his halo but still giving the sign of benediction, has undergone a similar metamorphosis, complete with shaved head and topknot. This picture is remarkable because the artist has adhered so carefully to the original yet made it a completely Chinese image, a transformation comparable to that of the Japanese *Madonna of the Snows* (fig. 35). Although it was likely intended as a Christian image, the slender body, delicate pose, and flowing gown of this Madonna make it very close to traditional images of Guanyin (fig. 46).

By far the most influential Christian devotional pictures of the period were prints and engravings, since their medium had an indigenous equivalent that oil painting lacked: woodblock printing. China had the world's earliest tradition of printing, reaching back to the Tang Dynasty in the tenth century, and by the Ming the technology of printing books had reached its height. Illustrated books were also very much in vogue in this period, with such prominent artists as the figure specialists Ding Yunpeng (d. 1638) and Chen Hongshou (1598–1652) producing preparatory drawings for woodblock prints. European prints were first translated into woodblocks during Ricci's lifetime, and four miscellaneous images that he provided were immediately and widely circulated in China. In 1606 Cheng Dayue and his brother Shifang published a widely popular and influential miscellany of designs for ink-cakes entitled *Master Cheng's Garden of Ink Cakes* (*Chengshi moyuan*), which included some of the earliest colour prints in China.[82] The illustrations themselves were produced by Ding in collaboration with Huang Lin (active ca. 1606–35). Cheng's miscellany included stone rubbings of fantastic phenomena relating to the heavens and earth, Confucianism, Buddhism, Daoism, as well as exotic and precious objects.

Cheng met Ricci through a mutual friend in Beijing in 1605, and asked him for some Christian pictures and samples of Latin script to add to his book after the sections on Confucianism and Daoism. As Spence has shown, Ricci was a little at a loss since he had very few prints, and the collection that would easily satisfy his needs, the lavishly illustrated volume of Nadal, was in Nanchang at the time.[83] Ricci provided Cheng, at short notice, with three engravings by Crispin de Passe and the Wierix brothers, and a Japanese engraving of the Virgen de la Antigua printed in the Seminary of Painters in 1597. Ricci also provided Chinese texts on 'Western Writings and Miracles' for all but the Japanese print, composed of biblical texts and moralist remarks tailored to the idiosyncrasies of each image. Although these engravings are far from elegant – the artist is uncomfortable with Western pose and gesture, and the figures are stiff and awkward – they are a true translation since they introduce Chinese motifs and use Chinese technique.

In *The Calling of Saint Peter* (fig. 49), the serpentine clouds and undulating waves with a scroll in the lower right recall decorative patterns with an ancient lineage in Chinese art, particularly in porcelains.[84] The figures, too, are drawn in a much cleaner, more linear way than the heavily shaded Flemish prototypes. In fact, shading is so alien to the whole conception of the picture that in the few places, such as Christ's calves, where Huang tries out Western hatching, it is used in a purely decorative way and ends up looking like hair. This unease with European modelling recalls a remark made in the eighteenth century by the Qing Emperor Qianlong that shading made figures look 'dirty.'[85] These same four woodblock prints appeared later in a similar miscellany called *Master Fang's Album of Ink Cakes* (*Fangshi Mopu*).[86] Despite Ricci's efforts, however, these ink impressions of christian themes were received as little more than exotica by Chinese society, and even for the publishers Cheng and Fang, Christianity itself was merely 'a marketing edge in the ruthless world of late Ming consumerism.'[87]

European engravings also had a limited influence on Chinese literati painting, particularly of a genre that naturally struck a chord with Chinese painters: topographical prints. However, their impact was subtle and never overt. Cahill and Sullivan have identified motifs from German and Flemish atlases, as well as landscape elements from Nadal, in the work of landscape painters such as Wu Bin (active ca. 1568–1626), Xiang Shengmou (1597–1658), Zhao Zuo (1600–30), Fan Qi (1616–ca. 1694), and Shao Mi (active ca. 1620–60).[88] European influences were limited to technique and incidental motifs, such as a bolder use of perspective and colour, the convention of the bird's-eye view, the appearance of reflections on water, smoking chimneys, unusual treatments of shorelines, and other topographical devices. A painting entitled *Whole View of the Zhi Garden* by the Suzhou painter Zhang Hong (1577–after 1652) resembles views of German and Dutch cities from Braun and Hogenberg's *Civitates Orbis Terrarum* (Cologne 1572–1616) with its aerial view, grid street pattern, and winding river.[89] Braun and Hogenburg's atlas has also been linked with the work of the prominent early Qing Nanjing painter Gong Xian (ca. 1617–89). Gong executed a famous landscape painting entitled *A Thousand Peaks and Myriad Ravines* (fig. 50), whose rugged topography and smoky chiaroscuro may show the influence of engravings of mountains in the German atlas (fig. 50).[90]

A new interest in naturalism and drawing from life is also attributed to European influence, and is perhaps most vividly displayed in Ding Guanpeng's (fl. ca. 1714–60) *Toy Seller at New Year*, with its subtle use of shading to suggest volume.[91] The work of other artists, however, has been less convincingly related to European art. The problem is that most of the influences are hinted at only subtly, and many of these supposedly novel features already existed in Song painting, which had a very sophisticated tradition of pictorial realism and atmospheric perspective.[92] Cahill suggests that what we are in fact witnessing is a revival of Song painting (fig. 43) – in other words, an acceptable indigenous prototype – *inspired* by exposure to European engravings with similar characteristics.[93] According to this theory, the ancient Chinese mode would be an acceptable one in which to explore the novelties of Western pictorial devices. Harrie Vanderstappen agrees: 'Surely Chinese artists could hardly have been unaware of Western illustrated books in their midst. And equally sure is it that Chinese painting of the past offered limitless pictorial models to match the newly seen or to put the new into acceptable Chinese formats.'[94] Therefore the artists, in a quintessentially Chinese solution to the problem, turned to *fang gu*.

The Jesuit Mission after Ricci, 1610–1773

In the twenty years after Ricci's death, the mission started to lose its esteemed position among the literati, as it became more overtly religious in nature. The scholars and merchants who supported Jesuit efforts when they seemed to be another school of Confucianism were now suspicious and found Christian ideas irreconcilable with Chinese ways of living and thinking. The most overtly doctrinal development in the Jesuit missions was the foundation of popular religious groups among the laity, which ignited a deep-rooted Chinese distrust of popular messianic movements.[95] These feelings led to periodic persecutions of the Jesuit missions between 1616 and 1620 by local authorities, who feared that Christians were an anti-government terrorist movement similar to the Buddhist White Lotus Society, a popular sect which did rebel openly at the end of the eighteenth century. Leadership of the five Jesuit residences was assumed by Niccolò Longobardi, who was never a supporter of Ricci's emphasis on Confucianism anyway, and the mission was increasingly focused at the popular level on ministry to the peasantry and small-time merchants and craftspeople.[96] In fact, Longobardo's mission had considerable success among these people, who were much more responsive than the literati to preaching about parables and miracles. The China mission grew to fifteen residences, with a congregation of between sixty and seventy thousand by the early 1640s, and the number rose to three hundred thousand by 1700.[97]

Meanwhile, Europe's attention was focused on the mission's efforts at court, which achieved little in the way of conversions but led to episode after dazzling episode of cross-cultural dialogue. Although during the Nanjing persecutions of 1616–20 the European Jesuits were forced to leave Beijing, they soon returned to establish an even greater presence there. After Ricci's death, the Fleming Nicholas Trigault left for Rome to advertise the mission by publishing Latin translations of Ricci's writings in 1615. These books became instant best-sellers, in the words of Dauril Alden, and led to a flood of applications by young men eager to join the Society and be sent to the Far Eastern missions.[98] They also persuaded the Pope to open his purse and – more importantly – to support Ricci's controversial accommodation methods. Twenty-two new recruits sailed for the Indies, of whom only eight actually arrived in China. Of the eight, however, were some of the most eminent scientists ever sent to the missions, including the German Johann Adam Schall von Bell (1592–1666) and the Italian Giacomo Rho (1592–1638). The scientific apostolate was to continue. Schall von Bell (Tang Ruowang) and his colleagues were appointed to revise the Imperial calendar, an extremely prestigious position which allowed them close contact with the court.

Even the overthrow of the much-weakened Ming regime in 1644 with the invasion of the Manchu Qing Dynasty did not threaten the exalted position of the Jesuit astronomers. Even though Schall himself had manufactured cannons for the desperate Ming forces in their final years, the Qing had no intention of treating such a useful scientific advisor as an enemy. Thus, in his first year of rule, the first Qing emperor, Shunzhi (1644–61), promoted Schall to head the Imperial Board of Astronomy, gave him mandarin status, and – unlike the relationship of Wanli to Ricci – became a frequent personal companion. Despite a period of persecution led by Buddhist and Confucian leaders following Shunzhi's death (1665–71), the next emperor, Kangxi (1662–1772), upon coming of age in 1668, welcomed the Jesuits back to the Imperial astronomical bureau, where they would remain well into the eighteenth century. Upon Schall's death, his assistant, the Fleming Ferdinand Verbiest (Nan huairen, 1623–88), took over the leadership of the Imperial Board of

Astronomy, and he in turn was replaced by a group of French scientists who were sent by Louis XIV as 'royal mathematicians' in 1688. These scientists founded the mission of the French Jesuits, officially independant of *Padroado* authority, which maintained separate bases from their Italian, German, and Iberian counterparts and were not always on the best of terms with them. The mission's success appeared to be guaranteed when the Kangxi Emperor promulgated his Edict of Toleration in 1692, allowing the Christians free worship in his realm.

The scientific apostolate lasted until the suppression of the Society of Jesus in 1773, but the Jesuits' real mission work met a tragic and much earlier end with the famous Chinese rites controversy.[99] After more than a century, Ricci's controversial policies had finally met their demise, largely at the hands of jealous mendicants who had been working in China since the 1630s. The Dominicans spearheaded the campaign in Rome. Two features of Ricci's accommodation, the use of the terms *tian* for 'Heaven' and *shangdi* for 'Supreme Lord' or 'God,' and his decision to allow certain Confucian ceremonies, including the veneration of ancestors, were decisively condemned by the Benedict XIV in 1742 after nearly a century of indecision and politicking. The procedures that led to the papal condemnation involved two particularly arrogant embassies to China in the first decades of the eighteenth century, in which the papal legates acted as if they could order the Emperor around. The Qianlong Emperor (1736–99) was not impressed with the antics of these 'outer barbarians' and told them that if they would not allow Ricci's version of Christianity, he would permit none at all. Needless to say, after 1742 the mission activities of the Society of Jesus were much reduced. Prohibited by Rome from pursuing an indigenized Christianity, the missions were marginalized, their congregation fell dramatically in number, and they were retained at court merely as Imperial servants. Ironically, it was precisely in this period that the artistic activity of the China mission reached its height. But first we must backtrack a little.

Artistic Acculturation after Ricci

The Jesuits pursued their first true policy of artistic acculturation just before Ricci's death and in the decades after, for both popular and cultured audiences. The popular classes, by now the foundation of the mission, were more receptive to devotional art than the literati or court had ever been. These people were more strongly Daoist and Buddhist – both of these faiths had rich traditions of figural imagery – and in this context the Confucian imperative was not so important. Consequently, devotional painting flourished throughout the next century and a half, primarily as adornment for private homes and community chapels. Since commoners seemed willing to replace their old gods with new Christian ones (in reality, they were often only adding them to the old as had the Nahua in New Spain), the Jesuits gave them images to do it with.[100] Longobardi made extensive use of devotional pictures when he preached, always taking care to provide the maximum dramatic effect, with curtains, candles, timed exposures, and other artifices. He also handed out copper images, medallions, and rosaries to the faithful, capitalizing on the Chinese commoner's respect for any object or image believed to possess magic powers: 'a transposition of Chinese attitudes and traditions relating to saintliness and the sacred.'[101]

We have no idea what these images looked like, but since Jesuit artists were mostly occupied at court they were probably made by Chinese artists and would consequently have been in a Chinese, if popular, style. Chinese authorship is especially likely when we consider the Chinese participation in the Society of Jesus itself – Chinese Jesuits constituted one-third of the total number of Jesuits in China by the mid-eighteenth century, a fact that has received little scholarly attention.[102] We know the name of only one Chinese Christian artist, Zhao Lun (late seventeenth century), who painted the Madonna.[103] An indigenous style is all the more likely since they were specifically being used to replace household gods, similarly to the Christian woodblocks made by Niwa to put in place of broadsheets of door gods. The increased dissemination of such imagery is reflected in the fact that Christian pictures started turning up in a wide range of Chinese media precisely during these years. One intriguing example of this popular imagery is an embroidered satin hanging depicting Saint Anthony of Padua, which was probably manufactured for the Christian community in China and which likely copied an engraving of Franciscan origin (fig. 51).[104] Much like the Nandogami images of the Hidden Christians in Japan, the iconography and pose of the figures is all that has survived from European art, the style having been completely indigenized and the composition enriched by details of Chinese landscape, flowers, and birds.

Meanwhile, the Jesuits launched a new offensive toward the literati in the print medium. Taking their cue from Ricci's small contribution to *Master Cheng's Garden of Ink Cakes,* they published the first illustrated lives of Christ in Chinese, this time adapting the images from Nadal's *Evangelicae Historicae Imagines.* The first were a series of fifteen woodblocks published in 1608 to illustrate a *Metodo de Rosario* (*Song nian zhu gui cheng*) by Ricci's colleague Juan da Rocha (1565–1623), and a later one was a set of fifty-seven prints to accompany a 1637 *Explanation of the Incarnation and Life of the Lord of Heaven* (*Tian zhu jiang sheng chu xiang jing jie*), by Guilio Aleni (1582–1649), another companion of Ricci, who also authored a treatise which tried to relate Aristotelian concepts to Confucianism.[105] Aleni, incidentally, founded the mission in the province of Fujian, which has recently been the focus of considerable scholarship owing to the survival of more relevant documentation than for any other Jesuit mission area.[106] The Chinese artists of these series are very accomplished, and within a decade of Ding and Huang's adaptations, the woodblock prints have become much more confident. The compositions are more balanced, elegant, and clear, and stand on their own as works of art.

The Aleni series uses European one-point perspective and shading (fig. 52). Also, like Nadal's original, Aleni's images use letters to key parts of the picture to the text in a way which Clunas suggests goes against the Chinese notions of how text relates to image.[107] Although the artist shows that he is quite comfortable with Western style through his meticulous and accurate rendition of complicated architectural and landscape features, he also chooses to translate some techniques into equivalent Chinese methods. For example, the artist replaces the cross-hatching of copper engravings with parallel lines resembling brush-strokes, which were drawn in the way traditional for Chinese block-cutters. In general there is an economy of line which relates to the medium; and the effect can be more satisfying than in the original, for example, in the calligraphic rabbits at the bottom of *The Temptation in the Wilderness*. He also resorts to specifically Chinese motifs; for example, when he uses the Chinese convention for depicting clouds with comma-like swirls or reduces the leaves in the trees to a painterly stippling effect. Nevertheless, the Aleni series is still predominantly European in style and less interesting than the Rocha cycle, whose subtle sinicization ranks it among the most thoroughly hybrid of Chinese Christian artworks. The Rocha version, incidentally, dispenses with the key letters.

Rocha's artist has gotten rid of figural shading altogether, choosing instead to render the images in an entirely linear manner (figs. 53, 54). Instead of reproducing the Flemish backgrounds, as was attempted by Ding and Huang, he has placed the figures in purely Chinese settings. Even his translation of clouds and waves into Chinese decorative motifs is more confident and assured. In fact, the very best of the illustrations to Rocha's treatise translate every feature of the original into its exact Chinese parallel, retaining only the poses of the figures and basic composition from their Flemish models. Even Albertian perspective – the bastion of Renaissance rationality – is abandoned in favour of the Chinese isometric method (see fig. 43). More so than on any other Jesuit mission, the China missionaries concluded that in order to communicate with the indigenous people they had to relinquish – reluctantly, I am sure – their 'well painted' and 'very beautiful' *maraviglie* from Rome, and learn more about the 'dead and lifeless' imagery of their host culture. With these images' success came the realization that God does not restrict His miracles to the products of the European Renaissance.

In Rocha's *Annunciation* (fig. 53), the principal figures remain in place, but the artist has transformed the entire setting and removed all secondary figures, such as the Calvary scene on the left (compare fig. 55). The brick Renaissance lean-to, meant to represent the Holy House of Loreto, is now a Chinese timber cantilevered pavilion, complete with lattice panels and a tile roof. The house trades in its Albertian perspective with a single vanishing point for Chinese isometric perspective with parallel vanishing points to the right.

References to the lifestyle of the wealthy scholar abound. The Virgin's *prie-dieu* is now a black lacquer table of the kind commonly found in the homes of Ming literati. In place of the Hill of Golgotha and the Flemish townscape above, the artist has introduced a simple Chinese landscape with a banana tree and scholar's rock – a favourite motif in Chinese painting and porcelains of the Jingdezhen kilns.[108] The artist has also opened up the pavilion and allowed it to look out onto a seascape in a manner very typical of Ming landscape painting (an example is the landscape at the Museum of Fine Arts, Boston, by Zhu Duan [1518]).[109] Even the figures' faces and drapery have been sinicized.

The most remarkable transformation of this picture, however, is the artist's treatment of the clouds surrounding the Virgin's shaft of light and the Angel's feet. Boldly Chinese, with lobed heads and tails of flame, these clouds are drawn in the traditional form used in China as vehicles for Daoist immortals or Buddhist Bodhisattvas, where they enclose or support the holy figures.[110] In the *Annuncia-*

tion, these clouds clearly denote the holy status of the Holy Ghost and the Angel, who himself resembles a Bodhisattva. This image is a remarkable example of convergence in action, since the artist has capitalized on a motif that serves a very similar role for both cultures. The diagonal shaft of clouds and light descending from the upper left is also very close to a Chinese convention used in depictions of the Eighth Lohan Vajraputra, in which a dragon rides down from the heavens (fig. 56).[111] It is also virtually identical, incidentally, to the Japanese Raigō paintings of Pure Land Buddhism.[112]

A similar composition underlies *The Agony in the Garden* (compare figs. 54 and 57), in which Christ appears very Lohan-like, indeed, sitting alone in a splendid landscape at the foot of a cave just as the Third Lohan Kanakabharadvaja does.[113] The craggy, rugged surroundings echo a kind of landscape traditionally associated with Bodhidharma, the Indian prince recognized by the Chinese as the founder of Chan Buddhism (whom we have already met in Japan as Daruma), and in the Buddhist tradition are meant to suggest an atmosphere of meditation. Every detail of the buildings in the landscape is sinicized, and the buildings are presented in isometric perspective; and again the very *apsaras*-like angel is accompanied by Chinese-style clouds.

In both of these woodblock prints, the anonymous Chinese author has presented Christian stories in a manner which was meant not only to play into traditional Buddhist imagery, but also to conjure up the world of the cultured literati. In the *Annunciation*, this is done by introducing the household objects and setting associated with the scholar. In *The Agony in the Garden*, it is done by evoking the grand landscape painting tradition, which resonates not only with Buddhism but even more so with the cultured world of *wenren hua*, literati painting. Rocha's illustrations, then, are a high point in artistic partnership, and are contemporary with an equally remarkable group of illustrated theological treatises produced at the Mughal court by Jerónimo Xavier (see chapter 5).

Heartened, no doubt, by their ability to synthesize with Chinese culture, the Jesuits continued to produce woodcuts throughout the seventeenth century. None of them, however, reached the heights of the Rocha illustrations. In 1640, Schall von Bell presented the last Ming Emperor Chongzhen with a 150-page vellum album in a silver binding containing forty-five prints of the life of Christ, which were later published as *Engravings Offered [to the Emperor]*, with forty-eight illustrations. Like the Aleni images, the figures have Chinese faces, but the architectural features are European.[114] In 1672, Aleni published a two-volume treatise on cosmography to accompany Verbiest's world map, containing images of animals and monsters, the Seven Wonders of the World, and the Roman Colosseum (after Heemskerck).[115] The Seven Wonders, in particular, became favourites in Chinese illustrated books. Michael Sullivan suggests that Verbiest himself taught perspective to the printmaker Jiao Bingzhen (ca. 1680–1720), best known for his *Illustrations of Rice and Silk Cultivation* (*Gengzhi tu*); however, judging from Jiao's work, he seems not to have adopted it, preferring instead the traditional isometric method.[116] Other Jesuit efforts in the fine arts included Francesco Sambiaso's (1582–1649) treatise on painting called *Answers about Painting* (*Huada*, 1629), with a preface by Ricci's colleague the scholar Li Zhizao.[117] But the future of Jesuit art in China was not to be in devotional art. It would be in the arts and crafts of the Imperial court.

An interesting footnote to this period of Jesuit artistic activity is the career of the painter Wu Li (1632–1718).[118] Wu is, by definition, the most distinguished Jesuit painter ever to live in China – although he is never recognized as such, and is overshadowed in the scholarship on mission art in China by his European Jesuit comrades. Wu is another example of the selective memory of historians of the missions; Chinese Jesuits made up one-third of the total number of Jesuits in China, outnumbering any other single nationality, yet they have received little press.[119] One of the Six Masters of the Early Qing, Wu was pupil of the great Qing traditionalist landscape painters Wang Jian (1598–1677) and Wang Shimin (1592–1680), and discussed art with Wang Hui. Wu's father died when the artist was a child, and he supported his poor family by selling his pictures. He established a wide reputation, working within the eclectic tradition of *wenren hua*. Wu is recognized by scholars of Chinese art as a painter of great originality, who sometimes worked in the Yuan landscape style of the fourteenth century, occasionally producing works of great visual realism, but who was also capable of very expressive works using a much freer brush-stroke (fig. 42). Like his Buddhist and Daoist compatriots, his art was a very personal means of expression and did not serve an overtly religious function. He even called himself the *Mojing daoren*, or 'Daoist of the Inkwell.'

As a result of further tragedy in his life – his mother and wife both died when he was thirty-one – Wu sought spiritual solace in Buddhism and other religions before arriving at Catholicism. He entered the Society of Jesus in 1682 and was ordained a priest in 1688 at the age of fifty-one, after six years as a scholastic in Macao (he left a fascinating account of life in that city). He devoted the rest of his life to missionary work in his native Jiangsu.[120] However, despite being not only a convert but a priest, he never for a moment considered adopting a European or European-inspired painting style, aside – possibly – from some superficial use of shading and perspective. Wu defended the Chinese landscape tradition when he wrote that it 'does not seek physical likeness [*xingsi*], and does not depend on fixed patterns; we call it divine [*shen*] and untrammelled [*yi*].'[121] Here we have an established artist, trained entirely in a non-European tradition, who becomes a Jesuit but keeps his artistic life separate from his religious vocation. There is even no evidence to suggest that Wu used his painting in his evangelization efforts even though he penned a large corpus of highly original and profoundly spiritual Christian devotional poetry, which has been called 'one of the boldest experiments in Chinese literary history.'[122] After all, as Craig Clunas points out, the notion of didactic art was, in the Chinese tradition, a contradiction in terms.[123] How can we reconcile Wu with *noster modus*?

Jesuit Artists at the Qing Court

With the advent of the Qing, the weakened prestige of the Christians among the educated classes was felt in the arts. Whereas in the late Ming the literati still showed a genuine, if distant, interest in European art, scholars under the Qing demonstrated increasing disdain as they launched verbal attacks on Western style. Although writers still conceded that Western art had some remarkable visual effects, they considered them mere tricks and below the notice of the educated painter. Jiang Shaoshu, for example, commented in 1720 that perspective 'did not correspond to scholarly taste, and consequently connoisseurs have not adopted it';[124] and Zhang Geng wrote in the middle of the century that the European style 'is not worthy of refined appreciation, and lovers of antiquity will not adopt it.'[125] In contrast, the Manchu court in Beijing greatly expanded its patronage of Jesuit art. But this was on its own terms, which never had anything to do with religion.

Ironically, the most active period of Jesuit artistic production in China was unrelated to Jesuit missionary aims, and remains an anomaly. In an surprising twist of fate, an impressive list of Jesuit artists and technicians from all over Europe – perhaps the greatest gathering of Jesuit artistic talent in mission history – spent nearly all of their time working for the Qing emperors as exalted domestic servants. Kangxi was the first to include Jesuits in his Zaobanchu, the group of craft ateliers under official supervision in the Yangxindian, or Hall for the Nourishment of the Spirit.[126] Just as he had welcomed Jesuit scientific advisors into his astronomical bureau, he and his successors Yongzheng (1723–35) and Qianlong pressed into service any Jesuits with knowledge in the arts to produce novelties ranging from fountains and palace pavilions to enamelled metalwork, ceramic ornament, and clocks.[127] One of the most important roles played by the best Jesuit artists was – to borrow James Cahill's term – as a kind of 'court photographer,' painting lifelike portraits of the Emperor, his concubines, favourite horses, and even lapdogs.[128]

The Emperor was so determined to have the latest Western techniques that he tried to enlist virtually every missionary who arrived in China, regardless of background. Soon these European 'specialists' included the Jesuits Father Luigi Buglio (1606–82), Brother Charles de Belleville (1656–after 1700), Father Joachim Bouvet (1660–1732), Father d'Entrecolles (d. 1741), Brother Cristoforo Fiori (in China, 1694–1705), Brother Giovanni Gherardini (in Beijing 1698–1707), Brother Giovanni Castiglione (Lang Shining, 1688–66), Father Denis Attiret (1702–68), Brother Gilles Thibault (1703–66), Father Ignatius Sichelbart (1708–80), Father Michel Benoist (1715–74), Father Pierre-Martial Cibot (1727–81), Father de Ventavon (1733–87), and Father Giuseppe Panzi (1734–1811, arrived 1772); as well as the diocesan priest Father Matteo Ripa (1682–1745) and the Augustinian Giovanni Damascèno Sallusti (d. 1781).[129] Some were professional artists, but others were obliged to take a crash-course in art after they arrived in Beijing. The court's use of Jesuit artists parallels much more rigidly the relationship of the Jesuits to the Mughal emperors Akbar and Jahangir more than a century earlier, with the significant difference that in India the emperors were actually interested in devotional art.

Although the Emperor wanted the benefits of Western artistic technology, he was not interested in European style. Everything had to be done within traditional Chinese parameters. In fact, the Chinese were forcing their Jesuit charges to glorify the Imperial Dynasty by practising the very artistic accommodation they had been developing for mission work. Father Ventavon, writing in 1769 about the Jesuit painter Attiret, said bluntly that 'it is necessary that he abandon his taste and his ideas in many aspects, so that he can accommodate to those of the country,' a situation he characterizes as 'embarrassing.'[130] In 1754 Attiret asked, famously, 'Will this farce never come to an end? ... I find it hard to persuade myself that all this is to the glory of God.'[131] The Qianlong Emperor explained in a poem that Western methods were only useful for capturing likenesses since they were contrary to traditional values, and fantasized about a synthesis between the painting styles of Castiglione and the Northern Song master Li Gonglin (ca. 1040–1106).[132]

Particularly draconian was the enamelling workshop, where artists like Castiglione and Ripa were obliged to manufacture enamelled trinkets using European techniques in what was described by Ripa as 'galley-slave' conditions.[133] Both Castiglione and Ripa performed badly on purpose so that they would be relieved of their duties. The Jesuit artists may also have been charged with painting undecorated Jingdezhen porcelains, although the ones which survive do not look as though they were painted by Europeans. As with other media since the seventeenth century, Christian devotional scenes became very fashionable in Jingdezhen production from the Kangxi to the Qianlong periods, although in porcelains made primarily for the export market. Scenes from Nadal and other engravings brought by the Jesuits were copied in grisaille or colour onto dishes.[134] Laufer published a Chinese album of drawings after Catholic engravings, which was possibly a book of cartoons for porcelain wares – and not, as Laufer contends, a work of the late Ming painter Dong Qichang (1555–1636).[135]

The most celebrated of the Jesuit painters at the Manchu court was Castiglione, by far the most talented European artist to reach China and the subject of three full-length studies.[136] A handful of paintings by this Milanese Jesuit survive in Genoa and Coimbra, which allow us to observe his original style.[137] The canvases are capable but unremarkable scenes of Jesuit visions in the Late Baroque style prevalent in Northern Italy at the time. Typical are a zigzag composition full of rolling clouds and sunbursts, a slight elongation of some of the figures, and an intensity of the mystical poses, possibly reflecting the influence of contemporary Venetian painters such as Giovanni Battista Piazzetta (1683–1754) and Antonio Balestra (1666–1740).

After the still young Castiglione arrived in Beijing in 1715, however, he was obliged to abandon his Late Baroque manner altogether in the works he produced for the Chinese court, reserving his Italian style exclusively for the few canvases he had time to produce for the Chinese mission churches. For the court, he produced paintings, designs for engravings, architectural plans, and objets d'art. Some of his work was merely decorative, while other projects – most notably his sketches for a 1765 set of engravings of the Emperor's conquest of Turkestan[138] – were fuel for Imperial propaganda. He remained in the service of the emperors for an astonishing fifty-one years, taught Chinese artists European oil painting technique, collaborated with court painters such as Ding Guanpeng, Qin Kun, and Tangdai, and made such a significant contribution to secular Chinese painting that he has been called 'one of the great court painters' of the Qing Dynasty.[139] But the best painters of the Qing were not court painters, and his impact on cultured Chinese painting (*wenren hua*) was negligible.

Castiglione's Chinese style, like that of the other Jesuits at court, was not purely Chinese, but a subtle hybrid of Eastern conventions and Western realism. After about seven years at court, Castiglione perfected this synthesis, fusing oil technique with those of traditional Chinese watercolour and ink painting, and producing works characterized by bright colours and extremely precise brush-work. He was also able to recreate the effects of oil painting on canvas by painting on layered Chinese paper – a very different method from that practised by the Japanese. Castiglione developed a style of painting referred to in court documents as *xianfa* ('line method'), which featured illusionistic conceits using linear perspective.[140] *Xianfa* became a separate branch of court painting, and Castiglione trained a number of pupils in this style.

Castiglione's mature style can be demonstrated by a signed work entitled *Imperial Procession* and *The Night Market at Yangcheng* (figs. 58, 59).[141] The landscapes, costumes, and subjects are Chinese, as is the medium, and at first glance they appear to fall completely within Chinese tradition. But a closer look reveals that they retain the most important features of Western technique. Castiglione uses one-point perspective in his architecture instead of the isometric perspective common in Chinese painting (compare fig. 43), and his landscapes incorporate the atmospheric effects of the Northern Renaissance and Leonardo. The artist shrouds the distant mountains in mist and gives them a bluish tint. Chinese literati painters often used mist in their mountain landscapes, but not to create an illusion of consistent spatial depth as Castiglione has done.

The surface of the trees in Castiglione are deeply modelled and textured. The reflections on water in the first painting and the slight shadows cast by the horses' hooves are also Western conventions. Although in some pictures Castiglione builds up his landscape elements with expressive, choppy brush-strokes in the Chinese manner (fig. 59), he never does so with his figures, whether human or animal. Castiglione's figures minimize the calligraphic line in favour of colour and a hint of shading, a three-dimensional effect which is at odds with traditional Chinese painting (compare fig. 42). He prefers three-quarters views and poses that emphasize movement and drama in a way that goes against Chinese conventions.

Vanderstappen has shown that Castiglione's portraits of horses – perhaps his most famous works – lose the vitality of traditional Chinese depictions by minimizing the expressive potential of the brush-stroke.[142] The taut, muscular lines which give the Chinese image the sense of being caught in mid-action is lost in the Italian Jesuit's quest for the third dimension. But this is a limitation of Western art, not of Castiglione's technique. In the final analysis, Castiglione was a consummate craftsman whose blend of East and West is one of the most successful ever attempted: 'In all, this is a brilliant synthesis, cleverly calculated to give the emperor enough of Western realism to delight him, but not enough to disconcert.'[143]

Castiglione also worked on architectural projects for the emperors. Although never trained as an architect, he collaborated in 1729 with the Chinese mathematician Nian xiyao on an adaptation of Andrea Pozzo's *Perspectiva Pictorum et Architectorum* (1693) called *Visual Learning* (*Shixue*), complete with diagrams on perspective architecture, for the benefit of Imperial architects.[144] The *Shixue* was acculturative, as well, including diagrams of the Chinese opera stage and Chinese animals. His largest and most extravagant project, however, was his collaboration with Benoist in the design of the European palaces (*Xiyanglou*) at the Imperial summer residence, the Yuanming Yuan or 'Garden of Everlasting Spring,' which now lie in ruins but are immortalized in a set of engravings made in the Jesuits' studio in Beijing (fig. 60). Perhaps best described as an Occidentalist theme park, this vast conglomeration of gardens, fountains, and pavilions, with its brightly coloured majolica tiles, automata, mirrors, and clocks, rivalled the excesses of the very Versailles court which sent such toys to China. Like Castiglione's paintings, this too was a mixture of East and West, but this time the European element was not quite so subtle. He used traditional Chinese hipped roofs and timber gates and a small army of Chinese masons and craftsmen, but his buildings, staircases, and fountains were done in the most extravagant French rococo style.

Many scholars have pointed to Italian villa architecture as the most important influence in the Yuanming Yuan pavilions because of Castiglione's own background.[145] But Castiglione was no architect, and he learned his craft in Beijing with whatever architectural manuals there were on hand. Judging by the style, it was French works, such as the treatise by Félibien, which exerted the strongest influence on Castiglione. Further evidence of a French inspiration can be found by comparing the Yuanming Yuan buildings to those of the so-called Turkish Baroque, an Occidentalist style in Ottoman architecture that flourished at exactly the same period.[146] Beginning in the reign of Ahmed III (1703–30), but especially prominent later in the century, this synthesis of French decorative motifs and Ottoman architectural forms was particularly common in water architecture such as fountains and riverside garden pavilions. Recent studies and my own research have shown that they were based largely on French and German designs taken from pattern books for fountains and grillwork, views of French palaces, and treatises by the likes of Antoine Watteau, Louis Fordrin, François Cuvillies, and Félibien, which the Ottomans obtained from merchants, ambassadors, and possibly missionaries.[147] The Yuanming Yuan pavilions have a striking affinity with their Turkish counterparts, particularly in the decorative details, betraying a similar origin.

Mission Architecture in the Qing

Even though the artists at the Manchu court were given virtually no time to work on mission art projects, they managed to build three substantial churches in Beijing, each with elaborate painted interiors. Perhaps in reaction to the enforced acculturation of their court efforts, the architects used emphatically European styles, specifically reminiscent of the Roman Late Baroque. The three churches were the North Church (Beitang, 1703), belonging to the French mission, the South Church (Nantang) of Nossa Senhora da Assunção founded by Schall in 1650 and rebuilt in 1703 (for which the Zhalan was the cemetery), and the Church of São José (Dongtang, 1729), where the library was housed.

São José was built by the Florentine Jesuit brother Ferdinando Bonaventura Moggi, and its vaulting and cupola were painted by Castiglione himself. Moggi compared it to no less a monument than Sant' Ignazio in Rome, particularly the high altar, which he said was like the one in the chapel of S. Luigi Gonzaga.[148] Moggi's reference to Sant' Ignazio was not entirely unwarranted since Pozzo's treatise on architectural perspective was one of the main models for his own church. Since it would have been very difficult and expensive to find someone to build a Western cupola in Beijing – and since a Christian church with a dome would have seemed arrogant to the Chinese – Moggi probably recreated Pozzo's illusionistic false dome in his church. There was even a diagram for such a dome in Castiglione and Nian's manual *Shixue*. Moggi's description also seems to confirm this, revealing that the church was low-slung and accommodated to a certain degree to Chinese architectural practices:

> ... the same can be said of the whole church which, in the manner that it differs from the architectural taste of Europe is to a large extent dissimulated to suit it to the genius of the Chinese, which likes a multiplicity of columns ... It is certainly true that in comparison with beautiful European churches its greatest defect, considering the whole, is that it is somewhat squat.[149]

São José was not the only church in Beijing that evoked Pozzo. As depicted in engravings, the Church of Nossa Senhora da Assunção (Nantang) was extremely ornate for its size, with multiple pilasters, volutes, and cartouches (fig. 61).[150] The exterior bears very little resemblance to Sant' Ignazio, other than in its coupled pilasters, and in fact it has distinctly Iberian features, such as the flanking towers and the *estípite* columns. The interior, however, reproduces Pozzo's trademark false dome, and – like São José – also evokes his design for the altar of S. Luigi Gonzaga. The church's only concession to acculturation was the Chinese temple gate and lions in the outer court, which led to the very Baroque gate in the main court.

The French Church of Saint-Sauveur also had aspirations to greatness. Built by Belleville, it was decorated by Gherardini, who, although from Bologna, had been working for the Duc de Nevers in Paris and reached China on a French ship.[151] Gherardini was especially renowned as a painter of architectural perspective, and it is tempting – and reasonable – to suppose that his painted cupola for Saint-Saveur also echoed Sant' Ignazio's illusionistic false dome. Perhaps this church also used Pozzo's design for the altar of S. Luigi Gonzaga for the high altar. Unfortunately, we have no record of what this church looked like.

It is well known that Andrea Pozzo's perspectival designs, especially his illusionistic ceiling, were disseminated throughout Italy and Central Europe. Pozzo himself painted such domes in places like Frascati, Mondovì, and Vienna, and artists such as Cosmas Damian Asam and Giovanni Marchini painted others in Southern Germany.[152] It may come as something of a surprise to scholars of Baroque art, however, that within a few decades of Pozzo's ceiling in Rome, as many as three churches in far-off Beijing may have boasted similar false domes, as well as copies of his altars. As the newest Roman flagship church of the Society of Jesus, Sant' Ignazio inherited the role played by the Church of the Gesù in the sixteenth and seventeenth centuries. Whereas in the early days, saying that a church was 'just like the Gesù' was just so much hyberbole, in this era, thanks to the increased dissemination of designs through Jesuit presses and a more modern notion of 'style,' a church on the other side of the earth could quite literally resemble one in Rome.

The China mission ended up as a high profile and extravagant failure, but not because of faults with the Jesuit approach to ministry; its pastoral fate was sealed primarily by the political back-stabbing of other Catholics in China. Artistically, too, the mission famously suffered, this time through the Jesuits' own lack of understanding of Chinese taste. Had the Jesuits made a greater effort in the time of Ricci to adapt to the painting tradition of the literati – and they had literati painter friends who could have helped them – they might have achieved an artistic synthesis on a par with Wu Li's Christian poetry. They did not and this was one reason why they failed to gain a foothold with the intellectual class.

Nevertheless, as was noted in chapter 2, most mission societies were complex, heterogeneous groups made up of contrasting audiences, and there was more to China than the literati. One audience was the Imperial court. No one can deny that Jesuit artists had luck with the Qing emperors, although the activities of Castiglione and his associates merely secured the Jesuits' influence without directly assisting with ministry. The Jesuits' greatest success, however, was on the level of the common people – merchants, farmers, and craftsmen – groups who have been little studied until now. These people were receptive to Christian imagery because of its similarities with Buddhist and Daoist iconography and because of a similar need for pictures in those religions and Christianity, and this convergence smoothed the way for conversion. But Christian imagery also made an impact on the wider popular society of the time in a way that had nothing whatever to do with religion. Late Ming and early Qing society was increasingly becoming a 'culture of curiosity,' ever more fascinated with exotica and foreign societies – in a similar way to Europe's own fad for *chinoiserie* – and this phenomenon formed part of a general expansion of all types of imagery in a wide range of media, as China itself reflected a more global awareness.[153] In their small but significant way, by serving as a conduit for European art and science during an era when little reached China by other means, the Jesuits helped pave the way for this awareness, and left a legacy – albeit a secular one – to Chinese visual culture.

5

'A Bright Assembly':[1] The Jesuit Mission to 'Mogor,' 1580–1773

European visitors to the palaces and tombs of the emperors of Mughal India ('Mogor' in Portuguese) between the 1590s and 1660s were amazed to find them prominently adorned with mural paintings depicting Christ, the Virgin Mary, and Christian saints executed in the styles of the Late Renaissance. To their astonishment, they also discovered Mughal artists at work on large numbers of miniature paintings, exquisite jewellery, and sculptures of the same subjects – including many which were apparently even being used as devotional images. Their wonderment led to false reports of the imminent conversion of the Muslim Emperors Akbar (1556–1605) and Jahangir (1605–27), and Portuguese governors, English merchants and clerics from all over the Catholic world hastened to forge alliances with a new Prester John. The catalyst for this extraordinary episode of cultural convergence was the Society of Jesus, whose Mogor mission facilitated what may well have been the most reciprocal artistic dialogue of any of their world missions.[2]

To a far greater extent than in China or Japan, the Mughal arts wholeheartedly embraced and openly appropriated Western styles and techniques – and, most unusually, Catholic devotional imagery. As in the case of early modern chroniclers, more recent scholars have tended to misinterpret these images, either as a sign of Mughal cultural capitulation to the West, or as a brief and superficial fad for exotica. Such views misunderstand the Emperors' intentions and underestimate their learning and shrewdness. The Mughals pressed Euro-Christian art into service as a vehicle for their message of universal supremacy and divinity; its use was erudite, and its meaning indigenous. Mughal India was the only sizeable Asian state to adopt European art on such a scale before the Industrial Age, and unlike other chapters in this book, therefore, most of my analysis will focus on works of art produced outside the mission by the mainstream artists of the Imperial court. However, like the art in the other missions, it is a true hybrid and ranges from works in a strongly European style to those with Christian subjects in a more traditional Indo-Islamic manner.

The Mughal Context for Cultural Exchange

Although an Islamic state, the Mughal Empire was ruled by a dynasty with Mongol roots, who inherited their forebears' religious tolerance and curiosity about

Christianity. The shamanist Mongol religion was open to borrowings from other faiths, and early Mongol rulers such as Chingis (Ghenghis) Khan (d. 1227) made it official policy to respect all religions without favouritism and to honour all priests and holy men.[3] In 1245, the widow of Chingis's son Ögedei (1229–41) welcomed a Franciscan mission from Italy, led by the sixty-five-year-old Franciscan Giovanni di Piano Carpini, to her court at Karakorum.[4] Fuelled by the legends of a benevolent Asian prince called Prester John, the Franciscans had travelled to Mongolia in a desperate last-ditch attempt to save the Crusades through an alliance with the Mongols. Although ultimately an extravagant failure, Carpini's mission, and later expeditions by the Dominican Andrew of Longjumeau (1248) and the Franciscan William of Rubrock (1253), brought Europe face-to-face with China and introduced to the East a few works of Western art, including an illuminated Bible and breviary.[5] The friars, however, were unwilling to show the same tolerance to the Mongols in return, and this, coupled with the paucity of gifts and their inability to debate convincingly with other religious leaders, thwarted this opportunity for cultural exchange.[6]

Akbar was also lenient toward different religions. Himself a Muslim, he ruled over a majority of Hindus, as well as Armenian Christians, Zoroastrians, and Jains, and for practical reasons maintained good relations with each group. One of the most prominent features of Akbar's tolerance, which also echoed his Mongol predecessors, was his initiation of interfaith debates in 1575. At first only including Sunni and Sufi Muslims, by 1578 the debates later welcomed 'learned men from Khorasan and Iraq and Transoxania and India, both doctors and theologians, Shi'ah and Sunnis, Christians, philosophers and Brahmins – indeed lords of all nations.'[7] When Akbar invited the Jesuits to his court in 1580, it was primarily to represent Western Christendom at these debates.

From the beginning, however, Akbar's intentions were not solely religious. Since the 1560s, royal artists had demonstrated an interest in Western art, particularly in its realism and visual drama, and probably also its devotional power. Akbar may well already have suspected that Catholic imagery had the potential to serve him as propaganda. By inviting the Jesuit mission to court, therefore, he was simultaneously assuring himself a constant supply of religious images from Western Europe and a group of men capable of explaining and theorizing about them. They came far better equipped than their thirteenth-century predecessors.

Although Islam is officially disinclined toward figural imagery, pictures of people and animals abounded in the Arabic and Persian painting traditions from which Akbar inherited his court art. Primarily designated for private enjoyment, these miniature paintings adorned poetry books, histories, and scientific manuals, and were gathered in albums. Traditional Indo-Persian painting was an extremely refined, aristocratic art on a miniature scale, favouring jewel-like colours, intricate detail, geometry, and, especially, balance and elegance (fig. 62). Artists had little interest in pictorial realism and similar optical effects before the time of Akbar, and tended toward stylization. Although virtually none of them still survive, figural mural paintings in a similar style had also decorated Islamic palaces for centuries, often including portraits of the rulers and their courts. Even biblical subjects, either from the Koran or from Judeo-Christian sources, were a fairly common feature of Islamic painting from North Africa to Central Asia, particularly portraits of prophets such as Solomon or the Queen of Sheba (fig. 62). But no other Islamic culture produced anywhere near the quantity of biblical subjects that would be executed by Mughal artists, nor do any earlier Islamic paintings depict saints who are not mentioned in the Koran, Hadith, or medieval Islamic literature.

The Mughal court almost certainly possessed a small number of European prints, including biblical scenes, prior to the first Jesuit mission in 1580, and even before the first recorded contact between the Mughals and the Portuguese in 1573.[8] In the chronicle of the Jesuit historian Fernão Guerreiro, for instance, Akbar makes a remark that suggests that his father collected European pictures: 'My father esteemed much things like this; and, if anyone had given it him, he would have granted him any boon he might have asked.'[9] The handful of engravings which Akbar's atelier probably possessed before the Jesuits arrived in 1580 included works by the German printmakers Georg Pencz and Hans Sebald Beham, some sixteenth-century German monogrammists, Flemish masters such as Allaert Claesz, and the Frenchman Delaune.[10] The initial reaction of Akbar's artists to Western art, however, was not especially sophisticated, it echoed that of the earliest Arab painters to Byzantine miniatures.[11] Like Arab painters, Mughal artists used the foreign pictures as models for technique and style, and quoted individual figures or compositions out of their original context, including poses, motifs, and costumes, as well as limited spatial effects such as primitive modelling, Breughel-like flocks of birds on the horizon, and the device of suggesting space by making background figures smaller.[12] By contrast, after the first Jesuit mission in 1580, Mughal artists began to show an enthusiasm for the subjects themselves, their meaning, and even their devotional significance.

In 1573, a delegation from Portuguese Goa met with Akbar at the northwestern port town of Surat and presented him with 'many of the curiosities and rarities of the skilled craftsmen of [Portugal].'[13] Akbar's appetite for curiosities was immediately whetted, and he responded by sending an embassy under Hajji Habibullah to Goa in 1575, which returned three years later with luxurious gifts, including textiles, Portuguese costumes, and musical instruments – as well as European musicians to play on them – one of which was a fancy pipe organ whose panels were painted inside and out with devotional images of Jesus and the saints.[14] The European costumes, furniture, pottery, and metalwork objects from these embassies quickly made their way into Mughal painting, just as Akbar himself donned Portuguese garb and listened to Renaissance madrigals. Shortly afterward, Akbar learned about another kind of European treasure: the legendary debating acumen of the Society of Jesus. He immediately sent another delegation to Goa, this time with the express goal of inviting some Jesuits to take part in his ongoing religious debates at the 'Ibādatkhāna, or Imperial debating hall.[15]

The First Two Jesuit Missions (1580–92) and the Arts

The Jesuits who would lead this first mission to a major Islamic power were based in Goa, the Portuguese colony in southwestern India which was rapidly becoming the largest European-style city in Asia. As we have already seen, the Jesuits had a special relationship with Goa, since the enclave had been the location of the Society's first mission in 1542. As the administrative and economic capital of Portuguese Asia, Goa was the staging ground for religious and cultural activities throughout the continent. Although the Jesuits were by no means the first missionary order to make Goa their home, they soon became one of the most prominent as they built monumental churches, colleges, and residences throughout the colony. These projects, together with those of the other religious orders, demanded legions of artisans, most of whom, as we have already seen, came from convert or Hindu families.

Although Goa would become a thriving centre for painting and sculpture in the later seventeenth century, in the sixteenth, the artistic life of the city was still meagre. From the very first years of Portuguese occupation, a few paintings had been sent from Lisbon to satisfy the needs of Goa and the other Portuguese settlements of Cochin, Daman, and Diu, but even fewer artists – Portuguese or otherwise – were active in Goa itself.[16] It was only during the next two centuries that artists would execute multitudes of panel paintings for the city's fifty churches and monasteries and over two hundred thousand inhabitants, carve exquisite ivory saints for domestic and export use (fig. 5), and craft intricate ivory-inlaid furniture called *certosina*, which was the pride of Portuguese castles and manors.[17] Since most of the artists active in seventeenth-century Goa were Indians or *mestiços*, Hindu motifs and Indian flora and fauna invaded their Christian imagery, and the result was fascinating blends of Christian content with indigenous patterns and approaches to symbolism. One haunting example is the 1683 death portrait of Sister Maria de Jesus, in the Convent of Santa Monica in Velha Goa (fig. 63). A gaunt former Mother Superior who received the stigmata, her face and wounds float as disembodied symbols above the flattened mass of her body, very much in the manner of the frontalized images found in Jain *yantra* diagrams or portraits of Hindu deities, and the carpet, incense-burners, and candlesticks below her coffin burst with verdant tropical flora. But when the first Jesuit missions brought art to Akbar, Goa was still an artistic backwater; set against the cultural barrenness of the Portuguese capital in the 1580s, therefore, the Mughal mission's precocity in the visual arts is all the more amazing.

The first Jesuit mission to the Mughal court (1580–3) was well apprised of Akbar's interests and wisely arrived with 'a large caravan laden with choice goods.'[18] The expedition was led by the the Italian aristocrat Rodolfo Acquaviva (1550–83), nephew of Father General Claudio Acquaviva (1593–1615), as well as the Spaniard Father António Monserrate (d. 1600) and a Persian convert Francisco Henriques. Their 'choice goods' included many printed books, some of which were illustrated, and some fine quality engravings, including a few late-sixteenth-century versions of Dürer's (1471–1528) *Small Passion* and *Virgin and Child*, and works by Philipp Galle (1537–1612) and his contemporaries.[19] They brought a few life-sized oil paintings, and statues, which were of sufficiently high quality to make a deep impression on Akbar – and he was no dilettante. These first oil paintings ever to reach the Mughal court included a retable of the Madonna,[20] a Crucifixion(?),[21] and a copy of the Saint Luke Madonna (fig. 1) painted by the Jesuit

Brother Manuel Godinho.[22] Godinho had copied an original sent from Rome to Goa in 1578 by Father General Everard Mercurian (1573–80).[23]

When the fathers exhibited the two paintings of the Madonna and Child at their chapel in Fatehpur Sikri in 1580, they supposedly caused an incredible stir as crowds thronged to see them. Akbar paid a personal visit, and brought 'a few of his intimates and his chief painter and other painters.'[24] The Emperor was so pleased with the paintings that he insisted on having one for himself, a request that could not be refused: 'On seeing how fond the King and his retinue were of the altar-piece of Fr. Martin da Silva, we presented it to him on behalf of the Fr. Provincial [Rui Vicente, 1574–83], as instructed by His Reverence.'[25] They also gave him a picture of Christ, and probably gave him the Godinho version of the Saint Luke Madonna when Acquaviva finally returned to Goa in 1583.[26] Akbar continued to send his best painters and artisans to the chapel to study the technique and subjects of these images,[27] and they produced paintings as well as replicas in gold and ivory.[28]

Despite his obvious delight in curiosities, the Emperor's interest in these paintings was not purely connoisseurly. Early on, he demonstrated a fascination with the ritual properties of the altarpiece by observing and imitating the behaviour of the Christians toward it; for example, when he himself prostrated before the image and made obeiances. Akbar and his court were impressed by the almost theatrical way in which the Jesuits used curtains, incense, and candles to enhance the spiritual power of their images.[29] Inspired by this behaviour, in 1581 a member of the royal family displayed the painting, draped with fine textiles, in Akbar's audience hall opposite his throne to celebrate his return from Kabul, and Akbar followed this lead by exhibiting it on other important state occasions, as well as annually on the Christian Feast of the Assumption (August 15), when he made his courtiers perform ritual obeiances before it (fig. 64).[30] He continued this practice after the Jesuit mission had already returned to Goa. Akbar's purpose was not simply to pay homage to the Virgin Mary, who is beloved by Muslims, but, as we shall see, also to enhance his own prestige and status by endowing his presence with reminders of divine approval.

On 3 March 1580, the fathers presented Akbar with seven of the eight volumes of Plantin's (1514–89) monumental Polyglot Bible (1567–72) and an atlas called the *Theatrum Orbis Terrarum* (1570), by Abraham Ortelius (1527–98), both of which contained numerous full-page engravings of the highest quality from the Antwerp workshop, and both of which were studied avidly by Mughal painters.[31] They also gave the Emperor an impressive library of books that appears to have been assembled specifically with Akbar's *'Ibādatkhāna* debates in mind, since it reproduced the kind of library owned by the great Jesuit preachers in Rome, who discoursed by means of commentary or *explication de texte*.[32] The collection was heavily scholastic, with an emphasis on works directed at non-Christians and texts justifying the use of images, and it also included the fundamental Jesuit writings, as well as some books on Portuguese history and law to satisfy Akbar's ongoing interest in that nation.

The library was inventoried in 1595 by the Jesuits of the third mission, who list the following works: additional bibles and concordances; four volumes of the

Summa Theologiae (1266–73), the *Summa contra gentiles* (1259–64) aimed at non-Christians, and a diatribe against Muslims, Jews, and Eastern Christians called *De Rationibus Fidei contra Graecos, Armenos et Saracenos*,[33] all by Saint Thomas Aquinas (1225–74);[34] a book by the sixteenth-century scholastic Domingo de Soto, who was a close follower of Aquinas; two copies of the *Summa Peccatorum*,[35] by the Dominican commentator on Aquinas, Cardinal Cajetan (1470–1534); a diatribe against Luther by Silvestro 'Prierius' Mazzolini;[36] two copies of the *Manual de confessores et penitentes*, by the Spanish priest Martín de Azpilcueta 'Navarro' (d. 1555);[37] the *Chronicles* (1454–9, a history of the world), of Saint Antonine of Florence;[38] a history of the popes, probably the *Liber de vita Christi ac omnium pontificum* (History of Christ and the Popes), by Bartolomeo Sacchi 'Platina' (1421–81);[39] a life of Saint Francis of Assisi (1182–1226), the *Spiritual Exercises* of Ignatius of Loyola, the *Constitutions* of the Society of Jesus, the Laws of Portugal, the *Commentaries* of Afonso de Albuquerque (1453–1515), and a Latin grammar by Father Manuel Alvarez.[40] Although most of these would not have contained pictures, several of them contained lengthy discussions of the use and potential of images, and we know that the Mughals read some of them because both Mughal and Jesuit sources cite translations of specific texts.[41]

The sources also reveal the way in which Mughal artists responded to the contents of the Jesuits' books. The fathers, who had been entrusted with the religious education of several children of the court, including Akbar's son Prince Murad, used an illustrated book of Christian doctrine during their lessons.[42] This was something like Father G. Baptista Eliano's *Dottrina Christiana* (Rome, after 1563), an example of a genre of catechism created by the Society for children or illiterates.[43] Akbar ordered his painters to attend closely to these lessons, and to 'paint all that [the missionary] should tell them.'[44] Another opportunity for teaching with illustrated books came during the weekly debates in the *'Ibādatkhāna*, during which the fathers would explain the tenets of Catholicism to men of all religions. Even when Akbar was on campaign in Afghanistan, Father Monserrate took the opportunity to explain Bible stories to him with engravings.[45]

The most colourful pageant for religious imagery was the mission's annual Christmas festival, when the Jesuits would adorn the crib with satin and velvet cloths, statues, and especially pictures.[46] This festival immediately became a favourite of the Emperor, who took his closest companions to the chapel to visit and showed a great curiosity about the story of the Nativity. From then on, Akbar, and later also Jahangir, would try to attend the spectacle every year, and usually lent the fathers Christian pictures from their own collections, including works by their own artists and portraits of themselves, for the event.[47] In these ways, the Imperial court and atelier became intimately acquainted not only with the visual images, but their narrative content, devotional and mnemonic power, and ritual context. Mughal artists would soon harness this potential for their own purposes.

The chapel at the Fatehpur Sikri mission, like those in the daimyos' castles in Japan, was simply a room inside the Imperial palace, and therefore obviously Mughal in style. In fact, the chapel had three locations in the palace during the Jesuits' stay there. The first was a room outside the palace in the *sarai* near the so-called Agra Gate, a location that became untenable because of the noisy market adjacent.[48] Next, it was moved to a room within the palace gates in the *hathyapol* complex where royal musicians were lodged (which can hardly have been much quieter). It was here that the Saint Luke Madonna was displayed in 1580. After the Jesuits had earned the enmity of the Muslims at court through their debating activities, Akbar moved the chapel one last time to a more secure chamber near his bedroom, or *khwābgāh*, and adjacent to the Divān-i 'Ām, which could access the palace through a secret passageway. Formerly a warehouse for perfume, this room was recently excavated by Muhammed, who showed that the Jesuits made some alterations to form a chapel.[49] The building has three chambers and a porch, the central chamber serving as a chapel, with three niches for altars to the North, South, and West. The high altar was likely in the Western niche, which would have been oriented toward Jerusalem. Muhammed suggests that the last room was the sacristy.

Akbar was openly disappointed when Acquaviva returned to Goa at the end of the first mission – the Jesuits had given up hope that Akbar would ever convert – and he soon made a serious effort to renew the defunct Mogor mission.[50] Encouraged, in part, by Akbar's ritual unveiling of the Madonna altarpiece during the Feast of the Assumption, the Jesuits sent a second mission, which lasted only for a couple of months in 1591. Although the missionaries, Fathers Duarte Leitão and Christoval de Vega and Brother Estevão Ribeiro, were entrusted with the education of the Emperor's son, we know almost nothing of their activities, and their impact on the arts seems to have been, at best, limited. Akbar only had three years to wait, however, for the most illustrious and longest lasting of the three Jesuit expeditions to Mogor.

Characteristics of Mughal Miniatures with Catholic Subjects: The Early Period

Most of Akbar's leading painters were inspired by the engravings and paintings brought by the first mission; however, four of them – all Hindus – came to specialize in this kind of image. Kesu Das (fl. ca. 1570–1590s) and Manohar (fl. 1582–ca. 1620) tended to favour overtly Christian images, while Basawan (fl. ca. 1560–ca. 1600) and Kesu Khurd (fl. ca. 1580–ca. 1605) preferred scenes of a more universal or allegorical nature based on biblical figures. Other painters who produced genre scenes featuring Christian and profane European figures include La'l (fl. before 1590), and the Muslim painters Miskin (fl. ca. 1580–1604) and Husain (fl. ca. 1584–98). Although directly inspired by the first Jesuit mission, most of these works were actually executed during the twelve-year hiatus between the missions, with Manohar's and Kesu Khurd's early work dating immediately before the arrival of the third mission in 1595.

Painters now went beyond the tentative experiments with Occidental style of the 1560s and '70s. They became fascinated by the power of images, with their ability to depict the spiritual, embody abstract ideas, stimulate the emotions, and aid the memory. On the one hand, artists such as Kesu Das closely reproduced the figures and composition of the original engravings, carefully emulating their spatial and modelling effects. On the other hand, he and other painters made pastiches from a variety of sources – a natural extension of the kind of excerpting common in earlier Islamic miniatures – which quickly became one of the most popular genres of the later 1580s and '90s. Their sources are very diverse, and often extremely difficult to identify. Some of them do not derive from prints at all, but are inspired by the actual Portuguese costumes, objects, and men brought to court by Akbar's embassies. Some of them are distinctly Christian in content, while others are not. Nevertheless, by the turn of the century, paintings and drawings in which Christian devotional images were the primary subject represented a major share of Mughal artistic production.

Mughal painters demonstrated an extraordinary aptitude for European style and subject matter in a very short period. Of all the artists, Kesu Das seems to have concentrated the most on acquiring the technique of European painting, and probably served as Akbar's specialist in the Occidentalist mode. He was probably also commissioned later on by Prince Salim (who would reign as Jahangir) to reproduce European images in his father's collection, since he made copies of many of his early works in the 1590s.[51] Kesu's Christian pictures are produced with an understanding and appreciation for their subjects, and a recognition of their devotional value. A careful draughtsman, Kesu restricted himself to a limited number of engravings, the style of each of which he painstakingly mastered. Sometimes he would produce a version of the whole engraving; at other times, he would combine figures from different sources, but he would infuse the image with his own personality, whether by altering the angle of the head, the pose of the arm, or the fall of the drapery.

Typical of his work is a signed copy of an engraving of Michelangelo's *Noah* from the Sistine Chapel, taken from the same Cartaro print we have seen copied in China (compare figs. 47, 65).[52] The nearly naked figure gives Kesu a rare opportunity to practise muscular modelling, a feature entirely alien to Indo-Islamic tradition, and one at which he excelled. The tree, horizon, and birds are typical of much of Kesu's later work, all of which had been incorporated into the standard Mughal repertory from Flemish prints. Characteristic of many Mughal versions of Christian pictures (as in Japan) is the prominence given to books: here, for example, he places a book in the man's hand even though it lies on the ground in the original. Books appear to serve as an attribute of sainthood.

Kesu also seems to have been the first painter in the Islamic tradition (although he was a Hindu himself) ever to paint a crucifixion – of all overtly Christian images possibly the most offensive to Muslims.[53] Kesu's finest *Crucifixion* is in the British Museum (fig. 66).[54] Here the painter has freed himself almost entirely from engraved models, and produces a record of Christian devotional practices that is augmented by his own observations from life. Kesu's crucifix itself is fairly generic, and Rogers points out that the heavy modelling suggests that it is copied after a sculpture.[55] However, the rest of the picture – for example, the vast and imaginative landscape, with its Indo-Flemish townscape – is purely the work of Kesu's imagination. The figures are especially interesting; dressed in European and Armenian clothing, they are like a group portrait of the fledgling Christian community of Fatehpur Sikri.[56] Kesu's attention to detail included dividing the worshippers into male and female groups, as they were divided in reality.[57] This fascination with manners of worship and devotion reflects Akbar's own interest in world religions; when entering the Jesuit chapel himself, he would show off his knowledge by performing his prayers before their images in the manners of the Muslims, Hindus, and Christians, respectively.[58]

In striking contrast to Kesu Das, the painter Basawan rarely moved beyond technical and stylistic borrowings. He also does not seem to have shared his colleague's reverence for saints; out of his handful of works in the Western style, only one can be identified as a Christian subject. Basawan's Occidentalist works are all variations on a single theme that particularly fascinated him: the woman as devotional object (fig. 67). Running the gamut from the Virgin Mary to an idolatrous sibyl, these fantasy studies of female religion and sainthood relate to other portraits by Basawan of male religious figures such as sheikhs, dervishes, and ascetics – displaying an interest in world faiths that was very much in sympathy with Akbar's own. Basawan's favourite model is the *Pietas Regia* (The Piety of the King) from the second title page of the Polyglot Bible.[59]

Most of Basawan's paintings of women as devotional objects are done in the *nīm-qalam*, or grisaille, style, a method which the artist introduced into Mughal painting and which may have been inspired by the absence of colour in European engravings.[60] Most of them maintain the pose of the *Pietas Regia* figure, and all wear the same long gowns with billowing sashes and a strap or gathering of cloth separating their breasts. In many cases, he adds leaves, twigs, and baubles to the hair to enhance their appearance as ascetics or wild women. In one version, the central figure is transformed into a dancing idol, with two imaginative versions of the same woman on either side kneeling in supplication and presenting her with offerings in bejewelled caskets (fig. 67).[61] In this drawing, their religious ardour is highlighted by a figure of God the Father, taken perhaps from an engraving by Crispin de Passe after Martin de Vos of *The Sacrifice of Noah*,[62] who emerges from a cluster of clouds in the sky to the right.

Basawan's son Manohar began his career in the 1580s, working in his father's shadow.[63] Born an intimate of the court, or *khānazāda*, Manohar collaborated with his father on manuscript illustrations, and also imitated his works in the European style. Manohar came to appreciate European paintings and engravings much more than his father, and by the advent of the third Jesuit mission in 1595, he appears to have succeeded Kesu Das as Akbar's chief specialist in Christian art. He later used his skills in pictorial realism to serve Jahangir as one of his principal portraitists. Distinct from his father's style is a tendency toward crisp, hard outlines and a more linear treatment of modelling, with less interest in spatial depth (figs. 68–9).[64] His drawings have a very finished, burnished appearance, which contrasts starkly with Basawan's sketchy, agitated brush-stroke; a natural draughtsman (like Kesu Das), he was better suited to working closely with engravings than his father, and he preferred a reticent elegance to the older painter's vigour.

Most of Akbar's painters at least dabbled in the new style, many of them in a way that makes their work virtually indistinguishable. One group of artists who produced lively genre scenes from 1590 onward with Christian characters included Kesu Khurd, La'l, and Miskin.[65] The trademark of this school are complex architectural settings, which look more like elaborate stage scenery than any real palace interior or townscape. Favourite props, echoing the pageantry of Akbar's embassies with Goa, include 'Savonarola' chairs, thin-necked bottles, bowls filled with mangoes, cats, and lapdogs.

Images of Christian saints in Mughal art were not limited to the private world of the album page or illustrated history book, but spread to the very walls of royal apartments, gardens, hunting palaces, and tombs – even to such a public location as a caravanserai. The first mural paintings depicting ostensibly Christian subjects were commissioned by Akbar at his palace at Fatehpur Sikri (ca. 1571–85), and may have derived from the Emperor's practice of publicly displaying European devotional oil paintings and large-scale Mughal copies during Islamic and Christian festivals.[66] The earliest reference to murals of Christian figures at Akbar's court was by Father Monserrate, who wrote in 1580 that Akbar had 'hanging pictures' (*ymagenes suspensas*) of Christ, Mary, Moses, and Muhammad in his dining-hall at Fatehpur Sikri.[67] Most of the wall paintings at Fatehpur Sikri with Christian subjects were of a more narrative type, however, as we read in this report by Jerónimo Xavier, who toured the already largely abandoned palace in 1600:

> Our tour demonstrated that [the palace buildings] had been sumptuous. They are of excellent stone, and are covered with beautiful illustrations. [These] include several pictures from the Old Testament, several of Our Lady, and others of Hindu subjects.[68]

All that remains of these figural murals today are a few intriguing fragments in what were most likely the private quarters of Akbar and his mother, Maryam Makani: the so-called *khwābgāh* (sleeping chamber) in the *mardāna*, or male quarters, and the building known as the Maryam-ki Kothi (Mary's House) or Sunahra Makān (Golden House) in the *zanāna*, or harem.[69] As well as being the most heavily inscribed areas of the palace outside the mosque, these two buildings had very similar mural cycles celebrating royal prestige and divine guidance, including the traditional Islamic motifs of the hunt, courtly pleasures, paradise gardens, literary scenes, and battles. Such themes are appropriate for buildings that house the two chief authorities of the palace, and give the royal complex a corresponding male and female axis. Both also featured images related to Judeo-Christian religious figures, which are all but destroyed today. Appropriately, the *khwābgāh* features illustrations of male prophets, such as Abraham, Jesus, and perhaps Jacob; whereas the Maryam-ki Kothi displays female figures closely related to prophets, Mary and Bilkis. Many of these characters are related to themes of parenthood and birth, even more closely linking the principal apartments of mother and son.

One painting from each building can illustrate this connection. One of the prophet murals in the *khwābgāh* very likely depicts the birth of Jesus.[70] It shows an angel holding a baby in its arms, rising from a grotto surrounded by a paradise garden of trees, flowers, and pairs of peacocks and herons or egrets. The baby has a fiery Islamic halo, and the angel is dressed in the typical post-Mongol manner with a flowing gown, long sashes, and a diadem with a feather (see fig. 62). While the style of the image is largely Persian, with very traditional costume and treatment of rockface, the composition of the figures points to a European depiction of the Virgin and Child such as Dürer's *Madonna* (fig. 77), which was popular at court and copied elsewhere.[71] The birth of Jesus is a very appropriate subject for Fatehpur Sikri. The palace was actually founded in thanksgiving by Akbar after he produced a long-awaited son by a woman named Mary through what he believed to be divine intervention.[72]

The most controversial picture in the Maryam-ki Kothi is a panel painting that was usually described to Victorian tourists as *The Annunciation*.[73] The scene depicts a pair of angels with Mongol-style wings and headdresses, one of whom is seated on a throne. The composition and landscape elements are again typical of contemporary Indo-Persian painting (fig. 62). But the pose and European drapery of the angel on the left derive from an engraving of Pencz's allegorical *Auditus*, an image commonly used elsewhere by Mughal painters to represent the Annunciation.[74] More importantly, the composition of the two figures points toward a European Annunciation scene. In Renaissance Annunciations, Mary is typically shown seated on a chair or before a *prie-dieu*, while the angel usually stands before her and gestures toward her with his hands.[75] Considering the probable subject of the *khwābgāh* painting – and keeping in mind that Xavier mentioned seeing images of Mary there in 1600 – it very likely does represent an Annunciation.[76] The subject appears in the Koran, and elsewhere in Islamic painting.[77] The pair of wings on the figure of Mary is a motif used elsewhere in Mughal painting simply to denote holiness (like a halo), and does not necessarily mean that she is an angel. Again, this scene would be very appropriate in the residence of a queen named Mary (Maryam is Arabic for Mary), whose son was anxious to compare his birth to that of Jesus.

The Third Jesuit Mission to Mogor (founded 1595) and the Arts

As we can see by the production of the royal atelier, the Emperor's enthusiasm for Euro-Christian art had only increased in the years since Rodolfo left for Goa, as had his curiosity about Christian religion and ritual. By this time, however, Akbar was not the only member of the Mughal royal family with an interest in Catholic culture. During the intervening years, Prince Salim (the future Jahangir) became a serious and enthusiastic connoisseur of the arts, with a taste for European art that rivalled that of his father. After ordering the court painters to reproduce the most important Occidental works of his father, such as the copies made by Kesu Das around 1590 of his own earlier paintings, Salim was as eager as his father to obtain new engravings and European paintings. The hunt was on.

Arriving in Lahore on 5 May 1595, and not departing until the suppression of the Society in 1773, the third mission was the most influential and longest-lasting European enterprise in Mughal India. Staffed initially by three of the Society's finest preachers and scholars, the third mission was the product of Valignano's reforms. Fathers Jerónimo Xavier (1549–1617) and Manoel Pinheiro (1544–?) and Brother Bento de Goes (1562–1607) were not only instructed to learn Persian and write catechisms in that language, but were accompanied by a professional Portuguese painter to serve the iconographical needs of the Mughal court.[78] Reorganized and invigorated, the mission placed renewed emphasis on ritual spectacle and display, as had the mission in Japan. Rich costumes and liturgical vestments, curtains and candles, flowers, singing and organ music, theatre, bell-ringing, fireworks, and the exhibition of pictures brought attention to events such as baptisms, funerals, Christmas, and Assumption Day.[79]

The fathers were not above using gimmicks and gewgaws to capture the imagination of the people; Xavier describes some of the decorations they used one year at the Christmas crib:

> ... an ape which squirted water from its eyes and mouth, and above it a bird which sang mysteriously ... and a globe of the world supported on the backs of two elephants ... and above this a large portrait of the King [Jahangir] which he sent us when he was a prince ... and next to this figure was placed a large mirror at the front of the crib ... [At the gates] were the Angel, i.e., Gabriel, with many angels, who were accompanied by placards proclaiming *'Gloria in Excelsis Deo'* or *'Nolite Timere'* in Persian. Around the Holy Infant in the crib were some sayings of the Prophets who pretold the coming of God into the World.[80]

One Easter a tightrope walker performed on a line tied between the Jesuits' chapel in Agra and their house, and another year the fathers hired a Neapolitan juggler to perform before the Emperor.[81] They succeeded in making a strong impression on the spectators, who sometimes exceeded ten thousand according to some hyperbolic reports,[82] but also incurred the wrath of their enemies, including the Muslim chronicler Badaoni, who wrote of 'the ringing of gongs ... and the showing of the figure of the Trinity and the Cribs ... and other childish playthings';[83] as well as the Protestant English factor Thomas Kerridge, who dismissed 'those prattling, juggling Jesuits.'[84] We will see below how these spectacles and plays directly inspired Mughal painting.

The third mission also quietly shifted its focus. Although it still paid close attention to the court and satisfied the whims of the emperors, the Jesuits realized that, pastorally speaking, this high profile ministry was bearing no fruit whatsoever – as would happen in China. Muslims, in general, particularly those in the upper echelons of society, demonstrated very little inclination for conversion, a phenomenon, incidentally, which was also remarked upon by missionaries to places such as Persia and Ottoman Turkey. Therefore, beginning in the time of Jeronimo Xavier and throughout the seventeenth and eighteenth centuries, the Mogor mission increasingly concentrated on commoners, particularly low-caste Hindus, as well as Armenian Christians, of whom there was a significant community in Agra. Except for the standard references to people being astounded by images, however, the sources make scarce mention of any artistic activity on this humbler level of ministry. The Jesuits appear never to have made any attempt to train their Hindu neophytes in the fine arts; perhaps they felt that the emperors' artists were providing Christian iconography with enough advertising already.

Meanwhile, Christian art thrived at the court. The third mission was extremely fortunate in having a copy of Nadal's *Evangelicae Historicae Imagines* (1593), whose magnificent illustrations – hot off the press – were of a completely new scale and lavishness. This was just as well since they failed to bring any new oil paintings, thereby incurring the wrath of Salim and inspiring him to send an embassy to

Goa expressly for that purpose.[85] Xavier also realized the seriousness of this oversight, and begged the Father Provincial in a 1595 letter for 'a beautiful and large picture of Our Lady or of the Nativity.'[86] Later, he added, 'For the love of God send us some good pictures on paper which depict stories such as the Life of Christ Our Lord, or some Saints, and some curious objects which we will give to the King.'[87] These requests echo those of Ricci in China, but with the Mughals they were aiming at a more appreciative audience. In 1596, Valignano himself, or his successor Nicolau Pimenta (1595–1613), sent to the Mughal mission an image of Jesus as Salvator Mundi, as well as another picture of Jesus and a portrait of Ignatius Loyola – all from Japan and almost certainly products of Niccolò's academy.[88] Other Japanese artworks included a dagger with a cross on the handle used by Xavier to discuss the Crucifixion with Salim in 1597; and a painting of Our Lady of Loreto on a copper panel (*calaim dourada*) – a type commonly produced by Niccolò's academy – was presented to Akbar by Xavier and Pinheiro in 1601.[89] The image of the Virgin of Loreto was a particular favourite of Akbar's.[90]

The earliest reports of the third mission also show that the Imperial collection of Christian devotional art had reached a fair size. One letter records that Akbar possessed 'several very fine images of Christ Our Lord and Our Lady, including beautiful panel paintings that came from Europe,'[91] and a 1598 letter specifically mentions a picture of the Man of Sorrows.[92] Prince Salim kept large pictures of Jesus and the Madonna in his sleeping chamber, 'which one day he exhibited at his window to prove that this was so,'[93] and also owned a 'carved image of Our Saviour on the cross with the two thieves hanging on either side,' which had been given to him by a Christian at court.[94]

Salim was jealous of his father and was not satisfied with the comparative insubstantiality of his own collection. One of the ways in which he compensated was simply to help himself to the parcels which arrived for the Jesuit fathers from the port of Cambay, taking any pictures which pleased him (including, unknowingly, ones that were actually meant for him).[95] Those pictures that he could not obtain in the original, Salim had copied. He achieved this by requisitioning the Portuguese painter and permitting him to work for no one but himself, ordering him to paint the devotional images in the Jesuit chapel and in Akbar's collection (fig. 70).[96] Xavier describes the artist's dilemma in a 1596 letter: 'The Portuguese painter who came with us has no time for anything except painting images for [Salim], of Christ Our Lord, and of Our Lady. He makes him paint the ones which his father owns.'[97] That same year, Dom Pedro Martins (1587–92), formerly the Provincial of Goa and now the Bishop of Japan, asked permission for the artist to go to Goa, possibly so that he could then move on to Japan. We hear nothing more about this painter, so that we can suppose he received his permission soon afterward. The Jesuits no doubt realized that his services were much more profitably employed in more promising fields (pastorally speaking), such as Japan.

Prince Salim was not discouraged, however, since he had legions of his own artists who could do the job just as well, even in other media. One of his favourites was sculpture in the round, which was completely at odds with Islamic tradition at that time but familiar, of course, to Hindu art. He ordered his artists to carve several ivory crucifixes and statues of the Infant Jesus copied from originals in the Jesuit chapel.[98] He also commissioned jewellery featuring Christian subjects for his personal adornment; for example, a crucifix carved into an emerald about the size of a man's thumb, which he had encased in a gold amulet and pierced to be hung around the neck on a gold chain.[99] A thumb ring survives from ca. 1615 bearing the face of Christ Pantocrator flanked by angels bearing offerings on the front side, and a bust of the Saint Luke's Madonna on the back.[100] As late as 1627, many years after he had become the Emperor Jahangir, he made a present of a bejewelled reliquary showing Calvary,

> with a Crucifix, about a cubit high, with our Lady and St. John on the sides and the Magdalen at the foot of the Cross, the whole of amber, [and] very rich. On the four corners of the cross, it has the figures of the four Evangelists in white amber. On all four sides of the mount, which is square, it has the chief scenes of the Passion, and the Resurrection, made with figurines of the same white amber; and they have their inscriptions in letters of gold, with sundry ornaments of Milan glasses and crystals ...[101]

The fathers even reported that Jahangir pressed the sealing wax onto his official letters with a pincer-like clamp whose presses were carved with pictures of Jesus and Mary:

> ... all of the decrees, provisions and letters that he sends – whether to Moors or Hindus or Christians – have his royal seal in the usual manner on the inside, but outside the seal is a figure of Christ Our Lord and Our Lady made in this manner: [with an instrument] with straight arms without fingers, the ends of which are impressed in sealing wax, one end bearing an engraved image of the Saviour and the other of Our Lady. It is like a golden forceps with emeralds encrusted at the ends like a fingernail, and square, on which are engraved the said figures, which impress, as I have said, into sealing wax with which the ends of the letter are stuck together. Could a very devout Christian King do any better?[102]

Salim/Jahangir also had many statues made of Christian figures and angels in ivory, alabaster, or white marble. For example, two European visitors to the Peri-mahal Palace in Lahore in the early eighteenth century saw a group of alabaster or marble statues of Jesus, Mary, other saints, and angels, which had been erected there in the last century.[103] A single statue of this type survives at the Old Cathedral at Agra, which I have published elsewhere (fig. 71).[104] The piece depicts the Virgin Mary, carved nearly in the round against a trefoil niche, standing on a lotus pedestal and leaning to the right with her hands in prayer. It can be dated by its close resemblance to Manohar's early studies of the Virgin (ca. 1590) (fig. 68), and, as I suggest in my article, it synthesizes the Christian image with elements of medieval Hindu carving. It is sensitively and skilfully executed, especially the drapery, and was probably the work of the Imperial atelier, perhaps under the direction of Manohar himself.

The Imperial court painters were also bidden by Salim to paint Christian pictures, either by executing smaller versions of large panels, making life-sized copies of engravings, or simply by filling in the original prints with colours.[105] Salim also demonstrated his interest in the technological side of art by repeatedly asking the fathers to have a printing press sent from Rome, along with some original copper plates carved with images, so that he could print his own engravings.[106] Although this desire was never satisfied (the Jesuit press was sent to the more fruitful missions in Japan, as we have seen), the Prince did order his artists to imitate the effects of engraving in their paintings, for example, cross-hatching.

Salim had a falling out with his father and moved to Allahabad, where he set up his own art studio between 1599 and 1605. During those years, the Jesuits kept a careful distance from the Prince so as not to threaten their relationship with his father. They showed all of their gifts and correspondence with Salim to Akbar first, and usually communicated with Salim via an Italian messenger by the name of Giovanni Filippo.[107] Since Salim modelled his court at Allahabad on Akbar's court at Lahore and Agra, he was anxious to have his own Jesuit mission, not only so that he could hold his own debates, but to further the education of his artists. Goa, however, declined. In the meantime, Xavier's mission was increased in number by the arrival of two new missionaries, the Italian Francesco Corsi (d. 1635) and the Portuguese Sebastião Barreto (1567–1625).[108]

The Mogor mission received a substantial infusion of artworks in the first decade of the seventeenth century, including several large-scale oil paintings, engravings, and sculpture, both from the Jesuit Provincial, Gaspar Fernandes (1605–9), and from an embassy sent to Goa by Jahangir under the leadership of Muqarrib Khan.[109] The most spectacular painting was another 'handsome image of Our Lady of Saint Luke,'[110] this time the *Madonna del Populo* from the church of Santa Maria del Populo in Rome (fig. 1). Like its predecessor, this image was transmitted by the Jesuits to places as diverse as Mexico and Goa,[111] and, according to the missionaries at least, it created a comparable stir in Mughal circles. The Jesuits recorded the usual riot, with tens of thousands of onlookers and miraculous conversions. After displaying it at Christmas of 1602, the fathers lent it to Akbar, Aziz Koka, and the Sultan of Qandahar, apparently so that they could show it to the women of their harems – the usual story. Akbar assembled his artists to make several copies of it, after which the fathers claim to have put it away 'for good and all.'[112] Another riot-inducing picture was a canvas painting of the Adoration of the Magi, sent along with a statue of the Virgin Mary by Father João Alvares from Goa, which supposedly caused a riot when it was first unveiled in Cambay.[113]

Jahangir and his atelier responded to these new images with renewed artistic activity. For example, the Emperor had his painters make an enlargement of a small engraving of the Man of Sorrows to serve as a cartoon for a silk tapestry, complete with a Persian caption of the subject.[114] He also had the unframed *Adoration of the Magi* from Cambay stretched out on a wooden frame and decorated on the borders with Christian subjects taken from engravings and perhaps pictures from the *Mirat al-Quds* books. The work was carried out, as before, by the Imperial artists working in close collaboration with the Jesuit fathers.[115]

In the first series of debates (Lahore, 1607) since the death of Akbar, Jahangir invited the fathers to his palace, and ordered his librarian to bring out his albums of engravings and Christian paintings by his own artists, so that he could learn not only their stories but also the significance of their symbols and allegories.[116]

Jahangir asked many pointed questions which demonstrate a keen interest in the role of images and the function of allegory in Christian art. For example, he found it difficult to separate the notion of honour from beauty; when shown a *Crucifixion*, he asked, 'Why, if [you] adored Christ Our Lord so much, did [you] paint him in such a dishonourable state?'[117] One of his nobles added, 'When we depict Christ we always paint him very beautifully and not on the Cross.'[118] When the fathers explained that it was a great honour because it showed that Christ had died for our sins, they also indicated the mnemonic value of the wounds as reminders of his sacrifice.[119] In another discussion, one of his nobles brought up the question of images as idols, asking them whether they pay homage 'before an image of the Virgin, or before the Virgin herself'? The fathers explained it in Mughal terms:

> Sire, we do not venerate the images for what they are, because we are well aware that they are merely paper or canvas with pigments; it is because of those whom they represent. Just as with your *fermāns* [decrees]: you do not touch them to your foreheads because they are papers covered in ink, but because you know that they contain your order and will.[120]

Jahangir was also curious about the function of symbols. When he was shown a picture showing God the Father surrounded by *putti*, for example, he asked the fathers to explain why the angels were placed there.[121] This must have struck the Emperor as an appropriate symbol of reverence and honour, since he subsequently had *putti* painted on many of his own portraits. Jahangir was also interested in the ability of a symbol to represent an abstract idea, and demonstrated his impressive knowledge of Christian stories and tenets by preaching with the assistance of devotional images.[122] Claudio Acquaviva himself could have done no better.

The Beginnings of a Catholic Literature in Persian

The most important development of the new century was the completion of the first of Xavier's Persian books. Begun as early as 1597, these editions of gospel stories, lives of Christ and the apostles, mirrors for princes, explanations of Christian life, and a psalter, constituted the first Catholic literature in the Persian language.[123] Written first in Portuguese and translated into Persian with the help of the court historian 'Abd al-Sattar ibn-Qasim Lahori, these manuscripts were presented to Akbar and Jahangir between 1602 and 1609. The most interesting is a work called *The Truth-Showing Mirror (Āyine-ye Haqq Numā)*, finished in 1609, written in the form of a debate between a priest, a philosopher (a thinly veiled reference to Jahangir), and a mullah, which not only records some of the actual terms of the debates held at the Mughal court but has a whole chapter on the use of images.[124] All of the manifold advantages of images according to post-Tridentine precepts are explained; for example, when comparing verbal speech to the 'speech' of an image, Xavier writes:

> ... the speech [of an image] is an abbreviated book and brief worship. It is something that

speaks without talking and is heard without the ear; something written that everyone understands; a letter that everyone can read; a book for the learned; an attribute that makes manifest things which are past and ancient; it is a mirror that reflects things held in trust [i.e., that is not actually part of it] ... an assistant to the temperament; a teacher of the intellect; and it depicts intention.[125]

The emphasis on mirror imagery, which appears elsewhere in the chapter as well, shows that Xavier was sensitive to the metaphorical language of Sufism.[126] In Sufi literature, paintings were often compared to mirrors, since they reflected an exact impression of their subject but did not themselves possess a soul.

Xavier also makes great use of the Aristotelian concept of the 'inner senses,' common both in Islamic and Western European literature. In this passage, he demonstrates how images are capable of penetrating deeper into these regions than speech:

Furthermore, those forms and media [i.e., images] pass deeper into all of the interior senses, and the more subtle they are the more easily they enter and take hold, until the intellect becomes aware of these things, like pictures and phantoms.[127]

To medieval Europeans, the 'interior senses' were the imagination, memory, and common sense, forces capable of interpreting the diverse data collected by the five senses. But this notion was also common in the Islamic world, thanks to Neoplatonic philosophers like al-Kindi (795–865) and members of the Brethren of Purity (ninth to tenth centuries). In Islam, the 'interior senses' were thought to act as a filter between the external senses and the intellect, and participated in artistic creation and aesthetic perception. Interior senses held perceivable data obtained from the senses in a 'treasury,' and used these to elicit emotional responses from the viewer. Xavier's own justification of images connects strongly with this tradition. He describes an image as a 'treasury ... in which worthy goods and parables are safely kept,' and later compares an image to the intellect, since it holds onto a 'perceivable thing' that has been gathered by the power of perception and conception.[128] This chapter gave the Mughal court the clearest affirmation of the power of devotional images that they had yet encountered, presented in a subtle, learned, acculturative package.

More directly relevant for Mughal painting was the *Mirror of Holiness (Mirāt al-Quds)*, finished in 1602, two copies of which were illustrated throughout with paintings (fig. 72).[129] With these paintings, Xavier moved toward an indigenization of Christian imagery similar to that of Rocha's catechism six years later in China. The lively miniature paintings were commissioned directly from Mughal artists under the leadership of Manohar in a style that was closer to the mainstream Indo-Persian idiom of the day, with its rich landscapes and jewel-like colours, than many of the Occidentalist paintings we have observed. In fact, they are painted in the style reserved for works of moralistic poetry, such as the *Lights of Canopus* (*Anvar-i Suhaili*) and *Breaths of Fellowship* (*Nafahāt al-Uns*) manuscripts (1590s and 1600s).[130] The style has been intentionally chosen because it is appropriate within Mughal culture for works of a pedagogical and religious nature. The

Lights of Canopus, for example, was very popular as a guide for leadership and proper moral behaviour for princes. The *Breaths of Fellowship* told the lives of famous saints and Sufis. The illustrations to the *Mirror of Holiness* do not even have much in common with traditional European Christological cycles, since they make use of legends and stories that were not in the Gospel but were a staple of mystery plays. They are charged with a dramatic energy that is enhanced by stage-like architectural settings, elaborate props, vibrant gestures, and a variety of *mis-en-scène* figures, such as priests and altar boys. All of these features reveal the pervasive influence of Jesuit theatre and liturgy, the most visible source of Catholic propaganda on the mission.[131]

Since Salim was not satisfied with the number of pictures in the original volume of the *Mirror of Holiness*, he had a luxury edition made with many more illustrations by his own studio, some of which he had copied from the engravings in Nadal:

> ... he ordered it transcribed in very fine letters on extremely costly paper and ordered paintings made of every scene that could possibly be depicted ... He was not content with the scenes that were engraved by Father Nadal; he [had] these painted, and many others. It was an extremely lavish book, and in Rome one would make a great effort to see it ...[132]

Salim even embellished the edition which the fathers had originally sent to him, painting a golden cross on the frontispiece and a crucifix by 'the best painter he had' on another page, as well as adding a Madonna and Child, with his arms around her neck, to a depiction of Christ's name, erasing the Portuguese caption and replacing it with a Persian translation.[133] A year after Akbar's death, in 1606, the fathers also gave Jahangir a Persian *Lives of the Apostles* 'interspersed with many illustrations of their labours.'[134] A few of these survive as loose miniatures, and are painted in a style consistent with the *Mirror of Holiness*.

The text of the *Mirror of Holiness*, which is primarily made up of New Testament stories, reflects a typically Jesuit emphasis on envisioning biblical characters in a visually accurate, immediate, and tangible way, a characteristic which can be traced back to the composition of place in the *Spiritual Exercises*.[135] The book describes in exacting detail the facial features of its principal characters; for example, stressing the importance of accuracy in the likeness of the holy face, such as in this depiction of the Virgin Mary, which sounds like instructions for a portraitist:

> Mary was a girl of medium height, wheaten-coloured and long-faced. Her eyes were large and inclined toward blue. Her hair was golden. Her hands and fingers were long. A pleasing figure. In everything well-proportioned. Her discourse was extremely mild. Her glance came from a modest and bashful face. Her apparel was humble and chaste. Such greatness and majesty appeared in her countenance that when the wicked and perplexed-hearted gazed upon her they pulled themselves together and became reformed. All of her companions knew of her goodness and agreeable nature and humility.[136]

The *Mirror of Holiness* also contains similar descriptions of other figures, such as

Jesus and John the Baptist. These reconstructions of holy faces are also acculturative, since they closely echo the Islamic tradition of *hilya*, verbal descriptions of the Prophet Muhammad's face, and the Hindu *silpasastras*, or image-making texts.

Architecture of the Third Mogor Mission

The third mission built the first Catholic architecture in Northern India, a harmonious hybrid of Indian and Western styles, two centuries before the foundation of the British Raj. From the very beginning, it appears to have been strikingly different from the architecture of Portuguese Goa. By the late sixteenth century, Goa was already densely built up, and its crowded plazas were dominated by sumptuous church buildings in the Portuguese Manueline style.[137] During the next century, when Goa was at its economic peak, a new wave of churches were built. Larger and grander than their provincial Portuguese predecessors, these monuments were built in a more classical Renaissance style, rife with quotations from Serlio – although more on the surfaces than in the plan. As David Kowal has pointed out, the buildings of this 'second phase' of Goan architecture were closer to Roman Late Mannerist architecture than were their counterparts in Portugal.[138] The most prominent example was the Sé Nova, or New Cathedral, built on the site of a demolished mosque.

The Jesuits, however, took the lead in this new classicizing trend. More than any other order, the Society of Jesus aimed to evoke the Renaissance tradition and its Italian heritage. Their first structure was the College of São Paulo (1560–72), the ruins of which are still standing in the jungle near Old Goa (fig. 73), a foundation which would become the greatest European university in the East and the training ground for missionaries bound for China, Japan, and Southeast Asia. In a bold statement of affiliation with Rome and the Italian tradition, the façade used rich composite orders rather than the plainer articulation favoured elsewhere in the colony, the very same order employed by Giacomo Della Porta on the Gesù (fig. 14).[139] In further contrast to Portuguese façades, which tended to be flanked by towers, São Paulo was towerless, as were Roman churches. The ultimate statement of the Jesuits' Italianate style in India was the Jesuit mother church in Asia, the Bom Jesus in Old Goa (1594–1604), built by the Jesuit architect Domingo Fernandes (fig. 45). Also lacking towers, the façade of Bom Jesus is richly adorned with Serlian oculi, pilasters, and a gabled top with fan-shaped volutes. While Kowal has shown that some of the pilasters' orders were already looking more hybrid in appearance, the whole effect is quite classical.[140] Bom Jesus, the final resting place of Saint Francis Xavier, would become a model for many other churches in the East, most notably in Macao (fig. 44), as we have already seen.

The tradition of emphatic classicism continued in later Jesuit structures in Goa and the other Portuguese strongholds in India, even though many indigenous design elements crept into façade ornamentation. This heavily articulated Serlian style can be seen in the churches in Salcete, a mission region under Jesuit supervision south of Goa. The Jesuit college in Salcete (begun 1606), in the town of Rachol, is a case in point (fig. 74). Although its interior ornamentation, particularly a cycle of images in the chancel of the life of Saint Ignatius, is profoundly acculturative with Hindu styles and even motifs, the façade seems to shout out its classicism.[141] Now framed between towers in a more Iberian manner, every compartment is framed by pilasters, entablatures, and pediments. This grandiose classicism typified the great number of parish churches built in the seventeenth and eighteenth centuries in Salcete, most of them grandiose in size as well as design and probably built by indigenous masons. An example is the parish church at Loutoulim, whose exterior is completely encased in pilasters and pediments.

In the North, things were different. Naturally, since the Jesuits were in someone else's territory, they could not build on the same scale as in the coastal strongholds. More importantly, they were more acculturative, since the Jesuits were careful not to offend local sensibilities by building structures that contrasted too strongly with local architecture. Although the Jesuits had churches in Lahore, Delhi, Agra, Cambay, and elsewhere, the only monuments that survive today are the Agra church and cemetery chapel (figs. 75, 76).[142] Mission headquarters was located in the northern part of the city in the present-day Old Cathedral. The first chapel, a simple affair attached to the Jesuits' residence, was built around 1598, the same year that Akbar announced in a decree that the Jesuits could build a church in the port city of Cambay.[143] In 1604 permission was granted for them to construct a larger church to accommodate their growing congregation, financed in part by Prince Salim himself.[144] Dedicated to Nossa Senhora, it was also given strong financial support by the Armenian community in Agra, who became the Jesuits' most important patrons in Northern India.[145] Only vaulted in 1613, this 'very spacious' church with a prominent tower and cross had three altars and was built in traditional materials of bricks and *chunam* clay: '... it was entirely vaulted [*toda de abóbada*] and had cost eleven or twelve thousand rupees, the greater part of which sum had been donated by an Armenian, a rich Christian merchant [Khwaja Martinus].'[146] Even the English visitor Nicholas Withington called it 'verye fayer.'[147] The building was damaged by fire in 1616, and shut down by the Emperors in 1614 and 1632, at the latter time being largely demolished.

A new, smaller church was built on the spot and maintained throughout the vicissitudes of the seventeenth century. Father Francisco Azevedo described this more humble chapel in 1632 as a 'not very large but pretty church' which was 'handsome and well ornamented,'[148] and Father António Botelho recorded that 'the fathers built in the place of the old one, a terraced building [*huma caza terreiza*] ... something quite big enough to have in it the Divine Offices.'[149] Decades later, in 1675, Botelho repaired the church inside and out, adding a dado of white stone [*pedra branca*] on the garden wall as high as a man, and, around the church, higher and 'of finer quality and much ornamented.' Although the church had only one altar and no retable, it did have more than ten smaller pictures of Christ and the saints, including one of the Saint Luke Madonna, and portraits of Saints Ignatius Loyola and Francis Xavier. Parts of the present church may survive from this second building, including the lower walls of the nave and some sandstone details.

The seventeenth-century church, heavily damaged in 1758 when the Persians sacked Agra,[150] was rebuilt ten years later by two German mercenary generals (one was the infamous Walter Reinhard, who always made sure his army fought on the winning side, even if this meant going against his patron) during the ministry of Father Wendel, the last of the Mogor Jesuits. The restoration took place in two stages, according to two inscriptions, one over the east door and one on the south wall of the nave, between 1769 and 1772. Most of the stucco decoration of the interior and the two exquisite sandstone doors on the side walls date from this restoration. The north door is entirely Mughal in style, reminiscent of such Jahangir-period architecture as the interior clerestory of the Tomb of Shaykh Pir, Meerut (1613).[151] Although the south door (fig. 75) appears at first glance to be built in the Portuguese colonial style, it is in fact a particularly eloquent synthesis of Mughal and European styles. The door is flanked by two columns topped by finials, and is surmounted by a raised classical pediment. The columns are of a Mughal type developed in the Shah Jahan period with a bulbous base and foliate decoration at both ends, known as the baluster column. Between the pediment and the door is a Mughal cartouche similar to those found on the north door, and the finials themselves resemble a Mughal artichoke form found, for example, at the springing of the arches at the Moti Masjid at the Red Fort at Delhi (1663). Both doors demonstrate the high quality of craftsmanship available in Agra at the time, and the absence of figural decoration shows that the builders were careful not to offend the aniconic sensibilities of the Muslim Mughal court. The façade, narthex, and transepts of the present church date from the early nineteenth century.

The most striking piece of hybrid architecture is the Padres Santos Chapel, built in 1611 in a cemetery north of the city founded by a decree of Jahangir in 1609 (fig. 76).[152] The chapel was the focus of an annual procession on the second day of November, and, like the Zhalan chapel in Beijing, was also the site of many Jesuit burials.[153] The patron was Khwaja Martinus, the same Armenian gentleman who helped build the 1604 church in Agra. Martinus was a man of considerable wealth and influence, and, by means of ancient Armenian trade networks, he visited Jerusalem and Rome.[154] The building is octagonal and built of brick, with a single door and two windows fitted with delicate sandstone *jalis* (grilles), the whole surmounted by a low, ribbed dome with a small lantern at the top. The chapel combines a traditional Mughal ground plan with a European elevation. The octagonal tomb with a square or cruciform interior and a dome – imported from Timurid Central Asia – was a common tomb type in early Mughal architecture and can be found, for example, at the Nila Gumbad at Delhi (1530s–1540s), but the dome and arches were always pointed. In contrast, the arches at the Padres Santos Chapel are round, and so is the dome, which is also ornamented with unusual vertical ribs. These features suggest that Khwaja Martinus, after his pilgrimage to the Eternal City, attempted to recreate one of the Baroque church domes that had begun to grace Rome's skyline in the second half of the sixteenth century – perhaps even Michelangelo's and Giacomo Della Porta's dome at St Peter's (1546–93), which owes its visual unity to those very ribs.

Characteristics of Mughal Miniatures and Mural Paintings with Catholic Subjects: The Later Period

As we have already seen, in the 1590s Prince Salim, soon to be Emperor Jahangir, emerged as a fully fledged patron of the arts, and quickly dominated the production of European-style paintings at court. More so than his father, Salim demonstrated a passion for exact, direct copies of engravings, because of a connoisseurly insistence on stylistic accuracy, an interest in categorizing exotica very much like the European phenomenon of the *Wunderkammer*, and an obsession with the identities of Jesus and Christian saints. Whereas Akbar had been content to allow Christian figures to populate his eclectic artistic landscape, at times in a religious context and at times in a more secular setting, Salim demanded that their devotional meaning and stylistic integrity be kept intact. His was an interest in the iconic and talismanic, the power of images as embodiments of the divine, and he showed less and less interest in their narrative aspect. Akbar, however, was increasingly concerned with pageantry and lavish architectural settings, which can be traced primarily to the larger, more elaborate engravings in Nadal's text.

The difference between works of the studios of Akbar and Salim can be seen at once. The leader of Akbar's studio was Manohar, who by the time of the third mission was the chief specialist in the European style. In the later 1590s, Manohar specialized in crowded, animated Christian scenes full of colour and pageantry. One such was the magnificent full-page miniature depicting the Last Judgment, executed in collaboration with the painter Nanhā (fl. 1589–1600s), which was bound incongruously in 1605 into a Persian poetic epic.[155] The picture does not follow the print figure for figure, as do the paintings of the Salim school, but uses the composition and poses of the original only as a guide, while the style of the individual figures is consistent with the mainstream figural painting style of the Mughal court.

Salim, by contrast, trained his artists to be exacting and consistent. Abu'l-Hasan (1584–ca. 1628), who became Jahangir's greatest painter and earned the name Nādir al-Zamān (Wonder of the Age), as well as legions of lesser artists, apprenticed in the European style by painting over actual engravings in colour.[156] An example in the British Museum (seventeenth century) of an engraving which is only half painted by a Mughal hand shows the way in which these were executed.[157] In addition to Abu'l-Hasan and Farrukh Beg, painters in this school included several women of the harem (Nini, Nadira Banu, and Raqiya Banu), reminding us that the artistic enterprises of the Mughal court were equally directed toward a female audience, and it is significant that art instruction existed within the harem, probably with women as teachers.[158] Nearly all paintings are of explicitly Christian subjects such as a colourful painting (fig. 77) after Dürer. Some painters, like Abu'l-Hasan, made masterly Occidental works of their own inspiration, while others worked closely within the parameters of the original engraving; nevertheless, all strived to emulate European style with an almost finicky accuracy.

The tradition of making pastiches found its ultimate expression in the margins (*hāshiyas*) of Salim's princely albums, which are like paper *Wunderkammern*. In two phases, the first between about 1598 and 1604 and the second around 1608–9, the Prince's (and later Emperor's) artists painted figural borders to adorn poetical texts, mostly written by the great Safavid Persian calligrapher Mir 'Ali. The earlier group, directed by Aga Reza and apparently including work by Basawan,[159] include a few Christian and other European images, which are interspersed with

Islamic and Hindu figures, probably to represent world religions (fig. 78). Their relationship to the mystical love poems which they frame is negligible; only rarely can a connection be drawn between the meaning of the verses and perhaps one or two of the figures in the margins, which suggests that the figures relate more to each other than to the text.[160]

The close adherence to engraved models also characterized mural painting commissioned by Salim after he became the Emperor Jahangir in 1605. Within three years, Jahangir had commissioned his first mural paintings of Christian saints and biblical subjects, and well before his death in 1627 they were to adorn the royal apartments of at least four palaces, several royal gardens, the tomb of Akbar, and also buildings belonging to prominent nobles and courtiers, including a palace and a caravanserai.[161] The earliest murals were executed at the Red Fort in Agra, immediately after the Emperor received a large package of engravings from Father General Claudio Acquaviva in 1607.[162] The next year, upon returning to Agra from Lahore, the fathers were conducted to the Public Audience Hall in the Imperial palace, where they beheld a vast array of Christian devotional images painted on the walls surrounding the throne and in several royal apartments. Jahangir had ordered his artists to enlarge the engravings onto cartoons, which were probably pounced for transferral onto the walls. The Jesuits were consulted by his artists on matters such as appropriate colouring.[163]

In two separate letters, Xavier describes images of Jesus, Mary, and a wide variety of male and female saints, scenes from the Acts of the Apostles and the Old Testament, as well as Jesuit fathers, Portuguese soldiers, and portraits of European kings and the Pope, painted on the walls and ceilings of the throne area of the Public Audience Hall,[164] the retiring room behind it, and other semi-public royal apartments: '[The Emperor] has painted images of Christ Our Lord and Our Lady in various places in the Palace where he spends most of his time, and there are so many different saints that ... you would say that it was more like the palace of a Christian king than a Moorish one.'[165]

The ceiling of the retiring room was dominated by a large image of Christ in Benediction surrounded by angels, and above and inside the throne were pairs of Mary and Jesus – in one case, the Saint Luke Madonna and Christ as the Salvator Mundi – with Jesus on the right and Mary on the left. Behind the *jharoka* (throne platform) of the Public Audience Hall, these images were accompanied by portraits of Jahangir's two sons. In an interior room, Jahangir had his muralists paint a group portrait of the Pope, Emperor, King Philip II of Spain, and the Duke of Savoy on their knees before the cross – probably the same one enlarged by the Chinese Emperor.[166] Xavier's description is partially corroborated by later travellers, including William Finch, William Hawkins, and Robert Coverte.[167] Two decades later, Father Francisco de Azevedo described the Christian murals at Agra Fort, and emphasized how they were painted in a row of chambers culminating in the Emperor's throne itself.[168] Pietro della Valle mentions similar images at the royal palace at Ahmadabad.[169]

Except for the *jharoka* wall of the Public Audience Hall, it is impossible to determine the exact location of these murals since these parts of the Agra Fort were torn down and rebuilt under Shah Jahan.[170] Our other source of evidence for the

Agra murals are two miniature paintings from the Jahangir and Shah Jahan periods (1620s–40s) showing durbar scenes (fig. 79).[171] Although they use a visual shorthand to represent the saints' images, illustrating only a fraction of the number indicated in the sources, the saints' images are generally consistent. These pictures invariably show a row of small saints' portraits in the frieze above the throne, usually with one or more images of Jesus on the Emperor's right and Mary on his left. The Virgin Mary is usually a version of the Saint Luke Madonna or the Madonna del Populo (fig. 1).

At roughly the same time, another major series of murals was being completed in the royal apartments of Lahore Fort. These were first mentioned by William Finch in 1610.[172] Finch describes a similar arrangement of small rooms linked by a corridor along the river which leads from the Hall of Private Audiences, 'wherein the King sits out all the first part of the night, commonly from eight to eleven,' to the *jharoka-i darshan* in the Kala Burj.[173] At Lahore, the Jesus and Mary duo were repeated over the *jharoka* doorway: '... on the right-hand of the King over the doore is the picture of our Saviour; opposite on this left-hand, of the Virgin Mary.'[174] Father Andrade left a description of the Lahore murals (1623) which mentions an unidentified Christian image in Jahangir's 'principal hall' – that was based on a painting sent by the Provincial in Goa. He also refers to a room similar to the retiring room in Agra that had a painting of Jesus on the ceiling.[175] Another Shah Jahan period miniature painting (ca. 1640) records the murals that once adorned the *jharoka* wall of the Hall of Public Audiences at Lahore.[176] These included the usual Jesus and Mary pair (in reverse order, with Jesus on the left and Mary on the right) inside the *jharoka* oriel itself, and a frieze of angels.

Most of the paintings we have discussed so far have been lost; however, cleaning in recent decades has revealed an angel vault in the male quarters of the Lahore Fort as well as a series of portraits of saints in a pavilion in the harem, all of which were likely part of a single painting campaign. The chamber with the angel vault was probably one of several, symbolic on a generic level as a microcosm of the heavenly sphere, referred to as the *qubbat al-khadrā'* in Islamic palace architecture.[177] Another ceiling of this type is the Christ ceiling in the retiring room at Agra Fort. The harem pavilion is a small structure known as the *sehdārī* ('three-doored [pavilion]') in Jahangir's Quadrangle. The small chamber overlooks the river on its north side, and was probably originally part of a row of painted rooms in the harem on the same axis as the painted chambers in the male quarters along the riverfront. The murals, found in the spandrels of the central chamber, include images of male and female saints copied from engravings by Wierix and others (probably the ones that arrived in 1607), in framed panels in a setting of floral arabesques and birds (fig. 80).[178] Painted before 1620, they were probably executed during an extensive palace renovation in 1612. Several of the *sehdārī* saints are shown holding books or trays of fruit, both common motifs for Mughal 'Christian' miniature paintings. The style is accomplished, with a mature understanding of modelling and colour and a haunting quality in the faces, although the hands' foreshortening is awkward. Ilay Cooper found the remains of a portrait of the young prince Khurram (Shah Jahan) in the central panel of the east wall, flanked by images of saints, and there may have been another royal portrait on the other side, similarly arranged.[179] In traditional Persian and Mughal painting, figures attending on monarchs are often shown bearing platters loaded with fruit; therefore, some of the saints are actually meant to be paying homage to members of the Mughal family.[180] This juxtaposition is a two-dimensional echo of the actual monarch's appearance among Christian holy images at his thrones.

Royal gardens also had wall paintings depicting saints. Very similar to the Lahore paintings is a series of murals including a figure of Jesus, probably by the same artists, in Queen Nur Jahan's Nur Afshan Gardens (Rambagh) at Agra, which were executed between 1613, when Nur Jahan became the Shah Begum (Queen consort), and 1621, when Jahangir visited the completed garden.[181] One of the most public manifestations of Christian imagery was at Akbar's tomb at Sikandra, completed between 1608 and 1614.[182] Unlike the locations mentioned so far, this gate was in full view of the public, and was the closest Jahangir ever came to commissioning such murals on religious architecture. According to four descriptions by European visitors, the octagonal interior chamber was painted with an angel vault in the ceiling, as at the Lahore Fort, and on a lower level with images of the Virgin Mary and Ignatius of Loyola adoring a large crucifix.[183] There was also a picture showing Jesuit fathers standing at the foot of Akbar's funeral bier. It is noteworthy that Jahangir commissioned a crucifix instead of a simple bust portrait of Jesus, since of all possible scenes from Jesus' life this one would have been most offensive to Muslims. The letters demonstrate his obsession with this image, which he had copied repeatedly.[184] It is illuminating to look at Persian references to this tomb. Jahangir's autobiography, for example, refers to it as 'the abode of angels,' or 'the circling-place of angels,'[185] a metaphor which echoes the *qubbat al-khadrā'* angel ceiling. If it resembled the angel ceiling at Lahore, which was enclosed in interlacing vaults, the concentric arrangement of angels would have given the impression of circular movement. The inscriptions on the gatehouse are also mostly concerned with paradise imagery, which is usual for tombs, including many references to Ridwan, the Islamic gatekeeper to heaven.[186] The scene of the fathers gathering at Akbar's funeral bier is suggested by an inscription on the interior tomb chamber: 'At the foot of his throne, eminent men of all kinds assembled.'[187]

Murals with Christian subjects also appeared in sub-Imperial structures, suggesting that the practice was fairly widespread, at least among members of the aristocracy. Asaf Khan, Nur Jahan's brother and one of the most powerful men in Jahangir's court, had a residence in Lahore in which the bathhouse contained wall paintings depicting scenes of the life of Saint John the Baptist and Noah's Ark.[188] These images were clearly chosen for the bathhouse because of their thematic relation to water, demonstrating that an underlying program often dictated the choice of saints' images. Although both John and Noah are in the Koran, there is no reference to John's baptisms, so that his association with the River Jordan (and hence water) must have come from knowledge of the Christian Bible. Both figures also heralded the coming of a New Age, and therefore fit into millennialist imagery that was popular at the Mughal court.

The most public appearance of Christian saint murals was at the caravanserai (begun before 1619) of the gentlewoman Mehr Banu Agha, the former head of

Jahangir's harem, in Delhi.[189] As at Akbar's tomb at Sikandra, the saints' murals adorn the interior of the main entrance gate and are accompanied by vegetal ornament, arabesques, and orthodox inscriptions such as repetitions of the Muslim *shahāda*, or credo. Only two fragmentary saints' murals survive, which were discovered in 1974.[190] One depicts a male(?) saint or Jesus in a state of ecstasy, with his eyes rolled heavenward and his head adorned with a fiery halo. The face is remarkably well preserved, and betrays similar modelling and colouring as the paintings from the *sehdārī*. The other depicts the Holy Family, and was in much better shape in 1981, when it was described as 'Mary and Joseph with Infant Jesus in Mary's lap ... Sunhaloes surround the three figures.'[191] The figure of the Virgin is the clearest today, with her typical headscarf and halo, while the outline of the child and of Joseph with their haloes can barely be discerned on the right. This subject was extremely popular in miniature painting.[192]

The Indigenous Element in Mughal-'Christian' Art

The Christian images which appeared in such proliferation that they moved the Jesuits to fall on their knees in gratitude included a large number of saints, but especially Jesus and Mary. Although it astonished European visitors and infuriated orthodox Muslims, this imagery is not as foreign to Indo-Islamic tradition as it might appear. Images of Jesus and Mary carried a rich range of relationships for their Mughal audience, and communicated messages related to moral leadership, divine guidance, and royal lineage. We know from contemporary texts that Mughal panegyrists openly alluded to both figures in prose and poetry to legitimate their leaders' right to rule. It naturally follows that Mughal artists instilled the same meanings into portraits of these holy figures. Let us investigate how they fit into the framework of Mughal culture.

Jesus and Mary both play an important role in the Koran and Islamic religious literature. About ninety verses of the Koran deal with Jesus, sixty-four of them with the Nativity. Koranic scripture pays special honour to Jesus as the product of a virgin birth and emphasizes his humility and piety.[193] He is also celebrated as one of few who returned to God alive at the end of their sojourns on earth, which is why the Koran denies his crucifixion and holds that another man was crucified in his stead.[194] The expansion of the role of Jesus and other Christian figures in the literature of the Muslim Middle Ages was fuelled partly by the presence of large indigenous Christian communities in major Muslim centres, and by the increasing familiarity of Muslim writers with Christian texts.[195] Even Christian icons made their appearance in Islamic literature. A famous passage from the medieval writer al-Azraqi (d. 858), for example, tells how the Prophet Muhammad singled out the portrait of Mary and Jesus for conservation when he ordered all of the other murals destroyed that originally adorned the interior of the Ka`bah at Mecca.[196] Later Muslim rulers, in imitation of the Prophet, showed great respect for images of the Madonna and Child.[197]

In Islamic literature, Jesus is frequently associated with abstinence and withdrawal from the world, and often appears as a kind of sheikh, or spiritual elder, who warns the worldly of their sins.[198] This is the principal sentiment in the writings of the great poet and philosopher al-Ghazzali (1058–1111), whose collection of Jesus' sayings was extremely influential in the Muslim world, including the Mughal court.[199] They dwell on the ascetic life of this man who 'wore for 20 years straight a tunic of wool,' and who had 'prayer for his speech, meditation for his silence and tears for his vision.'[200] As a moralistic recluse, Jesus was very popular among Sufis, and he became revered as a proto-master and ultimate contemplative saint.[201] Popular Sufi themes included the spiritual intoxication of the Eucharist wine (wine itself is a very important Sufi metaphor), Jesus as the life-giving and nurturing breath of God, and Jesus' emphasis on the heart as the principal organ of knowledge for spiritual truth.

A Mughal viewer at the turn of the seventeenth century would have recognized another very important role played by Jesus in Islamic legend: that of the Messiah. In a tradition dating back at least to the ninth century, it was believed that Jesus would descend into the Levant on the Day of Judgment, slay the Antichrist (*al-Dajjāl*), and reign as sovereign in Jerusalem.[202] This particular attribute of Jesus was also of prime importance to the ideology of the Mughal emperors, who tirelessly promoted themselves as messiahs, both in the Muslim and Hindu traditions.[203] Badaoni, for example, uses the example of Jesus to parallel Akbar's conquests with those of his predecessor Mahmud of Ghazni: 'Thou would'st say 'Isa [Jesus] has come forth to slay Dajjal.'[204] Monserrate records a session in which Akbar, showing a keen interest in Jesus' function as the Messiah, questioned him closely about 'the Last Judgement, whether Christ would be the Judge, and when it would occur,' to which the father replied, '[In a time of] wars and rebellions, the fall of kingdoms and nations ... and these things we see happening very frequently in our time.'[205]

The Koran is also generous in its texts about Mary. She is mentioned in no less than thirteen suras, and in Sura 19 (*Maryam*) and Sura 3 (*The Imrans*), she is the primary focus. She is the only woman mentioned by her proper name, and is said (3:42) to be exhalted 'above the women of the two (celestial and temporal) worlds,' and, like Jesus, to be a 'model' for Muslims (66:10–12). Mary was used as an explicit symbol of royal prerogative by Mughal panegyrists. Abu'l-Fazl compared her openly to a mythical Mongol proto-mother called Queen Alanqoa (meaning 'immaculate woman'), whom Akbar and Jahangir – following Mongol precedent – considered to be their direct ancestor.[206] According to Mongol legend, Alanqoa was impregnated by a divine light from God while sleeping in her tent and gave birth to the patriarch of the Mongol royal family. As Abu'l-Fazl wrote: 'The cupola of chastity became pregnant by that light in the same way as did her Majesty Mary ...'[207] It did not hurt that both Akbar's and Jahangir's mothers happened to have been called Maryam, or Mary, as we have already observed.

One of the most common types of Christian-inspired devotional images in Mughal painting was Jesus and Mary as a pair, usually with the adult Jesus on the left-hand side and the Virgin on the right. The prominent placement of this couple directly over Imperial thrones, on the Emperor's jewellery, and on his royal seal strongly implied a direct reference to monarchy or to the actual person of the Emperor. As I have hinted earlier, Jesus probably represented the Emperor himself, and Mary symbolized his genealogy through his female lineage. A pair of miniature portraits of Jahangir from around 1614 provides further evidence of this relationship. One of them, in the Musée Guimet in Paris, depicts the Emperor holding a portrait of his real father, Akbar, while its companion in the National Museum in New Delhi (fig. 64) shows him holding a portrait of his spiritual mother, the Virgin Mary.

This pairing also relates to earlier Sufi imagery. The medieval mystic Ibn al-'Arabi, for example, uses the Christian Annunciation (in his *Bezels of Wisdom*) to relate the celestial and earthly worlds to the male and female sex respectively, with Gabriel symbolizing heaven and the holy spirit with which God created Jesus, and Mary representing earth and water.[208] This also closely parallels an important Hindu symbol of kingship whereby the king is the husband of the earth, and together they are the father and mother of their people.[209] The Mughal Emperor's use of this saintly pair on his royal seal also recalls an old Islamic metaphor that referred to Muhammad as the 'Seal of the Prophets' (Jesus is a Prophet in Islam). Later Muslim writers also referred to themselves as seals; for example Ibn al-'Arabi, who boasted that he was the 'Seal of Muhammadan [*sic*] Sainthood.'[210] It is likely that Jahangir intended the pun raised by a seal bearing images of prophets.

Angels, often in the form of European-style *putti*, are ubiquitous in Mughal painting, and are usually shown inhabiting upper regions, whether the horizons of miniature paintings or the vaults and domes of architectural interiors. This is far from a capitulation to Catholic doctrine, however, since angels are as prominent in Islam as in Christianity, and medieval Sufi literature is full of references to angels. They are especially important as symbols of God's bestowal of wisdom on elect monarchs. Sufi sources even constructed complex hierarchies of angels in the form of revolving concentric circles, which echo the construction of actual Mughal ceiling vaults such as that at Lahore.[211]

More puzzling are the saints in Mughal painting that are not mentioned in the Koran and are often depicted in groups resembling Christ's apostles. The apostles do have a role in Islamic tradition, however, and are mentioned in medieval Islamic sources. The apostles were revered by many Muslims for their devotion to Jesus, and there is even an old Islamic tradition that they converted to Islam.[212] Sufis, in particular, honoured the apostles as role models for their own devotion toward their masters. It is possible that the appearance of the apostles, Jesus, and Mary in Mughal painting was also intended to serve as a paradigm for good behaviour. This brings us to a consideration of the intended audience of these images.

The male component comprised the royal family itself and the syncretic brotherhood known as the *Dīn-i Ilāhī* (the Divine Faith). Founded by Akbar in 1583, the Din-i Ilahi was an elite society of the Emperor's courtiers which has often been mistaken for a new religion. Combining Hindu and Muslim practices with a philosophy based on Illuminist Sufism and Mongol ancestor worship, the group practised devotion to the sun, abstinence, and religious debating, and experienced ecstatic visions. The inspiration came from several popular syncretic religious movements of the period.[213] The Din-i Illahi consciously abandoned open prayer and other formal aspects of orthodox worship as a way of uniting men of various religions and nationalities together in the service of their leader.[214] Members pledged their readiness to sacrifice the trappings of their culture and religion, as well as their property and life, to his service. The fraternity, which included the most important members of Mughal society, held its meetings in many of the very rooms adorned with Christian-inspired mural paintings.

The Catholic-inspired images we have been investigating are consonant with the ideology of the Din-i Ilahi. They manifest the same blend of esoteric Hindu, Muslim, and Mongol traditions, from esoteric Sufism to genealogical symbolism. They emphasize the central position of the Emperor in the celestial and temporal worlds, and set up his saintly and angelic servants as role models for personal obedience of the Emperor's devotees. They also underscore the Emperor's closeness to God and the semi-divine status of his ancestors. The most important connection, however, is the metaphor of Jesus – and hence the Emperor – as a Sufi sheikh, which was central to the tenets of the Din-i Ilahi. The society was directly modelled on the relationship between Sufi elders and their followers, with the Emperor as its *pīr*, or head, and his devotees as *murīds*, or pupils. Jesus, the ultimate *pīr*, with his apostles as his *murīds*, was therefore a powerful and appropriate symbol for this fellowship, combining fealty with religious devotion.[215]

What about the female audience? The women of the court, including the mother, wives, and family of the Emperor, and their attendants – as well as the women of the households of emirs who periodically visited the royal palace – formed a group ideologically parallel to the brotherhood of the Din-i Ilahi. Under the leadership of powerful women, such as Akbar's mother, Maryam Makani, and Jahangir's Queen Nur Jahan, the female community was divided into hierarchies very similar to those of the male sector. It is even possible that a master/disciple sisterhood based on the Din-i Ilahi existed there, especially since a woman always ruled opposite the Emperor as the head of the household, recalling Mongol traditions in which the queen and her attendants appeared in public with the male ruler, and enjoyed a higher public visibility than in later Islamic states. More symbolically relevant, this woman was also the guardian of two royal seals, including the *uzāk* (small seal), which bore the Emperor's name – this was affixed to domestic decrees, high appointments, and large disbursements – and the great seal, which was used on foreign correspondence.[216] The Jesus/Mary motif, which appears in both the male and female sectors of the palace and was also used on a royal seal, symbolized the male and female elements of kingship. The head of the harem controlled and participated in the same royal iconography as her male counterpart, the Emperor.

Just as the Din-i Ilahi went beyond ethnic and religious boundaries to unite subjects in the service of their monarch, Catholic devotional art provided a medium of expression that was perceived as culturally neutral, since it did not belong to any of the subcontinental faiths. Western Europe seemed sufficiently far away that it posed no immediate threat – unlike, for example, in the Ottoman Empire, where the contiguity of Imperial territories with the European frontier resulted in a much more reserved attitude toward European imagery, in spite of its availability in much greater quantities than in Mughal India. Catholic art was perceived as universal because of its naturalism; it had an immediacy which transcended cultural boundaries. It was also seen as intensely spiritual. Islam had virtually no tradition of figurative devotional imagery, and could not effectively compete with Hindu iconography. Catholic art, by contrast, possessed undeniable visual potency. Pictures of saints provided a safe and powerful substitute for Hindu gods in the devotions of the court's largest non-Muslim minority – devotions which resonated with the most ancient Indian traditions of kingship.

Another advantage to Christian iconography was its association with a rich tradition of stories and parables that not only formed part of Christian and Jewish tradition, but also of orthodox and Sufi Islam. This rich fabric of texts – biblical, Koranic, historical, mystical – provided many strands with which court propagandists could weave their new ideology. Through a careful selection and manipulation of images capable of striking a similar chord for different cultures, the Emperor elicited loyalty and devotion from all of his subjects. Linked intimately with the two most important elements of Imperial ideology – genealogy and divine right to rule – this powerful iconography happened to be perfectly suited to serve the ends of the Mughal regime at a period when it was faced with its most diverse and challenging citizenry.

The End of an Era: The Mogor Mission and the Arts after Jahangir

In the first years of the second decade of the seventeenth century, after almost forty years of ascendancy in the Imperial atelier, Catholic imagery began to lose its influence. Although Christian saints and other Catholic subjects continued to appear periodically in later Mughal painting, their role in royal propaganda began to diminish before 1625. This dramatic turnabout was the result of a number of rapid historical changes, not the least of which was the departure for Goa in 1614 of Jerónimo Xavier, the intellectual force behind the third Jesuit mission. During the same year, Jahangir temporarily shut down the Jesuit mission in retaliation for Portuguese actions at sea, and we know that the mission did not provide a single new work of European art for at least the next twelve years.[217] The fateful year 1614 also witnessed the arrival of the first documented piece of English art at the Mughal court, followed in the next year by the first official English ambassador, Sir Thomas Roe. After the Mughal court's exposure to the stunning pictorial realism and painterly skill of Jacobean miniatures – so close in size and technique to the Mughals' own miniatures – Protestant art gained an advantage over Catholic imagery, a development that echoed the military advances of English ships over Portuguese carracks. Nevertheless, the art of England, and later Holland, would never achieve the influence over Mughal art and ideology that Catholic art had exerted before them, for the conduit of high-level intellectual discourse had been shut off with the end of the *'Ibādatkhāna* debates.

Catholic art, however, had already penetrated so deeply into mainstream Mughal art and even architecture by this time that its basic ideas, compositions, and symbols were already a crucial ingredient of Mughal style and continued to inform the artistic production of Shah Jahan and subsequent rulers. This 'neutralized' persrverance of Catholic imagery is visible in a series of allegorical royal portraits called the 'Dream Pictures' (ca. 1618–25), an experimental and short-lived attempt to adapt the European Renaissance convention of the frontispiece to Imperial portraiture.[218] A true hybrid, these works borrowed elements from Catholic iconography and the newly arrived portraiture of the Jacobean Renaissance, yet they remained essentially Mughal and Islamic in content. Totally devoid of the Christian saints' images which were so important in earlier decades, these collages use European elements on a much more superficial level. Jahangir experimented with this mode of representation because it offered the means to express complex ideas – for example, moral choice – in a pithy, convenient package.[219] These conceits offered Jahangir a more expressive and immediate form of official propaganda.

Christian subjects remained popular in Mughal painting, to a much smaller degree and as one of a variety of modes of painting, well into the nineteenth century. Although very few new engravings were used as models, figures and themes popular under Akbar and Jahangir continued to appear among the work of Shah Jahani and later artists, and enjoyed an enthusiastic revival under the Nawabs of Oudh in late eighteenth-century Lucknow, particularly in the work of the school of Mir Kalan Khan. They remained a popular ingredient of albums, now common on the provincial level. Placed alongside European engravings in sections devoted to the Western mode, they were in turn sandwiched between sheaves of Deccani and Rajput paintings, as one of many exotic ingredients in these paper *Wunderkammern*.

The golden era of the Jesuit mission to Mogor had passed, but for another century and a half the mission faltered neither in its evangelizing and intellectual efforts, nor in the eminence of its personnel.[220] At times, Jesuits or their agents regained influence at court; for example, Henri Busi (1618–67), the Flemish confidant of the Mughal prince Dara Shukoh, or Juliana Diaz da Costa (d. 1734), a Portuguese lady who was close to Aurangzeb's son Prince Bahadur Shah and helped win favour for the Jesuits. The mission continued to be active in Indian diplomacy; for example, in the early eighteenth century, when the Jesuit superior Figueiredo accompanied Mughal embassies to Goa and arranged for the foundation of an influential Jesuit scientific mission at the court of the great Maharaja Sawai Jai Singh II Kachchwaha of Jaipur (1686–1743).[221] Even in the turbulent and factious climate of the late eighteenth century, figures such as Francis Xavier Wendel (d. 1803) managed to stay on the side of the winning armies and to win the generous patronage of victorious generals.

Great intellectuals continued to serve at the Mogor mission, such as the Italian mathematician and Sanskrit scholar Antonio Ceschi (1618–56); the Bavarian Heinrich Roth (1620–68), the first European to publish a Sanskrit grammar, who, upon return to Rome, assisted the eminent Jesuit scientist Athanasius Kircher with his influential book *China illustrata* (1667); and the Austrian Joseph Tieffenthaler (1715–85), who was simultaneously a mathematician, astronomer, geographer, and historian, and who has left a sizeable legacy of writings. The mission even expanded geographically. Already, in 1603, an expedition was sent from Agra to the Tibetan heartland; Eastern Bengal and Nepal were penetrated during the later seventeenth century; and a new base was set up in Narwar in Central

India in the eighteenth. The Mogor mission met its demise only with the suppression of the Society of Jesus in 1773 (it had even survived the Portuguese expulsion of the Society a few years earlier), and the last surviving fathers were turned into nomadic wanderers, seeking patronage from court to court. In the end, it was the Pope himself, not the Mughal Emperor, who terminated one of the world's longest-lasting Catholic missions in Muslim territory.

6

'The New Plant of the Primitive Church':[1] The Jesuit Reductions among the Guaraní in Paraguay, 1609–1768

Although most famous for their contributions to music, economics, and political theory, the Jesuit reductions (*reducciones*) in Paraguay were also the most prolific mission art enterprise ever undertaken by the Society of Jesus. Contemporary chroniclers raved about cathedral-sized churches in the rainforest sheltering hundreds of altarpieces adorned with thousands of gilt and painted statues – all produced by a vast network of indigenous workshops capable of supplying not only these architectural projects but also the extravagant processions which marked the days of the Christian year. In fact, the sheer extent of artistic production, based as it was on Euro-Christian models and created under the tutelage of European-trained missionaries, threatened to overwhelm indigenous visual culture to an extent that we have not seen in Asia. But Guaraní aesthetics did not disappear. Although many of the instructors were European, almost all of the artists and builders were indigenous. And just as the Jesuits adopted Guaraní economic, political, and ritual traditions when founding the reductions, they tacitly allowed indigenous style and even symbols to pervade mission art.

The Guaraní craftsmen indigenized Christian iconography on what might be described as the 'grass-roots' level: naturally and unofficially. Although the works of art they produced for their new religion adhered predominantly to European canons, they often interpreted Christian figures and symbols in a way that reflected their own artistic preferences and world-view. What makes this blending of styles so unusual – and so difficult to untangle compared to China, India, or Japan – was that the Guaraní had no figural arts tradition to start with, making their visual culture more alien to European art than any of the other civilizations discussed in this book. Nevertheless, this disparity meant that the two iconographies never clashed head-on (as the Virgin Mary did with Guanyin in China, for example), and were able to blend almost seamlessly. European missionaries considered the figural image to be the most important feature of a devotional picture and that was where they focused their attention. The Guaraní, however, were just as interested in patterns and rhythms, elements considered decorative by Europeans. Before contact with Europeans, they had shown a disinclination toward figural imagery, even when it was available to them for centuries through trade goods from the Andean highlands.[2] Art's goal was not to imitate nature but to reveal its essence by means of largely geometrical forms of expression. Their traditional patterns combined a variety of abstracted and stylized animal and floral motifs, such as the jaguar or passionflower (*mburucuyá*) arranged symmetrically and rhythmically. Therefore, as with the Andean peoples of Peru, the focus of indigenous artists was not just on the image itself, but on areas considered marginal or decorative by Europeans.

Surface patterns, and symmetrical and schematic renderings of their subjects, were very meaningful to the Guaraní. Artists also incorporated potent indigenous floral, feather, and faunal motifs into the 'ornamentation' of their saints, symbols which could be understood by their community in the context of indigenous religion. Therefore, while the Jesuits believed they were creating a perfect Christian art along largely European lines, Guaraní artists were interpreting Christian deities and demons as incarnations of their own gods and spirits, such as God the Creator, Ñanderuvusú, and the sylvan devil Añá. This understanding is completely in keeping with pre-contact Guaraní religion in which gods and spirits have many different incarnations and are constantly in a state of metamorphosis.

Even the act of carving a statue of a saint was not seen as creating a work of art in the European sense; image-makers quite literally believed that they were making saints and gods, as evidenced by their title *santo apohava* or 'saint maker.' This veneration of the object itself is often evident in the wealth of symbols and stylistic details which allowed for many different levels of interpretation. The result, in much of the sculpture of the Paraguay reductions, is a unique and powerful testament to cultural partnership that goes far beyond a blending of styles and involves a synthesis of two very different concepts of the sacred. First, however, let us put Guaraní reduction art in context by reviewing trends in mainstream Spanish South American colonial art and architecture from this period.

The Art and Architecture of Seventeenth-Century Spanish South America

European colonization in South America south of the Caribbean got off to a slow start, thanks to the civil wars which raged in the Andes for decades after the conquest of the Inca Empire during 1531–2. Therefore there was little in the way of colonial architecture before Viceroy Toledo's tenure began in 1570. In the early seventeenth century, European settlement was focused for the most part in small metropolitan centres where life went on much as it had in Spain. The most densely populated areas in the Andean region were the Peruvian and Ecuadorian coast and highlands and Alto Peru (today Bolivia), where major cities such as Lima, Cuzco, and Quito were built or rebuilt according to the principles of Renaissance urban planning. Further south, in what is present-day Argentina and Paraguay, European settlement began as early as the 1550s, resulting in a string of colonial towns such as Santiago del Estero, Mendoza, Tucumán, Córdoba, Santa Fé, and Salta by the end of the century. Buenos Aires, although founded in 1536, was destroyed and rebuilt only in 1580, and even then did not really gain any size or importance until the last quarter of the eighteenth century, when it became the capital of the new Viceroyalty of the River Plate (1776). The two principal cities were Córdoba, the cultural capital and later episcopal seat, and Asunción (founded 1537), now the Paraguayan capital and at one time the bishopric for the whole region.

As we would expect, the art and architecture of these Andean and Southern towns was Iberian in style – primarily Andalusian since the principal ports for the voyage to America were found in Southern Spain. Early colonial architecture showed very little evidence of acculturation with indigenous forms, even though Amerindian artists, craftsmen, and even architects were common. A recent study of the earliest colonial architecture of Peru has concluded that it was even more conservative and classicizing than architecture in Spain at the time, and often demonstrated Serlian influence.[3] During the golden age of colonial architecture in Cuzco in the second half of the seventeenth century, stone churches and houses went up in an emphatically Spanish style, so that even today the cupolas and facades are reminiscent of Valencia, Salamanca, or Toledo. Nevertheless, this confident Spanish Renaissance culture was humbled as many of the stone structures in Peru were destroyed in earthquakes during the seventeenth and eighteenth centuries. Ironically, colonists in Lima and along the coast turned to indigenous techniques as the great churches were rebuilt using the lightweight technique of *quincha* (mud and rushes).[4]

In contrast to the Andean region, Argentina was always on the frontier, not unlike the 'Wild West' in nineteenth-century America, and consequently its cities were small and their architecture humble adobe structures built in a provincial Peruvian style. Even in the later seventeenth century, when larger churches such as Córdoba Cathedral or the convent church of San Francisco in Santa Fé were being rebuilt, they were still constructed of more basic materials. Nevertheless, wood in the northern forests was strong and plentiful, and consequently some elaborate roofing techniques were possible, such as the Islamic-derived *mudéjar* style of flat panels over transverse beams. San Francisco in Santa Fé possesses one of the finest roofs in Argentina. Sometimes this natural wealth in hardwood encouraged woodwork carving of extraordinary richness, such as the eighteenth-century doorway to the Carmelite *convento* of San Bernardino in Salta. It was this same resource which made it possible for Guaraní reduction sculpture and architecture to flourish.

South American sculpture of the sixteenth and early seventeenth centuries also followed Spanish sixteenth-century styles, showing a noticeable Flemish influence that was also felt in Spain itself. Quito was an exceptionally creative centre of sculpture in the seventeenth century, especially benefiting from Franciscan efforts.[5] Unlike in Italy, the sculpture in South America was almost all wood or gypsum, which was gilded and tooled (*estofado*) with rich, textile surface patterns, or polychrome painted. Sculpture was also a more prominent feature of Spanish colonial churches than in Italy, where painting enjoyed primacy. Sculptures were made, not to stand in the round, but to form parts of elaborate retables, or altarpieces, which incorporated sculptures, paintings, and carved decoration in a profusion of ornament, often taking up the entire end wall of the chapel. These complex structures involved careful planning between designers, sculptors, painters, and woodworkers, and are in reality more like architecture than sculpture.

The retables of Peru are perhaps the closest to metropolitan Spanish examples, many having been made by Andalusians and encorporating sculptures by such peninsular masters as the Sevillian Juan Martínez Montañés (1564–1649).[6] In addition to the polychromy and *estofado* decoration, the feature most typical of Spanish colonial sculpture is the emphasis on expressive realism, much of which focused on penitence and pain. Images of Christ and martyrs, whose ivory white skin contrasted with horribly realistic wounds and garish streams of blood, were not meant to delight but to excite pathos (fig. 89). Some scholars have suggested that the South American enthusiasm for gory images of the Passion reflects the Amerindians' projection of their own sense of oppression onto that of Christ; nevertheless, these images enjoyed similar popularity in Spain.[7] Unlike in early colonial New Spain, scholars have found virtually no traces of indigenous motifs or styles in Andean sculpture of the early Colonial period, a phenomenon which they trace to the relatively unimportant position of figural art in Inca society. However, scholars generally acknowledge that a process of indigenization had begun by the end of the seventeenth century.[8]

Peru was the capital of painting in the early colonial period, with two distinct schools located in Lima and Cuzco.[9] We have already seen how this tradition began with the Jesuit Bernardino Bitti, and his Italian Mannnerism, with a hint of Flemish style, prevailed throughout the seventeenth century (figs. 15, 16). As well as Bitti's many students and assistants – I have already mentioned fellow Jesuit Pedro de Vargas – other Italian painters, such as Angelino Medoro (1565–1632) and Matteo da Leccio (1547–ca. 1616), helped create a remarkably international style in the early years of the colony. Leccio was particularly distinguished; he was active in Rome and also executed surviving works in Malta and Seville before going to Lima at the invitation of the Jesuits around 1588.[10] Nevertheless, like everyone in the colonies, his paintings used engravings as models; for example, the print of Raphael's *Virgin of the Oak* found pasted on the back of an oil-on-copper painting by Leccio, *The Virgin of the Milk* (1583), in a private collection in Lima, which reproduces the facial features of the former.

In addition to these Italians, and to the many Spanish painters working in South America at the time, some remarkable indigenous people contributed to the artistic climate of the day. The first is the chronicler Guaman Poma de Ayala (1534–1615), whose history of Peru is accompanied by hundreds of subtly acculturative drawings by the author. This manuscript, now at Copenhagen, has become the most popular focus of study in recent scholarship on cultural hybridity in Peru.[11] Another artist of Andean ancestry, Diego Quispe Tito (1611–81), has also attracted considerable attention, not so much for introducing indigenous traits into his art as for his originality of vision.[12] Quispe Tito relished expansive landscapes, a feature lacking in most of the other painting of the period, and even though they, too, derived from prints of Flemish masters such as the Sadelers, the artist has infused them with an other-worldly quality which anticipates later work in Cuzco. In the eighteenth century, Cuzco became the centre of a school of painting that has been widely recognized as incorporating indigenous motifs and sensibilities into Christian religious imagery.

I have already discussed earlier (chapter 2) the important role played by Jesuit artists and architects in South America. The Society founded important bases in all of the major metropolitan centres, including major colleges such as San Pablo in Lima, and were among the most prominent patrons of the arts. In many regions, especially those whose colonial style blossomed for the first time in the eighteenth century, the Jesuits' contribution was foundational. This is true, as we have already seen, in Chile and Argentina.[13] The Jesuits were even prime movers in cosmopolitan Quito in the eighteenth century, and are responsible for giving Quiteño art of that era a markedly Italian and German stamp. Although there was nothing like a 'Jesuit style' in South America, many of the major Jesuit architectural foundations there – especially the early ones – are characterized by a late Italian Mannerist style which makes them quite different from other churches in the same city. Typical are flat, Serlian façades divided by pilasters and bearing little sculptural decoration. This is true of the church of the college of San Pablo (now known as San Pedro, 1638) in Lima (fig. 13), San Ignacio at Bogotá (begun 1625), the eighteenth-century Compañía in Salta (fig. 81), and even Bianchi's façade at Córdoba Cathedral (begun 1729). This severe style also characterized Jesuit foundations in Brazil, for example, the Jesuit collegiate church at Salvador (1657–72). The Jesuits' international blend of styles, dominated by a reverence for Italian classicism and later the Roman and German Baroque, was to be even more characteristic of the Guaraní missions.

Culture and Art of the Guaraní before the Arrival of the Jesuits

The Guaraní were a semi-nomadic people related to the Tupí of Brazil who entered the lowlands in present-day Paraguay, northern Argentina, and southern Brazil during A.D. 1000–1200.[14] At the time of the Spanish conquest in 1537, greater Paraguay was home to many different tribes, including several Guaraní subgroups, as well as the Payaguá and Guaycurú peoples, who had arrived about five hundred years before them. Guaraní society was centred on the village, each one containing a number of extended households called *teyy*, built around a plaza and communal house, or *teyy-óga*.[15] Political power rested in the hands of a village chief, who passed it on through patrilineal inheritance. The Guaraní had virtually no political organization beyond the village level, although groups of villages would meet at agricultural festivals, and a complex system of alliances existed for survival in times of crisis or war.

The Guaraní religion was – and still is – animist, since they depended upon natural forces for their livelihood of hunting and agriculture. It divided natural phenomena into positive and negative forces, and was not based on theology, or knowledge of the gods.[16] In stark contrast to Catholicism, Guaraní religion possessed no figural iconography, being based instead on oratory and dance. As one anthropologist writes, 'their culture is not a culture of images, but one of words.'[17] Among the Guaraní, the Word was equated with the human soul – making naming an essential aspect of identity – and every critical stage of a person's live was marked by a word.[18] In the Guaraní creation myth, the Great Father, Ñanderuvusú, founds human language with a fragment of his divinity, conceiving a sacred chant even before he created the earth itself.[19]

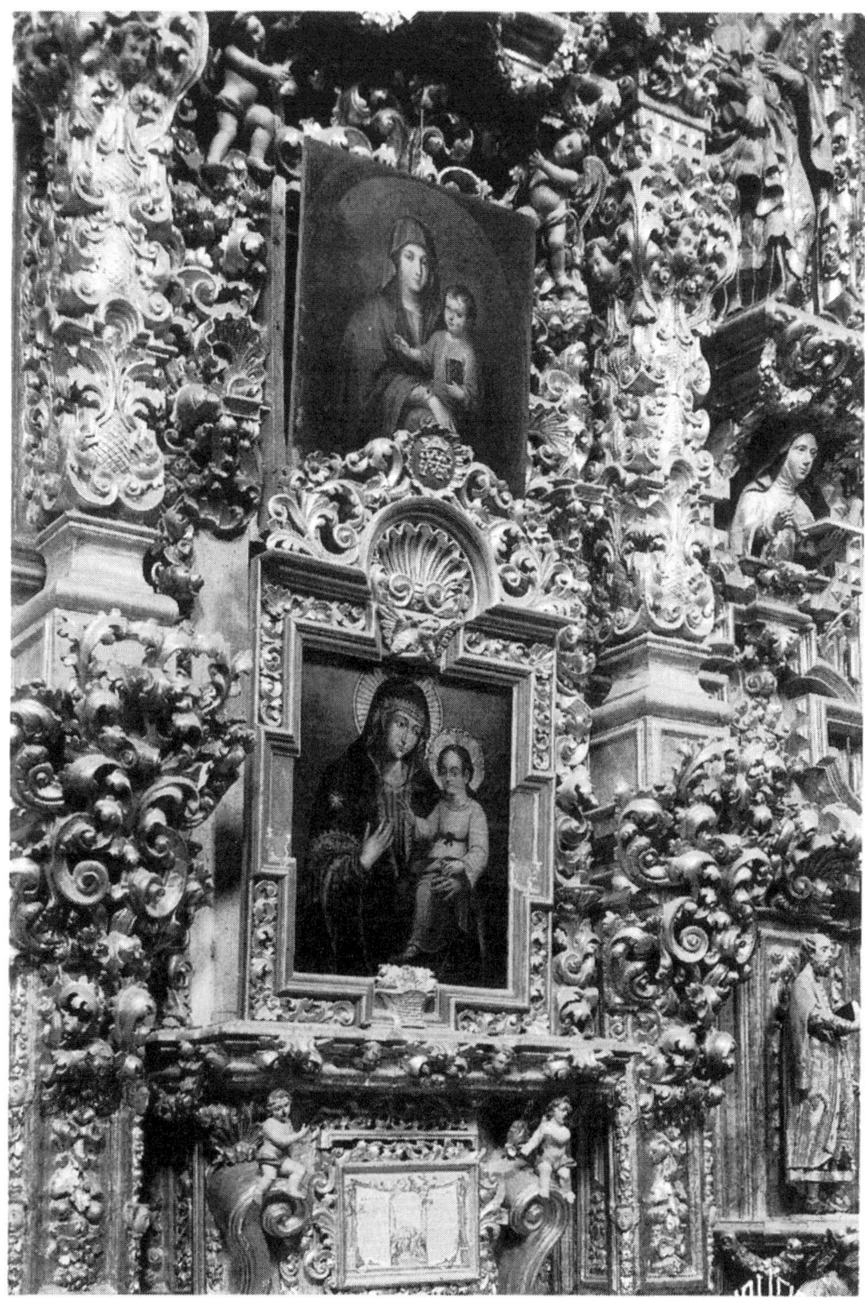

1 Mexican copies of the miraculous images *Salus Populi Romani* (top) and *Madonna del Popolo* (bottom), both supposedly painted by Saint Luke and in the churches of Santa Maria Maggiore and Santa Maria del Popolo in Rome. Former Jesuit College of San Martín, Tepotzotlán (Mexico State, Mexico). From a postcard of ca. 1910. Collection of the author.

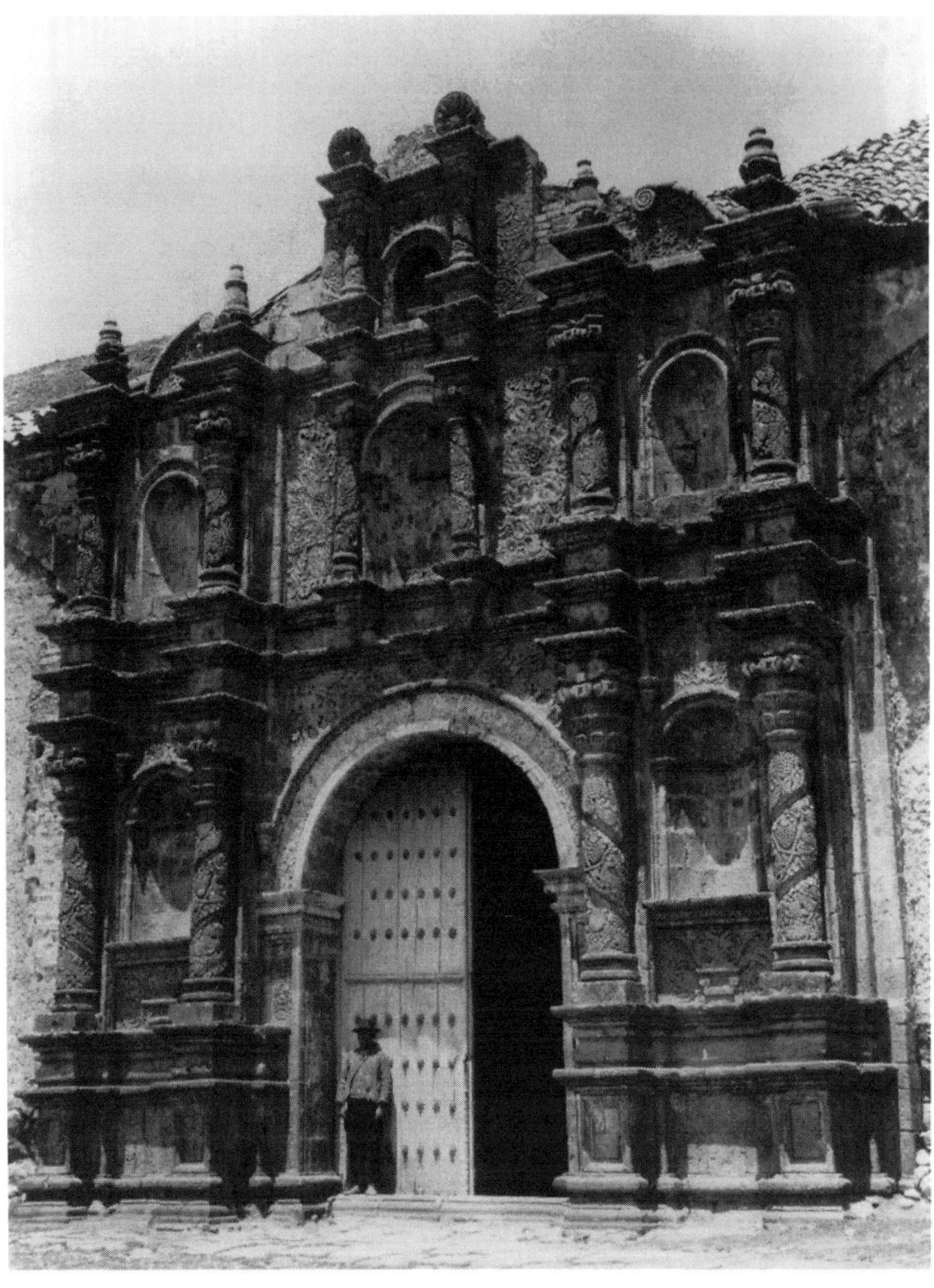

2 Jesuit mission church of San Juan, Juli (Chucuito, Peru). Side portal in planimetric *'estilo mestizo'*, 18th century. Juli was one of the original reductions of the Society of Jesus, founded in 1578. Photograph of the late 19th or early 20th century. Courtesy Visual Collections, Fine Arts Library, Harvard University.

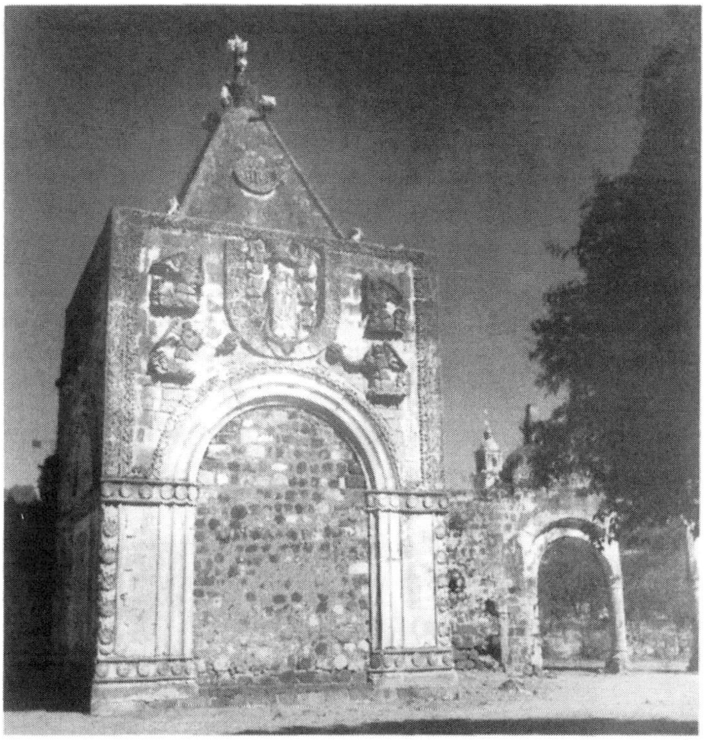

3 Northeast *posa* chapel of the Franciscan mission church of San Andrés, Calpan (Puebla, Mexico), founded 1548. Note the planimetric carved decoration over the doorway. Photograph of the early 20th century. Courtesy Visual Collections, Fine Arts Library, Harvard University.

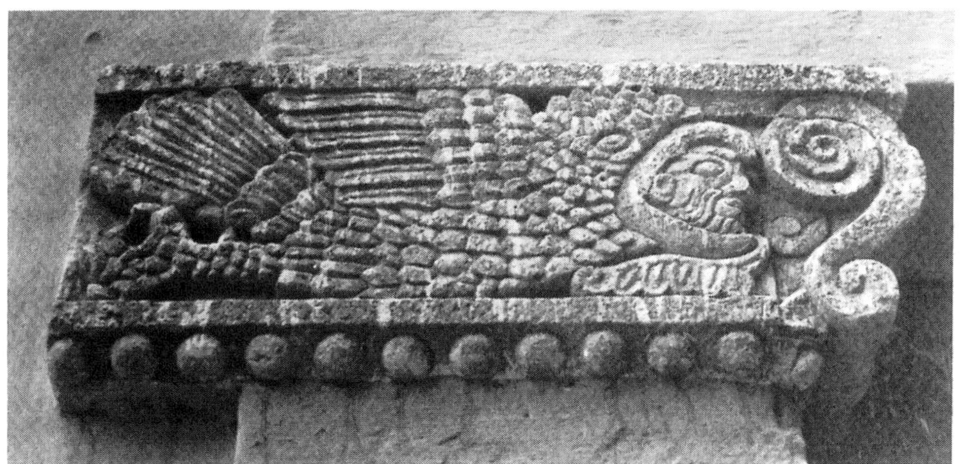

4 Doorjamb of an early colonial period house with an image of an Aztec eagle knight, Cholula (Puebla, Mexico). An example of planimetric '*tequitqui*' ornamentation. Courtesy Visual Collections, Fine Arts Library, Harvard University.

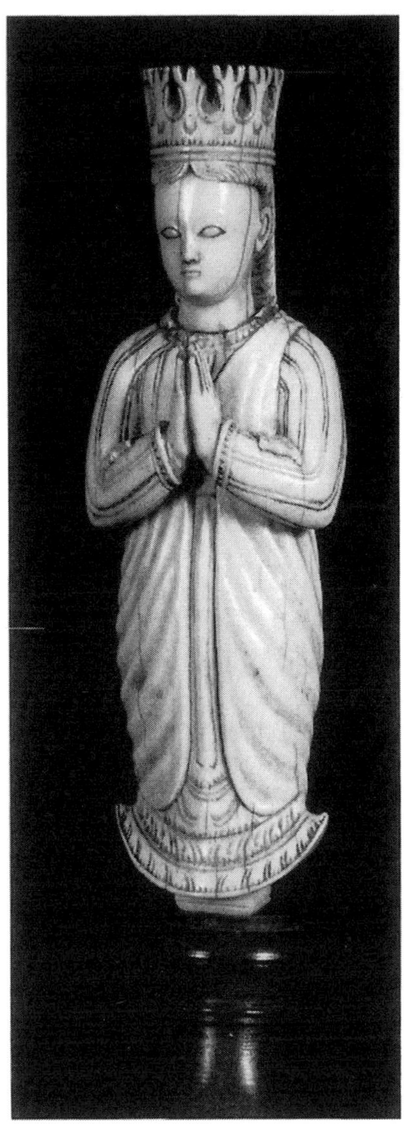

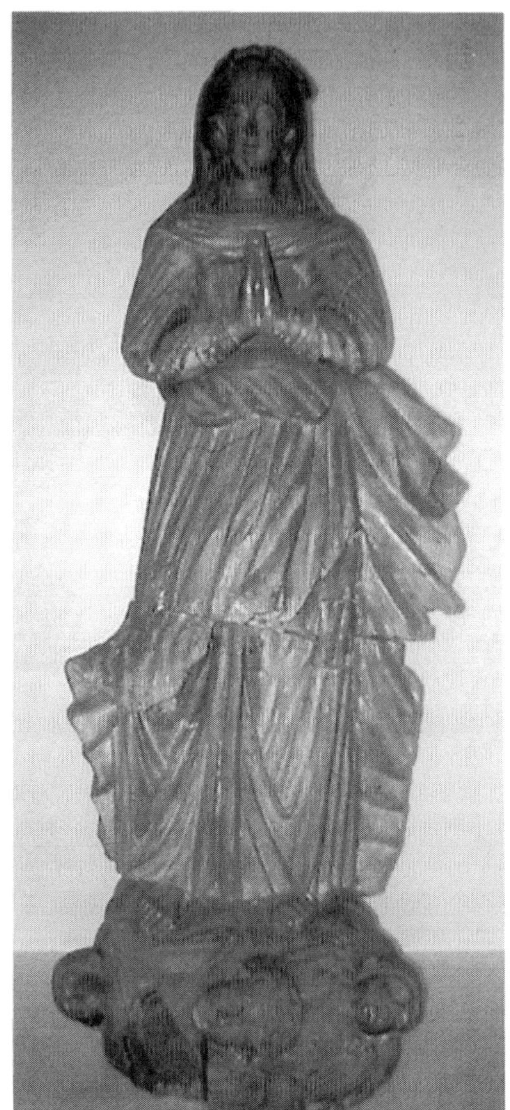

5 *Immaculate Conception*, ivory. Indo-Portuguese, 17th–18th century (15 cm). Távora Sequeira Pinto Collection, Oporto.

6 *Immaculate Conception*, wood. Guaraní, 17th–18th century (1.25 m). São Miguel, Brazil.

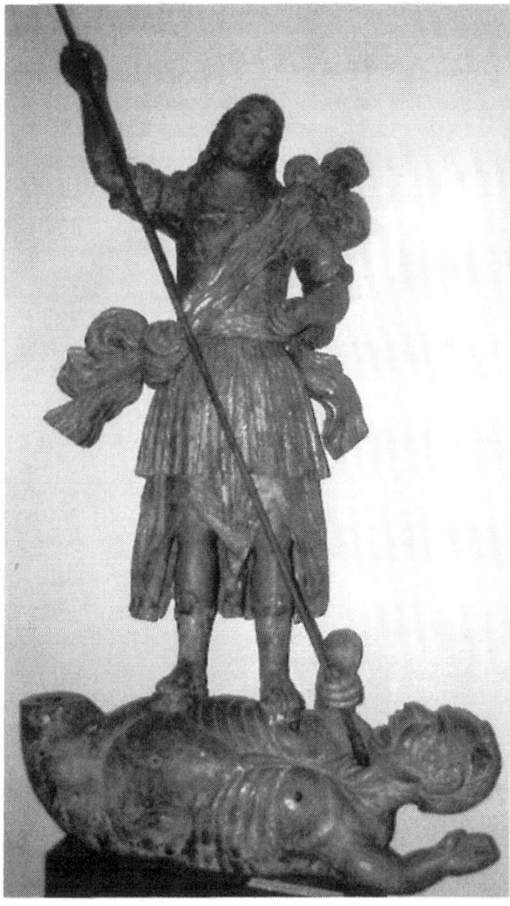

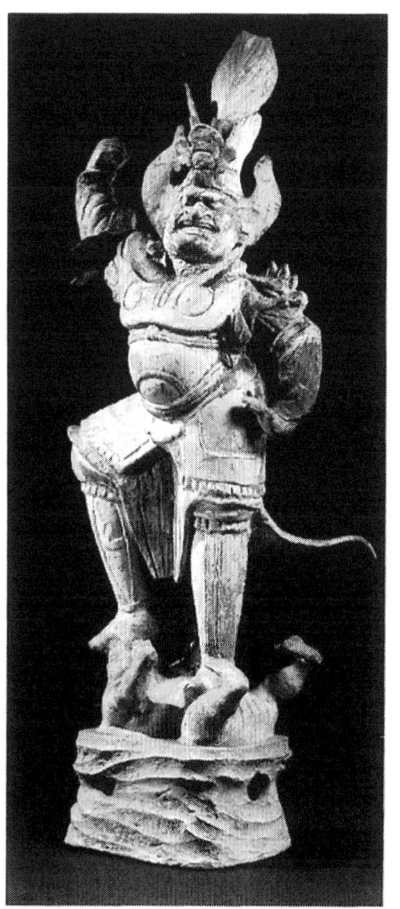

7 *Saint Michael Slaying the Devil*, wood and gold with traces of polychrome (1.30 m). Guaraní, 17th century. San Ignacio Museum, Paraguay.

8 *Buddhist tomb guardian trampling a demon*, clay. Chinese, Tang dynasty, 8th century (56.5 cm). Royal Ontario Museum, Toronto, 918.21.316, George Crofts Collection.

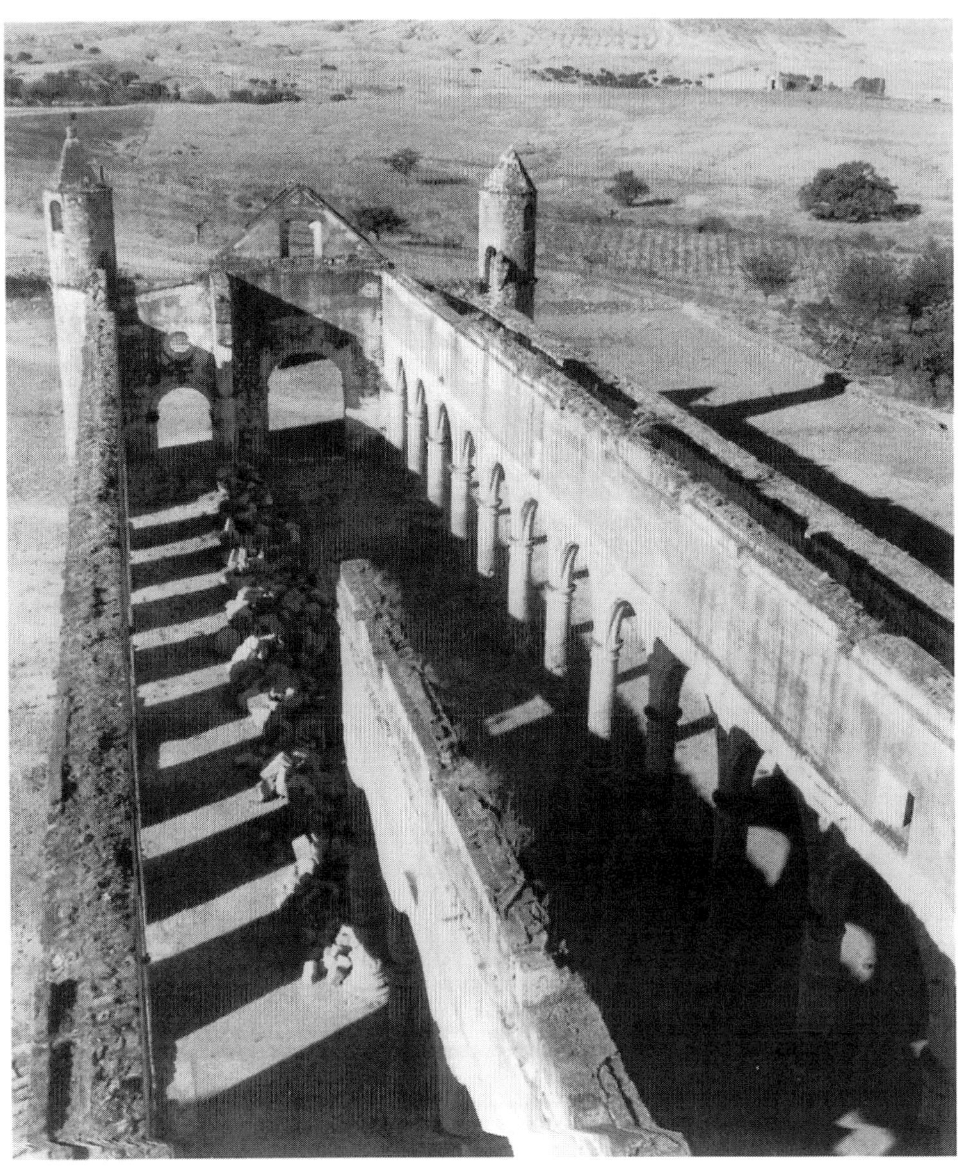

9 Dominican mission 'basilica' open chapel of Santiago Apóstol, Cuilapan (Oaxaca, Mexico), begun 1555 by Antonio de Barbosa. Three-aisled basilican churches were typical of the early mission period. Photograph of the early 20th century. Courtesy Visual Collections, Fine Arts Library, Harvard University.

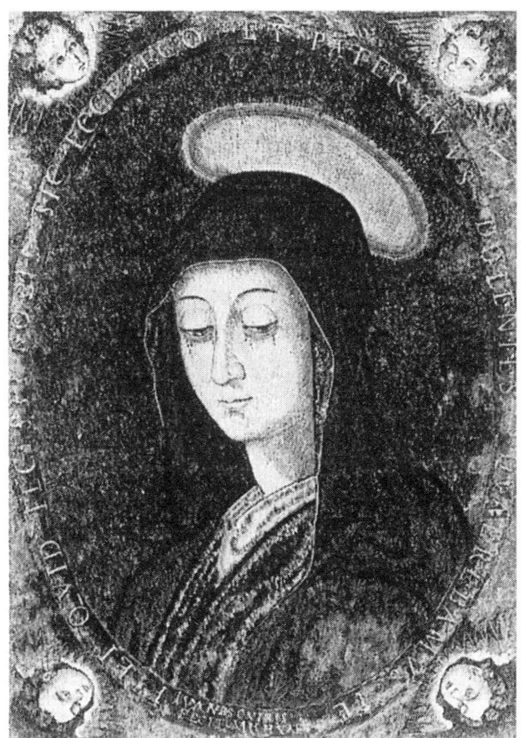

10 Juan Baptista Cuiris: *La Virgen de los Dolores* (New Spain, Nahua technique), feather mosaic, Michoacán 1550/80 (25.4 × 18.2 cm). Kunsthistorisches Museum, Vienna, cat KK. Kap.322.

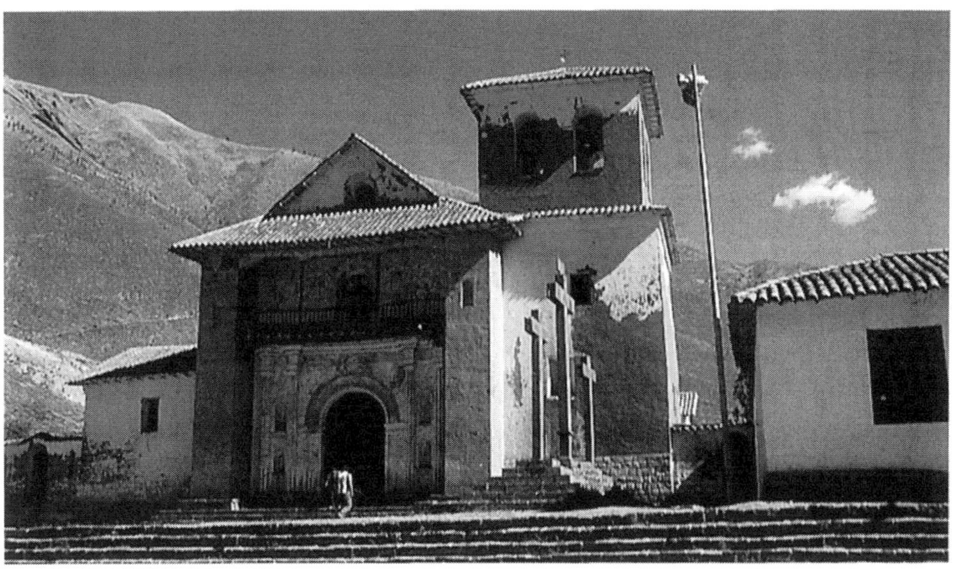

11 Reduction church of San Pedro Apóstol, before 1626, Andahuaylillas (Peru).

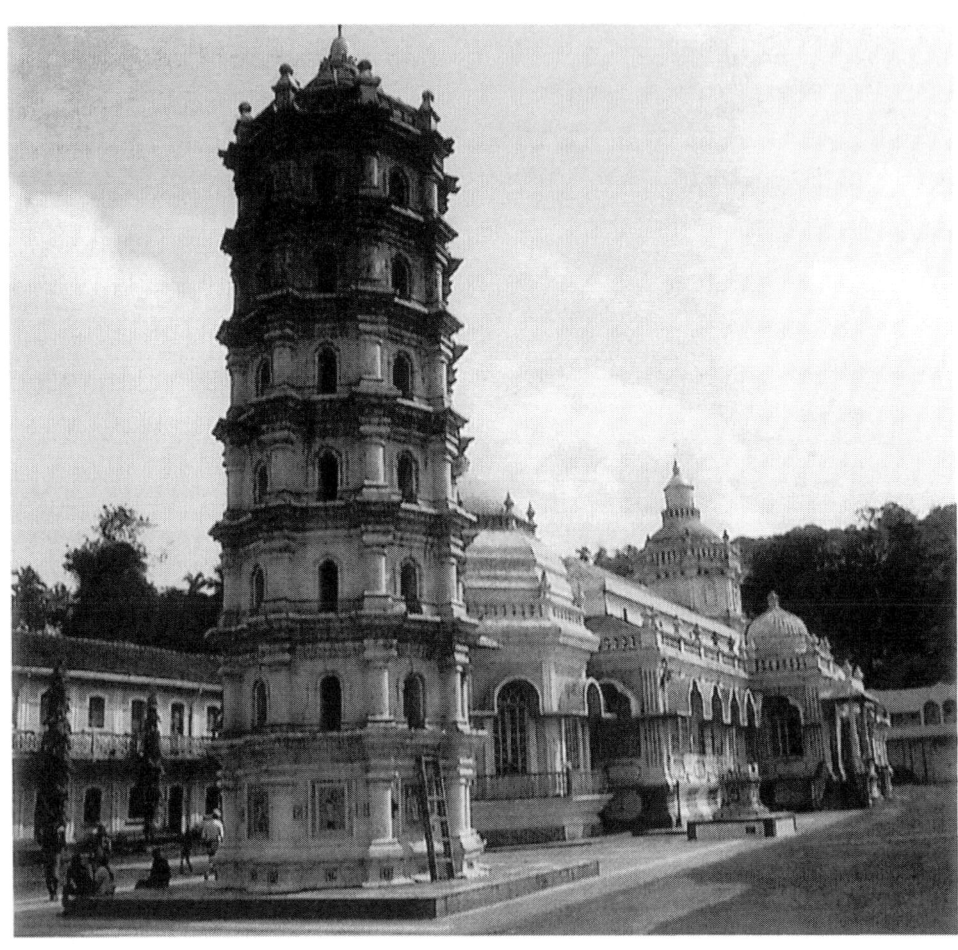

12 Shri Manguesh Temple, Priol (Goa, India), 18th century.

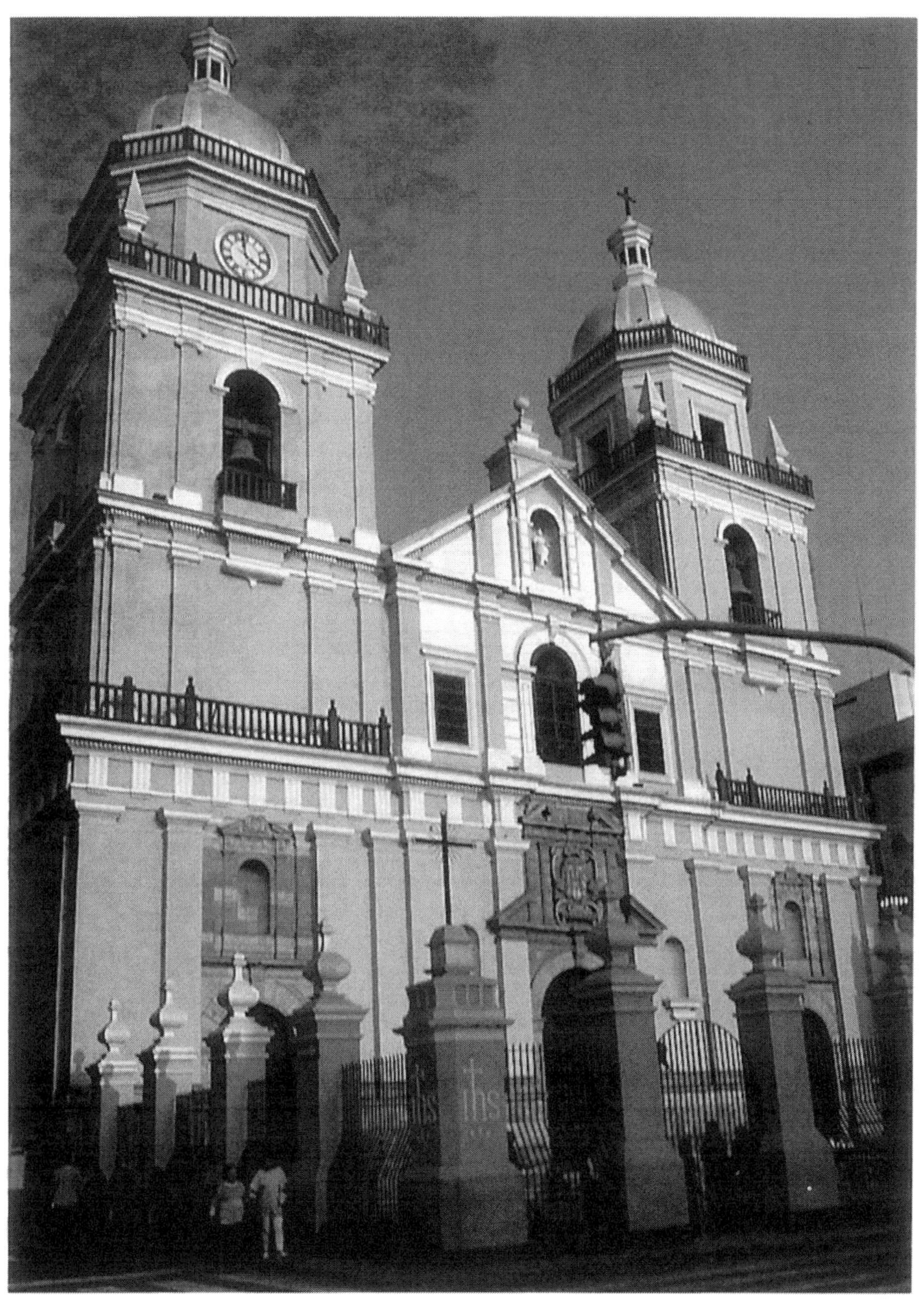

13 Jesuit church of San Pedro, formerly the collegiate church of San Pablo, Lima (Peru), finished 1638. The façade was heavily restored in the 19th and 20th centuries.

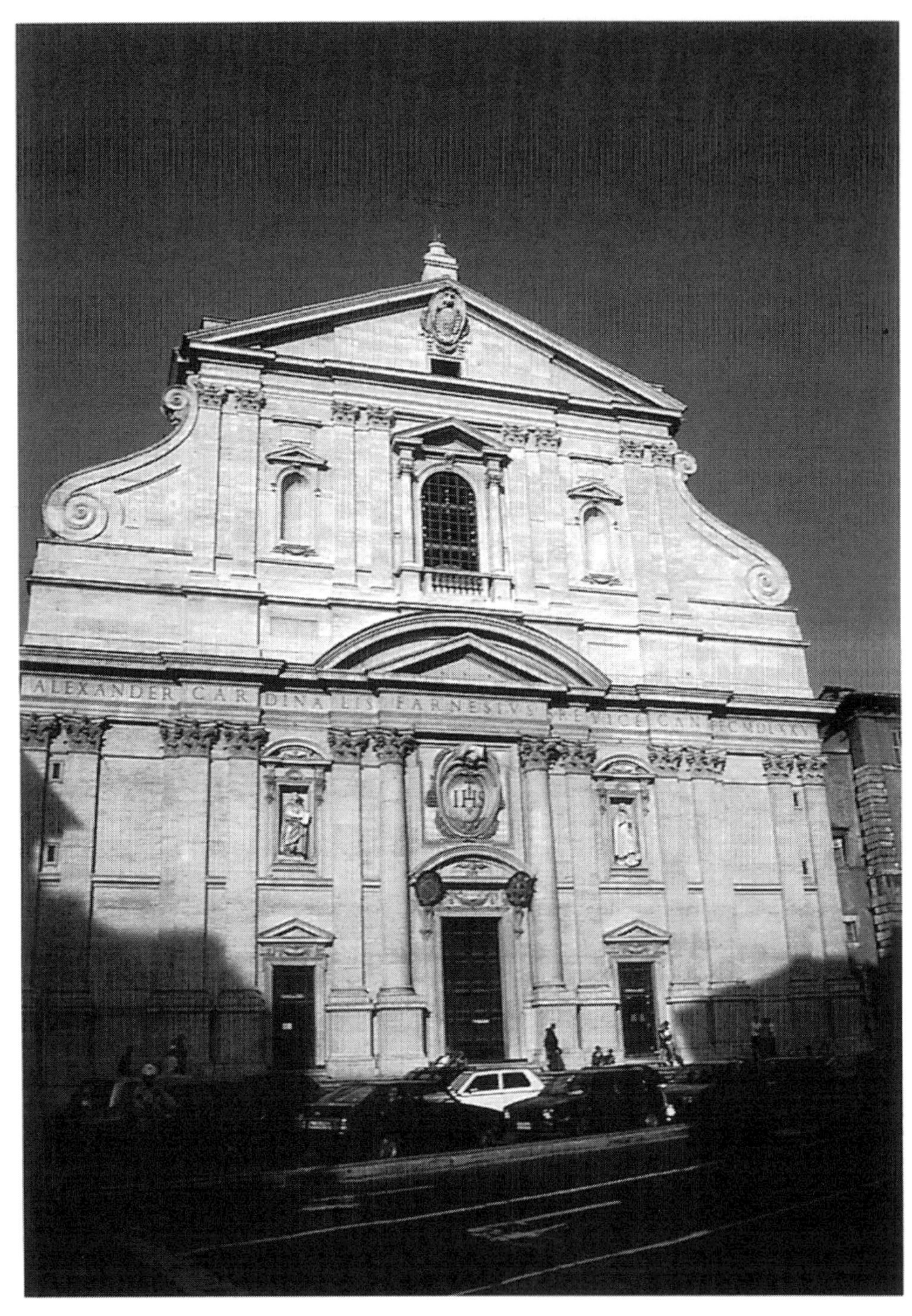

14 Church of the Gesù, Rome. Façade by Giacomo della Porta, 1571–2.

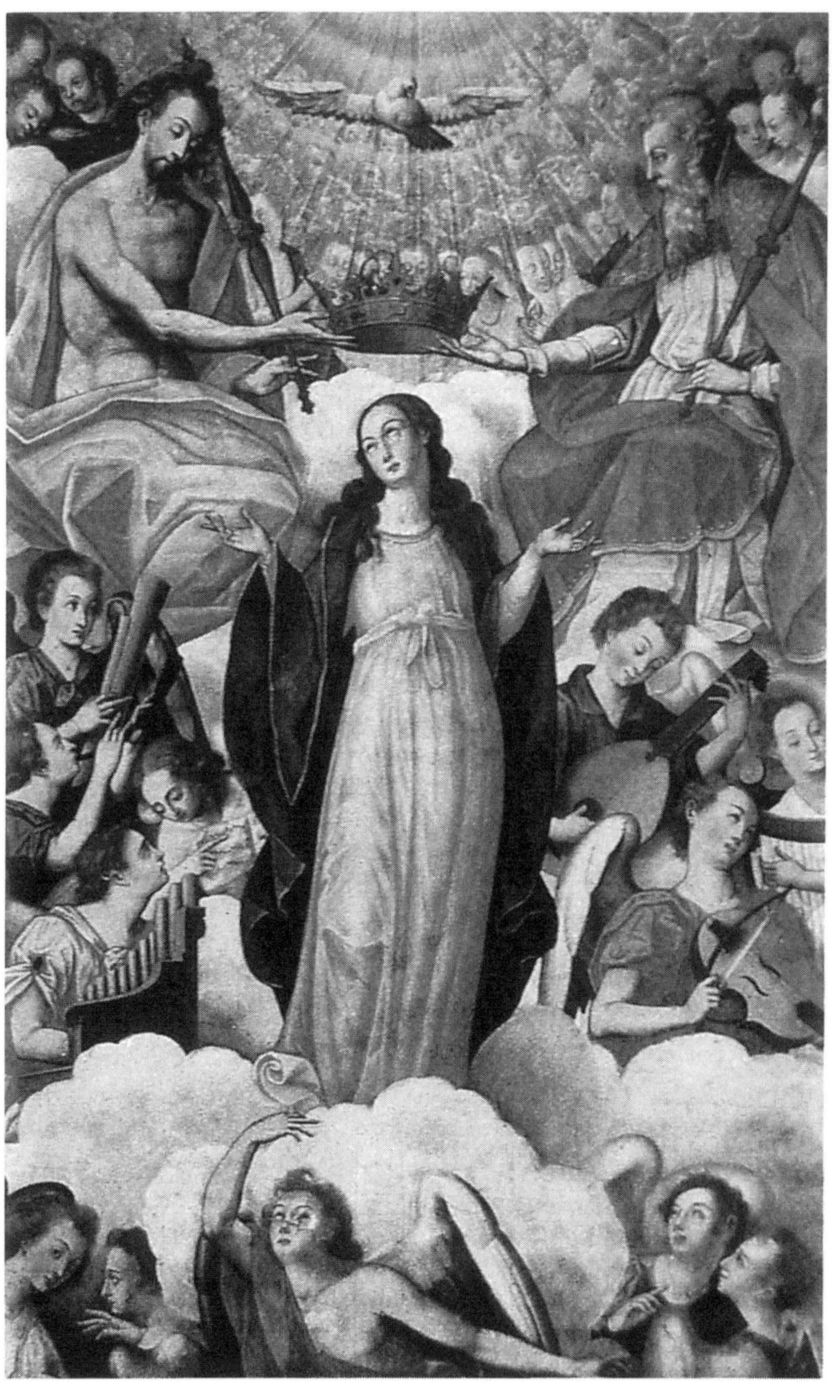

15 Bernardino Bitti, S.J., *Coronation of the Virgin*, oil on canvas, ca. 1595–1600. Monastery of La Merced, Cuzco (Peru).

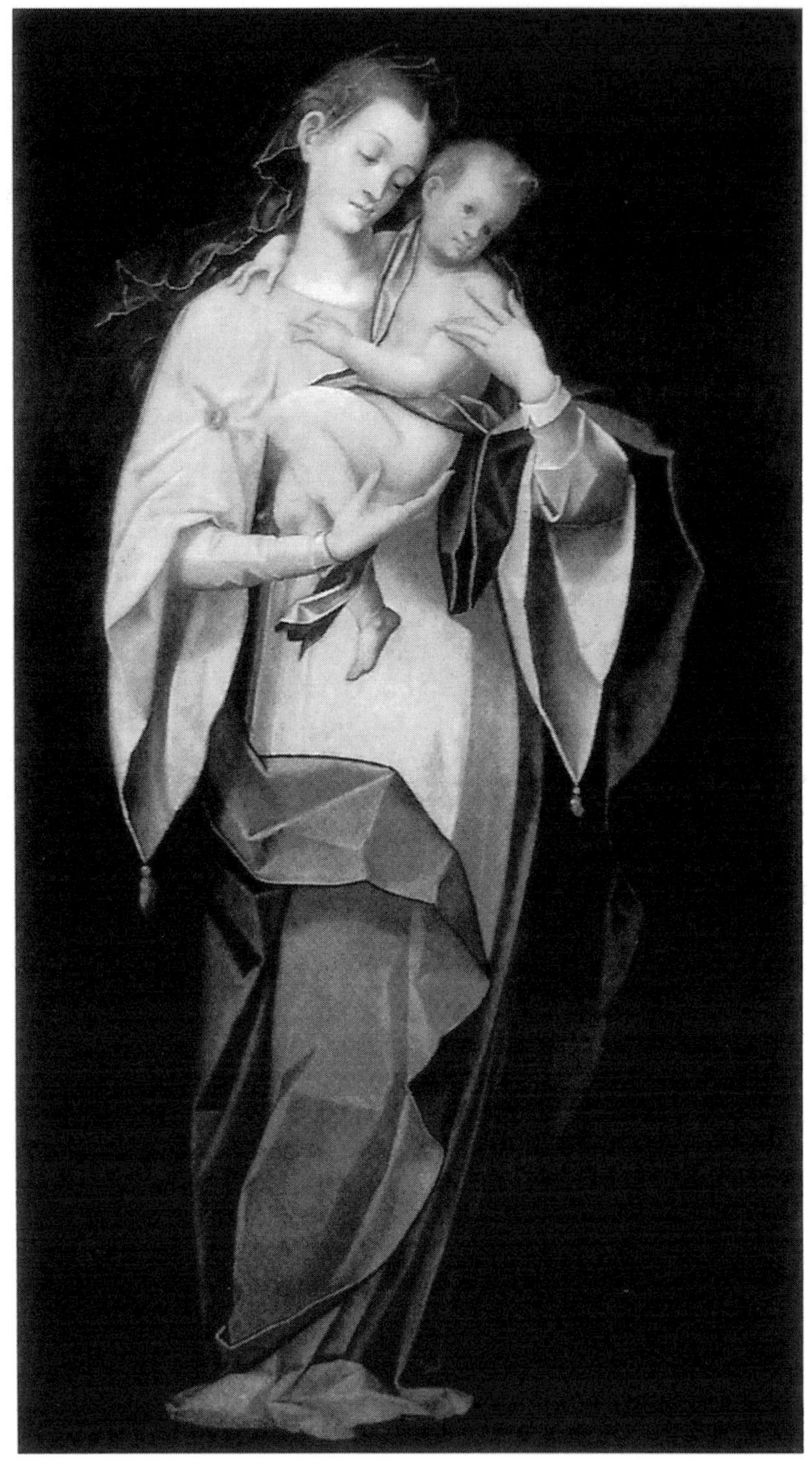

16 Bernardino Bitti, S.J., *Madonna and Child*, ca. 1595–1600. Compañía, Arequipa (Peru).

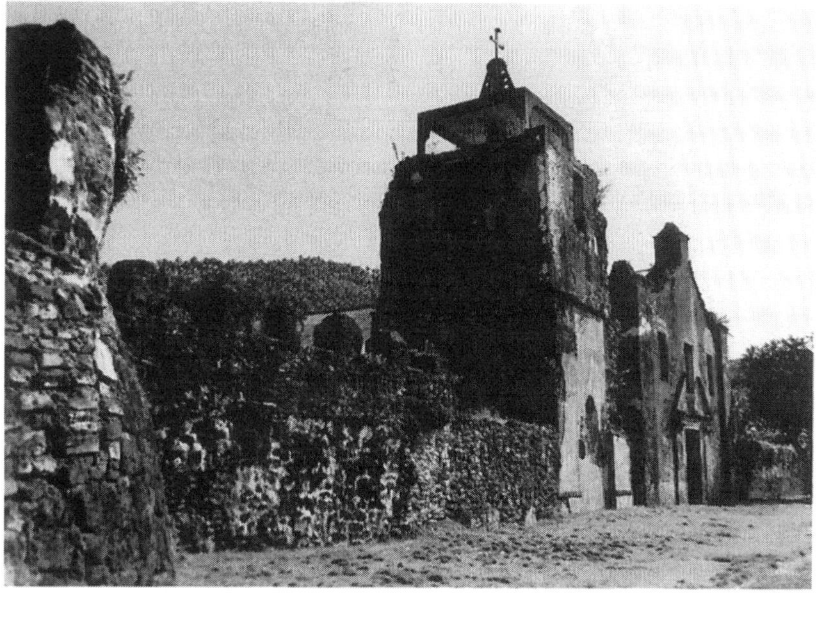

17 Jesuit mission church and fortress of San Ignacio, Capul Island (Philippines), founded 1616, present church 18th century. This complex shows the continuation of the Jesuit tradition of fortification architecture, which began in the Philippines with Antonio Sedeño in the late 16th century. Photograph courtesy of René Javellana.

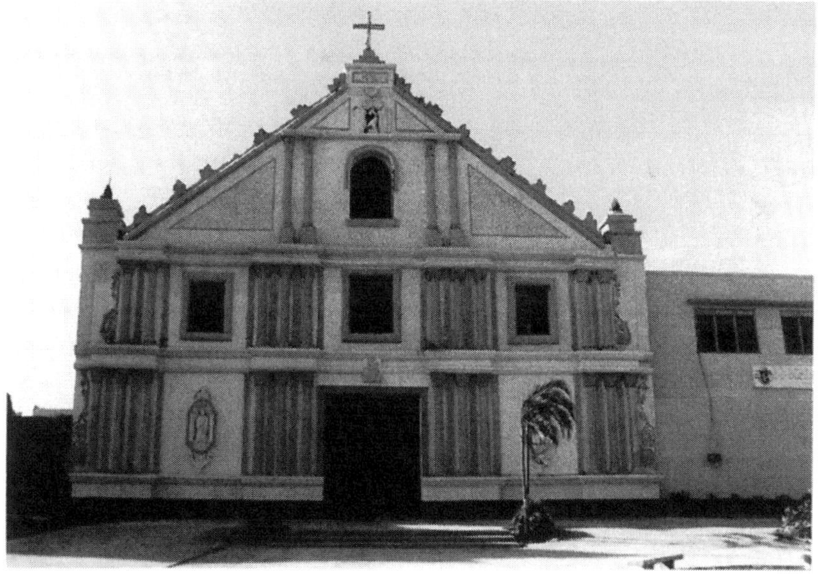

18 Jesuit mission church of the Immaculate Conception, Guiuan, Samar Island (Philippines), founded 1595, present church ca. 1700. Photograph courtesy of René Javellana.

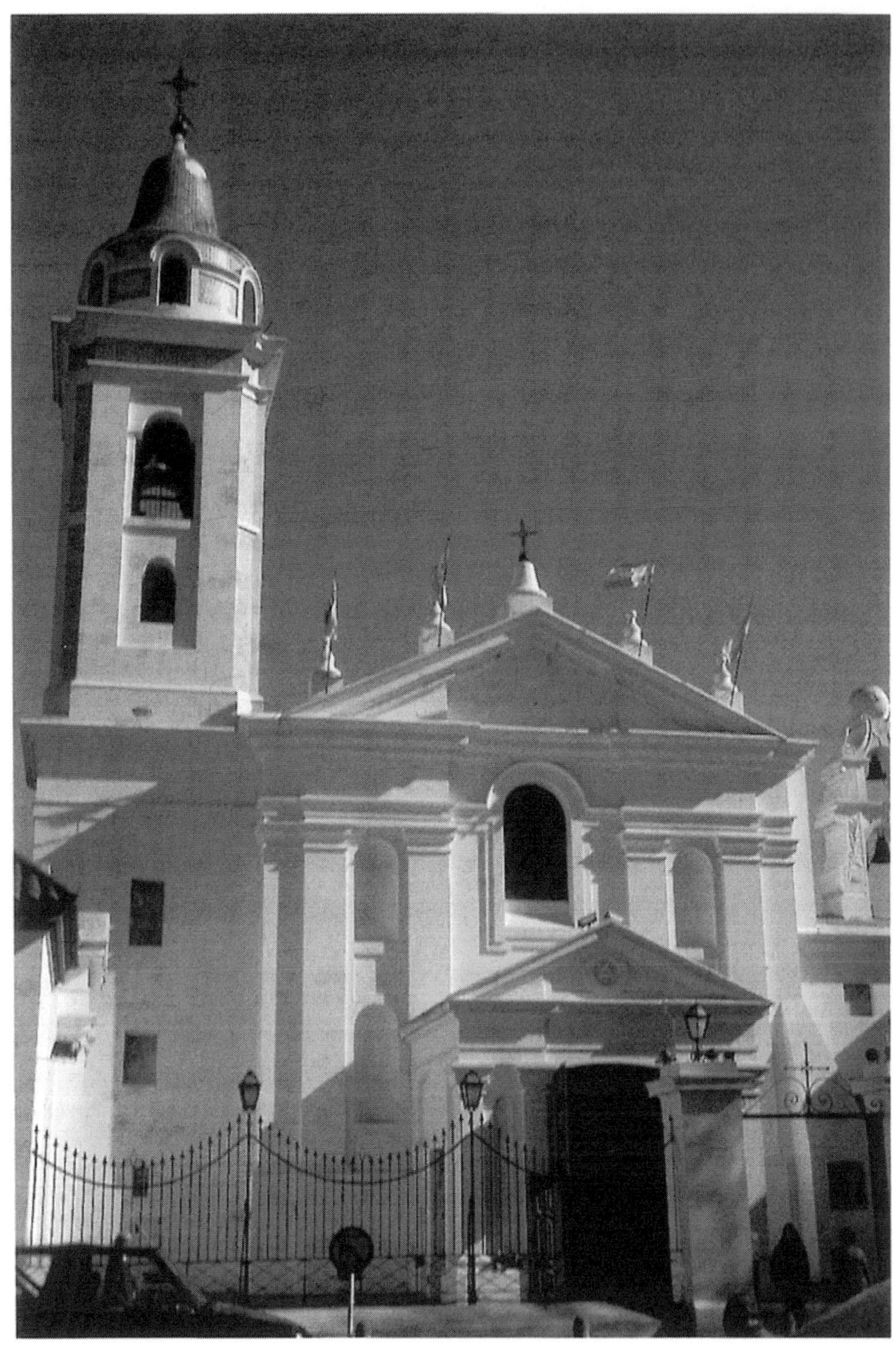

19 Church of Nuestra Señora del Pilar, Buenos Aires (Argentina), 1716–32. By Andrea Bianchi, S.J.

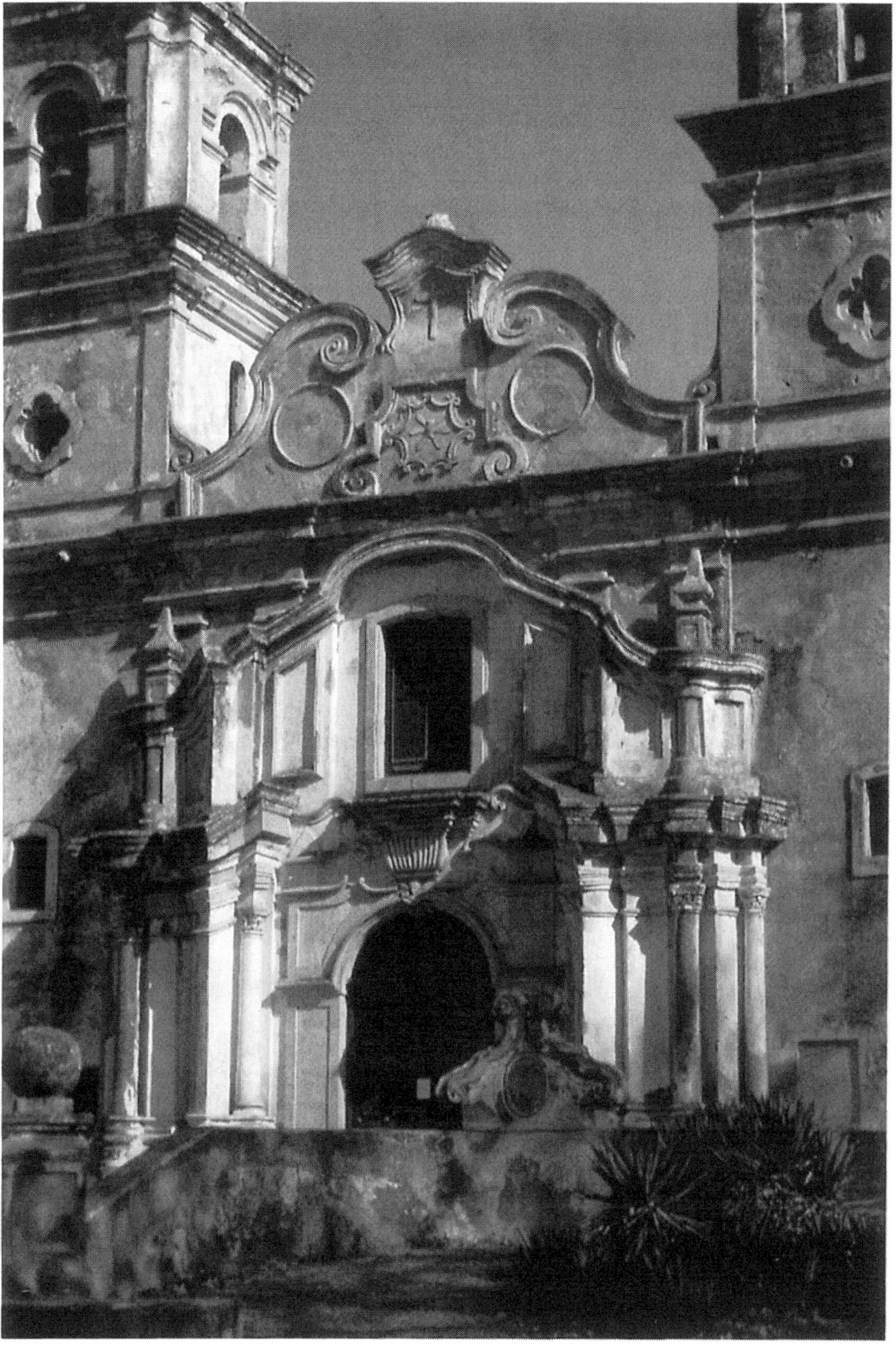

20 Jesuit *estancia* church of Santa Catalina, Sierras de Córdoba (Argentina), begun first third of 18th century. Façade by Anton Harls, S.J. (?).

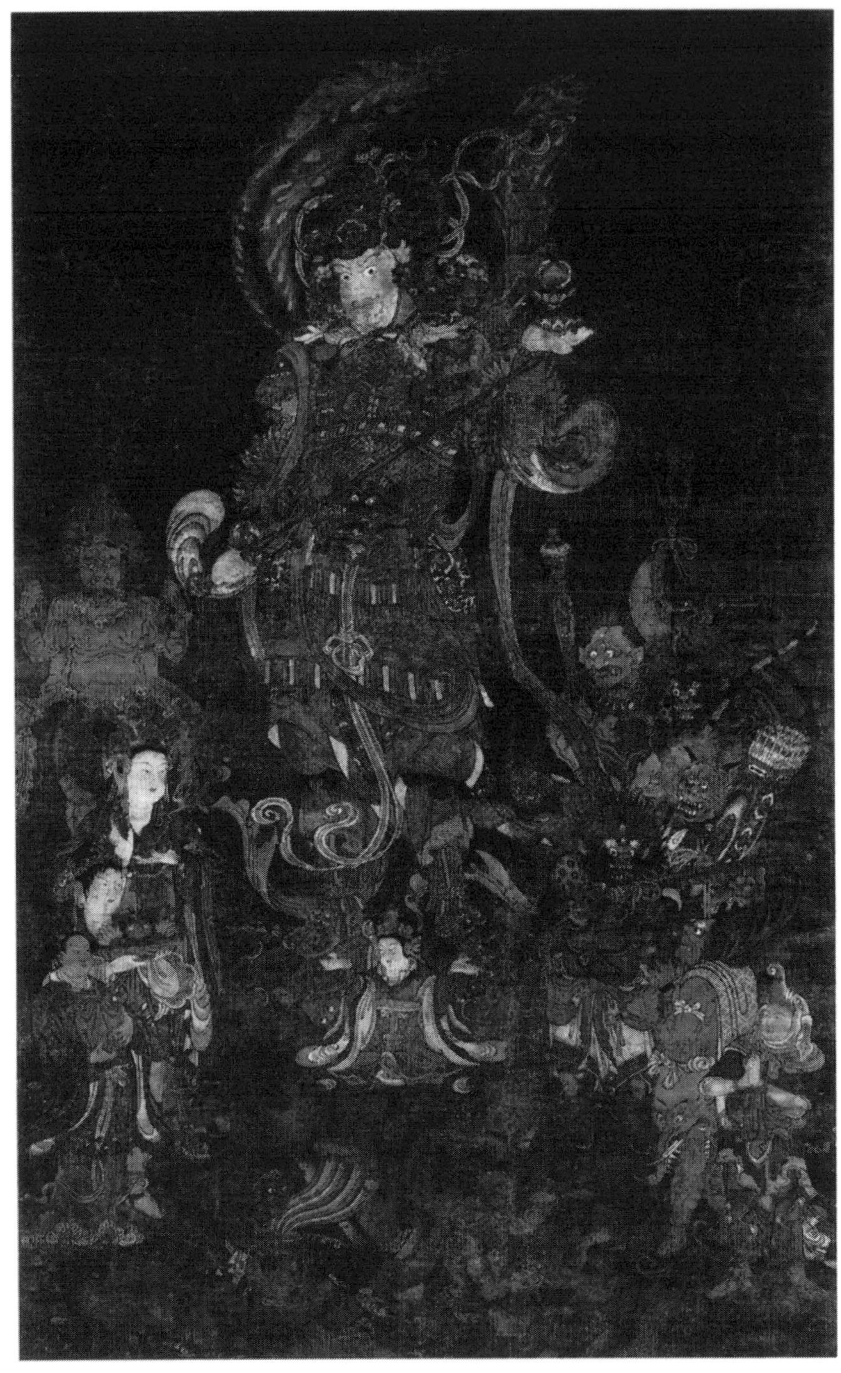

21 *Divine Guardian of the North with His Retinue (Tobatsu Bishamon-ten).* Japan, Kamakura Period, late 12th to early 13th century. Panel; ink, colours, and gold on silk (119 × 68 cm). Museum of Fine Arts, Boston, 05.202, Special Chinese and Japanese Fund. Courtesy Museum of Fine Arts, Boston.

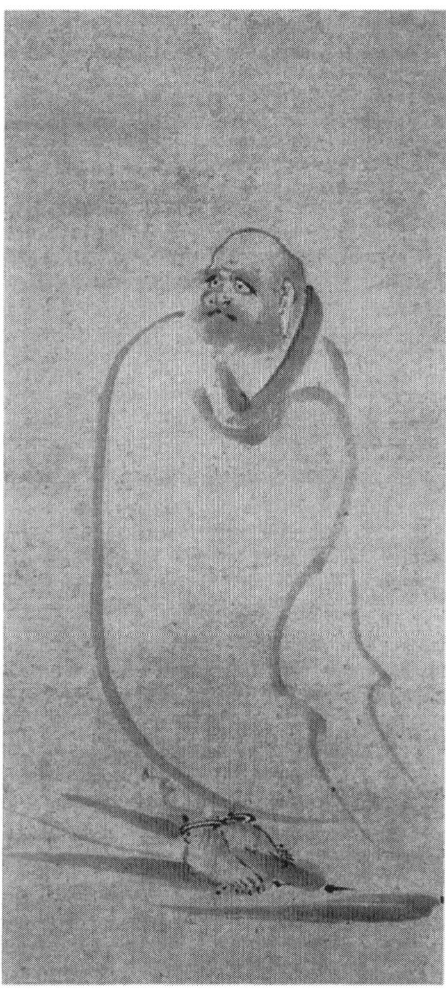

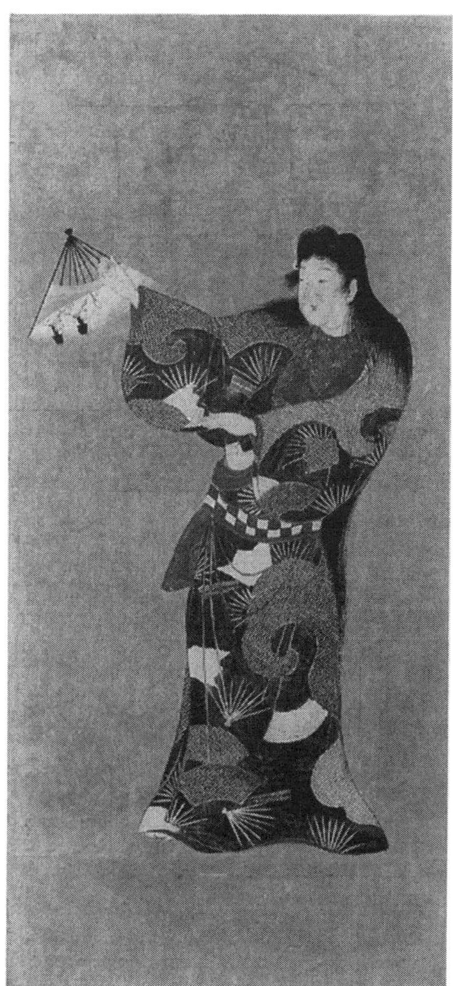

22 Fūgai (1568–1654): *Standing Daruma* (detail). Japan, Edo Period, 17th century. Hanging scroll; ink on paper. Private collection.

23 *Dancer.* Japan, Edo Period, 17th century. Folding screen (byōbu). Panel from a set of eleven; ink, colours, and gold on paper (75.5 × 36.9 cm). Museum of Fine Arts, Boston, 17.1091. Denman Waldo Ross Collection. Courtesy Museum of Fine Arts, Boston.

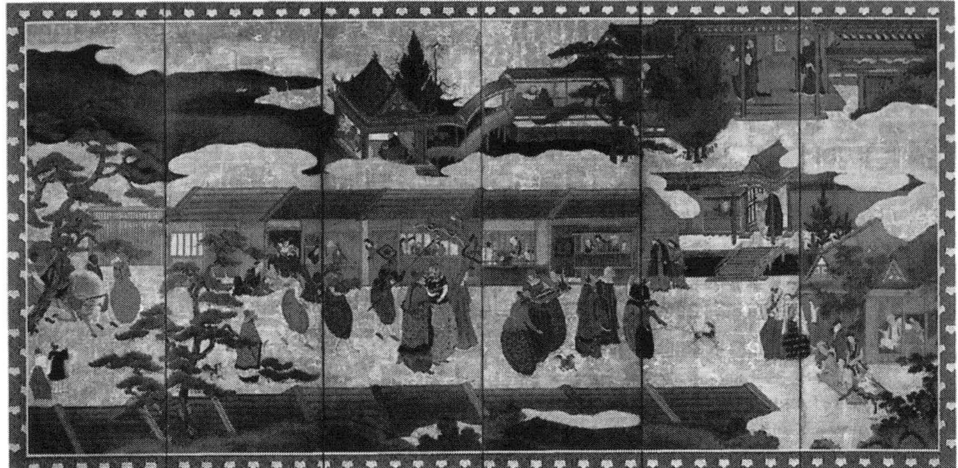

24 One of a pair of six-panel *namban byōbu*, early 17th century (Momoyama Period), colours and gold leaf on paper (each screen 1,530 × 3,310 cm). Courtesy of the Freer Gallery of Art, Washington. The complex on the upper right is a Jesuit church and mission.

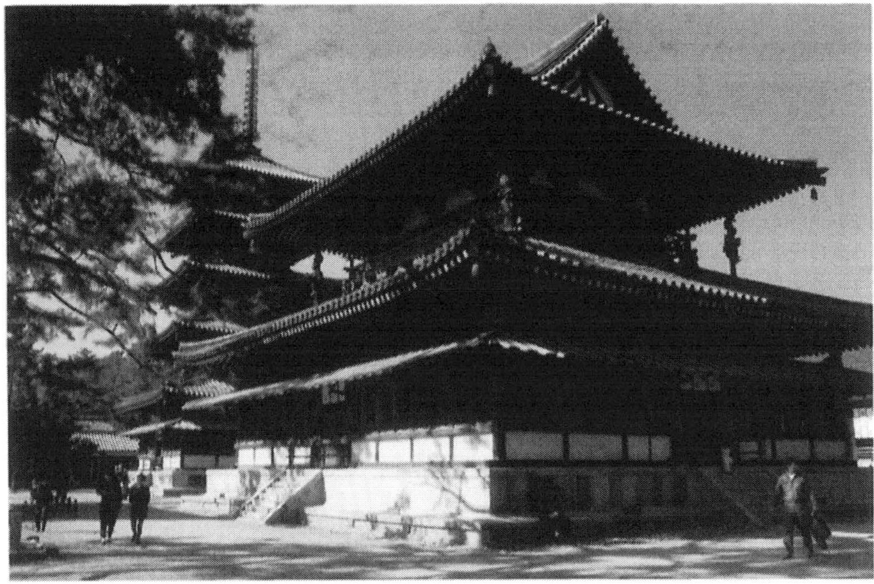

25 Hōryūji (Nara, Japan). Temple courtyard from the southeast showing the *kondō* (main worship hall, in later temples called *hondō*) and pagoda, 7th century. Built in a style imported from China, this is the prototype for Japanese Buddhist temples. Although predating the Jesuit encounter by centuries, its profile is virtually identical with that of the Jesuit church in Kyoto, the so-called Nambandera or Southern-Barbarian Temple.

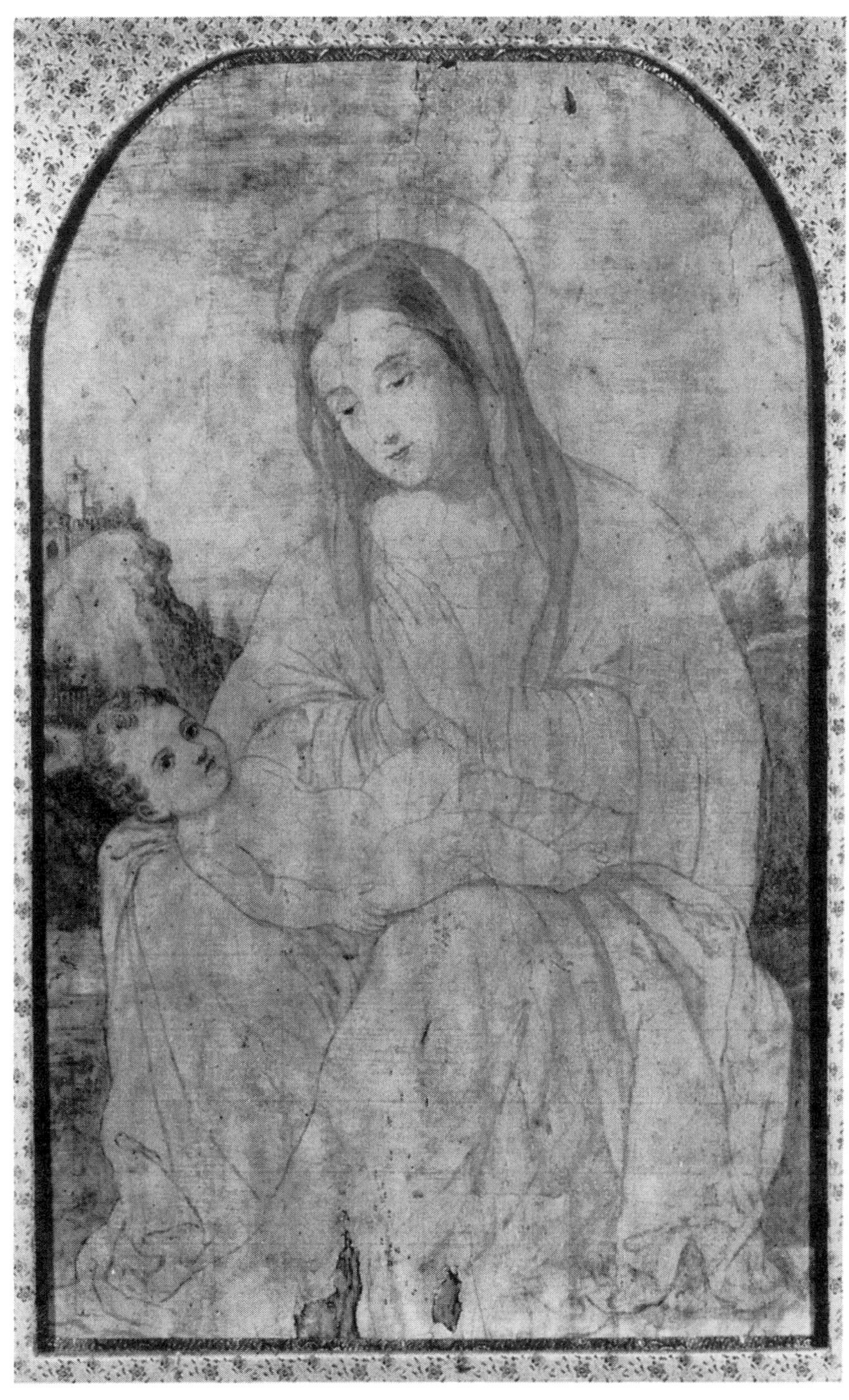

26 Giovanni Niccolò, S.J.: *Madonna and Child*, after 1583, *bozzetto*, oil on wood panel (58 × 36 cm), Nanban Bunka-kan, Osaka.

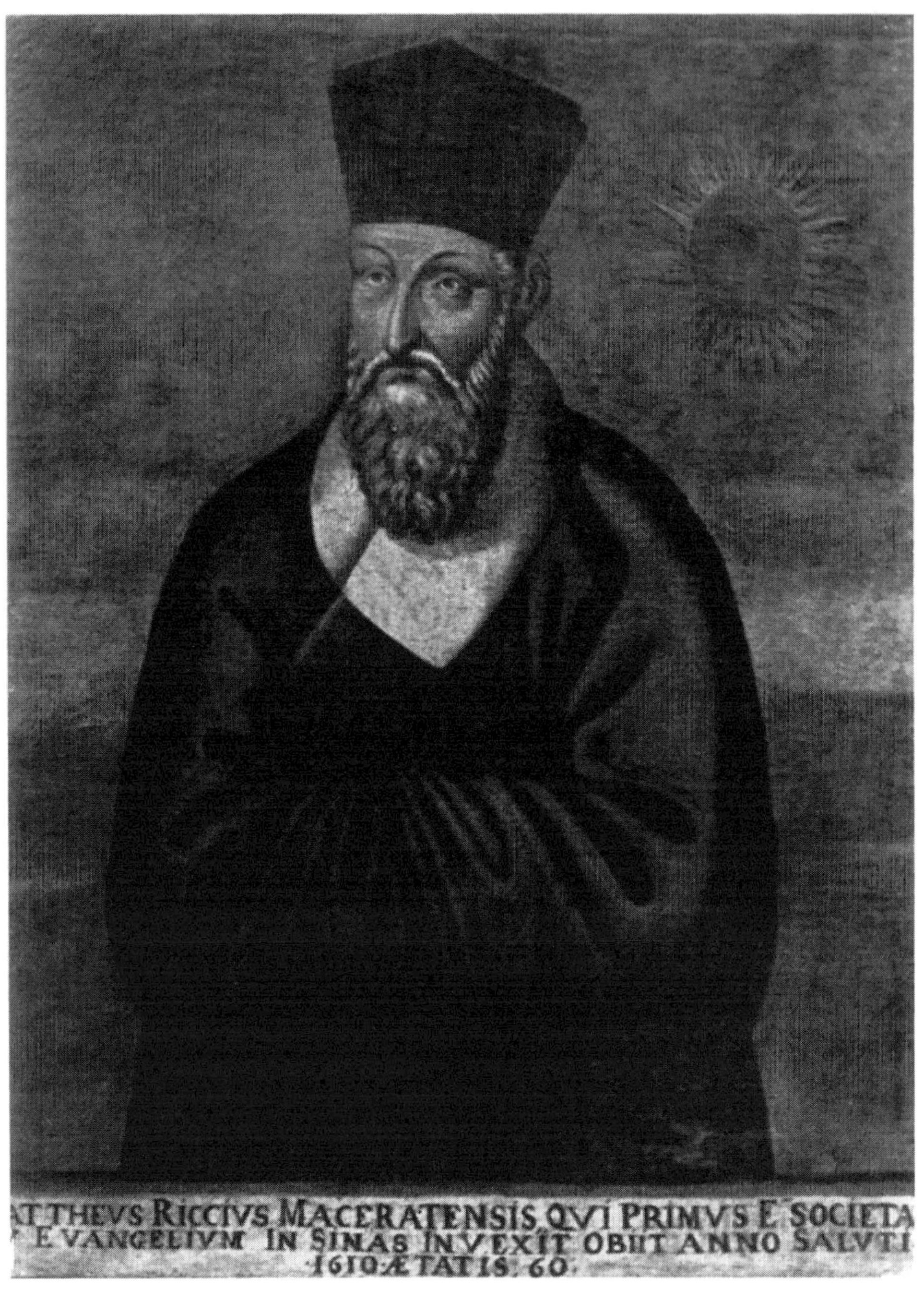

27 Yu Wenhui (Emanuel Pereira), S.J.: *Portrait of Matteo Ricci*, oil on canvas, ca 1610. Photograph courtesy of the Italian Province of the Society of Jesus.

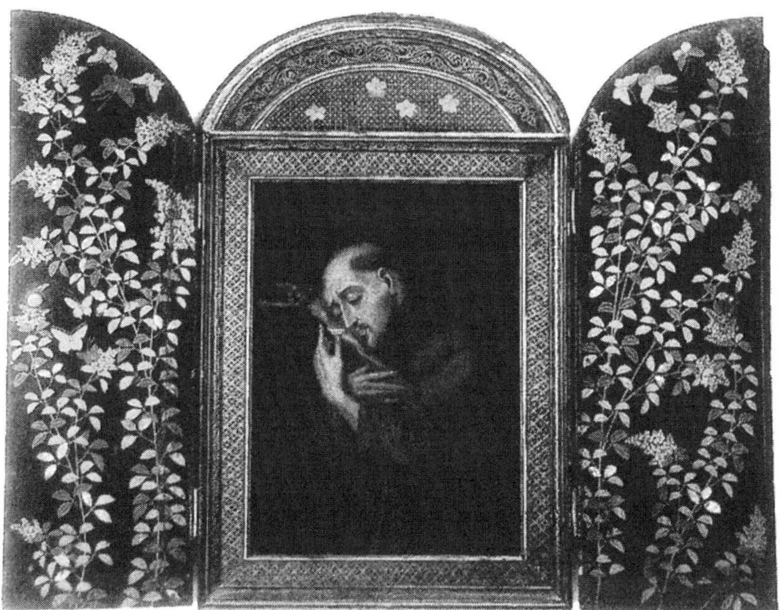

28 Niccolò school: *Saint Francis of Assisi*, ca. 1597, oil on wood panel (57 × 73 cm, open). *Namban* shrine, sold at Sotheby's, 'Japanese Works of Art, Prints, and Paintings' (13 June 1986), lot 726. Photograph courtesy of Sotheby's.

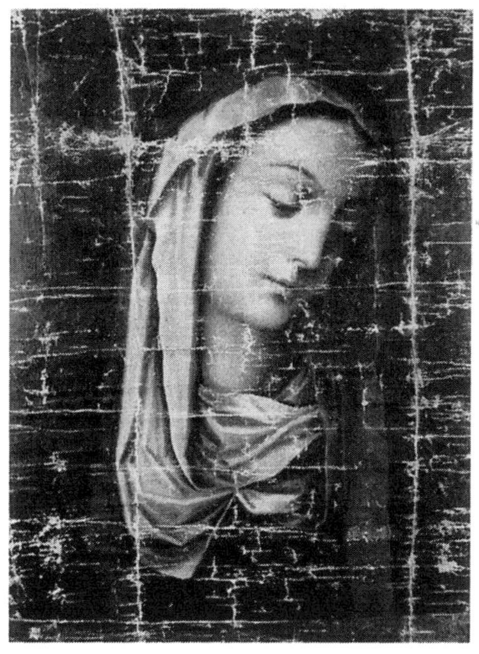

29 Niccolò school: *Dolorosa*, after 1583, oil on canvas (52.5 × 40 cm). Namban Bunka-kan, Osaka (see fig. 69).

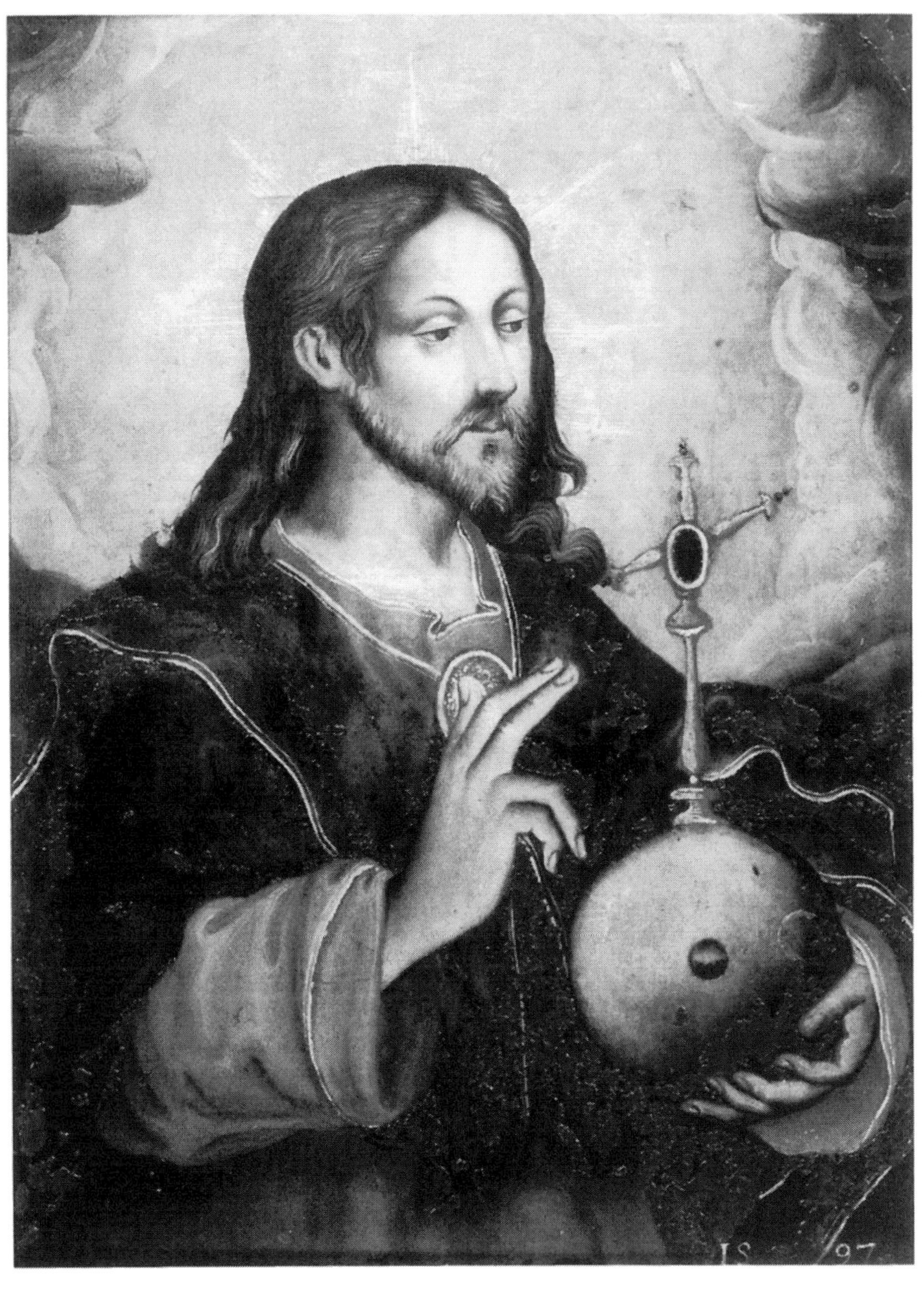

30 Signed Sacam Iacobus: *Salvator Mundi* (23 × 17 cm), dated 1597, oil on copper panel. General Library, University of Tokyo Library System. A100: 1649.

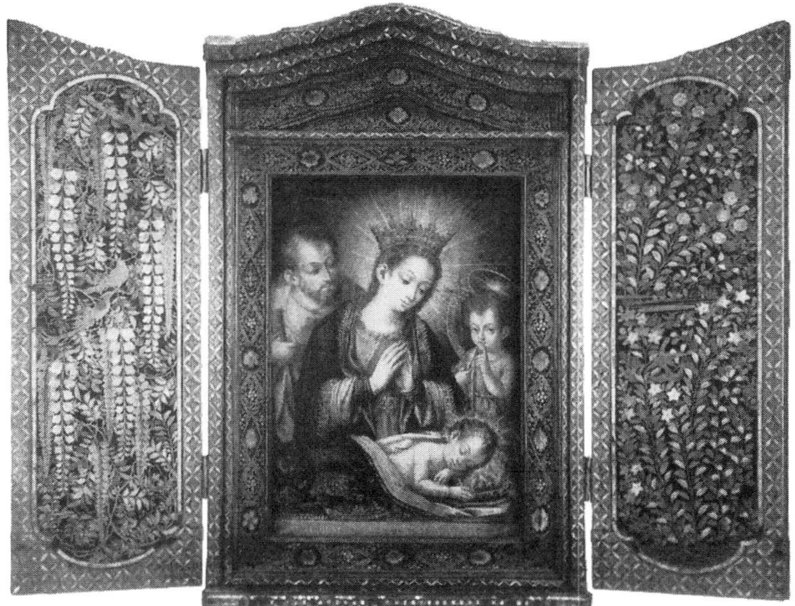

31 Niccolò school: *Holy Family with St John the Baptist*, ca. 1597, oil on copper. *Namban* shrine (39.5 × 61.5 cm), private collection. Sold at Sotheby's, 'Japanese Works of Art' (13 Nov. 1985), lot 52. Photograph courtesy of Sotheby's. The same artist executed figures 32 and 33.

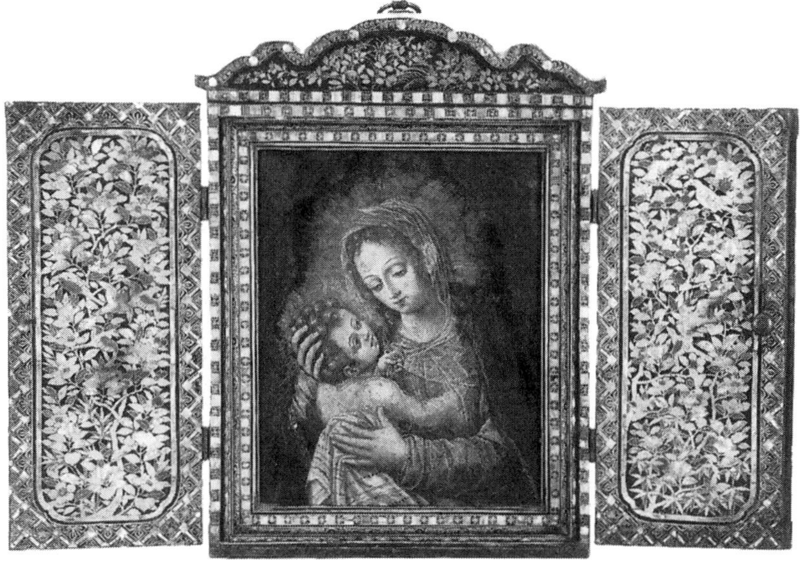

32 Niccolò school: *Madonna and Child*, ca. 1597, oil on wood panel. *Namban* shrine (38 × 55 cm). Sold at Sotheby's, 'Important Japanese Works of Art, Ceramics and Swords' (12 June 1985). Photograph courtesy of Suntory Museum of Art, Tokyo.

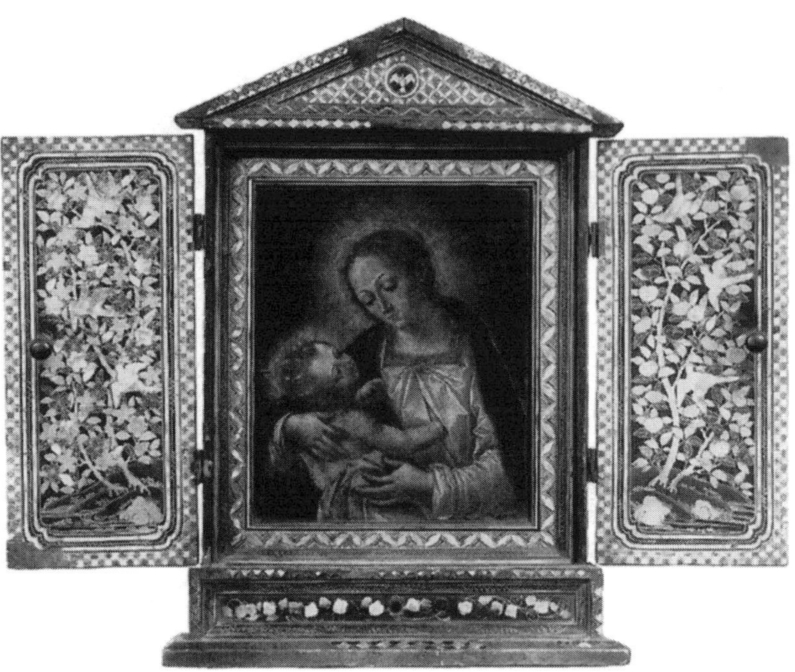

33 Niccolò school: *Madonna and Child*, ca. 1597, oil on wood panel. *Namban* shrine (20.5 × 17.5 cm), Museum Catharijneconvent, Utrecht, ABM s00093.

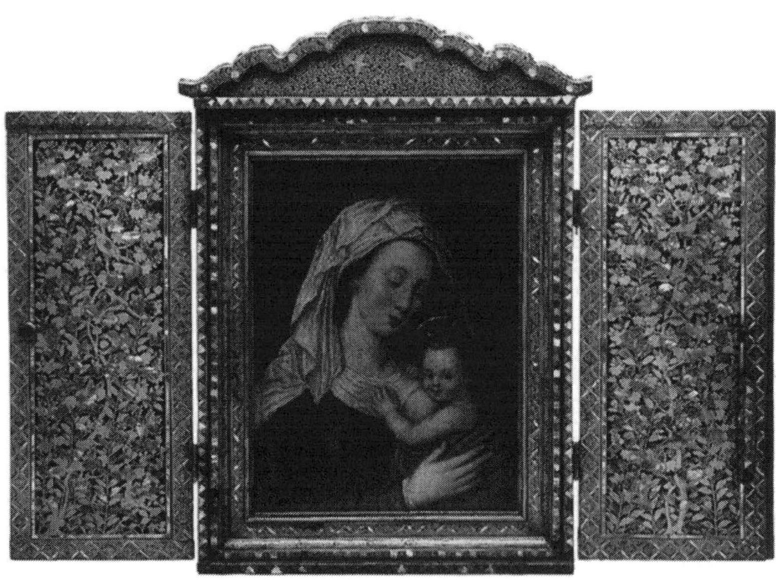

34 Niccolò school: *Madonna and Child*, ca. 1597, oil on wood panel. *Namban* shrine (45.5 × 32 × 4.5 cm), private collection. Sold at Christie's (New York), 'Japanese Art' (24 April 1997), lot 183. Photograph courtesy of Christie's.

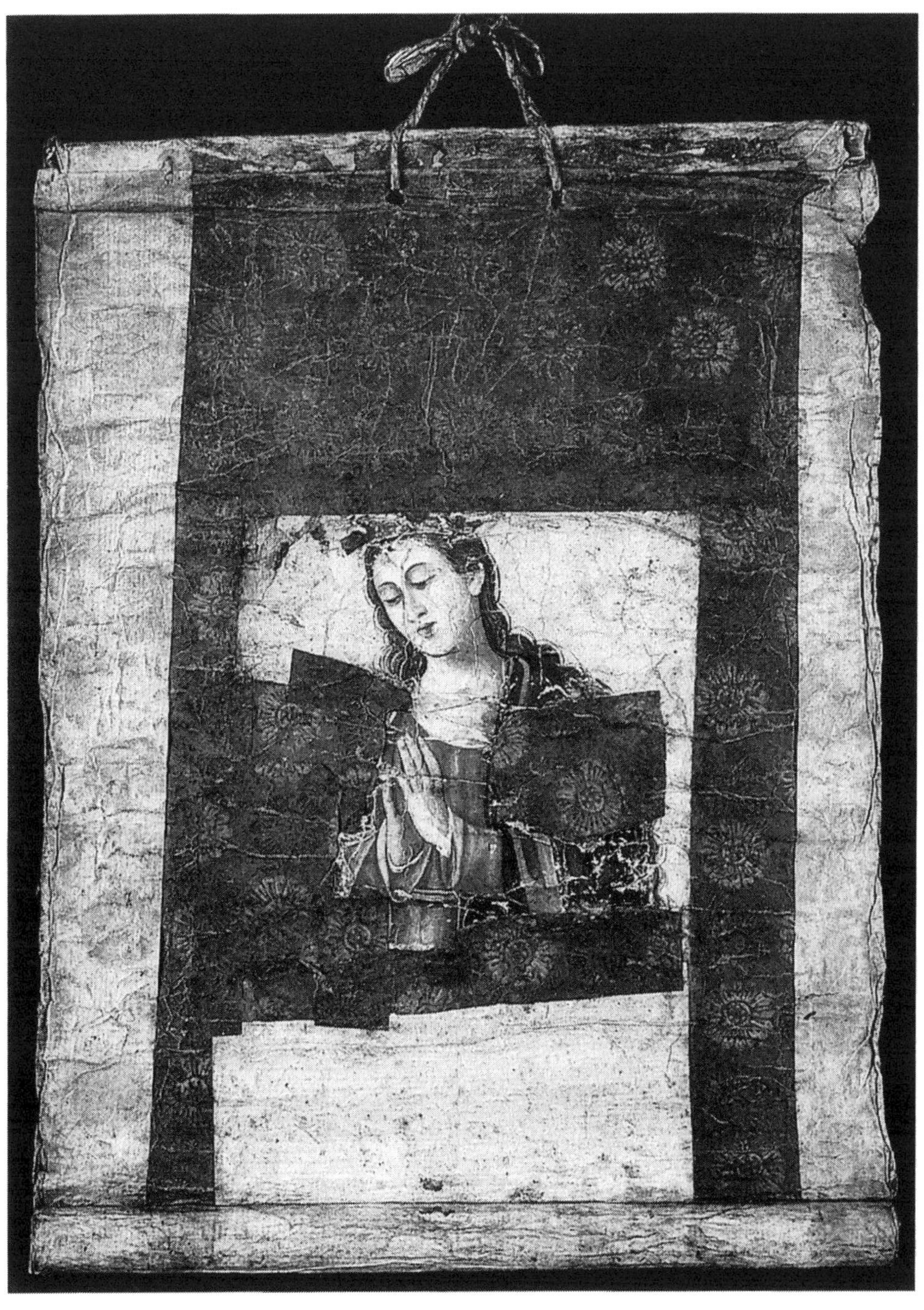

35 Niccolò school: *Madonna of the Snows*, after 1583, oil and Japanese colours on paper, mounted on a hanging scroll (17 × 12 cm). Twenty-six Martyrs Museum, Nagasaki. Photograph courtesy of Diego Yuuki, S.J.

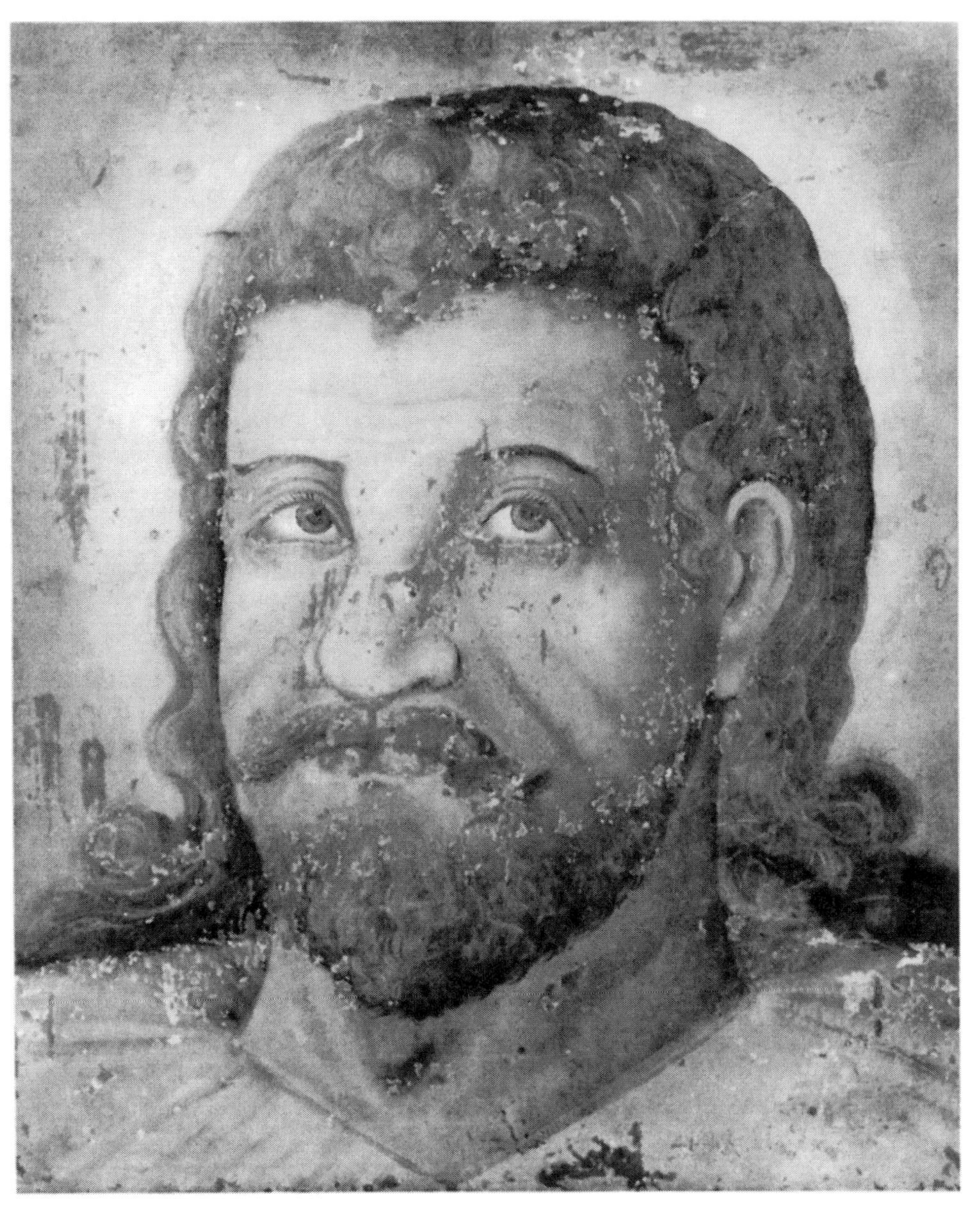

36 Niccolò school: *Salvator Mundi* (?), oil on copper panel, first or second quarter of 17th century (48 × 40.5 cm), courtesy of the Tokyo National Museum.

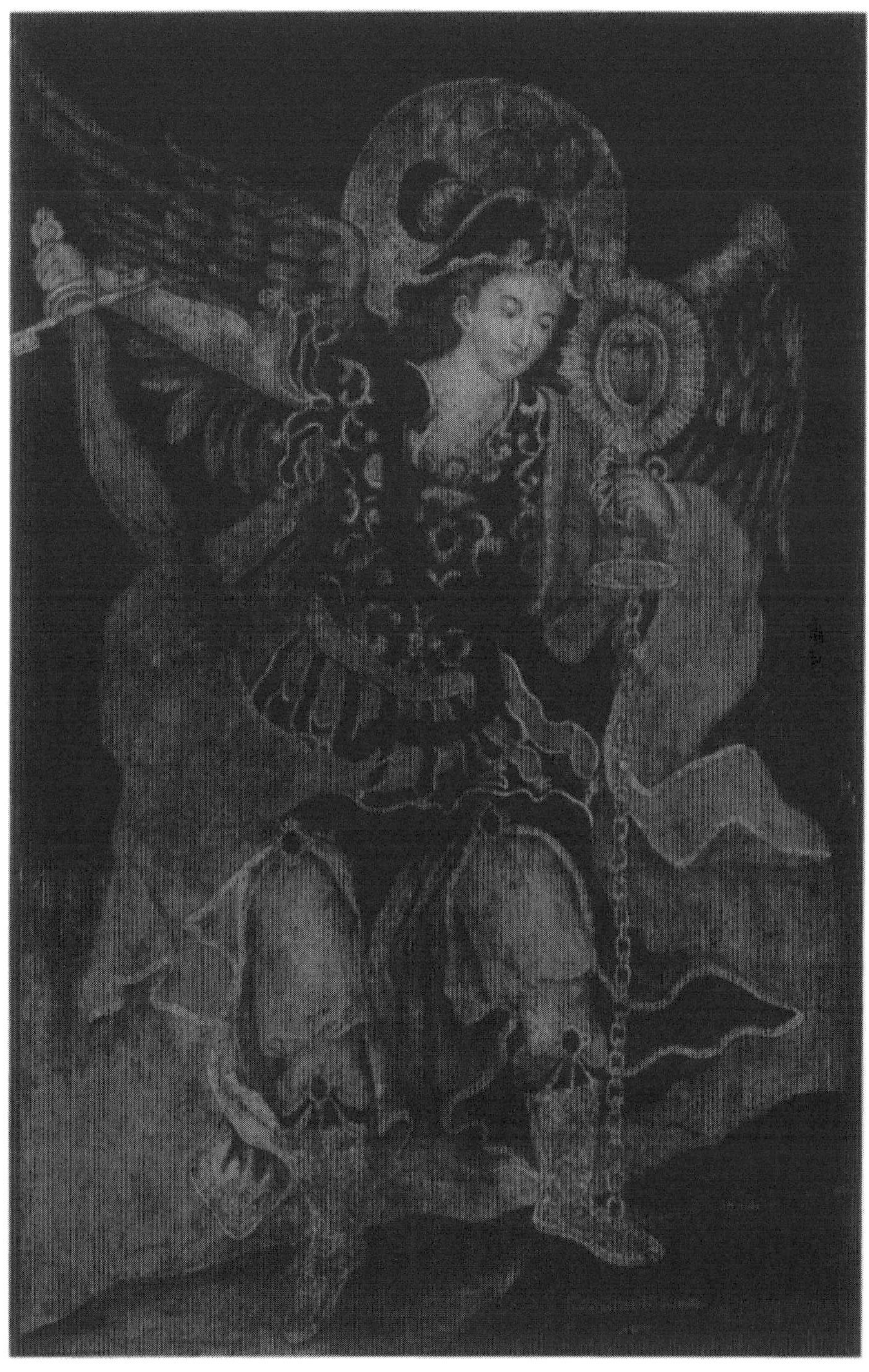

37 Niccolò school: *Saint Michael Slaying the Dragon*, oil on wood panel, probably ca. 1630s (202 × 133 cm). Seminario de São José, Macao.

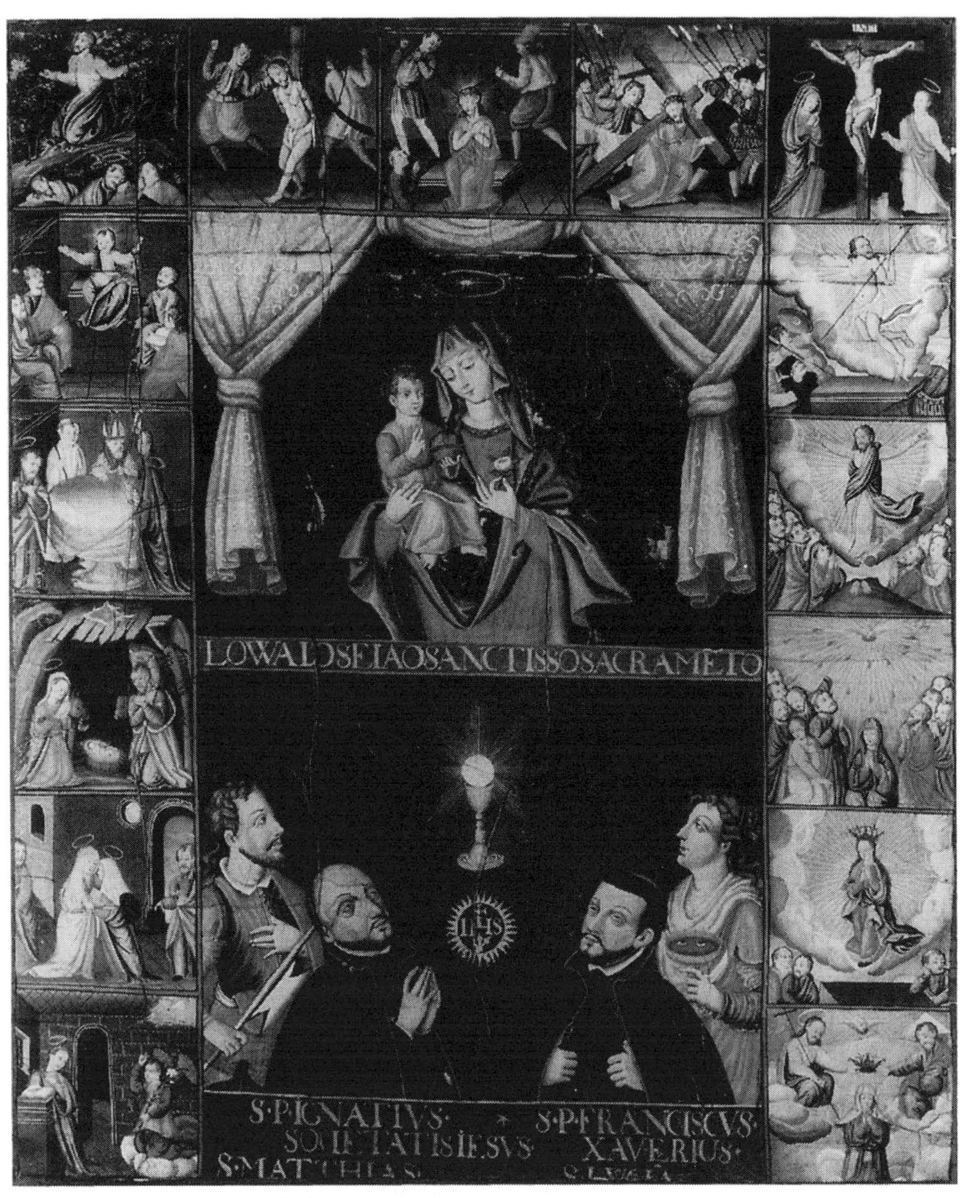

38 Niccolò school: *Mysteries of the Rosary*, ca. late 1640s, oil and Japanese colours on paper (81.6 × 64.8 cm). Courtesy of the Kyoto University Natural History Museum.

SANCTOS
NOGOSAGVEONO
VCHINVQIGAQI
quan dai ichi.

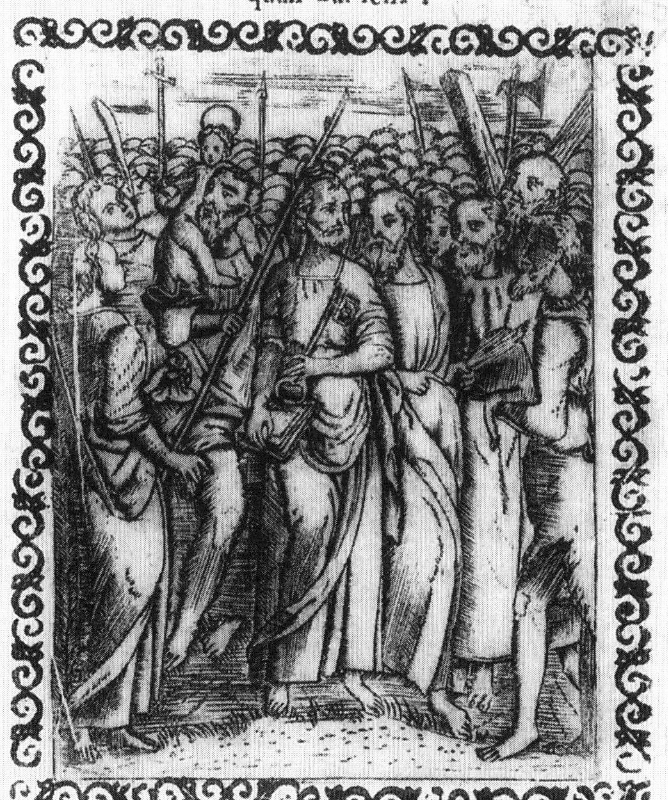

FIIENNOCVNITACACVNOGVN
IESVSNOCOMPANHIANOCOLLEGIO
Cazzuſa ni voite Superiores no von yuruxi uo cò
muri core uo fan to naſu mono nari. Goxuxxe irai
MDLXXXXI.

39 Title page from *Sanctos no Gosagueo no Uchi Nuquigaqi* (Selections from the Acts of the Saints), printed in Katsusa in 1591. The Bodleian Library, University of Oxford, Arch Bf.69.

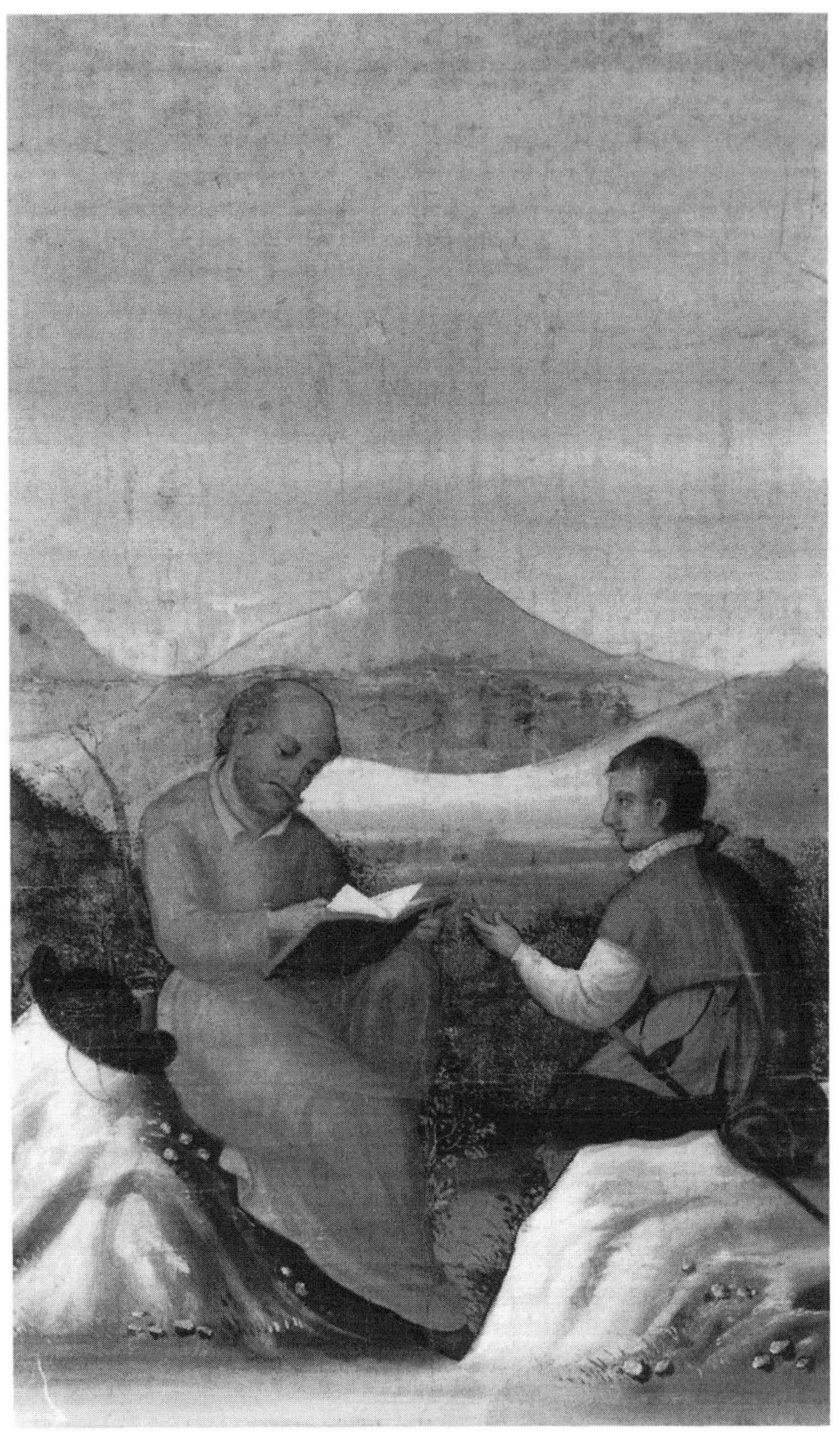

40 Kanō school: Western genre scene with a young man and a hermit. Section of a folding screen, colours on paper (126 × 48.7 cm). Namban Bunka-kan, Osaka.

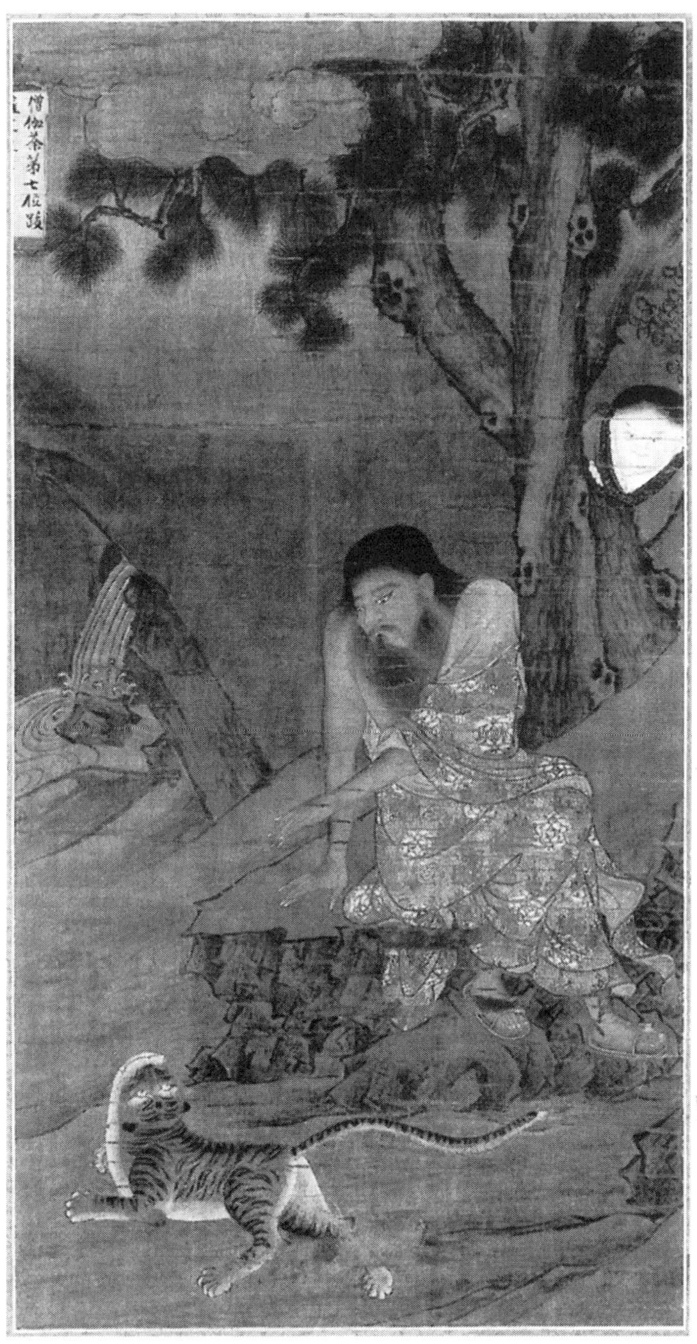

41 Lu Xinzhong: *The Seventh Lohan Bhadra*. China, Southern Song Dynasty, late 12th century. Hanging scroll mounted as panel; ink, colour, and gold on silk (80 × 41.5 cm). Museum of Fine Arts, Boston, William Sturgis Bigelow Collection. Courtesy Museum of Fine Arts, Boston.

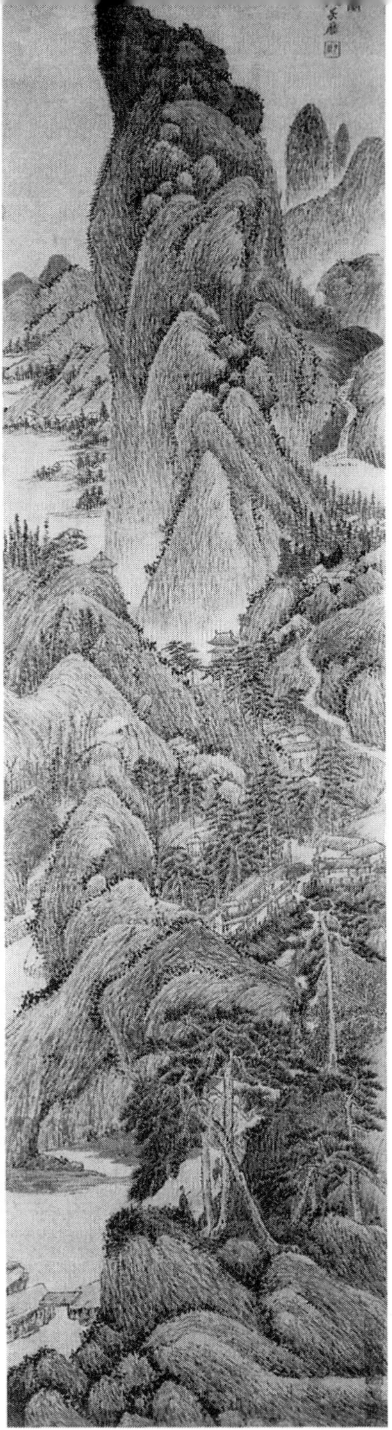

42 Wu Li, S.J. (1632–1718): *Pine Winds from Myriad Valleys*. China, Qing Dynasty, undated, ca. early 18th century. Hanging scroll, ink on paper (10.5 × 25.5 cm). Cleveland Museum of Art, John L. Severance Fund, 1954.584. © The Cleveland Museum of Art.

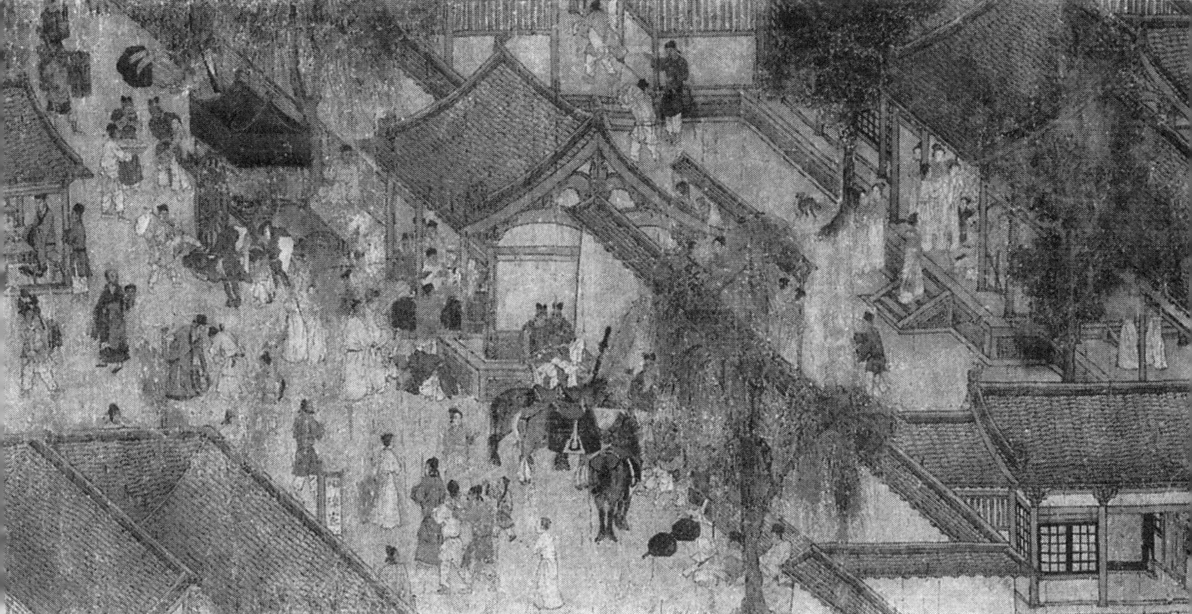

43 *Lady Wenji's Return to China: Wenji Arriving Home.* China, Southern Song Dynasty, second quarter of 12th century (25 × 55.8 cm). Museum of Fine Arts, Boston, 28.65. Denman Waldo Ross Collection. Courtesy Museum of Fine Arts, Boston.

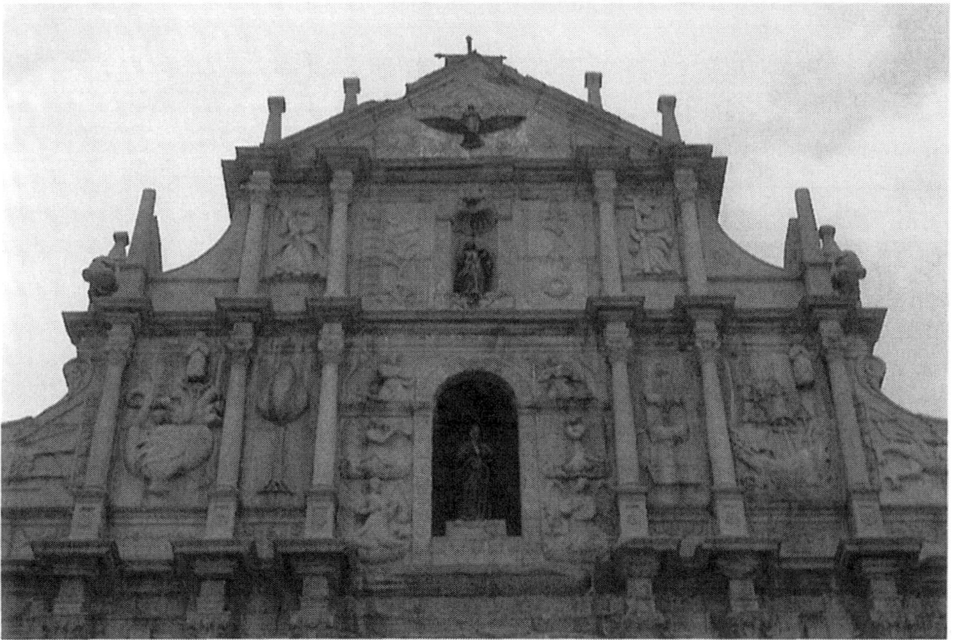

44 Jesuit collegiate church of Nossa Senhora da Assunção or Madre de Deus, Macao, popularly known as São Paulo; façade, begun 1601 (detail of upper part). The angels flanking the central niche resemble Buddhist *apsasas* figures.

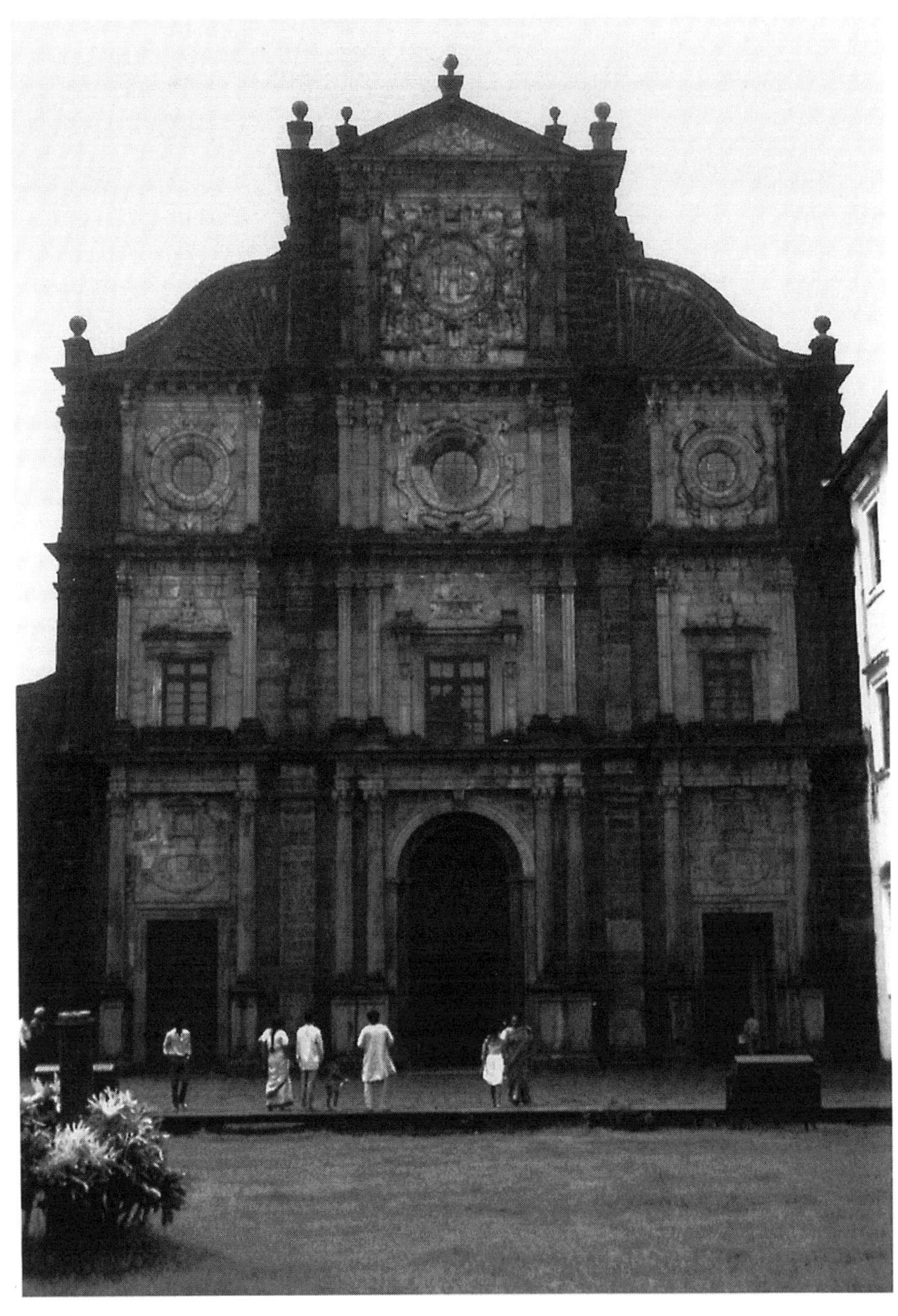

45 Jesuit church of Bom Jesus, Goa (India), built 1594–1605.

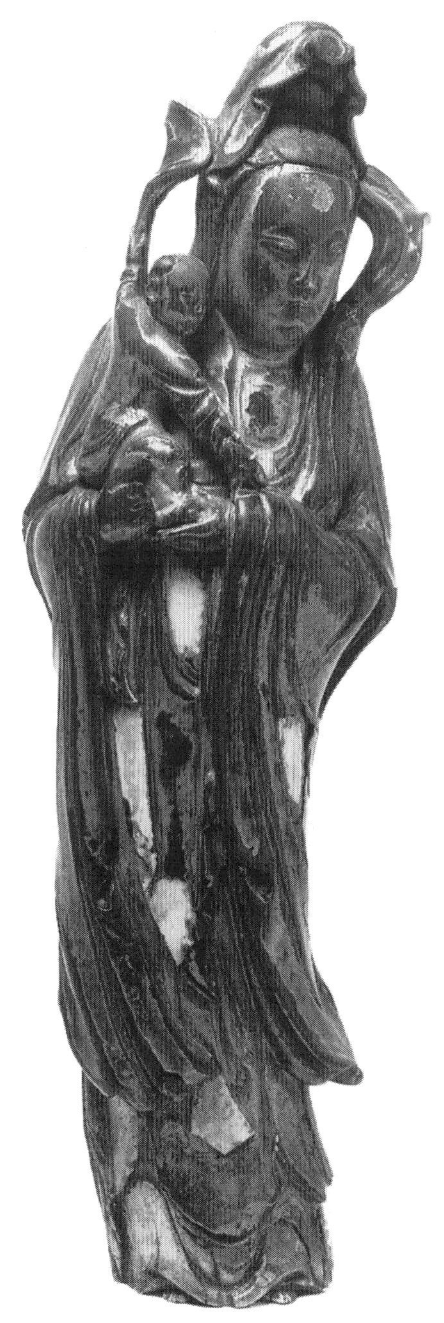

46 *Guanyin as 'Bringer of Sons.'* China, Ming Dynasty, ca. 1580–1640. Lacquered and gilt ivory (h. 32 cm). Victoria and Albert Museum, London, A15.1935. © The Board and Trustees of the Victoria and Albert Museum.

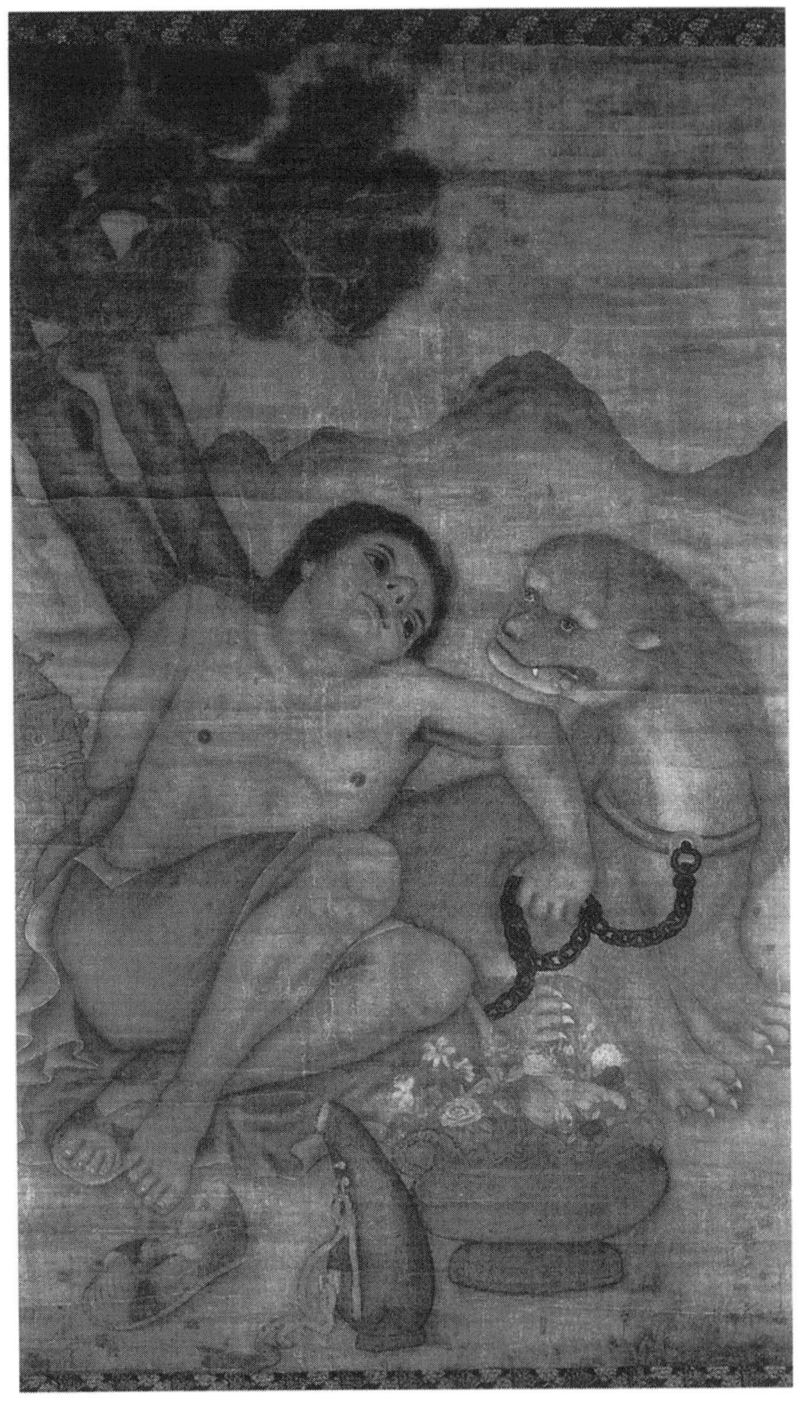

47 *The Seventh Lohan Bhadra (?)* China, Ming Dynasty, early 17th century (?) Ink and colours on silk. Private collection, Japan. Photograph courtesy of the Machida City Museum of Graphic Arts.

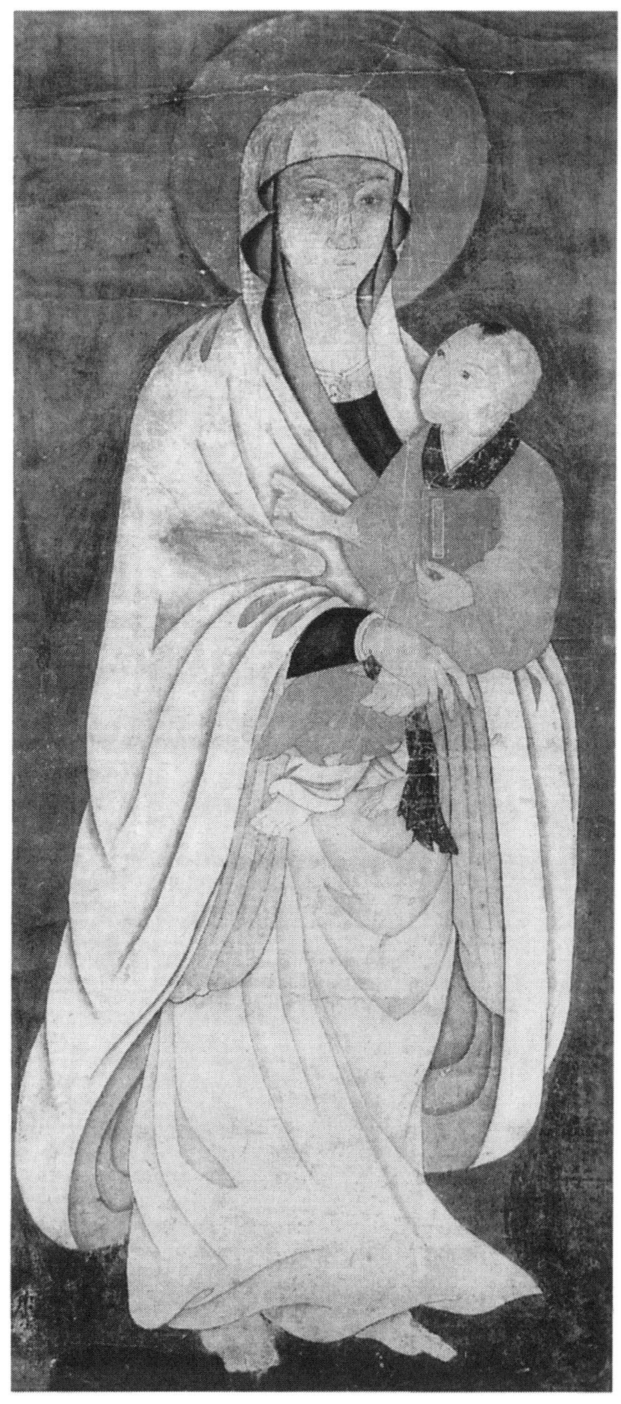

48 *Madonna of Saint Luke*. China, Ming Dynasty, late 16th to early 17th century. Ink and colours on silk. © The Field Museum, Chicago, IL., neg. # C5A33288.

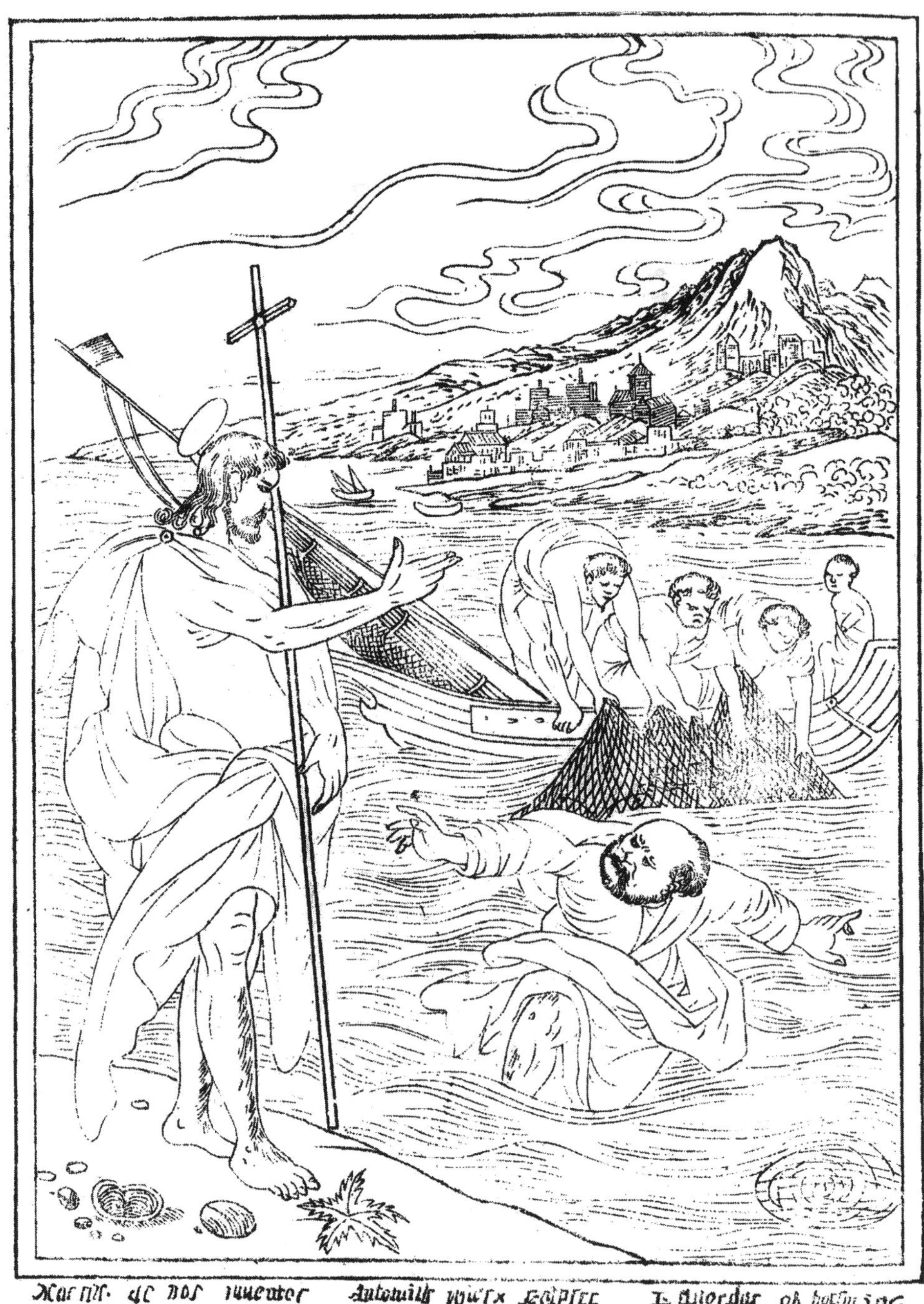

49 *The Calling of Saint Peter*. Woodblock print from Cheng Dayue and Cheng Shifang, *Master Cheng's Garden of Ink Cakes* (*Chengshi moyuan*), 1606. After an engraving by Wierix. By courtesy of the Percival David Foundation of Chinese Art, London.

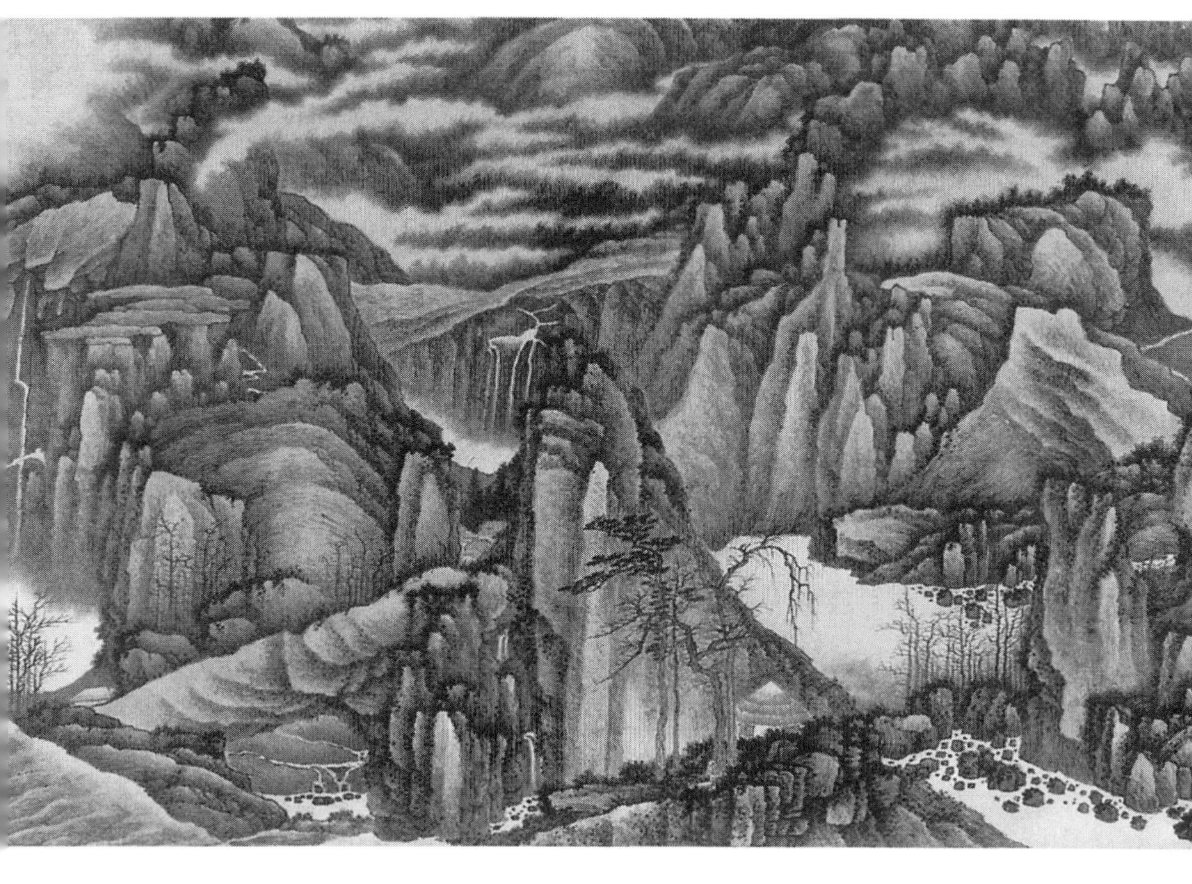

50 Gong Xian (ca. 1617–89): *A Thousand Peaks and Myriad Ravines*. China, late Ming or early Qing Dynasty, mid-17th century. Ink on paper. Museum Reitberg, Zürich, Drenowatz Collection. Photograph courtesy of Wettstein & Kauf.

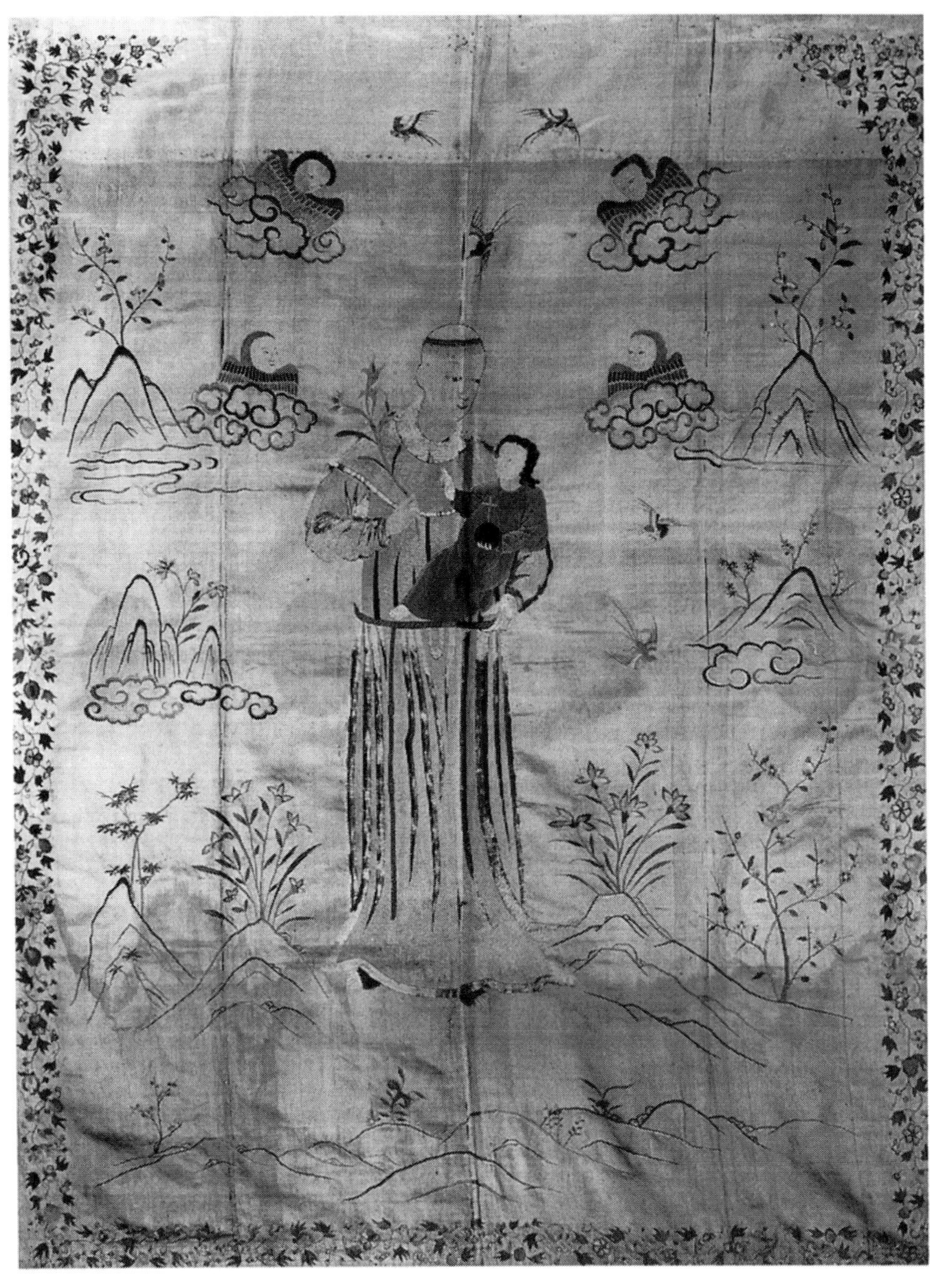

51 *Saint Anthony of Padua*. China, Qing Dynasty, late 17th century. Embroidered satin hanging. Victoria and Albert Museum, London, T246-1921. © The Board and Trustees of the Victoria and Albert Museum.

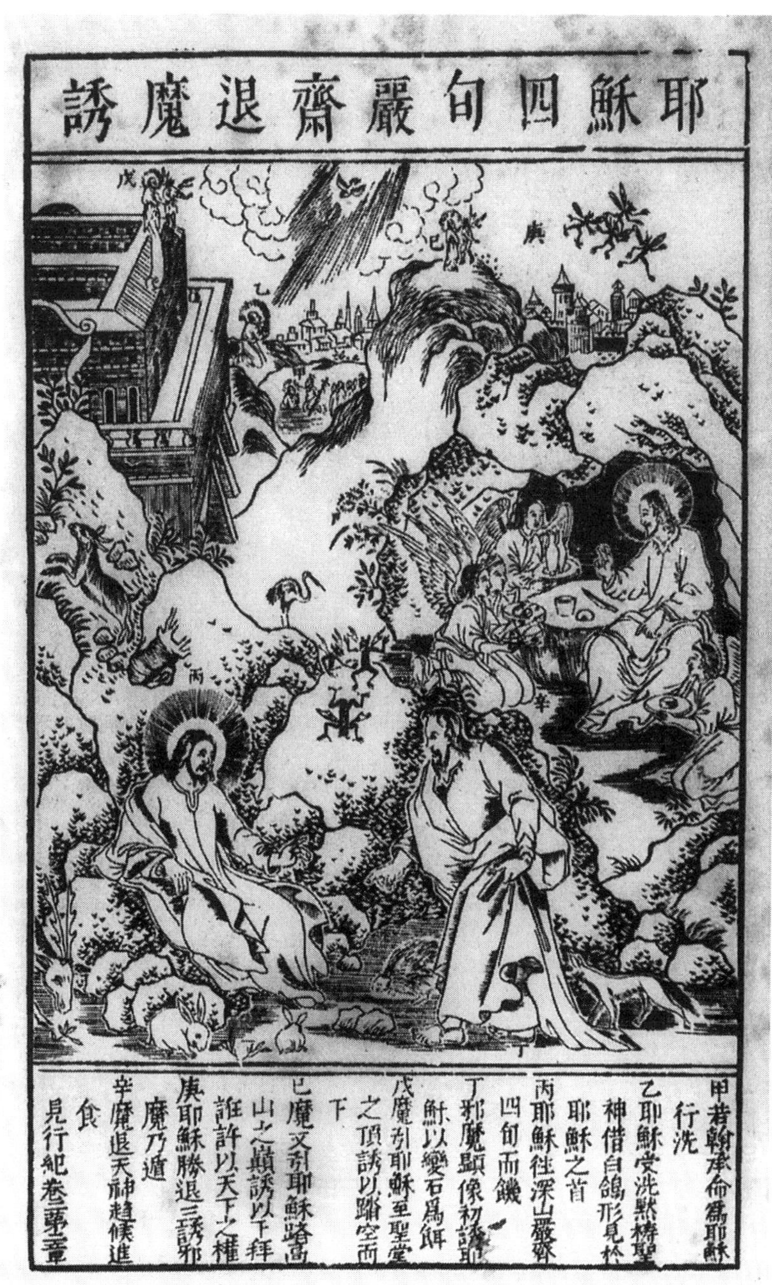

52 *Temptation in the Wilderness*, woodblock print. One of a series of fifty woodblocks to accompany the *Illustrated Explanation of the Incarnation of the Lord of Heaven (Tian zhu jiang sheng chu xiang jing jie)*, by Guilio Aleni, S.J. (Jinjiang, Fujian Province, China, 1637). Bibliothèque Nationale, Paris, Chinois 6750.

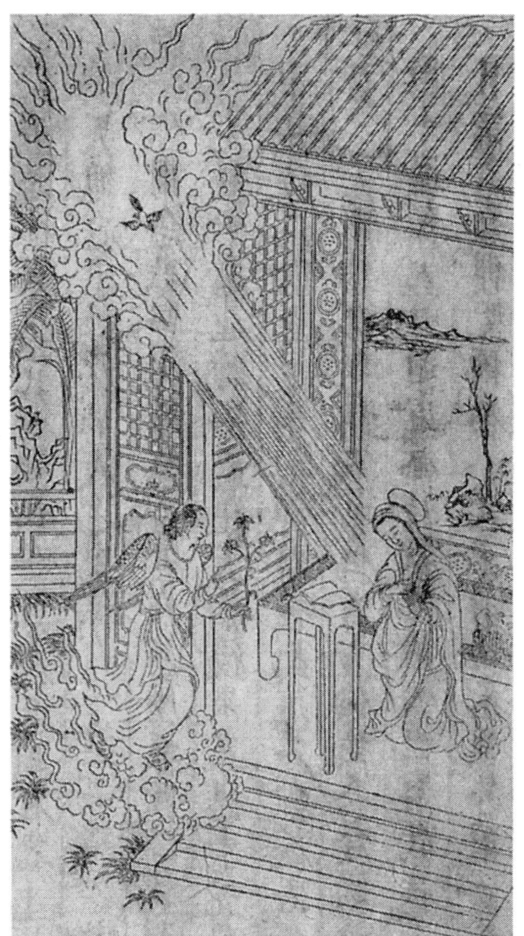

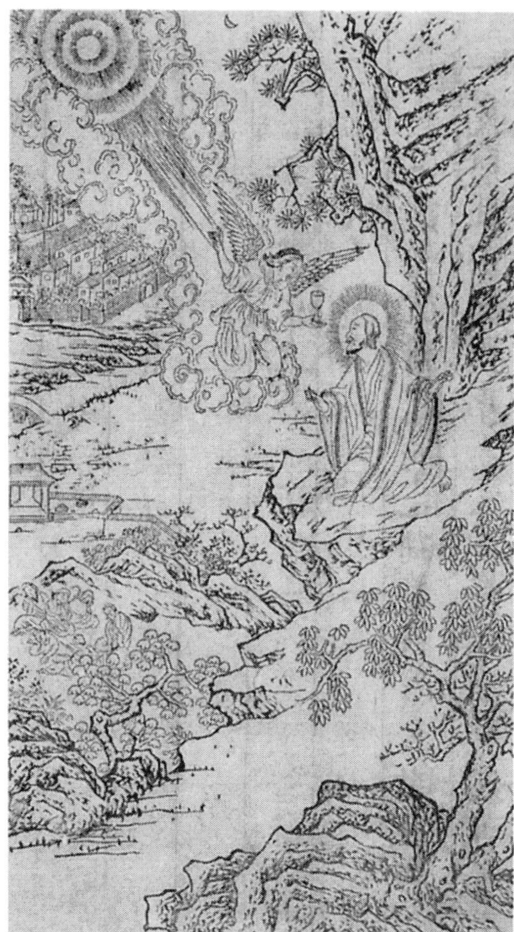

53 *Annunciation.* One of a series of fifteen woodblocks printed in 1608 to illustrate a *Metodo de Rosario (Song nian zhu gui cheng)*, by Ricci's colleague Juan da Rocha, S.J. (China). ARSI, Rome, Jap-Sin I, 43. Courtesy ARSI.

54 *The Agony in the Garden.* Woodblock print from Rocha (1608). ARSI, Rome, Jap-Sin I, 43. Courtesy ARSI.

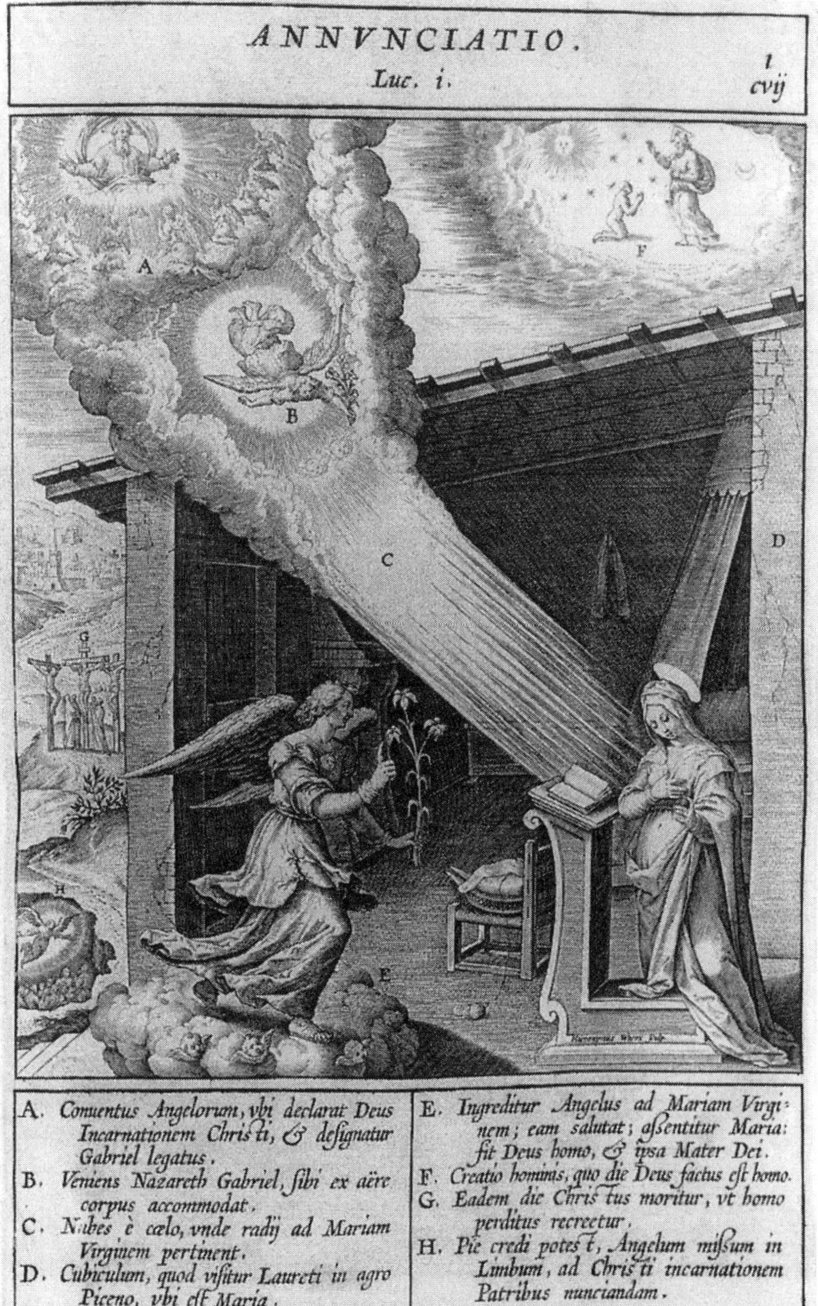

55 *Annunciation*. Engraving from Jerome Nadal's *Adnotationes et Meditationes in Evangelia* (Antwerp, 1593). Courtesy John J. Burns Library, Boston College.

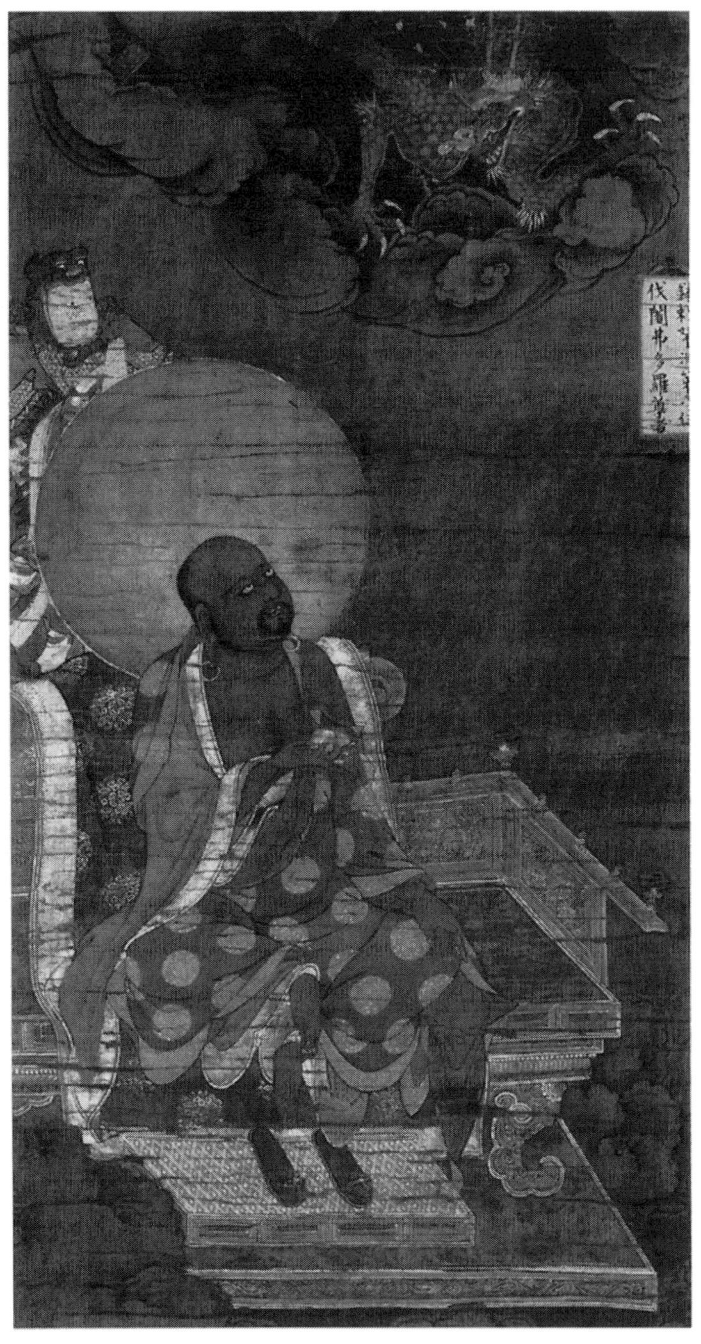

56 Lu Xinzhong, *The Eighth Lohan Vajraputra*. China, Southern Song Dynasty, late 13th to early 14th century. Hanging scroll mounted as panel; ink, colours, and gold on silk (80 × 41.5 cm). Museum of Fine Arts, Boston, 11.6124. William Sturgis Bigelow Collection. Courtesy Museum of Fine Arts, Boston.

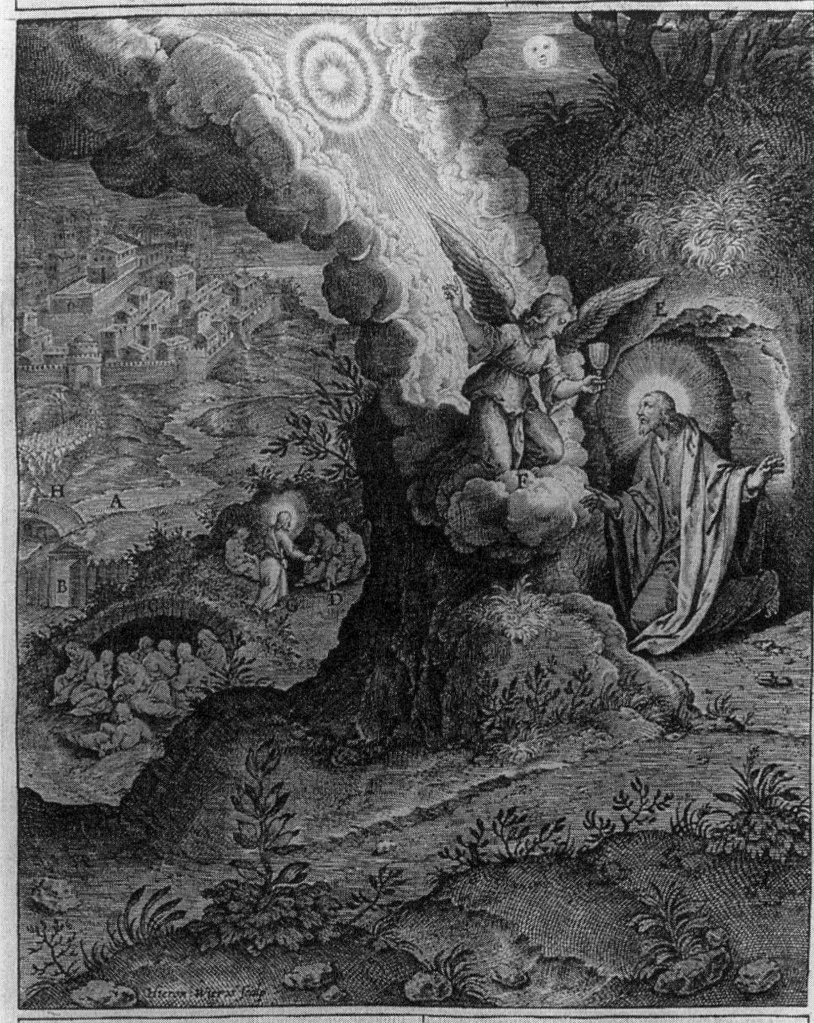

57 *The Agony in the Garden*. Engraving from Nadal (1593). Courtesy John J. Burns Library, Boston College.

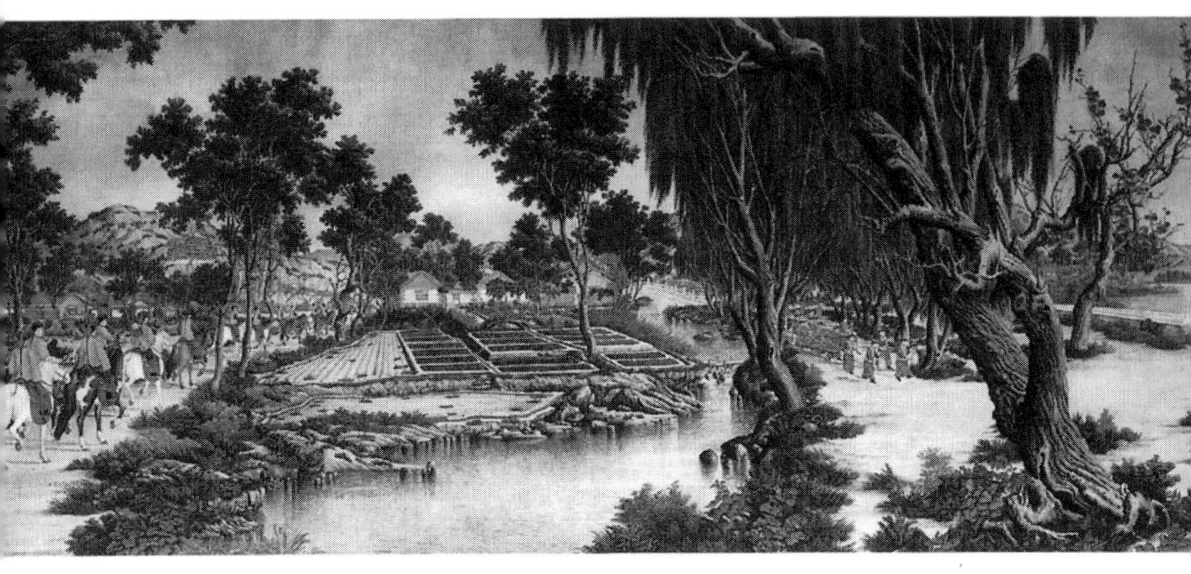

58 *Imperial Procession*, signed Giuseppe Castiglione, S.J. (detail), before 1766. Horizontal scroll; ink and colours on silk. Courtesy Freer Gallery of Art, Washington.

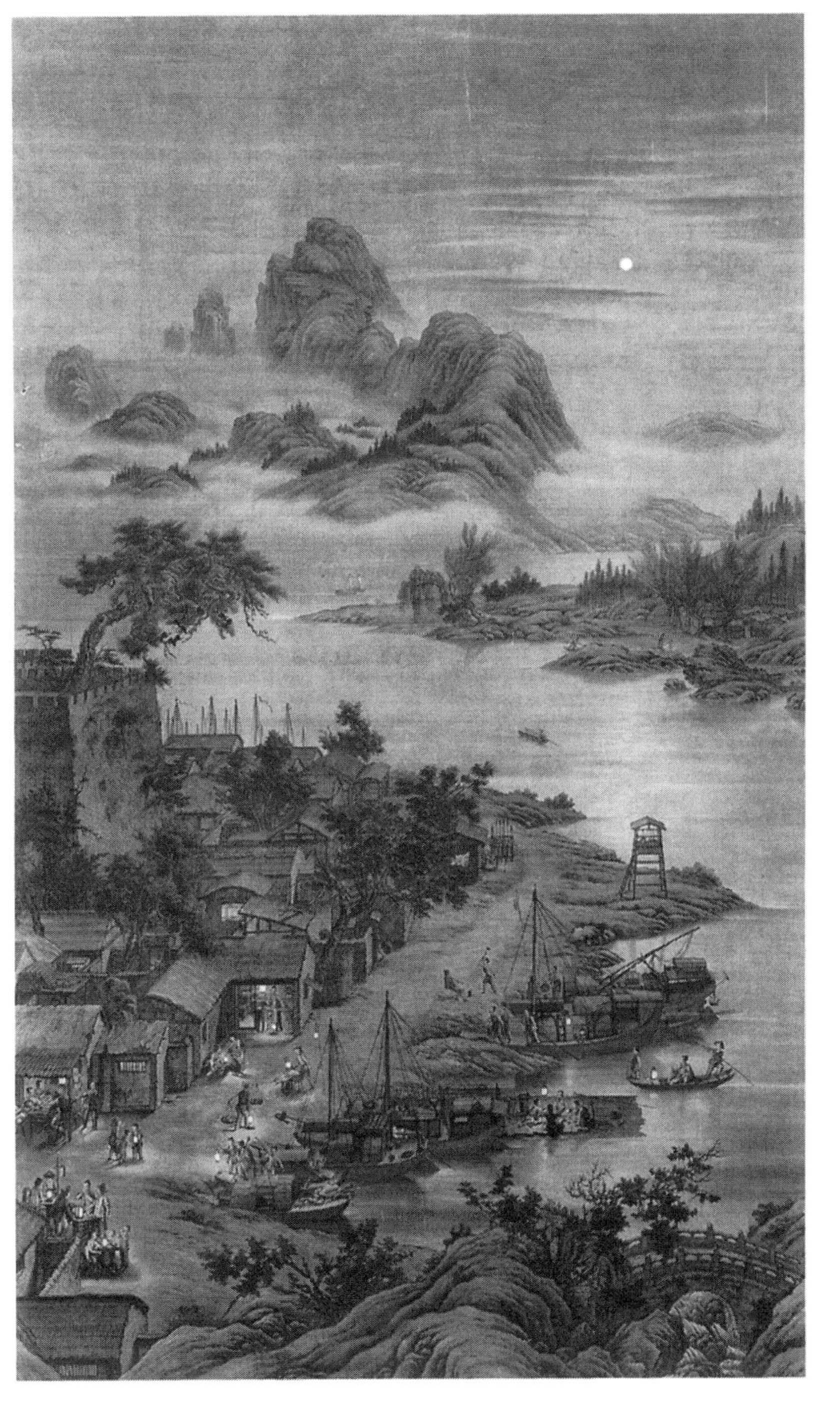

59 *The Night Market at Yangcheng*, attributed to Giuseppe Castiglione, S.J., 1736. Hanging scroll, colours on silk. Courtesy of Carmen M. Christensen.

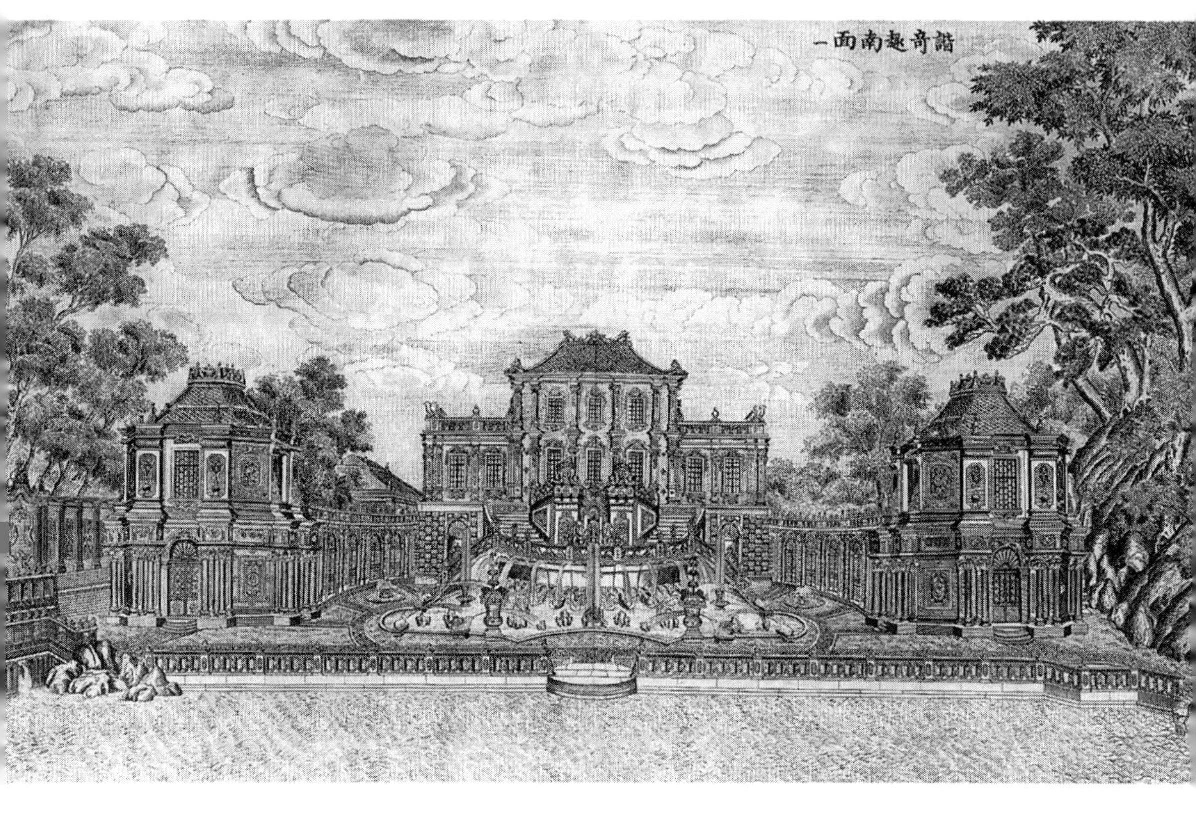

60 After Giuseppe Castiglione: *The Palace of Delights and Harmony*, engraving. China, Jesuit school, Qing Dynasty, ca. 1785. Bibliothèque Nationale, Paris.

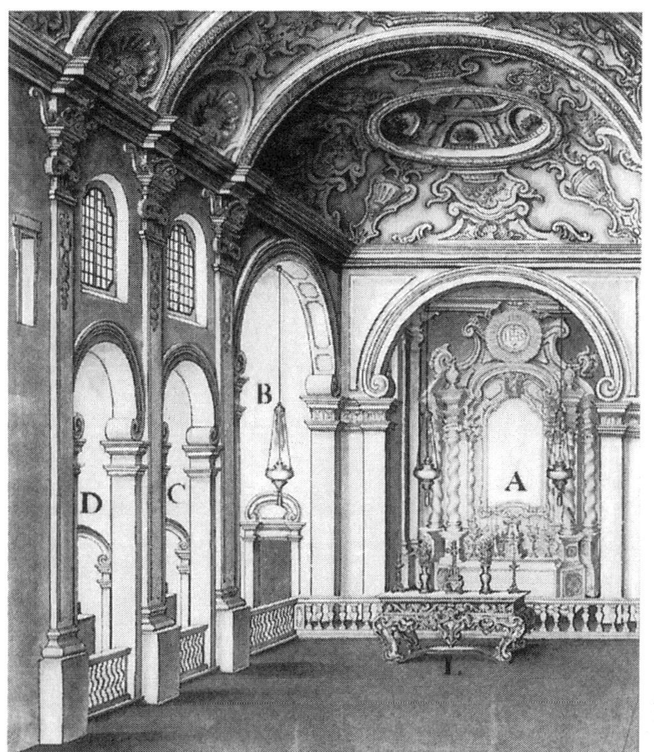

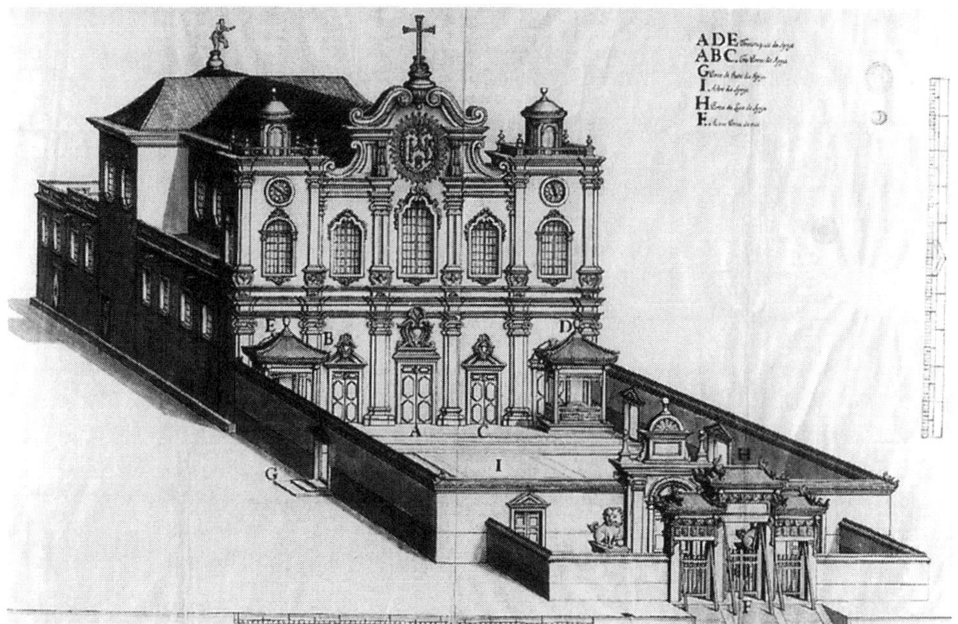

61 Jesuit church of Nossa Senhora da Assunção, 1703, Beijing. Engraving, 18th century. Arquivo Histórico Ultramarino do Instituto de Investigação Cientifica Tropical, Lisbon, Cart. MS-XI.CM 758-759. Photographs courtesy of Cintra e Castro Caldas.

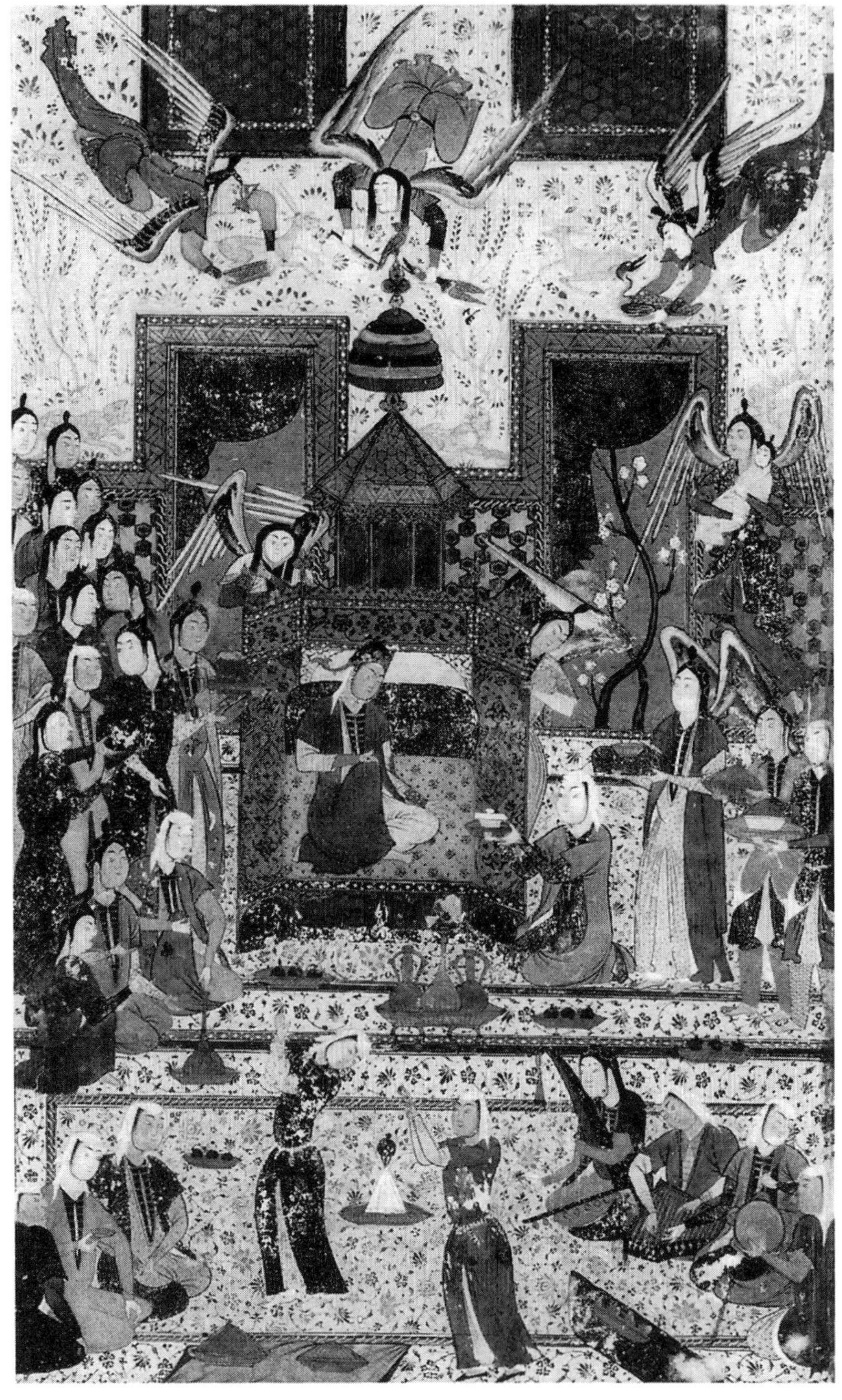

62 *Bilkis, Queen of Sheba, Attended by Angels*. Shirazi illustration from Sa'di's *Kulliyāt*, dated 1566. Colours on paper (21.6 × 13.5 cm). British Museum, London, Add. 24944 (3a).

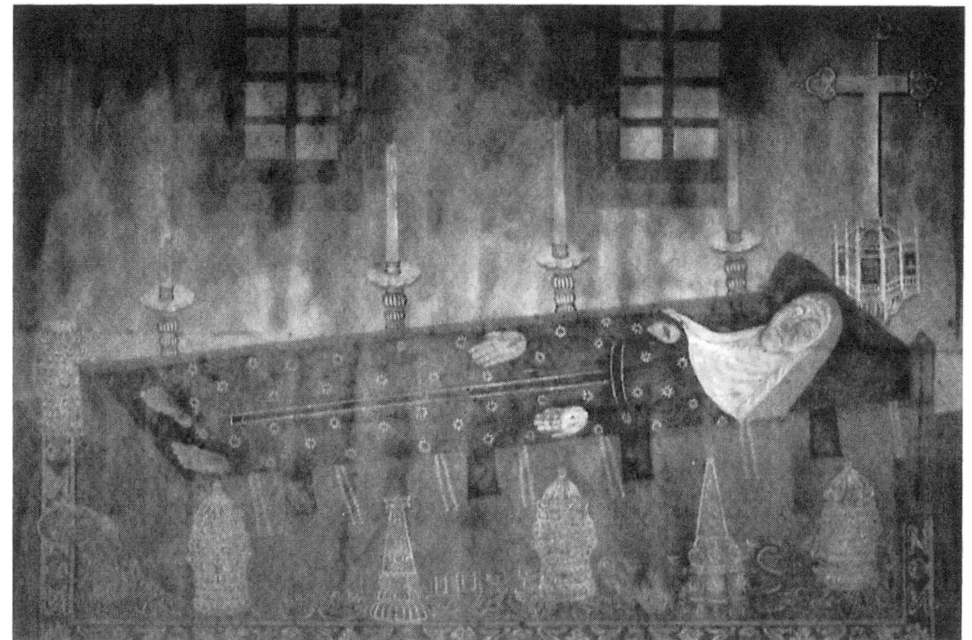

63 *Death Portrait of Sister Maria de Jesus*, oil on canvas. Goan, ca. 1683. Convento de Santa Monica, Velha Goa, India.

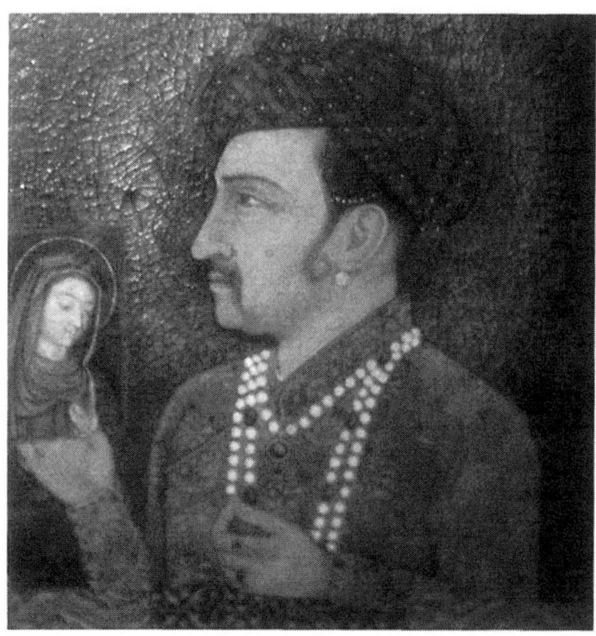

64 *Jahangir Holding an Image of the Virgin Mary*, attributable to Manohar, ca. 1614. Colours and gold on paper. National Museum of India, New Delhi. By reverencing the Virgin Mary, Jahangir continued a tradition of his father, Akbar. Compare the image of the Virgin with that in figure 69.

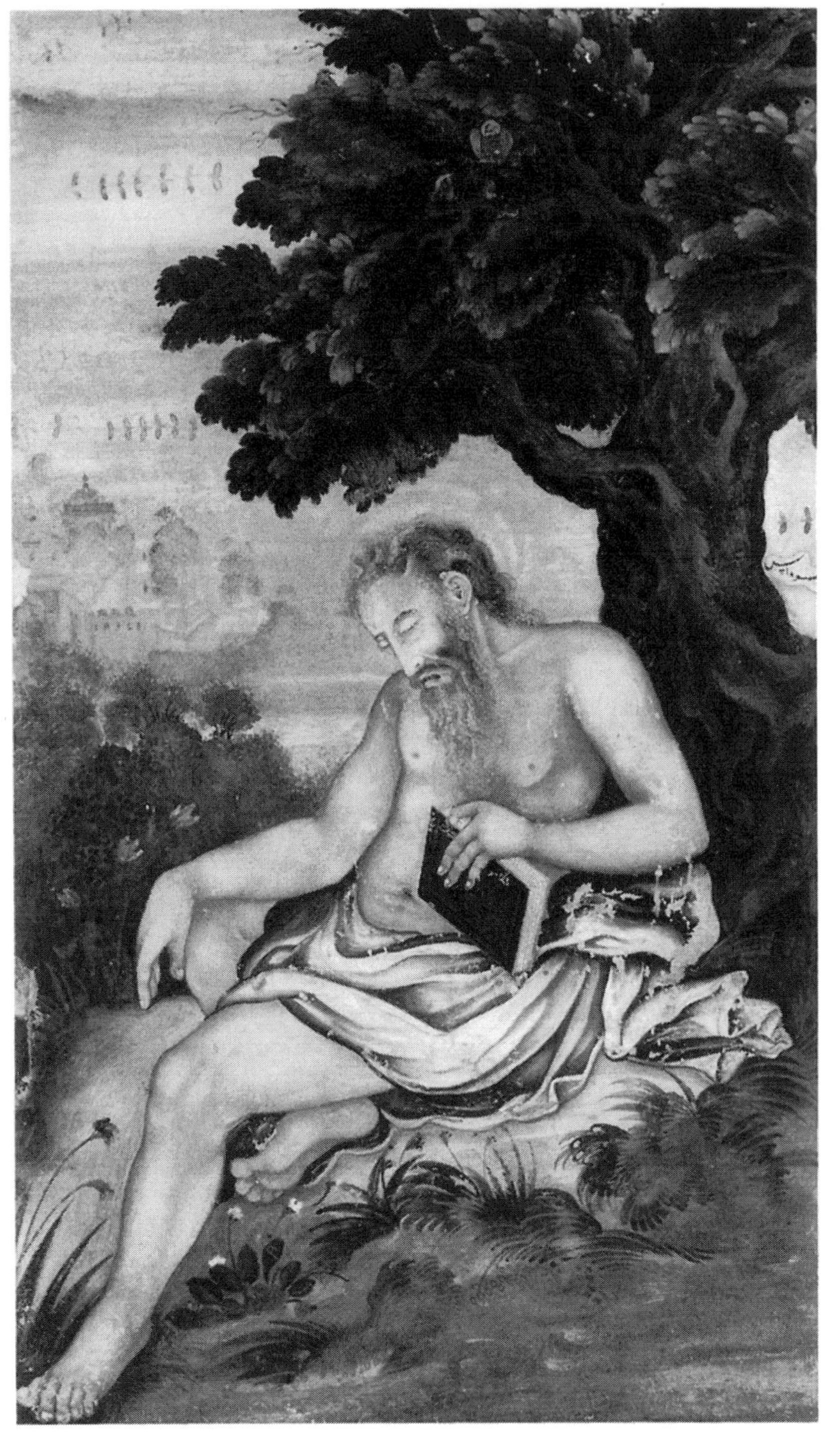

65 *Saint Jerome*, signed by Kesu Das, ca. 1580–5. Colours on paper (17 × 10 cm). Musée Guimet, Paris, MA2476. Courtesy of the Réunion des Musées Nationaux, Agence Photographique.

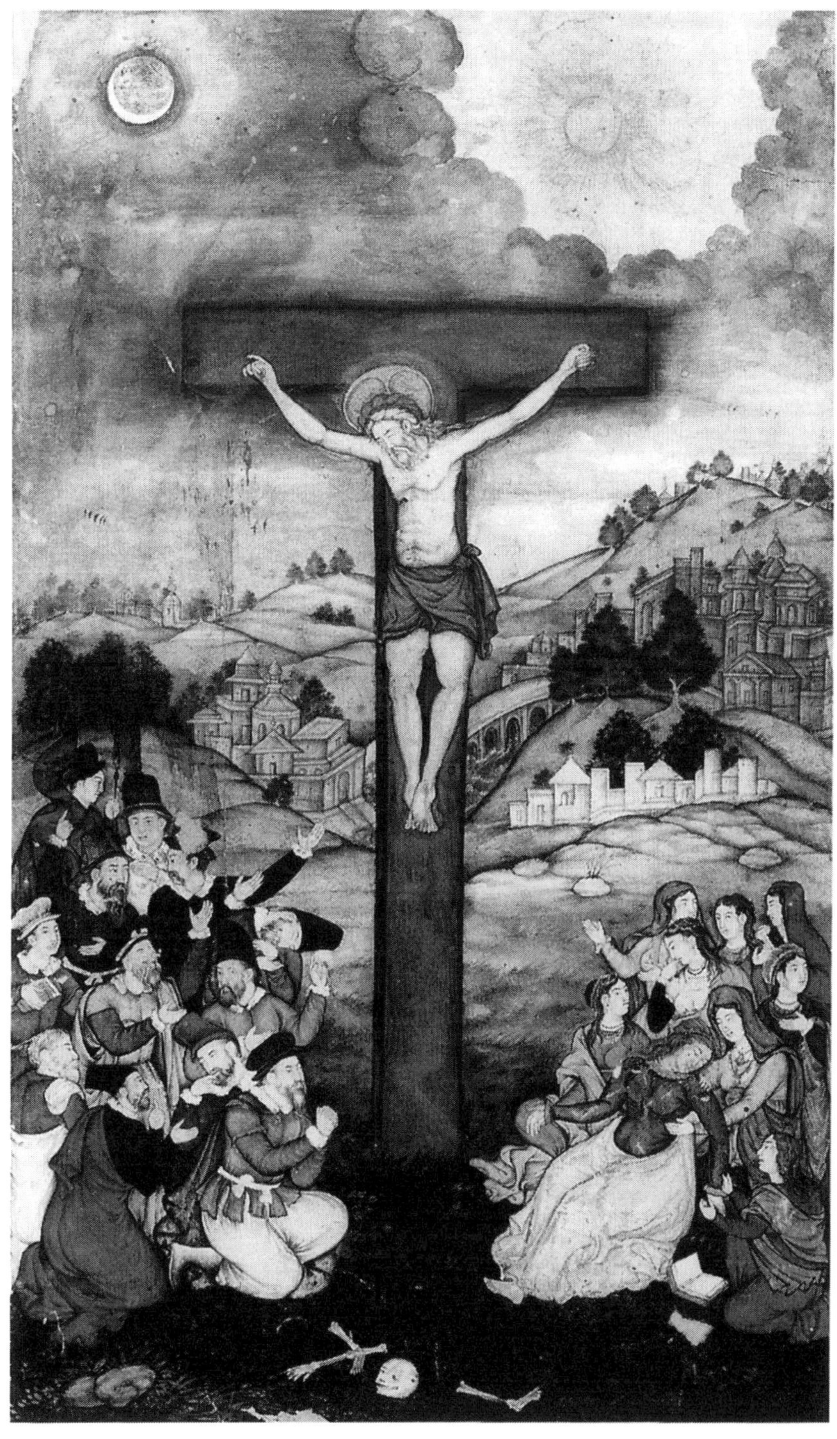

66 *Crucifixion*, attributed to Kesu Das, ca. 1585–90. Colours on paper (19.5 × 17.8 cm). British Museum, London.

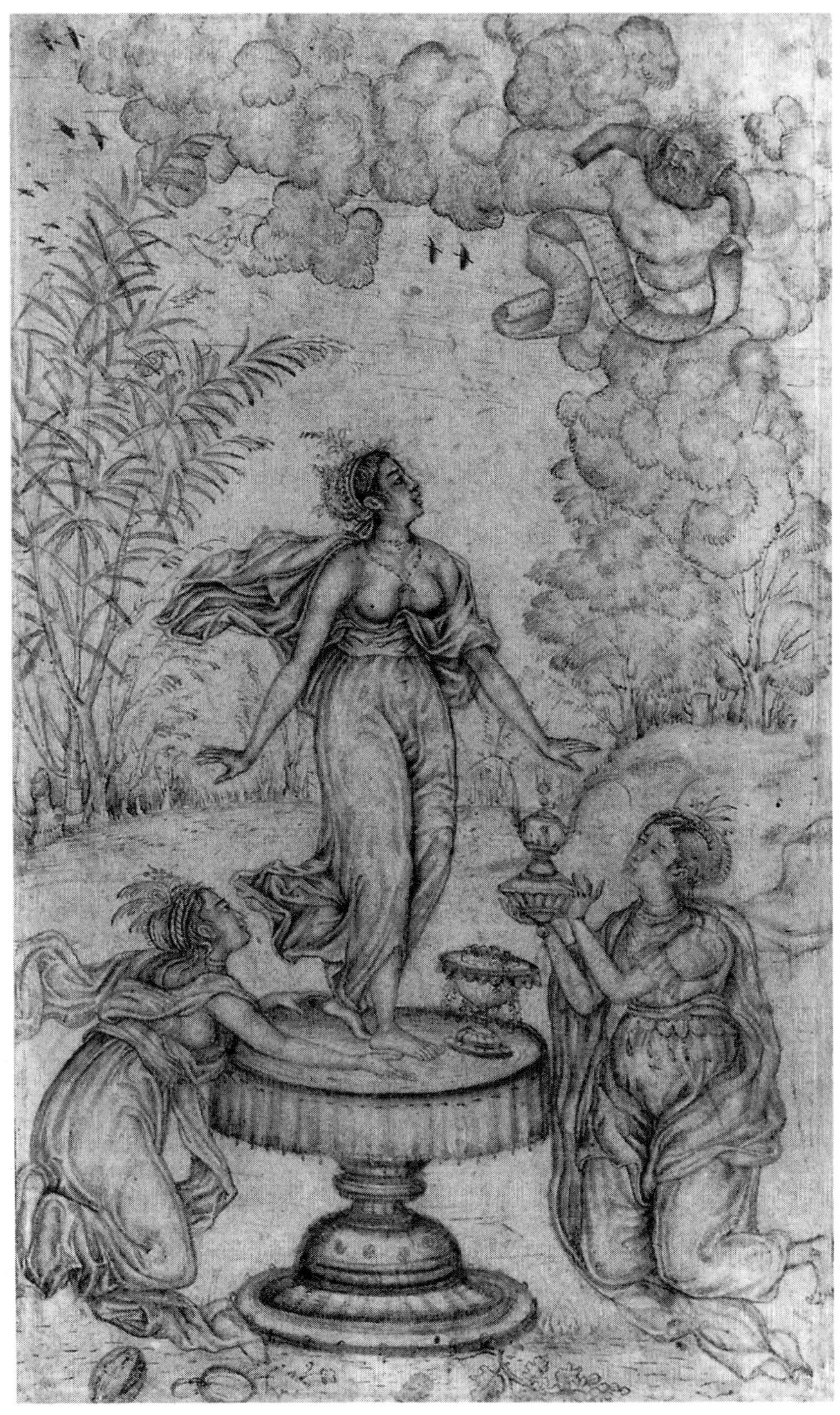

67 *Allegorical Figure*, signed by Basawan, ca. 1585–90. Ink on paper (19.8 × 11.8 cm). Musée Guimet, Paris, No 3619, J, a. Courtesy of the Réunion des Musées Nationaux, Agence Photographique.

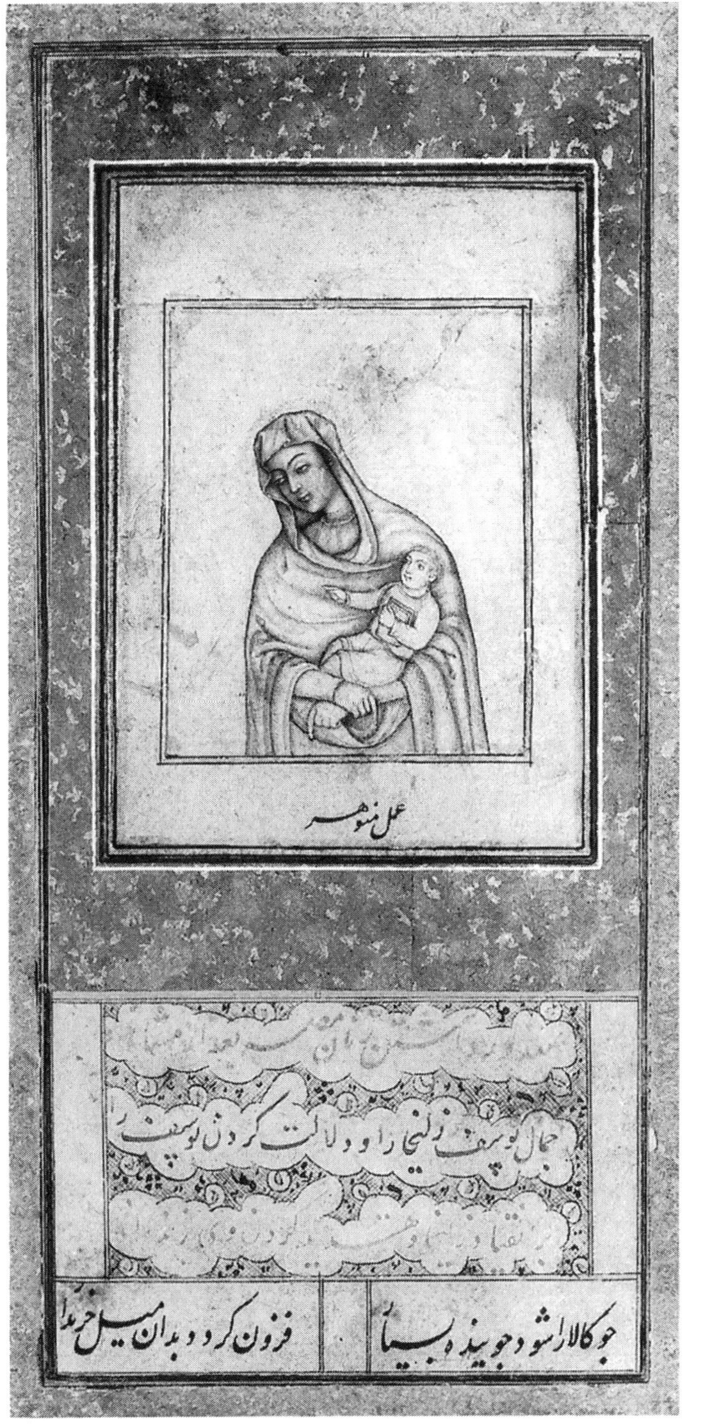

68 *The Virgin Mary*, signed by Manohar, ca. 1590–5. Ink on paper (7.5 × 5.3 cm, miniature only). Institut Néerlandais, Paris, Collection Frits Lugt, 1974-T.67.

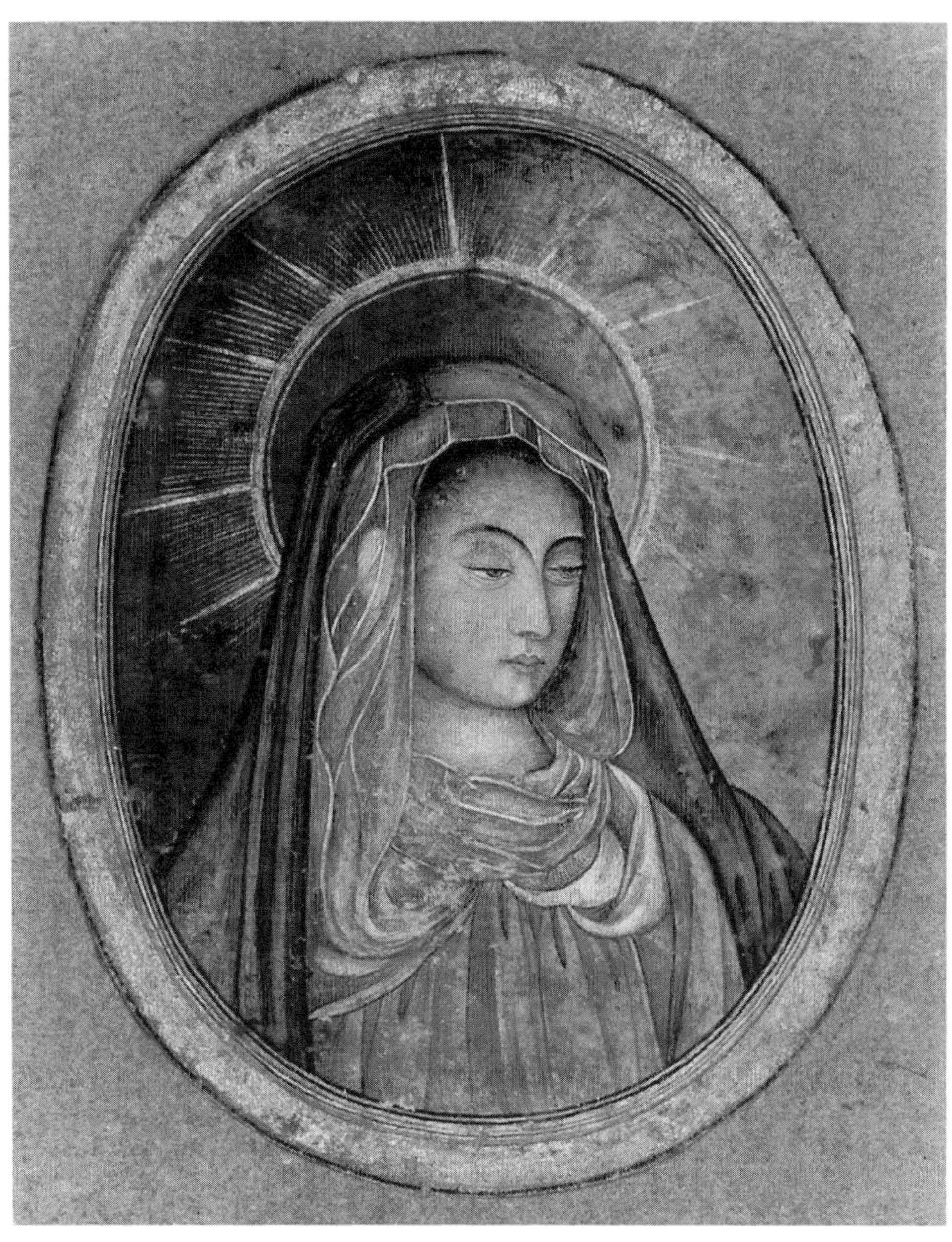

69 *The Virgin Mary*, school of Manohar, ca. 1590–5. Ink, colours, and gold on paper. Victoria and Albert Museum, London, IS 133-1964. © The Board and Trustees of the Victoria and Albert Museum.

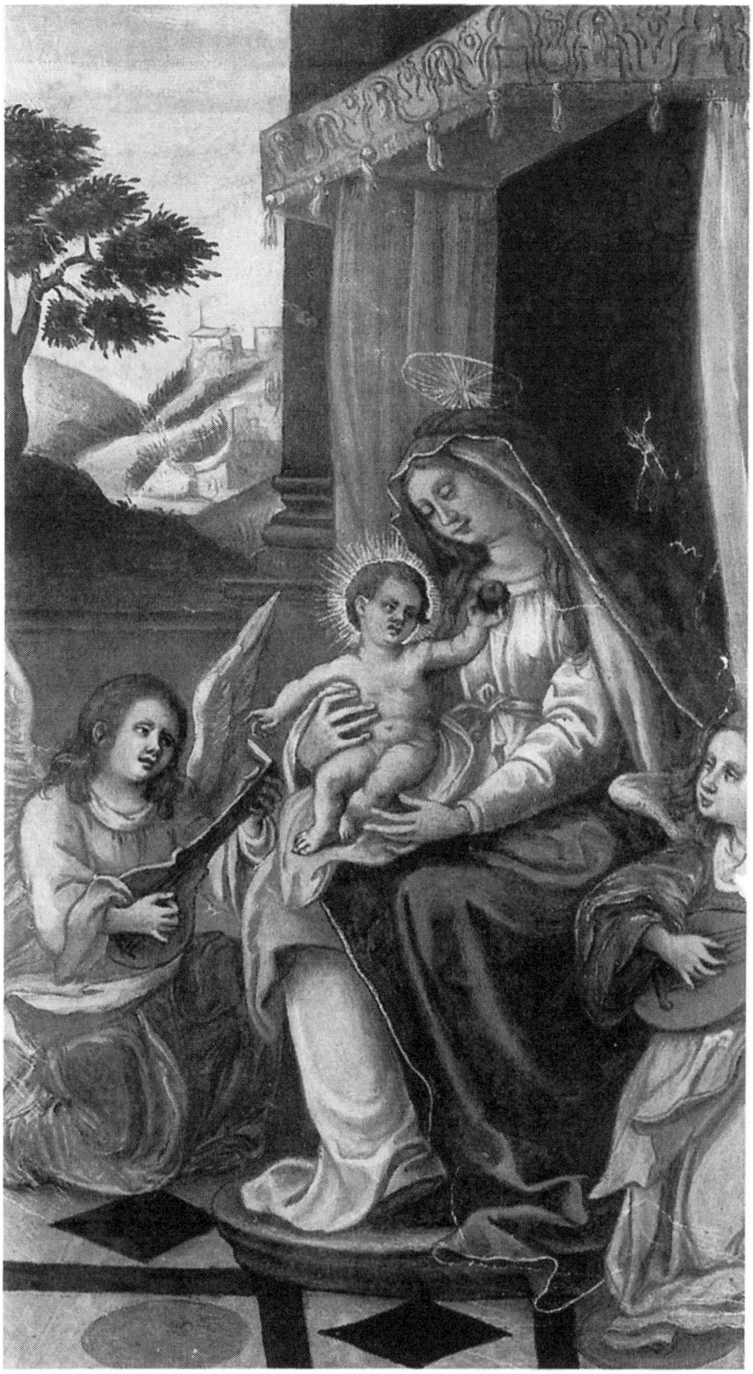

70 'Portuguese Painter' (?): *The Virgin and Child with Angels*, oil on paper, ca. 1595. Arthur M. Sackler Museum, Harvard University. Copied from *The Virgin and Child with Angels*, by Antoon Wierix after Martin de Vos, dated 1584. Courtesy of the Arthur M. Sackler Museum, Harvard University Art Museums, gift of John Goelet, 1958.233.

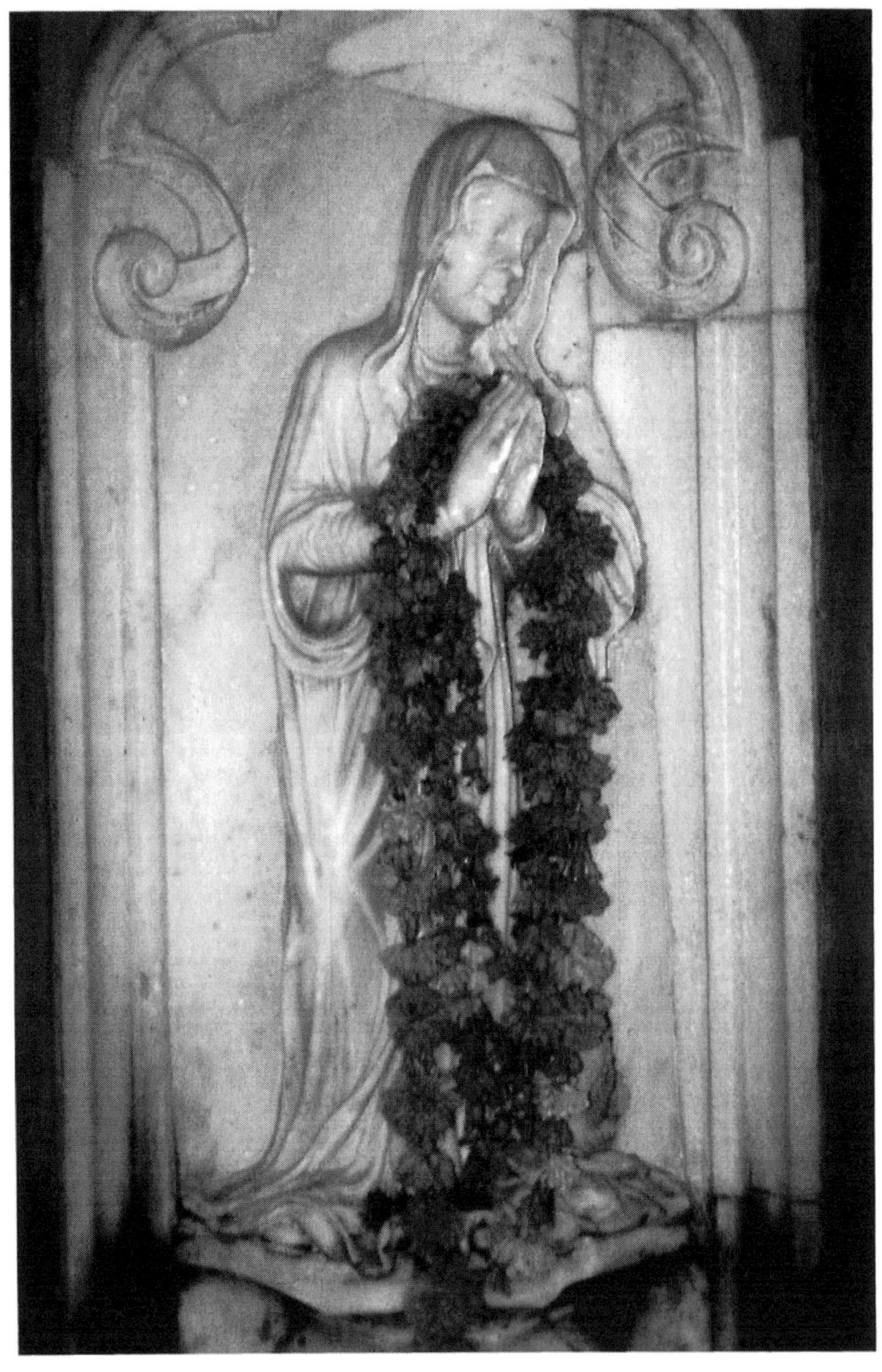

71 *Madonna*, white marble statue, after Manohar, ca. 1590. Agra, Old Cathedral.

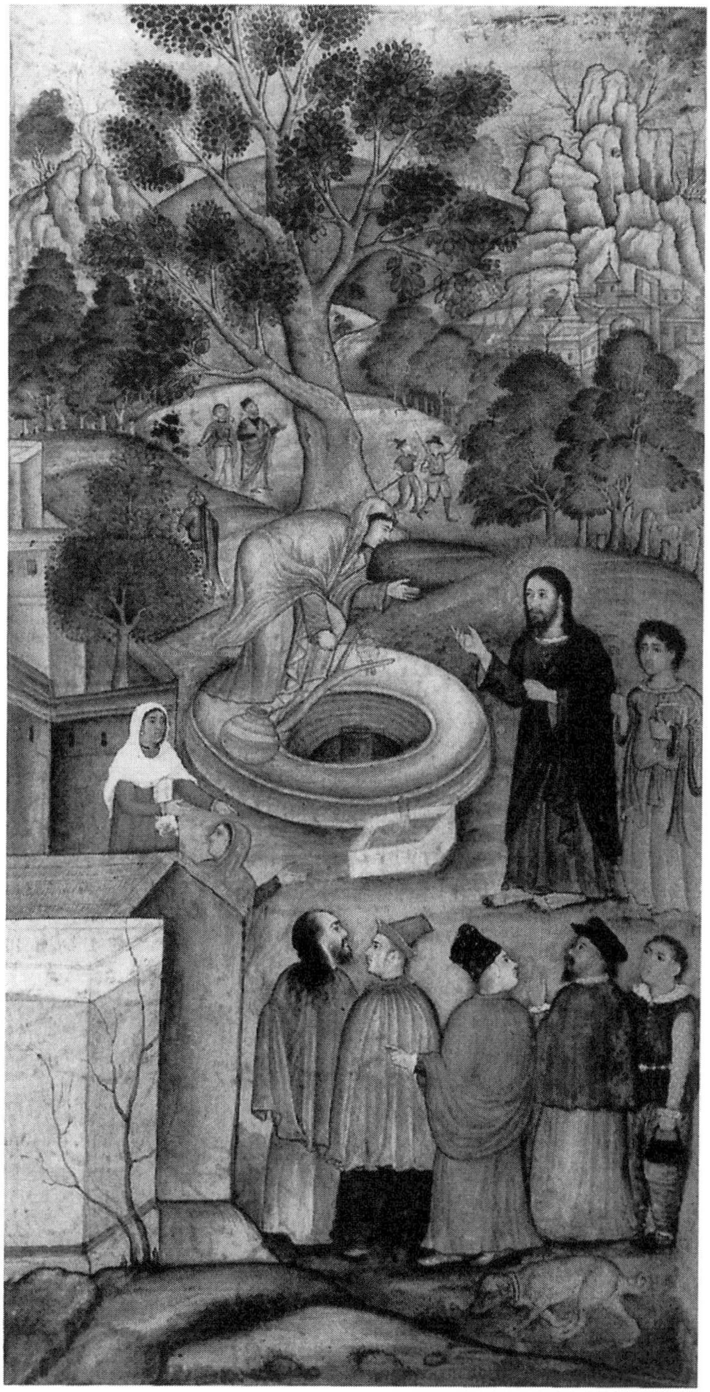

72 *Christ and the Woman of Samaria*, attributable to Manohar, ca. 1600–2. Colours on paper (26.3 × 14.5 cm). Institut Néerlandais, Paris, Collection Frits Lugt.

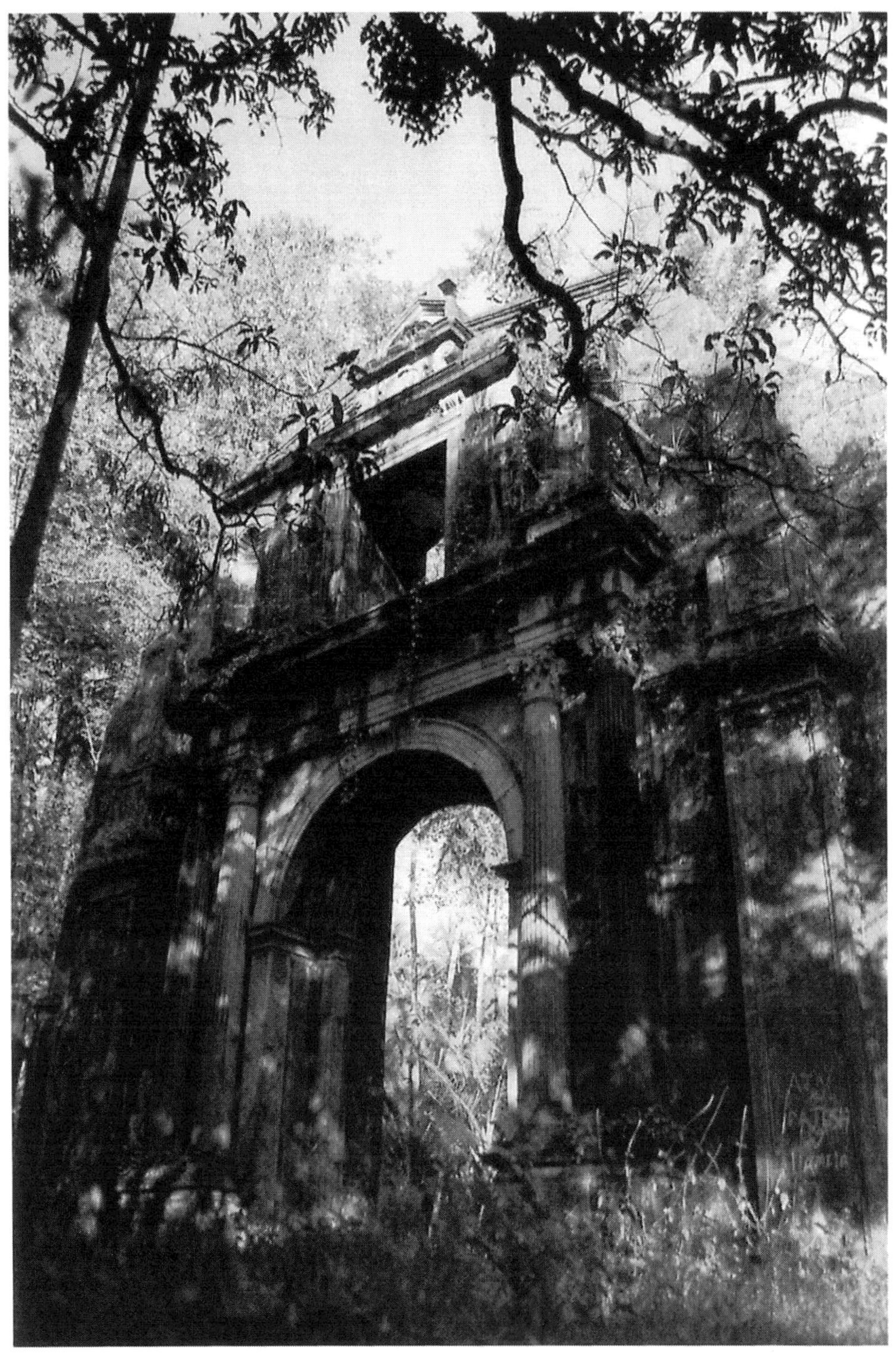

73 Jesuit collegiate church of São Paulo, Goa (India); central part of façade (1560–72).

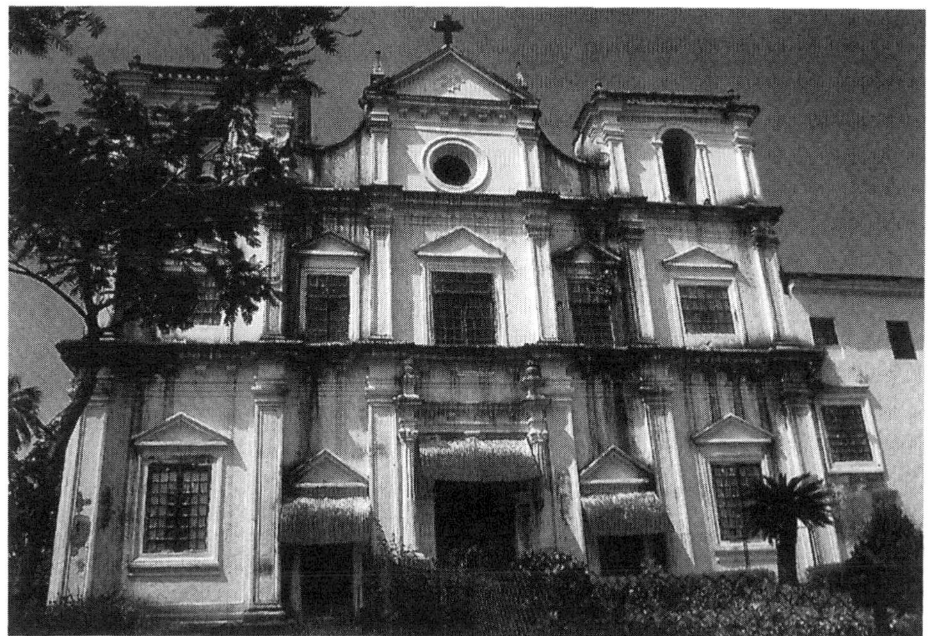

74 Jesuit College, Rachol, Salcete (India), begun 1606.

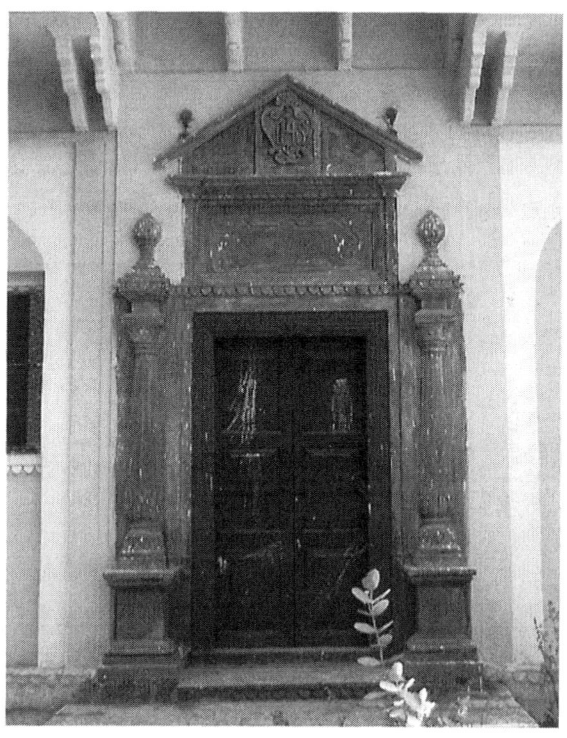

75 Jesuit mission church or 'Old Cathedral,' Agra (India), founded 1599. South door, 1769.

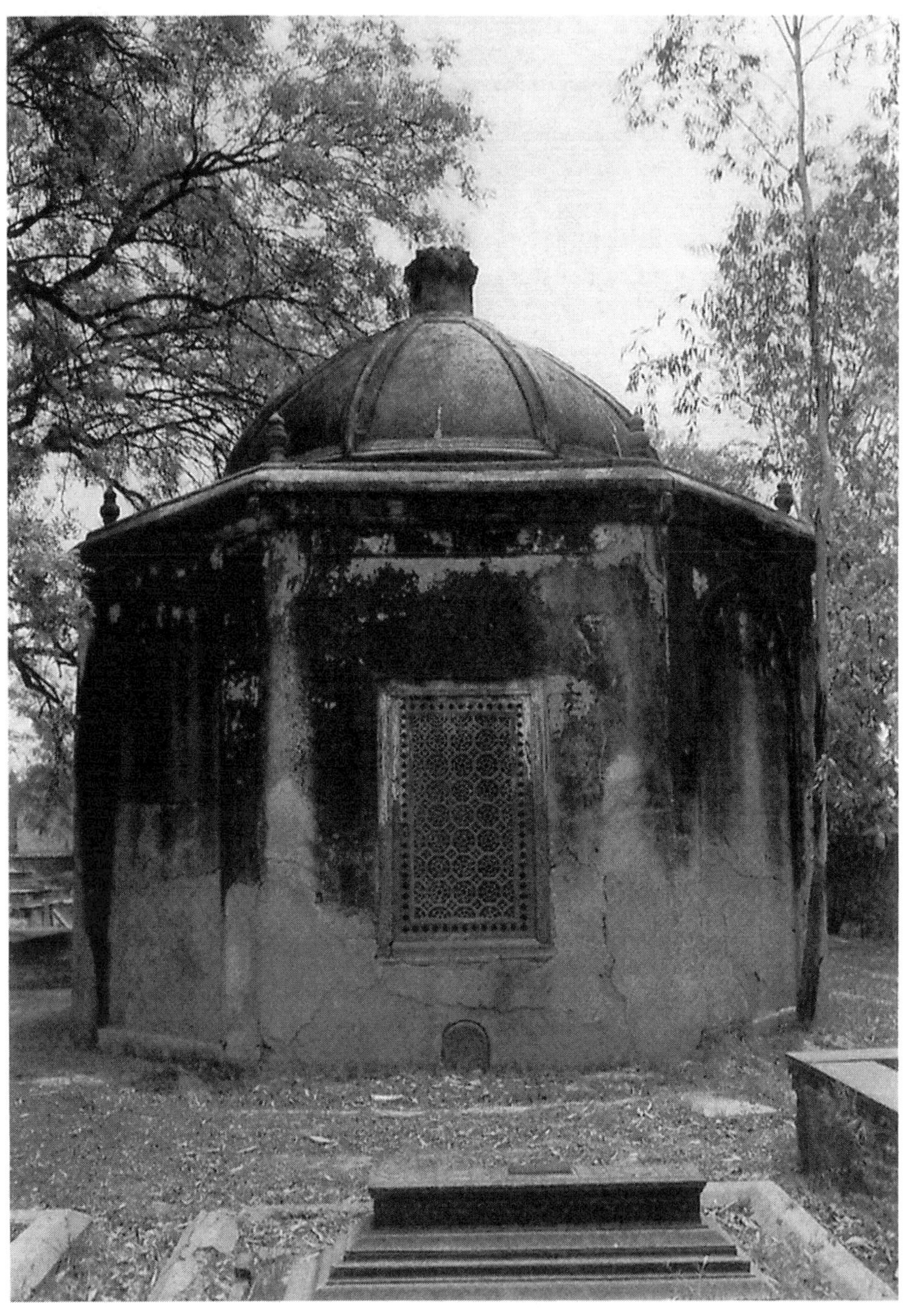

76 Jesuit funerary chapel known as the 'Padres Santos Chapel,' Agra (India), 1611.

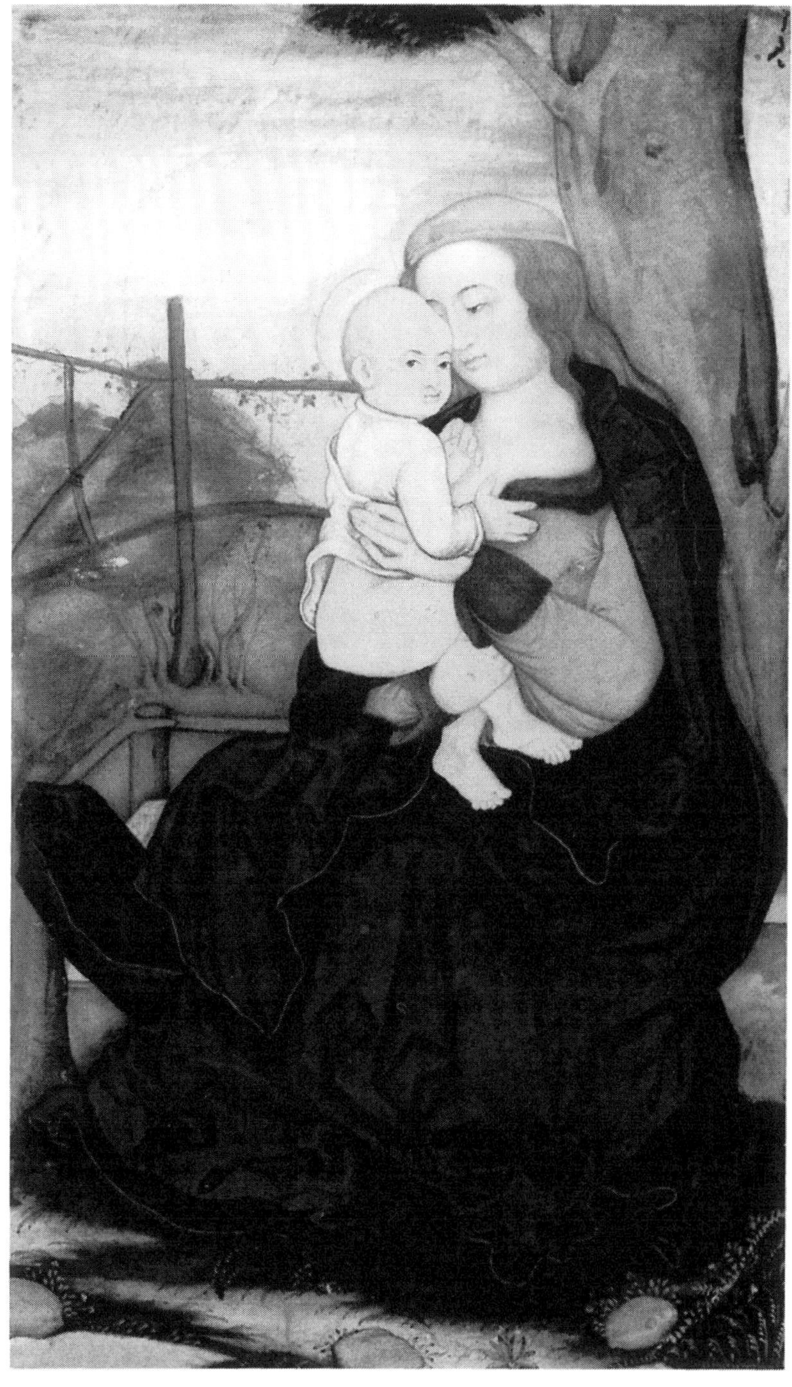

77 *The Virgin and Child*, Salim Studio after Dürer, ca. 1599–1604. Colours on paper. Windsor Castle. The Royal Collection © Her Majesty the Queen.

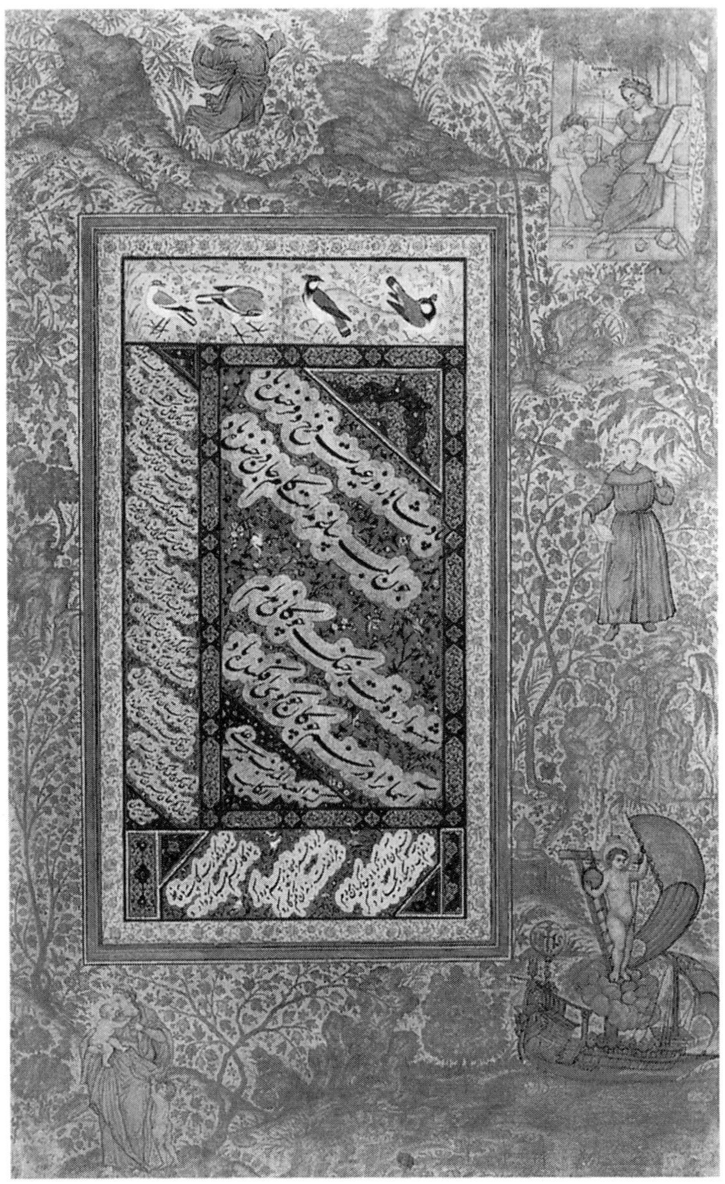

78 Marginalia, school of Aga Reza, ca. 1599–1604. Ink, colours, and gold on paper (42.5 × 26.6 cm). Arthur M. Sackler Gallery, Washington.

Translation of verses in central panel:

Oh King! May you be happy and fortunate on your day of `īd [Islamic festival at the end of Ramadan]!
Like the lip of a cup, may wine put a smile on the mouth of your soul;
The horseman of your realm is continually on the polo pony;
May the celestial sphere be thrown like a ball in the curve of the polo mallet!

The miserable slave Mīr `Alī the scribe wrote this.

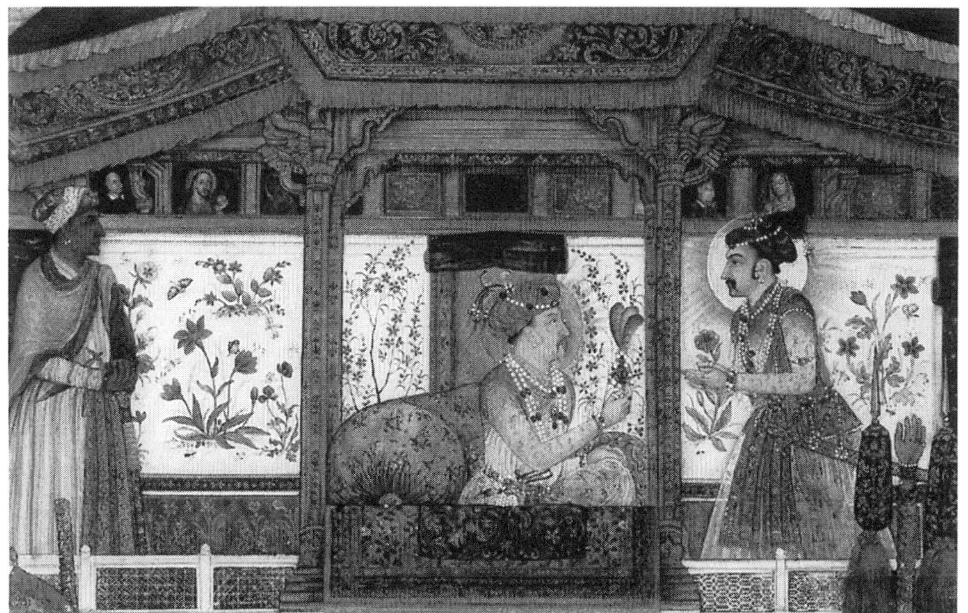

79 *Jahangir Presents Prince Khurram with a Turban Ornament.* Mughal, mid-17th century, from the *Padshahnama* manuscript. Colours and gold on paper (detail). Windsor Castle, Holmes binding 149, page 389, f. 195a 1005025 OMS 1641v. The Royal Collection © Her Majesty the Queen. Note the saints' portraits in the frieze above the throne. Compare the figure of the Virgin at far right to that of figure 69.

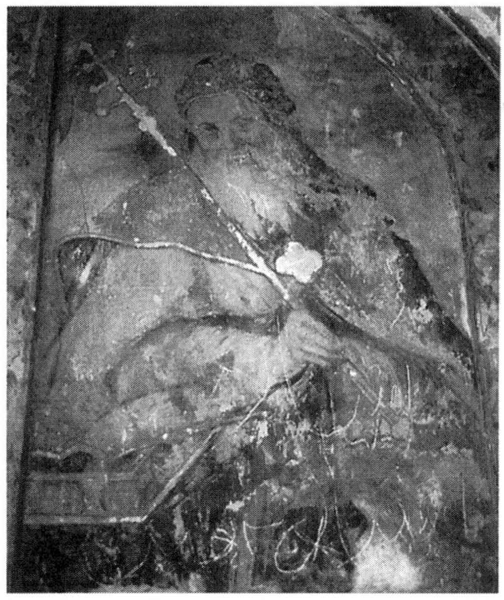

80 *Saint Gregory the Great.* Mural painting on the north spandrel of the west wall of the Sehdārī pavilion (approx. 140 × 60 cm), Lahore Fort, ca. 1610–20.

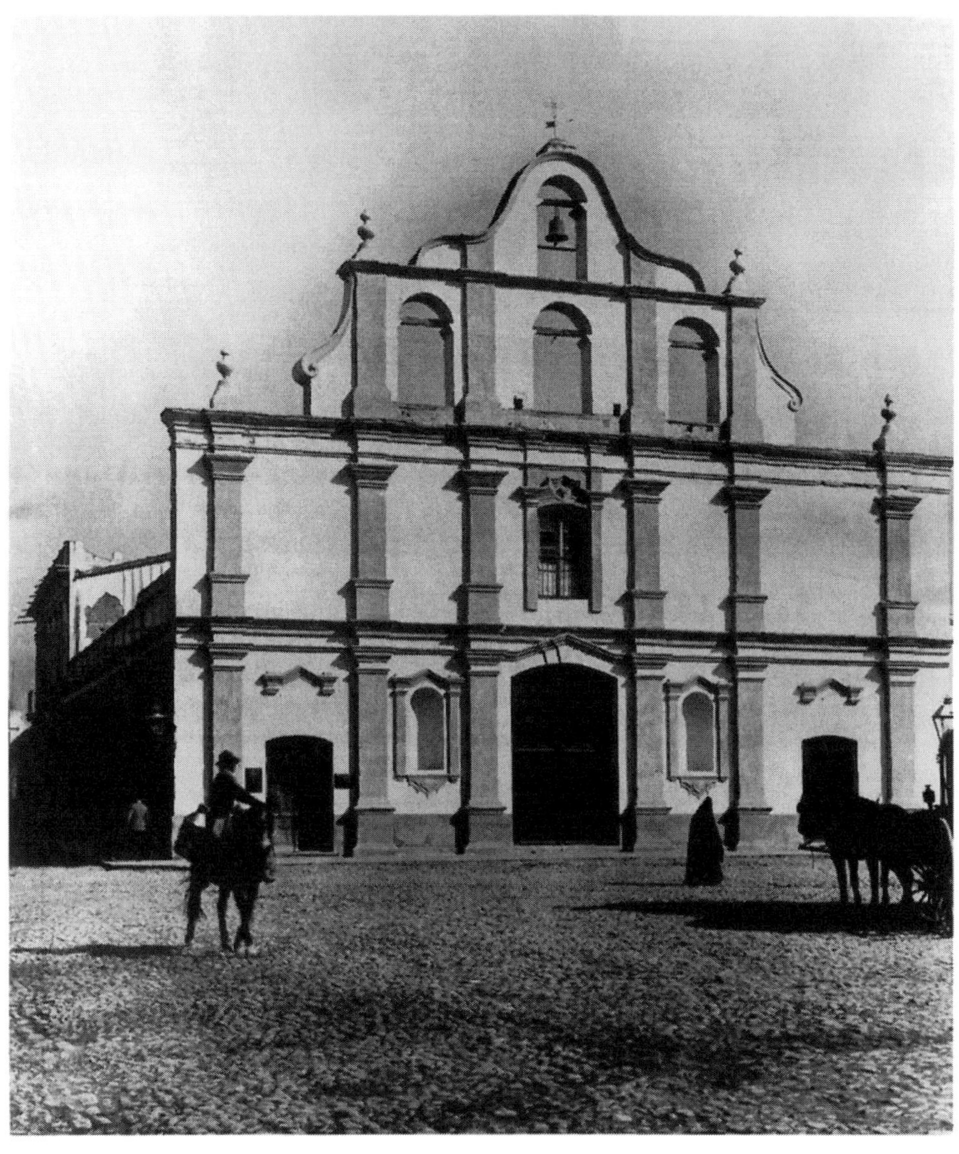

81 Jesuit church of the Compañía, Salta (Argentina), 18th century. Destroyed 1910. From a photograph of the late 19th century. Courtesy Visual Collections, Fine Arts Library, Harvard University.

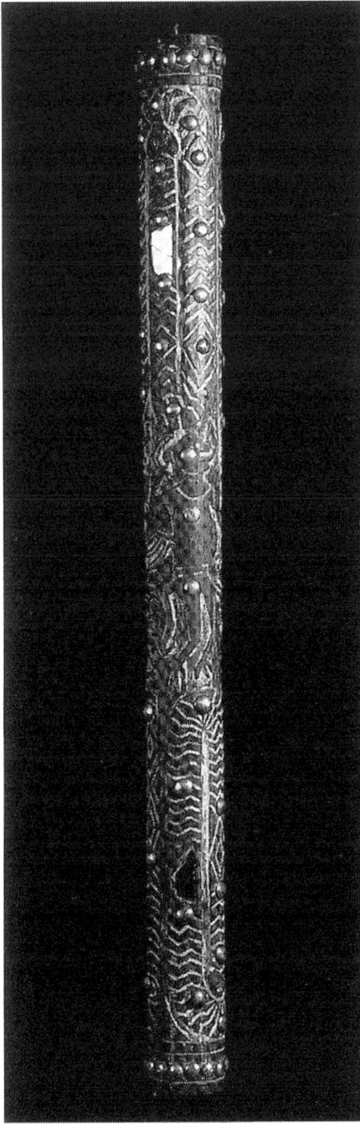

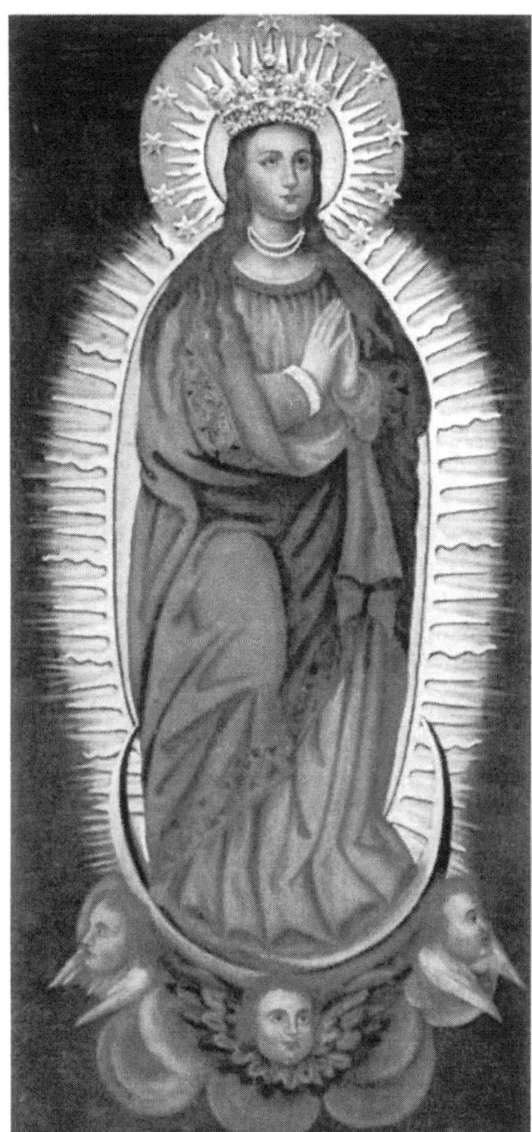

82 Wooden shamanic pipe with geometric, figural, and animal ornament. Tupi-Guaraní, late 18th or early 19th century. Museo de América, Madrid, 13322.

83 *Virgen de los Milagros ('La Conquistadora')*, by Louis Berger, S.J., ca. 1618. Church of La Compañía, Santa Fé, Argentina.

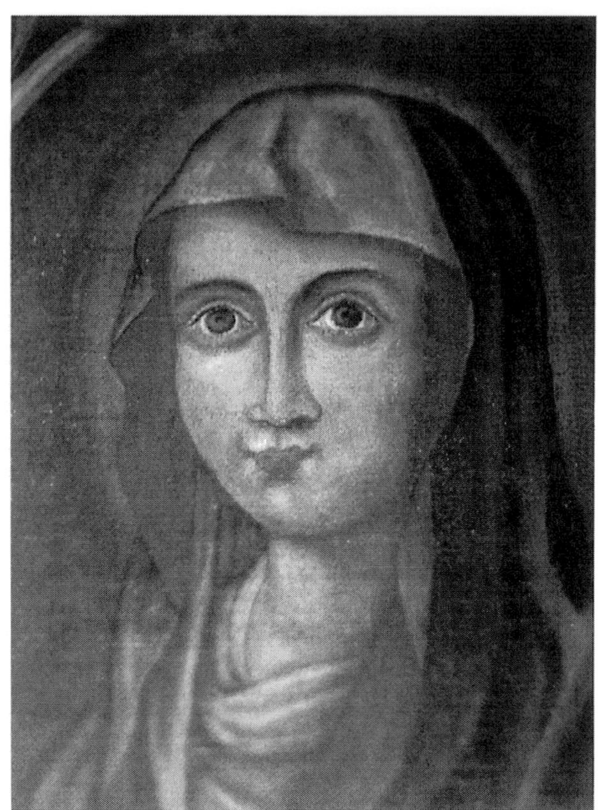

84 *Madonna of Saint Luke*, by José Habiyú (detail), over drawing attributed to Louis Berger, S.J., oil on canvas, 1618 (20.2 × 24 cm). Museo Enrique Udaondo, Luján, Argentina.

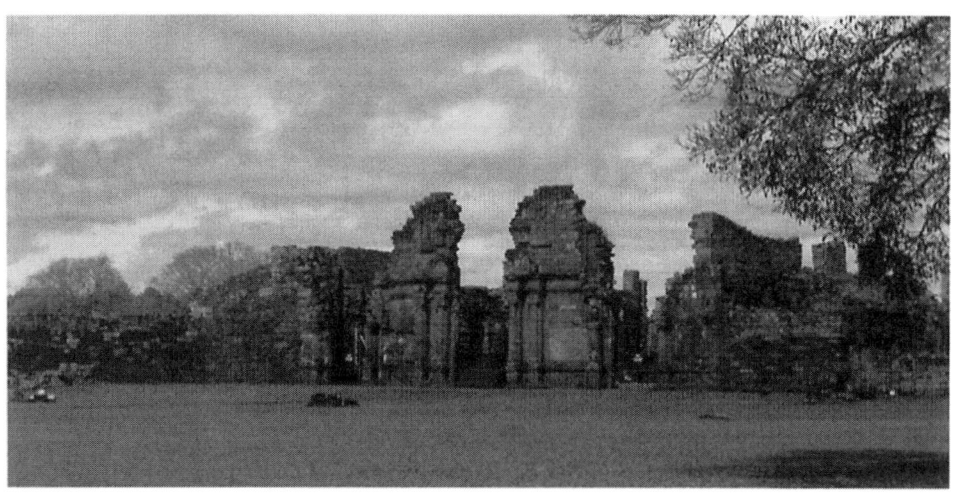

85 Reduction church and mission ruins, San Ignacio Miní (Argentina), by Giuseppe Brasanelli, S.J., and Angelo Camillo Petragrassa, S.J.; finished 1727.

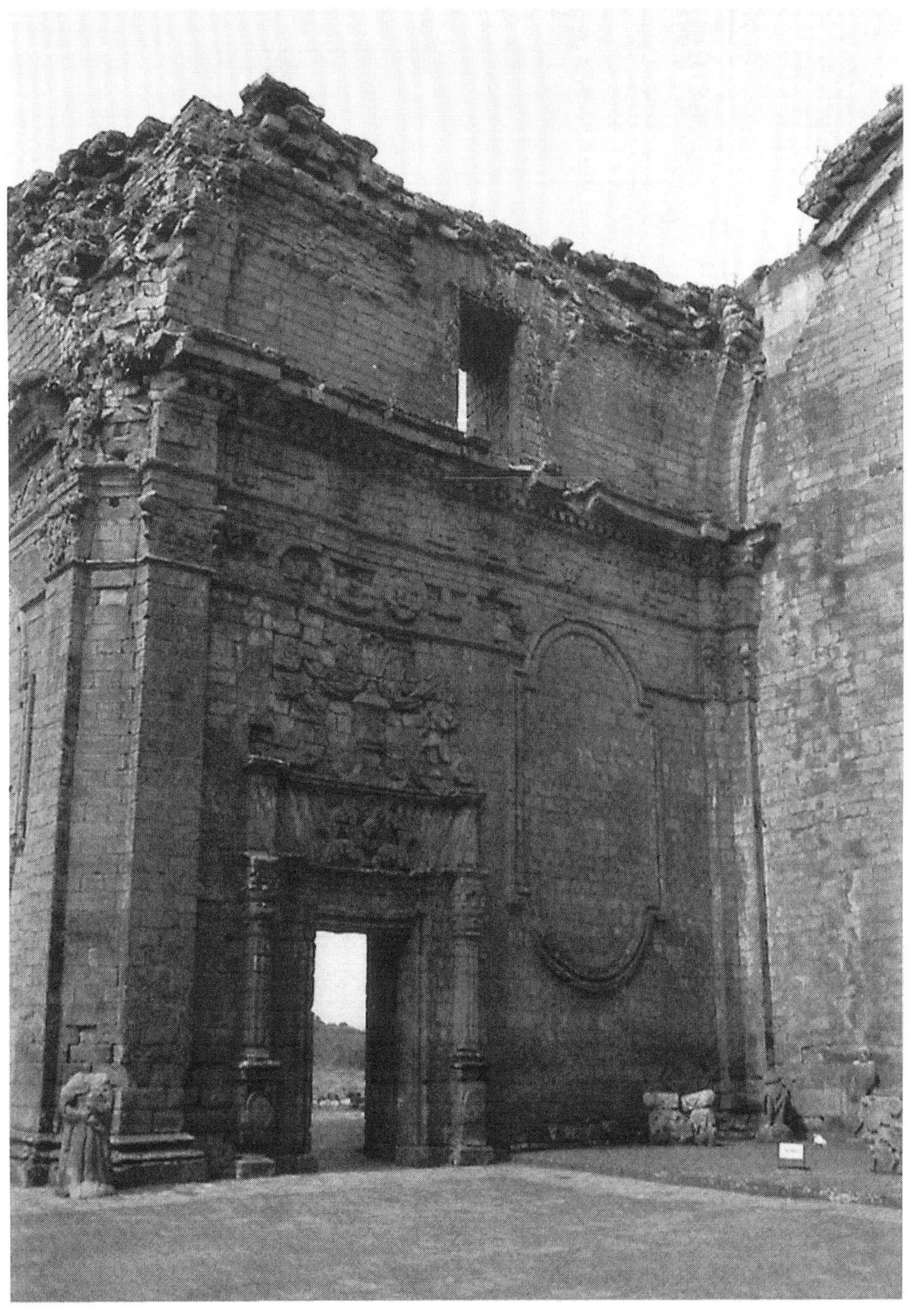

86 Reduction church, Trinidad (Paraguay); interior of nave looking east, by Giovanni Battista Primoli, S.J. (1673–1747). Note the angel frieze in the entablature above.

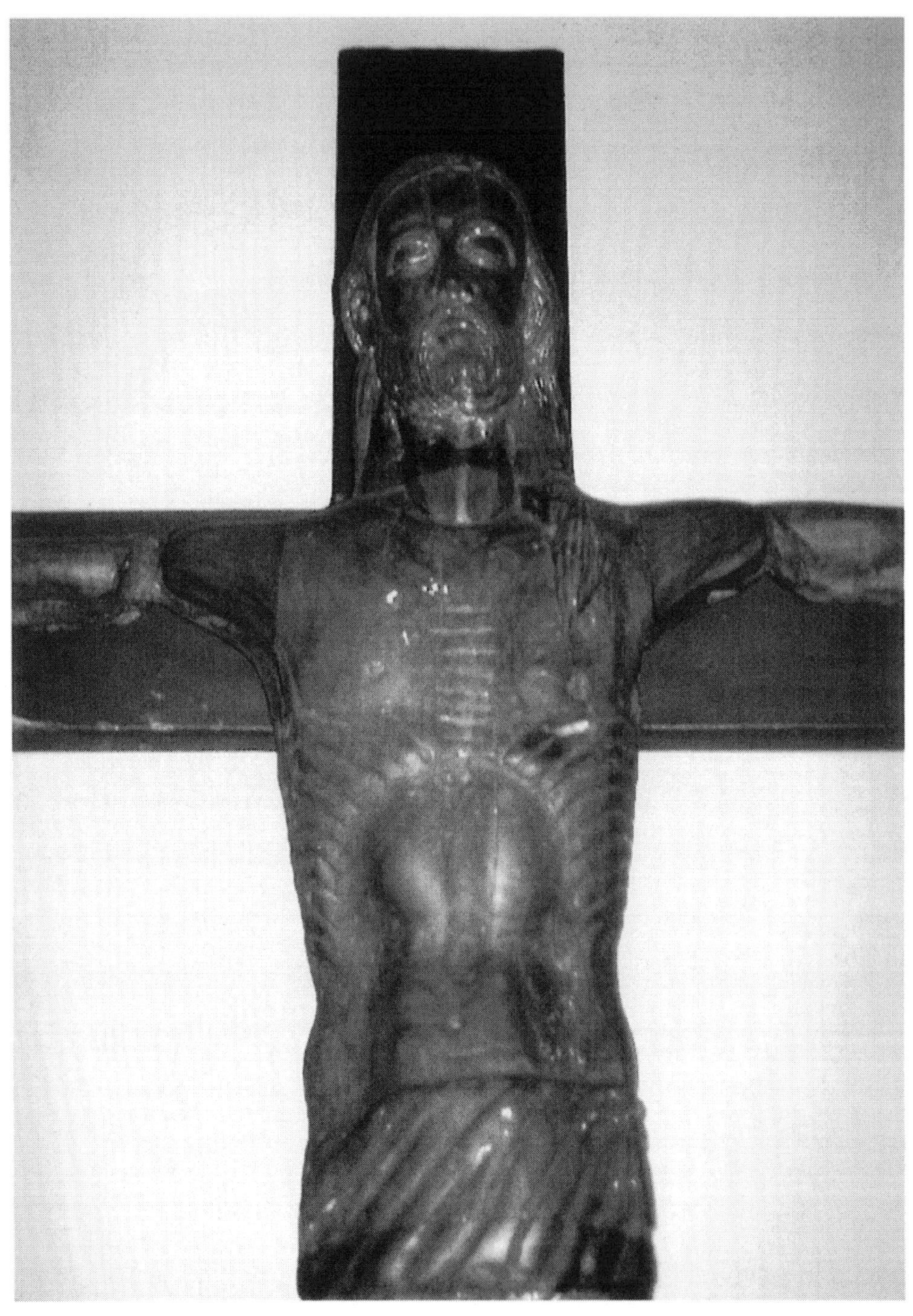

87 *Crucifixion*, wood with traces of polychrome, 17th century. Museo Fernandez Blanco, Buenos Aires.

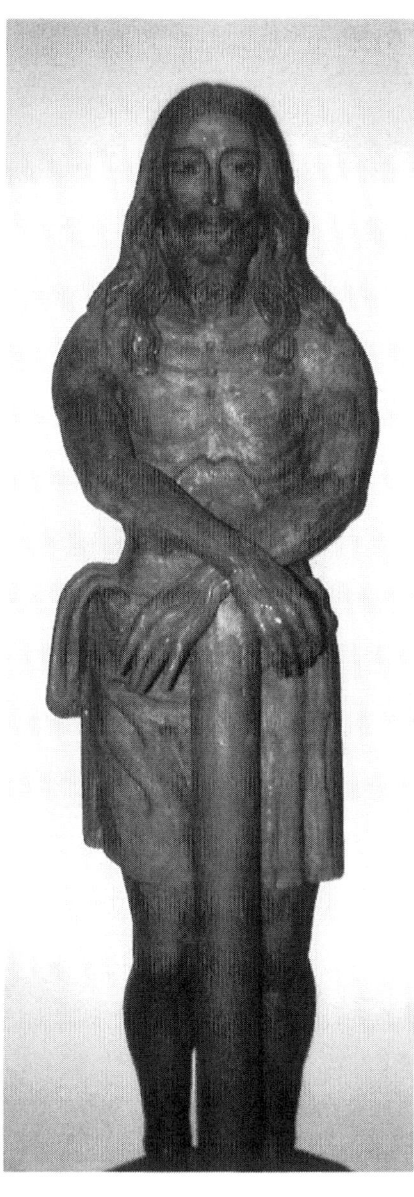

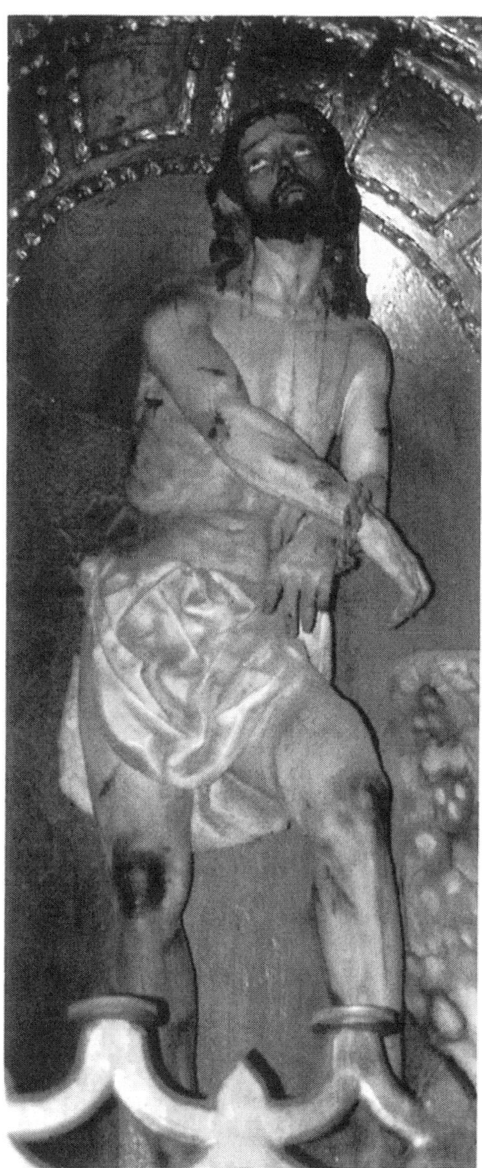

88 *Man of Sorrows*, wood with traces of polychrome, 17th century (1.35 m). Santa María Museum, Paraguay. Such statues of Christ's passion featured prominently in Holy Week celebrations.

89 *Man of Sorrows*, wood polychrome, 17th century, Lima. Lima, San Pedro, Altar del Cristo de la Contrición.

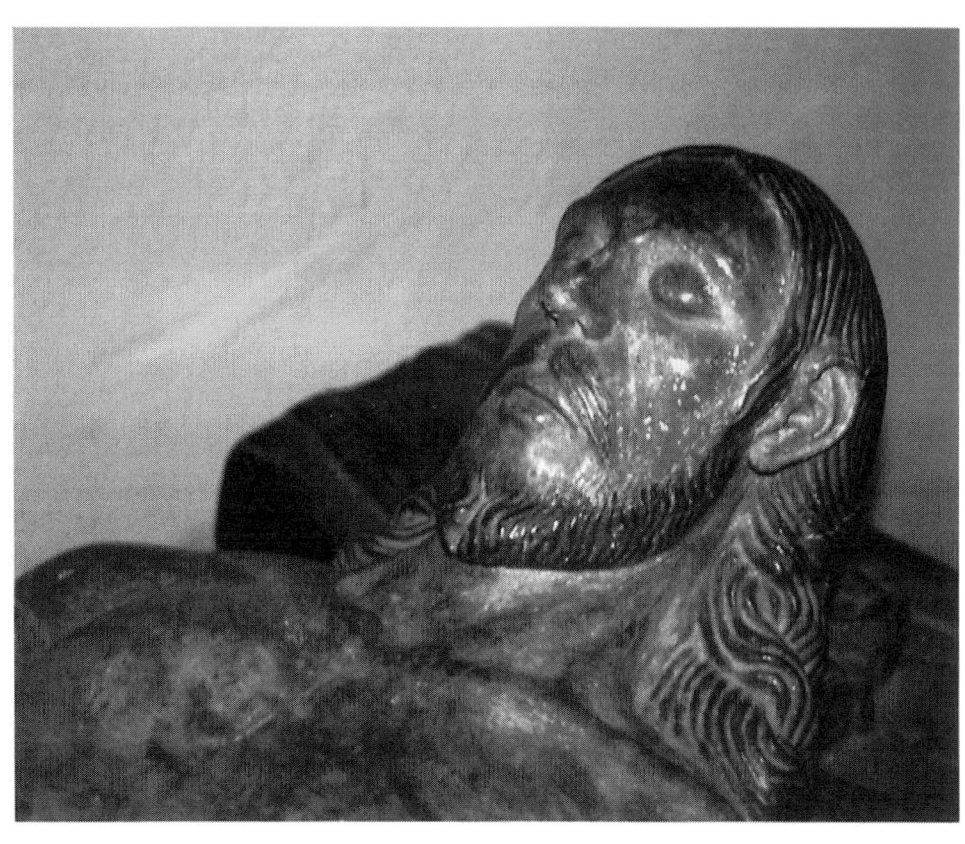

90 *Dead Christ*, wood with traces of polychrome, 17th century (detail). Santa María Museum, Paraguay.

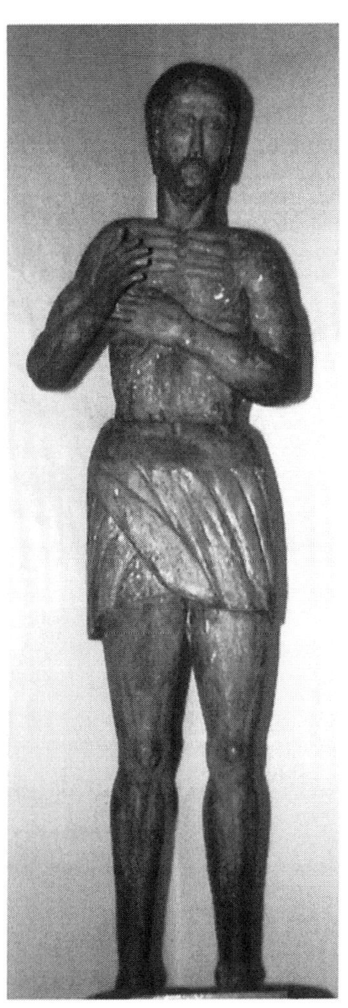

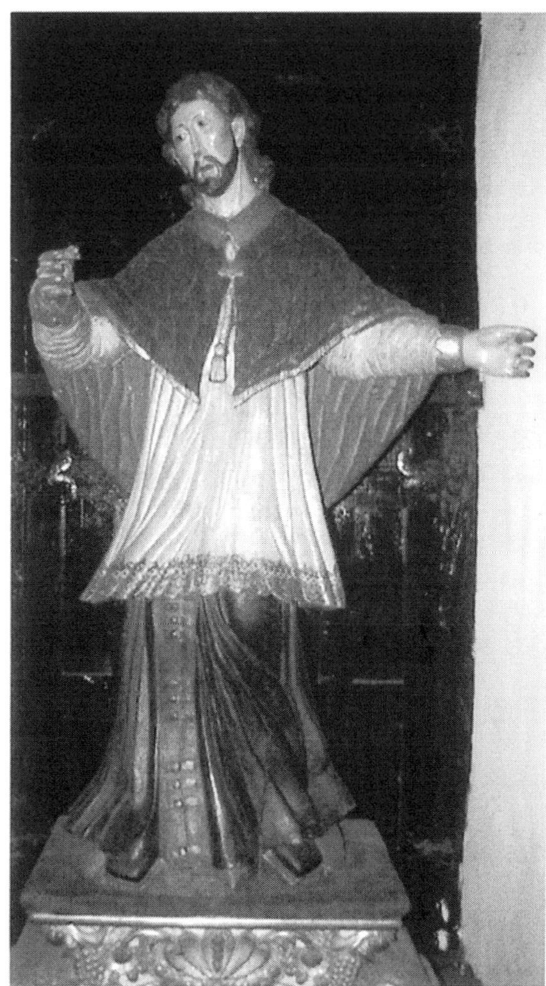

91 *Christ Bearing the Cross*, wood with traces of polychrome, 17th century (1.25 m). San Ignacio Museum, Paraguay.

92 *Saint John Nepomuk*, wood polychrome, 18th century. Santa Fé Provincial Museum, Argentina.

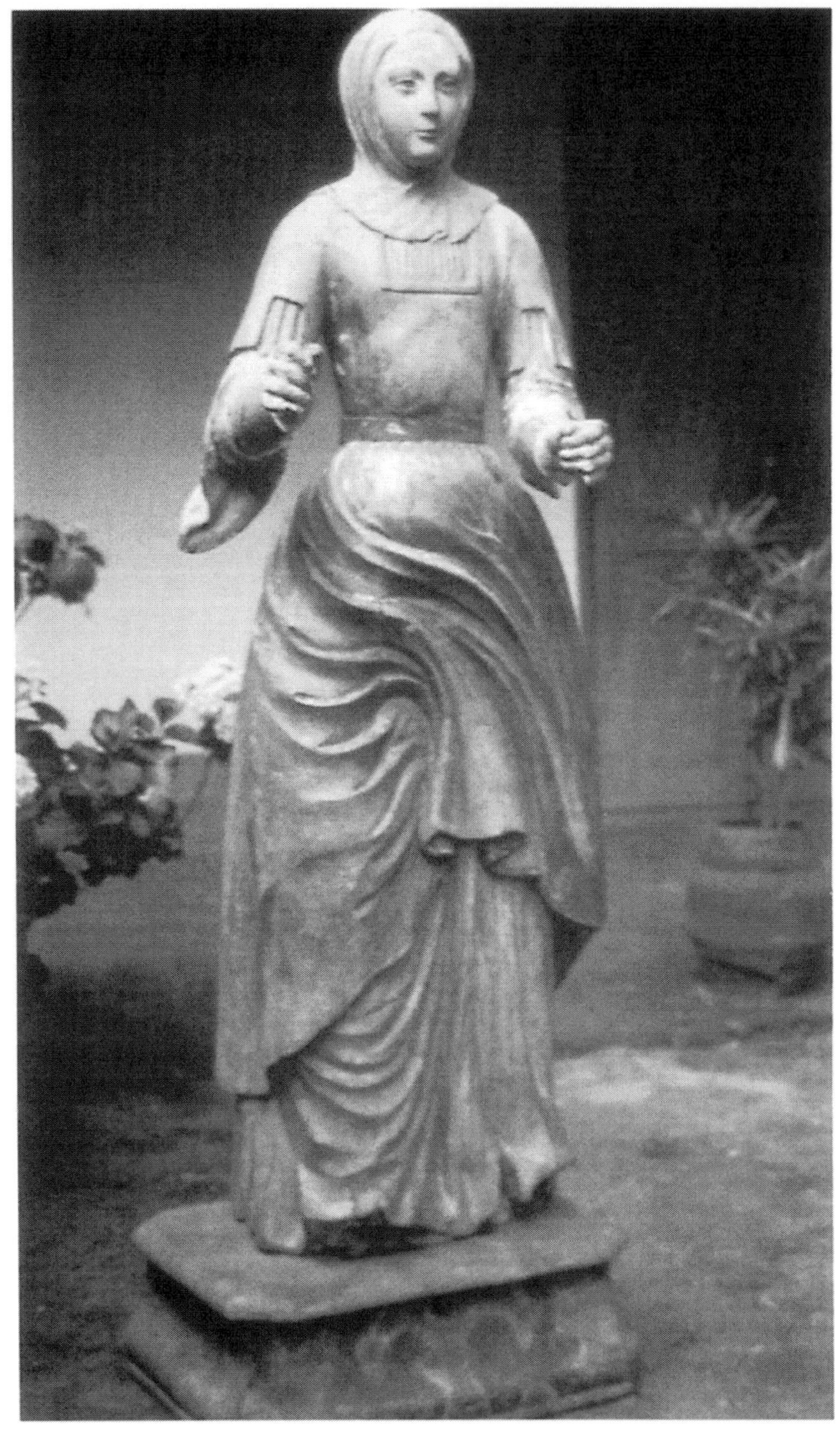

93 *María de la Cabeza*, wood polychrome, late 17th century. Santiago Museum, Paraguay. Photograph courtesy of Paul Frings.

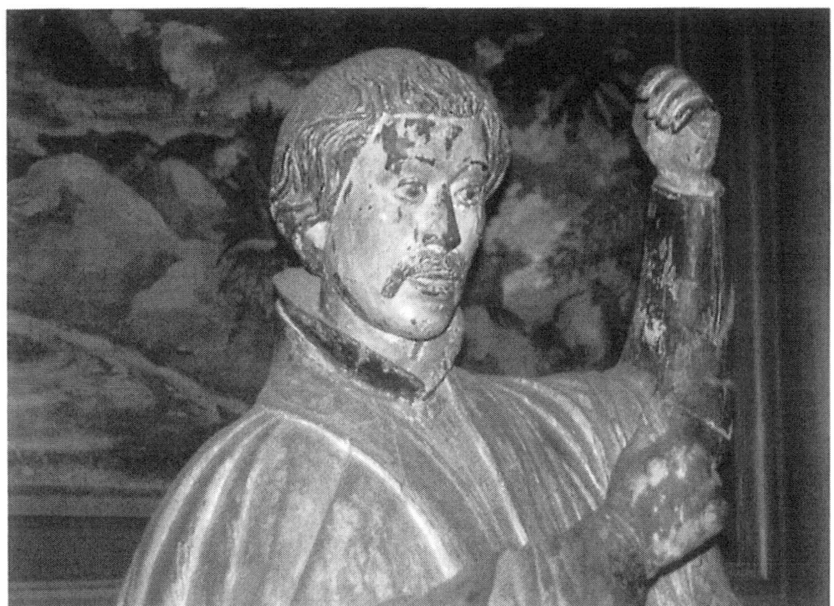

94 *Saint Francis Xavier*, here attributed to the Trinidad Master; wood polychrome, mid-18th century (detail). Museo Francisco Pascasio Moreno, La Plata, Argentina.

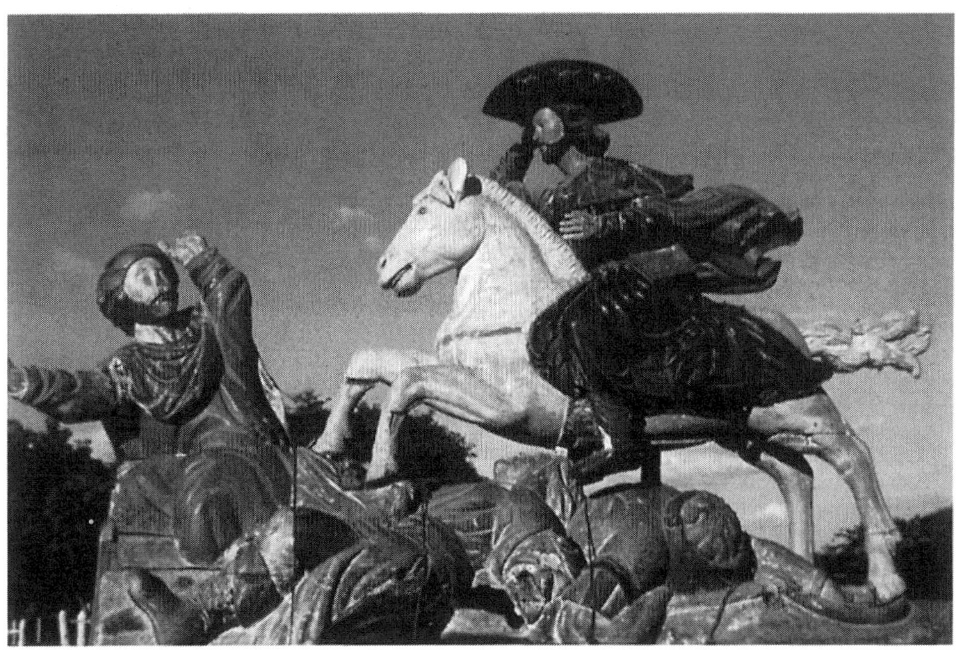

95 *Santiago Matamoros*, here attributed to the Trinidad Master; wood with traces of polychrome, after 1737 (2.12 × 1.26 m). Santiago Museum, Paraguay. Photograph courtesy of Paul Frings.

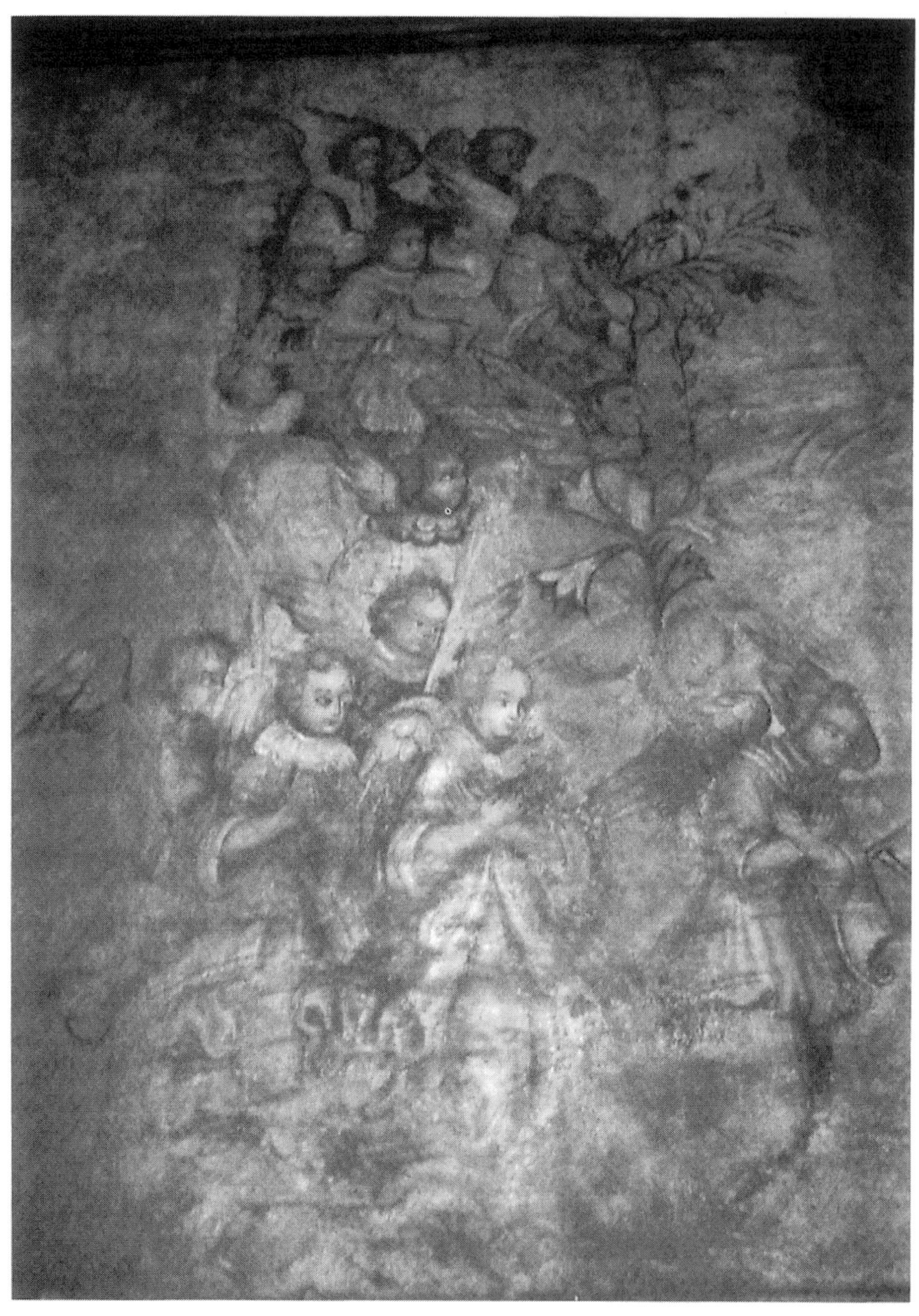

96 *Last Judgment* (detail), mural painting, 18th century. Loreto Chapel, Santa Rosa Museum, Paraguay.

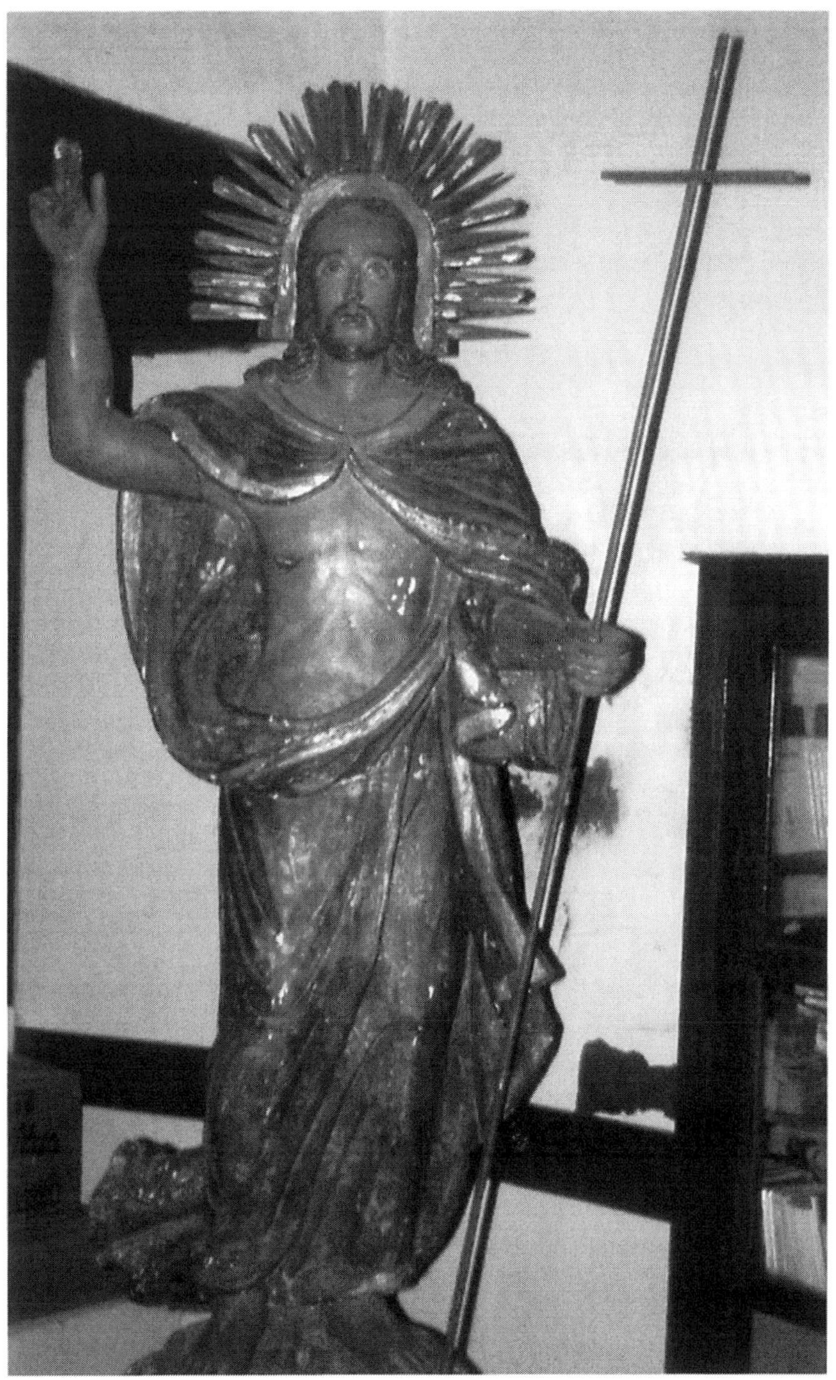

97 *Risen Christ*, wood polychrome, 17th century. San Ignacio Museum, Paraguay.

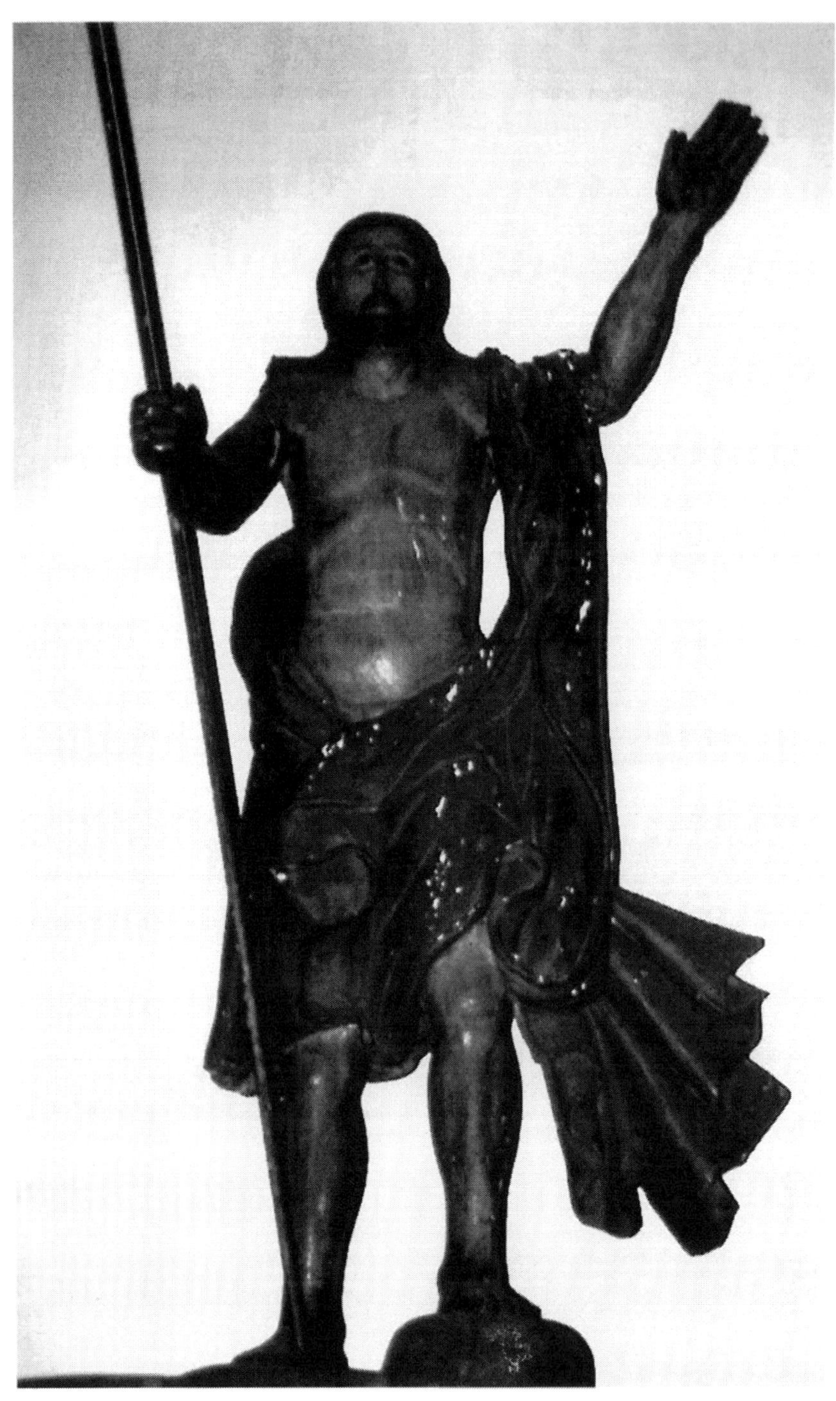

98 *Risen Christ*, wood polychrome, 17th century. Santa María Parish Church, Paraguay.

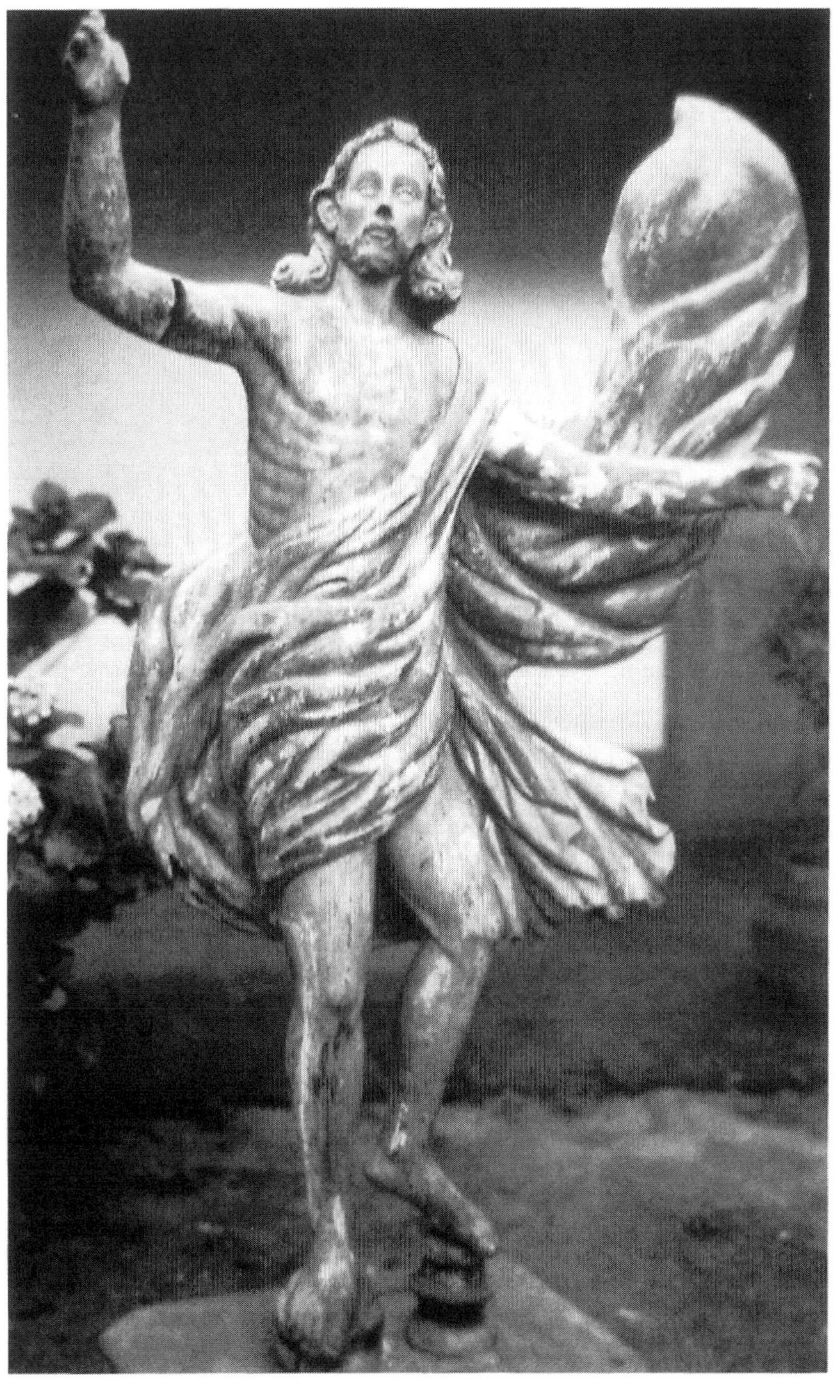

99 *Risen Christ*, wood polychrome, second quarter of 18th century. Santiago Museum, Paraguay. Photograph courtesy of Paul Frings.

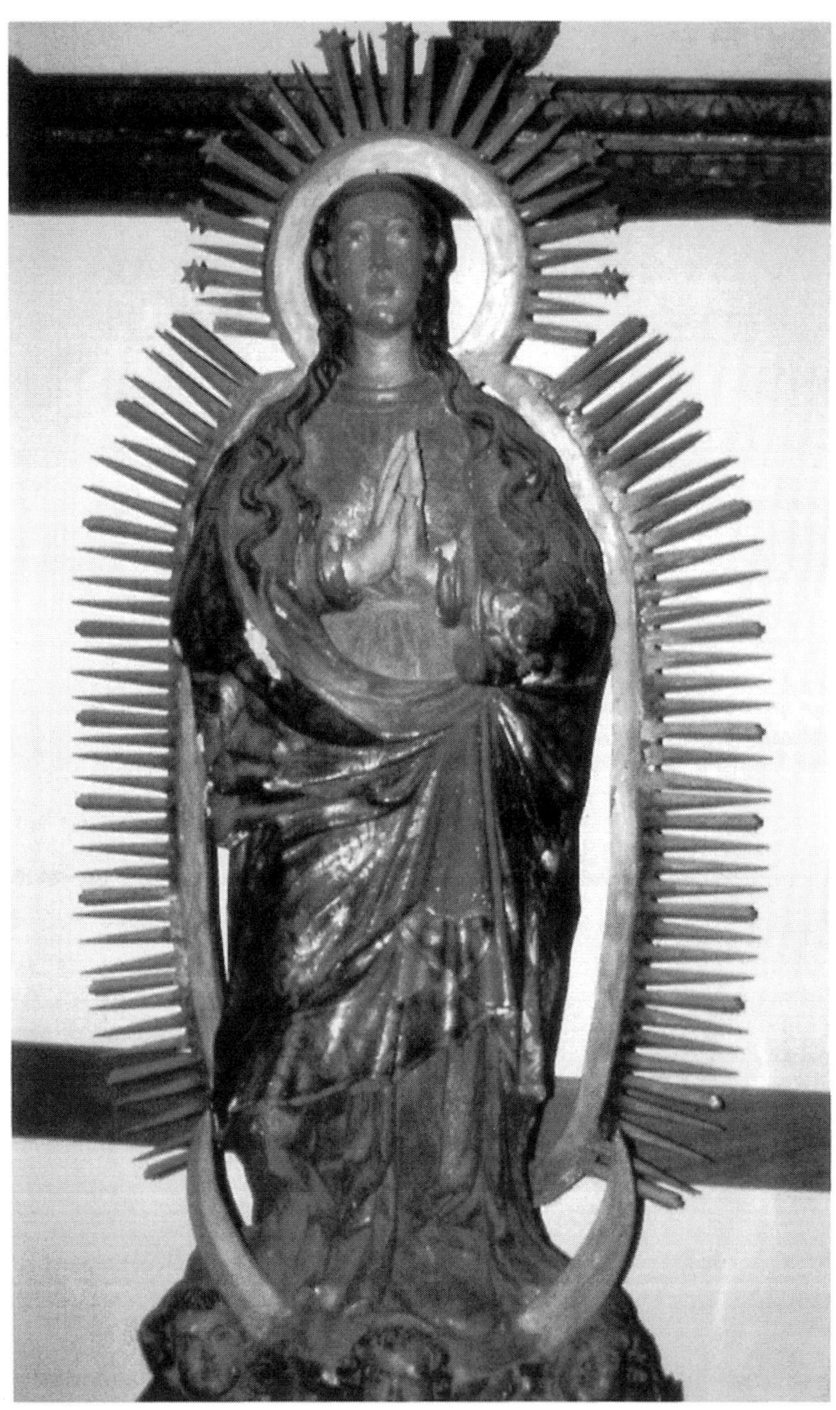

100 *Nuestra Señora de los Milagros ('La Conquistadora')*, wood polychrome with gold, 17th century; after Louis Berger, S.J. San Ignacio Museum, Paraguay.

Religious authority was the only kind capable of operating beyond the village level. Its hierarchy was based on an individual's capacity for sacred chant, or 'beautiful words' (*ñe'é porá*), which combined dance, spoken words, sung chants, and wordless melodies.[20] Anyone with this gift could achieve a certain degree of religious authority according to the number of sacred chants and curative abilities he or she possessed. The highest level belonged to the shamans (*payé*), who could lead collective dances in sacred rituals and festivals, and especially the great shaman (*karai*), who presided over the great collective dance (*Nimongarai*) celebrated every year between January and March when the corn began to ripen.[21] Like Christian anchorites, the *karai* lived an ascetic life in isolation from society, and were uniquely able to move from village to village, even passing unharmed through enemy territory.

In fact, the *karai* were so influential that their authority clashed directly with that of the chiefs. This contradiction was a fundamental weakness in Guaraní society. The only way that a great shaman could manifest his power was by disrupting the sedentary social order of the village in favour of a nomadic, spiritual life with strong messianic overtones. In Brazil, among the Tupí-Guaraní, great shamans led extraordinary pilgrimages toward a distant paradise beyond the mountains or the sea known as the 'Land-without-Evil.' During 1539–49, for example, ten to twelve thousand people left their farms in coastal Brazil in a march toward the headwaters of the Amazon, where a mere 300 survivors finally reached their destination.[22] Among the Guaraní of Paraguay, who did not attempt giant migrations until the nineteenth century, these messianic phenomena took the form of resistance movements against the Spanish settlers.[23] It was their role as heralds of the Land-without-Evil that gave the great shamans the highest authority. That place, often equated with the Christian heaven, was a land of verdant richness which was attainable without dying but which was nevertheless related to imminent cataclysm.

It is no surprise that a people whose pantheon was composed of the forces of nature and whose worship was based on the Word would have little place for the human figure in their visual culture. Unfortunately, virtually no pre-contact Guaraní art survives today, other than a few ceramic burial vessels with corregated or cross-hatched patterns found in excavations. Almost everything we know about Guaraní art before the arrival of the Jesuits comes from descriptions and illustrations in European texts, and, most importantly, the post-contact art of the unconverted Guaraní peoples. Many pre-contact traits continued to flourish in the art of these indigenous peoples in the Paraguayan interior, as can be seen in the tightly knit meander patterns and concentric whorls found on Tupí-Guaraní shamanic pipes from the late eighteenth or early nineteenth century (fig. 82). We will return to these and other colonial-period objects, which also borrow and interpret elements of European art, later in this chapter.

Guaraní art was not merely aniconic, but anti-mimetic.[24] The reality of things was not expressed by imitating their visual appearance, as in European art, but by capturing their essence. Guaraní style is schematic and geometric, conceptual rather than perceptual. It is based on stylized, simple forms, themselves taken from patterns found in nature which are endowed with strong symbolic meaning.

Rather than reproducing the entire appearance of an object or animal, for example, the Guaraní would quote an attribute of it that they felt captured its inner meaning. Ticio Escobar gives the example of ceramic vessels decorated with a fingerprint motif that signifies an armadillo by resembling its skin, or basketry patterns that recall snakeskin.[25] This mode of representation – like an ideogram, the symbol connotes rather than denotes – is completely opposed to Renaissance conceptions of the image and had important implications for reduction art. Thus, Guaraní art was a reflection of the natural and mythological world in which these people lived, and its apparently abstract forms (to a European) were in fact highly meaningful. This is why a surface pattern on a reduction sculpture could mean as much to its sculptor as the image itself.

Like many non-European art traditions, Guaraní visual culture was deeply integrated with other cultural forms – in this case, primarily dance and oratory – and was also involved with everyday utility and sustenance. Remarkably, for a people who would later excel in the production of wooden and stone statuary, the Guaraní had no tradition of wood or stone carving. Their principal media were ceramics, basketry, featherwork, and body painting, the latter two being particularly significant since they adorned the human body.[26] Featherwork played the most important role in Guaraní ritual, and was related closely to the powers of the shamans. In general, patterns and motifs derived from the material of the object. Thus featherwork was the main source of floral imagery, since the feathers resembled petals in both shape and colour, and woven basketry favoured geometrical ornament.[27] This trueness to material later surfaced in reduction sculpture in wood, whereby the shape and grain of the wood would sometimes dictate the final form and pattern of the sculpture.

The First Jesuit Reductions and the Guaraní Reaction

As in Asia and other outlying areas of Latin America, the Jesuits were chosen in 1609 to lead the Guaraní missions because of their expertise at the frontier. Although officially falling within the jurisdiction of the Viceroy of Peru, most of greater Paraguay in reality lay outside of colonial control. The warlike Guaraní remained politically independent – living *'a modo de bestias por los campos,'*[28] according to one contemporary description – except in the environs of Asunción and the territory of the Franciscan missions to the east and southeast of the city, and they posed a constant threat to the Spanish regime, particularly during the *karai* uprisings of the later sixteenth century. Paraguay also owed some of its freedom to being a buffer zone between Spanish Peru and Portuguese Brazil (this position, however, would later have tragic consequences for the Guaraní). As a semi-independent region, therefore, the territory of the Jesuit reductions on the Paraná and Uruguay riverbanks and in Guairá to the northeast was comparable to Jesuit mission regions in Asia that lay outside of colonial control. Although the threat of European force was more immediate for the Guaraní than it was for the Japanese or Mughals, they managed by an accident of history to remain effectively beyond the arm of Spanish rule.

Contrary to popular opinion, the Society did not arrive in Paraguay with a utopian reduction system planned out in advance. It was – like all of their missions – the product of trial and error, and involved selective adaptation of specific local indigenous traditions. In fact, the reductions were still adapting to local circumstances well into the eighteenth century.[29] Even the Utopian and Arcadian character that has been ceaselessly attributed to the reductions has more to do with the romantic associations of later historians than with the reality of the time.[30] The Paraguay reductions were not even unique. The first missions were based loosely on the Jesuit *aldeias* among the Tupí of Brazil and the *doctrinas* in Juli (in fact, the Jesuit Provincial at the time of the first Paraguay reductions was Diego de Torres, who had been Superior at Juli).[31]

The Jesuits also learned many important lessons from their predecessors in the area. As we have already seen in chapter 2, the earliest Spanish settlers in Paraguay capitalized on indigenous networks of kinship bonds when they allied with Guaraní groups against their Guaycurú, Payaguá, and Yapirú foes in ways which the Jesuits would adopt later on. The Franciscans, however, were the primary model. The Order of Saint Francis founded their first missions in the Asunción region in 1575 and openly adopted the role of *karai*, acquiring the great shamans' traditional authority as messiah. They also introduced Guaraní concepts of landownership into their missions – most famously the division of property into communal and private territory (*tupá mba'e* and *avá mba'e*), a process popularly credited to the Jesuits. Even the most significant improvement introduced in the Jesuit missions – their freedom from the exploitative colonial *encomienda* system enforced in 1556– was made possible by Franciscan efforts in the Synod and Ordinances of Asunción (1603) and the Ordinances of Alfaro (1611).[32]

In spite of the relative freedom and autonomy of the Guaraní hinterlands, many scholars insist that the Society of Jesus was such a forceful presence in the region that the reduction Guaraní were more quickly and completely cut off from their past than even their colonized kinsmen in the colonial towns.[33] This view is partly influenced by contemporary Jesuit sources, which – as we have seen elsewhere – tended to exaggerate the European character of their missions to impress authorities in Rome. The earliest Jesuit missionaries came to Paraguay fuelled with the spirit of palaeochristian revival. As do similar sources in Mexico and Peru, letters from the period equated the Guaraní with antediluvian man, and represented the fathers as heirs to the Early Christians – as the quotation included in the title of this chapter attests. As a result, reports from as late as the eighteenth century cast the Guaraní as Simple Natives, '*barbaros desnudos*,'[34] whose passiveness and innocence made them a *tabula rasa* for conversion.[35] A remark by the Paraguayan missionary Anton Sepp is typical of this paternalistic attitude. Writing at the end of the seventeenth century, he commented that the Guaraní loved the Jesuit fathers 'like a child loves his father. We clothed them, instructed them, and educated them. They are very docile and imitate everything that they see.'[36] This attitude – 'a paradoxical blend of pride and disdain'[37] – coloured the Jesuits' descriptions of Guaraní mission arts, as well, so that indigenous artists ended up being portrayed as derivative copyists incapable of creativity or originality.

Recent work on the social and economic structure of the reductions, however, is challenging the assumption that the reduction Guaraní lost touch with their indigenous past, and is revealing the extent of their own contribution to reduction culture.[38] In fact, the Jesuits could have done nothing without their willing cooperation; the handful of missionaries were completely at their mercy. Just as in the great Asian empires, the Jesuits could only ingratiate themselves among this virtually autonomous people by gaining their respect as equals. The first Guaraní converts consented to join the fathers, not because they were impressed with the superiority of European civilization, but, rather, because they admired the Jesuits' ability to express authority within the parameters of their own culture. The Jesuits always relied heavily on Guaraní converts to spread the word to their unconverted brethren. Even within the reductions, authority was mild and usually exercised through Guaraní chiefs. Guaraní acceptance of Christian routine was also very slow and not without resistance, both passive and active as we will see.[39]

The Jesuits immersed themselves in Guaraní society. Taking their cue from the Franciscans, the first fathers adopted the role of *karai*, or great shamans. As we have seen, within Guaraní society this position is associated with messianic hope and a disruption of existing norms. As great shamans, therefore, missionaries were able to uproot villagers in a quest for heavenly salvation without transgressing traditional conventions. But unlike the Guaraní great shamans, the Jesuits were able to unite universal spiritual authority with that of the secular chief. They led people away from their villages toward the 'Land-without-Evil,' but here it was an actual village (the reduction), which offered the earthly benefits of sustenance and protection together with the spiritual ones of oratory, music, and dance. The Jesuits owed their astonishing success to this unique combination of spiritual and temporal power, which had been unattainable in traditional Guaraní society.[40]

The Jesuits borrowed extensively from indigenous culture. As practitioners of 'beautiful words,' they enticed people to follow them using oratory, the most sacred and potent feature of Guaraní religion – the same method that had won them the respect of Confucian scholars and the Mughal Emperor. As at Akbar's debating hall in Fatehpur Sikri, the Jesuits did not defeat rival *karai* by brute force but through public debate.[41] Another concession to Guaraní beliefs was the importance given to religious visions in reduction life. Visionary experience provided a convenient point of convergence for the two cultures, since it was an essential feature both of Guaraní religion, in which people acquired religious authority through divine revelations of 'beautiful words,' and of early modern Catholicism. In one of the most remarkable examples of religious syncretism in the history of the Catholic missions, the early Jesuits and the Guaraní shared apparitions and dreams. Not only did the Jesuits report having the same dreams as Guaraní *caciques*, but they placed value even on the prophecies of unconverted shamans.[42] Visions also provided the most prominent forum for the indigenous people to come to terms with Christianity. A common miracle recounted by Jesuit writers told of a convert having a vision who, fuelled by the gift of Christianized 'beautiful words,' preached in a trance for hours or even days at a time. Such an intense spirituality, reminiscent of nineteenth-century tent revival meetings in the United States, renders ridiculous the assumption that the Guaraní were a simple people, embodied in comments like this one by Sepp: '... our Indians have in reality little aptitude for anything invisible or not placed directly before their eyes, namely the spiritual and abstract, but they have much capacity for all of the mechanical arts.'[43]

The predominance of dance, music, and costume in Christian reduction life was another acquiescence to the predelictions of Guaraní religion. But most of all, the reductions celebrated the Word. Again building on the efforts of Franciscans such as Fray Luis Bolaños, who wrote the first Guaraní catechism during 1585–6,[44] the Jesuits made the Guaraní language the foundation of their missionizing efforts. Often cited as the most significant survivor of pre-contact culture, Guaraní is still an official language in Paraguay, and possesses a thriving literature even today. Better known to historians is the adoption of Guaraní political and social institutions, such as the communal work regimen popularly known as *comunismo misional*, and the organization of reduction society into twenty or thirty *cacicatos* (a Caribbean term equivalent to the Guaraní *teyy*), combined with the democratic Spanish concept of the *cabildo*, or town council.[45] In reality, this system was far from communistic, and recent studies cited in chapter 2 have revealed a discrepancy between the rights and possessions of the Guaraní elites and commoners.

The Jesuits did not hesitate, either, to synthesize elements of Guaraní religion with Christianity – even if these substitutions were not always accurate.[46] The Guaraní had an extensive mythology populated by gods, culture heroes, and animal spirits. The missionaries' first dilemma was which of their many benificent gods to equate with the Christian God. Their choice of Tupá,[47] the lord of thunder and the west wind, was a notoriously bad one. Barely appearing in the great Creation Myth, Tupá was a destroyer god who was 'neither creator of the world nor transformer, nor culture hero,'[48] and was therefore the antithesis of the Christian God, although he did share the role of master of human destiny. For the Devil, missionaries chose the sylvan imps named Añá and Yurupari, whose role is to persecute men and doom them to failure. The Jesuits also capitalized on the existence of flood myths (*iporun*) in Guaraní religion, although there is some evidence that they did not have the importance for Guaraní religion that later converts claimed.[49] Christ was cast as a great shaman (the same role taken on by the fathers themselves), and given the name Pai Guazú, or 'great father.'[50] As in India, Mexico, and Peru, the Jesuits also equated an indigenous culture hero with the apostle Thomas, this time using the figure Zumé, or Pai Tumé, a Guaraní and Tupí-Guaraní patriarch who appeared mysteriously, introduced agriculture and civilization to mankind, and disappeared over the eastern ocean – that is, toward Europe.[51] Missionaries drew upon native baptism and confession rites (although naturally without the cannibalism associated with the former), and even allowed the persistence of featherwork in dances, although these costumes admittedly were confined to characters portraying unconverted *indígenos*.[52]

While the Jesuits were appropriating aspects of indigenous religion, society, and culture, the Guaraní were perpetuating their traditions on their own. Throughout the Jesuit era, the reduction Guaraní maintained contact, through trade, diplomacy, and mutual emigration, with unconverted Guaraní tribes such as the Caremás and Apyterés (ancestors of today's Mby'a, Chiripá, and Pai

Tavyterá), who lived in the mountains on the periphery of reduction territory.[53] These autonomous *ta'a*, or mountain, tribes (also known as Caaiguá, or 'people of the forest') preserved the rites, symbols, and myths of pre-contact religion. They still do today. In one astonishing testament to the persistence of pre-contact beliefs, the Avá-Katú-Eté (Chiripá) returned to the mountains in the eighteenth century after 150 years of Jesuit tutelage with the essence of their original religion and myths largely intact.[54] One explanation for the persistence of indigenous beliefs is that most Guaraní never really completely internalized Christianity. Many believe that they only accepted the exterior and superficial aspects of Christianity, such as ceremonial, because its doctrine was alien to their belief system but its pageantry was akin to the expressive nature of the 'beautiful words.'[55] Another way to look at this, as I have suggested in chapter 2, is that they indigenized Christianity and made it their own.

The Guaraní – both the converts and *ta'a* tribes – adopted aspects of Christianity that made sense in their own world. They could do this either in sympathy with Christianity or as a challenge to it. The latter attitude was especially prevalent during the Guaraní resistance movement, when indigenous leaders capitalized on the traditional shamanistic ability to take on attributes of an enemy to outmanoeuvre him.[56] Shaman leaders such as Yuapití, Miguel Artiguaye, and Guyraverá wore costumes inspired by Catholic vestments, performed mock masses with altars, manioc cake and maize wine, episcopal benedictions, crosses, and anti-baptisms.[57] Shaman leaders related a Guaraní tradition in which *karai* were virgin-born to Christ's birth by the Virgin Mary.[58] They equated the Christian concept of Hell with the shamanic *Ñandeyára*, which punishes and rewards, and used it to prophesize a punishment for Christian converts.[59] Some resistance movements, such as that of the shamans Yeguacaporú and Yaguarobí, even presided over a body of twelve shamans in imitation of Christ's apostles.[60]

The most visible adoption of Christian forms by the Guaraní anti-Christian movement was the erection of mock chapels and anti-reductions in the hills of Guairá beyond mission territories. These chapels, described here by Ruiz de Montoya, were in fact shrines housing the bones of shamans, important objects of worship in Guaraní religion:

> They found the temple alone and unguarded ... [it] was spacious and well fitted out. In the interior was a dark, two-doored compartment, in which the corpse was suspended on a net or hammock between two poles. The ropes were decorated with a variety of brilliant feathers. The hammock was covered with two precious cloths of colored feathers, striking to the eyes. There were devices for perfuming the place. No one dared enter it but the priest who posed questions in the people's name to this oracle. In the front part of the temple were numerous benches where the people sat and listened to the replies given by the devil. Hanging from the walls and beams all over the temple were numerous offerings of fruits of the earth in curiously worked baskets.[61]

Surrounding the chapel were little 'hermitages,' where fleeing neophytes would meet periodically to hear the speeches and oracles of the shaman. Shaman resistance leaders would chastise them for leaving the fold and invite them to abandon Christianity in a manner that closely resembled the Jesuits' own proselytizing.[62]

The motif of hung offerings of food used in the anti-chapels was later adopted by reduction Guaraní for the Christian cause. Reductions frequently decorated ritual walkways with cornucopian triumphal arches to punctuate liturgical celebrations, one of which was described in a letter of 1643. Woven from tree branches into the form of a tripartite Roman triumphal arch, the central arch was draped all over with

> dried and fresh fish, dried and fresh wild game, live pullets in cages, hens tied by the neck, ostrich eggs ... colourful birds which are in great abundance in the region, and foxes and dogs ... The [lateral] arches, columns, and plinths are similarly adorned; they have hung [from them] tigers, serpents, and the greatest variety of wild skins, which are stuffed to regain their former appearance, so that they look alive. Interspersed between these are bags stuffed full of food ... [Elsewhere are hung] clothing, bows, arrows, quivers and furthermore all kinds of household furnishings ...[63]

Few structures are more symbolic of the dialogue between cultures than these two ephemeral monuments of the earliest days of the Paraguay reductions.

Jesuit Artists at the Paraguay Reductions

Although several decades passed before the missions could produce works of art on a massive scale, Jesuit fathers and brothers began training Guaraní converts in the fine arts from the very beginning. Taking the lead from the humble art ateliers that had been founded in the reductions in Juli as early as 1577, the first missionaries taught the rudiments of painting, architecture, and probably sculpture.[64] Over the next century and a half, the Jesuit teachers represented a wide variety of nationalities and professional backgrounds, making the European component of reduction art more international than anywhere else in the River Plate region – and much of Latin America.[65] One of the first artists to set foot in reduction territories was French, and he was followed not just by Spaniards from all over the Peninsula, but by Italians, Germans, Flemings, Central Europeans, and Peruvians. Typical of the international make-up of the Paraguay reductions is the boatload of Jesuit missionaries with whom the artist and musician Anton Sepp reached Buenos Aires from Europe in 1693: 'There were forty-four of us missionaries from a variety of nations: Spaniards, Italians, Dutch, Sicilians, Sardinians, Genoese, Milanese, Romans, Bohemians, Austrians ...'[66]

As we have seen in their missions around the world, most of the Jesuit artists in Paraguay were jacks of all trades, capable of an extraordinary variety of activities, ranging from carpentry and music to medicine and astronomy.[67] Although some of the later missionaries were professional artists or architects in their own right, most of the earliest ones could best be described using Francisco Xarque's characterization of 1687: 'some Brother, who understands something of carpentry, of using a paintbrush, of proportion, perspective, and similar arts, under whose direction, and the study of a few books, the fathers were able to accomplish such churches.'[68]

Even the first Paraguay reductions were remarkably active artistically, especially in the realm of architecture. Already by 1618, less than a decade after the arrival of the Jesuits, the Paraná mission of San Ignacio Guazú ('the Greater,' founded 1609) and the Guairá reduction of Loreto (founded 1610) had functioning art workshops and handsome three-aisled churches.[69] By the late 1620s, all thirteen of the Guairá missions, soon to be destroyed during 1632–6 by the Brazilian slave raiders known as 'Mamelucos,' boasted 'beautiful churches, of which I have not seen better in the countries I have passed through, from Peru to Chile,'[70] according to a contemporary visitor. Most of the early missionaries put their hands to architectural projects, including José Cataldino, one of the first two Guairá missionaries, Antonio Ruiz de Montoya, the martyr Roque González de Santa Cruz, Pedro de Espinosa, Silverio Pastor, and Ignacio Henart.[71] We know much less about sculpture or painting from this period, but since retables framing statues and pictures were standard features of even the most rudimentary mission architecture of the period, they must have been produced as well. There were enough statues in Guairá in 1639 for the Mamelucos to smash them to pieces, 'chopping up and smashing the holy images, as if they were Lutheran statutes.'[72] Because of their location in the safer Paraná region, the reductions of San Ignacio Guazú and Itapuá (founded 1615) appear to have had the most consistently active art ateliers during this pioneer era.[73]

Very little remains of the work of the first Jesuit artists on the reductions. The earliest Jesuit painter to work there was the Andalusian brother Bernardo Rodríguez (in the reductions, 1615–20; d. 1650), who was sent by Torres from Peru in 1606 and also painted canvases for Jesuit foundations in colonial cities such as Santa Fé. Before his arrival, most of the religious painting at the missions had been on paper.[74] Shortly afterward, the reductions were given a boost by the arrival of the French brother Louis Berger (1590–1643). Born in Abbeville, Berger was the first missionary to have a professional art background, having trained in art academies in Paris, Rouen, and the Low Countries before coming to Paraguay.[75] Like Rodríguez, Berger divided his time between Jesuit foundations in colonial centres such as Tucumán and the reductions, since Jesuit artists were scarce in the entire River Plate region. Typically for mission artists everywhere, he was a man of 'many skills,' which also included those of doctor, sculptor, musician and instrument-maker, and goldsmith.[76] Jesuit chroniclers affirmed his astonishing popularity with the indigenous people of the region; or, as his obituary asserted: 'it is difficult to believe how many Indians he led to piety.' In 1623 he was at San Ignacio, where he had built and 'beautifully decorated' the church and had just begun the house.[77] Three years later, a report remarked that he was not only painting, but teaching the Guaraní to paint and play musical instruments, an activity at which he was a great success.[78]

One of Berger's canvases survives today, albeit in a heavily restored state. His 1634 *Virgen de los Milagros* in the Compañía at Santa Fé (fig. 83) is an elegant *inmaculada* in the Flemish style, whose sharp pleats of drapery recall the work of Bitti in Peru, although the figure lacks the winsomeness of Bitti's madonnas. Like most reduction art, it is almost certainly inspired by an engraving.[79] Berger is also known to have painted many other oil paintings, including *Portrait of Charles Borromeo* (1633), *The Sixty Archangels* (1624), another *Inmaculada*, and the *Cuatro Novísimos*.[80] Berger taught painting at the reductions of Itapuá and San Ignacio Guazú, and at the missions along the Uruguay. At Itapuá he taught one of the few

Guaraní artists who signed his work. José Habiyú, whom we will explore further below, painted an oil portrait of the Virgin Mary in 1618 over a pencil sketch that has been attributed to Berger himself (fig. 84). The miniature painting copies the figure from a version of the St. Luke Madonna that was in the Jesuit College in Córdoba – the very image that had so enthralled Asia (fig. 1).[81] The underdrawing is delicate, and again exhibits the angular lines and frontal pose of the Flemish school. Habiyú's overpainting, although rudimentary, accurately executes the drapery and *chiaroscuro* of its model, as Plá has noted.[82]

In the early 1630s, the Mamelucos from São Paulo devastated the thirteen Guairá missions in their ruthless drive for slaves, forcing the entire population to move in a vast migration four hundred miles downriver past the thundering cauldron of Iguazú Falls. Only after the Spanish Crown permitted the reductions to bear arms were they able to put an end to the terror at the victory of Mbororé in 1641. The survivors were divided among the remaining missions in the safer territory of the Paraná and Uruguay, and soon began to rebuild their towns again, giving them the same names as their lost homes in Guairá. Such a tremendous scale of new building activity demanded a new generation of artists and architects. Among the first painters to answer the call was Louis de la Croix (Luis de la Cruz, 1600–69) from Flanders, who specialized in mathematics and perspective at his college in Europe.[83] De la Croix almost singlehandedly supplied the new churches as well as colonial foundations with retable paintings: 'The residences, colleges, and reductions are all full of canvases which he has left us with his marvellous brush.'[84] This enthusiastic praise for de la Croix's interior of the Church of San Lorenzo (1647) shows that the artist's lack of materials did not prevent him from evoking a Italian Renaissance style:

> The greatest praise goes to the high altar which is adorned with a fine wooden gilt throne just recently arrived from Spain [with] the holy image of Loreto. The rest of the main chapel is adorned with an elegant series of holy pictures, as well as columns, urns, crowns, and stylobates, [all] painted to look like jasper and various marbles.[85]

The letter goes on to describe a 'skilfully made' tomb for the body of Christ done in the same style. De la Croix's work at San Joseph was similarly ornate; despite the most meagre resources, the walls around the high altar were adorned with gilt columns, urns, and crowns, focusing on his own painting of the titular saint.[86]

The actual church buildings were erected by a brother who worked on the same grandiose scale. The first trained architect to join the reductions, the Andalusian brother Bartholomé Cardeñoso (1596–after 1656), who was described as a 'megalomaniac,' built such extravagant churches that he became something of an embarrassment to the Society in Europe.[87] Cardeñoso would not have been able to do this work without considerable assistance, both from the Guaraní and from other Jesuit carpenters. The latter may have included the Catalan Juan Terrer (b. 1597), Juan de Morales (b. 1606) from Lima, Claudio Flores (b. 1576), and the Paraguayan native Juan de Cardenas (b. 1593), all of whom came to the Paraguay province in the 1620s or '30s, just in time for this building expansion.[88] Other painters and sculptors at the reductions in the mid-seventeenth century included two Flemings, Philippe Viveros (van der Vyvere, 1605–79) and Philippe Lemaire (1608–69), mentioned already in chapter 2. The painter van der Vyvere is known to have worked at Yapeyú, Loreto, and Encarnación; and the architect and woodworker Lemaire was quite active on the reductions after entering the Society in 1640.[89] Two Spanish artists of the same period, Antonio de la Cuesta and Brother Cañigual, established a school for painting, sculpture, and carpentry at the reduction of San Luis in 1650.[90]

By 1646 witnesses made glowing reports of the extent of the Society's work, which had reached an astonishing scale when we consider the missions' financial circumstances and their distance from colonial centres:

> [The churches are] very well adorned with the cleanliness and order which [exists] in all parts of Spain ... the forementioned fathers of the Company [of Jesus] ... keep the retables and church furniture well ornamented and in every one of the forementioned reductions there are sacristies and inside those are their treasuries of church plate.[91]

Similarly, in 1648, a glowing *real cédula* proclaimed:

> [The Jesuits] fertilized the land in such a way that one can see such settlements very properly founded with churches, music, and every adornment pertaining to the Divine Faith ... such that this new plant imitates the Primitive Church.[92]

The legend of the grandeur and abundance of the reductions, later to be used against them by writers such as Voltaire, had already taken root.

Reduction art briefly lost its international character during the later seventeenth century, after the Spanish Crown stopped allowing foreigners to join the Paraguay province.[93] Few artists of any kind arrived during this period, exceptions being the *sevillano* Jesuit Anselmo de la Mata (fl. 1674–1732), who ran a workshop at the reduction of San Nicolás, Domingo de Torres (1607–after 1687), a brother who worked as an architect at San Carlos and San Nicolás, the Castillian sculptor Juan Castaño (b. 1640), and the Argentine brother Blas Gómez (b. 1632), a '*pictor et sculptor*' from Santa Fé.[94] This period of Iberian cultural domination ended dramatically in the last decade of the century, however, with the arrival of a new wave of Jesuit artists from Italy and Germany. For the first time in the history of the Paraguay reductions, these men included artists who could have held their own in Europe.

Opening the floodgates of the Baroque, Giuseppe Brasanelli (1659–1728), Angelo Camillo Petragrassa (1656–1729), and Anton Sepp (1655–1733) introduced the Guaraní to the triumphalist style of late-seventeenth-century Roman and Bavarian art – in particular, the great Jesuit artistic projects of the vaulting and altar of St. Ignatius at the Gesù (1699) and the Church of Sant' Ignazio (1693–4), conceived by Giovanni Battista Gaulli (Baciccio) and the Jesuit Andrea Pozzo. Especially influential for later reduction art was the new iconography of Jesuit saints, standardized for the first time with a new dose of *magnificenza*, not only by Baciccio and Pozzo but by Ciro Ferri and Pierre Legros on their projects for the same Roman commissions.[95]

The first decades of the eighteenth century were by far the most international and cosmopolitan era of reduction art history to date. This period witnessed a new generation of churches which surpassed their predecessors in grandeur, including new foundations such as San Borja (1692) and San Juan Bautista (1697), as well as older reductions that moved to new locations, such as San Ignacio Miní ('the Lesser,' moved 1695) and Loreto (moved 1696).[96] They also saw a reformation of Jesuit iconography within the reductions, inspired by the new images from Rome. This campaign was led by the Visitor Luis de la Roca in the 1710s and '20s, who replaced outdated images of Jesuit saints, such as these ones at Santiago in 1714: 'They are to procure some [new] statues of St Xavier and St Borgia for the main altar, because those which are now there are not fitting. The same is true for the statues of the Chapel of All Souls.'[97]

Brasanelli (1659–1728) was the greatest Jesuit artist in Paraguay, and the leading force behind the renewal of reduction visual culture. A man of incredible energy, Brasanelli divided his time between the missions, building churches, executing paintings, sculptures, and altarpieces,[98] and leading workshops in San Borja (1696–1705), Concepción (1705–15), Itapuá (1718–24), Santa Ana (1720–4, 1728),[99] San Francisco Xavier (1725), San Ignacio Miní (1724–8) (fig. 85),[100] and Loreto.[101] A contemporary description of Brasanelli's projects at Itapuá in 1718 depicts a man of Herculean, even frenetic energy:

> The church has begun. The greater part of the foundations have been completed, the pillars of the chancel have been raised, and much wood is being worked, all under the direction of Brother Joseph Brasanelli, who is responsible for the work, and simultaneously exercises all of his skills. He is directing the sculptors and the painters in producing a life of Our Saintly Father [Ignatius], which is to be divided into panels to be set up in the corridors of our residence. They have already finished eleven panels without defects, except for the lack of decent colours, because one cannot obtain them.[102]

Sometimes Brasanelli collaborated with Petragrassa, who himself worked on San Joseph, San Borja, Santo Thomé, Concepción, and San Xavier.[103] Of Italian origin, Petragrassa was no less active than his Italian collaborator, which may have hastened his untimely death in 1729. Visitor Roca makes several references to Petragrassa's work, indicating that he was a respected technician. In 1725, for example, the Visitor suspended all work on the church at San Joseph until the workers could consult with Petragrassa, 'whose recommendations will be followed to solve [the problem].'[104] Perhaps he took care of most of the technical matters and left the stylistic ones to Brasanelli.

Anton Sepp, another companion on the ship from Europe who himself founded art workshops in San Juan Bautista,[105] declared that the work of the apprentices of this 'Italian brother' would have been much appreciated in Rome.[106] Although Brasanelli was extremely prolific, and several extant sculptures have been attributed to him, only a single statue survives which can be definitely linked by documentation to the Italian maestro. A partially mutilated image of Saint Francis Borgia in a church in the former reduction town of that name in Brazil has been identified by Darko Sustersic as Brasanelli's, thanks to a reference in a letter by the Jesuit Jaime Oliver.[107] An ecstatic image in the tradition of Gianlorenzo Bernini and Gaulli, this statue and others like it became the model for a whole series of reduction statues of Jesuit saints *'a la Italiana'*[108] that were produced by Guaraní artists to meet Roca's demands for a new iconography. Owing both to the work's medium and to its intended location in a Spanish-style retable, Brasanelli's sculpture is polychrome painted, which is very un-Italian. Nevertheless, the expressive pose, windswept drapery, and mystical facial expression relate it to currents in contemporary Roman Baroque sculpture.

During the last remaining decades before the expulsion in 1767, reduction art experienced a final flowering, especially in architecture when complete stone churches were built for the first time. The hero of this age was the great Italian architect Giovanni Battista Primoli (1673–1747), who worked on three of the most magnificent stone churches ever to grace the reductions: San Miguel, Trinidad (fig. 86), and Concepción, as well as projects in Buenos Aires.[109] The Milanese architect entered the Society in 1716 and was sent the next year to the province of Paraguay, where he was immediately put to work designing buildings. The Catalán José Grimau (b. 1718) designed the equally astonishing churches at Jesús (never completed) and the dome at Trinidad, and also painted and directed art workshops at San Miguel (1745–9), San Luis (1749), Santa Rosa (1765), and Candelaría (1767).[110] His one surviving canvas, the *Virgen de las Lágrimas* at Salta Cathedral, however, is the work of a competent but second-rate painter, yet another example of reduction painting not excelling in the same way as sculpture and architecture.[111] Grimau was assisted at Jesús and perhaps also San Luis by Antonio Forcada, a builder who reached the reductions in 1759.[112]

We do not read of much sculptural activity in this period, probably because the minor arts were overshadowed by the great architectural commissions, but as I will point out below many of the great Guaraní sculptures which survive today are datable to the 1740s and 1750s. We know that reduction sculpture workshops were directed in this period by the Andalusian brother Salvador Conde (b. 1697), who worked in Candelaría (1742), Santo Angelo (1752), and Concepción (1765–8), and other art training was carried out by missionaries such as Acacio Negle (arrived 1749).[113] The new churches would have required large numbers of new statues for their retables, as well as stone sculpture to adorn their exteriors. These works in stone, of which many survive today, all date from this later period when the Guaraní had for the first time the metal tools capable of carving them.

Guaraní Artists and Workshop Practice

Although the Jesuit artists are better known and receive the most attention, the fact remains that the Guaraní themselves were responsible for the majority of reduction art. Without the idiosyncratic hand of the indigenous artist, Jesuit art in Paraguay would have been an – albeit international – blend of largely second-rate European art. The extraordinary aptitude of the Guaraní for the fine arts amazed contemporary viewers:

> I have seen several crafts made by the Indians (with the industry and care of the fathers) which deserve as much esteem as if they had had *maestros* to teach them. No one surpasses

them. It is worthy of every praise and admiration. I want to encourage and promote those who show an aptitude in these things, so that they do not waste these skills and learn others, since for the time being there is no other way to obtain these trades and ensure that the missions have them.[114]

The skill of the Guaraní artists also gladdened the hearts of their Jesuit supervisors, whose comments ranged from 'not bad at all' to 'comparable to the best work of Europe,' and even – in one gush of enthusiasm – mistakable for Rubens.[115]

Calling themselves simply *santo apohava* ('saint maker') and *retablo apohava* ('retable maker'), Guaraní artists worked in small groups of less than ten under apprenticeship to a Jesuit or an indigenous maestro called an *alcalde*, usually in the second patio of the reduction next to the church.[116] Similarly to European workshops of the period, groups of artists worked on a single painting or statue according to their skill level, with the faces and hands reserved for the masters. Xarque, writing in 1687, describes a lively workshop reminiscent of Niccolò's Seminary of Painters in Japan or the Calera de Tango in Chile, with various projects in different media going on at once:

There are carpenters for the heavy work, joiners who make retables, and carve curiosities onto them. There are other sculptors, who manufacture holy statues of every kind for the churches and altars. They also make out of iron everything that is necessary for the buildings, and the tools which serve for every trade. They found bells, and other things of smaller size, they build organs, clarinets, *chirimias*, and every kind of musical instrument. They paint icons, and holy mysteries, with which they adorn their temples. They know how to gild, and adorn their altar and retables with *estofado* work.[117]

Unlike Japan or Chile, however, this description only covers a single mission among dozens. Thanks to legions of indigenous artists, the volume of art production in Paraguay is unequalled by any other Jesuit mission enterprise anywhere in the world.

Only a handful of names of Guaraní artists have come down to us, since the communal nature of workmanship did not lend itself to personal signatures. It should be noted, incidentally, that even the Jesuits did not sign their works; we only know about their contributions from written records and their titles in the triennial catalogues of the Society. Plá has suggested that the Guaraní artists who did sign their work were *caciques*, and therefore had a higher social status.[118] Aside from José Habiyú (fl. ca. 1618), Berger's student at Itapuá, they include another of Berger's apprentices called Esteban (fl. 1644), whose Guaraní name is lost, the engravers Juan Yaparí (fl. ca. 1705) and Thomas Tilcara (fl. ca. 1728), the silversmith and musician Ignacio Paica (fl. first quarter of eighteenth century), and the 'celebre pintor' from San Borja named Ignacio Albae (fl. second half of eighteenth century).[119] A few names of young apprentice artists survive from the post-expulsion period; for example, Romualdo Payeyú from Yapeyú, who was sent to Buenos Aires in 1770 to study sculpture and retable making with a certain Don Isidro de Lorea, and his companions from the same village Ignacio Yaciberá, León Panayú, and Estanislao Fañuirá, who learned iron- and silver-smithery in the same city.[120]

Although most reductions housed workshops by the end of the seventeenth century, some of them excelled in certain media, and their work was sought after by other missions. The finest statuary was made at various times at Santa María la Mayor, Santa Rosa, San Juan, and San Nicolás; San Miguel and Itapuá were renowned for painting; and Santa María la Mayor, Loreto, and San Xavier were leading centres of painting and engraving.[121] Expulsion documents list inventories of sculpture workshops at Cruz, San Lorenzo, Mártires, and San Joseph,[122] and painting ateliers, at Trinidad, Candelaría, Apóstoles, and San Nicolás.[123]

Sometimes young artists from reductions with lesser workshops would be sent to apprentice at better ones; for example, in 1722 when Visitor Joseph de Aguirre recommended that 'they send some skilled youths with good aptitude to the towns where they have good painters and smiths to learn to paint and work with metal.'[124] Occasionally artists would be brought over from other reductions during building projects, as well; for example, when the new church was being built at Itapuá and the Visitor recommended that 'if they need an Indian skilled in that craft, he can be sought from another town.'[125]

Production took place on such a vast scale that the reductions were plagued by surplus statuary, paintings, and supplies. We must keep in mind that the arts were considered a vital means for preventing laziness among the Guaraní, and so artists were encouraged to increase their productivity even when the art was not required. Since natural hardwood abounded, and so did native skill, sacristies began to look more and more like storage warehouses. Visitor Roca recommended in 1714, for example, that retable makers in Santa Ana go ahead and use some extra wood that had been cut for a retable even though they did not need one, or at least to send it to be made at another reduction.[126] In July 1735 there were so many unused statues in a storage facility in Yapeyú and San Miguel that the Visitor Gerónimo Herrar was obliged to give them away to other chapels that needed them, so that they would not get profaned and used for the wrong purpose.[127]

Remarkably, given that the reductions had the most skilled and productive workshops in the entire River Plate region, their aim was self-sufficiency and they were therefore not actively involved with colonial trade – except for retables and textiles.[128] They did a burgeoning trade in retables, however, supplying colonial centres all over the southern cone of the continent, as well as other Jesuit enterprises such as the *estancias* in the Sierras de Córdoba and the Pampas missions south of Buenos Aires.[129] This untapped resource finally came to play a central role in colonial culture only after the expulsion, when ex-reduction workshops furnished the towns and cities of the new Viceroyalty of Río de la Plata. Documents from the 1770s and 1780s attest to the continuing production on a large scale of retables and paintings, with metropolitan centres taking over the role of apprenticeship.[130] Many workshops also migrated to the Franciscan missions near Asunción, where Guaraní Christian art had a last flowering during the great Franciscan construction projects of the late eighteenth century in places such as Yaguarón and Capiatá.[131]

As was standard for Jesuit missions worldwide, Guaraní artists learned their craft studying from engravings, which they at first copied directly and then used only as an inspiration for more original work, as we have seen elsewhere. In very few cases, however, are they slavish copies. Whether closer to European canons or the indigenous mentality, Guaraní art is consistently creative and original – in contradiction to contemporary claims to the contrary. The European prints were predominantly the work of the great Antwerp engravers of the late sixteenth century such as Wierix, Collaert, Cort, and Sadeler, but also included eighteenth-century Flemish prints, as well as Spanish, Italian, German, and probably Mexican work.[132]

Again, however, the sources provide us with few additional details. Sepp specifically mentions that he asked Guaraní artists to paint and sculpt copies of an engraving of the Virgin of Altötting which he had brought from Germany, as did the Consultor of the Jesuit College of Asunción, Francisco Bautista (b. 1696), who had a local painter copy engravings of the martyr Julian Lizardi on paper to send to the missions.[133] Since many of the images were copied in reverse, artists probably traced the image or used some optical instrument like the *Pantographica* designed by the Jesuit scientist Christoph Scheiner (1575–1650), which enabled one to make either an enlarged or reduced copy of an image simply by tracing over the original picture.[134] Although engravings were by far the most common model used, artists also studied imported European statues and paintings, as well as *bozzetti* of wax or clay.[135] Sepp himself brought over a hundred little clay devotional figures with him from Spain.[136]

Many original artworks from Europe and Peru reached the reductions, although they were never able to compete in number with indigenous works. At the beginning, the main sources for imported art objects and '*cosas al servicio del culto divino*' throughout the River Plate region were Andean centres such as Cuzco, which was solicited by Paraguay missionaries in 1621 and 1639 for church plate, bells, vestments, *ornamentos*, and paper.[137] The first recorded painting ever to appear at the reductions was an image of the Virgin Mary by the Peruvian Jesuit artist Hernández, which Roque González carried with him from village to village.[138] As we have seen elsewhere on the missions in chapter 2, it was standard practice in the pioneering days to have on hand a large canvas of the Virgin, Christ, or archangels (ranging from half a yard high to two yards high), which was unfurled as a banner of spiritual conquest in tandem with the large crosses which were raised at the foundations of new reductions.[139] Another early form of European art to reach the Paraguay province were bejewelled reliquaries containing the bones of martyrs, several of which would have been sent to the reductions. One such piece was sent from the treasury at St Moritz in Switzerland by the Jesuit Peter Aldenhoven in 1621, and another from Camarina, Sicily, by Giovanni Battista de Alterii in 1641.[140] These were often exquisitely worked and bejewelled objects, frequently composed of figural sculpture, painted scenes, metalwork, and elaborate architectural frames, and they deserve to be considered works of art in their own right.

However, before the eighteenth century, European art came only in a trickle. In 1646 the Procurator General of Paraguay ordered '36 *figuras de alabastro*' directly from Lisbon, as well as a number of books, including a mathematical text, and in 1661 a larger shipment of art arrived from Seville, including four statues of Nuestra Señora de Concepción, five of the infant Jesus, two Saint Francis Xaviers, and statues of Saint Peter, Saint Paul, Saint Nicholas, and 'Santo Rey Negro' (one of the Magi), as well as prints, medallions, and paintings.[141] Other European artworks are mentioned in the early eighteenth century as belonging to the reductions; for example, a book of the life of Saint Ignatius with engravings (probably the edition by Collaert), and a large Roman painting of Saint Ignatius writing the *Exercises* before the Virgin Mary.[142]

From the 1740s onward, a flood of paintings, sculptures, and engravings arrived on the boat from Europe. Sources record several grocery lists of such artworks. For example: four statues and '*demas adornos*' from Barcelona in 1740; 'six chests of wooden statues arrived from Napoli' in 1740; a shipment including a painting and 1,540 *novenas* of Nuestra Señora de Belén, 900 engravings of the heart of Jesus, 80 other engravings of various sizes, a marble crucifix, two paintings of the heart of Jesus and one of Christ on canvas, and an Our Lady of Peace with two or three engravings on paper in 1744; and a variety of goods including books, engravings on paper, paintings on copper, oil paintings, reliquaries, bronze and other crucifixes, medallions and paper medallions from Rome, a statue of Christ and of the Agnus Dei.[143] Despite such shipments, however, the inventories drawn up at the time of the expulsion in 1768 show that before their demise, the reductions had acquired a comparably small number of imported artworks. These included large Italian Baroque paintings of a variety of saints, a series of large Cuzco paintings, statues of the infant Jesus from Naples and Spain, other statues from Spain, and a European baptismal font.[144] Everything else was made on site.

The reductions were also well equipped with European treatises on the arts, apparently already at an early period. Although the Bishop of Asunción complained to the King, just a year before the first reduction was founded in 1608, that in the whole of Paraguay 'there isn't a single book in Latin, never mind on Philosophy or Theology,' the reduction architect Bartolomé Cardeñoso was already ordering books on such specialized topics as architecture from Europe as early as 1631.[145] Almost a century later, we read that Father Bartolomé Jimenez wrote to Europe for '*libros de pintura y arquitectura*.'[146] There were probably many orders in between. At the time of the expulsion, reduction libraries had a substantial collection of the leading art and architectural treatises of the Renaissance and Baroque, including Alberti's (1404–72) *De architectura* (Yapeyú); Cesare Ripa's (fl. 1600) *Iconologia* (San Nicolás and Itapuá); Giovanni Domenico Ottonelli's (1584–1670) *Trattato della pittura e scultura: uso e abuso loro*, which he wrote with Pietro da Cortona (San Ignacio Miní); Jan Vredeman de Vries's (b. 1527) *Architectura* (Yapeyú); and numerous unidentified books on architecture, painting, sculpture, and geometry, including a two-volume Italian illustrated book on the wonders of ancient and modern Rome (Apóstoles), perhaps the one by Theodore de Bry owned by the Japan mission.[147]

Characteristics of Reduction Art and Architecture

Sculpture

The art of the Guaraní reductions is at once eclectic and unmistakable. Josefina Plá and others have characterized its style as '(Hispano-)Guaraní Baroque'; however, it is more complicated than such a term would suggest.[148] It is best exemplified in sculpture. Many of these images of saints and angels possess a formal beauty and spiritual presence that rank them among the great works of world art. Most of them cannot be confused with the product of any other region, except for later work by other Guaraní missions, such as the Franciscan *doctrinas* near Asunción – who inherited artists from the Paraguay reductions after their suppression – and the eighteenth-century Jesuit reductions among the Chiquitos in Bolivia.[149] Nearly all of them are anonymous. Surviving objects include pieces which adhere closely to European canons (back jacket), but in a bouquet of styles ranging from Iberian and Flemish to Italian and German, reflecting the international make-up of the mission personnel – and, more directly, of the engraved models they studied. They also include objects – often scenes of Christ's Passion – whose European features look more like a skin stretched over an autonomous form from another world. These latter raise again the issue, which I will address at the end of this chapter, whether they are just the result of bad copying by artists unfamiliar with European canons, or whether they are a testament to indigenous creativity and even the persistence of pre-contact forms. I am not the first to raise this question. Paraguayan art historian Josefina Plá asks:

> Was the Indians' manifest inability to reproduce the model in its plastic, canonical and rhythmic entirety the logical result of the form of his artistic apprenticeship ... or does it reflect, on a deeper level, the fight between the rhythms imposed by the imported culture, on the one hand, and the indigenous artisan's formal will ... on the other?[150]

And her countryman art historian/anthropologist Ticio Escobar similarly observes:

> ... in the simple primitivism of the Paraguayan [there is] an expressive validity and an originality that is absent in the diligent and mechanical copy of the masters.[151]

Such questions again force us to go beyond concepts such as 'folk' or 'primitive' art and examine how these works might represent a distinctive dialect of the common Late Renaissance and Baroque language that is equally indigenous and part of that global phenomenon. In order to do this, we must consider how these works of art might be a genuine and unique statement of Guaraní culture.

The stylistic disparities of Guaraní sculpture have prompted many scholars to attribute the more canonic ones to European artists and European-born Jesuit maestros, and the more unusual ones to indigenous hands.[152] Some have even managed to trace a handful of statues through documentation to Europe or Jesuit artists. However, as we have already observed for New Spain and elsewhere, it is very dangerous to assume that the artists' style was determined by their ethnic background. The documents tell us that the vast majority of sculpture, painting, engraving, and architectural ornament produced in the thirty reductions that eventually settled on the Paraná and Uruguay river valleys and beyond was the work of Guaraní artists. The same sources also praise their skill at adopting the European manner. Therefore, just as I have proposed for the *urushi* shrines in

Japan, there is little doubt that these men could produce works in the *Cuzqueño* style of the Altiplano or of Baroque Rome just as easily as works that possessed an essence as genuinely Guaraní as the Nimongarai harvest dance.

Any summary of the style of Guaraní reduction art runs the risk of oversimplification, since there is no way to generalize about objects of such diversity. It is possible, however, to make some remarks about a sizeable body of them that possess a sensitivity more alien to European conventions. All of these are works of sculpture, the finest product of the Guaraní reduction workshops. On the formal side, these statues are exceptionally robust and solid – more so than most contemporary sculpture elsewhere in Latin America. Often crafted of imposing, monumental blocks of wood or stone (75 per cent of them are more than a metre tall),[153] reduction sculptures are rigid and elemental, with heavy, rounded modelling (fig. 87). The wooden statues manifest a trueness to their material in which the shape and texture of the log – unencumbered by the metal, porcelain, glass, and human hair that give some Latin American sculpture a doll-like appearance – often dictate form and line. Many statues are carved primarily from a single log. This quality, along with their tendency toward frontal poses and deep, bevelled carving, has reminded some scholars of the sculpture of the Northwest Coast Amerindians of North America.

Drapery, hair, and other surface lines are schematized and reduced to geometric, rhythmic patterns, as can be seen in the ribcage and drapery of the *Crucifixion* at the Museo Fernandez Blanco (fig. 87). Sometimes these patterns, which one writer calls 'vital arabesques,'[154] recall palm fronds, ferns, petals, or other plant forms, such as the tendril-like pleats of hair on the *Man of Sorrows* at the Museum of Santa María (fig. 88) – although, as I have pointed out in chapter 2, this hair motif also appears (albeit more naturalistically) in Iberian sculpture of the period. This schematization in Guaraní sculpture contrasts strongly even with contemporary work in the rest of Latin America. Compare, for example, the symmetrical, regularized hair, veins and ribcage of the Santa María *Man of Sorrows* (fig. 88) with the same image in a seventeenth-century Limeño version (fig. 89), with its irregular, naturalistic treatment of hair and musculature. Even the pose of the Paraguayan image is straighter and more rigid than that of its Altiplano counterpart, whose flaccid *contrapposto* and bent head emphasize Christ's crippling pain. Although representing human forms and sometimes even echoing the high cheekbones and long hair of Guaraní physiognomy, these sculptures often seem to have less to do with mere mimicry of nature or movement than with a world of expressive geometric forms.[155]

The expressive possibilities of drapery in particular were explored by many Guaraní artists, resulting in works of exceptional originality and vigour. One such statue is the *Santa María de la Cabeza*, an image of the pious wife of the popular Spanish agrarian saint Isidro Labrador, at the Santiago Museum (fig. 93). Popularly revered as a saint in Spain and Latin America, this farmer's wife would have struck a common chord with the agricultural community of the Guaraní reductions. In this image, the saint stands perfectly still, her body rigid and frontal, her face blank save for a Mona Lisa smile, and her hands reaching out stiffly toward her husband, who would have been standing across from her. But the static nature of this figure is completely counteracted by her garments. Her dress churns with concentric energy, drawn into a whirlpool that is driven by powerful, wavelike folds, yet nevertheless remains perfectly contained and tightly controlled. The mood conveyed is one of quiet fervour and devotion; without drawing on either gesture or facial expressions, two of the standard resources of European art, the indigenous sculptor communicates her piety through abstract patterns. On the other end of the scale from the control of the *Saint Elizabeth* is a *Risen Christ* (fig. 99), also at Santiago. Spinning as if on a pirouette, the body of this triumphant Christ is still fairly rigid and expressionless. But this does not matter since he is engulfed in a massive, windswept garment which encircles him and flies out in three directions as though it were giant tongues of flame. Few sculptures anywhere summon up the explosive glory of the Resurrection quite like this. It is true that both artists may have learned how to use expressive drapery from someone who knew about Bernini and Roman High Baroque conventions, but they go far beyond any European examples, and the controlled symmetry of the patterns recall the geometricality of non-Christian Guaraní models (fig. 82).

Other aspects of Guaraní sculpture could best be described as spiritual. Guaraní saints and angels possess a calmness and serenity that is very different from both the pained, emaciated realism of much Iberian and Latin American religious art and the ecstatic frenzy of the Roman Baroque. The two *Man of Sorrows* just compared illustrate this characteristic (figs. 88, 89). In addition, we also see the contrast between the solidity and monumentality of the Paraguay version and the delicate Andean sculpture with its gaunt cheeks and weakened pose.[156] The gaze of the Guaraní figure has an aloofness which suggests that the figure has advanced beyond human pain to a higher order of existence. Elsewhere in Guaraní sculpture this serenity is expressed through piercing stares of an unsettling intensity. Although there is no lack of sorrow in Guaraní sculpture, as in the statues of Christ's Passion in the museums at San Ignacio Guazú (fig. 91), Santa María, and São Miguel, particularly the deeply moving *Dead Christ* at Santa María (fig. 90), it is always a resigned sorrow, with the barest minimum of expression or gore. This characteristic recalls the triumphalist quality in Guaraní spirituality, both before contact with the Jesuits and after. The Guaraní paradise is a place that can be reached in this life, by abandoning one's earthly trappings and following the great shaman. Consequently, Christ as the great shaman was celebrated more for his messianic qualities than for his suffering, and for the forbearance he represented more than for the sadness of his Passion. This attitude is very different from the emphasis on pathos, pain, and penitence seen elsewhere in Latin America.[157]

The triumphalism in Guaraní reduction sculptures is further enhanced by their ubiquitous Mona Lisa smiles, remarked upon by many writers (e.g., figs. 7, 93). Even when depicted in a swoon or ecstacy, or bent forward in deference, the saints react with a dancer's grace. In fact, these dance-like poses and gestures are among the most striking features of Guaraní statues, and recall the importance of dance in Guaraní religious life and the role played in ritual and processions by these very statues. Some of the most striking dancers are the images of priests; for example, the *Saint John Nepomuk* at the Provincial Museum of Santa Fé, with his twisted stance (fig. 92), or the *Saint Francis Xavier*, by the Trinidad Master, who spins forward weightlessly on his right foot (fig. 94). Similar is the balletic Christ we have already seen (fig. 99).

Guaraní sculpture can also inspire awe. Many of the statues of Christ the Redeemer, and especially the images of God the Father or the Trinity, possess a stern majesty worthy of a Byzantine Pantocrator (e.g., figs. 87, 91). In this category also are the authoritative church fathers divided between La Plata and Luján, and the Trinity groups at Trinidad and La Plata, easily inspiring exhaltation in their beholder. Although it is only a myth that the Jesuits used to hide in the holes in the back of these sculptures to scare their audiences into submission like the Wizard of Oz,[158] these statues testify to the importance of astonishment in the religious art of the period. As Sustersic remarks:

> The sculptor was called *santo apohava*, or 'saint maker.' His office was a shamanic condition which consisted of evoking in a treetrunk, and later in a stone, the figures of a superior power capable of eliciting the experience of the sacred in its audience ... [and exhalting] everything that can appear as a sign of astonishment and power.[159]

Such images are made to evoke visions, the basis of the Guaraní religious experience.

In addition to these images of majesty and power, Guaraní artists were also extremely adept at depicting evil – even if it is a more human kind of wickedness. Many images of Saint Michael the Archangel show the protagonist slaying churlish devils who manifest a theatrical malice which verges on the burlesque (fig. 7). These figures recall the impish forest demons, or Añá, who inhabited Guaraní mythology more than the European devil, whose malignant powers are much more formidable. The best examples writhe in agony with an energy equalled only by those trampled by Buddhist warrior kings in China and Japan, and are more expressive and ghastly than Iberian or other Latin American versions of the same image. One of them is even carved to resemble a Mameluco. Guaraní reduction sculpture did not inhabit a world of childlike innocence and humility as is so often stated. These saints, gods, and angels represent the complex, sometimes conflicting, pantheon of a warlike yet intensely spiritual people who adapted Christian deities to their own cosmology.

Considering that each church had four or more altarpieces, and that even the secondary chapels tended to be 'easily comparable to the parish church in their retables, paintings, ornamentation, and cleanliness,'[160] it is little wonder that reduction ateliers produced such an extraordinary number of statues. Some believe that as many as four thousand wooden and stone statues were made before the expulsion, of which only a scant four hundred have survived natural disasters and the even more disasterous wars of the early Independence period.[161] Most reduction sculpture is made with *igary* cedar, a material of critical indigenous religious significance, but a wide variety of other native hardwoods were used, some of them as hard as iron.[162] The subjects of these statues were fairly limited. Based on a survey of existing statues, Maeder and Gutiérrez found that 47 per cent of them depicted saints, of whom 27 per cent were non-Jesuit and

12 per cent Jesuit, with 9 per cent [*sic*] representing female saints.[163] The rest were primarily of Jesus (25 per cent), Mary (16 per cent, particularly the Assumption), and angels and Trinities (12 per cent).

To complement these results, I made a similar calculation based on the approximately 834 statues listed by name in the expulsion inventories.[164] Most of these depicted saints, with Saint Joseph the most frequent, followed by the Jesuit founders Ignatius and Francis Xavier, Saint Barbara, Saint Isidore, Saint Anthony of Padua, Saint John the Evangelist, Saint John the Baptist, Saint Rock, and the Jesuit saints Saint Aloysius Gonzaga, Saint Stanislas Kostka, Saint John Nepomuk, and Saint Francis Borgia.[165] Saint Stanislas was so popular, in fact, that when the unconverted Mbyá in the mountains created a syncretic Jesus figure for their own religion they called him Pai Tani (Father Stanislas).[166] Less common were Saints Peter and Paul, Saints Anne and Joachim, and the four Church Fathers, who were followed by a wide range of saints who only appear once or a couple of times.[167] Surprisingly, considering their popularity in Europe at the time as a symbol of penitence, virtually no Magdalenes and only a handful of Peters are listed in the inventories, supporting the common scholarly belief that penitence was not an important aspect of Guaraní Christian life. Another unusual lacuna is the paucity of images of Saint James Matamoros – with one notable exception (fig. 95) – a fantastically popular image of Christian conquest elsewhere in Latin America. Perhaps the Jesuits did not stress the symbolism of Euro-Christian conquest, choosing instead to favour an ideology of friendly partnership and mercy.

The predominance of Joseph images goes hand-in-hand with this approach since Joseph is valued especially as a figure of compassion, almost a female Mary. Joseph was especially favoured by the Society of Jesus. He was venerated by Ignatius, and his cult was actively promoted by the Society on their missions to Asia and Latin America.[168] It is less surprising that the most common individual represented was Jesus. The Pai Guazú (Great Father) of the Guaraní was shown as an infant and in various stages of the Passion and Resurrection. He is followed closely in number by images of the Virgin Mary, who appeared in various versions, and finally angels, particularly Michael, who is shown slaying the devil.[169] Many of the images were meant to go together in groups, such as the *Annunciation* at Santa Rosa (back jacket) or the lavish *Adoration of the Magi* set at Santa María, which has no less than fifteen separate statues of holy figures, kings, attendants, and animals, including the local *coatí*, or coatimundi.

Architecture, Painting, and Other Media

Reduction ateliers worked in all of the principal media of European art, including architecture, sculpture, painting, and engraving. All of the missions had a church (over seventy-five of them in total by one count),[170] which by the middle of the seventeenth century was usually quite large and divided into three or five naves in imitation of the Primitive Church. In addition to references to Early Christian architecture, these buildings also incorporated traditional Guaraní building techniques, as recent work in Argentina is revealing, and capitalized on Guaraní traditions of communal construction[171] – although the architects were always Jesuits.

As well as the principal church, each mission also had a plethora of independent chapels, including a Loreto chapel (which Diego de Torres decreed for each reduction),[172] a pair or four processional chapels in the corners of the plaza like Mexican *capillas posas*,[173] wayside chapels on the roads to *estancias* (ranches),[174] chapels in *estancias* themselves, and cemetery chapels, including an octagonal one built by Sepp at San Juan Bautista which recalls the Padres Santos Chapel at Agra and the funerary chapel at Zhalan.[175]

Nothing survives of the earliest reduction architecture, but from written sources we can reconstruct three distinct structural phases over the missions' 250-year history. The earliest churches (1609–90) were wooden structures very similar to those in the Chiquitos missions today. They were very simple three-aisled buildings with wooden columns supporting a pitched roof and walls of adobe or brick. The second phase (ca. 1690–1725) was characterized by the introduction of stone facades and walls, often very ornate but with wooden roofs, like the reconstructed church of San Cosmé y San Damián. The churches which stand in ruins today date from the third stage (1725–67), when the entire church was made of stone, including the stone vaulting and cupolas (figs. 85, 86).[176]

As is the case for the sculpture of the Paraguay reductions, the style of their architecture was something of a mixed bag. The stone buildings which survive in ruined form feature flat, Serlian pilasters, more exuberantly carved Baroque details with engaged columns, and Spanish *mudéjar* features, such a cusped arches.[177] They are all longitudinal churches, with or without transepts. Although most of them have flush walls, Primoli's church at São Miguel has a genuine Roman Baroque façade with concave bays like Borromini's San Carlo alle Quattro Fontane (1665–7) in Rome and its progeny. It is the only façade which survives relatively complete, so that we have no way of knowing whether or not it was an anomaly. The sculptural ornament on the reduction churches is often profuse, although usually only around the doorways and windows, and is strongly planimetric, in the same way as the sculpture of the Mexican *conventos* or the 'mestizo' style of seventeenth- and eighteenth-century Peru. Although there are figural bas-relief carvings, such as the famous angels and the *Purgatory* panel at Trinidad, most of them are strictly vegetal, with some birds and animals.

Although we do not have the space to consider it here, urban design in the reductions has also been the subject of considerable interest. Ramón Gutiérrez was the first to propose that the plans of the reductions were innovative and departed considerably from those of Spanish colonial towns, which were decreed by Philip II of Spain in 1573. He calls these new city plans, which owe something to indigenous tradition as well as other factors, the 'Jesuit model.'[178]

Painting on the reductions, although apparently extensive, rarely equalled the quality of sculpture, according both to contemporary accounts and the meagre handful of works which survive today. One of the reasons was that good pigments were very hard to come by in Paraguay. Xarque wrote in 1687: 'In that place colours are rare that turn out well without adulteration, and because of this paintings are dead, or else quickly lose their vitality.'[179] Reduction workshops produced mural paintings, such as the fragmentary murals in the Loreto Chapel at Santa Rosa (fig. 96), panel paintings on wood, examples of which can be seen also at Santa Rosa and at La Plata, and paintings on canvas, such as the image of the Virgin by Habiyú at Luján (fig. 84). Most of these paintings are unremarkable. The Loreto murals, although crude by Mexican or Andean standards (and even more crudely restored), are the most imaginative and delicate of surviving work. Depicting the legend of the holy house of Loreto and the Last Judgment, they are a pastiche of early seventeenth-century book engravings, including works such as Orazio Torsellini's *Laurentiae historiae libri quinque* (Rome, 1597), and the Marian imagery by Theodor Galle in *Pancarpium Marianum* (Antwerp, 1607). Another important source is the *Imago Primi Saeculi Societatis Iesu* (Antwerp, 1640), an album published to celebrate the centenary of the Society, whose images of men and angels at workbenches were adapted by the muralists in their lively depictions of the construction and translation of the holy house. As we are warned by the written sources, the palette in the Loreto murals is limited, with a predominance of blues and reds.

Their quality notwithstanding, paintings were produced in large quantities, as is attested by expulsion inventories, which list a large number of paintings of apparently local manufacture, as well as earlier accounts. A 1736 list of paintings from the *estancia* of San Ignacio, for example, shows that they favoured the same images as sculpture, such as Jesuit saints, various versions of the Virgin, and Saint Joseph.[180] As well as depicting religious images, reduction painters occasionally copied portraits of the Spanish kings and other secular officials, again taken from engravings which were circulated among the missions.[181]

In addition to their architectural role, sculptures and paintings played a focal part in processions and ritual, possibly more so than in other missions owing to the Guaraní propensity for communal dance and song. Often sculptors would be commissioned at the last minute to produce whatever statues were required for an event. For the 1747 Holy Thursday procession at Santa Ana, the Visitor Nussdorfer ordered that 'if something should be lacking for the sepulchre of Our Lord or whatever is needed for the other stations, the carpenters and sculptors who live in this town can make them.'[182] Perhaps, like the ephemeral structures they often adorned, they were not meant to last.

The most common of these ritual structures were temporary altars or triumphal arches, which were set up to celebrate special occasions. I have already mentioned a kind of cornucopian triumphal arch found on all the missions decorated with birds, fruit, and game. Others, however, were built more along European lines. In a very early example (1612), Diego de Torres himself was received on the riverbank by Miguel Ateguaye, the principal *cacique* of San Ignacio Guazú, who led a procession with crosses through many triumphal arches.[183] Three decades later, the Visitor was welcomed at several missions by elaborate celebrations for the Jesuit centenary held in 1641, involving triumphal arches, statues, and painting.

For this celebration, the mission of Itapuá set up a triumphal arch covered with paintings of emblems and bordered with one hundred holy wafers, whose program was based on an allegory of the Society of Jesus in the frontispiece of the centenary volume of the Society, the *Imago Primi Saeculi*. The church decorations themselves were arranged in a similar vein. The high altar was lit by one hundred lights and had one hundred tributes to the Society affixed to it. Above the church were placed three statues: 'The middle one [a female image] represented the Society with this epigram: *centenarium societatis iesu triumphat*, and the side ones [represented] Piety and Wisdom with the following inscriptions: *pietate duce*, and *sapientia comite*.'[184] At the Xavier mission, the people constructed, in addition to many triumphal arches, 'a beautiful pulpit, elaborately painted, of a variety of woods; it was adorned with the image of Saint Xavier.'[185]

Few displays of ephemera equal that witnessed toward the end of the century by Francisco Xarque, who wrote about a splendid festival celebrated with triumphal arches and altars combining European and traditional Guaraní imagery, each housing many statues or paintings:

> Some of them took the form of triumphal arches, with a distance between them of ten or twelve paces, and each was linked with the next with curious railings, all made out of cane and wood, all beautifully carved and painted. In the principal part of each arch there was a wooden sculpture or painting, accompanied by others of smaller size, and the rest of the arch and railings are decorated, in place of garlands, with the most beautiful and exquisite birds of the type which populate the air in this province named Paraguay ... next to each [arch] there was altar, not full of silver or gold but decently arranged, with holy pictures and statues of saints, steps, and other works of sculpture, all gilt and ornamented with *estofado* work, which were accompanied by bouquets and flowers, both man-made and natural.[186]

Detailed reports such as these, rare as they are, show us how much we lose in our ignorance of the statues' original locations and functions. Aside from triumphal arches, statues were a crucial ingredient in Christmas and Holy Week processions, as evidenced in this precious account in the expulsion inventory for Itapuá, which describes in some detail the function of a variety of statues:

> There is the sepulchre of Our Lord Jesus Christ which is used in the Good Friday procession. There is also a large Christ which is used in the procession on Holy Thursday, and during Lent on Ash Wednesday and Good Friday in the church for the *exemplo, miserere*, and doctrine ... There are various statues of the Passion of Our Lord Jesus Christ for the Holy Thursday and Good Friday processions ... there is the statue of Our Lady and of Saint Joseph and the three kings and everything else that is used on that day [Christmas].[187]

Religious images were also instrumental in mission foundation ceremonies, and possibly even in combat.[188]

As in the Japan mission, the Paraguay Jesuits were anxious to have a printing press to produce catechisms in the Guaraní language. As early as 1632, missionaries wrote to the Father General asking for an experienced brother from France, Germany, or Flanders to help them set one up.[189] Since, unlike in Asia, their prayers would not be answered for another seventy years, they made do with the next best thing. In a remarkable testament to the indomitability of human will, they trained Guaraní artists to make painstaking pen-and-ink copies of Flemish and other European printed books, complete with accurate typefaces and imitation engravings, which were so well executed that they could fool an observer into thinking they were genuine.[190]

The technology for a printing press arrived at the turn of the eighteenth century, with the Jesuit printers José Serrano and Juan Bautista Neumann.[191] Although there has been some dispute among scholars about the number of presses in the reductions, contemporary documents strongly suggest that, as in Japan, there was only a single one, which travelled from mission to mission.[192] Nevertheless, trained Guaraní printers and engravers resided at several missions. All of the materials used in making and running the press were local, except for the paper.[193] At first, engravings were done on wood; only later on were metal plates used. Guaraní artists had a greater aptitude for engraving than for painting, and surviving images are extremely intricate and well made.

The first published book was a Guaraní-language edition of the *Martirologio Romano* (1700), followed by a translation of the *Flos Sanctorum* of Rivandeneira that included original sermons by the Guaraní writer Nicolás Yapuguay, an author who, like his Japanese counterpart Brother Romão Nishi, provided compelling evidence of indigenous creativity.[194] Almost all of the surviving engravings come from a Guaraní edition of Juan Eusebio Nieremberg's *De la diferencia entre lo temporal y lo eterno*, published at Santa María la Mayor in 1705. Many of the forty-three engravings are closely adapted from the illustrations by Dirk Bouttats in the 1684 Antwerp edition,[195] as well as pictures from Nadal's *Evangelicae Historiae Imagines*,[196] María Eugenia de Beer's frontispiece to F. Aguado's *Sumo Sacramento de la Fé* (Madrid, 1640),[197] an English portrait of Father General Tirsio González, and Italian(?) images of Hell, which were copied later in the century by the Mexican printer Villavicencio from Puebla.[198] Although inspired by models, some of these Guaraní adaptations of earlier prints are quite imaginative – the plate after Nadal, for example, combines two of Wierix's images in a single scene, much as we have seen in the Chinese illustrations to Rocha's catechism.

The last known Guaraní print is an image of Saint John Nepomuk from 1728 by Tomas Tilcara, a delicate and lilting portrait in which the saint seems to be dancing. This image, along with several other engravings produced on the reductions, were in turn used as models in painting and sculpture workshops. The Tilcara print was probably the inspiration behind the statue of Nepomuk at Santa Fé (fig. 92), and an image of the Virgin of Passau from the frontispiece to another Guaraní book was later copied in oils. Although Cardiel mentions the press as late as 1747, we have no evidence of any printing later than 1730.[199]

Chronology of Reduction Sculpture

Almost none of the dates and origins of Guaraní reduction art are known, and archival references are scanty and confusing. Many scholars date existing sculptures and paintings on the principle that the cruder or less European-like pieces are earlier and those which fall more within Western canons are later. Some believe that the most 'correct' images were the work of the Jesuits, and the most 'primitive' the product of Guaraní workshops.[200] Some even suggest that many of the 'correct' works are of European provenance, which is extremely unlikely given that European works represented only a small fraction of the art in the missions, and the art which survives today is a very small fraction of that.[201] Others see the seventeenth century as an era of imitation, and the eighteenth as one of creativity, yet I have found that engravings were equally inspirational in both periods.[202] Still others propose that there was no stylistic development at all, and, to be safe, curators assign most existing images to the eighteenth century.[203] The truth is much more complicated. In reality, the two styles – works with a more marked Guaraní inflection and those with more purely European ones – were likely produced side by side throughout the period of the reductions. Furthermore, as Escobar suggests, many of the simplest, 'folkish' images probably date from the late eighteenth and nineteenth centuries after the workshops had dispersed and the skill level declined.[204]

Only one scholar, Sustersic, has attempted a more scientific general chronology that links archival research with stylistic analysis.[205] He also introduced the evolutionary principle of '*cabezas de series*,' or single models that spawned copies in the manner of a family tree. I will build on Sustersic's foundations by tracing reduction sculpture to specific, datable European models, mainly engravings. Dated models do not always tell us much, however, since Guaraní ateliers consistently favoured late sixteenth- and early seventeenth-century Antwerp engravings right up to the last years of the reductions. Apparently the number of engravings used was relatively limited, and individual prints enjoyed wide circulation. Therefore, in dating these objects, I also must consider stylistic traits which relate to trends in Rome and the Iberian world. Finally, where applicable I will compare Paraguay reduction work with related art in the Chiquitos missions, which is known to date from the eighteenth century.

A large number – perhaps a full third – of surviving sculptures probably predate the arrival of Brasanelli and the international Baroque style in 1693. Since this period was dominated by Flemish and Iberian art, and especially the style of the Altiplano workshops of Peru and Ecuador, we can assign to this period any works which do not betray the influence of the Italian or German Baroque. This group is large and distinctive, and is represented especially well in the museums at São Miguel, San Ignacio Guazú, and Santa María. Lacking any trace of the exuberant drapery and movement of the Italian Baroque, these images are the most static, frontal, symmetrical, and iconic – although we must bear in mind that, as we have seen, these very characteristics were also imposed to a lesser degree on Baroque models right through the eighteenth century. Like much Latin American sculpture of the period, many of them have heavy drapery and elaborate *estofado* decoration, or gilt and painted fabric-like ornament.[206] Nevertheless, as I have noted above, Guaraní versions lack the hyper-realism typical of the Iberian and Latin American schools of the seventeenth century. They are also more solid and monumental, particularly when viewed from the side.

The earliest group of Guaraní sculptures predominantly depict Christ, the Virgin Mary, and angels, and are characterized at least in the Christ images by an interest in the semi-nude human body. They range from pieces that demonstrate a deft understanding of anatomy to examples like the Crucifixion at the Fernandez Blanco Museum which are as elemental as Greek *kouroi* (fig. 87). They are the most frontal and serene of all reduction sculpture. Most typical is a series of scenes of Christ's Passion divided between San Ignacio and Santa María, which Sustersic dates to the 1680s (figs. 88, 90, 91).[207] Whether shown *yacente* (recumbent) or *a columna* (as the Man of Sorrows), Christ is rigid but calm, his hands crossed before him. As we have seen already, these figures' musculature, bones, hair, beard, and even wounds are reduced to geometrical patterns of strict symmetry when compared to contemporary Andean sculpture. This tendency is even more obvious when we compare them to their printed models.

A series of *cristo triunfantes* also at San Ignacio and Santa María are adapted from engravings by Wierix and others after Martin de Vos, perhaps the most influential Flemish artist in early colonial Latin America. One version, in San Ignacio (fig. 97), is a close rendering of a Wierix print of Martin de Vos's *Mitigat accensam divini numinis iram* (1585).[208] Despite its reliance on the model, however, the figure has been straightened out so that the head faces the viewer, and the benediction is similarly directed forward. The hair is arranged in regular layers of ringlets, and the ribcage is simplified. The sweep of the drapery is both bolder and more controlled than in its model. Another *cristo triunfante*, in the parish church at Santa María (fig. 98), is inspired by Vos's *Legis Perfectio Christus ad Iustificationem Omni Credente*. Here the artist has taken the expressiveness of the drapery one step further.[209] Although the Christ retains the *contrapposto* of the print, the head is again turned to face the viewer – like a Greek Pantocrator – the chest and ribcage are regularized, and the hair restrained. The exuberant mass of drapery, however, is the most ambitious yet. This time the artist has gone beyond a reliance on the drapery lines of the original, and has allowed them to take on a life of their own. The cloak becomes an independent organism, surging over the body with great weight and thrusting outward at the lower right to counteract the direction of the cross. We are only a step away from the Triumphant Christ we have already looked at in figure 99.

Martin de Vos also inspired a group of angel sculptures in this period, and his influence lasted well into the eighteenth century (fig. 7).[210] These statues were based loosely on Wierix versions of Vos's *Grandia spirantes sumo de vertice coeli* (1584), *Quis Sicut Deus?*, and *S. Michael*, reproducing their helmets, their costume, with its characteristic neckline, and boots.[211] Again, the Guaraní sculptors have rendered their images in a more frontal and static way than their models, and have regularized the drapery. In most cases, they have also chosen the long hair of the Amerindian over the tight curls of their European prototypes. The devil in figure 7 is adapted from a series of engravings of Hell which not only influenced later images of Saint Michael, but also the illustrations to *De la diferencia entre lo temporal y lo eterno* (1705). These sculptures probably also show the impact of seventeenth-century Andean sculpture, especially in their garments, with the double skirts tucked up between the knees, and their characteristically bent head and small, raised wings. They are also relatable stylistically, as Sustersic has pointed out, to a Guaraní drawing of an angel datable to the 1680s.[212]

In the mid-seventeenth century, Guaraní artists also produced images of Jesuit saints – well before the arrival, with Brasanelli, of Jesuit imagery from Late Baroque Rome. Even in Europe, Jesuit imagery in the first half of the seventeenth century was eclectic and irregular. Developed mostly outside of Rome, the imagery of the Order's founders was not standardized until the second half of the century.[213] The most common images of Ignatius and Francis, those used on the Guaraní reductions, were derived from a scattered collection of early sources. They included a pair of early portraits made for the Gesù which were thought until recently to be by Anthony Van Dyck in 1622; the first illustrated life of the blessed Ignatius entitled *Vita B.P. Ignatii de Loyola* (1609), some of whose drawings were designed by Rubens and engraved by the Galle workshop; Orazio Torsellini's 1606 *Vita* of Francis Xavier with an engraved frontispiece; the frontispiece to Jean de Courbes's *Pratica de la frequencia de la sagrada comunión* (Madrid, 1622);[214] and Rubens's own double portrait of the two founders executed during 1619–20 for the Jesuit church in Antwerp.[215] These images reached Paraguay mostly in Flemish and Spanish books.

Early Guaraní images of Ignatius and Francis are extremely frontal and use a minimum of gesture, sometimes so much so that the drapery of their gowns resembles a fluted classical column. Examples include a Saint Ignatius at São Miguel, several Saint Francis Xaviers in Asuncíon and elsewhere, and, at the Santiago museum, a Saint Ignatius praying, after the scene of Ignatius seeing the soul of Diego Hoces from Galle's life of Ignatius of 1609.[216]

Other saints were similarly adapted from two-dimensional models, such as a Saint Peter at San Ignacio, taken from the frontispiece by Alardo de Popma to A. Zapata's *Novus Index Librorum Prohibitorum* (1632),[217] and an image of Nuestra Señora de los Milagros at San Ignacio, done by the same artist who did the *cristo triunfante* of figure 97, and taken from Louis Berger's painting at Santa Fé (compare figs. 83 and 100) – one of many examples of copying within the reductions of images produced on the reductions.[218]

The Baroque revolution began in 1693 and lasted until the end of the reductions in 1768. Many of the sculptures in this style probably date from the beginning of this period (1700–30), under the energetic tutelage of Brasanelli, when statues were made to supply the new churches erected in the first half of the eighteenth century. Brasanelli's school also introduced the new iconography of Jesuit saints to replace the earlier, eclectic statues that we have seen. Here we find the dramatic gesture and movement, ecstacies, dance-like poses, and flowing drapery of the new generation of Roman sculptors (figs. 92, 94). Every reduction had a retable with Jesuit saints, including Saint Ignatius, Saint Francis Xavier, Saint Francis Borgia, Saint Luigi Gonzaga, Saint Stanislas Koska, and Saint Francis Regis. Guaraní sculptors worked from *bozzetti* and imported statues – such as the Saint Ignatius at the San Ignacio museum, which many believe to be Italian – as well as engravings of the new Jesuit Roman commissions. Most of the Saint Francis Xavier statues from this period are inspired by a slightly earlier frontispiece by Marcos Orozco to *Labor evangélica ... de la Compañía de Jesús* (Madrid, 1663),[219] where the saint is transformed from the submissive martyr of earlier imagery to a triumphant apostle to the Indies, with his cross held high (e.g., fig. 94). Especially popular with reduction artists were the lace borders and shimmering folds of his gown – features which also appeared on images of Saint Luigi Gonzaga.

Even though they were now executed in the Late Baroque manner with sweeping gestures and windswept drapery, a new series of angel statues still sought inspiration from Martin de Vos, testifying to the independence of style and model in reduction art. Ironically, these are closer to their early seventeenth-century models in their hair, costume, and movement.[220] The devils are also carved with a more intense feeling of horror and anguish than before, reflecting perhaps the renewed influence of these images with the 1705 series of *de la Diferencia* illustrations.[221] Stylistically, this series of Saint Michaels also resembles examples in the Chiquitos missions, which have to date after 1690, giving further indication of an eighteenth-century date.

Many of the statues of the eighteenth-century approach European canons so closely that they might be accused of not being sufficiently Guaraní. Throughout this period, however, reduction workshops continued to produce works of more indigenous character, and the second quarter of the century witnessed a revival of Guaraní style, as we have already seen in the drapery of figure 99, which probably dates from this period, and also the *Immaculate Conception* we have looked at already in chapter 2 (fig. 6), whose gown exhibits a similar combination of panache and controlled geometry. The most dramatic examples are the angel figures on the friezes at Trinidad Church (fig. 86).[222] Inspired in part by the illustrations to the *Imago Primi Saeculi* (1640), these planimetric, frontal images would appear to be earlier than the more canonic, Italianate angels on the façade of San Ignacio Miní (fig. 85). Nevertheless, they are among the last commissions of the reductions (finished 1763) and postdate the San Ignacio angels by almost four decades. The most impressive tribute to the indigenous voice in the mid-eighteenth century, however, was a sculptor in wood – in my opinion, one of the greatest sculptors ever to work in the reductions.

Although occasionally two or three statues can be assigned to the same hand, it is rare to find a large body of work that bears the unmistakable stamp of a single master. Such an artist flourished in the second quarter of the eighteenth century in Trinidad (after 1737–ca. 1763) (figs. 94, 95). Almost certainly an indigenous artist, this man was one of the greatest geniuses ever to emerge from the reductions and is of the calibre of the great Baroque sculptor Aleijadinho of Brazil (1738–1814). I call him the Trinidad Master.[223] The key to the Trinidad Master's genius is his ability to synthesize the frontal, static, and symmetrical elements I have identified as being characteristically Guaraní with the mimetic, dynamic Italianate style introduced by Brasanelli. Immediately recognizable trademarks of his art are the sharp lines of definition on the faces, especially around the hair and beard and the eyes and eyebrows, and the high cheekbones and almond eyes of indigenous physiognomy. Staring with slightly bulging eyes, the lips are pursed, the hair is thick and wavy, and the costumes are made of heavy cloth with wide borders. Very frontal and iconic, these statues are among the most elaborate ever produced on the reductions, and even the smallest of them possess an unmistakable majesty. Often they seem to emerge from a bulging mass of clouds, angels, or other figures, hewn out of several blocks of wood. Although all are apparently inspired by engravings, there is nothing derivative or mechanical about them.

The most splendid of all of the Trinidad Master's work is the great Santiago group (fig. 95), which is precisely datable by its model, a 1737 edition of Plantin's *Missae Propriae Sanctorum Hispaniorum*, which was also copied frequently in Mexico, Ecuador, and Peru.[224] The Trinidad Master brings his model into the third dimension with solid, rounded forms, and a treatment of drapery that manages at the same time to suggest movement and to delight in its own patterns. The heavily bevelled carving gives the ensemble an intensely plastic and tactile quality. The Trinidad Master also executed a series of monumental Trinities. A God the Son at Santiago and a full Trinity at La Plata are inspired by a print by Johannes Sadeler I entitled *Sedet ad Dextram Maiestatis*,[225] and a God the Father at Santiago is freely adapted from a print of the crowning of the Virgin by the same printmaker entitled *Deposuit potente de sedes* [sic] *et exaltauit humiles*.[226] The Trinidad Master also executed a Saint Francis Xavier after Orozco (fig. 94), and a series of Doctors of the Church taken from engraved frontispieces. The artist has confined the movement and gesture of these prototypes, and made the images slightly more frontal and symmetrical, but he has also achieved a truly dynamic drapery and has given the hair and beard a more naturalistic wave. The faces are more animated – almost confrontational – than the printed models, which do not always look the viewer in the eyes. Few artists were as successful in evoking awe.

The Indigenous Element in Guaraní Reduction Art

After seeing how creatively Guaraní artists interpreted engraved models, we can no longer take seriously statements about the Guaraní's lack of originality, such as this one by Sepp:

> They are absolutely incapable of inventing or creating anything by means of their own imagination or thought. Even for the simplest work imaginable the father has to be there guiding them; he has to give them above all a model and example. If they have one, then he can be sure that they will imitate the work exactly. They are indescribably talented as imitators.[227]

Neither can we accept the belief, inspired by such remarks, that the reductions constituted a negation of indigenous culture.[228] I also do not believe, despite the tone of reports like Sepp's, that the Jesuits were not interested in acculturating religious art on the reductions and opposed the adaptation of indigenous elements. The challenge is to show that these characteristics that I have been describing are in fact indigenous. By indigenous I do not necessarily mean pre-contact, although some features may well have ancient lineages. Perhaps we can only hope to find mere hints and suggestions of the Guaraní world hidden in a dominant and more familiar European matrix. We are also thwarted by our ignorance about how these images were used in mission ceremonial. But the exercise is worth the effort, since it compels us to look at the art from the point of view of its makers.

One place to look for supporting evidence is among the unconverted Guaraní and related tribes in the mountains and hinterlands, who, like their missionized brethren, also adopted elements of European Late Renaissance and Baroque art, and achieved their own syncretism by the eighteenth century.[229] The *ta'a* people demonstrate how the Guaraní would have reacted to Euro-Christian art entirely on their own terms, since they were free from either missionaries or colonists. Here we find many of the same features we have observed in reduction sculpture but in a much more pronounced way. The *Caaiguá* and their descendants showed little interest in mimesis or figural imagery, transformed all alien symbols by geometricizing them and making them more symmetrical, and showed a preference for surface patterns.[230] The *ta'a* people considered surface ornament to be the most significant manifestation of an object's or person's essence.[231] They did not depict volume in their art, favouring instead linear, two-dimensional symbols. Typical are highly schematic floral, animal, celestial, and occasionally human forms incorporated into ceramics, ceremonial gourds, and body painting.[232]

One fascinating example is the shamanic pipe of the related Tupí-Guaraní people, made during the late eighteenth or early nineteenth century (fig. 82).[233] These cylindrical pipes were very important ritual instruments of the shaman, and are long tubes of about fifty centimetres in length which are profusely ornamented with engraved patterns, animals, monsters, and biblical themes. As we have seen earlier in this chapter, shamans often adopted Christian images or customs to harness their spirituality for their own ends (not unlike what we have seen in Mughal India). In this case, the biblical figures and animals are taken from Euro-Christian images, and they have been made subservient to tightly woven indigenous geometrical patterns and interspersed with stylized local flora and fauna in a way reminiscent of the *Book of Kells*. Even the figures themselves are made into patterns, reduced to their most elemental forms and placed in frontal or profile views. They have been indigenized to such an extent that their origins in European visual culture are virtually impossible to trace, and they become part of the natural and supernatural surroundings of their makers.

Owing to their intimate relationship to the ritually significant art of featherwork, flowers and flower symbols tended to invade much of the borrowed Euro-Christian material in *ta'a* imagery, including floral motifs borrowed from European art. As a means of identifying themselves in the face of Christianity, mountain tribes assimilated crosses and Christian altar imagery using featherwork and even ritual canoes.[234] Especially potent were the 'flowery crosses' (*kurusu poty*), symbols of religious authority carried by shamans which united the most powerful emblems of Christianity and the Guaraní religion, and are reminiscent of the syncretic forms developed by the shamans who revolted against the Jesuits in the early seventeenth century. On a more fundamental level, the introduction of floral elements into alien artforms was a mark of identity.

The art of the *ta'a* Guaraní and other post-contact indigenous groups in the area provides compelling evidence that many of the features which make reduction art unique derive from indigenous traditions, some descending diachronically from pre-contact roots and others adopted synchronically through interaction with these very tribes in the colonial period. The naturalistic figural depictions of their engraved models are tamed, reduced, and regularized because that is how the Guaraní make sense of their world. Despite their exceptional aptitude for copying their models, many sculptors persisted in making frontal, iconic, almost expressionless statues right through the eighteenth century. They did this because it is precisely their unrealism and indifference which made them holy. Surface patterns, especially the folds of the garment, provide such a lively counterpoint to the figure because they were as important as the image itself; they may possibly have signified concepts or abstract notions that are beyond our understanding.

The importance of drapery patterns may particularly be linked to the tradition of body painting. Unconverted Guaraní and related tribes practised elaborate bodypainting well into the twentieth century, which often involved completely covering the body with geometrical patterns similar to those found in their other arts (and in reduction sculpture), ranging from simple dots, parallel lines, and circles, to meander patterns, whorls, zig-zags, and elaborate interlaces.[235] These patterns, apparently decorative and random to the European viewer, were in fact highly symbolic of personal identity and kinship. The indigenous people of Paraguay did not wear these patterns lightly; scholars have demonstrated hierarchies of patterns, with some having more potency than others, as well as specific links with tribal identity. An interesting illustration is the way in which some tribes used borrowed European patterns from Baroque engravings in their body art. Such intrusions were relegated to secondary parts of the body and were only used temporarily; they never put such patterns on their faces, for example, and the few tribes who practised the more permanent form of tattooing (the Guaraní did not tattoo) never introduced such foreign ornament into their tattoos. For the indigenous people of Paraguay, human beings were bearers of pattern, carriers of meaning; it was not the figure who counted as much as the message he or she wore.

Anthropological and literary evidence suggests that Christian saints, gods, and angels did not simply replace Guaraní deities on the reduction but were interpreted as versions of them and incorporated into their cosmology. I will not claim, as some scholars have in other areas of South America,[236] that the Guaraní were secretly worshipping their own gods unbeknownst to the Jesuits: the situation is more complex than that. Guaraní artists were interpreting Christian deities and demons as *versions* of their own gods and spirits, such as God the Creator, Ñanderuvusú, and the sylvan devil Añá – as we know they did in their oral literature – but not in an attempt to undermine Christianity. This approach is completely in keeping with pre-contact Guaraní religion in which gods and spirits have many different avatars and are constantly in a state of transformation. Gods, culture heroes, and devils graduate back and forth between the human, animal, aviary, vegetal, and even mineral worlds. It is a sign of their divinity. Therefore, why should the Christian saints not also share in this transformative ability?

There are also indigenous elements in reduction art with a more immediately symbolic value. Like their brethren in the mountains, the reduction Guaraní showed a propensity for flower imagery – especially a kind of rosette – which they may have added to Christian pictures and architectural ornament to enhance their ritual power.[237] Often this floral imagery is found on the wooden columns and pilasters used on retables to frame holy images, or it is inserted into the spaces between figural images in carved reliefs. Another much rarer shamanic symbol is the bow and arrow, mentioned already in the description of the cornucopian triumphal arches, but which was also carved on the paving stones inside the churches of San Ignacio Miní and Trinidad to preserve the memory of dead *caciques*.[238] Although these could be discounted as merely decorative, the importance of such symbols in pre-contact Guaraní religion suggests that they could be more meaningful. A more obvious symbol, which have been related by Josefina Plá to indigenous mythology, are the devil figures that were so popular both in sculpture and in Guaraní engravings.[239]

A final indigenous feature in reduction art which has caused considerable debate among scholars is the translation of European flora and fauna into their local equivalents in ornament and background scenery.[240] Roses become passion flowers, oxen become jaguars, and the architectural ornament of buildings such as the churches at San Ignacio Miní and Trinidad is smothered in a profusion of carved jungle vegetation. Although in many cases this transformation was likely an unconscious switch on the part of Guaraní or indigenized Jesuit artists, recent work on early contact period Augustinian murals in Mexico compels us to take these symbols more seriously.[241] By studying them closely, we may even be able to identify a vegetal iconographic program parallel to the figural one. Many of the plants represented played very important roles in Guaraní religion and myth.

The passion flower (*mburucuyá*), for example, had an important place in the Guaraní Creation Myth. It was the favourite plant of the Sun and one also favoured by shamans for its ability to induce trances.[242] Passion flower was also associated with rebirth and resurrection; for example, in the Mbyá version of the Creation Myth, the older of the Hero Twins, Kuarahy (the Sun), uses it to revive his dead mother. The tobacco plant had even greater religious significance. It was an elixir of oracles and visions and the main vehicle of communication with the Divine.[243] Tobacco is called 'the deadly mist' (*tatachina reko achy*) and is the source of life and knowledge, as well as a protection against evil. Finally, corn stalks, often shown hung as garlands in architectural or retable ornament, were hung on trees during the great pre-contact inter-tribal conventions, such as the Nimongarai, to symbolize international fraternity.[244] Corn is also related directly with divinity, since it was created by the Creator God Ñanderuvusú himself. Although some of these plants also had European meanings – as its name suggests, the passion flower was associated with Christ's Passion – many of them did not resonate within Euro-Christian tradition.

All of these plants could conceivably be linked to an overall indigenous program of Salvation, which would have been perfectly consonant with their Christian context, as well. They all relate to resurrection, rebirth, and divine creation. They are also the plants of the Guaraní paradise, and therefore could be seen as uniting the Christian Heaven with the indigenous concept of the Land-without-Evil. The reductions were founded, after all, as a replacement for the latter in people's aspirations. These plants also relate to oratory and community, both of which are particularly appropriate for a church setting, especially given the emphasis on rhetoric, singing, music, and other active rituals in reduction church life. Similar connections could be made for the imagery of the jaguar, coatimundi, parrot, and other indigenous animals that appears in Guaraní reduction art.

These elements of pre-contact symbolism kept alive the memory of an indigenous reality, a world in which flora and fauna participated in the cosmology. Whether on a palpably symbolic level or more on the level of general *mentalité*, reduction sculpture presents compelling evidence that the Guaraní embraced Christianity but indigenized it, making it a true successor to their own religion and adding its saints to their own pantheon. The result, in much of the sculpture of the Paraguay reductions, is a unique and powerful testament to cultural partnership that goes far beyond a blending of styles and involves a synthesis of two very different – but not necessarily uncomplementary – concepts of the sacred.

7

Conclusion: On the Partnership

In the Jesuit church of the Compañía in Cuzco, a curious seventeenth-century painting greets the visitor on the left side of the main door upon entering. Amid great pageantry, we see two marriages taking place, one set before a crowd of Inca nobility in their feathers and finery, dressed in Inca textiles and holding heraldic shields, and the other in front of a more solemn crowd of hidalgos and European ladies in taffeta, lace, and velvet. The Incas are seated in phalanx-like rows in front of an architectural backdrop which resembles the early colonial architecture of the Cuzco region. The Europeans stand before the portal of a grander church and the loggia of a palazzo, perhaps meant to evoke a European city. In between these two scenes, in the dead centre of the canvas, are Saint Ignatius of Loyola and Saint Francis Borgia, looking sombre in their black cassocks and holding a copy of the *Constitutions* and a human skull respectively. Above them the skies burst open with the Jesuit emblem, IHS. This picture will stop even visitors familiar with the usual run of Jesuit imagery dead in their tracks.

The happy couple on the left is composed of a young European dandy with a starched lace collar and an Inca woman, dressed in a European gown decorated with an Inca heraldic device and prominently hemmed with brilliant Andean textiles, not only on the gown but on her mantle and tunic. The inscription tells us that we are witnessing the marriage of Don Martín de Loyola, Governor of Chile and descendant of Saint Ignatius's older brother Don Beltrán de Loyola, to Doña Beatriz Ñusta, 'Princesa del Perú' and niece to Don Diego Inca (Tupac Amaru), the last of the Incas. Since Don Diego's brother, Don Felipe, died without a son, Doña Beatriz was nothing less than the heir to the Inca throne. This most holy of matrimonial ties would be impressive enough for the Society of Jesus. But there is more.

The inscription goes on to describe the couple on the right, this time in Europe and, consequently, dressed in European costume. It now appears that the lady is the daughter of the happy union on the left, a woman named Doña Lorenza Ñusta de Loyola, who went on to marry a certain Excelentísimo Señor Don Juan de Borja. Señor Borja just happens to be the son of Saint Francis Borgia, as well as the Spanish ambassador to Germany and Portugal. The inscription concludes: 'With this Marriage the Royal house of the Inca Kings of Peru was united with those of Loyola and Borja.' I can think of no document which better expresses the affinity which the Jesuits felt with their cultural partners. In its contrived but endearing way, this anonymous canvas can serve as a metaphor for the partnerships we have seen in this book.

This book is not meant to be an exhaustive treatise on the art of the Jesuit missions or the cultural exchanges engendered by the Society of Jesus around the world. I have not looked at comparably uncharted areas in Africa, New France, and Southeast Asia, and even the scholarship on the art of the missions I have examined is so skeletal that it merits much more attention, particularly the study of indigenous-language texts. More work needs to be done in China, for example, where scholars are reassessing the reception of European philosophy and Ricci's Confucianism, and are also finding new sources which refer to the Jesuits and Western art and to the workshop practices of the Jesuit artists of the Qing Dynasty.[1] In Japan, a team of scholars at the Kirishitan Bunko Library at Sophia University are recovering new manuscripts from Japan's Christian century, which are now being published, and scholars such as Antoni J. Üçerler are reconsidering the role of Alessandro Valignano and Jesuit humanist education in Japan.[2] Sanskrit and Tamil specialists such as Francis Clooney are translating and assessing early Jesuit catechisms and indigenous documents in those languages in South India, which will balance out our knowledge of Islamic-language sources in the North.[3] Finally, in Paraguay scholars are translating colonial-period Guaraní texts, mostly late eighteenth-century legal documents, but potentially testimonies of great value for rediscovering the Guaraní voice, as James Lockhart, Kevin Terraciano, and Matthew Restall have shown for New Spain, and George Urioste and Frank Salomon for Peru.[4]

I have also been very selective with the works of art I have chosen – they illustrate trends but do not flesh out the whole picture. I have confined myself to the images which have the greatest aesthetic and cultural significance, objects which deserve recognition as masterpieces of world art but which also most clearly reflect the intercultural dialogue. Some of the missions treated in this book – for example, Mughal India and Paraguay – have produced such a plethora of artworks that we are perforce only able to look at a representative selection. This study aims to suggest the range of Jesuit artistic activity and, more importantly, of indigenous response. It is less about 'mission art' than it is about art made possible by the missions. I am tired of tracing influences and inspirations, of sifting artworks into their component ingredients, whether Italian, Flemish, or Chinese. Identifying these strains is important, to be sure, but it overlooks the creative genius and composite magic of these artworks. This book is really about a partnership or a dialogue between peoples – friendly or antagonistic, overt or secretive, conscious or unconscious – and the novelty of artistic expression made possible by the fusion of their traditions, what Jacques Lafaye, referring to mythology, calls 'the birth certificate of a new culture.'[5]

Now it is time to look back over the four missions in this book and ask ourselves some questions about motive. Although we have seen much clash and resistance, we have also seen an often amicable relationship develop between the Jesuits and various non-European peoples, representing the widest range of cultures and social groups. We have seen people of astonishing creativity on both sides willing to take a step into the unknown to learn more about the 'Other.' We have seen negotiation, compromise, adaptation, and accommodation between unrelated groups in an age before the onslaught of modern armies, industrial monotony, and mass popular culture, when this kind of rapprochement was still possible. Finally, we have seen the originality and innovation made possible by this partnership. Small wonder philosophers and historians in the past have spoken in terms of Utopia.

The Jesuit reductions of Paraguay are the most famous of such literary Arcadias, although Japan and China enjoyed similar treatment in the sixteenth and seventeenth centuries. Ever since the eighteenth century, when the normally critical Voltaire called the reductions a 'triumph of humanity' and Chateaubriand spoke of the 'marvels' of this 'Christian republic,' Enlightenment philosophers, socialists, Marxists, economists, and Hollywood directors have outdone one another in depicting these South American missions in paradisical terms.[6] Ennio Morricone's haunting soundtrack for the 1986 film *The Mission*, starring Jeremy Irons and Robert De Niro, became the favoured background music for the 'environmentally friendly' age of the early 1990s and was imitated countless times in advertisements for products meant to conjure up Arcadian rainforests. I can count on the fingers of one hand the number of popular books printed on the Paraguay missions that do not have the word *Utopia* or *Arcadia*, or an oblique reference to Milton's *Paradise Lost*, in the title.[7] Of course, as I pointed out in chapter 6, this romanticism says much more about the ideology of the historians than it does about the missions themselves: I refer to people such as R.B. Cunninghame-Graham, author of *A Vanished Arcadia* (1900), who was inspired by this supposed 'Christian republic' to found the Scottish Labour Party. All of these sources praise the Jesuits as paternalistic heroes and the Guaraní Indians as noble but naïve children. The much-vaunted egalitarian society of the reductions was seen as all the more praiseworthy because it *replaced* the savage paganism of native America with a perfect society based on classical ideals. The reality, as we have seen, was much more complicated.

So, if we are not dealing with Utopia, how can we explain what happened on these and other missions around the world? In chapter 2 we have already reviewed various explanations for such phenomena in the colonial sphere. In areas such as New Spain and the Andes, where Euro-Christian culture was imposed by force, scholars have explained the accommodation of the missionaries, on the one hand, in terms of both idealism and opportunism; on the other hand, they see the conversion of the indigenous peoples and their participation in colonial culture in largely pragmatic terms as a way to maintain a stable environment and negotiate within the new society. Given that the four missions treated in this book are lacking the element of force present in the Iberian colonies, must we explain everything in such Machiavellian terms? Only in Paraguay is there anything resembling a colonial situation, since Spanish and Portuguese forces were not far off and the Jesuits provided mediation with, and protection against, them. But even there the Jesuits did not arrive at the head of armies.

Before trying to answer this question, we should ask what conditions, factors, and social groups either facilitated and thus created possibilities for the partnership, or – alternatively – made problems for it. Let us first assume the pessimistic view of human nature by which people only cooperate for the sake of personal benefit. Given a choice, societies would rather have nothing to do with each other unless there was a tangible advantage to be gained through cooperation. Following this argument, it therefore must have been for purely political or material gain that the host societies put up with the Jesuits. They were either motivated by competition with other groups, operated out of fear, or saw the missionaries as a convenient way to gain a trade monopoly on silks, guns, or artworks. This is – at least on the surface – a very convincing argument.

We might also ask whether these cultural fusions were only the purview of a small group of the rich and powerful, and therefore not representative of the people at large. It is no secret that the Jesuits focused on elites; it was their policy right from the beginning. In his instructions to future missionaries in the *Constitutions* (1552), Ignatius of Loyola exorted Jesuits to focus their energies on princes and other 'important and public persons,' and even singled out 'great nations such as the Indies.'[8] The idea was that if the Society could convert the prince, then his subjects would naturally follow, and they could more easily win the souls of an entire nation. Although idealistic, this plan had occasional successes, such as with the Christian daimyos in Japan. The Jesuits' presence at the top would also make their activities more visible and provide much needed advertising, even if they failed to move the monarch, as we saw with the 'Christian' mural paintings in Mughal India. In addition, Ignatius knew from personal experience working in Rome how important it was to obtain the financial support of wealthy patrons, and he instructed his followers to make wise use of such potential benefits. Thus, we might suppose that the Jesuits were merely early modern social climbers who were tolerated by a handful of royal patrons because they provided a few trinkets and gewgaws. Prattling, juggling Jesuits.

Let us put these assumptions to the test, first with Japan. In Japan the Jesuits arrived at a time of civil war and cosmopolitanism. They were immediately associated with three kinds of 'merchandise' made very desirable by that political climate: guns, riches, and exotica. The Jesuits allied themselves with the merchant ships from Macao, made no secret of their involvement in the silk trade, and provided access to cannon and musketry. They also brought with them a colourful and alluring art style which appealed to the *nouveau-riche* taste for the fantastic and was briefly but brilliantly in vogue in the Japanese art community. And, as one would expect, the Jesuits concentrated on the rich and famous. Their main targets and most prominent supporters were the warlord class, men whom they described as 'lords' and 'kings' in their letters, men who had the most to gain by the material and political advantages provided by the missionaries. The Jesuits served as adjuncts to their courts, travelled with them on campaigns, and lived within their castle walls.

Yet how do we explain that thousands of ordinary Japanese gladly suffered torture and death of the most horrible conceivable kind rather than abjure Christianity? Some were beheaded or crucified, others were roasted alive, and others still were bound, the skin on their faces slit with a knife, and hung upside-down for days over a pit of excreta. But unlike European *auto da fés*, the Tokugawa authorities only cared about apostasy; if the victims denounced Christianity, they would be released immediately. Yet so many Japanese chose death, an alternative that even some European Jesuits were unwilling to accept; for example, the former Vice-Provincial Cristóvão Ferreira (1580–1650), who converted to Shintoism in 1633 and went on to help Japanese officials torture other Christians.[9] These people were not elites, but villagers, peasants, fishermen, and merchants. They would not have enjoyed the same political or financial benefits as the warlords by allying with the Jesuits, and if they had converted for opportunistic reasons we would expect them to apostatize when it was no longer to their advantage to remain Christians. It looks, therefore, as if we are dealing with genuine religious fervour at the grass-roots level.

Perhaps it was only the rich and powerful who converted to Christianity for opportunistic reasons. Yet even some of them seem to have felt the same way as their subjects about the new faith. George Elison, who is very unsympathetic toward the Jesuits and is a major proponent of the opportunism model, conceded that the daimyo of Bungo, Ōtomo Sōrin Yoshishige (1530–87), who converted in 1578, did so out of genuine admiration for Christianity.[10] Similarly, the Christian lords of Takatsuki, Takayama Hidanokami (converted 1563) and his son Takayama Ukon (succeeded 1573), did not merely accept Christianity but founded charitable confraternities which conducted funerals and burials for rich and poor alike.[11] Since burial was a job usually given to social outcasts, the participation in funerals by the elite goes against the grain of the Japanese class system and would seem to me to be evidence of genuine Christian sentiment on the part of these nobles.

It was not only in the dramatic example of the persecutions that we can witness the power of Japanese Christianity. Japanese confraternities, Catholic lay religious organizations, were introduced into Japan by Francis Xavier and allowed the relatively few Jesuits more effectively to manage the 215,000 Japanese Christians who made up the mission community by 1593.[12] But they went much further than administration, revitalizing the Christian community and providing it with charitable and spiritual services. It was the confraternities, more so than the Jesuits themselves, who founded and maintained the Church among the Japanese people. After the persecutions started in 1587, these groups went underground, developing into devotional confraternities, based on devotions to the Holy Eucharist and Saint Mary. Much of the Christian art produced by Niccolò's academy was probably aimed at confraternities, who would have their own chapels or at least religious pictures. These underground movements assisted Christians during the persecutions and laid the groundwork for the 'Hidden Christian' phenomenon. Confraternities were entirely run by lay people, including people of all ages and both sexes, and were completely voluntary.

There was also an intellectual dimension to the Jesuit-Japanese partnership. After Valignano's recommendations were implemented and the seminaries were founded, prominent families sent their young sons to be educated in the humanist tradition and even to enter the Society. The benefits of language study, rhetoric, and art provided by these colleges evidently appealed to people. Jesuit teachers, including Japanese, lectured not only on Christianity and Christian theology and morality, but also on Japanese culture and religion, cosmography, and human nature. The Japanese sent their children there, not to become little Europeans, but because the schools offered a well-rounded education in Japanese civilization as well as in contemporary European and classical studies. We see this reflected in the visual arts as well, if only subtly. Many of the artists of Niccolò's academy borrowed from Japanese stylistic traditions as well as Euro-Christian ones, and no doubt would have continued to do so had they not been stopped by the expulsion. And artists from the Kanō school went to train there so that they could bring new techniques of shading, perspective, and colour to their otherwise purely secular paintings. The Japanese Church worked only because it was able to be relevant within Japanese cultural parameters. By adopting Japanese social customs, cleanliness, dignity, and architecture, the Jesuits were accepted into Japanese society. The mission was cut off too early for us to assess whether this process of indigenization would continue; however, I have little doubt that it would have done so.

In China the political situation was very different, and the Jesuits had much less success with the ruling class, at least in matters of religion. Ming China was a time of peace, and its culture was decidedly uncosmopolitan; in fact, it was Ming policy to reverse the position of their Mongol Yuan predecessors, who had allowed a significant foreign presence in Chinese culture and politics. Therefore, the Jesuits' link with Europe and Western trade was not an important card to play, as it had been in Japan. The Ming had little interest in Macao and the Portuguese, and European culture was considered, for the most part, beyond contempt. Only during the years prior to the Ming-Qing interregnum, when the Middle Kingdom was plunged into civil war, did their foreignness gain the Jesuits a strong foothold with the Imperial household; their scientific and military knowledge was now in demand, a situation which would persist to an even greater degree under the Qing.[13] The Qing were a foreign (Manchu) dynasty and, unlike the Ming, showed an interest in foreign cultures that eventually gave rise to the fad for exotica and Western artistic techniques that possessed the courts of Kangxi, Yongzheng, and Qianlong in the eighteenth century. However, the much-vaunted episode of the Jesuits at the Qing court was not really a high intellectual dialogue, much less a conversation among equals. Imperial interest operated on a largely superficial level, in contrast to the learned nature of Ricci's dialogue with the literati. This dichotomy highlights the difference between an alliance of convenience and genuine intercultural partnership.

Genuine intercultural partnership existed in China only when both sides were on more equal ground. It was also only possible when the Jesuits were willing to accommodate. Ricci's remarkable friendship with the literati only worked when he operated within Chinese cultural traditions. This is made evident by comparing his successes not only with the failures of the Eurocentric approach of the Macanese, but also with his own earlier attempts in the Buddhist mode. But there was a built-in problem, relating to what scholars have seen as the inherent incompatability of Christianity and Confucianism. Ricci taught Christianity as a Confucianist philosophy, without concepts such as a personal God or specific ideas about the afterlife, retribution, miracles, or a priesthood. Recently, Qiong Zhang has shown that the literati did not even believe in the immortality of the soul, making it very difficult for the missionaries to convince them 'that there are souls to be saved in the first place.'[14] Erik Zürcher points out that Ricci's method failed with the literati as soon as the missionaries proclaimed a basically irrational doctrine based on mysteries of faith and a personal God.[15] These concepts went against Chinese orthodoxy (*zheng*) and resulted in marginalization for Christianity; by contrast, Christianity and Japanese Buddhism had many institutional and theological similarities. Nevertheless, the Jesuits did win converts among the Chinese elite, so that this barrier was not always insurmountable. Ricci also owes his success partly to something he had which the Chinese particuarly valued: namely, his gift for memory. One of the main reasons he was such a welcome guest at the literati soirées was that he was entering a mileu based on memorization and examination of the classics.

Ricci's was not the only true partnership to exist in the China mission, as we have seen already. Another flourished between the Jesuits and quite another level of society in places such as Fujian: that of popular Daoism and Buddhism – which was reflected in the arts. As in Japan, the new religion had a strong appeal for the common people, with its mysteries, miracles, and charismatic preaching. And, as in Japan, their success is borne out by impressive numbers; 300,000 Chinese called themselves Christians by 1700. Perhaps popular Christianity was successful only because its adherents were the poor and forgotten, a people who, as Gernet puts it, were willing to try anything new.[16] Christianity gave them hope. This theory is supported by the fact, noted by many scholars but not yet satisfactorily explained, that Christianity was more successful in China in periods of political and economic disunity, and less so when things were going well.[17] This phenomenon sounds very similar to the situation in Japan, and I will return to it later.

The fate of Jesuit art projects in China are reflected in these two spheres of missionary activity. The failure of the Jesuits' mission art at the high intellectual level has partly to do with their insistence on concentrating on the Imperial household, a cultural milieu looked upon with disdain by the true taste-makers, the literati. However, it was also brought about by their stubborn refusal to accommodate stylistically in the crucial first years. With the exception of a few selected artworks, most notably the series of woodblock prints illustrating Rocha's treatise, the Jesuits in China pursued the policy of impressing the Chinese with the superiority of European art, a legacy from Ricci's time. They also – astonishingly – completely ignored the crucial role played by calligraphy in Chinese art. It was only after the Qing emperors compelled Jesuit artists to work in Chinese styles that widespread acculturation took place on the higher level, but it was too late to do any good, pastorally speaking. Even in the arts, the Jesuits were up against a concept Zürcher refers to as the Chinese 'cultural imperative,' or the necessity for foreigners to conform to orthodoxy (by which he means Confucianism).[18] In a delightful mock dialogue, Nicolas Standaert defines just how imperative it is:

> One can express the force of cultural imperative in another way. Jesuit accommodation is often described by a sentence attributed to Ignatius of Loyola: 'enter through the door of the other so as to make them leave through our door.' Cultural imperative means that Chi-

> nese say to the Jesuits: 'You should enter through our door (and you will have to prove it). Moreover you should remain inside, and you cannot leave without permission. Anyway, we have no intention to leave through your door.'[19]

One can almost hear the Qianlong Emperor saying this to Castiglione, as he toiled away painting portraits of his mistresses. But the court was not the only place the Jesuits were producing or promoting art. Christian art flourished at the popular level because imagery and mystery were not only acceptable here but an integral part of popular Daoist and Buddhist tradition. It also appealed to a much wider popular interest in curious things, not unlike that in Japan in the late Momoyama Period. It was also at this level that the Jesuits got off their cultural high horse and promoted full-scale accommodation, especially in the realm of inexpensive woodblock prints and other household images. Unfortunately for us, however, these often ephemeral works of art are mostly lost, and we are left with the court art.

Mughal India shares aspects of both the Japan and China missions. Here, the nation was united and peaceful under a single ruler, as in China, yet it was extremely cosmopolitan, even more so than Japan. The cosmopolitanism was built into the society in a way it was not in China or Japan. The Mughal 'people' were a mixture of many different, and not always complementary, cultures from all over South, Western, and Central Asia. As usual, the Jesuits concentrated on the elite; however, unlike in China, the Mughal emperors were actively involved in high culture and were arbiters of taste. In fact, the emperors united the power of the Chinese emperor with the high level of intellectual discourse of the literati. Unlike in Japan or China, the Jesuits were actually invited to court, by the Emperor himself, and he facilitated the dialogue. In fact, I get a strong feeling from both Persian and European-language sources that if the Emperor and his family had not presided over the debates, the Muslim mullahs would have had the Jesuits lynched. It was not at all like the polite gatherings of the literati in China. Yet, in striking contrast to China, there was no 'cultural imperative' at play in India. Akbar and Jahangir encouraged the Jesuits to act as differently as possible from Indian culture. What the emperors did with it, however, was another matter.

Akbar's motives for having the missionaries at Fatehpur Sikri were a combination of opportunism and genuine interest. He wanted the Jesuits as a possible pawn in the growing competition at sea among the Portuguese, English, and Dutch (Akbar had nothing to worry about yet by land). As with the Japanese daimyos and Qing emperors, he also wanted a steady source of exotic items such as clocks, musical instruments, and bejewelled daggers for his *Wunderkammer*. Here he was acting like a whole series of Eastern potentates, from the Sultan of Turkey to the King of Siam. Yet he also wanted the Jesuits to participate in his exploration of world religions and his quest for a universal spirituality. And, as a true art connoisseur determined to forge a dynastic style that could address a cosmopolitan audience, he needed the Jesuits as a source of European Renaissance visual culture and as artistic advisors. Of course, as we have seen, these motives, too, were tied to propagandistic aims. But the two impulses are not necessarily incompatible; the partnership between the Mughals and the Jesuits shows that both parties of a dialogue can be interested in gaining mutual advantages yet remain genuinely interested in one another.

As in the Far Eastern missions, it was not at the court but among the commoners that the Jesuits had their greatest pastoral successes. The emperors never converted, of course, and only continued to tolerate the Jesuits after the death of Jahangir because they provided periodic diplomatic services and still served as a conduit for information and trinkets from increasingly powerful Western nations. And, for the most part, Muslims also did not convert. Perhaps Muslims and Christians knew too much about each other, and the two religions were so closely linked with a history of antagonism and mutual hatred. The Jesuits were no exception; the disgust with which the missionaries regarded Islam and the Prophet Muhammad in their letters has no parallel in Asia and approaches the mendicants' revulsion toward Aztec mass sacrifice. Most of the converts to Catholicism were Armenian Christians, low-caste Hindus, and poverty-striken Muslims. They were either already Christians, or they were the poor and untouchable. So again we have people in unhappy circumstances turning to Christianity, people from underprivileged social groups.

In Mughal India, the art inspired by the missions was almost entirely produced by non-Christians for their Muslim Emperor, and its context remained largely Islamic. Thus the situation was very similar to that of Qing China, except that the art was explicitly religious, and appeared at least on the surface to be Christian. As in China as well, the art that has come down to us is mostly tied to the court and other elite groups, unlike in Japan, where much of what survives probably comes from confraternities and private households. The Jesuits were probably very active in what could be more accurately described as 'mission art,' very likely merging Hindu iconographic traditions with those of Christianity. Again, however, we have little evidence to show us what such an art might have looked like, since it was probably largely ephemeral and would not have survived the civil wars that tore Northern India apart in the eighteenth century. Even at the end, the Jesuits were wasting their time shooting for the stars; for example, in the eighteenth-century Jesuit-sponsored scientific mission to the Maharaja of Jaipur, at the time the most powerful potentate in the Mughal Empire.[20]

The Guaraní are fundamentally different from the other three mission cultures in this book: they were not a complex, literate culture; they lack a centralized political focus; and they had absolutely no foreknowledge of Christianity. Mughal India and China already had Eastern Christian populations, and even Japanese sailors would have encountered Nestorian Christian traders in places like Canton. However, the Guaraní also had many similarities with these Asian cultures. They had an elite class. They had their own religion, strongly characterized by rhetoric and spirituality, and an extensive mythology. And they had political and material advantages to be gained by a partnership with the Jesuits. As in Japan, the Jesuits were valued as allies against competing tribes, and they had the added advantage of being able to provide protection against the potential onslaught of Spanish or Portuguese forces. When the Portuguese Mamelucos proved too much for the reductions to withstand, the Jesuits were able to provide the Guaraní with the latest European weaponry. So the Jesuits were eminently useful to them.

The Jesuits also allowed for an improvement in the standard of living. Their reductions made available a political stability lacking in pre-contact Guaraní society, linking the spiritual with the temporal in a single site. And as they grew, the reductions became centres of great material prosperity, tied to more efficient forms of agriculture and above all to the colonial trade network. The only way the Jesuits could afford their elaborate churches was through a brisk trade in the region's natural resources, not to mention man-made products. The latter recalls the Jesuits' role in the Macao silk trade in Japan. Even in the reductions, the Jesuits paid the greatest attention to the elites, cultivating alliances and giving out special favours to what constituted the ruling class in Guaraní society. This was no communistic society, but, as usual, there was more than pure opportunism at play.

As did Akbar, the Guaraní gained intellectual satisfaction from the Jesuits' rhetorical skills. Guaraní culture is based on the spoken word, and the oral debates and mutual interpretation of dreams that took place during early contacts with the fathers indicate that an intercultural dialogue of great subtlety and complexity prospered on the mission.[21] They also – famously – shared a passion for music, and even before the Jesuits organized indigenous orchestras and choirs and premiered operas during the eighteenth century, it was their love for melodies which enticed the Guaraní out of the rainforest to participate in their 'beautiful words.' The Jesuits and Guaraní also shared a similar spirituality. Even in Europe, the Jesuits sought what they called a 'mystical theology,' which merged neatly with the Guaraní's own visionary tradition. Many scholars have pointed out the affinity between the early modern Catholic taste for prophecy and spectacle and that of the Guaraní. As in the Asian missions, the Guaraní admired the Jesuits' ability to manifest authority within the parameters of their own culture. In particular, the Guaraní were attracted to the Christian idea of Paradise, which coexisted with their own Land-without-Evil.

The subtlety of the cultural synthesis is also expressed in the visual arts. This blending was not as obvious as in Asia, where the cultures had figural arts traditions of their own, but it can be perceived in elements of style and by relating figures to Guaraní culture and the Guaraní world-view. As in Mughal India, artistic hybridization occurred both in 'mission art' and in the art of unconverted peoples – in this case, the *ta'a* tribes of the mountains. The tradition also lived on after the expulsion of the Society of Jesus in 1767 where Guaraní artistic traditions prospered in the colonial towns outside Asunción and on a few of the original mission sites.

While we are looking at issues of reception, and specifically the factors which made non-European societies respond favourably to the Jesuits, let us focus more closely on the art they brought with them. If we can say, as I think this book has demonstrated, that a wide range of non-European societies found something remarkable or at least intriguing about European Late Renaissance and Baroque art, we must ask ourselves why this was so. What values did European art have in the early modern period to which so many different civilizations responded? We cannot simply assume, as Europeans did then, that it was inherently superior. Most non-Europeans, most notably the Chinese, would have had a bone to pick with that notion. Yet there has to have been something in European art which most other art styles did not have.

First, in spite of the Plinian hyperbole of some Jesuit reports, it is clear that most people were impressed primarily by the lifelike qualities of European art. Even in indigenous-language texts, references to mirrors abound, and the comment is made repeatedly that European figures look as though they are breathing, moving, and occupying real space. We have seen examples of these reactions throughout this book. I might add to them this remark by Akbar's Muslim historian Abu'l-Fazl, in a famous passage on the art of painting:

> ... the European painters ... have attained world-wide fame. The minuteness in detail, the general finish, the boldness of execution, etc., now observed in pictures, are incomparable; even inanimate objects look as if they had life.[22]

It seems, therefore, that above all it was the Renaissance technique of pictorial realism which gave European art appeal to the rest of the world. Specifically, the most popular features were the anatomical realism of the human body, the realism and humanity of gesture, and the effects of *chiaroscuro*, all from the Italian tradition, together with the Northern Renaissance convention of atmospheric perspective in landscape. In contrast, Albertian one-point perspective received a (predictably) cold reception, even in China, where it was refracted through Pozzo's treatise and the illusionistic domes of the Jesuit mission churches. Perhaps it was far too contrived and mathematical to gain universal appeal.

Equally important, at least in some places – notably Mughal India and possibly Japan – was the ability of European art of this period to communicate pathos, psychological insight, and mood. Many people responded to the drama, immediacy, and sentimentality of the tradition of Raphael, Correggio, and their successors in the Baroque. People found this emotive quality approachable and understandable. Abu'l-Fazl spoke for most of his contemporaries when he wrote:

> ... painters, especially those of Europe, succeed in drawing figures expressive of the conceptions which the artist has of any of the mental states, so much so, that people may mistake a picture for a reality.[23]

These same qualities, of course, help explain the popularity of *arte sacra* in Europe itself; such art was invading Italy at the very time that the world missions of the Jesuits were getting under way. The new *arte sacra* (it is also called 'counter-*maniera*') contrasted sharply with much of the elite religious art produced in Italy at the time, which was dominated by erudite late Mannerist sensibilities. A more consciously classicizing current within *maniera* painting, *arte sacra* developed in the later 1550s in the wake of the Council of Trent, was visible in the late Pontormo (1494–1557), and was well developed in artists such as Marcello Venusti (1512–79) and the later work of Jacopino del Conte (ca. 1510–98). It would later mature into the 'timeless' art of Scipione Pulzone, Giuseppe Valeriano, and other artists working for the Jesuits in Rome in the 1590s, and finally help fuel the classicizing and naturalistic trends of the early Baroque. Sidney

Freedberg even credits the Jesuits directly with helping popularize this style.[24] Similarly to the art we have seen on the missions, the simple, bright, and optimistic images of *arte sacra* featured large figures, centralized compositions, and a minimum of narrative detail or action. They were primarily images of meditation and piety and were therefore strongly iconic and minimally expressive, with little in the way of setting. There was also a strong emphasis on miraculous images, such as the various Madonnas supposedly painted by Saint Luke and the Madonna of Loreto. By contrast, much of the mainstream *maniera* painting in Rome of the period was characterized by smaller figures and complex compositions and settings, and scenes were brimming with narrative activity, erudite symbolism, and ornament.

The evidence in this book makes a compelling case, I believe, that many non-European peoples considered Renaissance art techniques to be universal phenomena which went beyond cultural parameters. They were not merely aspects of European 'style.' Although scholars such as Cecilia Klein have rightly pointed out that European pictorial realism achieved universal status in the Americas 'in part because native modes of visual expression were often discouraged, if not stamped out, by the European,'[25] her comment does not explain situations in which the Europeans did not have the upper hand, for example in independant Asian countries, where no European could ever get away with the hubris of domination. Although this kind of pictorial realism was invented by the Europeans, once it spread overseas it did not belong to them any more than the musket or cannon – it was a technology, not an aspect of culture. When non-European cultures borrowed European conventions, it was not an acknowledgment of the superiority of European art. It is telling that, with the possible exception of the Mughals, none of the cultures examined in this book valued pictorial realism as much as their own traditions.

Perhaps the best parallel for the social position of European art outside of Europe can be found in the history of photography. In nineteenth- and early twentieth-century Europe, photography was received with enthusiasm as a scientific marvel, interpreted as an accurate recorder of visual data, and used to entertain peoples' curiosity, but it was held in disdain when compared to the 'fine arts' of painting, sculpture, and architecture. This comparison is especially apt in the later Chinese mission, where the Qianlong Emperor kept the Jesuit artists in his palace in a capacity best equated with that of court photographers. Even the Mughals did not esteem pictorial realism (or any representational art) as highly as beautiful calligraphy, a legacy not only of Islamic law but also of a long-standing Chinese influence. As Abu'l-Fazl wrote: '... pictures are much inferior to the written letter, inasmuch as the letter may embody the wisdom of bygone ages, and become a means to intellectual progress.'[26] The art of the missions itself sends us the same message. The ultimate legacy of European art in mainstream Mughal painting or Qing court painting was pictorial realism alone, shorn of European cultural conventions such as costume, subject matter, or symbolism. It was, to quote Samuel Edgerton, 'an absolute scientific truth, universal to all men regardless of cultural background or historical period.'[27]

If non-European peoples found something interesting about Late Renaissance and Baroque art, did the Europeans reciprocate? Throughout this book, we have been looking at what is surely only one side of the equation. Certainly the Jesuits on the missions themselves demonstrated, to varying degrees, a genuine desire to understand non-European art traditions, but rarely do we have a sense that they were interested in those traditions for aesthetic reasons – that is, beyond a purely practical desire to use them to help bring Christianity to the natives. Valignano's enthusiasm for Japanese architecture is one notable exception. Perhaps, as seems to have been the case with the letters describing the lack of indigenous creativity, missionaries were simply keeping their enthusiasm in check to appease audiences in Europe. This may have been so. However, it is one of the ironies of the entire 'Age of Exploration' that the Europeans were quite zealous about exporting their own culture, but aside from an acquisitive interest in curious objects for their *Wunderkammern*, they learned virtually nothing from Asian or American art. The Jesuits, who served as one of the main conduits for Europe of information and objects from the outside world, were no exception – beyond the periphery of the mission enterprise.

This intransigence at the centre meant that even though European *arte sacra* could be made to accommodate with a plethora of cultures outside Europe, it was not allowed to serve correspondingly as a means of bringing those cultures back home. Other than an interest in exotic flora and fauna, and a superficial enthusiasm for selective foreign symbolism and ornament, Europe closed its eyes to the art of the outside world. As Donald Lach observed about Asia and implied about America, 'The revelation of Asia did not fundamentally transform any of the European art forms.'[28]

Scholars in the past have found this inflexibility hard to accept. Many have argued, for example, that the Manueline style of architecture prevalent in sixteenth-century Portugal borrowed motifs and styles from Hindu temple architecture. But the two merely share a taste for surface ornament, and the so-called Indian symbols in Manueline façades and doorways are in reality only maritime themes such as ropes, shells, or aquatic animals. In one particularly creative hypothesis, it was even argued that the Jesuits created the Baroque by infusing an Indian and Chinese delight for ornament into Portuguese architecture of the 1540s to 1580s, thereby igniting the Italian Baroque via the Gesù in Rome.[29] Would that they had.

There are a few exceptions to this European blind-spot. It is true that Dürer famously showed genuine admiration for Aztec metalwork, which he was able to see in Europe, but he was not an average European by any stretch – and, besides, he never incorporated a single Aztec motif into his own art. Yet Dürer engravings were taken up with enthusiasm by the Emperor Akbar a few decades later – as works of art. Rembrandt also demonstrated a brief interest in non-European art, this time Mughal miniatures, which he copied in a series of well-known and sensitive drawings that even evoke the style of the originals. But other than a bit of exotic costume, we do not see what he learned appearing in his paintings – especially nothing in terms of style. This unwillingness at home to come to terms with the essence of Asian and American art is much to Europeans' discredit, and shows that despite their muskets and galleons they were still far behind many of the non-European cultures we have been observing in terms of intellectual curiosity and openness. The Jesuits, alas, were cut of the same cloth. But this is the subject of another book. Let us go back again to the missions.

We have so far been concentrating on the factors which made the partnership work between the Jesuits and non-European cultures. Equally important are those which hindered the exchange. We should first divide the kinds of exchanges possible into two categories, discarding those based purely on opportunism (alliances, guns, trinkets, and baubles). In all four missions, the *intellectual*, as opposed to *spiritual*, exchange seems to have fewer restrictions. Purely cultural dialogue seems possible in situations of peace and prosperity (Mughal India, Ming China) as well as war and discord (Japan). All that is required is a little curiosity and tolerance. Religious dialogue, by contrast, seems much more confined. In every region except Paraguay, an indigenous Christianity prospered mainly in times of strife or among the poor, imperilled, or forgotten. Christianity is a religion of salvation, and offered hope to a people in need, as well as an identity to people lacking status. Even in Paraguay, where the mission populations expanded prodigiously in peacetime (after the Battle of Mbororé kept the Mamelucos at bay), the Guaraní had adopted Christianity because it offered more stability than their indigenous *teyy* system and kept them out of the hands of the colonists.

Neither kind of partnership – intellectual or spiritual – could work when the Jesuits refused to operate within indigenous cultural traditions – when they did not accommodate. Thus, Christian art was a failure in elite China, and missionaries got nowhere in Japan while the policies of Cabral were still in place. Both intellectual and spiritual exchanges flourished when the Jesuits were willing to make the requisite overture to native culture. The literati applauded Ricci as a Confucianist, not as a Christian, and conversions increased everywhere in direct proportion to the extent of the Church's indigenization. The Jesuits' corporate strategy – flexibility – was the only path open to them.

Now let us return once more to the people we started with: the Jesuits themselves. What were their motives, and, in the language of current Jesuit scholarship, what was their 'mode of proceeding.' Depending on whether their authors were sympathetic to the Jesuits or not, histories of the Jesuit missions tend to depict their protagonists as either saints or diabolical propagandists. Was their policy on the missions entirely polemically determined, doctrinal, and anti-intellectual, as Elison would have it? He writes that 'the intellectual Jesuit is a cliché' and that they 'came to convert Japan, not to enlighten it.'[30] Yet Japanese studies and Buddhism, as well as pagan authors such as Aristotle and the classics, were the cornerstone of Jesuit education in Japan.[31] Were they only acting out of self-interest? Was their motto *Ad Maiorem Dei Gloriam* itself a cliché?

I was attracted to the Jesuits as a subject in the first place because they seemed to me to be one of the most compelling examples of the indomitability of the human will. This zeal also struck Lord Macaulay, whom I quoted earlier – certainly no friend of the Jesuits, but one who nevertheless admired their stamina: '... with what vehemence, with what policy, with what exact discipline, with what dauntless courage, with what self-denial, with what forgetfulness of the dearest private ties, with what intense and stubborn devotion to a single end ... the Jesuits fought the battle of their church.'[32] Against all odds, these men traversed the earth even when they had so few brethren and so little money that they could barely hold down the fort in Rome. In the words of Jean Lacouture,

> ... the founders of the Society of Jesus and ... those of their successors who remained faithful to their message [are] the pioneers of a human adventure in the heart of a world taken on board in its totality, the preservers of a dynamics of life which seeks and exalts the glory of God through that of man, and not in the execration of created things.[33]

In a time when most Italians were still not quite clear about the location of places like Portugal or Poland, the Jesuits had established rudimentary bases on all five continents of the known world. For the most part, they did it for completely unselfish reasons, as well. Although the very notion of going on a mission to convert non-European people to Christianity is recognized by many today as being chauvinistic and Eurocentric, we cannot judge the sixteenth-century Society according to twentieth-century mores. The Jesuits were honestly convinced that they were bringing God's truth to fellow human beings the world over. As in Europe, their ultimate goal – albeit achieved by approaching princes first – was the consolation of the poor, needy, and wretched. And they had great success in those areas, bringing the message of Christian salvation to more than three-quarters of a million people in the four missions of this book alone. Even when they realized that their most cherished missions were not living up to their expectations, and faced the truth that most non-Europeans had no interest in becoming Christians, they continued to give with all of their heart. It is this generosity on the part of so many Jesuits that I find striking.

In particular, they invested Herculean energies into elaborate cultural projects when a simpler and more basic approach would probably have sufficed – if not indeed worked better. Almost as powerful as their love for God was their love for high culture. In China, Christianity prospered at the popular level while the extravagant court mission of Castiglione and his companions foundered. The Guaraní did not require the glories of Baroque Rome, the extravagances of Primoli's stone masterpieces, to be convinced of God's love. Jerónimo Xavier knew he was getting nowhere with Akbar and should devote his attention to the lower-caste Hindus and Armenians who made up his congregation, yet he sacrificed most of his time to debating and mastering the baroque intricacies and nuances of court Persian so that he could engage the intelligentsia of the Mughal court.

Bluntly put, why did they waste their time? Because even though they were missionaries, they were not above enjoying the sheer thrill of intellectual engagement. Just as in Europe, where the Jesuits' commitment to education and flexibility got them more deeply involved in secular society and humanism than any order which came before them, the Jesuits on the missions felt the passion of high culture – European and non-European – and wanted to communicate this enthusiasm to their audiences. This is why, even though the Jesuits were well aware of their pastoral limitations, they were content to prolong the dialogue at any cost, even if only on the cultural plane. And this is why they did not shrink from confrontations like that of Francis Xavier and the Swahili noble, in which it was clear that both parties were going to remain in disagreement. For surely it is the conversation itself, the intellectual exercise with its basic reaffirmation of human affinity, that is the ultimate attraction and final legacy of the Jesuits' mission enterprise.

Notes

Abbreviations for Archives

AGN	Archivo General de la Nación, Buenos Aires
AHPT	Archivo Historico de la Provincia de Toledo de la Compañía de Jesús, Madrid
ARSI	Archivum Romanum Societatis Iesu, Rome
BL	British Library, London
BNP	Biblioteca Nacional del Perú, Lima
CBL	Chester Beatty Library, Dublin
GSA	Goa State Archives, Panjim (India)
HIL	Heras Institute Library, Bombay
IOL	India Office Library, London
LNM	Lahore National Museum (Pakistan)
NAI	National Archives of India, New Delhi
NAP	National Archives of the Philippines, Manila
NLM	National Library of Macao

1: Introduction

1 Martin, *Miniature Painting and Painters*, 1:85.

2 Federico Zeri spoke in terms of 'timelessness' when he referred to the revolution in Italian painting that took place in the 1580s and 1590s at the Church of the Gesù in Rome, particularly the work of Scipione Pulzone (Federico Zeri, *Pittura e contrariforma*, 54–5). Although the scope of the present volume extends well into the period of the High Baroque in Europe, the majority of the art sent to the missions before 1700 still fell firmly within the canons of the late *maniera* or proto-Baroque art of the last decades of the sixteenth century in Rome. See Bailey, 'The Jesuits and Painting in Italy.'

3 The comment is by Jerónimo Nadal, one of the most prominent of Ignatius's companions. Ignatius sent Nadal to promulgate the Constitutions of the Society in Italy, Spain, Portugal, Germany, and Austria. He served as the Society's Visitor in several provinces and founded schools. He is best remembered for his highly influential illustrated book of meditations on the Gospel, the *Evangelicae historiae imagines* (1593), which was also the earliest imagery associated with the Jesuits. The comment is quoted in O'Malley, *The First Jesuits*, 80.

4 *The Constitutions of the Society of Jesus*, 68.

5 Sweet, 'The Ibero-American Frontier Mission in Native American History,' 9.

6 On the history of 'inculturation' during and after Vatican II, see Kapola, *The Zairian Mass*. Vatican Council II, or 'Vatican II,' was a series of ecumenical council sessions held between 1961 and 1964 through which there has been a liturgical revision of the Mass and the Sacraments in which the vernacular and a new approach make them more meaningful to the Christian.

7 The term was coined by Jean Lacouture in his *Jésuites: Une multibiographie* (Paris, 1992); its first appearance in English was in John Bossy's review of Lacouture's book: 'Global Humanists?' *Times Literary Supplement*, no. 4662 (7 Aug. 1992).

8 D'Elia, *Fonte Ricciane*, 1:cxlii.

9 See the discussion in Spence, *The Memory Palace of Matteo Ricci*, 1–12.

10 On the Borghese Madonna, see Mâle, *L'art religieux après le Concile de Trente*, 23–5; Cellini, *La madonna di San Luca*; and d'Elia, 'La Madonna di S. Maria Maggiore in Cina.' On the cult of Loreto in Europe, see Grimaldi, *Il santuario di Loreto*. On the *acheiropoieton*, see Jones, *Federico Borromeo and the Ambrosiana*, 169.

11 On the Litany of Loreto in New Spain and Germany respectively, see Bargellini, 'Jesuit Devotions and Retablos in New Spain'; and Smith, 'The Art of Salvation in Bavaria.'

12 Kennedy, '*Candide* and a Boat.'

13 Dean, 'The Renewal of Old World Images,' 171.

14 Frois, *Die Geschichte Japans*, 267. Later on, Frois mentions the same incident: 'After this fiend had taken the picture away, he put it in his room and struck out the eyes with ink and did other blasphemies, and showed it out of mockery to people who came to his house for entertainment' (p. 308).

15 Ruiz de Montoya, *The Spiritual Conquest ... of Paraguay*, 152ff.

16 NAP, Temporalidades, bundle II.

17 See Pilar, 'Philippine Painting'; and José, *Images of Faith*, 15–20.

18 Jones, *Federico Borromeo and the Ambrosiana*, 2ff.

19 See my 'Le style jésuite n'existe pas.'

20 Characteristically, however, *Circa 1492*, the largest museum exhibition ever to celebrate this mutual discovery, assiduously avoided works of art that actually resulted from the encounter, except for African art. See Levenson, *Circa 1492*. For a critique of post-1992 literature, see Cummins and Boone, *Native Traditions*, 1–9.

21 For example, Hiromitsu Kobayashi at Sophia University, Catherine Pagani at the University of Alabama, and Hui-hung Chen at Brown University, all working on the impact of the Jesuits on Chinese art.

22 *The Namban Art of Japan*, 8.

23 Boone, 'Pictorial Documents and Visual Thinking in Postconquest Mexico,' 158.

24 Macaulay, 'Ranke's History of the Popes,' 20.

25 Parry, *The Spanish Seaborne Empire*, 154ff; Lippy et al., *Christianity Comes to the Americas*, 8–10, 67; Alden, *The Making of an Enterprise*, xxx.

26 Lippy et al., *Christianity Comes to the Americas*, 10. This organization is often mistakenly believed to be a Jesuit foundation. For example, Rudolf Wittkower, in his introduction to *Baroque Art: The Jesuit Contribution*, writes about Borromini's building for the Congregation in Rome as if it were a Jesuit institution.

27 Parry, *The Spanish Seaborne Empire*, 186.
28 See Maldavsky, 'Langues indigènes et mission.'

2: The Origins of the Partnership

1 See summary in Cummins and Boone, *Native Traditions*, 5. For New Spain, see also Koyabashi, *La educación como conquista*; and Ricard, *La conquista espiritual de México.* and For Portuguese Asia, see several works by C.R. Boxer, such as *Portuguese India in the Mid-Seventeenth Century.* A classic refutation of the conquest mentality in the scholarship about Portuguese Asia is Panikkar, *Asia and Western Dominance.*
2 On Paraguay, see Necker, *Indios Guaraníes y Chamanes Franciscanos*, 34. For accommodation in the *encomienda* system, see next note.
3 Lockhart, *Nahuas and Spaniards*, 21. See also Gibson, *The Aztecs under Spanish Rule*, 102ff; and Fraser, *The Architecture of Conquest*, 93.
4 Lippy et al., *Christianity Comes to the Americas*, 58.
5 The adherence to pre-contact religion and 'idolotry' was extremely widespread, as the literature of extirpation makes clear. For a survey of this phenomenon in the Andean highlands, where it was especially prevelant, see Duviols, *La lutte contre les religions autochtones dans le Pérou colonial.*
6 Ricard, *La conquista espiritual de México*, 396–7; Gruzinski, *The Conquest of Mexico*, 18–19.
7 Hanke, *Aristotle and the American Indians*, 20; Gibson, *The Aztecs under Spanish Rule*, 98; Gruzinski, *The Conquest of Mexico*, 14.
8 Dibble, 'The Nahuatlization of Christianity'; Klor de Alva, 'Spiritual Conflict and Accommodation in New Spain'; Gruzinski, *The Conquest of Mexico.*
9 Acosta, *De Procuranda Indorum Salute*, 113ff (my translation).
10 For New Spain, see Clendinnen, *Ambivalent Conquests*; Klor de Alva, 'Spiritual Conflict and Accommodation in New Spain'; Burkhart, *The Slippery Earth*, 23; and Gruzinski, *The Conquest of Mexico*, 150, 170. For Central America, see Markman, *Architecture and Urbanization of Colonial Central America*, 99ff. For Peru, see Martín, *The Intellectual Conquest of Peru*, 125; and MacCormack, *Religion in the Andes*, 205, 388. For China, and a comparison with Peru, see Gernet, *China and the Christian Impact*, 41. In 1596, the Annual Letter from Peru is very concerned with the rise of 'superstition' among the Andean people of Cuzco, reflecting how widespread it was in the region (ARSI, Peru 12 I, f. 129ff).
11 GSA, 9529: Provisões a favor da cristandade (1595), ff. 53a–54b; see also Ferrão de Taveres, *Imaginária Luso-Oriental*, xxi.
12 Lockhart, *Nahuas and Spaniards*, 22. See also Klein, 'Editor's Statement: Depictions of the Dispossessed,' 107.
13 Block, *Mission Culture on the Upper Amazon.*
14 Sweet, 'The Ibero-American Frontier Mission in Native American History,' 32.
15 See Dibble, 'The Nahuatlization of Christianity.'
16 For the reference to Actopan, see Baird, *The Churches of Mexico 1530–1810*, 83.
17 Neumeyer, 'The Indian Contribution to Architectural Decoration in Spanish Colonial America,' 105.
18 Fraser, *The Architecture of Conquest*, 162.
19 Burkhart, *The Slippery Earth*, 189. See also Gruzinski, *The Conquest of Mexico*, 118–20.

20 For New Spain, see Gibson, *The Aztecs under Spanish Rule*, 118; and Burkhart, 'Pious Performances.' For the Philippines, see Trota José, *Simbahan*, 31–2.

21 Quoted in MacCormack, *Religion in the Andes*, 252.

22 Frois, *Die Geschichte Japans*, 262–3; Bourdon, *La Compagnie de Jésus et le Japon, 1547–1570*, 587.

23 Lockhart, *The Nahuas after the Conquest*, 207; Kiracofe, 'Architectural Fusion and Indigenous Ideology in Early Colonial Teposcolula.'

24 Fraser, *The Architecture of Conquest*, 5. Fraser claims that although the Indians did all the work, they had 'no say in the appearance of the product.'

25 Herskovits, *Man and His Works*; Kroeber, *Anthropology*; Drucker, *The Native Brotherhoods*.

26 Foster, *Culture and Conquest*, 10–11; Glick and Pi-Sunyer, 'Acculturation as an Explanatory Concept in Spanish History.'

27 For example, see Ortiz, *Contrapunteo del tabaco y el azúcar*; and Gutièrrez, *Pintura, escultula y artes útiles*, 11–24. For a discussion of the literature, see Escobar, *La belleza de los otros*, 34–5.

28 Escobar (*La belleza de los otros*, 34) calls hybrid art an 'elogio de la impureza.'

29 See Sahlins, *The Islands of History*; and Homi K. Bhabha's collected essays in *The Location of Culture*.

30 Gruzinsky, *The Conquest of Mexico*; Lockhart, *Nahuas and Spaniards*. Lockhart writes: 'A partially unwitting truce existed in which each side of the cultural exchange seemed satisfied that its own interpretation of a given cultural phenomenon was the prevailing, if not exclusive one. Elsewhere, I have called this the process of Double Mistaken Identity ... The essence of the matter is that each side naively underestimates the complexity and idiosyncrasy of phenomena as seen from the other side and imperviously marches ahead in its own tradition' (*Nahaus and Spaniards*, 22).

31 Farago, 'Editor's Introduction,' 12.

32 Tedlock, *The Spoken Word and the Work of Interpretation*, 324–34; Burkhart, *The Slippery Earth*, 185–8. This understanding also agrees with that of Glick and Pi-Sunyer, and of James Clifford, who see cultures as constantly changing in reaction to others (Glick and Pi-Sunyer, 'Acculturation as an Explanatory Concept in Spanish History'; Clifford, *The Predicament of Culture*).

33 Francis Xavier, letter of 20 September 1542, in Costelloe, ed., *The Letters and Instructions of Francis Xavier*, 48.

34 It is easy to get bogged down with these terms. See, for example, George Kubler's elaborate system of categorizing degrees of artistic convergence in Kubler, 'On the Colonial Extinction of the Motifs of Pre-Columbian Art,' 68.

35 Kubler was one of the most firmly opposed to the acculturation model, believing that nearly all symbolic expressions of indigenous origin were suppressed and replaced by both colonials and the colonized indigenous elites (Kubler, 'On the Colonial Extinction of the Motifs of Pre-Columbian Art,' 67). More recently, scholars are demonstrating a long-lasting persistence of indigenous elements in colonial Latin American art and culture. For New Spain, see Anderson et al., *Beyond the Codices*; 1976; Klor de Alva, 'Christianity and the Aztecs'; Lockhart and Schwartz, *Early Latin America*; 'Spiritual Conflict and Accommodation in New Spain,' in Gollier, ed., *The Inca and Aztec States: 1400–1800*, 345–66; Gossen, 'Mesoamerican Ideas as a Foundation for Regional Synthesis'; Lock-

hart, *Nahuas and Spaniards* and *The Nahuas after the Conquest*; Gruzinsky, *Painting the Conquest*; Peterson, *The Paradise Gardens of Malinalco*; Kiracofe, 'Architectural Fusion and Indigenous Ideology in Early Colonial Teposcolula'; as well as several articles in Farago, *Reframing the Renaissance*, and in Cummins and Boone, *Native Traditions in the Postconquest World*, esp. 5ff.

For Peru, see MacCormack, 'From the Sun of the Incas to the Virgin of Copacabana,' 'The Heart Has Its Reasons,' 'Pachacuti: Miracles, Punishments, and Last Judgment,' *Religion in the Andes*, and 'Art in a Missionary Context,' Cummins, 'Abstraction to Narration' and 'Representation in the Sixteenth Century and the Colonial Image of the Inca'; Cummins and Rappaport, 'Between Images and Writing'; and Damian, *The Virgin of the Andes*.

36 Wethey, *Colonial Architecture and Sculpture in Peru*, 21.

37 The term is contemporary with the period. The Jesuit Ignacio Alzina, for example, referred to Filipino churches that used indigenous structural forms as '*arquitectura mestiza*' in the 1660s (Trota José, *Simbahan*, 32).

38 Guido, *Fusión hispano-indígena en la arquitectura colonial*; and *Redescubrimiento de América en el arte*, 18ff, 91ff.

39 For example, Wethey wrote: '*mestizo* or creole art is the most original contribution of the Hispanic colonial period. Its distinguishing and flavorsome qualities were those of the Indian's heritage' (*Colonial Architecture and Sculpture in Peru*, 21). Kubler also proposed the term *criollo* ('On the Colonial Extinction of the Motifs of Pre-Columbian Art,' 77). Angulo Iñiguez, Marco Dorta, and Mario J. Buschiazzo (*Historia del arte hispanoamericano*, 3:421) refer to this style as 'Andean Baroque' or 'planimetric decoration.' José de Mesa and Teresa Gisbert use the term 'mestizo' regularly; for example, see their 'Renacimiento y manierismo en la arquitectura "mestiza"' and 'Determinantes del llamado estilo mestizo.' See also Gisbert, *Iconografía y mitos indígenas en el arte*; Flores Ochea, *El Cuzco: Resistencia y continuidad*; and Adorno and Adorno, eds, *Transatlantic Encounters*.

40 Bayón, *History of South American Colonial Art and Architecture*, 155ff.

41 Kubler and Soria, *Art and Architecture in Spain and Portugal and Their American Dominions*, 92; Gasparini, 'Análisis critico de las definiciones de "arquitectura popular" y "arquitectura mestiza."'

42 Wethey, *Colonial Architecture and Sculpture in Peru*, 21.

43 Neumeyer, 'The Indian Contribution to Architectural Decoration in Spanish Colonial America.' John McAndrew was also fond of this term and used it to refer to what he called an 'indian quality' (*The Open-Air Churches of Sixteenth-Century Mexico*, 174). More recently, Elizabeth Wilder Weismann also uses the term (*Art and Time in Mexico*, 4, 22).

44 Villa Moreno, *La escultura colonial mexicana*, 16; McAndrew, *The Open-Air Churches of Sixteenth-Century Mexico*, 197–9; Vargas Lugo, 'Sobre el concepto tequitqui'; Grizzard, *Spanish Colonial Art and Architecture of Mexico and the U.S. Southwest*, 14. Wilder Weismann (*Art and Time in Mexico*, 25) comments: 'It is fair to call this tequitqui (instead of poor drawing) because the symbolic, flat, two level relief with tape-like edges resembles (in style) preconquest examples.'

45 Reyes Valerio, *Arte indocristiano*. Reyes inventoried 120 Nahua motifs which survived the conquest.

46 George Kubler, 'Introduction'; Kubler, 'On the Extinction of the Motifs of Pre-Columbian Art,' 67; Gibson, *The Aztecs under Spanish Rule*, 100. See also Gonzáles Galván, 'Influencia por selección de América en su arte colonial'; and Manrique, 'La estampa como fuente del arte en la Nueva España,' 57. Kubler remarks: 'Such survivals are so few and scattered that their assembling requires an enormous expenditure for a minimal yield, like a search for the fragments of a deep-lying shipwreck' ('On the Extinction of the Motifs of Pre-Columbian Art,' 66).

47 See Gombrich, 'In Search of Cultural History.'

48 See Kaufmann, 'Italian Sculptors and Sculpture outside of Italy,' 50–1.

49 For a summary of this literature in Russia, Poland, and Turkey, see Cracraft, *The Petrine Revolution in Russian Architecture*, 88ff; Kaufmann, 'Italian Sculptors and Sculpture outside of Italy,' 50ff; Mamboury, 'L'art Turc du XVIIIème siècle'; and Aslanapa, *Turkish Art and Architecture*, 321–32.

50 Kaufmann, 'Italian Sculptors and Sculpture outside of Italy,' 51.

51 Gruzinsky, *The Conquest of Mexico*, 187; Kubler and Soria, *Art and Architecture in Spain and Portugal and Their American Dominions*, 164.

52 Kaufmann, 'Italian Sculptors and Sculpture outside of Italy,' 57.

53 Cracraft, *The Petrine Revolution in Russian Architecture*, 88. Cracraft paraphrases the work of B.R. Vipper.

54 On this problem even within Italy, see Brown, 'Painting and History in Renaissance Venice' and *Venetian Narrative Painting in the Time of Carpaccio*; and Welch, *Art and Society in Italy 1350–1500*, 9ff. New surveys of Italian Renaissance art try to move away from the Florentine-Roman paradigm and look at such other places as Milan, Modena, and Naples; for example, see Paoletti and Radke, *Art in Renaissance Italy*.

55 Rice, 'The Conflux of Influences in Eighteenth-Century Russian Art and Architecture,' 280.

56 Wilder Weismann, *Art and Time in Mexico*, 3.

57 Kaufmann, 'Italian Sculptors and Sculpture outside of Italy,' 51.

58 Kuran, 'Eighteenth Century Ottoman Architecture,' 315.

59 Kuban, 'Influences de l'art européen sur l'architecture Ottomane au XVIIIème siècle,' 149.

60 Cracraft, *The Petrine Revolution in Russian Architecture*, 88.

61 Kubler, 'Introduction,' 145–6. Kubler is speaking of planimetric architecture in colonial Latin America, in particular.

62 Compare the facial features and pose of this statue to the sixteenth-century Hindu sculptural group representative of the Vijayanagara culture of Southern India, and compare the drapery and stance to the great Buddha at Avukana in Sri Lanka, both published in Harle, *The Art and Architecture of the Indian Subcontinent*, figures 267 and 357.

63 Kubler, 'On the Colonial Extinction of the Motifs of Pre-Columbian Art,' 68; Peterson, *The Paradise Garden Murals of Malinalco*, 8ff.

64 'When a ... figure such as the Virgin Mary was accepted as an object of veneration by the Christianized Andean people, the figure itself may have been relatively unimportant. Rather, the ceremonial garments and attributes which accompanied it delivered a more significant message based on Non-Western aesthetics' (Damian, *The Virgin of the Andes*, 31).

65 See MacCormack, *Religion in the Andes*.

66 Kubler, *The Art and Architecture of Ancient America*, 37.
67 Klein, 'Editor's Statement'; Furst, 'The nahualli of Christ,' 209.
68 On the Cuzco school, see Damian, *The Virgin of the Andes*, 10. On syncretism in the Virgin of Copacabana, see MacCormack, 'From the Sun of the Incas to the Virgin of Copacabana.' On the controversial issue of syncretism in the Virgin of Guadalupe in colonial New Spain, see Lafaye, *Quetzalcóatl and Guadalupe*; and Peterson, 'The Virgin of Guadalupe.'
69 Gruzinsky, *The Conquest of Mexico*, 118.
70 For New Spain, see Grizzard, *Spanish Colonial Art and Architecture of Mexico and the U.S. Southwest*, 17ff. For the Philippines, see Javellana, *Wood and Stone for God's Greater Glory*, 25.
71 Fraser, *The Architecture of Conquest*, 6.
72 Kubler and Soria, *Art and Architecture in Spain and Portugal and Their American Dominions*, figs. 135 and 140(B). See also Plá, *El barroco hispano Guaraní*, 125; and Escobar, *Una interpretación de las Artes Visuales en el Paraguay*, 1:247.
73 Moura Sobral, 'L'estampe anversoise et la peinture portuguaise au début du XVII siècle,' 57–8; Serrão, *O Manierismo e o Estatuto Social dos Pintores Portugueses*, especially 'Os anos de servidão e aprendizagem,' 190–204.
74 Brown, *Images and Ideas in Seventeenth-Century Spanish Painting*, 51.
75 I would like to thank Pamela Jones for bringing this relationship to my attention.
76 See Kris and Kurz, *Legend, Myth, and Magic in the Image of the Artist*; Goldstein, *Visual Fact over Verbal Fiction*; Rubin, *Giorgio Vasari*, especially chapter 4; and Gardner, '*Homines non nascuntur, sed figuntur:* Benvenuto Cellini's *Vita* and Self-Presentation of the Renaissance Artist.'
77 Maravall, 'La Utopia politico-religiosa de los Franciscanos en Nueva España'; Hanke, *Aristotle and the American Indian*, 6, 14, 20–1; Burkhart, *The Slippery Earth*; Moffitt Watts, 'Languages of Gesture in Sixteenth-Century Mexico.'
78 Wethey, *Colonial Architecture and Sculpture in Peru*, 29ff; Foster, *Culture and Conquest*, 17; Baird, *The Churches of Mexico 1530–1810*, 86–7; Gibson, *The Aztecs under Spanish Rule*, 99; Toussaint, *Colonial Art in Mexico*; McAndrew, *The Open-Air Churches of Sixteenth-Century Mexico*, 181; Kubler, 'On the Colonial Extinction of the Motifs of Pre-Columbian Art,' 67; Weismann, *Art and Time in Mexico*, 10, 19ff; Trexler, 'Aztec Priests for Christian Altars'; Burkhart, *The Slippery Earth*; Fraser, *The Architecture of Conquest*, 64ff; MacCormack, *Religion in the Andes*, 205, 368; MacCormack, 'Art in a Missionary Context.'
79 It is still a matter of debate why in Mexico most of these three-aisled basilicas were later replaced with single-aisled 'fortress' style churches. For an early typology, see Kubler, *Mexican Architecture of the Sixteenth Century*, 2:292ff. See also Bargellini, 'Jesuit Devotions and Retablos in New Spain' and 'Representations of Conversion,' 96. On the Early Christian Revival in late sixteenth-century Rome, see Abromson, *Painting in Rome during the Papacy of Clement VII*; Zuccari, *Arte e committenza nella Roma di Caravaggio*; and Macioce, *Undique Splendent*.
80 Langer and Jackson, *The New Latin American Mission History*, 2.
81 Parry, *Spanish Seaborne Empire*, 160–1.
82 See Hanke, *Aristotle and the American Indian*; O'Gorman, *The Invention of America*; and Pagden, *The Fall of Natural Man*.
83 Pagden, *The Fall of Natural Man*, 181.

84 Gruzinsky, *The Conquest of Mexico*, 67.
85 See Wright, *The Counter Reformation*, 32ff; and Gruzinsky, *The Conquest of Mexico*, 67, 264.
86 Ross, *A Vision Betrayed*, especially the Introduction; Alden, *The Making of an Enterprise*, 56ff.
87 Schütte, *Valignano's Mission Principles for Japan*, 1:293.
88 'The conflict between the Jesuits and the settlers, therefore, concerned Indian *custody* more than it did freedom as that concept is understood today' (Alden, *The Making of an Enterprise*, 500).
89 The words are Ricci's own, used to describe the reaction of a local Chinese governor and his people to the Madonna of Saint Luke (d'Elia, ed., *Fonti Ricciane*, 1:127).
90 Ricci's own term, used in a letter (d'Elia, ed., *Fonte Ricciane*, 1:127).
91 See Edgerton, *The Renaissance Rediscovery of Linear Perspective*. Edgerton applied the idea of moralist linear perspective to the New World in his lecture 'Leon Battista Alberti vs. Quetzalcoatl: The Role of Italian Renaissance Art Theory in the Sixteenth-Century "Conversion" of Mexico,' delivered at the symposium 'Cultural Transmission and Transformation in the Ibero-American World, 1200–1800,' at Virginia Polytechnic Institute and State University, 21 October 1995.
92 Pelliot, 'La peinture et la gravure européenes en chine au temps de Mathieu Ricci' (my translation from the French).
93 This same comment was made by early mendicants in New Spain, for example, in Tlatelolco, where Nahua artists were praised for their ability at 'imitating the models presented by their masters' (Gruzinsky, *The Conquest of Mexico*, 47). See also McAndrew, *The Open Air Churches of Sixteenth-Century Mexico*, 194; and Wilder Weismann, *Art and Time in Mexico*, 14. For the Philippines, see José, *Images of Faith*, 19.
94 Already, in the first half of the sixteenth century, Bernal Díaz del Castillo, the historian of the conquest of Mexico, compared Nahua artists to Apelles, Michelangelo, and Berruguete (Wilder Weismann, *Art and Time in Mexico*, 36). One and a half centuries later, the Paraguayan Jesuit Anton Sepp compared Guaraní artists to Rubens (see chapter 6).
95 Kris and Kurz, *Legend, Myth, and Magic in the Image of the Artist*, 42–3.
96 Acosta, *De Procuranda Indorum Salute*, book 5, chapter 24 (my translation).
97 Alden, *The Making of an Enterprise*, 77.
98 Bhabha, *The Location of Culture*, 116.
99 The pioneer of mission history is Hubert Eugene Bolton, whose article 'The Mission as a Frontier Institution in the Spanish-American Colonies' was the foundation of the field. Bolton is now regarded as being too hispanophile, but he and his generation of 'boltonians' set the perameters of the field by focusing on the institutional setting and organization of missions, and their ideology. Where Bolton and his school are weak is in social and economic history. For a good recent survey of the literature, see Langer and Jackson, *The New Latin American Mission History*, x–xi, 2–3.
100 The literature on peripheral missions includes Bolton, 'The Mission as a Frontier Institution in the Spanish-American Colonies'; Spicer, *Cycles of Conquest*; Ramon, ed., *Bolton and the Spanish Borderlands*, 188–21; Mörner, *La Corona Espanola y los foráneos en los pueblos de indios de América*; Ybot León, *La Iglesia y los eclesiásticos en la empresa de indias*; Egaña, *Historia de la Iglesia en la América española*; Polzer, *Rules and Precepts of the Jesuit Missions of Northwest New Spain*; Necker, *Indios Guaraníes y chamanes franciscanos*, 12ff; and Block, *Mission Culture on the Upper Amazon*.

101 Gibson, *The Aztecs under Spanish Rule*, 98; Polzer, *Rules and Precepts of the Jesuit Missions of Northwest New Spain*, 5.
102 Lippy, Choquette, and Poole, *Christianity Comes to the Americas*, 19, 39.
103 Weismann, *Art and Time in Mexico*, 33.
104 Polzer, *Rules and Precepts of the Jesuit Missions of Northwest New Spain*, 7.
105 Wethey, *Colonial Architecture and Sculpture in Peru*, 6; Fraser, *The Architecture of Conquest*, 11; MacCormack, *Religion in the Andes*, 140.
106 Polzer, *Rules and Precepts of the Jesuit Missions of Northwest New Spain*, 47–9.
107 Ibid., 49.
108 Acosta devotes a chapter to this, advising that priests should preserve their hands for serving God since corporal punishment would ruin peoples' respect for them (Acosta, book 4, chapter 19).
109 Lippy et al., *Christianity Comes to the Americas*, 68–9.
110 Burkhart, *The Slippery Earth*, 12; Gibson, *The Aztecs under Spanish Rule*, 114. Important work on this field in Peru is being done by Aliocha Maldavsky; for example, her unpublished article 'Langues indigènes et mission: Recherches sur la crise de l'apostolat chez les jésuites de la province péruvienne au tournant des XVIe et XVIIe siècles.' I am grateful to Professor Maldavsky not only for this article but for considerable assistance in the Roman Archives in finding Peruvian materials relating to the arts.
111 Pagden, *The Fall of Natural Man*, 181; Alden, *The Making of an Enterprise*, 417.
112 Martín, *The Intellectual Conquest of Peru*, 5; Pagden, *The Fall of Natural Man*, 184; Lockhart, *The Nahuas after the Conquest*, 5ff; Trota José, *Simbahan*, 19.
113 Burkhart, *The Slippery Earth*; Moffitt Watts, 'Languages of Gesture in Sixteenth-Century Mexico,' 149; Burkhart, 'Pious Performances.'
114 MacCormack, *Religion in the Andes*, 247.
115 See Pagden, *The Fall of Natural Man*, 189; Burkhart, *The Slippery Earth*, 22; Cummins, 'From Lies to Truth,' 163. Cummins also spoke on this topic recently at a symposium at the City University of New York in February 1997. For more on the cross-cultural impact of Nahua and Inca systems of writing, see Boone and Mignolo, *Writing without Words*.
116 Gruzinsky, *The Conquest of Mexico*, 30; Boone, 'Pictorial Documents and Visual Thinking,' 161.
117 Block, *Mission Culture on the Upper Amazon*, 119.
118 Kubler and Soria, *Art and Architecture in Spain and Portugal and their American Dominions*, 164; Wilder Weismann, *Art and Time in Mexico*, 26; Grizzard, *Spanish Colonial Art and Architecture of Mexico and the U.S. Southwest*, 57.
119 Estrada de Gerlero, *Nueva España*, 75–6.
120 MacCormack, 'Art in a Missionary Context,' 103.
121 For both sides of the argument, see Toussaint, *Colonial Art in Mexico*; McAndrew, *The Open Air Churches of Sixteenth-Century Mexico*, 207ff; Baird, *The Churches of Mexico*, 86ff; Kubler, 'Non-Iberian European Contributions to Latin American Colonial Architecture,' 81; and Wilder Weismann, *Art and Time in Mexico*, 26ff. Samuel Edgerton recently gave a talk on this subject, with new evidence from the Yucatan (Edgerton, 'Missionaries and Indians in Sixteenth-Century Mexico').
122 See Gisbert and de Mesa, *La tradición bíblica en el arte virreynal*, 3–18; and Lara, 'God's Good Taste.'

123 Trota José, *Simbahan*, 13.

124 See Kowal, 'The Evolution of Ecclesiastical Architecture in Portuguese Goa'; and his lecture 'Innovation and Assimilation.' On Jesuit architecture in Goa, see Chicó, 'Algumas observações acerca da arquitectura da Companhia de Jesus no distrito de Goa.'

125 Hanke, *Aristotle and the American Indian*, 19; Gibson, *The Aztecs under Spanish Rule*, 99; Pagden, *The Fall of Natural Man*, 189; Wilder Weismann, *Art and Time in Mexico*, 33; Gruzinsky, *The Conquest of Mexico*, 60.

126 Martin, *The Intellectual Conquest of Peru*, 4; Fraser, *The Architecture of Conquest*, 96.

127 Lippy et al., *Christianity Comes to the Americas*, 10.

128 In addition to the literature cited above on border missions, see Dunne, *Pioneer Jesuits in Northern Mexico*; Roca, *Spanish Jesuit Churches in Mexico's Tarahumara*; Konrad, *A Jesuit Hacienda in Colonial Mexico*; *Arquitectura en el desierto: Misiones jesuitas en Baja California*; Block, *Mission Culture on the Upper Amazon*; and Polzer, *Kino: A Legacy*.

129 Umberger, 'The Monarchía Indiana in Seventeenth-Century New Spain,' 55. The basic source on Jesuit activities in New Spain is Decorme, *La obra de los jesuitas mexicanos durante la época colonial*.

130 Spicer, *Cycles of Conquest*; Polzer, *Rules and Precepts of the Jesuit Missions of Northwest New Spain*, 11. On the Jesuits in Mexico, see also Dunne, *Pioneer Jesuits in Northern Mexico*; Konrad *A Jesuit Hacienda in Colonial Mexico*; and Díaz, *La Arquitectura de los Jesuitas en Nueva España*.

131 Block, 'Priests and Providers.' See Lehnertz, 'Lands of the Infidels.'

132 See Gruzinski, *The Conquest of Mexico*, 188ff; and his 'Délires et visions chez les Indiens du Mexique.' See also chapter 6 of the present volume.

133 On Acosta, see Lopetegui, *El Padre José de Acosta S.I. y las misiones*; Martin, *The Intellectual Conquest of Peru*; Pagden, *The Fall of Natural Man*; and MacCormack, *Religion in the Andes*. Claudio Burgaleta has recently made an important reassessment of Acosta's acculturation policy in his 1996 Ph.D. dissertation for Boston College (Burgaleta, 'The Jesuit Theological Humanism of José de Acosta').

134 *De Procuranda Indorum Salute*, book 5, chapter 18 (my translation, as are all of the selections from Acosta).

135 Alden, *The Making of an Enterprise*, 73, 476.

136 Burgaleta, 'The Jesuit Theological Humanism of José de Acosta.'

137 *De Procuranda Indorum Salute*, book 2, chapter 12; see also book 4, chapter 6.

138 Ibid., book 2, chapter 24.

139 Ibid., book 4, chapter 2.

140 Ibid., book 3, chapter 2.

141 The text exists in an Elizabethan English translation. The work was preceded by Bartolomé de las Casas's *Apologetica Historia* (first printed 1588), which was the first detailed comparative analysis of Amerindian culture (Pagden, *The Fall of Natural Man*, 146).

142 Pagden, *The Fall of Natural Man*, 146, 149–50.

143 Ibid., 159–60; MacCormack, *Religion in the Andes*, 267. Burgaleta maintains that by the time Acosta wrote his Third Catechism, he had revised his earlier views and praised Amerindian civilizations more highly (personal communication given at thesis defence, Boston College, Fall 1996).

144 Pagden, *The Fall of Natural Man*, 163. In *De Procuranda Indorum Salute*, Acosta also

stressed the important role images played in easing the transition of neophytes into Christian life, by making them familiar with Christian customs (book 5, chapter 11).

145 Francis X. Clooney, 'True God, False Gods: Roberto de Nobili's Understanding of Religion and Hinduism in the Dialogue on Eternal Life and Inquiry on God'; and René Javellana, 'The Jesuits and the Indigenous Peoples of the Philippines,' lectures delivered at the symposium 'The Jesuits: Culture, Learning, and the Arts, Boston College, 29 and 30 May 1997.

146 For a summary of the literature, see my *'Le style jésuite n'existe pas*: Jesuit Corporate Culture and the Visual Arts.' The classic literature on this subject includes Serbat, 'L'architecture Gothique des Jésuites au XVIIe siècle'; Braun, *Die belgischen Jesuitenkirchen*, *Die Kirchenbauten der Deutscher Jesuiten*, and *Spaniens alte Jesuitenkirchen*; Poncelet, *Histoire de la Compagnie de Jésus dans les Anciens Pays-Bas*, 21:575–83; Kirschbaum, 'La Compagnia di Gesù e l'arte'; Galassi Paluzzi, *Storia segreta dello stile dei Gesuiti*; Dainville, 'La légende du style jésuite'; Barrett, 'A "Jesuit Style" in Art?'; Moisy, *Les églises des Jésuites de l'ancienne Assistance de France*; Charpentrat, 'Jésuite (Art)'; Wittkower and Jaffe, eds., *Baroque Art: The Jesuit Contribution*; and Gómez, 'Polémica en torno a los orígines de la arquitectura de las Jesuítas y la posible aceptación de un estílo.'

147 Some, following the example of Vallery-Radot et al., seek a definition that can be equated with a corporate orientation or, as Joseph Connors puts it, a 'corporate strategy.' Others go further and seek to identify basic common architectural and iconographic forms, even reviving the discussion over 'Jesuit style' itself. One is Richard Bösel, who seeks architectural commonalities (*ordensintern entwickelter Bautypen*) between Jesuit foundations (Bösel, *Jesuitenarchitektur in Italien 1540–1773*, Bösel and Garms, 'Die Plansammlung des Collegium Germanicum-Hungaricum'; Bösel, 'La chiesa di S. Lucia'; Bösel, 'Die Nachfolgebauten von S. Fedele in Mailand'). Sandro Benedetti uses the often-quoted rule from the First General Congregation of the Society of Jesus (1558) calling for practicality and plainness in Jesuit foundations to demonstrate an underlying ideal of poverty (Benedetti, *Fuori dal Classicismo*).

148 Díaz, *La arquitectura de los jesuitas en la Nueva España*, 186–96. See also Decorme, *La obra de los jesuitas mexicanos durante la época colonial*.

149 Hibbard, '*Ut picturae sermones:* The First Painted Decorations of the Gesù.'

150 Ignatius Loyola himself was credited with the invention of this term, by Jerónimo Nadal (O'Malley, *The First Jesuits*, 8). The best recent survey of the use of this term is Isabella Balestreri, 'L'architettura negli scritti della Compagnia di Gesù.'

151 Dainville, 'La légende du style jésuite,' 7.

152 The classic study of the pre-modern concept of the copy is Krautheimer, 'Introduction to an Iconography of Medieval Architecture.'

153 ARSI, Peru.12 II, f. 12a.

154 See Haskell, 'The Role of Patrons,' especially 54ff, and his *Patrons and Painters*, chapter 3; Moore, 'Pellegrino Tibaldi's Church of S. Fidele in Milan'; Robertson, *'Il Gran Cardinale': Alessandro Farnese, Patron of the Arts*; and her 'Two Farnese Cardinals and the Question of Jesuit Taste.'

155 The original Latin text reads: 'De ecclesiis tamen nihil dictum est, et hanc rem totam magis considerandum esse videbatur' (*Examen et Constitutiones Decreta Congregationum Generatium Formulae Congregationum*, 182–3).

156 Abromson, *Painting in Rome during the Papacy of Clement VIII*, 239.

157 Wittkower, 'Problems of the Theme,' in Wittkower and Jaffe, eds, *Baroque Art*, 12.

158 Pirri, *Giovanni Tristano e i primordi della architettura Gesuitica*, 164; Kubler and Soria, *Art and Architecture in Spain and Portugal and Their American Dominions*, 46; Rodriguez Gutiérrez de Ceballos, *Bartolomé de Bustamente y los Origines de la Arquitectura Jesuitica en España* (Madrid, 1961), 4, 7; Pirri, *Giuseppe Valeriano*, 4.

159 For a discussion of Jesuit imagery in Italy in the sixteenth and seventeenth centuries, see Bailey, 'The Jesuits and Painting in Italy.'

160 Mâle, *L'art religieux après le Concile de Trente*, 109–12; Röttgen, 'Zeitgeschichtliche Bildprogramme der katholischen Restauration unter Gregor XIII'; Lotti and Lotti, *La Comunità Cattolica Inglese di Roma*, 125–8; Buser, 'Jerome Nadal and Early Jesuit Art in Rome'; Monssen, 'Rex Gloriose Martyrum'; Zuccari, *Arte e Committenza nella Roma di Caravaggio*, 37; Herz, 'Imitators of Christ,' 65, 67; Lucas, *Saint, Site, and Sacred Strategy*, 186–91.

161 Haskell, *Patrons and Painters*, 86–93; Haskell, 'The Role of Patrons,' 57ff; Hibbard, '*Ut picturae sermones*: The First Painted Decorations of the Gesù,' 30ff; Macioce, *Undique Splendent*, 22ff; Levy, 'A Noble Medley and Concert of Materials and Artifice,' 51ff.

162 On the Lisbon cycle on the life of Saint Francis Xavier, see Serrão, 'Quadros de Vida de S. Francisco Xavier.'

163 Braun, *Die belgischen Jesuitenkirchen*, 12; Pirri, *Giovanni Tristano e i primordi della architettura gesuitica*; Kubler and Soria, *Art and Architecture of Spain and Portugal and Their American Dominions*, 19ff; Vallery Radot, *Le recueil de plans d'édifices de la compagnie de Jésus conservé a la Bibliothèque Nationale de Paris*, 125ff; Rodriguez Gutiérrez de Ceballos, *Bartolomé de Bustamente y los Orígenes de la arquitectura Jesuítica en España* (1961); Alfonso Rodriguez Gutiérrez de Ceballos, *Bartolomé de Bustamente y los Orígines de la arquitectura Jesuítica en España* (1967); Pirri, *Giuseppe Valeriano*; Wittkower, Introduction to Wittkower and Jaffe, eds, *Baroque Art*, 5; Moore, *Pellegrino Tibaldi's Church of S. Fedele in Milan*, 231; Bösel, 'Typus und Tradition in der Baukultur Gegenreformatorisher Orden,' 246ff.

164 'It seems good that the style and plans for any building proposed for construction by Ours should be submitted to Reverend Father General so that, according to the decree in the latter *acta* of the previous congregation, he may decide what he deems proper in the Lord' (Decree 84, Congregation 2, 1565; Padberg, O'Keefe, and McCarthy, *For Matters of Greater Moment*, 129.

165 Wittkower, Introduction to Wittkower and Jaffe, eds, *Baroque Art*, 7–8; Bösel, *Jesuitenarchitektur in Italien*, 11; Bösel, 'Typus und Tradition in der Baukunst gegenreformatorischer Orden,' 245; Vallery Radot, *Le recueil de plans d'édifices de la compagnie de Jésus*, 6ff.

166 Baglione, *Le vite de' pittori*, 353–4. Laire specialized in images such as the Saint Luke Madonna and the Madonna del Populo. He was laid in state in the Jesuit church of Santo Stefano Rotondo, and was buried in the Capella di San Giuseppe di Terra. I am grateful for Pamela Jones and Joseph Connors for bringing this reference to my attention.

167 Hibbard, *Caravaggio*, 161, n. 18.

168 McNaspy, 'Art in Jesuit Life,' 95. On Brazilian Jesuit architecture, see Costa, 'Arquitetura dos Jesuitas no Brasil'; Ferreira Santos, *O barroco e o jesuítico na arquitetura*

no Brasil; Smith, *Arquitectura jesuítica no Brasil*; Carvalho, *O colegio e as residencias dos jesuitas no Espirito Santo*; and *A forma e a imagem: Arte e arquitetura jesuítica no Rio de Janeiro colonial*.

169 Lundberg, *Jesuitische Anthropologie und Erziehungslehre in der Frühzeit des Ordens*, 232–5; Porteman, *Emblematic Exhibitions at the Brussels Jesuit College*; Rice, 'College Art.'

170 Sierra, *Los Jesuitas germanos en la conquista espiritual de Hispano-America*, 248.

171 BNP, Manuscrito C-58, Diversos asuntos de las misiones de Moxos y Chiquitos 1681–1765, letter of 12 March 1696. See also letter of 26 September 1695.

172 Sierra, *Los Jesuitas germanos en la conquista espiritual de Hispano-América*, 255.

173 Vargas Ugarte, *Ensayo de un diccionario de artifices coloniales de la America Meridional*, 62–4; Soria, *La Pintura del siglo XVI en Sud America*, 45–72; Kubler and Soria, *Art and Architecture in Spain and Portugal and Their American Dominions*, 321–2; Mesa and Gisbert, *Bernardo Bitti*; Martín, *The Intellectual Conquest of Peru*, 20; Castedo, *The Cuzco Circle*, 20; Mesa and Gisbert, *Historia de la pintura cuzqueña*, 56–62; Bayón and Marx, *History of South American Colonial Art and Architecture*, 103–5.

174 There is an example at San Pedro, the Jesuit church in Lima, of a guardian angel statue executed by Pedro de Vargas after designs by Bitti. It is incorporated into the later Altar de los Reliquias (1661). Vargas himself describes his method of working with Bitti in a letter of 1585 (see also below). Vargas built the huge main altar and two collateral altars at the Compañía in Cuzco, using designs drawn by Bitti for the panels (ARSI, Hisp. 129, f. 275a).

175 ARSI, Hisp. 129, f. 275a.

176 This painting is in the Museo de Arte in Lima.

177 Zeri, *Pittura e controriforma*. See also Bailey, 'The Jesuits and Painting in Italy,' 107ff.

178 ARSI, Rom. 171c, f. 30.

179 ARSI, FG 1488, 22a.

180 ARSI, Hisp. 121, ff. 214b, 242a; Hisp. 129, ff. 275a, 288a; Peru 4 I, ff. 11b, 17a, 24b, 31a, 35a, 53b, 55a, 60a, 78a, 93b, 120a; Peru 12 I, ff. 206b, 286b, 338a, 392.

181 Benavente Velarde, *Pintores Cusqueños de la Colonia*, 1–16.

182 Javellana, *Wood and Stone for God's Greater Glory*, 20.

183 Ibid., 20, 22; ARSI, Philipp. 2 I, ff. 4a, 13b, 19a, 24a.

184 Sierra, *Los Jesuitas germanos en la conquista espiritual de Hispano-America*, 248.

185 Bayón and Marx, *History of South American Colonial Art and Architecture*, 24, 261.

186 Sierra, *Los Jesuitas germanos en la conquista espiritual de Hispano-America*, 257.

187 Ibid., 258. See also Gonzalez Echenique, *Arte colonial en Chile*, especially 39ff.

188 Sierra, *Los Jesuitas germanos en la conquista espiritual de Hispano-America*, 238.

189 For example, Walter Hanisch Espindola, in his *Historia de la Compañía de Jesús en Chile*, says in one place that Bitterich arrived in Chile in 1711 (pp. 109–10); but later on in the same book, he is just leaving Germany in 1715 (p. 120). The archival records show that Bitterich only reached Chile in 1720 (and late enough that his records were placed in an addendum at the end of the catalogue) (ARSI, Chil. 2, ff. 302b, 310b).

190 ARSI, Chil. 2, ff. 218a, 237a, 254a, 275a-b, 279b, 302a, 305a, 306a, 322b, 324a, 326a-b, 323a, 328b, 330a; Chil. 3, ff. 24b, 51b. Hanisch Espindola mistakenly writes that Millet arrived much later, in 1724 (Hanisch Espindola, *Historia*, 109).

191 Sierra, *Los Jesuitas germanos en la conquista espiritual de Hispano-America*, 243–51; Ferrari Peña, 'La influencia de los jesuitas bávaros en la arquitectura y el arte chileños del

siglo XVIII'; Bayón and Marx, *History of South American Colonial Art and Architecture,* 233.

192 ARSI, Chil. 3, ff. 70a, 241b, 245b, 246a, 249b, 251b, 252a, 255b, 256a.

193 Javellana, *Wood and Stone for God's Greater Glory*, 22ff.

194 On the Silang church, see Javellana, *Wood and Stone for God's Greater Glory*, 103–4.

195 Ugarte, *Ensayo de un diccionario de artifices coloniales de la América Meridional*, 174–7; Bayón and Marx, *History of South American Colonial Art and Architecture*, 47. Wethey and others do not agree with this attribution, although it appears to be supported in the sources.

196 Sierra, *Los Jesuitas germanos en la conquista epiritual de Hispano-America*, 260; Bargellini, 'Jesuit Devotions and Retablos in New Spain.'

197 Bayón and Marx, *History of South American Colonial Art and Architecture*, 24, 261.

198 Sierra, *Los Jesuitas germanos en la conquista espiritual de Hispano-America*, 257.

199 Bayón and Marx, *History of South American Colonial Art and Architecture*, 129, 137, 139.

200 ARSI, Paraq. 6, ff. 173b, 151a, 214b, 227b. Schmidt is first mentioned in the Paraguay catalogues in 1735.

201 *Martin Schmid 1694–1772.*

202 Vargas Ugarte, *Ensayo de un diccionario de artifices coloniales de la America Meridional*, 336 (my translation). Even though the quotation names Primoli, Vargas has proven that the writer has confused the two Italian architects.

203 ARSI, Paraq. 4II, ff. 480b, 481a; Paraq. 6, ff. 2a, 20a, 40a; Vargas Ugarte, *Ensayo de un diccionario de artifices coloniales de la America Meridional*, 315.

204 ARSI, Paraq. 6, ff. 42a, 59a, 65a, 78b, 91a, 116b, 122a, 177b, 183a, 214a, 223b, 252a, 261b, 286b, 297a, 344a, 354a; Vargas Ugarte, *Ensayo de un diccionario de artifices coloniales de la America Meridional*, 357–8.

205 Kubler and Soria, *Art and Architecture in Spain and Portugal and Their American Dominions*, 98; Bayón and Marx, *History of South American Colonial Art and Architecture*, 189.

206 Javellana, *Wood and Stone for God's Greater Glory*, 20. See also Trota José, *Simbahan*, 148.

207 Block, *Mission Culture on the Upper Amazon*, 95 156, 160ff.

208 BNP, Manuscrito C-58, Diversos asuntos de las misiones de Moxos y Chiquitos 1681–1765, letter of 26 September 1695.

3: The Jesuit Mission to Japan, 1549–1622

1 From a letter of Alessandro Valignano: 'Your Paternity should understand that this is, beyond a doubt, the greatest enterprise that there is in the world today' (Moran, *The Japanese and the Jesuits*, 51).

2 From a letter of Francis Xavier, 5 November 1549 (Costelloe, ed., *The Letters and Instructions of Francis Xavier*, 297).

3 Moran, *The Japanese and the Jesuits*, 96–7.

4 Pastor, *The History of the Popes*, 20:448.

5 For a classic survey of the impact of the Aztecs on early modern Europe, see Keen, *The Aztec Image in Western Thought*.

6 'There be many Iesuites and Franciscan friars in this land, and they have converted

many to be Christians and have many churches in the land' (Boxer, 'Some Aspects of Portuguese Influence in Japan, 1542–1640,' 19).

7 Boxer, *The Christian Century in Japan*, 114.
8 Ross, *A Vision Betrayed*, 87.
9 Moran, *The Japanese and the Jesuits*, 51.
10 Ibid., 26–7.
11 Boxer, *The Christian Century in Japan*, 117–21; Moran, *The Japanese and the Jesuits*, 43.
12 Kawamura, 'Jesuit Confraternities in Japan.'
13 Costelloe, ed., *The Letters and Instructions of Francis Xavier*, 338.
14 Elison, *Deus Destroyed*, 28.
15 Moran, *The Japanese and the Jesuits*, 102.
16 Ross, *A Vision Betrayed*, 55–6.
17 Elison, *Deus Destroyed*, 94–5.
18 For example, the missionary catalogue of 1592 lists 207 churches for Japan and 24 residences (BL, Add. MSS 9860, ff. 1–6).
19 Ross, *A Vision Betrayed*, 27; Frois, *Die Geschichte Japans*, 6, 14, 85, 95, 106, 110–11, 124, 132, 146–7, 148, 149, 171, 173–7, 198, 254, 265, 271, 310, 313, 375, 404, 465, 478, 483.
20 Bourdon, *La Compagnie de Jésus et le Japon 1547–1570*, 582–6.
21 Hickman, *Japan's Golden Age*, 151.
22 Bourdon, *La Compagnie de Jésus et le Japon*, 584–5.
23 Ibid., 582–3.
24 Ibid., 582–3; Ross, *A Vision Betrayed*, 52.
25 Boxer, *The Christian Century in Japan*, 65; Sansom, *A History of Japan*, 417. A contemporary depiction of this church on a fan is in the Kobe City Museum (*Namban Arts Selection*, cat. no. 1).
26 McCall, 'Early Jesuit Art in the Far East (IV),' 52–3.
27 Ovalle, *Historia relatione del regno di Cile*.
28 Cooper, ed. *The Southern Barbarians*, 147.
29 Costelloe, ed., *The Letters and Instructions of Francis Xavier*, 306.
30 McCall, 'Early Jesuit Art in the Far East (I),' 124. In a 1578 letter from Bungo, the Jesuit missionary Antonio Prenestino told Antonio Possevino about the Japanese interest in drawings of knights in armour, horsemen, and land and sea battles (ARSI, Jap/Sin 8 I, f. 212a).
31 ARSI, Jap/Sin 46, f. 69b. The annual Letter for 1588 records that on a group of islands 'everyone has in their houses beautifully executed crosses painted on paper, which they made themselves using their own abilities, since the Japanese are all devoted to the cross, and also because they have no other images.'
32 Bourdon, *La Compagnie de Jésus et le Japon*, 586.
33 Frois, *Die Geschichte Japans*, 255, 435; Schurhammer, 'Die Jesuitenmissionare des 16. und 17. Jahrhunderts und ihr Einfluss auf die Japanische Malerei'; McCall, 'Early Jesuit Art in the Far East (I),' 124; Bourdon, *La Compagnie de Jésus et le Japon*, 586–7.
34 Pirri, *Giuseppe Valeriano*, 235
35 Shimmura, 'Christian Relics Found at Mr. Higashi's House,' pl. VI.; McCall, 'Early Jesuit Art in the Far East (I),' 137; *The Namban Art of Japan* (1986), cat. nos. 14–38.
36 Mentioned in Frois, *Die Geschichte Japans*, 14, 55, 120, 125, 157, 159, 162–3, 175, 191, 201, 233, 242, 254–5, 267, 273, 297, 428, 435, 440, 464, 504; Schurhammer, 'Die Jesuitenmis-

sionare des 16. und 17. Jahrhunderts und ihr Einfluss auf die Japanische Malerei,' 770–1; McCall, 'Early Jesuit Art in the Far East (I),' 124.

37 McCall, 'Early Jesuit Art in the Far East (I),' 124–5.

38 Schütte, *Valignano's Mission Principles for Japan,* 1:236. Mach, or Maech was by his own estimation 'quite skilful at [making crucifixes], as my products testify; indeed, the best ones in Asia and Japan, etc., are made by me ... My crucifixes are much appreciated in Italy and the rest of Europe; I have, to my great consolation, supplied all the colleges and brothers here with them ...' The Society took away his tools because they wanted him to concentrate on his spiritual work and were concerned with their image of poverty. The original letter of 1591 is in ARSI, Goa 14, ff. 395a-6b.

39 Maza, *El Pintor Martín de Vos en México;* Zweite, *Martin de Vos als Maler.*

40 Schütte, *Valignano's Mission Principles for Japan,* 1:337.

41 See Uçerler, 'Jesuit Humanist Education,' 16–19.

42 Ross, *A Vision Betrayed,* 50.

43 Uçerler, 'Jesuit Humanist Education,' 19.

44 The quote is from a 1598 letter to Father General Claudio Acquaviva (Ross, *A Vision Betrayed,* 112; Boxer, *The Christian Century in Japan,* 204).

45 Moran, *The Japanese and the Jesuits,* 13.

46 Schütte, *Valignano's Mission Principles for Japan,* 2:112. The original letters are in ARSI Jap-Sin 8 I, f. 178a (Miyako, 29 Sept. 1577); and ARSI, Jap-Sin 8 I, f. 122b (Miyako, 21 Sept. 1577).

47 Moran, *The Japanese and the Jesuits,* 22.

48 According to Ross, Valignano's methods 'broke fundamentally and decisively with the approach of the propagation of the Christian faith by missionaries under the authority of the Spanish and Portuguese crowns' (Ross, *A Vision Betrayed,* xi).

49 He discusses the importance of higher education in his 1582 *Sumario* (ARSI, Jap/Sin 51, ff. 204a ff).

50 ARSI, Jap/Sin 51, ff. 199b-201a; Ross, *A Vision Betrayed,* xii.

51 Uçerler, 'Jesuit Humanist Education,' 23–30.

52 The first Japanese priests were ordained in 1601. By 1614 there were fourteen Japanese priests (Moran, *The Japanese and the Jesuits,* 115).

53 In the Annual Letter of 1582, Valignano suggests that it would be a good idea to send an embassy (ARSI, Jap/Sin 46, f. 82a).

54 Boxer, *The Christian Century in Japan,* 314. An oil portrait survives of the ambassador, Hasekura Tsunenaga (1561–1622), which was made during his stay in Rome (Okamoto, *The Namban Art of Japan,* fig. 49). See the recent exhibition at the Suntory Museum of Art, *Date Masamune and His Mission to Rome.*

55 The original Portuguese text, with an Italian translation, can be found in Valignano, *Il ceremoniale per i missionari del Giappone.*

56 Moran, *The Japanese and the Jesuits,* 56.

57 Ross, *A Vision Betrayed,* 64. The Jesuits continued to wear Japanese sandals and *tabi* (socks).

58 '... Como tãobem sua fabrica hé tão dyfferente da que nós outros usamos em Europa e hé tão diferente o trato e agazalhado que se há em nossas casas de fazer aos forasteiros, não podemos nós outros por nós mesmos traça-las bem ...' (Valignano, *Il ceremoniale,* 270).

59 ARSI, Jap/Sin 51, f. 183a.

60 Pacheco, 'Iglesias de Nagasaki durante el "Siglo cristiano" 1568–1620'; Kawamura, 'Jesuit Confraternities in Japan before 1587.'

61 '... porque na forma das igrejas não convem imita-los, pois as suas são sinagogas de satanas e as nossas igrejas de Dios ...' (Valignano, *Il ceremoniale*, 278).

62 ARSI, Jap/Sin 46, f. 85a.

63 Schütte, *Valignano's Mission Principles for Japan*, 1:343. For a plan of Nagasaki model, see Pacheco, 'Iglesias de Nagasaki,' 56.

64 From a letter of 1596, in Pérez, 'Cartas y relaciones del Japón,' 234. On the artistic activity of the Franciscan and Dominican missions in Japan, see McCall, 'Early Jesuit Art in the Far East (I),' 135–6, 294.

65 Pérez, 'Cartas y relaciones del Japón,' 229 (letter of Blázquez, 1595); and Cooper, *Rodrigues the Interpreter*, 129–30 (letter of Fray Martín de la Ascención, 1596).

66 Schütte, *Valignano's Mission Principles for Japan*, 1:143 (the original text is in ARSI, Goa 47, f. 52b).

67 Schütte, *Valignano's Mission Principles for Japan*, 2:93.

68 According to the Annual Letter of 1594, the embassy returned with 'algumas imagens das mais perfeitas que trouxerão de Roma os Japões Fidalgos' (ARSI, Jap/Sin 52, f. 20a). See Boxer, 'Some Aspects of Portuguese Influence in Japan,' 38; McCall, 'Early Jesuit Art in the Far East (I),' 136; and Moran, *The Japanese and the Jesuits*, 12.

69 ARSI, Jap/Sin 51, ff. 187b–188a.

70 Ibid., f. 189.

71 He deemed the prized *Raku* ceramics used for the tea ceremony as worthy of being placed in a bird cage, for example (Schütte, *Valignano's Mission Principles for Japan*, 1:289; 2:234, 2:274–5. ARSI, Jap/Sin 51, ff. 187a–189a).

72 ARSI Jap/Sin 9 II, f. 329a; Jap/Sin 9 II, f. 240b, 329a.

73 ARSI Jap/Sin 10 II, ff. 123a–123b; Jap/Sin 12 I, ff. 112a–113a.

74 The fault lies with John McCall, who gave this art workshop the fanciful title 'Academy of St. Luke,' following a remark made by Pelliot in 1935 that the Japanese academy was the 'successor to the "academies" of the Italian painters,' such as the Accademia del Disegno of Florence, or the Accademia di San Luca of Rome, which had been founded five years earlier, in 1577. McCall went on to use this term as if it were historical, and subsequent writers such as Sullivan and Hickman have accepted the name as factual. In reality, not a single source mentions this name, referring to the workshop simply as a school or seminary for painters. See Pelliot, 'La Peinture et la Gravure Européennes en Chine au Temps de Mathieu Ricci,' 208; McCall, 'Early Jesuit Art in the Far East (I),' 124–30; Sullivan, *The Meeting of Eastern and Western Art*, 8; and Hickman, *Japan's Golden Age*, 255.

75 On the seminaries, see McCall, 'Early Jesuit Art in the Far East (I),' 126; Elison, *Deus Destroyed*, 68, 460; Schütte, *Valignano's Mission Principles for Japan*, 1:346–54; and Moran, *The Japanese and the Jesuits*, 12–13.

76 ARSI, Jap/Sin 25, ff. 2a, 3a, 12b–13a, 19b, 234b, 29a, 61a, 61b, 86a, 94b, 99a, 104a, 109a, 110b, 114a, 128b, 132b; Schurhammer, 'Die Jesuitenmissionare ... und ihr Einfluss auf die Japanische Malerei,' 771; McCall, 'Early Jesuit Art in the Far East (I),' 126–7; d'Elia, *Le origini dell'arte cristiana chinese*, 23–4.

77 Okamoto, *The Namban Art of Japan*, 100–1.

78 *The Namban Art of Japan*, cat. no. 2; Sakamoto et al., *An Essay*, cat. no. 62.

79 They are the earliest students mentioned in the records (they entered the Society in 1592), and the only ones listed as learning to paint before 1596 (ARSI, Jap/Sin 25, f. 23b). They may well have studied with Niccolò as pupils at the Seminary before entering the Society. Pedro João entered the Society even earlier, in 1585.

80 Üçerler, 'Jesuit Humanist Education,' 33–5.

81 ARSI, Jap/Sin 25, ff. 23b, 29a–b, 35a, 56a, 57a, 61b, 70a, 81a, 86a, 90b, 110a; Guerreiro, *Relaçam Annual das cousas que fezerem os padres da Companhia de Jesus na India, & Japão, 1600–01* (Evora, 1603), 122–3; *Relaçam Annual das cousas que fezerem os padres da Companhia de Jesus nas partes da India Oriental* (Lisbon, 1605), 9; *Relaçam Annual das cousas que fezerem os padres da Companhia de Jesus nas partes da India Oriental, 604, 605* (Lisbon 1607), 4; Schurhammer, 'Die Jesuitenmissionare ... und ihr Einfluss auf die Japanische Malerei,' 771; McCall, 'Early Jesuit Art in the Far East (I),' 132–4.

82 The missionary catalogues for Nagasaki during 1606–7 refer to him as a 'painting instructor' (BL, Add MSS 9860, ff. 112–13). We know that the atelier produced paintings on copper from references from the Mughal mission (see chapter 5).

83 ARSI, Jap/Sin 9 II, f. 329a; Jap/Sin 10 II, ff. 223a–223b; BL, Add. MSS 9860, ff. 8–12; Schurhammer, 'Die Jesuitenmissionare ... und ihr Einfluss auf die Japanische Malerei,' 776; Boxer, 'Some Aspects of Portuguese Influence in Japan,' 43–5; 'Portuguese Influence in Japanese Screens from 1590 to 1614,' 79–85; McCall, 'Early Jesuit Art in the Far East (I),' 128–31; Schütte, *Valignano's Mission Principles for Japan*, 264, 268–9.

84 ARSI, Jap/Sin 51, f. 362a. The first book was printed in 1591 in Katsusa.

85 ARSI, Jap/Sin 52, f. 20a. A part of it is translated in McCall, 'Early Jesuit Art in the Far East (I),' 132.

86 ARSI, Jap/Sin 12 II, f. 270b; Schütte, 'Christliche Japanische Literatur,' 263. Later scholars, such as Boxer, have concluded from these sources that the Japanese painters did not show any originality, merely producing 'more or less slavish copies of European art' (Boxer, *The Christian Century in Japan*, 200).

87 Letter of Francisco Pasio, September 1594 (BL, Add. MSS 9860, ff. 8–8b); Boxer, 'Aspects of Portuguese Influence in Japan,' 47; Schurhammer, 'Die Jesuitenmissionare ... und ihr Einfluss auf die Japanische Malerei,' 772.

88 ARSI, Jap/Sin 52, f. 97a.

89 Ibid., f. 193a.

90 ARSI, Jap/Sin 46, f. 283a.

91 Ibid., f. 283b.

92 Ibid., f. 283b. The painting is also mentioned in Schütte, 'Christliche Japanische Literatur,' 263–4; and McCall, 'Early Jesuit Art in the Far East (I),' 133.

93 Gregory Martin describes the popular veneration for the Madonna picture at Santa Maria Maggiore in Rome in 1581 (Martin, *Roma Sancta*, 39).

94 The original copy is in the death-room of Stanislas Kostka at S. Andrea al Quirinale. See Bernard, 'L'art chrétien en Chine du temps du P. Matthieu Ricci,' 203; d'Elia, 'La Madonna di S. Maria Maggiore in Cina,' 30–1; Wittkower and Jaffe, eds, *Baroque Art*, 56; Jennes, *Invloed der Vlaamsche Prentkunst in Indie, China en Japan*, 49; and Baumstark, ed., *Rom in Bayern*, cat. no. 158. The painter would have been someone like Sigismondo Laire (1550–1639), who specialized in religious imagery for overseas export (see chapter 2).

95 Besides having a strong impact on Chinese and Japanese painting, this picture was also very popular in Latin America. See, for example, d'Elia, 'La Madonna di S. Maria

Maggiore in Cina,' 31–2; McCall, 'Early Jesuit Art in the Far East (IV),' 47; and Sullivan, *The Meeting of Eastern and Western Art*, 43. I have seen versions at the São José Seminary in Macau, in collections in Manila, and in several foundations of the Jesuits in Mexico, Peru, and Paraguay. Copies survive in the Church of Saint Stephen (1613–14) and Saint John the Baptist (1621) in New Julfa (near Isfahan), implying that the Society brought them to Persia after their establishment in that city in 1653 (Carswell, *New Julfa*, pl. 29c; Hakhnazarian, *Nor Djulfa*, pls. 42/43, 72/74).

96 ARSI, Jap/Sin 25, ff. 57a, 86a, 90b; McCall, 'Early Jesuit Art in the Far East (I),' 135.

97 Guerreiro, *Relaçam Annual das cousas que fezerem os padres da Companhia de Jesus nas partes da India Oriental, 604, 605*, 9 (summarized in Pagés, *Histoire de la religion crétienne au Japon*, 1:45).

98 BL, Add. MSS 9860, f. 36a; ARSI, Jap/Sin 25, f. 70a.

99 BL, Add. MSS 9860, f. 45b.

100 ARSI, Jap/Sin 51, f. 362a. In 1595 Gomez sent to Rome an oil painting of the Crucifixion by a twenty-year-old Japanese pupil, and boasted about how European his style was (ARSI, Jap/Sin 12 II, f. 270b).

101 Guerreiro, *Relaçam annual das cousas que fezeram os padres da companhia de Iesus nas partes da India Oriental* (Lisbon, 1609), 5ff.

102 Some references refer to them as *dojucus pintores* (BL, Add. MSS 9859, ff. 98–192; Add. MSS 9860, f. 8–8b). Several Japanese brothers went to Manila, both in 1614 and in 1624, including at least one painter, Brother Thaddeus (ARSI, Jap/Sin 25, f. 139b; Philipp. 2 I, f. 7b). McCall makes reference to Japanese Christian sculptors moving to Peru, but unfortunately he gives no source for this statement other than personal communications from his colleagues in Latin American history (McCall, 'Early Jesuit Art in the Far East (III),' 299). It is certainly possible that they migrated to the Americas; the Manila galleons were a very strong link between Latin America and the Far East in that period, and many Asians moved to Mexico and Peru. See my own article on a Mughal woman who moved to Puebla and became a prominent Christian mystic under Jesuit patronage (Bailey, 'A Mughal Princess in Baroque New Spain').

103 ARSI, Jap/Sin 25, ff. 61b, 98a, 118b; Schurhammer, 'Die Jesuitenmissionare ... und ihr Einfluss auf die Japanische Malerei,' 774; McCall, 'Early Jesuit Art in the Far East (I),' 130.

104 A Crucifixion, possibly by him or by Taichiku, was sent to Rome in 1595 (ARSI, Jap/Sin 25, ff. 62a, 86a,, 94b, 97a, 99a; Schurhammer, 'Die Jesuitenmissionare ... und ihr Einfluss auf die Japanische Malerei,' 773; McCall, 'Early Jesuit Art in the Far East (I),' 130).

105 ARSI, Jap/Sin 25, ff. 86a, 89a, 97b.

106 Ibid., ff. 95a, 97a, 99a; Pagés, *Histoire de la religion crétienne au Japon*, 1:302.

107 ARSI, Jap/Sin 25, ff. 61b, 87a, 95b, 97a, 111a, 118b, 129a, 137b; Philipp. 2 I, 7b, 16a; Schurhammer, 'Die Jesuitenmissionare ... und ihr Einfluss auf die Japanische Malerei,' 774; McCall, 'Early Jesuit Art in the Far East (I),' 131.

108 BL, Add. MSS 9860, f. 3; ARSI, Jap/Sin 25, f. 23b, 29b, 35a, 81a, 86a, 95a, 99a, 105b.

109 ARSI, Jap/Sin 25, f. 61b; Jap/Sin 46, f. 327a; Moran, *The Japanese and the Jesuits*, 146.

110 ARSI, Jap/Sin 25, f. 61b.

111 BL, Add. MSS 9860, f. 3a.

112 Ibid., ff. 2, 113.

113 ARSI, Jap/Sin 12 II, f. 200b.

114 Prunier, 'Des peintures à fouler aux pieds,' fig. 9; Cooper, *The Southern Barbarians*, fig. 62. The example in Prunier is after a Wierix print of the subject, but the Cooper one is strikingly Byzantine in style and may be a European or Goan copy of the original in Rome. The first is also reproduced in *The Namban Art of Japan* (1986), cat. no. 4, along with a third, cat. no. 5. See also Sakamoto et al., *An Essay*, cat. no. 276.

115 See, for example, Sakamoto et al., *An Essay*, cat. nos. 54–90.

116 De Sousa, 'A Arte Cristã de Goa'; Serrão, 'A Pintura na Antiga India.'

117 Boyer, *Japanese Export Lacquers*, 23; Christie's [New York], *Japanese Works of Art* (23 June 1982), lots 756, 757; *Christie's Price Review 1982* (London, 1982), p. 371; Sotheby's [New York], *Japanese Works of Art, Property of Gretchen Kroch Kelsch and Other Owners* (11 April 1985), lot 158; Christie's, *Japanese Works of Art from the Age of Western Influence* (22 May 1985), lot 1; Sotheby's, *Fine Japanese Works of Art* (13–14 June 1985), lot 235; Sotheby's, *Japanese Works of Art* (12 Nov. 1985), lot 52; Christie's, *Review of the Season 1988* (London, 1988), 40; *Art Namban* (Brussels, 1989), cat. nos. 43–5; Mendes Pinto, *Lacas Namban em Portugal*; *Suntori Museum of Art Collection*, cat. no. 39; *Via Orientalis*, cat. nos. 170, 185; De Kesel, *Japanese Export Lacquers*, cat. no. 9; Hickman, Japan's Golden Age, cat. no. 124, Christie's [New York], *Japanese Art* (24 April 1997), lot 183; *The Beauty of Momoyama*, cat. no. 15. Two of the known examples were discovered in Central America.

118 Okamoto, *The Namban Art of Japan*, fig. 78; *The Namban Art of Japan* (1986), cat. no. 1; Sakamoto et al., *An Essay*, cat. no. 62.

119 *The Namban Art of Japan* (1986), cat. no. 11; *Via Orientalis* (1993), cat. no. 177; Sakamoto et al., *An Essay*, cat. no. 54. The Wierix original is in Mauquoy-Hendrick, *Les estampes des Wierix*, vol. 1, cat. no. 493.

120 Sotheby's, *Japanese Works of Art* (12 Nov. 1985), lot 52.

121 *The Namban Art of Japan* (1986), cat. no. 41. There is some doubt about the reading of the seal 'Nobukata.'

122 Sotheby's, *Important Japanese works of Art, Ceramics and Swords* (12 June 1985), lot 235; de Kesel, *Japanese Export Lacquers*, cat. no. 9, *Suntory Museum of Art Collection*, cat. no. 39.

123 The image appears in Christie's *Review* (1982) (29 cm wide; 10.5 cm high).

124 *Yearbook of the Society of Jesus 1995* (Rome, 1995), 69, Sakamoto et al., *An Essay*, cat. no. 65.

125 Diego Yuuki, personal communication.

126 *The Namban Art of Japan* (1986), cat. no. 6; Sakamoto et al., *An Essay*, cat. no. 77.

127 *The Namban Art of Japan* (1986), cat. nos. 73–84; Sakamoto et al., *An Essay*, 227–69.

128 *The Namban Art of Japan* (1986), cat. nos. 68–70, 73–7.

129 *As ruinas de S. Paulo* (1994), cat. no. 111; Sakamoto et al., *An Essay*, 321. I am grateful to Father Manoel Teixeira for allowing me to examine this painting.

130 Shimmura, 'Christian Relics Found at Mr. Higashi's House,' pls. 3–4; Tei Nishimura, 'Study on the Fifteen Mysteries of St. Mary in Japan'; McCall, 'Early Jesuit Art in the Far East (III),' 284–92; Okamoto, *The Namban Art of Japan*, 128; *The Namban Art of Japan* (1986), cat. nos. 12, 13; Sakamoto et al., *An Essay*, cat. no. 67–1; *University Museum Faculty of Letters, Kyoto University* (1987), 49. See also Nagayama, *Collection of Historical Materials Connected with the Roman Catholic Religion in Japan*; Wakakuwa, 'The Image of Saint Francis Xavier'; and Vlam, 'The Portrait of St. Francis Xavier in Kobe.'

131 See Mason, *History of Japanese Art*, 169ff.

132 Okamoto, *The Namban Art of Japan*, figs. 88–92, 133, 135–6; *The Namban Art of Japan* (1986), cat. nos. 39–40; *Via Orientalis* (1993), cat. nos. 163, 164, 178.
133 Sullivan, *The Meeting of Eastern and Western Art*, fig. 35.
134 Prunier, 'Des peintres à fouler aux pieds'; Okamoto, *The Namban Art of Japan*, fig. 50; *Objects Relating to Early Christian Faith in Japan* (1972), cat. nos. 1–10; *Surviving Early Christian Art in Japan* (1973), cat. nos. 24–30; Nishimura, *Namban Art, Christian Art in Japan, 1549–1639*, figs. 136–43, 147–50; *Art Namban* (1989), cat. nos. 48, 49.
135 Dr Lewis is presently preparing for publication a catalogue which will include two European bronze plaquettes which were copied by Japanese artists. I am grateful to Dr Lewis for generously sharing information and sources regarding these plaquettes, on which the following paragraph is based.
136 Münsterberg, 'Die Darstellung von Europäern in der japanischen Kunst,' 210ff; McCall, 'Early Jesuit Art in the Far East (II),' 216ff; Sullivan, *The Meeting of Eastern and Western Art*, 11ff; Okamoto, *The Namban Art of Japan*, cat. nos. 36–42; *The Namban Art of Japan* (1986), cat. nos. 41–65; *Selected Masterpieces of Asian Art* (1992), cat. no. 45; Hickman, *Japan's Golden Age*, cat. no. 39; *Twelve Centuries of Japanese Art from the Imperial Collections* (1997), cat. no. 32.
137 Okamoto, *The Namban Art of Japan*, 144–5; Sakamoto et al., *An Essay*, 154–225.
138 Especially Abraham Ortelius's *Teatrum Orbis Terrarum* (1579) and G. Braun's *Civitaties Orbis Terrarum* (1576).
139 Boxer, 'Some Aspects of Portuguese Influence in Japan,' 31.
140 Ibid., 31–2.
141 Sakamoto and Ochi, 'Classification of Folding Screens.'
142 Ibid.
143 Sakamoto, 'Christian Art.'
144 Alden, *The Making of an Enterprise*, 137. At the time of the expulsion of the Jesuits from Portuguese territory in 1759, the Japan mission owned considerable property in India, according to the account books of the Society in the Goa Archives (GSA, 859; 7602, ff. 108–21; 7670, ff. 190–8).
145 See Prunier, 'Des peintures à fouler aux pieds.'
146 Endo, 'The Final Martyrs,' 33.

4: The Jesuit Mission to China, 1561–1773

1 Ricci's description in his *Commentary* of his own translations into Chinese of letters addressed to the Chinese Emperor supporting the foundation of Jesuit mission, 'tutto secondo lo stile della Cina ... scritta con molta galantaria e ornamento' (Tacchi Venturi, ed., *Opere storiche del P. Matteo Ricci*, 1:172)
2 The court artist Zou Yigui, quoted in Sullivan, *The Meeting of Eastern and Western Art*, 80.
3 For more on the Jesuit blind spot about calligraphy, see Ledderose, 'Chinese Influence of European Art.'
4 Spence, *The Search for Modern China*, 7–8.
5 Sickman and Soper, *The Art and Architecture of China*, 204.
6 Teixeira, *A fachada de S. Paulo*; Guillen-Nuñez, *Macau*; Lee Yuk Tin, *Olhar as ruínas*; Marreiros, 'Traces of Chinese and Portuguese Architecture'; Couseiro, 'L'Eglise de Notre-

Dame de l'Assomption ... à Macao et l'Art de la Compagnie de Jésus en Chine'; Couseiro, *A Igreja de S. Paulo de Macau*; Regina Valente, *Igrejas de Macau; As ruinas de S. Paulo.*

7 ARSI, Jap/Sin 46, f. 318b.

8 Kowal, 'Innovation and Assimilation.'

9 The classic study is Spence, *The Memory Palace of Matteo Ricci*. See also Dunne, *Generation of Giants*, 21–107; Goodman and Grafton, 'Ricci, the Chinese, and the Toolkits of Textualists'; and, for a more recent assessment, Alden, *The Making of an Enterprise*, 68ff. The primary source material for Ricci has been published for some time, in Venturi, *Opere storiche del Matteo Ricci*; d'Elia, *Fonte Ricciane*; and Gallagher, *China in the Sixteenth Century*.

10 Jesuit cartography in China has been the subject of much debate recently. See Yee, 'Traditional Chinese Cartography and the Myth of Westernization'; and Clunas, *Pictures and Visuality in Early Modern China*, 172–3; and Pagani, 'One Continuous Symphony.'

11 On the Late Ming persecutions of Christians, who were given the subversive label 'White Lotus' along with other heretical groups, see Haar, *The White Lotus Teachings in Chinese Religious History*. See also Dudink, 'Christianity in China,' 1–176.

12 On the encyclopaedic efforts of Li Zhizao in translating and publishing the works written by Ricci and other Jesuit missionaries in China, see Chen, 'Li Chih-tsao and the *T'ien-hsüeh ch'u-han*.'

13 Although scholars such as Pasquale d'Elia and Gonçalo Couseiro consider Ricci himself to have initiated the process of artistic adaptation, their definition differs from my own. Couseiro, for example, gives as evidence of acculturation Chinese artists executing Christian art and European missionaries writing catechisms in Chinese. Such processes by no means guarantee that Ricci himself was interested in a hybridization of artistic styles or techniques. See d'Elia, *Le origini dell'arte christiana-cinese*, especially chapter 2; and Couseiro, 'Pintores jesuítas na China,' 93.

14 Pelliot, 'La peinture et gravure europées en Chine au temps de Mathieu Ricci,' 5–6; Bernard, 'L'art chrétien en Chine du temps du Matthieu Ricci, 201; Tacchi Venturi, *Opere storiche del Matteo Ricci*, 1:16; Cahill, *The Compelling Image*, 74; Mungello, *Curious Land*, 53–4.

15 See Standaert, 'Jesuit Corporate Culture as Shaped by the Chinese.'

16 Clunes, *Art in China*, 128–9.

17 Bernard, 'L'art chrétien en Chine du temps du Matthieu Ricci,' 205–6; d'Elia, *Le origini dell'arte cristiana cinese*, 125–7; Tacchi Venturi, *Opere storiche del Matteo Ricci*, 2:60; McCall 'Early Jesuit Art in the Far East (I),' 129; McCall, 'Early Jesuit Art in the Far East (IV),' 48; Spence, *The Memory Palace of Matteo Ricci*, 246–8; Vanderstappen, 'Chinese Art and the Jesuits in Peking,' 107; Masini, ed., *Western Humanistic Culure Presented to China by Jesuit Missionaries*, 141. See also the reaction of Yang Guang-xian (1597–1669) in his anti-Christian treatise in Wu, *Literature of Catholicism to the East*, 3:1135–42.

18 Gernet, *China and the Christian Impact*, 124.

19 Bernard, 'L'art chrétien en Chine du temps du Matthieu Ricci,' 212; Tacchi Venturi, *Opere storiche del Matteo Ricci*, 2:474–5.

20 Goodman and Grafton, 'Ricci, the Chinese and the Toolkits of the Textualists,' 116.

21 Translation is by Clunas (*Pictures and Visuality in Early Modern China*, 177); see also Vanderstappen, 'Chinese Art and the Jesuits in Peking,' 107.

22 Gernet, *China and the Christian Impact*, 87.

23 Ibid.
24 Ibid.
25 The famous report is by Fray Toribio de Benavente (Motolinía). See Palmer and Pierce, *Cambios*, 75.
26 Bernard, 'L'art chrétien en Chine du temps du Matthieu Ricci,' 213; Tacchi Venturi, *Opere storiche del Matteo Ricci*, 1:287–8; d'Elia, *Le origini dell'arte cristiana cinese*, 28.
27 Pelliot, 'La peinture et la gravure européenes en Chine au temps de Mathieu Ricci,' 13; Tacchi Venturi, *Opere storiche del Matteo Ricci*, 2:272.
28 Pelliot, 'La peinture et la gravure européenes en Chine au temps de Mathieu Ricci,' 9–10; Bernard, 'L'art chrétien en Chine du temps du Matthieu Ricci,' 214–15; Tacchi Venturi, *Opere storiche del Matteo Ricci*, 1:350.
29 Bernard, 'L'art chrétien en Chine du temps du Matthieu Ricci,' 218; Tacchi Venturi, *Opere storiche del Matteo Ricci*, 2:475.
30 For a list of artworks, see Bettray, *Akkomodationsmethode*, 51–65.
31 Bernard, 'L'art chrétien en Chine du temps du Matthieu Ricci,' 210; d'Elia, *Le origini dell'arte cristiana cinese*, 18; Tacchi Venturi, *Opere storiche del Matteo Ricci*, 2:60, 398, 404, 419.
32 d'Elia, *Le origini dell'arte cristiana cinese*, 24; Tacchi Venturi, *Opere storiche del Matteo Ricci*, 2:421.
33 ARSI, Jap/Sin 13, f. 319b. Cited in d'Elia, *Le origini dell'arte cristiana cinese*, 31.
34 ARSI, Jap/Sin 13, f. 359a. Cited in d'Elia, *Le origini dell'arte cristiana cinese*, 32.
35 It reached Macao in 1581 (BL, Add. MSS 9859, f. 6b; ARSI, Jap/Sin 10 II, ff. 223a–223b, 329a). See also Tacchi Venturi, *Opere storiche del Matteo Ricci*, 1:127, 132. 2:405; Schurhammer, 'Die Jesuitenmissionare ... und ihr Einfluss auf die Japanische Malerei,' 771; Bernard, 'L'art chrétien en Chine du temps du Matthieu Ricci,' 203; d'Elia, *Le origini dell'arte cristiana cinese*, 22; McCall, 'Early Jesuit Art in the Far East (I),' 127–8; and McCall, 'Early Jesuit Art in the Far East (IV),' 47.
36 Tacchi Venturi, *Opere storiche del Matteo Ricci*, 1:339; Bernard, 'L'art chrétien en Chine du temps du Matthieu Ricci,' 214; d'Elia, *Le origini dell'arte cristiana cinese*, 32.
37 Tacchi Venturi, *Opere storiche del Matteo Ricci*, 1:157–8, 287–8; Pelliot, 'La peinture et la gravure européenes en Chine au temps de Mathieu Ricci,' 7; Bernard, 'L'art chrétien en Chine du temps du Matthieu Ricci,' 211; d'Elia, *Le origini dell'arte cristiana cinese*, 28.
38 Tacchi Venturi, *Opere storiche del Matteo Ricci*, 1:298; Bernard, 'L'art chrétien en Chine du temps du P. Matthieu Ricci,' 214; d'Elia, *Le origini dell'arte cristiana cinese*, 30; McCall, 'Early Jesuit Art in the Far East (IV),' 48.
39 Tacchi Venturi, *Opere storiche del Matteo Ricci*, 1:125–6, 157–8.
40 Ibid., 1:157–8, 2:159, 176, 186, 210; Bernard, 'L'art chrétien en Chine du temps du Matthieu Ricci,' 213; d'Elia, *Le origini dell'arte cristiana cinese*, 26.
41 Dudink, 'Christianity in China,' 177–226; Masini, *Western Humanistic Culture*, 127–42.
42 Tacchi Venturi, *Opere storiche del Matteo Ricci*, 1:339; Pelliot, 'La peinture et la gravure européenes en Chine au temps de Mathieu Ricci,' 6; Bernard, 'L'art chrétien en Chine du temps du Matthieu Ricci,' 214; d'Elia, *Le origini dell'arte cristiana cinese*, 32; McCall, 'Early Jesuit Art in the Far East (IV),' 48; Sullivan, *The Meeting of Eastern and Western Art*, 42; Dudink, 'Christianity in China,' 127.
43 Tacchi Venturi, *Opere storiche del Matteo Ricci*, 1:359–60; Bernard, 'L'art chrétien en

Chine du temps du Matthieu Ricci,' 216. The Italian text reads: 'un molto bello crucifisso intagliato in legno e pinto col sangue.'

44 Wyngaert, *Sinica Franciscana*, 2:36–7; Bernard, 'L'art chrétien en Chine du temps du Matthieu Ricci,' 203; McCall, 'Early Jesuit Art in the Far East (IV),' 47; Spence, *The Memory Palace of Matteo Ricci*, 189.

45 During the anti-Christian persecution in Nanjing during 1616–17, an inventory was drawn up by Chinese officials of the contents of the mission there, which included four feather-pictures of the Four Seasons which had supposedly been offered as tribute to the Wanli Emperor in 1600 (Masini, *Western Humanistic Culture*, 127–42).

46 Spence, *The Memory Palace of Matteo Ricci*, 188–9.

47 Christie's, New York (23, 24, 28 June 1982), lot 757; Lach, *Asia in the Making of Europe*, 1:18.

48 Bernard, 'L'art chrétien en Chine du temps du Matthieu Ricci,' 219; McCall, 'Early Jesuit Art in the Far East (IV),' 48; Sullivan, *The Meeting of Eastern and Western Art*, 43.

49 ARSI, Jap/Sin 13, f. 319b; Tacchi Venturi, *Opere storiche del Matteo Ricci*, 475, note 2; Bernard, 'L'art chrétien en Chine du temps du Matthieu Ricci,' 218; d'Elia, *Le origini dell'arte cristiana cinese*, 31, 80; Spence, *The Memory Palace of Matteo Ricci*, 11. The same was true for Japan and Mughal India. The Italian Jesuit Marco Ferraro asked the General in 1587 for a copy of Nadal, saying that another illustrated book he possessed of the life of Christ had been extremely well received (ARSI, Jap/Sin 10 II, ff. 286a–286b), and the superior of the Mughal mission, Jerónimo Xavier, also asked for a copy of Nadal in 1603, which he eventually received (ARSI, Goa 46I, f. 52b).

50 O'Malley, *The First Jesuits*, 164. On Nadal's *Evangelicae Historiae Imagines*, see Buser, 'Jerome Nadal and Early Jesuit Art in Rome'; Mauquoy-Hendricks, 'Les Wierix illustrateurs de la Bible de Natalis'; Wadell, 'The *Evangelicae Historiae Imagines*: The Designs and Their Artists'; Wadell, *Evangelicae Historiae Imagines: Entstehungsgeschichte und Vorlagen*; Rheinbay, *Biblische Bilder für der inneren Weg*; and my 'The Jesuits and Painting in Italy.'

51 Buser, 'Jerome Nadal and Early Jesuit Art in Rome,' 425.

52 Wadell, 'Designs and Their Artists,' 282; Wadell, *Entstehungsgeschichte*, 31–42.

53 Tacchi Venturi, *Opere storiche del Matteo Ricci*, 2:283–4; Bernard, 'L'art chrétien en Chine du temps du Matthieu Ricci,' 219; d'Elia, *Le origini dell'arte cristiana cinese*, 82; Spence, *The Memory Palace of Matteo Ricci*, 62–3.

54 Pelliot, 'La peinture et la gravure européenes en Chine au temps de Mathieu Ricci,' 6–7; Bernard, 'L'art chrétien en Chine du temps du Matthieu Ricci,' 211; d'Elia, *Le origini dell'arte cristiana cinese*, 34–5; Loehr, *Giuseppe Castiglione*, 78; Vanderstappen, 'Chinese Art and the Jesuits in Peking,' 103–4; Sullivan, *The Meeting of Eastern and Western Art*, 46. See also the catalogue of the Pei-t'ang Library, *Catalogue de la Bibliothèque du Pé-t'ang*.

55 McCall, 'Early Jesuit Art in the Far East (IV),' 62; Ross, *A Vision Betrayed*. 123, 136.

56 Tacchi Venturi, *Opere storiche del Matteo Ricci*, 2:484.

57 Ibid., 1:613, note 2; Bernard, 'L'art chrétien en Chine du temps du Matthieu Ricci,' 226–7.

58 Tacchi Venturi, *Opere storiche del Matteo Ricci*, 1:613, note 2.

59 D'Elia, *Le origini dell'arte cristiana cinese*, 42.

60 Bernard, 'L'art chrétien en Chine du temps du Matthieu Ricci,' 226–7; McCall, 'Early Jesuit Art in the Far East (IV),' 68.

61 See Malatesta and Gao, eds, *Departed, Yet Present*, especially 13–55.
62 Pelliot, 'La peinture et la gravure européenes en Chine au temps de Mathieu Ricci,' 13; McCall, 'Early Jesuit Art in the Far East (IV),' 68. On the Christian cemetery in Beijing, see Malatesta, and Gao, eds, *Departed, Yet Present.*
63 Malatesta and Gao, eds, *Departed, Yet Present*, 33.
64 Clunas, *Pictures and Visuality in Early Modern China*, 176; *The Compelling Image*, 171; Vanderstappen, 'Chinese Art and the Jesuits in Peking,' 107. It should be pointed out, however, that Gu may simply have been parroting what Ricci told him, since he continued by reporting Ricci's speech verbatim, as we have just seen above.
65 Hsiang Ta, 'European Influences,' 164, note 23; Vanderstappen, 'Chinese Art and the Jesuits in Peking,' 107.
66 d'Elia, *Le origini dell'arte cristiana cinese*, 42.
67 Pelliot, 'La peinture et la gravure européenes en Chine au temps de Mathieu Ricci,' 15; Hsiang Ta, 'European Influences,' 156; Sullivan, *The Meeting of Eastern and Western Art*, 43. This translation is by Clunas (*Pictures and Visuality in Early Modern China*, 177).
68 Sullivan, *The Meeting of Eastern and Western Art*, 63.
69 ARSI, Jap/Sin 25, ff. 128b, 136b, 141b.
70 Schurhammer, 'Die Jesuitenmissionare ... und ihr Einfluss auf die Japanische Malerei,' 773; Bernard, 'L'art chrétien en Chine du temps du Matthieu Ricci,' 220–1; d'Elia, *Le origini dell'arte cristiana cinese*, 36–8; McCall, 'Early Jesuit Art in the Far East (IV),' 49–51.
71 Such images can be seen in Kobayashi et al., *Exhibition of Western-Style Paintings of China*, 106–7.
72 Pelliot, 'La peinture et la gravure européenes en Chine au temps de Mathieu Ricci,' 17.
73 Tacchi Venturi, *Opere storiche del Matteo Ricci*, 2:254; Pelliot, 'La peinture et la gravure européenes en Chine au temps de Mathieu Ricci,' 11.
74 Tacchi Venturi, *Opere storiche del Matteo Ricci*, 1:439; 2:300, 304; Pelliot, 'La peinture et la gravure européenes en Chine au temps de Mathieu Ricci,' 10–11; Bernard, 'L'art chrétien en Chine du temps du Matthieu Ricci,' 220–1; d'Elia, *Le origini dell'arte cristiana cinese*, 38ff; McCall, 'Early Jesuit Art in the Far East (IV),' 51–3.
75 'On y void Jesus-Christ nostre Sauueur & Redepteur assis en vn throsne magnifique, les Anges en haut, les Apostres en bas semblent de chaque costé l'escouter, comme s'il les enseignoit' (Riquebourg-Trigault in Pelliot, 'La peinture et la gravure européenes en Chine au temps de Mathieu Ricci,' 13). See also Tacchi Venturi, *Opere storiche del Matteo Ricci*, 1:645.
76 Cahill, *The Compelling Image*, 114.
77 Bernard, 'L'art chrétien en Chine du temps du Matthieu Ricci,' 212; d'Elia, *Le origini dell'arte cristiana cinese*, 46; McCall, 'Early Jesuit Art in the Far East (IV),' 56.
78 D'Elia, *Le origini dell'arte cristiana cinese*, 19; McCall, 'Early Jesuit Art in the Far East (IV),' 49; Kobayashi et al., *Exhibition of Western-Style Paintings of China*, 25, 117–22.
79 Wu Tung, *Tales from the Land of Dragons*, cat. no. 54.
80 Moltedo, *La Sistina Reprodotta*, fig. 3a.
81 Laufer, 'A Chinese Madonna'; Pelliot, 'La peinture et la gravure européenes en Chine au temps de Mathieu Ricci,' 222–3; d'Elia, *Le origini dell'arte cristiana cinese*, 51; McCall, 'Early Jesuit Art in the Far East (IV),' 60; d'Elia, 'La Madonna di S. Maria Maggiore in Cina'; Kobayashi et al., *Exhibition of Western-Style Paintings of China*, 110.

82 Pelliot, 'La peinture et la gravure européenes en Chine au temps de Mathieu Ricci,' 2; Bernard, 'L'art chrétien en Chine du temps du Matthieu Ricci,' 220; Sickman and Soper, *The Art and Architecture of China*, 304–5; Spence, *The Memory Palace of Matteo Ricci*, 11, 64; Vanderstappen, 'Chinese Art and the Jesuits in Peking,' 104; Sullivan, *The Meeting of Eastern and Western Art*, 53. See also Guarino, 'The Interpretation of Images in Matteo Ricci's Picture for Chengshi Moyuan.'

83 Spence, *The Memory Palace of Matteo Ricci*, 63–4.

84 See my chapter on Chinese ceramics in Bailey, Golombek, and Mason, *Tamerlane's Tableware*, 7–16, and fig. 4.1.

85 *Three Thousand Years of Chinese Painting* (1997).

86 Vanderstappen, 'Chinese Art and the Jesuits in Peking,' 104.

87 Clunas, *Pictures and Visuality in Early Modern China*, 174.

88 Cahill, *The Compelling Image*, sections 1 and 3; Vanderstappen, 'Chinese Art and the Jesuits in Peking,' 109; Sullivan, *The Meeting of Eastern and Western Art*, 50–67. See also Yoshiho, *Painting of the Ming Dynasty*, 31–2.

89 See Sullivan, *The Meeting of Eastern and Western Art*, figs. 33 and 34.

90 Ibid., 59–9; Kobayashi et al., *Exhibition of Western-Style Paintings of China*, 137.

91 Sullivan maintains that this picture demonstrates 'unmistakable signs of European influence' (Sullivan, *The Meeting of Eastern and Western Art*, 42, 63, fig. 44).

92 See Vanderstappen, 'Chinese Art and the Jesuits in Peking,' 109–11.

93 Cahill, *The Compelling Image*, 76; Cahill, 'Late Ming Landscape Albums'; Sullivan, *The Meeting of Eastern and Western Art*, 63; Goodman and Grafton, 'Ricci, the Chinese, and the Toolkits of the Textualists,' 143–4.

94 Vanderstappen, 'Chinese Art and the Jesuits in Peking,' 114.

95 Gernet, *China and the Christian Impact*, 43; Haar, *The White Lotus Teachings in Chinese Religious History*, 241.

96 Recently, scholars have begun to focus on these local-level Christian communities. See Mungello, *The Forgotten Christians of Hangzhou*; and Entenmann, 'The Establishment of Chinese Catholic Communities in Early Ch'ing Szechwan.' For an assessment of new approaches to Chinese Christian history, see Standaert, 'New Trends in the Historiography of Christianity in China.'

97 Alden, *The Making of an Enterprise*, 144, 149.

98 Ibid., 141. There is an edition of Trigault's *Entrata nella China de' Padri della Compagnia del Gesu* (Augsburg, 1615) in the Library of the Historical Archives of Macao (NLM).

99 For a recent assessment of this well-documented event, see *The Chinese Rites Controversy* (1994).

100 Gernet, *China and the Christian Impact*, 83, 86–7.

101 Ibid., 87. As Gernet comments, 'traditional Chinese ways of behaving may have been taken for striking proof of the effects of grace.' Compare Pelliot's remark quoted in chapter 2. For more on Jesuit activities at the level of popular culture and magic, see Standaert, 'Chinese Christian Visits to the Underworld.'

102 Standaert, 'The Jesuit Presence in China.'

103 Chaves, *Singing of the Source*, 41.

104 Clunas, *Picture and Visuality in Early Modern China*, 182–3.

105 D'Elia, *Le origini dell'arte cristiana cinese*, 7, 67ff, 121ff; McCall, 'Early Jesuit Art in the

Far East (IV),' 57; Cohen and Monnet, *Impressions de Chine*, 112; Couseiro, 'Pintores jesuítas na China,' 93; Clunas, *Pictures and Visuality in Early Modern China*, 180. For both complete sets of illustrations and an insightful discussion of the artists' use of perspective and shading, see Kobayashi et al., *Exhibition of Western-Style Paintings of China*, 73–106; 475–80. On Aleni, see Zhang, 'Cultural Accommodation or Intellectual Colonization'; and Zhang, 'Translation as Cultural Reform.'

107 Clunas, *Pictures and Visuality*, 181.

108 See Bailey, Golombek, and Mason, *Tamerlane's Tableware*, fig. 4.6.

109 Sickman and Soper, *The Art and Architecture of China*, 215.

110 Rawson, *Chinese Ornament*, 139; Sickman and Soper, *The Art and Architecture of China*, fig. 118. See also Steinhardt, 'Zhu Haogu Reconsidered,' fig. 22.

111 Vanderstappen, 'Chinese Art and the Jesuits in Peking,' fig. 4.3 (by Wu Bin, 1601); see also Wu, *Tales from the Land of Dragons*, cat. no. 55 (by Lu Xinzhong, Southern Song, late twelfth century).

112 See Mason, *History of Japanese Art*, fig. 198.

113 Wu, *Tales from the Land of Dragons*, cat. no. 50.

114 D'Elia, *Le origini dell'arte cristiana cinese*, 122–4; Vanderstappen, 'Chinese Art and the Jesuits in Peking,' 106; Wu, *Literature of Catholicism to the East*, 3:1135–42.

115 Sullivan, *The Meeting of Eastern and Western Art*, 53.

116 Loehr, *Giuseppe Castiglione*, 61; Vanderstappen, 'Chinese Art and the Jesuits in Peking,' 108; Sullivan, *The Meeting of Eastern and Western Art*, 56 (fig. 39).

117 Pelliot, 'La peinture et la gravure européenes en Chine au temps de Mathieu Ricci,' 5; Vanderstappen, 'Chinese Art and the Jesuits in Peking,' 108; Sullivan, *The Meeting of Eastern and Western Art*, 53.

118 On Wu Li, see Sickman and Soper, *The Art and Architecture of China*, 344–7; Sullivan, *The Arts of China*, 237–8; *One Thousand Years of Chinese Painting* (1997), 264.

119 See Standaert, 'The Jesuit Presence in China.'

120 Chaves, *Singing of the Source*, 48.

121 Cahill, *The Compelling Image*, 35; Sullivan, *The Meeting of Eastern and Western Art*, 56–8. The original text is in Ch'in Tsu-yung, ed., *Hua-hsüeh hsin-yin* (1866), ch. 4, 47a.

122 Chaves, *Singing of the Source*, 10.

123 Clunas, *Art in China*, 130; *Pictures and Visuality in Early Modern China*, 181.

124 Although, admittedly, he also commented about European painting that 'it is of a majesty and elegance which the Chinese painters cannot match' (Sullivan, *The Meeting of Eastern and Western Art*, 56).

125 Cahill, *The Compelling Image*, 72.

126 Loehr, 'Missionary-Artists at the Manchu Court,' 51.

127 For recent work on clockmaking in China during this period, see the following articles by Pagani: 'One Continuous Symphony'; 'The Clocks of James Cox'; 'Clockmaking in China under the Kangxi and Qianlong Emperors'; and 'Most Magnificent Pieces of Mechanism and Art.'

128 Cahill, *The Compelling Image*, 72.

129 Listed in Beurdeley and Beurdeley, *Giuseppe Castiglione*, 194–7. For a recent, extremely detailed study of Ripa's sinicizing style, see Comentale, 'Les recueils de gravures sous la dynastie des Ch'ing.'

130 *Lettres Edifiantes et Curieuses* (Toulouse, 1810), 4:129. Quoted in Loehr, 'Missionary-Artists at the Manchu Court,' 64; and Couseiro, 'Pintores jesuítas na China,' 100.

131 Sullivan, *The Meeting of Eastern and Western Art*, 68.

132 Cahill, *The Compelling Image*, 72.

133 Loehr, 'Missionary-Artists at the Manchu Court,' 55.

134 See the exhibition catalogue from the Museu de São Roque in Lisbon: *Reflexos: Símbolos e Imagens do Cristianismo na Porcelana Chinesa* (1997).

135 Pelliot, 'La peinture et la gravure européenes en Chine au temps de Mathieu Ricci,' 2; Laufer, 'Christian Art in China' McCall, 'Early Jesuit Art in the Far East (IV),' 57–8; Sullivan, *The Meeting of Eastern and Western Art*, 49. This book is in the Natural History Museum in New York.

136 Loehr, *Giuseppe Castiglione*; Beurdeley and Beurdeley, *Giuseppe Castiglione*; Zoratto, *Giuseppe Castiglione*. See also Picard, *Les peintres jésuites à la cour de Chine*; the special number of *Orientations* (19, no. 11 [1988]) devoted to Castiglione; and Kobayashi et al., *Exhibition of Western-Style Paintings of China*, 190–226.

137 Beurdeley and Beurdeley, *Giuseppe Castiglione*, 11–12; Couseiro, 'Pintores jesuítas na China,' 94–5.

138 Vanderstappen, 'Chinese Art and the Jesuits in Peking,' 119; Sullivan, *The Meeting of Eastern and Western Art*, 74.

139 Yang Boda, former Vice Director of Beijing Palace Museum, calls him 'one of the great court painters of the Qing dynasty' (Yang Boda, 'Castiglione at the Qing Court,' 44). See also Sullivan, *The Meeting of Eastern and Western Art*, 72.

140 Yang Boda, 'Castiglione at the Qing Court,' 46.

141 Beurdeley and Beurdeley, *Giuseppe Castiglione*, cat. nos. 17, 104.

142 Vanderstappen, 'Chinese Art and the Jesuits in Peking,' 121.

143 Sullivan, *The Meeting of Eastern and Western Art*, 71.

144 *Le Yuanmingyuan* (1987); Pirazzoli-t'Serstevens, 'A Pluridisciplinary Research on Castiglione and the Emperor Ch'ien-lung's European Palaces'; Sullivan, *The Meeting of Eastern and Western Art*, 54; Hou Renzhi, 'Yuanmingyuan'; Durand and Thiriez, 'Engraving the Emperor of China's European Palaces'; *The Delights of Harmony* (1994). For the complete set of illustrations to *Shixue*, see Kobayashi et al., *Exhibition of Western-Style Paintings of China*, 449–71.

145 For example, see Pirazzoli-t'Serstevens, 'The Emperor Qianlong's European Palaces.'

146 On the 'Turkish Baroque,' see Mamboury, 'L'Art Turc du XVIIIème siècle'; Kuban, *Türk Barok Mimarisi Hakkında bir Deneme*; Arel, *Onsekizinci Yüzyıl Mimarisinde Batılılaşma Süreci*; Artan, 'Architecture as a Theatre of Life'; and İrez, 'Topkapı Sarayı Harem Bölümündeki Rokoko Süslemenin Batılı Kaynakları.' For other images of Istanbul fountains in this style, see H. Orcün Barışta's two surveys of Istanbul fountains, *İstanbul Çeşmeleri: Bereketzade Çeşmesi*; and *İstanbul Çeşmeleri: Beyoğlu Cihetindeki Meyva Tabağı Motifleriyle Bezenmiş tek Cepheli Anıt Çeşmeler*.

147 İrepoğlu, 'Topkapı Sarayı Müzesi Hazine Kütüphanesindeki batılı Kaynaklar Uzerine Düşünceler,' especially 62–9. İrepoğlu publishes fourteen engravings mounted on card and coloured, and twenty-four books, which probably entered the collection in the first half of the eighteenth century. The engravings include six views of the Palace of Versailles and eight views of various of the fountains in the gardens, including Les Bains d'Apollon, the Bassin de Neptune, the Fontaine de Latone, the Theatre d'Eau,

the Colonnade, the Fontaine de Flore, and the Fontaine de Ceres. They represent the work of Menant, Charles Lebrun, and F. Delamance, and some of them bear the date 1714. The books are the following: *Les Divertissements de Versailles donnez par le Roy a toute sa cour au retour de la conqueste de la Franche-Comté en l'année M.DC.LXXIV* (Paris: De l'Imprimerie Royale, 1676); *Veues de Maisons Royales et de Villes* (no provenance; engravings date from 1667–80); *Plans, Veues et Ornements de Versailles* ... (no provenance; engravings date from 1673–82); *Description Générale de L'Hostel des Invalides Etablé par Louis le Grand, dans la Plaine de Grenelle près Paris. Avec les Plans, Profils et Elevations de ses Faces, Coupes et Appartements* (Paris, 1683); *Description de la Grotte de Versailles* (1679); Carlo Fontana, *Ultilissimo Trattato dell' Aque Correnti Diviso in Tre Libri* (Rome: G. Francesco Buagni, 1696); François Blondel, *Cours d'Architecture* (Paris, 1698); *Nouveau Theatre d'Italie, ou Déscription exacte de ses Villes, Palais, Eglises. Et les Cartes Geographiques de toutes ses Provinces* (Amsterdam, 1704); Andrea Palladio, *The Architecture of A. Palladio: In Four Books* (2 vols.; London, 1721); *Le Grand Escalier de Versailles* (no provenance, undated); *Plans Lhôte des Ynyal; Plans L'Hôtel Royal des Invalides* (no provenance, undated); *Livre de Dessins de Cheminées* (no provenance, undated); Johann David Flücken, *Neue Gartenlust, oder Völliges Ornament* (no provenance, undated); *Labyrinte de Versailles, suivant la Copie de Paris A la Hate, Chez Rutgert Albert* (Paris, 1724); *L'Architecture Françoise* (Paris, 1727); James Gibbs, *A Book of Architecture Containing Designs of Buildings and Ornaments* (London, 1728); James Gibbs, *Rules for Drawing. The Several Parts of Architecture* ... (London, 1732); *Architecture Françoise* (Paris, 1738); Antoine Watteau, *Figures de differentes Caractères de Paysages et Etude Dessinées d'Après Nature* (Paris, 1726–8); *Les Oeuvres D'Architecture* (Paris, undated); Louis Fordrin, *Nouveau Livre de Serrurerie, Contenant toutes sourtes de grilles d'un goût nouveau, propres pour les coeurs d'eglises, portes de vestibules, péristiles et de jardins, tant pour les maisons royales, que pour celles des seigneurs et particuliers. Rampes, port enseignes, balcons riches et simples, et autres de différents desseins* (Paris: G. Duchange, 1723); album of French and German engravings of furniture, and household architecture, including designs by Watteau and François Cuvillies; and two anonymous books of garden and park plans.

148 ARSI, Jap/Sin 184, f. 41a; Loehr, 'Missionary Artists at the Manchu Court,' 61–2.

149 Loehr, 'Missionary Artists at the Manchu Court,' 61–2.

150 *As Ruinas de S. Paulo* (1994), cat. nos. 65, 66. A British engraving of ca. 1860 is reproduced in Malatesta and Gao, *Departed, Yet Present*, pl. 37.

151 Loehr, 'Missionary Artists at the Manchu Court,' 52.

152 Wilberg, 'Le finte cupole e la loro recezione nella Germania meridionale.'

153 Clunas, *Pictures and Visuality in Early Modern China*, 173–81.

5: The Jesuit Mission to 'Mogor,' 1580–1773

1 From a mystical poem about the Emperor Akbar by his court biographer Abu'l-Fazl:

The Lover and the Beloved (i.e., worshipper and his god) are in reality one;
Idle talkers speak of the Brahmin as distinct from his idol.
There is but one lamp in this house, in the rays of which,
Wherever I look, a bright assembly meets me.

(Abu'l-Fazl 'Allami, *The Āīn-i Akbari*, 1:162)

2 Bailey, *The Jesuit and the Grand Mogul*.

3 Dawson, *Mission to Asia*, xiii–xiv.
4 Saunders, *The History of the Mongol Conquest*, 92; Abu Lughod, *Before European Hegemony*, 162; Dawson, *Mission to Asia*, xv.
5 Dawson, *Mission to Asia*, xix, 162–80. The khans had also captured Western European artisans; for example, the Parisian goldsmith family of Buchier and William of Paris, a furniture maker who carved a statue of the Virgin for the friars 'sculptured after the French fashion' (ibid., 180).
6 Wyngaert, *Sinica Franciscana*, 1:289–97; Dawson, *Mission to Asia*, 188–94.
7 Shaykh Nur al-Haqq, *Zubdat al-Tavārīkh* (BL, Ethé 290 f. 157a).
8 See Beach, *The Imperial Image*, 180; and Beach, *Mughal and Rajput Painting*, 55.
9 Translation by Sir Edward Maclagan (*The Jesuits and the Great Mogul*, 231).
10 The identifications were made by Nancy Graves Cabot of the Museum of Fine Arts, Boston (see Beach, 'The Gulshan Album and Its European Sources').
11 Michael Brand and Glenn D. Lowry, in *Akbar's India*, point out that 'prior to the time of Fatehpur-Sikri, European prints occupied a rather modest position in the Mughal collection. They were used more as source material for his artists than admired by Akbar as precious objects in their own right' (p. 97).
12 Beach, 'The Mughal Painter Kesu Das,' 39; Beach, *The Imperial Image*, 181; Beach, *Early Mughal Painting*, 17. Examples are found in the *Hamzanāma* (Story of Hamza, ca. 1562–77) and *Tūtīnāma* (Tales of a Parrot, 1556–60) illustrations.
13 Abu'l-Fazl 'Allami, *Akbarnāma*, 3:37, 207; Biker, *Collecção de Tratatos*, 25–6; Du Jarric, *Akbar and the Jesuits*, 219, note 12.
14 *Akbarnāma*, 207, 322; Al-Badaoni, *Muntakhāb ut-Tawārīkh*, 2:299. Two depictions of this organ in contemporary Mughal paintings show that it was painted with a variety of religious images: *Plato Playing to the Animals* from a *Khamsa* of Nizami, ca. 1590 (BL, Or. 12208 f. 298r); and a margin drawing from the Berlin Album of Jahangir (see Kühnel and Goetz, *Indian Book Painting from Jahangir's Album in the State Library Berlin*). Badaoni's description makes it sound as though the instrument had mechanical figures who marched in and out of it as it played (Elliot, *Bibliographical Index to the Historians of Muhammadan India*, 1:250).
15 See *Akbarnāma* 3:349–51; Pierre Du Jarric, *Akbar and the Jesuits*, C.H. Payne, trans., 14–15; Badaoni, *Muntakhāb ut-Tawārīkh*, 215; Maclagan, *The Jesuits and the Great Mogul*, 24.
16 Serrão, 'A pintura na antiga India,' 104–5.
17 José, *Images of Faith*, 9–10.
18 *Akbarnāma*, 3:1027.
19 Most of these have been identified previously. See, for example, Kühnel and Goetz, *Indian Book Painting from Jahangir's Album in the State Library Berlin*; and Beach, 'The Mughal Painter Kesu Das.' See also below.
20 The picture was sent from Rome to Goa by Father Martin da Silva (Correia-Afonso, *Letters from the Mughal Court*, 33, 48). Although Correia-Afonso believes that this picture is the Borghese Madonna, I think it is another one. Another letter differentiates it from 'the one of St. Luke' (Correia-Afonso, *Letters from the Mughal Court*, 33).
21 Maclagan, 'Jesuit Missions to the Emperor Akbar,' 50. The sources only say that it is a picture of Christ, but it was likely a Crucifixion, given Akbar's predeliction for that subject.
22 Correia-Afonso, *Letters from the Mughal Court*, 31, 60.

23 Jennes, *Invloed der Vlaamsche Prentkunst in Indie, China en Japan*, 49.
24 Correia-Afonso, *Letters from the Mughal Court*, 30–1, 33.
25 Ibid., 33; Monserrate, *The Commentary of Father Monserrate*, 49.
26 Maclagan, 'Jesuit Missions to the Emperor Akbar,' 50.
27 Ibid.; Maclagan, *The Jesuits and the Great Mogul*, 227.
28 Correia-Afonso, *Letters from the Mughal Court*, 33, 59.
29 For example: Correia-Afonso, *Letters from the Mughal Court*, 33–4; Monserrate, *The Commentary of Father Monserrate*, 59–60.
30 Maclagan, *The Jesuits and the Great Mogul*, 228; Monserrate, *The Commentary of Father Monserrate*, 176.
31 Monserrate, *The Commentary of Father Monserrate*, 28, 37; Maclagan, *The Jesuits and the Great Mogul*, 225; Correia-Afonso, *Letters from the Mughal Court*, 29, 42, 58. The engravings brought by the Jesuits were not 'cheap woodcuts' (Arnold, *The Old and New Testaments in Muslim Religious Painting*, 40), as many have claimed, but the work of the finest engravers of the day. The Antwerp Polyglot, for example, which was commissioned by Philip II of Spain himself, had pictures by Pieter van der Heyden after sketches by Pieter van der Borcht, Jan Wierix, Geeraert van Kampen, Pieter Huys, and Philip Galle (*Biblia Sacra Hebraice, Graece & Latine* [Antwerp, 1569–72]; Jennes, *Invloed der Vlaamsche Prentkunst in Indie, China en Japan*, 46–7). Ortelius's Atlas contained maps by Franz Hagenberg (1540–90).
32 Many of the books were the key texts used for lecturing and preaching by Jesuits, such as Polanco and Nadal in Italy in the sixteenth century. In Rome, these were 'the most important and influential texts of the day' (O'Malley, *The First Jesuits*, 146).
33 Identified by Arnulf Camps (*Jerome Xavier, S.J., and the Muslims of the Mogul Empire*, 163).
34 Father Pinheiro's letter of 3 September 1595 lists the '*Summa* of St. Thomas, one work against the heathen and another against the Jews and Saracens, etc.' (Maclagan, 'Jesuit Missions to the Emperor Akbar,' 68). Father Xavier's letter of 8 September 1596 adds: 'parte de S. Thomas contra gentes' (ARSI, Goa 46I, f. 30a). Camps shows that Xavier used Aquinas's *Summa contra gentiles* in preparing his own *Āyine-ye Haqq-Numā* (Camps, *Jerome Xavier*, 163).
35 Pinheiro's letter does not give the title of Cajetan's book, but the *Summa Peccatorum* was one of the key confessional books of the early Jesuits (O'Malley, *The First Jesuits*, 146).
36 Not Pope Sylvester II, as Maclagan suggests (Maclagan, 'Jesuit Missions to the Emperor Akbar,' 69).
37 Again, Pinheiro does not give the title, but this manual for confessors was one of the most prominent texts used by the Jesuits in Europe (O'Malley, *The First Jesuits*, 146).
38 This is Saint Antoninus Pierozzi, or Forciglioni (1389–1459), whose *Chronicles* (1454–9) are a history of the world, containing the lives of Greek and Roman kings and philosophers, as well as the history of various European nations. The ten printed editions date from 1484 to 1587, the last two of which (1586, '87) were edited by a Jesuit, Peter Maturus, S.J. (see Walker, *The 'Chronicles' of Saint Antoninus*). This work was quoted extensively by Akbar's court historian 'Abd al-Sattar ibn Qasim Lahori (see below). Akbar may also have possessed the *Summa confessionalis* by the same author, since it was a popular work with the early Jesuits in Europe (O'Malley, *The First Jesuits*, 146).
39 Pinheiro refers to it only as 'Historium Pontificum' (Maclagan, 'Jesuit Missions to the

Emperor Akbar,' 69), but O'Malley proposes that Platina is the most likely author. An Italian humanist and historian, Platina was the Vatican librarian under Sixtus IV (1475). In addition to the history of the popes, he wrote works on politics, philosophy, and rhetoric (O'Malley, personal communication; *Webster's New Biographical Dictionary* [1988], 874).

40 Pinheiro's letter from Lahore, dated 3 September 1595 (Maclagan, 'Jesuit Missions to the Emperor Akbar,' 66–7); Xavier's letter from Agra, dated 8 September 1596 (ARSI, Goa 46I, f. 30a). See also Du Jarric, *Akbar and the Jesuits*, 63.

41 The sources tell us that Akbar had at least some of his European works translated; for example, the history of Saint Antonine (1454–9), which he had rendered into Persian by his court historian 'Abd al-Sattar ibn Qasim Lahori as part of the latter's *Thamrat al-Falāsafa* (The Fruit of Philosophy), written in Lahore in 1603 (the original text can be found in NAI, 2713; and IOL, Or. 5893). That same work included material 'mixed in from other histories' and from the Gospels (NAI, 2713, f. 3b; IOL, Or. 5893, f. 7). Xavier and 'Abd al-Sattar collaborated on several catechisms in Persian (see below), which Camps has shown rely heavily on Saint Thomas (Camps, *Jerome Xavier*, 163).

42 Monserrate, *The Commentary of Father Monserrate*, 52–3. As was the practice in Italy, the fathers spent the lessons teaching the 'Our Father,' the 'Hail Mary,' the Decalogue, remedies for sin, the works of mercy, and the Beatitudes (O'Malley, *The First Jesuits*, 120). They also taught the children the Roman alphabet, which they drew out in coloured ink. For a contemporary description of the daily routine on the Mogor mission, see ARSI, Goa 46I, ff. 83a–85a.

43 It could also have been Diego de Ledesma's *Dottrina Christiana* (mid-sixteenth century), written in two versions, one for the 'very ignorant' and another for the 'less ignorant'; or Francis Xavier's *Doutrina Christam* (Goa, 1556), the first book ever published in Goa (O'Malley, *The First Jesuits*, 115, 124, 189; Miller and Roth, *Aussereuropäische Druckereien im 16. Jahrhundert*, 39).

44 Correia-Afonso, *Letters from the Mughal Court*, 85.

45 Monserrate, *The Commentary of Father Monserrate*, 138.

46 Badaoni mentions these cribs (Badaoni, *Muntakhab ut-Tawarikh*, 2:304).

47 For example, the years 1580, 1598, 1599, 1600, 1607, and 1627 (Monserrate, *The Commentary of Father Monserrate*, 59; ARSI, Goa 46I, f. 77b; Maclagan, 'Jesuit Missions to the Emperor Akbar,' 81, 85; Hosten, 'Three Letters of Fr. Joseph de Castro,' 151; BL, Add. MSS 9854, f. 64b). See also Allen, 'Four Letters by Austin of Bordeaux,' 15; and BL, Add. MSS 9854, f. 64a. The emperor also sent pictures to the mission to adorn the church during the Feast of the Assumption (ARSI, Goa 14, f. 288a).

48 Heras, 'The Jesuit Dwelling at Fatehpur-Sikri,' 297–8; Narayan, *Aquaviva and the Great Mogul*, 92; Correia-Afonso, *Letters from the Mughal Court*, 48; Muhammed, 'Excavation of a Catholic Chapel at Fatehpur Sikri,' 3.

49 Muhammed, 'Excavation of a Catholic Chapel at Fatehpur Sikri,' 7ff.

50 Correia-Afonso, 'The Second Jesuit Mission to Akbar (1591),' 73.

51 This was first suggested by Beach (*The Grand Mogul*, 56).

52 For example: Beach, 'The Mughal Painter Kesu Das,' 38–9; Okada, *Indian Miniatures of the Mughal Court*, 97. Michelangelo's work was published in a 1515 engraving by Agos-

tino Musi (Veneziano), which identified the figure as *Diogenes*, and another version was made in 1564 by Mario Cartaro as *Saint Jerome* (Moltedo, *La Sistina Reprodotta*, fig. 3). The latter print was also used in Japan, as we have seen in chapter 3.

53 Muslims deny that Jesus was crucified.

54 British Museum, 1983.10-15.1. This image is published in Rogers, *Mughal Miniatures*, pl. 44; and also in Artemis Group, *Indian Painting 1525–1825*, fig. 5.

55 Rogers, *Mughal Miniatures*, 68.

56 Kesu Das, or someone working in his style, also produced individual life studies of an Armenian priest and Portuguese character types (see Okada, *Miniatures de l'Inde impériale*, cat. nos. 60–1; and Gahlin, *Indian Miniatures from the Collection of the Fondation Custodia*, cat. nos. 4, 5).

57 This was at least true during the time of the third mission (Hosten, 'Mirza zu-l-Qarnain, a Christian Grandee of Three Great Mughals,' 153.

58 Correia-Afonso, *Letters from the Mughal Court*, 58–9.

59 Okada ('Les Baigneuses du musée Guimet, 85) was first to make this identification, although she only makes it for one of the drawings.

60 Okada, 'Basawan,' 11. See Welch, *Indian Drawings and Painted Sketches*; Atil, *The Brush of the Masters*; and Swietochowski and Babaie, *Persian Drawings in the Metropolitan Museum of Art*.

61 Published in Okada, *Indian Miniatures of the Mughal Court*, fig. 85.

62 Published in Beach, 'The Gulshan Album and Its European Sources,' fig. 8a.

63 Lowry, 'Manohar,' in Beach, *The Grand Mogul*, 130–1; Beach, *The Imperial Image*, 112; McInerney, 'Manohar,' 54; Okada, *Indian Miniatures of the Mughal Court*, 136.

64 As identified by Lowry in Beach, *The Grand Mogul*, 130.

65 As Beach indicated in the only article to deal with this enigmatic artist, Kesu Khurd held a secondary position within Akbar's atelier, since he was most often assigned to paint illustrations for manuscripts designed by more prominent artists (Beach, 'The Mughal Painter Kesu Das,' 46). See also Pal, *Indian Painting*, 237. The painter La'l, listed immediately after Kesu Das in the *Āīn-i Akbari*, 1:114.

66 ARSI, Goa 14, f. 288a; Maclagan, *The Jesuits and the Great Mogul*, 228.

67 Monserrate, *The Commentary of Father Monserrate*, 29.

68 ARSI, Goa 55, f. 20b.

69 Smith, *The Moghul Architecture of Fathpur-Sikri*, vol. 1, pls. XI, XII, XIII, XV (a,b,c), CIX, CX, CXI, CXII, CXIII, CXIV, CXV, CXVI, CXVII, CXVIII, CXIX, CXX. For the debate on the function of the rooms, see Heras, 'La casa de la Señora María'; Rizvi and Flynn, *Fathpur-Sikri*, 56; and Muhammed, 'Excavations at Fatehpur Sikri.'

70 Smith, *The Moghul Architecture of Fathpur-Sikri*, vol. 1, XV(b); Bailey, 'Counter-Reformation Symbolism and Allegory,' fig. 245.

71 The grotto setting is echoed in a number of paintings of Rustam slaying the White Div from the *Shāhnāma*; for example, Baysunghur's *Shāhnāma* from 1430 (Binyon, Wilkinson, and Gray, *Persian Miniature Painting*, pl. XLVIII-B.49). Close is another image from the *Shāhnāma* showing the Simurgh restoring the child Zal to his father, but here it is clearly an angel, and no other characters are present (Lentz and Lowry, *Timur and the Princely Vision*, cat. no. 43 [Iran, ca. 1444]). In the Istanbul albums at the Topkapi Sarayi Museum (H.2152, f. 69a) there is a *Mirājnāma* picture, attributed to Ahmad Musa, show-

ing an angel swooping down with an adult man in his arms, but the position is different (*Islamic Art*, vol. 1, fig. 10).

72 The palace was founded on the site of the *dārgāh* of Salim al-Din Chisti, to whom Akbar had made pilgrimages and whom he credited with the miraculous late birth of his son, Salim, by Maryam (Mary) al-Makani. See Brand and Lowry, *Fatehpur Sikri*, 1–2.

73 A tradition that Maclagan accepts with caution, Smith dismisses as a fabrication aimed at 'extra *bakhshish*,' and Rizvi and Flynn call 'plausible nonsense' (Maclagan, *The Jesuits and the Great Mogul*, 237; Smith, *The Moghul Architecture of Fathpur-Sikri*, 1:31; and Rizvi and Flynn, *Fathpur-Sikri*, 54).

74 This scene relates to a whole series of Akbar-period genre scenes depicting men and women in a garden pavilion. The poses and dress are also very close to one of the so-called 'Tobias and the Angels' pictures (Brand and Lowry, *Akbar's India*, cat. no. 64), itself likely copied after an Annunciation.

75 As we can see in an *Annunciation* by Titian (1520) in Treviso (Freedberg, *Painting in Italy, 1500–1600*, fig. 58). For earlier Flemish examples and a version by the Safavid painter Sadiqi Beg Afshar, see Bailey, 'In the Manner of the Frankish Masters.' Another Mughal example is painted on an early seventeenth-century box (London, Victoria and Albert Museum, IS 142-1984).

76 It is unlikely, however, that Xavier visited this building since it was still inhabited by Maryam Makani until 1601, and by other members of the harem for some years afterward (Brand and Lowry, *Sourcebook*, 4).

77 For example, in a painting from Ilkhanid Persia illustrated in Binyon, Wilkinson, and Gray, *Persian Miniature Painting*, pl. XV-A.8.

78 This anonymous painter is only mentioned in one published letter (Maclagan, 'Jesuit Missions to the Emperor Akbar,' 67), and in the history of Du Jarric (Du Jarric, *Akbar and the Jesuits*, 67). I have found two additional letters that mention him (ARSI, Goa 14, f. 288a; and Goa 46I, f. 30b).

79 BL, Add. MSS 9854, f. 64b, Add. MSS 9855, f. 43b; ARSI, Goa 46I, f. 78a-b; Hosten, 'Mirza zu-l-Qarnain,' 158; Maclagan, *The Jesuits and the Great Mogul*, 317; Camps, *Jerome Xavier, S.J., and the Muslims of the Mogul Empire*, 226–39; Bailey, 'The Catholic Shrines of Agra,' 136.

80 BL, Add. MSS 9854, f. 164b.

81 Ibid., f. 168; Sainsbury, *Calendar of State Papers*, 256.

82 Camps, *Jerome Xavier, S.J., and the Muslims of the Mogul Empire*, 230.

83 Badaoni, *Muntakhāb ut-Tawārīkh*, 2:304.

84 Sainsbury, *Calendar of State Papers*, 255.

85 ARSI, Goa 14, f. 288a; Maclagan, 'Jesuit Missions to the Emperor Akbar,' 66.

86 ARSI, Goa 14, f. 288b; Maclagan, 'Jesuit Missions to the Emperor Akbar,' 66–7; Maclagan, *The Jesuits and the Grand Mogul*, 226. Jesuit letters sent from the Mughal mission include a litany of requests for pictures, whether retables, large and small engravings, illustrated books, or even a copper plate from which to make engravings (e.g., ARSI, Goa 14, f. 288a [20 Aug. 1595]; f. 344a (18 Aug. 1597); Goa 46I, f. 64a [24 Sept. 1607]). The last letter shows that when some engravings finally arrived in 1607, they created a sensation.

87 ARSI, Goa 46I, f. 36a.

88 The *Salvador Mundi* was intended for the church, although Akbar got hold of it before-

hand and showed it to the women of the harem. The other two were intended as gifts to Akbar (letter of 8 Sept. 1595 [ARSI, Goa 46I, f. 36b]). The Japanese pictures of Christ and Ignatius Loyola were given to Akbar by Father Xavier (Maclagan, 'Jesuit Missions to the Emperor Akbar,' 76).

89 ARSI, Goa 55, f. 32b; Maclagan, 'Jesuit Missions to the Emperor Akbar,' 74, 85; Du Jarric, *Akbar and the Jesuits*, 111; Maclagan, *The Jesuits and the Great Mogul*, 226.

90 ARSI, Goa 46I, f. 48a. There are two *calaim dourada* pictures in the State Museum, Panjim, donated by Don Martin of Porvorim.

91 Xavier's letter from Lahore, dated 20 August 1595 (ARSI, Goa 14, f. 288a). A later Latin version of this letter reads: 'He has images of Our Lord Christ and of the blessed Virgin, which are of the best kind of those which are brought from Europe, and he keeps them with respect and reverence' (Maclagan, 'Jesuit Missions to the Emperor Akbar,' 66, 68). In another letter, we hear that '(Akbar) demonstrates such a taste for images of Christ Our Lord and Our Lady that when his painters wish to present him with some piece of work for a gift that will please him, they bring an image of Christ Our Lord or of Our Lady, which pleases him very much' (ARSI, Goa 46I, f. 30b).

92 Maclagan, 'Jesuit Missions to the Emperor Akbar,' 77; Maclagan, *The Jesuits and the Great Mogul*, 226.

93 de Dieu, *Narratio brevis rerum*, 127; Maclagan, 'Jesuit Missions to the Emperor Akbar,' 73.

94 Maclagan, 'Jesuit Missions to the Emperor Akbar,' 73.

95 ARSI, Goa 46I, f. 31a; Maclagan, 'Jesuit Missions to the Emperor Akbar,' 75.

96 ARSI, Goa 14, f. 288; ARSI, Goa 46I, f. 30b; Maclagan, 'Jesuit Missions to the Emperor Akbar,' 67.

97 ARSI, Goa 46I, f. 30b.

98 ARSI, Goa 14, f. 288b; Maclagan, 'Jesuit Missions to the Emperor Akbar,' 67. Salim had two ivory crucifixes and infant Jesuses made after originals in the Jesuit chapel (ARSI, Goa 14, f. 288b; ARSI, Goa 46I, f. 30b; Maclagan, 'Jesuit Missions to the Emperor Akbar,' 67).

99 ARSI, Goa 46I, f. 53a; London, BL, Add. MSS 9854, f. 11a; Maclagan, 'Jesuit Missions to the Emperor Akbar,' 92. Salim continued this practice throughout his reign as Emperor Jahangir. In 1610, for example, a slave in the seal-cutting department made him an amulet out of carved ivory set inside the shell of a filbert. Each compartment was sculpted with a scene, including wrestlers, a prince, and rope dancers, and 'in the fourth compartment ... a tree, below which the figure of the revered [*hazrat*] Jesus is shown. One person has placed his head at Jesus' feet, and an old man is conversing with Jesus and four others are standing by' (*Tūzuk-i Jahangīrī*, 1:200–1).

100 Welch, *India!* cat. no. 134. It is made from Narwhal ivory (Maharaja Sawai Man Singh II Museum, Jaipur, S.1950).

101 Hosten, 'Three Letters of Fr. Joseph de Castro, S.J., and the Last Year of Jahangir,' 156. See also 161.

102 BL, Add. MSS 9854, ff. 72a–b.

103 Ketelaar, *Journaal*, 155; *Viaggi*, 158–9.

104 Bailey, 'The Catholic Shrines of Agra,' 133, 135. It was found during excavations at the Red Fort, Agra, in the mid-nineteenth century.

105 Salim presented the fathers with a painting of Christ which was executed by his own

artists, along with a portrait of himself 'which is very lifelike' (ARSI, Goa 46I, ff. 36a–b). The letter goes on to say: 'I am not able to get his father's portrait, since he did not send it to me.' This portrait is the same one used years later in the Christmas crib decorations mentioned above. Both were finally sent to General Acquaviva in Rome in 1607 (ARSI, Goa 46I, ff. 68a–b).

106 ARSI, Goa 46I, ff. 36a–b, 64b, 68a.

107 ARSI, Goa 55, f. 20b; BL, Add. MSS 9854, f. 11a; Maclagan, 'Jesuit Missions to the Emperor Akbar,' 88; Maclagan, *The Jesuits and the Great Mogul*, 69. In 1600 and 1604, Xavier visited Salim while he was residing at Fatehpur Sikri.

108 Hosten, 'List of Jesuit Missionaries in "Mogor,"' 528.

109 ARSI, Goa 46I, f. 64b; BL, Add. MSS 9854, f. 64a; Guerreiro, *Jahangir and the Jesuits*, 44; *Tūzuk-i Jahāngīrī*, 1:167.

110 ARSI, Goa 33I, f. 78a. Other references to paintings are in ARSI, Goa 55, f. 23b, 32b; Maclagan, 'Jesuit Missions to the Emperor Akbar,' 86; and Maclagan, *The Jesuits and the Grand Mogul*, 226.

111 For example, Tepotzotlán, Mexico, where there is an example from the late seventeenth or early eighteenth century (fig. 1). On this and others, see Museo Nacional del Virreino, Tepotzotlán, *Pintura Novohispana*, cat. no. PI/0048.

112 ARSI, Goa 33I, f. 78a; Maclagan, 'Jesuit Missions to the Emperor Akbar,' 87–8; Maclagan, *The Jesuits and the Great Mogul*, 228–34.

113 BL, Add. MSS 9854 ff. 72a–72b; *Tūzuk-i Jahāngīrī*, 1:144, 153.

114 '... the image of Christ Our Lord *a columna* ... he ordered copied from a small engraving onto a large panel, with its colours beautifully executed, to serve as a pattern to make a silk cloth with those figures, like an *arras* silk. He ordered that the caption on this paper be written in Persian to be woven into the cloth in the same manner' (BL, Add. MSS 9854, f. 72a).

115 'Afterward he sent [the *Adoration of the Magi*] to Father Francesco Corsi to decorate it as he saw fit, and to this end he ordered his artisans to be at his service. It was stretched out on a wooden frame, so that it would not become damaged through constant rolling and unrolling, and on the border at the sides he drew some scenes in outline, which were taken from the illustrations in our books and pictures. [The King] was very pleased with the drawings, and ordered that a golden frame be made for it and at the same time to paint his own portrait among these scenes in a place that the Father left empty for it' (BL, Add. MSS 9854, ff. 72b–73a). This method of framing with little episodes was a common European practice, and we have also seen it in Japanese Christian art (see chapter 3).

116 BL, Add. MSS 9854, f. 66a

117 Ibid., f. 66b.

118 Ibid., f. 68a.

119 Ibid.

120 Ibid., f. 67a.

121 'He asked, "What is this?" I replied, "It is an image of God, not only because he looks like this, but also in order to demonstrate some of his attributes using this picture. For example, for this purpose angels are depicted as boys with wings, although He has none of these, etc. And in this manner He appeared to several Prophets ... Everyone painted Him as he saw Him"' (BL, Add. MSS 9854, f. 67a).

122 BL. Add. MSS 9854, ff. 72a–b.
123 Listed in Camps, *Jerome Xavier, S.J., and the Muslims of the Mughal Empire*, 14–39. See my article 'The Truth-Showing Mirror.'
124 BL, Harley 5478, ff. 278a–290a ('On the Uses of Images and Their Veneration, and an Explanation of the Rationality of Them, and the Advantages of [Pictures of Christ] and of the Rest of the Saints'). The quote in the text appears in f. 280a.
125 BL, Harley 5478, f. 280b.
126 See Soucek, 'Nizami on Painters and Painting,' 14.
127 BL, Harley 5478, f. 281b
128 Ibid., ff. 282a–282b.
129 Maclagan, 'Jesuit Missions to the Emperor Akbar,' 87. Many copies were made of this work, two of which bear Akbar's seal, but only the Lahore one has its pictures intact. The original edition, presented to Akbar, is now in the National Museum in Lahore, and has ten of its illustrations intact; the copy sent to Salim may be the one in the Bodleian, which no longer has any illustrations other than the illuminated cross mentioned in the sources (LNM, M-645/MSS-46; Camps, *Jerome Xavier, S.J., and the Muslims of the Mughal Empire*, 15).
130 Compare with Beach, *Mughal and Rajput Painting*, 72ff.
131 See Bailey, 'The Lahore *Mirat al-Quds* and the Impact of Jesuit Theater on Mughal Painting.'
132 ARSI, Goa 46I, ff. 52b–53a. See also ARSI, Goa 33I, f. 126a.
133 ARSI, Goa 46I, f. 53a; Maclagan, *The Jesuits and the Great Mogul*, 226.
134 ARSI, Goa 46I, f. 64a; Guerreiro, *Jahangir and the Jesuits*, 32, 44; BL, Add. MSS 9854, f. 64a; Add. MSS 9854, f. 53a.
135 Wittkower and Jaffe, eds, *Baroque Art: The Jesuit Contribution*, 12; O'Malley, *The First Jesuits*, 37–50.
136 The complete Persian text appears in De Dieu, *Historia Christi*, 31.
137 For an assessment of Goan architecture, see Chicó, 'Algumas observações.' More recent discussions, including a classification of styles, are found in Kowal, 'The Evolution of Ecclesiastical Architecture in Portuguese Goa'; and Kowal, 'Innovation and Assimilation: The Jesuit Contribution to Architectural Development in the Portuguese Indies.'
138 Kowal, 'The Evolution of Ecclesiastical Architecture in Portuguese Goa,' 5.
139 As noted by Kowal, 'Innovation and Assimilation.'
140 Ibid.
141 Ibid.
142 See Bailey, 'The Catholic Shrines of Agra.'
143 The decree is in the episcopal archives, Agra, and a translation has been published in Brand and Lowry, *Akbar's India*, cat. no. 80. It does not refer to the Agra cathedral directly, as Maclagan and others contend (Maclagan, *The Jesuits and the Great Mogul*, 313).
144 Hosten, 'Mirza zu-l-Qarnain,' 170.
145 The first church at Agra (after the small chapel built under Akbar) was built in 1604, under the patronage of Jahangir, Khwaja Martin, and Mirza Sikandar, two Armenian grandees (Hosten, 'Mirza zu-l-Qarnain,' 179).
146 BL, Add. MSS 9855, f. 42b; Hosten, 'Mirza zu-l-Qarnain,' 156; Maclagan, *The Jesuits and*

the Grand Mogul, 313–14. The French traveller François Bernier mentions the steeple: 'A high steeple stood upon this church, with a bell whose sound was heard in every part of the city.' Also '... the steeple ... contained a clock heard in every part of the city' (Bernier, *Travels in the Mongol Empire*, 177, 286–7) Niccolò Manucci also mentions a 'bell-tower' (Manucci, *Storia del Mogol*, 1:195). For the reference to the three altars, see Botelho's letter in BL, Add. MSS 9855 f. 145a.

147 'The 9th of June, 1614, I visited the Jesuites which remayned in Agra; whoe have a verye fayer church buylte them by the Kinge, and a howse allsoe' (Nicholas Withington, 1614, in Foster, *Early Travels to India*, 222).

148 Father Azevedo, writing in 1632 (Wessels, *Early Jesuit Travellers in Central Asia*, 282–3.

149 BL, Add. MSS 9855, f. 43a.

150 *Akbar's Church* [an anonymous leaflet printed by the Agra Diocese, apparently composed of an article by Father Felix, in *Agra Diocesan Calendar* (1907), 204ff; and another by Father H. Hosten, 'The Armenian Inscription of the Central Jail Compound, Agra,' in *Journal of the United Provinces Historical Society* 2 (1919), Part 1, 40–50], 3.

151 See Koch, *Mughal Architecture*, fig. 77.

152 The decree is quoted in full in Tirmizi, *Mughal Documents*, 83.

153 Father Botelho, quoted in Hosten, 'Mirza zu-l-Qarnain,' 156.

154 Father João de Velasco, S.J., in a letter of 1612 (Hosten, 'Mirza zu-l-Qarnain,' 183).

155 Losty, *The Art of the Book in India*, pl. XXXI, cat. no. 77.

156 Das (*Mughal Painting during Jahangir's Time*, 30), is one of the few who suggest that many of Salim's Occidentalist works may be overpaintings: 'Many of these were colored or copied, in some cases with minor variations, by his painters.' Skelton also writes that 'in some cases Mughal painters simply coloured over a print' ('Europe and India,' 35). Seyller says of the Mughal tradition of overpainting in general that 'the Mughals demonstrated a remarkable inclination to rework all kinds of paintings' ('Recycled Images: Overpainting in Early Mughal Art,' 64).

157 Rogers, *Mughal Miniatures*, fig. 71.

158 Das, *Mughal Painting during Jahangir's Time*, 46. This theory has been championed by others; for example, see Soustiel and Soustiel, *Miniatures orientales de l'Inde*, 15. The inscription appears in Wilkinson and Gray, 'Indian Paintings in a Persian Museum,' 174. See also Godard, 'Un album des princes timourides de l'Inde,' fig. 110.

159 Beach is the only source who mentions signed marginalia by Basawan, which he noted on f. 84b of the Gulshan album in the Golestan Library, Tehran (Beach, *The Grand Mogul*, 183, n. 6).

160 Beach, 'The Gulshan Album and Its European Sources,' 73.

161 The list of monuments is well known to specialists. Most of the sources are listed in Maclagan, *The Jesuits and the Great Mogul*, 237–41.

162 Letter of 24 September 1607 (ARSI, Goa 46I, f. 64b). Earlier requests for images are legion; for example, in a letter of 16 September 1603, Xavier asked for engravings 'since they are so useful here, and cost so little' (Goa 46I, f. 53b).

163 'He ordered that (his artists) inquire of the Fathers what colours to give to their clothing, and that they not stray from the words of the Fathers because whatever they instruct them to do is written. The King himself chose the images to be painted from among the engravings he owns, as well as their location. He also ordered his painters to sketch on paper on a large scale all of the engravings that he wanted to be painted,

and the Fathers then told them how they should be painted' (BL, Add. MSS 9854 ff. 71a–72a).

164 The letter clearly indicates that the setting was not the *jharoka-i darshan*, as some scholars have assumed, but the *jharoka* of the Hall of Public Audiences, which is consistent with contemporary miniature paintings. Because of Maclagan's ommision, some scholars, such as Ebba Koch ('The Influence of the Jesuit Mission on Symbolic Representations of the Mughal Emperors,' 26), have claimed that these paintings were placed on the outer walls surrounding the *jharoka-i darshan*. Contemporary miniature paintings depict the saints' pictures only in the Hall of Public Audiences, and not the *jharoka-i darshan*, which is shown unadorned in the famous *Jahangirnama* painting in the Sadruddin Aga Khan Collection in Geneva (Acc. # M.141).

165 Letter of 9 July 1609 to Juan Ximenez de Oco (AHPT, 104.12 (896) f. 1b). The much longer description from Xavier's letter of 24 September 1608 is in BL, Add. MSS 9854, ff. 71a–72a:

> When he came from Lahore, he discovered that the palace had been very beautifully ornamented and painted with several pictures that were already finished, and others awaiting completion, both on the interior and exterior of a varanda upon which he ascends every day *ad populum*. In the centre of it he is seated alone, on his two flanks (are) his two sons, and behind them some domestic servants. All of the Captains and Grandees stand below, and when *ad tempus* he summons one of them forward, he proceeds and then returns. On the inner side, where he retires at night and sits before he wishes to enter the *janela* or varanda in front, he has a large varanda. At the top of the ceiling of this there is painted in the centre Christ Our Lord, very fine, with some angels in a circle with his aureola. On the walls of this, i.e., the hall, there are some Portuguese very well painted on a large scale, and some saints on a small scale, for example: Saint John the Baptist, Saint Anthony, Saint Bernard of Siena and others, both male and female, beautifully executed. What shall I say about the outer *janela*? On the sides of the place where the King sits when he appears *ad populum*, some of the King's favourites had been painted very naturalistically. A few days later, he ordered them all rubbed out and replaced with some Portuguese soldiers, armed in a very bizarre manner, and life-sized so that one can see them from the whole square. There are three to a side, and above them on the right-hand side is painted Christ Our Lord with a globe of the world in his left hand and giving the blessing with the other.
>
> On the other side there was (a picture of) Our Lady very nicely painted. However, after he saw an Our Lady of Saint Luke that we have in our church, he ordered that the former be rubbed out and the latter painted in its stead, in order that it be naturalistic. To the sides of Christ Our Lord and Our Lady are some saints (depicted) as if in prayer. In the oriel of the varanda, or *janela*, where he sits, his two sons are painted on the sides of the same wall, very richly dressed and life-like, above one of which is Christ Our Lord on a small scale together with a Father with a book in his hand, and above the other is Our Lady. In the same niche of the oriel are Saint Paul, Saint Gregory, Saint Ambrose – because these are so small and behind the oriel, one can barely see them from below, but all the others are visible ... Behind it, in various rooms, he had various pictures of the mysteries of Christ Our Lord and some of the scenes from the Acts of the Apostles painted on the walls

and ceilings, taken from the book of their lives that we gave to him, of Saint Anne, Susanna, and various other histories ... In another wall of a room, he ordered the Pope, the Emperor, King Philip, and the Duke of Savoy to be painted naturalistically, all on their knees adoring the Holy Cross in the middle of them, which conforms to a print which he has of this. The King is very well informed about the uses of these images and with the customs that were told to him concerning all the Mysteries of Our Lord and of Our Lady.

166 According to Sullivan, a print of this description appears at the end of Abraham Ortelius's *Theatrum Orbis Terrarum*, which the Mughals possessed, but I have not been able to find it in any of the sixteenth-century editions of this work (Sullivan, *The Meeting of Eastern and Western Art*, 12.

167 Foster, *Early Travels to India*, 115, 185; Coverte, *A True and Almost Incredible Report*, 40; *Tuzuk-i Jahangiri*, 1:177.

168 'Upon entering the court, one proceeds toward the King through several rooms, small but well executed, gilt, and curiously painted. Among various images one sees there one is of Our Saviour, of the Lady, of the Magdalene, and others of famous world leaders, but not of Muhammad, for whom the King holds no devotion whatever. Between these tiny rooms, and corresponding ones that house the women, of the same size and beauty, there is a grand and beautiful patio ...' (Wessels, *Early Jesuit Travellers in Central Asia*, 284).

169 Pietro della Valle mentioned an image of the Virgin Mary in the Imperial palace at Ahmedabad: 'Some said that a while ago in one of the Balconies stood expos'd to publick view an Image of the Virgin *Mary*, plac'd there by *Sciah Selim* (i.e., Jahangir), who, they say, was devoted to her, and to whom perhaps it was given by one of our Priests, who frequent his Court out of a desire to draw him to the Christian faith; but the Image was not there now, and possibly was taken away by *Sultan Chorrom* his Son, (reported an Enemy of the Christians and their affairs) since his coming to the Government of those parts of *Guzarat*' (Valle, *The Travels of Pietro della Valle in India*, 1:98).

170 Asher, *Architecture of Mughal India*, 111.

171 Both of these pictures are in Shah Jahan's *Padshahnama* and are illustrated in *King of the World: The Padshahnama* (1997), cat. nos. 38, 39. The second one is also illustrated in my *The Jesuits and the Grand Mogul*, fig. 1.

172 They therefore predate Jahangir's extensive renovations in 1612, which included rooms 'adorned (*munaqqash*) and embellished (*musawwar*) with paintings by rare artists [*ustadan-i nadirah-kar*]' (*Tūzuk-i Jahāngīri* 2:183). Finch's description was the basis of a later report by Thomas Herbert (1626), who never actually visited Lahore (Vogel, *Tile-Mosaics of the Lahore Fort*, 50).

173 Koch, 'Jahangir and the Angels,' 177. I agree with Cooper, who has suggested that the painted rooms were probably in a row adjacent to the river (Cooper, 'Sikhs, Saints and Shadows of Angels,' 15).

174 Foster, *Early Travels to India*, 163.

175 'The King ordered them to paint an image of Christ our Saviour on the ceiling of a handsome varanda in his apartments, just as he has ordered to be painted in his principal hall, which had been newly made, an image that Your Reverence gave to me when I departed from India [i.e., Goa]. It appears that in the cartoon prepared for the painting there was a dove over the head of the image of Christ, but the painter, either

because he did not know any better – or out of malice, which is more likely – painted an owl in place of the dove over the head of the image of the Saviour. Whereupon the King became very angry and ordered that the painter be beaten, and that he paint the dove in place of the owl. He stopped short of ordering his execution only because he was convinced that he had done it out of ignorance' (letter of Father Andrade, 1623, BL, Add. MSS 9854, f. 98a).

176 Bodleian Library, Ouseley Add. 173 #13. Attributed to Payag (Pal, *Master Artists in the Imperial Mughal Court*, 5). Apparently, no one has noticed these images, which cannot be made out from any photograph, but which are clearly visible in the original.

177 See Koch, 'Jahangir and the Angels'; Bloom, 'The *Qubbat al-Khadra'* and the Iconography of Height in Early Islamic Architecture.'

178 Cooper has dated them to ca. 1617–20, based primarily on Koch's dating of the Bagh-i Nur Afshan at Agra, but we do not know the date of the construction of that garden, nor of its murals; the sources only tell us that Jahangir rested there twice in March of 1621. The *Tuzuk-i Jahangiri* does not say what parts of the palace were completed, and there are at least two different building campaigns, in 1612 and 1617–20. Asher is more cautious with dating. (*Tuzuk-i Jahangiri*, 2:183; Koch, 'Notes on the Painted and Sculptured Decoration of Nur Jahan's Pavilions at Ram Bagh,' 51; Koch, *Mughal Architecture*, 86; Asher, *Architecture of Mughal India*, 129; Cooper, 'Sikhs, Saints, and Shadows of Angels,' 27). We can only say with assurance that the harem murals were executed before 1620, when the renovations at Lahore Fort were brought to a conclusion.

179 Cooper 'Sikhs, Saints, and Shadows of Angels,' 27. He suggests it is Shah Jahan as a young man of about twenty-five, and uses this to date the paintings. The drawing is very indistinct, and could represent any of the princes. The one on the other side is missing.

180 See, for example, Beach, *Mughal and Rajput Painting*, fig. 73 (Mughal, ca. 1605).

181 *Tuzuk-i Jahangiri*, 1:232. A miniature painting from c. 1617 showing Nur Jahan entertaining Jahangir and his son in her garden has been proposed by Koch as a 'visual paraphrase' of the Bagh-i Nur Afshan pavilion, and includes the familiar Jesus and Mary pair in the frieze above (Das, *Mughal Painting during Jahangir's Time*, 157; Beach, *The Imperial Image*, 206; Koch, 'Notes on the Painted and Sculptured Decoration of Nur Jahan's Pavilions at Ram Bagh,' 60–1) See also my *The Jesuits and the Grand Mogul*, fig. 2.

182 Asher, *Architecture of Mughal India*, 106.

183 Manrique, *Itinerario*, 229–30; BL, Add. MSS 9855 f. 21a; Tavernier, *Travels in India*, 1:91; Manucci, *Storia del Moghol*, 1:137.

184 For example, ARSI, Goa 14, fol. 288a.

185 *Tuzuk-i Jahangiri*, 2:101.

186 Nath, *A History of Mughal Architecture*, 373–80.

187 Nath, *A History of Mughal Architecture*, 388 (I have altered Nath's translation).

188 Manrique, *Itinerario*, 257–8.

189 A sandstone inscription on the great eastern gate notes that the founder was 'Mehr Banu, an old servant of Jahangir Shah's' (*Mehr Bānū qadīmī-yi Jahāngīr Shāh*); although it bears no date, Jahangir wrote in 1619 that it had already been in construction 'for some time past' (*Tūzuk-i Jahāngīri*, 2:111).

190 Nath, *A History of Mughal Architecture*, 196. The caravanserai murals were published

shortly after their discovery by K.A. Thomas, who went so far as to suggest that the building served as a Catholic church (Thomas, 'Christian Paintings on a Mughal Monument,' 30).

191 Thomas, 'Christian Paintings on a Mughal Monument,' 30.

192 Kühnel and Goetz, *Indian Book Painting*, B.35, Vergl. Tafel 41.

193 Cragg, *Jesus and the Muslim*, 26, 43; Parrinder, *Jesus in the Qur'an*, 30–53.

194 'They denied the truth and uttered a monstrous falsehood against Mary. They declared: "We have put to death the Messiah Jesus the son of Mary, the apostle of Allah." They did not kill him, nor did they crucify him, but they thought they did. [Or, literally, he was made to resemble another for them.]' (*The Koran*, trans. N.J. Dawood [1983], 382).

195 Many biblical stories concerning Jesus, Mary, and John found their way into the biographical and historical writings of Ibn Ishaq (d. 768), al-Tabari (d. 923), al-Mas`udi (d. 956), and Ibn al-Athir (1160–1234), including the identification of Jesus' trade as carpentry and his birthplace at Bethlehem, as well as the stories of the manger, the Magi (who were from Persia), Herod's plot to kill the innocents, the Flight into Egypt, and the preaching and murder of John the Baptist. The teachings of Jesus find a more central place and explicit citation in the writings of Abu 'Abdallah Harith al-Muhasibi (ninth century), in his *Kitāb al-Wasāyā* (Book of Commandments), a work which coincided with the first translations of the New Testament into Arabic (Watt, *Muslim-Christian Encounters*, 38–48).

196 The interior of the shrine was decorated throughout, each column bearing portraits (*suwar*) of the Prophets – including a portrait of Ibrahim as an old man divining with arrows, a picture of Jesus, and one of Mary – as well as depictions of angels and trees. Azraqī wrote:

> The day of the conquest of Mekka, the Prophet entered the Ka'ba and sent for al-Fadl ibn 'Abbās – who brought water from Zemzem, and he ordered him to bring a rag soaked in water and efface the pictures (*suwar*) which he did. They say that the Prophet put his two hands on the picture of 'Īsā bin Miryam and His Mother and said: 'Efface all these pictures except these under my hands.' He then raised his hands from above 'Īsā and his Mother. (Creswell, *Early Muslim Architecture*, 1:2–3)

197 This devotion was consciously echoed by later Muslim rulers, including several of the Ottoman emperors who honoured images of the Virgin. See Raby, 'El Gran Turco,' 103.

198 This is an especially prominent theme in the writings of the Koran exegete Al-Zamakhshavi (1075–1144), Al-Baidawi (d. 1286), and Fakhr al-Din al-Razi (1149–1209), where he appears as a kind of sheikh who warns the worldly of the sins of this world (Cragg, *Jesus and the Muslim*, 47; *'Ilm al-Akhlāq*, trans. M.S.H. Ma'sumi (1969]).

199 Especially his Jesus sayings in his famous work *Ihyā' 'Ulūm al-Dīn* (Religion: Its Meanings and Practice Revitalized). Al-Ghazzali mined many sources, including the Gospel of Saint John (Cragg, *Jesus and the Muslim*, 46).

200 Cragg, *Jesus and the Muslim*, 4, 49, 167.

201 Ibid., 60.

202 Parrinder, *Jesus in the Qur'an*, 124.

203 Many scholars have stressed the predominance of the Messianic metaphor in the propaganda of Akbar and Jahangir; Rizvi, for example, shows how Akbar harnessed

Muslim enthusiasm for the thousandth anniversary of the Hijra (1591–2) for his own purposes (Rizvi, *The Wonder That was India*, 2:196). Subrahmanyam pointed out that millenarianist expectations were a universal development in the sixteenth century that affected both Portugal and India (Subrahmanyam, 'Sixteenth-Century Millenarianism from the Tagus to the Ganges').

204 Badaoni, *Muntakhāb ut-Tawārīkh*, 1:369.

205 Monserrate, *The Commentary of Father Monserrate*, 129.

206 Richards, 'The Formulation of Imperial Authority under Akbar and Jahangir,' 265. For a Timurid medallion scroll descending from an image of Alanqoa, see Lentz and Lowry, *Timur and the Princely Vision*, fig. 37.

207 *Akbarnama*, 1:179, 182.

208 Ibn al-'Arabi, *The Bezels of Wisdom*, 176. He also uses an Adam and Eve metaphor: 'As representative of Heaven, as mouthpiece of the divine Word, man is male, while as representative of Earth, man is female, so that just as Earth or the Cosmos came forth from God the Creator, so did Eve, the woman, come forth from Adam' (ibid., 35).

209 Inden, 'Ritual, Authority, and Cyclic Time in Hindu Kingship,' 30.

210 Ibn al-'Arabi, *The Bezels of Wisdom*, 38.

211 More directly pertinent to the Mughal depiction of saints and angels in vertical layers is a prevalent Sufi doctrine that depicted the heavens as consisting of horizontal tiers of these heavenly creatures who transmitted God's light downward to cognizant mortals. Finding its ultimate expression in the twelfth-century Persian metaphysician Shihabuddin Suhrawardi Maqtul (1153–91), the founder of the Eastern or Ishrāqī School of philosophy, this view of the universe was highly influential at the Mughal court under Akbar and Jahangir, although it never enjoyed the unqualified approval of all Sufis or of orthodox Muslims (Richards, 'The Formulation of Imperial Authority under Akbar and Jahangir,' 265–6; Ibn al-'Arabi, *The Bezels of Wisdom*, xiv).

212 Hodgson, *The Venture of Islam*, 1:72.

213 Richards, 'The Formulation of Imperial Authority under Akbar and Jahangir,' 34.

214 Ibid., 267; Rizvi, *The Wonder That Was India*, 195.

215 Richards, 'The Formulation of Imperial Authority under Akbar and Jahangir,' 48; Subrahmanyam, 'Sixteenth-Century Millenarianism from the Tagus to the Ganges,' 8. Shah Isma'il of Persia also created a system of arcane rituals based on Sufi practices and shamanistic ritual which compares with Akbar's synthetic creed.

216 Rizvi and Flynn, *Fathpur-Sikri*, 45.

217 In 1627, Father Joseph de Castro, who replaced Xavier as head of the mission, wrote: 'What makes us sorry is that we have nothing to give in return, owing to the little help we have either from (Portuguese) India or from anyone else ... for more than twelve years now I have not seen anything from anyone, nor the things which Your Reverence says you send; nothing until now has reached us here, except an amber image of our Lady for Mirza [Zū-l Qarnain, an Armenian Catholic courtier]' (Hosten, 'Three Letters of Fr. Joseph de Castro, S.J., and the Last Year of Jahangir,' 156–7).

218 The literature on these paintings includes Ettinghausen, *Paintings of the Sultans and Emperors of India in American Collections*, pls. 11–14; Ettinghausen, 'The Emperor's Choice'; Welch, *Imperial Mughal Painting*, 80–3; Das, *Mughal Painting during Jahangir's Time*, 213–28; Beach, 'The Mughal Painter Abu'l-Hasan and Some English Sources for

His Style'; Beach, *The Imperial Image*, 167–72; Koch, 'The Influence of the Jesuit Mission on Symbolic Representations of the Mughal Emperors'; Skelton, 'Imperial Symbolism in Mughal Painting'; and Okada, *Indian Miniatures of the Mughal Court*, 45–59.

219 Koch, 'The Influence of the Jesuit Mission on Symbolic Representations of the Mughal Emperors,' 19–21. Ettinghausen comments: 'In view of this mentality, it is not surprising that at times the court art of this Emperor should show a reflective and critical point of view; that he should come to see life in depth. Thus, his court painters were the first to cope in Muslim painting with the issue of moral choice and to reveal a deliberate consciousness of time and the limits it sets on mortal man' ('The Emperor's Choice,' 99).

220 The following is taken from Maclagan, *The Jesuits and the Great Mogul*, 99–147; Bailey, The Catholic Shrines of Agra,' 131–9; and Bailey, 'A Portuguese Doctor at the Maharaja of Jaipur's Court.'

221 See my 'A Portuguese Doctor at the Maharaja of Jaipur's Court.'

6: The Jesuit Reductions among the Guaraní in Paraguay, 1609–1768

1 The title is a paraphrase of a reference in a *Real Cédula* of 1648 which describes the success of the new reductions in Paraguay: 'fertilizó la tierra de manera ... que es imitadora aquella nueva planta de la primitiva Yglesia ...' (AGN, IX.6–9–3, f. 486b).

2 Escobar, *Una interpretación*, 1:84.

3 Fraser, *The Architecture of Conquest*.

4 Kubler and Soria, *The Art and Architecture of Spain and Portugal and Their American Dominions*, 83; Bayón and Marx, *History of South American Colonial Art and Architecture*, 55.

5 Escudero de Terán, *América y España en la escultura colonial Quiteña*; Americas Society, *Barroco de la Nueva Granada*.

6 There is a statue by the Spanish master, for example, in the Altar del Cristo de la Contrición in the Jesuit church of San Pedro in Lima.

7 Kubler and Soria, *Art and Architecture in Spain and Portugal and Their American Dominions*, 164.

8 Palmer and Pierce, *Cambios*, 23.

9 On colonial painting in Peru, see Soria, *La Pintura del siglo XVI en Sud America*; Benavente Velarde, *Historia del Arte Cusqueño*; Castedo, *The Cuzco Circle*; Banco de Credito del Perú en la Cultura, *Pintura Virreynal*; Mesa and Gisbert, *Historia de la pintura cuzqueña*; Mujia Pinilla, *Angeles apócrifos en la América virreinal*; Damian, *The Virgin of the Andes*; and Americas Society, *Potosí: Colonial Treasures and the Bolivian City of Silver*.

10 Baglione, *Le vite de' pittori*, 31–2; Mancini, *Considerazioni sulla pittura* 1:222; Bayón and Marx, *History of South American Colonial Architecture*, 105. Leccio was known in Peru as Matteo Pérez de Alesio.

11 The classic study is Adorno, *Cronista y príncipe: La obra de Don Felipe Guaman Poma de Ayala*. For a recent symposium dedicated to Guaman Poma's work, see The Americas Society, *Guaman Poma de Ayala: The Colonial Art of an Andean Author*. See also MacCormack, 'Time, Space, and Ritual Action.'

12 Bayón and Marx, *History of South American Colonial Art and Architecture*, 110–12.

13 See also Bravo, *El Barroco Jesuita Chileño*; Eugenio Pereira Salas, *Historia del arte en el reino de Chile*; González Echenique, *Arte colonial en Chile*; Ferrari Peña, 'La influencia de los jesuitas bávaros en la arquitectura y el arte chilenos del siglo XVIII'; and Buschiazzo, *Estancias jesuíticas de Córdoba*.
14 Susnik, *Los aborigines del Paraguay*, 9ff; Escobar, *Una interpretación de las artes visuales en el Paraguay*, 1:14.
15 Susnik, *Los aborigines del Paraguay*, 18.
16 'The originality of the Tupí-Guaraní religion lies in the fact that it does not unfold within the "element" of theology, or knowledge of the gods' (Clastres, *The Land-Without-Evil*, 22).
17 Melià and Blinder, 'Aquellos Pai-Tavytera que por primera vez dibujaron,' 59.
18 Melià, *El Guaraní*, 32; Clastres, *The Land-Without-Evil*, 74.
19 Clastres, *The Land-Without-Evil*, 74.
20 Hill, 'Foreword,' in Clastres, *The Land-Without-Evil*, x.
21 Susnik, *Los aborigines del Paraguay*, 17; Clastres, *The Land-Without-Evil*, 25–30.
22 Melià, *El Guaraní*, 14; Clastres, *The Land-Without-Evil*, x, 24, 26–7, 57.
23 Susnik, *Los aborigines del Paraguay*, 13.
24 Neolithic art is characterized by a tendency toward synthesis and representation with basic, schematic geometry (Escobar, *Una interpretación*, 14, 20, 104). Escobar's is virtually the only art-historical study of Guaraní art; the rest are anthropological. Escobar's study is also the most sensitive and intelligent study to date of the indigenous impact on the art of the Jesuit reductions in Paraguay.
25 Escobar, *Una interpretación*, 27.
26 Ibid., 21, 36. Unlike other Amerindian peoples of the region, the Guaraní did not tatoo.
27 Escobar, *Una interpretación*, 21; Pallestrini and Perasso, *Jeguakáva*, 28.
28 AGN, IX.6–9–3, f. 452b (1648).
29 Escobar, *Una interpretación*, 56; Gutiérrez, 'The Jesuit Missions,' 2; Necker, *Indios Guaraníes y Chamanes Franciscan*, 34; Carbonell de Masy, *Estrategias de desarrollo rural en los pueblos guaraníes*.
30 Morales, 'New Directions in Research on the Paraguay Reductions, 1610–1767.' The utopian reputation of the reductions dates back to the time of Voltaire. For a discussion of utopian treatments, see my article '*Le Style Jésuite n'existe pas*.' The classic literature includes Cunninghame Graham, *A Vanished Arcadia*. Some of the most glowingly utopian recent literature includes Abou, *La republica jesuítica de los guaraníes y su herencia*; Bulgheroni, *Summa Chaqueña-Argentina*.
31 Gutiérrez, *The Jesuit Guaraní Missions*, 2; Necker, *Indios guaraníes y chamanes franciscanos*, 210–13.
32 Necker, *Indios guaraníes y chamanes franciscanos*, 14–16.
33 Susnik, *Los aborigines del Paraguay*, 124; Escobar, *Una interpretación*, 56–76.
34 AGN, IX.6–9–3, f. 182a (1630).
35 For example: Father Cardiel, in Furlong, *José Cardiel, S.J., y su Carta-Relación*, 125. See also Escobar, *Una interpretación*, 62; Clastres, *The Land-Without-Evil*, 12.
36 Sepp, *Relación de viaje a las misiones jesuíticas*, 121.
37 Mörner, 'The Role of the Jesuits in the Transfer of Secular Baroque Culture to the River Plate Region.'
38 For a review of the literature, see Necker, *Indios guaraníes y chamanes franciscanos*, 12ff.

39 'In the new reduction villages which the Jesuits founded, not all of the reduction Guaraní were always inclined to abandon all of their traditions; they were not prepared for a radical change from their old customs' (Susnik, *Los aborigines del Paraguay*, 129; my translation).
40 Clastres, *The Land-Without-Evil*, 68.
41 The *payé* was not just a magic worker but a visionary. He battled with the Jesuits using spectacle and oratory, elements of central importance both to Guaraní religion and Christianity. The *payé* led the traditional dances of 'psychic exhaltation' and showed off rhetorical skills to outdo the sermons of the missionaries (Susnik, *Los aborigines del Paraguay*, 166–7).
42 Melià, *El Guaraní*, 108; Ruiz de Montoya, *The Spiritual Conquest ... of Paraguay*, 121–2; Clastres, *The Land-Without-Evil*, 30.
43 Sepp, *Continuación de las labores apostólicas*, 270.
44 Necker, *Indios guaraníes y chamanes franciscanos*, 84.
45 Plá, *El barroco hispano guaraní*, 42–4; Susnik, *Los aborigines del Paraguay*, 129.
46 For their syncretic efforts, the Jesuits were vilified by Don Bernardino de Cardenas, the seventeenth-century Franciscan Bishop of Paraguay (Plá, *El barroco hispano Guaraní*, 34; Clastres, *The Land-Without-Evil*, 9–18, 37).
47 The Franciscans were the first to make this choice (Necker, *Indios guaraníes y chamanes franciscanos*, 84).
48 Clastres, *The Land-Without-Evil*, 18.
49 Ibid., 17.
50 Bartolomé, *Chamanismo y religion entre los Ava-Katu-Ete*, 72.
51 Ruiz de Montoya, *The Spiritual Conquest ... of Paraguay*, 74–84.
52 Cadogan, *Ayvu Rapyta*, 99–110; Pallestrini and Perasso, *Jeguakáva*, 40; Melià, *El Guaraní*, 60.
53 Escobar, *Una interpretación*, 82; Clastres, *The Land-Without-Evil*, 3–4.
54 Bartolomé, *Chamanismo y religion*, 70.
55 Susnik, 'El rol de la Iglesia en la educación indígena colonial,' 154; Plá, *El barroco hispano Guaraní*, 149; Susnik, *Los aborigines del Paraguay*, 255; Escobar, *Una interpretación*, 66. Some, with Melià (quoted in Escobar, 66), even propose that since the Guaraní religion is based on words which operate on a formal and expressive level, rather than semantically, that it was naturally very open to Baroque influence and the external elements of Christianity as presented by the Jesuits.
56 Susnik, *Los aborigines del Paraguay*, 123, 167; Melià, *El Guaraní*, 25.
57 Susnik, *Los aborigines del Paraguay*, 166–7; Ruiz de Montoya, *The Spiritual Conquest ... of Paraguay*, 53, 152.
58 Clastres, *The Land-Without-Evil*, 32.
59 Susnik, *Los aborigines del Paraguay*, 168.
60 Ruiz de Montoya, *The Spiritual Conquest ... of Paraguay*, 176.
61 Susnik, *Los aborigines del Paraguay*, 169–71; Ruiz de Montoya, *The Spiritual Conquest ... of Paraguay*, 86, 153, 175.
62 On a number of occasions, Montoya, Mendoza, Cataldino, and Domenec were obliged to destroy these shrines publicly (Susnik, *Los aborigines del Paraguay*, 169–70; Ruiz de Montoya, *The Spiritual Conquest ... of Paraguay*, 86; Clastres, *The Land-Without-Evil*, 14).
63 ARSI, Paraq. 8, f. 360b.

64 Plá, *El barroco hispano Guaraní*, 63.

65 'Whereas the north of the Virreinato lived in a zone profoundly influenced by Hispano-Peruvian art, in the litoral under the shelter of the Jesuit missions in the seventeenth and eighteenth centuries an art developed of deep realist influence' (Ribera and Schenone, *El arte de la imaginería en el Río de la Plata*, 54; my translation). See also Mörner, *La Corona Española y los foráneos en los pueblos de indios de América*.

66 Sepp, *Relación de viaje a las misiones jesuíticas*, 1:123–4.

67 Plá, *El barroco hispano Guaraní*, 66; Plá, 'Rasgos generales de un barroco desconocido,' 309.

68 Xarque, *Insignes misioneros*, 341.

69 Furlong, *Misiones y sus pueblos de Guaraníes*, 526; Plá, *El barroco hispano Guaraní*, 36.

70 Plá, *El barroco hispano Guaraní*, 82. Already in 1633 there were twenty reductions, each with a 'iglesia decente y buena, con provisión de ornamentos y lo necesario al culto divino y administración de sacramentos' (Pastells, *Historia de la Compañía de Jesús en la Provincia del Paraguay*, 490).

71 Furlong, *Misiones y sus pueblos de Guaraníes*, 526.

72 Pastells, *Historia de la Compañía de Jesús en la Provincia del Paraguay*, 34.

73 Sustersic, 'Imaginería,' 169.

74 Vargas Ugarte, *Ensayo de un diccionario de artífices coloniales de la América meridional*, 258; Furlong, *Misiones y sus pueblos de Guaraníes*, 496; Ribera, 'La pintura en las misiones jesuíticas de guaraníes,' 506. On the Jesuit college in Santa Fé, see Furlong, *Historia del Colegio de la Inmaculada.* (Santa Fé, 1962).

75 ARSI, Paraq. 4 I, ff. 67b, 76b, 86a, 97b, 114a, 117b, 122a, 133b, 139a; Paraq. 8, ff. 236a–b; 307b–309; Vargas Ugarte, *Ensayo de un diccionario de artífices coloniales de la América meridional*, 280; Ribera, 'La pintura en las misiones jesuíticas de guaraníes,' 507.

76 ARSI, Paraq. 8 ff. 236a–b; Plá, *El barroco hispano Guaraní*, 66.

77 ARSI, Paraq. 4 I, f. 89b.

78 Ibid., ff. 109b, 114a.

79 Schenone, *Historia general de arte en la Argentina*, 62. Plá suggests that both the Berger and Habiyú pictures are after engravings (Plá, *El barroco hispano Guaraní*, 195).

80 Furlong, *Misiones y sus pueblos de guaraníes*, 496; Plá, *El barroco hispano Guaraní*, 185; Ribera, 'La pintura en las misiones jesuíticas de guaraníes,' 507–13.

81 Sustersic, 'Presencia de una imagen hispano-bizantina en America,' 15.

82 Plá, *El barroco hispano Guaraní*, 195.

83 ARSI, Paraq. 4 I, ff. 142b, 149b, 153a, 160b, 168a, 175b, 193a, 199a, 214a, 221a; Paraq. 4 II, ff. 240b, 249a, 251b, 260b; Paraq. 9, ff. 173a–b; Furlong, *Misiones y sus pueblos de Guaraníes*, 498; Ribera, 'La pintura en las misiones jesuíticas de guaraníes,' 513.

84 ARSI, Paraq. 9, f. 173a: 'Omnesque Reductiones imaginibus referta quas ille mira penicilli elegantia.'

85 ARSI, Paraq. 8, f. 454b.

86 Ibid., f. 456a.

87 ARSI, Paraq. 4 I, ff. 93a, 117a, 133a, 142a, 153a, 159b, 167a, 170a, 192a, 194b; Vargas Ugarte, *Ensayo de un diccionario de artífices coloniales de la América meridional*, 139; Furlong, *Misiones y sus pueblos de Guaraníes*, 530.

88 ARSI, Paraq. 4 I, ff. 97a, 114a, 117a–b, 119a, 133b, 138b, 142a, 145b, 147a, 149a, 152a–b, 153a, 155a–b, 159b, 160b, 167a, 168a, 170b, 175b, 192a, 193a, 195a, 199a.

89 ARSI, Paraq. 4 I, ff. 142a, 147a; Paraq. 9, ff. 174a–b; Ribera, 'La pintura en las misiones jesuíticas de guaraníes,' 515.

90 Plá, *El barroco hispano Guaraní*, 186.

91 '... muy bien adornados con la limpieza y polizia que en todas las partes de España ... tienen los dichos Padres de la Compañía ... tienen muy bien adorno de retablos y ornamentos y en todos las dichas reducciones ay sagrarios y dentro dellos sus custodias de plata ...' (AGN, IX.6–9–3, f. 334a). These comments were made by Father Cristóbal de Asesti, Bishop of Paraguay (1646), during his visit to the five reduction churches of San Ignacio, Encarnación, Natividad, Corpus, and Santa María.

92 '... fertilizó la tierra de manera, que ya se veen dichas poblaciones muy bien fundadas con Yglesias, musica, y todo ornato perteneciente al culto divino ... que es imitadora aquella nueva planta de la primitiva Yglesia ...' (AGN, IX.6–9–3, f. 486b [1648]).

93 For the *real cédula* with this decree (1651), see Pastells, *Historia de la Compañía de Jesús en la Provincia del Paraguay*, 2:264.

94 Furlong, *Misiones y sus pueblos de Guaraníes*, 532; ARSI, Paraq. 4 II, ff. 337b, 338b, 354b, 365b; Paraq. 4 II, ff. 247b, 248b; Paraq. 4 I, ff. 213b, 216a; Sustersic, 'Imaginería,' 165; Ribera, 'La pintura en las misiones jesuíticas de guaraníes,' 515.

95 See Bailey, 'The Jesuits and Painting in Italy,' 112–20.

96 Plá, *El barroco hispano Guaraní*, 265–9.

97 'Procuranse unas Estatuas de S. Xavier y S. Borja para el Altar mayor: porque las que estan aora no son decentes. Lo mismo de las Estatuas de la Capilla de las Animas' (AGN, IX.6–9–5, f. 540a).

98 ARSI, Paraq. 4 II, ff. 419a, 431b, 451a, 462b, 474b, 480b, 482a, 493b; Paraq. 6, ff. 2a, 18b, 45a, 67b, 77b, 87a, 91a, 122a, 119a. This remark by Visitor Roca depicts Brother Brasanelli at work on an altarpiece in Santa Ana in 1724: 'Para el altar mayor se hará otro retablo, que ideará el H(erman)o Joseph Brazaneli, y el que ahora sirve se empleará en otro nicho' (AGN, IX.6–9–6, f. 88).

99 Brasanelli executed a considerable amount of work at Santa Ana. Visitor Roca here describes the brother leading a group of indigenous architects in rebuilding the church dome and nave: 'Emprendasse la obra de la media naranja, y de la prolongación de la Iglesia, con todo lo qual correrá el H(erman)o Joseph Brazaneli cuya dirección se seguirá assi en esto como en el numero de los peones, que an de trabajar' (AGN, IX.6–9–6, f. 161a).

100 Roca describes here Brasanelli's work at the Church of San Ignacio Miní: 'Se haran los lugares en el sitio señalado, y se acontará la pieza que ha de servir de trassacristia; uno, y otro con la dirección del H(erman)o Joseph Brazaneli' (AGN, IX.6–9–6, f. 81a).

101 Furlong, *Misiones y sus pueblos de Guaraníes*, 532; Ribera, 'La pintura en las misiones jesuíticas de guaraníes,' 516–17; Sustersic, 'José Brasanelli,' 268–9.

102 'Empézose la Iglesia; se ha hecho la maior parte de los cimientos, levantándose los pilares del Presbiterio, y labrándose mucha madera, todo con la dirección del H(erman)o Joseph Brasaneli, que tiene la obra a su cargo, y a un tiempo exercita todas sus habilidades, dirigiendo a los estatuarios y a los pintores en la vida de N(uestro) S(an)to P(adr)e (Ignacio) que ha para sacar en quadros para poner por los corredores de N(uest)ra casa; estan ya acabad(os) onze quadros sin otro defecto, que el de colores finos, porque no se hallan' (letter from Ignatio de Astudillo to Luis de la Roca, Itapua, 25 April 1718, AGN, IX.6–9–5, f. 711a).

103 ARSI, Paraq. 4 II, ff. 480b, 481a; Paraq. 6, ff. 1a, 18a, 43b, 67a, 77a, 86a, 90a, 116b, 121a; Furlong, *Misiones y sus pueblos de Guaraníes*, 547.

104 'Suspéndase la obra de la Iglesia hasta consultar al P[adr]e Petragrassa cuyo dictamen se seguirá para el remedio' (AGN, IX.6–9–6, f. 186). He is also mentioned at San Xavier: '... se levantará el Presbiterio segun la angaba para todo lo qual se consultará al P[adr]e Angelo Camilo Petragrassa, o al H[erman]o Brazaneli, o otra Persona inteligente' (AGN, IX.6–9–6, f. 191); and at San Borja: 'Cópanse las gotteras de la Yglesia, y su Portico, y al Corredor della, que cae al patio de nuestra casa desele corrientes, consultando antes al Angelo [Petragrassa]' (AGN, IX.6–9–6, f. 205).

105 AGN, IX.6–9–5, f. 60; ARSI, Paraq. 4 II, ff. 418a, 429b, 450a, 461b, 479a, 481a, 494b; Paraq. 6, ff. 1a, 18a, 44a, 67a, 77a, 87b, 90a, 121a, 118a, 146b, 150a, 156a; Furlong, *Misiones y sus pueblos de Guaraníes*, 525. In San Juan Baptista alone, Sepp trained personally six sculptors and ten painters (Sepp, *Relación de viaje a las misiones jesuíticas*, 2:267).

106 Sepp, *Jardín de flores Paracuaria*, 180.

107 Sustersic, 'José Brasanelli,' 269 (see also 275ff); Sustersic, 'Imaginería,' 172; Sustersic, 'Antigua devoción,' 51–62. Sustersic has convincingly attributed a *cristo yacente* from Corrientes Cathedral to Brasanelli, but there are no written documents to confirm this attribution.

108 This term was used by the author of the suppression document written in 1767 to describe a statue of the titular saint at the mission of San Luis Gonzaga: 'el Santo Patron que está a la Italiana con Roquete y Santo Christo en las manos con dos Angeles a dos lados el uno con el escudo de su cassa y el otro floreciéndole la flor de Lis y regulas' (AGN, IX.22–6–3, no. 3, f. 2b).

109 ARSI, Paraq. 6, ff. 90a, 91a, 82a, 83b, 112b, 114a, 121a, 122a, 139b, 148b, 151a, 172a, 173a, 177b, 186a, 213a, 214b, 218b, 221a, 245a, 252a, 258a. Bianchi, who was the better theorist, did not do any work on the reductions, focusing instead on colonial centres such as Buenos Aires (Furlong, *Misiones y sus pueblos de Guaraníes*, 551). Primoli is mentioned as being in San Miguel in 1735 (AGN, Bib. Nac. 69, ff. 40a, 81a, 86b). In a 1742 catalogue of the Society in Paraguay, he is listed as 'Architectus' (AGN, IX.6–9–7, f. 702).

110 ARSI, Paraq. 6, ff. 214, 219b, 252a, 262a, 287a, 300b, 344a, 359a; AGN, IX.6–10–1, f. 244; IX.22–6–3, no. 13, ff. 1a–1b; Maeder and Guttiérrez, 'La imaginería jesuítica en las misiones del Paraguay,' 93; Ribera, 'La pintura en las misiones jesuíticas de guaraníes,' 518–19. Apparently these were not the full extent of his talents. The catalogue for 1742 lists Grimau as living in San Miguel and serving as a grammatician (dat opera in grammatica) (AGN, IX.6–9–7, f. 702).

111 The Salta virgin is itself a copy of one in Córdoba (Plá, *El barroco hispano Guaraní*, 186). For an illustration of this painting, see Schenone, *Historia general de arte en la Argentina*, 59.

112 Brother Antonio Forcada came to the missions in 1759 (Furlong, *Misiones y sus pueblos de Guaraníes*, 558, 561).

113 ARSI, Paraq. 6, ff. 177b, 215a, 225b, 252b, 263b, 286b, 300b, 345a, 359a. Conde is listed as a 'pintor y bordador' (Ribera, 'La pintura en las misiones jesuíticas de Guaraníes,' 517). On Negle, see Ribera, 'La pintura en las misiones jesuíticas de Guaraníes,' 517–18; and Schenone, *Historia general de arte en la Argentina*, 59.

114 'He visto algunas obras mechanicas hechas por los Indios (con la industria y cuydado

de los P[adres]) que merecian toda estimación, si uvieran tenido maestros, que los enseñassen, y no aviendo quien les vaya delante, es cosa digna de toda alabanza, y admiración. Deseo se fomenten, y adelanten los que señalan en estas obras, porque no se malogren estas habilidades, y aprenden otros; pues por ahora no ay otro modo de lograr estos oficios, y assegurarlos en los Pueblos' (AGN, IX.6–10–1, f. 540).

115 Sepp, *Relación de viaje a las misiones jesuíticas*, 1:210, 215; Hernández, *Organización social de las doctrinas guaraníes de la Compañía de Jesús*, 298.

116 Maeder, *Misiones del Paraguay*, 39, 40; see also Plá, 'Los talleres misioneros.'

117 'Ay carpinteros de obra gruesa, ensambladores, que hazen retablos, y los entallan curiosos. Otros esculptores, que forman estatuas sagradas de todas suertes para las Iglesias, y Altares. Labran tambien de hierro todo lo necessario para los Edificios, y las herramientas que sirven para cada officio. Funden campanas, y otras cosas de menor porte; hazen organos, clarines, chirimias, y todo genero de instrumentos musicos. Pintan Imagenes, y Misterios Sagrados, con que adornan sus Templos; saben dorar, y estofar sus Retablos, y Altares' (Xarque, *Insignes misioneros*, 306).

118 Plá, 'The Missionary Workshops,' 2.

119 Sepp, *Continvación de las labores apostólicas*, 2:271; Ribera, 'La pintura en las misiones jesuíticas de Guaraníes,' 513; AGN, IX.11–8–7. The name Tilcara is not a Guaraní one, according to Plá (Plá, *El barroco hispano Guaraní*, 172).

120 AGN, IX.17–4–2.

121 Plá, *El barroco hispano Guaraní*, 82. Some missions were more renowned than others for particular media: San Nicolás, for example, was praised by Sepp as being the best place for statues, and he went there to buy some for his new mission at San Juan Bautista (Sepp, *Continuación de las labores apostólicas*, 2:257).

122 AGN, IX.22–6–3, no. 9, ff. 6a–7a; (San Lorenzo) IX.22–6–3, no. 16, ff. 7b–8a; (Mártires) IX.22–6–3, no. 4, f. 12b; (San Joseph) IX.22–6–3, no. 28, f. 18b.

123 The artists' materials listed in suppression inventories include stones for grinding colours, and a variety of powdered colours such as yellow (*amarillo*), verdigris (*cardenillo*), cochineal (*grana*), carmine (*carmin*), vermilion (*vermellon*), blue colour (*color azul*), light blue (*celeste*), crude varnish (*esmaltes bruto*), and lead white (*albayalde*) (AGN, IX.22–6–3, no. 8, ff. 24a–b [Trinidad]; IX.22–6–3, no. 13, f. 17b [Candelaría]; IX.22–6–3, no. 1, ff. 11a–b [San Juan Baptista]; IX.22–6–3, no. 29, f. 24a [Apóstoles]; IX.22–6–3, f. 33a [San Nicolás]). See also Ribera, 'La pintura en las misiones jesuíticas de Guaraníes,' 519–20.

124 '... embiense à los Pueblos donde hai buenos Pintores, Herreros, algunos muchachos habiles, y de buen natural para que aprendan à pintar y de herrería' (AGN, IX.6–9–5, 931, f. 1a).

125 'Si se necessitaré de algun Indio ni intelligente en la materia, se pidirá de otro Pueblo.' (AGN, IX.6–9–5, 923, f. 2a).

126 AGN, IX.6–9–5, 529, f. 1b.

127 AGN, Bib. Nac. 69, f. 39b.

128 Ribera, 'La pintura en las misiones jesuíticas de Guaraníes,' 523; Maeder, *Misiones del Paraguay*, 40.

129 In 1687, for example, the Cathedral of Asunción ordered a retable from Santa María de Fé (Sustersic, 'Imaginería,' 170). New Jesuit missions also ordered retables and statuary from older missions; for example, when Sepp founded San Juan Baptista (see

above) and when new missions were founded in the Pampas in the eighteenth century: 'The Jesuit workshops were able to satisfy to a great extent the religious art needs of this part of the continent' (Ribera and Schenone, *El arte de la imaginería en el Río de la Plata*, 75–6, 79).

130 AGN, IX.17–6–4; IX.17–6–2; Ribera, 'La pintura en las misiones jesuíticas de Guaraníes, 524, 526–7. Documents from the later 1770s show that large quantities of retables and paintings were made and sold, and that paint supplies were still being purchased. In the 1780s, some of the villages no longer had any *maestros* to teach painting or other arts, and local boys were sent to apprentice with artists and craftsmen in Buenos Aires. This was true of Yapeyú, for example, a town which sent several boys to the capital to learn a variety of trades, including painting, building, silver-smithery, and carpentry.

131 See *El espejo salvaje* (1992).

132 Sepp, however, did not have such a high opinion of the engravings that he had available to him at San Juan Baptista: ' ... an amateur like Bauttas (Bouttats), Tu Merlen or Cols would be here considered equal to a Gallisch (Galle? Gallis?), a Wurx (Wierix ?) or other *maestro* of this caliber' (Sepp, *Relación de viaje a las misiones jesuíticas*, 1:165; my translation).

133 Sepp, *Relación de viaje a las misiones jesuíticas*, 1:145; 2:131–2, 256. Sepp brought the image of Our Lady of Altötting to South America in 1693. A popular German pilgrimage icon, Our Lady of Altötting also became an important reduction image, thanks to the tireless efforts of Sepp, and was reported to have caused several miracles (*Continuación de las labors apostólicas*, 123–5, 127–8, 131–2).

In a letter of 1743, Francisco Bautista, S.J. (b. 1696), Consultor of the College of Asuncion, described to Joseph Martin, S.J. (b. 1698), at the mission of San Miguel, an engraving he had copied by a local (probably Guaraní) painter of a portrait of the martyr Julian Lizardi in which the artist added new additions appropriate for an Amerindian setting: 'flechando, hize pintar à sus lados 6 indios flechandole, y sobre su cabeza, dos Angeles con la guirnalda en una mano, y en la otra una palma, y flechas, y este epigrafe en medio: *Veni coronaberis*.' Bautista asked Martin whether he wanted to order a copy 'en dos, o 3 medio pliegos de papel ordinario, come el de esta carta, o semehante, &c.' (AGN, IX.6–9–7, f. 792). According to Xarque, the college at Asunción regularly sent prints, medallions, and rosaries to the various missions in the Paraguayan outback (Xarque, *Insignes misioneros*, 193).

134 The pantograph, a mechanical device for tracing designs, was promoted by the German Jesuit astronomer Christoph Scheiner (1573–1650) in his *Pantographice* (Rome, 1631).

135 Such models were used by other South American artists in the period; for example, the Brazilian sculptor Aleijadinho (1738–1814) (Plá, *El barroco hispano Guaraní*, 86).

136 He also brought some 'pequeños regalos' of the type used for catechisms, and a few small ceramic statues of the Virgin Mary made in Seville (Sepp, *Relación de viaje a las misiones jesuíticas*, 1:139, 143).

137 AGN, IX.6–9–3, ff. 73a, 300a.

138 Plá, *El barroco hispano Guaraní*, 185.

139 When, at the height of his exodus, Ruiz de Montoya was leading his flock around the falls at Iguazú, he sent a delegation off to Itatín with the bells, pictures, and other

heavy objects from the mission (Ruiz de Montoya, *The Spiritual Conquest ... of Paraguay*, 93–8, 106, 108, 120, 161).

140 The sources do not indicate whether these went to the reductions or stayed in Asunción (AGN, IX.6–9–3, ff. 169a, 310a). Other relics were more specifically Jesuit: Fernando de Valdez, the Provincial of Toledo, sent a book of letters by Ignatius of Loyola to Diego de Boroa, the Provincial of Paraguay, in 1639 (IX.6–9–3, f. 304a). For a large collection of reliquaries from the period in the Jesuit house in Lisbon, see the recent exhibition catalogue *Esplendor e Devoção: Os relicários de S. Roque* (1998).

141 AGN, IX.6–9–3, f. 412a; José Torre Revello, 'Un envio de imágenes con destino a las misiones jesuíticas,' 29–30.

142 AGN, IX.6–9–6, f. 360a. The painting is described as a: 'pintura de Roma, de quando la Virgen le dichava los exercicios' (IX.6–9–7, f. 206).

143 AGN, IX.6–9–7, no folio number, f. 510. On the picture of Our Lady of Peace: 'una N. Sra de la Paz, embuelta en una havana con dos, u, tres Estampas de papel' (IX.6–9–7, ff. 1158 ff; IX.6–10–6, no folio numbers).

144 AGN, IX.22–6–3, no. 8 (Trinidad), f. 5b; no. 28 (San Joseph), f. 4a; no. 17 (Itapuá), ff. 4b, 5b; no. 2 (San Carlos), f. 3b; no. 7 (Santa María la Mayor) f. 6a; no. 21 (Corpus), ff. 2a, 3a, 3b; no. 22 (Santa Rosa), f. 36a; no. 20 (Santa Ana), ff. 2a, 3a; no. 6 (Santiago), f. 12b; no. 9 (la Cruz), f. 2a; IX.22–6–4, no. 20 (Santo Angel), f. 8b.

145 Pastells, *Historia de la Compañía de Jesús en la provincia del Paraguay*, 127; Furlong, *Misiones y sus pueblos de Guaraníes*, 530.

146 Ribera, 'La pintura en las misiones jesuíticas de Guaraníes,' 506.

147 AGN, IX.22–6–3, no. 27 (Yapeyú), ff. 13a–13b; no. 15 (San Nicolás), f. 27b; no. 17 (Itapuá), ff. 10b–16a; no. 24 (San Ignacio Miní), f. 22a; no. 21 (Corpus), f. 8b; no. 27 (Yapeyú), ff. 13a–12b; no. 18 (Yapeyú), f. 17a; no. 29 (Apóstoles), f. 14a.

148 Plá, *El barroco hispano Guaraní*; McNaspy and Blanch, *The Lost Cities of Paraguay*, 134–57; Abramo, 'Barroco misionero.'

149 Scholars have repeatedly made this observation. See, for example, Sustersic, 'Imaginería y patrimonio mueble,' 158; and Sustersic, 'La escultura en el Río de la Plata durante el periodo colonial,' 274. For recent publications with photographs of the mission art of the Franciscan missions in Paraguay and the Chiquitos missions in Bolivia, see *El espejo salvaje* (1992); and Querejazu, ed., *Las misiones jesuíticas de Chiquitos*.

150 Plá, 'The Mission Workshops,' 25.

151 Escobar, *Una interpretación*, 250 (my translation).

152 Typically, scholars have labelled as European the sculptures that fall more clearly within European canons. See, for example, Sustersic, 'Una antigua devoción misionera,' 53.

153 According to one survey undertaken in 1970 (Maeder and Gutiérrez, 'La Imaginería jesuítica en las misiones del Paraguay').

154 Sustersic, 'Imaginería,' 162.

155 'Primary geometrical forms are the basis of their visual and psychic world; the surfaces are the sensory epidermis which expresses with its planimetric writing the deeper forms within' (Sustersic, 'Imaginería,' 161; my translation).

156 Escudero de Terán, *América y España en la escultura colonial Quiteña*, pl. 52.

157 Commenting on the proliferation of images of the Resurrected Christ, Sustersic considers that this triumphal aspect separates Guaraní reduction art from Spanish sculp-

ture or European sculpture, in general, although to my mind there are few art forms as insistently triumphalist as Italian Baroque sculpture (Sustersic, 'Antigua devoción,' 59).

158 The hollowed-out backs served to prevent cracking (a technique used all over the world, for example, in Nara Period Japanese Buddhist sculpture), and also helped make the statues lighter so that they could more easily be lifted onto high retables. See Plá, *El barroco hispano Guaraní*, 150. The myth that the Jesuits would get inside the statues and move their arms to make them look alive is in the same tradition as the tales of Jesuit mines and hidden treasures which proliferated in such places as eighteenth-century France.

159 Sustersic, 'Imaginería,' 158–60.

160 Xarque, *Insignes misioneros de la Compañía de Jesús en la Provincia del Paraguay*, 344.

161 Plá, *El barroco hispano Guaraní*, 181.

162 Ribera and Schenone, *El arte de la imaginería en el Río de la Plata*, 61–2; Maeder and Gutiérrez, 'La imaginería jesuítica en las misiones del Paraguay,' 97.

163 Maeder and Gutiérrez, 'La imaginería jesuítica en las misiones del Paraguay,' 97–8.

164 AGN, IX.22–6–3; IX.22–6–4.

165 In order of frequency, they are: Saint Joseph (43); Saint Francis Xavier (28); Saint Ignatius of Loyola (28), including the Vision of Ignatius (1); Saint Barbara (19); Saint Isidore (17); Saint Anthony of Padua (15); Saint John the Evangelist (15); Saint Aloysius Gonzaga (15); Saint Stanislas Kostka (14); Saint John the Baptist (13) (although it is not always clear which John is meant); Saint John Nepomuk (11); Saint Rock (11); and Saint Francis Borgia (10).

166 Melia, *El Guaraní: Experiencia religiosa*, 60.

167 In order of frequency: Saint Peter (8); Saint Anne (7); Saint Joachim (7); Saint Agustine (6); Martyrs of Japan set (6); Saint Paul (6); Saint Francis Regis (6); Saint Thomas (6); Wise Men set (6); Saint Ambrose (5); Saint James Matamoros (5); Saint Rose of Lima (4); Trinity set, one with a crowned Virgin Mary (4); Saint Gregory (3); Saint Leon (3); Saint Nicholas (3).

The rarest subjects are the complete set of Apostles (2); the complete set of Evangelists (2); Saint Francis of Assisi (2); God the Father (2); Saint Elizabeth (2); Saint Mary Magdalene (2); Saint Peter of Alcantara (2); Saint Sebastian (2); Saint Simeon (2); Saint Andrew (1); Saint Charles (1); Saint Catherine of Alexandria (1); Saint Cecilia (1); King David (1); San Diego de Alcalá (1); Saint Eustache (1); Saint Francis Solano (1); Saint Julian (1); Livorio (1); Saint Laurence (1); Saint Martin (1); Saint Monica (1); Saint Sebastian (1); Saint Stephen (1); Saint Theresa (1); Saint Ursula (1); a Virgin Saint (1); Saint Zachary (1).

168 For more on the Jesuits and the cult of Saint Joseph, see the catalogue *Patron Saint of the New World: Spanish American Colonial Images of Saint Joseph* (1992).

169 The Christ statues total 223, of which: the infant Jesus (41); Crucifixion (35); Resurrection (15); Christ of the Column (15); Carrying the Cross (9); Ecce Homo (8); Sepulcher (8); Ascension (7); Nazarene (6); on the Mount of Olives (3); Good Shepherd (2); Christ as a Youth (1); Circumcision (1); Good Counsel (1); and The Veronica (1).

Statues of the Virgin total 109, of which: Virgin of Sorrows (14); Immaculate Conception (9); Virgen del Rosario (8); Nuestra Señora del Purificación (3); Virgin and Child

(3); Nuestra Señora de Belén (1); Nuestra Señora de Candelaría (1); Virgen de Loreto (2); Nuestra Señora del Pilar (2); Nuestra Señora de Mbororé (1); and Nuestra Señora de Soledad (1).

Angel statues total 81, of which: Michael (33); Raphael (5); Gabriel (1); and Guardian (1).

170 Plá, *El barroco hispano Guaraní*, 107.

171 Gutiérrez, 'The Jesuit Missions,' 9–10; Maeder, *Misiones del Paraguay*, 43; Maeder, 'Historia de las misiones jesuíticas'; Norberto Levinton, personal communication. See also Levinton, 'Recursos de información para la restauración de las obras de arquitectura de las misiones jesuíticas.' Contemporary reports show that building projects involved a 'great number' of indigenous people (Visitor Ignatio de Arteaga, 1725, at San Miguel AGN, IX.6–9–6, f. 201).

172 Plá, *El barroco hispano Guaraní*, 109.

173 An order survives by Visitor Luis de la Roca, S.J., to build two chapels in the corners of the plaza for the dead at Itapuá in 1714 (AGN, IX.6–9–5, f. 534).

174 The same Visitor, Roca, ordered that 'la Capilla, o hermita que esta en el campo' at San Carlos mission be completed (1714) (AGN, IX.6–9–5, f. 526).

175 Visitor Roca ordered one built for the mission of San Nicolás in 1714, and at Santa María la Mayor in 1725, when he wrote: 'Hágase una Capilla en el cementerio para cantar en ella las missas a constumbradas por los difuntos' (AGN, IX.6–9–5, no. 518, f. 1b; IX.6–9–6, no. 190). Anton Sepp mentions building an octagonal cemetery chapel (a copy of one at Altötting) at S. Juan Bautista (Sepp, *Continuación de las labores apostólicas*, 256). I would like to thank Norberto Levinton for bringing this to my attention.

176 These phases were first set out by Buschiazzo (Kubler and Soria, *Art and Architecture in Spain and Portugal and Their American Dominions*, 100). See also Furlong, 'La arquitectura en las misiones jesuíticas'; Furlong, *Arquitectos argentinos durante la dominación hispanica*; Busaniche, *La arquitectura en las misiones jesuíticas guaraníes*; Buschiazzo, 'La arquitectura en madera de las misiones del Paraguay'; and Bruxel, *Los treinta pueblos guaraníes*.

177 Norberto Levinton has recently spoken about the latter ('Pervivencias mudéjares').

178 Gutiérrez, *Evolución urbanística y arquitectónica del Paraguay 1537–1911*; *The Jesuit Guaraní Missions*; 'The Jesuit Missions: City Planning, Architecture and Art'; 'La planificación alternativa en la Colonia.' An early work on reduction urbanism is Ruiz Moreno, 'El urbanismo en las misiones jesuíticas.'

179 'Raros son los colores que llegan alli finos, y sin adulterar; por lo qual son muertas las pinturas, ò presto pierdan su viveza' (Xarque, *Insignes misioneros*, 306).

180 'Un quadro grande de los Desposorios de N(uestra) S(eño)ra, sin marco; otro quadro mediano de N(uestra) S(eño)ra, de la Annunciación, sin marco ... un quadro grande de N(uestro) P(adr)e San Ignacio, de: *Ego vobis Roma Dra*. sin marco; un quadro mediano de la Concepción de N. Sra., con su marco dorado, y pintado; otro quadro mediano de San Joseph, con su marco dorado, y pintado; un quadro pequeño de la Virgen del Carmen, con su marco pintado; otro quadro pequeño de San Ant(oni)o de Padua, con su marco pintado; un quadro pequeño de N(uestro) P(adr)e San Ignacio, con su christal, nicho, y cortinas; ... un San Juan de Dios, dorado y pintado' (AGN, IX.6–9–7, 206).

181 Ribera, 'La Pintura en las misiones jesuíticas de guaraníes,' 532. See also the document cited in the previous note.

182 'Si faltaré algo para el sepulcro del Señor y para los otros passos, que se usan, lo podran hacer los carpinteros, y estatuarios, que ay en el pueblo' (AGN, IX.6–10–1, f. 73b).
183 Pastells, *Historia de la Compañía de Jesús en la Provincia del Paraguay* 1:154.
184 ARSI, Paraq. 8, f. 384a. A slightly different version, in Spanish instead of Latin, is published in Pastells, *Historia de la Compañía de Jesús en la provincia del Paraguay*, 2:322ff, which refers to them as paintings.
185 Pastells, *Historia de la Compañía de Jesús en la provincia del Paraguay*, 2:322ff.
186 Xarque, *Insignes misioneros*, 350.
187 'Ay ... el sepulcro de N(uest)ro Señor Jesu-Christo, que se usa en la processíon de el Viernes Santo; Ay tambien un santo christo grande que se usa el Juebes Santo, en la procession, y en tiempo de cuaresma, los miercoles, y viernes en la Igl(esi)a para el exemplo, Miserere, y disciplinas. Hay en otro Lugar otras cinco estatuas de santos ... Ay varios estatuas de la Pasión de N(uest)ro Señor Jesu-Christo para las processiones de Juebes, y Viernes santo ... ay la estatua de N(uestr)a S(eñor)a de San J(ose)ph y de los tres reyes y todas las demas que se suelen usar en tal dia [Christmas]' (AGN, IX.22–6–3, no. 17, f. 6a). Other references to statues used for Holy Week include a Crucifixion at Trinidad, three large Christs at San Nicolás, and unidentified statues at Xavier (AGN, IX.22–6–3, no. 8, f. 7b; IX.22–6–3, no. 26, f. 20a; IX.22–6–3, no. 15, f. 18b).
188 Sustersic, 'Imaginería,' fig. 118.
189 Furlong, *Misiones y sus pueblos de guaraníes*, 566.
190 Sepp, *Relación de viaje a las misiones jesuíticas*, 1:121, 188; Plá, *El barroco hispano Guaraní*, 162. The same was true in Japan, where acolytes prepared handwritten tracts before the arrival of the first printing press in the 1580s (see chapter 3).
191 On the press, see Furlong, *Historia y bibliografia de las primeras imprentas rioplatenses 1700–1850*.
192 No two books exist with the same date that were printed in different places. Ignacio de Arteaga wrote about the press in June of 1727 making it clear that there was only one: 'mantengase aqui la imprenta cuidando de ella para lo que se ofreciere adelante' (AGN, IX.6–9–6, f. 349).
193 Furlong, *Misiones y sus pueblos de Guaraníes*, 589.
194 Plá, *El barroco hispano Guaraní*, 161.
195 Furlong, *Misiones y sus pueblos de Guaraníes*, 512; Susana Fabrici, 'Un antiguo libro en Guaraní.'
196 For example, plates 74 and 75 from Nadal.
197 *Summa Artis* 31:317. None of the forty-three images is entirely original, despite many scholars' comments to the contrary. Furlong, for example, writes that 'at least a third' of the images are pure creations of the indigenous artists (Furlong, *Misiones y sus pueblos de Guaraníes*, 587), and Ribera considers many of them to be 'absolutely creations of the indigenous illustrators' (Ribera, 'La pintura en las misiones jesuíticas de Guaraníes,' 503).
198 *El grabado en la ciudad de Puebla de los Angeles* (1933), 686, fig. 53.
199 Furlong, *Historia y bibliografia de las primeras imprentas rioplatenses 1700–1850*, 38.
200 Furlong notes perceptively: 'It is an error to consider the works with the finest features and highest merit to be of European provenance and to consider those which are most primitive and crude to be of indigenous manufacture. All of these statues, as one can

conclude from the material used, are of American origin' (Furlong, *Misiones y sus pueblos de Guaraníes*, 494; my translation). This still leaves open the question of who made them, however, and Furlong uses the very same criteria himself to attribute the more 'correct' statues to the Jesuits.

201 See, for example, Plá, *El barroco hispano Guaraní*, 123, 198ff, 207.

202 See, for example, Gutiérrez, 'The Jesuit Missions'; and Furlong, *Misiones y sus pueblos de Guaraníes*. For a criticism of this view, see Escobar, *Una interpretación*, 222–4.

203 Plá, *El barroco hispano Guaraní*, 124; Escobar, *Una interpretación*, 70; Sustersic, 'José Brasanelli,' 267.

204 Escobar, *Una interpretación*, 155, 158.

205 Sustersic's categorization is divided into four basic periods: 1610–50, 1650–1700, 1700–30, and 1730–68. My dates will differ slightly from his, but are based on the same general guidelines (Sustersic, 'Imaginería,' 164ff; Sustersic, 'Antigua devoción,' 54).

206 Compare, for example, a statue of the Virgin Mary and a fully clothed Christ the Redeemer from Santa María, with their thick drapery and close, regular vertical folds, to contemporary versions from Quito (Escudero de Terán, *América y España en la escultura colonial Quiteña*, pls. 5, 6, 16, 26).

207 Sustersic, 'Imaginería,' 158.

208 Zweite, *Martin de Vos als Maler*, fig. 218.

209 Ibid., fig. 217.

210 These also relate closely to Quiteño examples datable to the seventeenth century (Escudero de Terán, *América y España en la escultura colonial Quiteña*, 59). Typical is the double skirt tucked in between the legs, the raised small wings, and the bent head. Details of the costume also relate to Cuzqueño painted angels from the same period (e.g., Gutiérrez, *Pintura, escultura, y artes útiles*, 57).

211 Mauquoy-Hendrik, *Les Estampes des Wierix*, vol. 2, cat. nos. 1260–2.

212 Sustersic, 'Imaginería,' 170.

213 See Bailey, 'The Jesuits and Painting in Italy,' 112–20.

214 Vetter, *Die Kupferstiche zur Psalmodia Eucharistica des Melchior Prieto von 1622*, fig. 43.

215 For a discussion of the development of the imagery of Jesuit saints, see my 'The Jesuits and Painting in Italy.' See also ARSI, FG 545, 2v; Lucas, *Saint, Site, and Sacred Strategy*, 225; Angeli, *Sant'Ignazio di Loyola nella vita e nell'arte*; Held, 'Rubens and the *Vita Beati Ignatii Loiolae* of 1609'; König-Nordhoff, *Ignatius von Loyola*; Papi, 'Le tele della cappellina di Odoardo Farnese della Casa Professa dei gesuiti a Roma'; 71–80; Simson, *Peter Paul Rubens*; and Baumstark, *Rom in Bayern*, cat. nos. 34, 35.

216 Mauquoy-Hendrik, *Les estampes des Wierix*, vol. 2, cat. nos. 142, 1049.

217 Vetter, *Die Kupferstiche zur Psalmodia Eucharistica des Melchior Prieto von 1622*, fig. 30.

218 This was first noted by Sustersic in 'Imaginería,' 169. Others include a plaque in the museum of Luján, which is taken from an image in the Guaraní version of Juan Eusebio Nieremberg's *De la diferencia entre lo temporal y lo espiritual* (1705).

219 Rios, *Repertorio de grabados españoles en la Biblioteca Nacional*, cat. no. 1545.

220 Compare, for example, the statue of Saint Michael from Santa María Museum with Wierix's version of Vos's angel (Mauquoy-Hendrik, *Les estampes des Wierix*, vol. 2, cat. nos. 1260, 1262). Sustersic attributes this angel directly to Brasanelli (Sustersic, 'José Brasanelli,' 276).

221 The devil in the Saint Michael from Santa María is taken from the depiction of Jeremiah 3:16 from that book.

222 As indicated by Sustersic in 'La fachada de San Ignacio Miní entre hallazgos y nuevos enigmas.' For the classic study on San Ignacio Miní, see Nadal Mora, *San Ignacio Miní.*

223 Today his works are divided between the museums at Trinidad and Santiago in Paraguay, and La Plata and Luján in Argentina.

224 Kelemen, *Baroque and Rococo in Latin America*, pl. 139c. This image was frequently copied in Ecuador, Peru, and New Spain, as well. There is also a 1761 version of the same frontispiece (ibid., pl. 191[i]), but the sculpture group is much closer to the earlier version. Sustersic dates the Santiago sculptural group to before 1700, and Plá proposes that it is by the same hand as the Christmas group at Santa María (Sustersic, 'Imaginería,' 170; Plá, *El barroco hispano Guaraní*, 214).

225 Hollstein, *Dutch and Flemish Etchings, Engravings and Woodcuts*, vol. 22, cat. no. 261. For the La Plata collections, see Barrio, 'Las colecciones de las Misiones Jesuíticas del Paraguay existentes en el Museo de La Plata,' *Revista del Museo de La Plata.*

226 Hollstein, *Dutch and Flemish Etchings, Engravings and Woodcuts*, vol. 22, cat. no. 159.

227 Sepp, *Relación de viaje a las misiones jesuíticas*, 1:215. See also Xarque, *Insignes misioneros*, 306; Escobar, *Una interpretación*, 159, 221; Sustersic, 'Imaginería,' 160; and Plá, 'Rasgos generales de un barroco desconocido,' 309.

228 Many believe that reduction art represented a complete break with pre-contact Guaraní culture and that the Jesuits actively prevented acculturation: 'The old forms and symbols of the Indian were not admitted into the institutions of the new colonial order ... the Jesuits never tried to promote a genuinely missionary art and were opposed to the possibility of the indigenous people developing any creative impulse' (Escobar, *Una interpretación*, 55, 245). This is a surprising remark coming from Escobar, who, in fact, has made the most sensitive assessment to date of the indigenous content in reduction art. For similar comments, see Plá, *El barroco hispano Guaraní*, 109; and Schenone, *Historia general de arte en la Argentina*, 13.

229 One of the greatest contributions Ticio Escobar made to the field was to consider all Guaraní art – Christian and non-Christian – as reflecting aspects of a single cultural group, which he does in his 1980 book.

230 Escobar, *Una interpretación*, 81–127. One of the most telling reactions of these tribes to European art was their consistent disinclination toward figural imagery, despite its availability in such large amounts.

231 The human body was considered merely a bearer of patterns, whether through body-painting or featherwork. Corporal ornament was perceived as the sole feature separating humans from animals. When a missionary in the eighteenth century asked a Caduveo (Mbyá) from the Chaco why he wore paint on his body, he said: 'What about you? Why do you not paint yourself? Do you want to look like the animals?' (Escobar, *Una interpretación*, 36–9). The notion of human figures as bearers of ornament may carry over into reduction sculpture.

232 Escobar, *Una interpretación*, 88–9.

233 There seems to be some disagreement about these objects' provenance. Escobar states that these pipes were made by the Payaguá people, also of Paraguay (Escobar, *Una interpretación*, 2:94); however, the catalogue *Un camino hacia la Arcadia* (pp. 28–9) and the Museo de América, which owns them, call them Tupí-Guaraní.

234 Escobar, *Una interpretación*, 85, 110–12. Escobar comments elsewhere: 'A culture capable of confronting and expressing new situations from within, and of absorbing other symbols while remaining faithful to its own interpretation, has more chance of becoming revitalized and renewing its traditions' (Escobar, *Una interpretación*, 122; my translation).

235 Escobar, *Una interpretación*, 2:85–7.

236 Damian, *The Virgin of the Andes*, 10.

237 I originally coined the term 'floreation' to refer to the transformation of various kinds of Chinese ornament into floral and plant ornament by Persian potters in the fifteenth and sixteenth centuries (Bailey, 'The Dynamics of Chinoiserie in Timurid and Early Safavid Ceramics'; and Bailey, Golombek, and Mason, *Tamerlane's Tableware*, 57ff). Floral motifs (*poty* in Guaraní) appear at all three levels of colonial period Guaraní art (non-Christian, those who lived in colonial towns, and reduction Guaraní), and are very prevalent (Escobar, *Una interpretación*, 30–5; 76). The non-Christian Guaraní would add *poty* decoration to everyday objects to increase their ritual significance, often transforming them into a shamanic item.

238 Maeder, *Misiones del Paraguay*, 37.

239 These imaginary animals include a dog-fish (*pez perro*) type, which she relates to an important animal in Guaraní mythology called a *pirá yaguá* (Plá, *El barroco hispano Guaraní*, 138). She also writes about the fearsome devils that appear in the Saint Michael archangel statues: 'En estos demonios verdugos vino por otra parte a encontrar el indio cauce sublimado a sus reprimidas creencias tradicionales: se hizo lícita para él la evocación de los genios y fantasmas habitantes de sus bosques y esteros del mismo modo que en los rostros radiantes de cierta iconografía anterior al XVI (estampas góticas) hallaron identificación para sus símbolos cosmogónicos aherrajados los artistas del Altiplano' (Plá, *El barroco hispano Guaraní*, 172).

240 Some, with Plá and Ribera, believe that these transformations derive from indigenous culture (Plá, *El barroco hispano Guaraní*, 137; Ribera, 'La pintura en las misiones jesuíticas de guaraníes,' 502). Escobar is more cautious, admitting that such motifs do come from Guaraní tradition, but he plays down their symbolic significance. Norberto Levinton told me that he does not believe that they are representative of indigenous culture, and proposes that the Jesuits themselves introduced such motifs in an attempt to make Christianity more palatable to the Guaraní.

241 See Peterson, *The Paradise Garden Murals of Malinalco*.

242 Bartolomé, *Chamanismo y religion entre los Ava-Katu-Ete*, 25, 46.

243 Cadogan, 'Some Plants and Animals in Guaraní and Guayakí Mythology,' 102; Clastres, *The Land-without-Evil*, 89.

244 Bartolomé, *Chamanismo y religion entre los Ava-Katu-Ete*, 25; Susnik, *Los aborigines del Paraguay*, 17; Clastres, *The Land-without-Evil*, 37–8.

7: Conclusion

1 For a summary of the literature, see Standaert, 'New Trends in the Historiography of Christianity in China,' 602–11. For references to work on Chinese texts by Hui-hung Chen and Catherine Pagani, see chapters 1 and 4.

2 *Compendium catholicae veritatis*, 3 vols. (1997), including Üçerler's 'Jesuit Humanist

Education in Sixteenth-Century Japan,' in volume 3. Uçerler is also preparing a critical edition of Alessandro Valignano's rules for Japan for his doctoral dissertation at Oxford University.

3 Clooney, 'Christ as the Divine Guru in the Theology of Roberto de Nobili'; 'Roberto de Nobili, Adaptation and the Reasonable Interpretation of Religion'; 'Translating the Good: Roberto de Nobili's Moral Argument and Jesuit Education Today'; 'Religious Memory and the Pluralism of Readings'; and 'Roberto de Nobili's Dialogue on Eternal Life and an Early Jesuit Evaluation of Religion in South India.'

4 I was shown photocopies of these documents by Norberto Levinton in Buenos Aires. A team of scholars, including Bartolomeu Melià, are working on these sources at the Centro de Estudios Antonio Guasch in Asunción. For the references to New Spain and Peru, see Lockhart, 'Three Experiences of Culture Contact.'

5 Lafaye, *Quetzalcóatl and Guadalupe*, 301.

6 Voltaire, *Essai sur les moeurs* (Paris, 1756), chapter CLIV; Chateaubriand, *Génie du christianisme* (Paris, 1802), fourth part, fifth book, chapters IV and V, 'Missions du Paraguay.'

7 Some examples: Cunninghame-Graham, *A Vanished Arcadia*; McNaspy and Blanch, *Lost Cities of Paraguay*; Caraman, *The Lost Paradise* (London, 1976); *Paradise Lost: The Jesuits and the Guarani South American Missions 1609–1767* (New York, 1988); Duviols and Bareiro Saguier, *Tentación de la Utopia; Un camino hacia la Arcadia* (Madrid, 1995); Reiter, *They Built Utopia*.

8 Lucas, *Saint, Site, and Sacred Strategy*, 124–5.

9 Alden, *The Making of an Enterprise*, 136. This is the central story in Shusaku Endo's novel *Silence*.

10 Elison, *Deus Destroyed*, 28.

11 Kawamura, 'Jesuit Confraternities in Japan before 1587.'

12 Ibid.

13 See Struve, *Voices from the Ming-Qing Cataclysm*.

14 Zhang, 'Translation as Cultural Reform.' See also her PhD dissertation, 'Cultural Accommodation or Intellectual Colonization?'

15 Zürcher, 'Giulio Aleni et ses relations dans le milieu des lettrés chinois au XVIIème siècle,' 135.

16 Gernet, *China and the Christian Impact*, 83.

17 Standaert, 'New Trends in the Historiography of Christianity in China,' 590.

18 Zürcher, 'Jesuit Accommodation and the Chinese Cultural Imperative.'

19 Standaert, 'Jesuit Corporate Culture As Shaped by the Chinese.'

20 Bailey, 'A Portuguese Doctor at the Maharaja of Jaipur's Court.'

21 de Montoya, *The Spiritual Conquest ... of Paraguay*; Gruzinski, 'Délires et visions chez les Indiens du Mexique.'

22 Abu'l-Fazl 'Allami, *The Āīn-i Akbari*, 1:113–14.

23 Ibid., 1:103.

24 Freedberg, *Painting in Italy 1500–1600*, 600.

25 Klein, 'Editor's Statement,' 108.

26 Abu'l-Fazl 'Allami, *Āīn-i Akbari*, 1:103.

27 Edgerton, *The Renaissance Rediscovery of Linear Perspective*, 6. See also Freedberg, *The Power of Images*, 236–45.

28 Lach, *Asia in the Making of Europe*, 1:186.

29 Ibid., 1:62–3.

30 Elison, *Deus Destroyed*, 250–2.

31 See *Compendium catholicae veritatis* (1997).

32 Macaulay, 'Ranke's History of the Popes,' 20. By the way, the words that have been elided in this quotation show the other side of Macaulay's views on the Jesuits: '... with what unscrupulous laxity and versatility in the choice of means ...'

33 Lacouture, *Jésuites: Une multibiographie*, 8.

Bibliography

Abou, Sélim. *La republica jesuítica de los guaraníes y su herencia*. Buenos Aires, 1995.
Abramo, Livio. 'Barroco misionero.' *IV Bienal de São Paulo* (Sept. to Dec. 1961), pp. 304–15.
Abromson, Morton Colp. *Painting in Rome during the Papacy of Clement VII*. New York, 1981.
Abu'l-Fazl 'Allami. *The Āīn-i Akbari*. Trans. H. Blochmann. 2 vols. Calcutta, 1873.
– *Akbarnāma* Trans. H. Beveridge. 3 vols. Calcutta, 1902–39.
Abu Lughod, Janet. *Before European Hegemony*. Oxford, 1989.
Acosta, José de. *De Procuranda Indorum Salute*. Ed. and trans. Francisco Mateos. Madrid, 1952.
Adorno, Rolena. *Cronista y príncipe: La obra de Don Felipe Guaman Poma de Ayala*. Lima, 1989.
Adorno, Rolena, and Adrian Adorno, eds. *Transatlantic Encounters*. Berkeley, 1992.
Ahmed, Khalid Anis. *Intercultural Influences in Mughal Painting*. Lahore, 1995.
Akbar's Church. Agra, n.d.
Akiyama, Terukazu. 'First Epoch of European Style Painting in Japan.' *Bulletin of Eastern Art* (1941).
Albarnoz, Dilma, and Miriam Legaureta. *Comunidades aborígenes de América*. 2 vols. Buenos Aires, 1987.
Alden, Dauril. *The Making of an Enterprise: The Society of Jesus in Portugal, Its Empire, and Beyond, 1540–1750*. Stanford, 1996.
Allen, P.S. 'Four Letters by Austin of Bordeaux.' *Journal of the Punjab Historical Society* 4, no. 1 (1916): 1–17.
Americas Society. *Barroco de la Nueva Granada*. New York, 1992.
– *Guaman Poma de Ayala: The Colonial Art of an Andean Author*. New York, 1992.
– *Potosí: Colonial Treasures and the Bolivian City of Silver*. New York, 1997.
Anderson, Arthur J.O., et al. *Beyond the Codices*. Berkeley and London, 1976.
Angeli, D. *Sant'Ignazio di Loyola nella vita e nell'arte*. Lanciano, 1911.
Angulo Iñiguez, Diego, Enrique Marco Dorta, and Mario J. Buschiazzo. *Historia del arte hispanoamericano*. 3 vols. Barcelona, 1945–56.
Araneda Bravo, Fidel. *El Barroco Jesuita Chileño*. Santiago, n.d.
Arel, Ayda. *Onsekizinci Yüzyıl Mimarisinde Batılılaşma Süreci*. Istanbul, 1975.
Arnold, Thomas W. *The Old and New Testaments in Muslim Religious Painting*. London, 1932.
Arquitectura en el desierto: Misiones jesuitas en Baja California. Mexico City, 1986.
Art Namban. Brussels, 1989.

Artan, Tülay. *Architecture as a Theatre of Life: Profile of the Eighteenth Century Bosphorus.* Doctoral dissertation, Massachusetts Institute of Technology, 1989.

Artemis Group. *Indian Painting 1525–1825.* London, 1982.

Asher, Catherine. *Architecture of Mughal India.* Cambridge, 1992.

Aslanapa, Oktay. *Turkish Art and Architecture.* London, 1971.

Atil, Esin. *The Brush of the Masters.* Washington, 1978.

Azevedo, Carlos de. *Arte crista na India Portuguesa.* Lisbon, 1959.

– *A arte de Goa, Damão e Diu.* Lisbon, 1970.

Al-Badaoni. *Muntakhāb ut-Tawārīkh.* Trans. and ed. George S.A. Ranking. Calcutta, 1898.

Baglione, Giovanni. *Le vite de' pittori, scultori et architetti.* Rome, 1642.

Bailey, Gauvin Alexander. 'The Dynamics of Chinoiserie in Timurid and Early Safavid Ceramics.' In *Timurid Art and Culture.* Ed. Lisa Golombek and Maria Subtelny. Leiden, 1992, pp. 179–90.

– 'The Catholic Shrines of Agra.' *Arts of Asia* 23, no. 4 (1993): 131–9.

– 'In the Manner of the Frankish Masters: A Safavid Drawing and Its Flemish Inspiration.' *Oriental Art* 40, no. 4 (Winter 1994/95): 29–34.

– 'A Portuguese Doctor at the Maharaja of Jaipur's Court.' *South Asian Studies* 11 (1995): 51–62.

– 'Counter-Reformation Symbolism and Allegory in Mughal Painting.' PhD diss., Harvard University, 1996.

– 'A Mughal Princess in Baroque New Spain: Catarina de San Juan (1606–1688), the *china poblana.*' *Anales del Instituto de Investigaciones Estéticas* 71 (1997): 37–73.

– 'The Lahore *Mirat al-Quds* and the Impact of Jesuit Theater on Mughal Painting.' *South Asian Studies* 13 (1997): 95–108.

– 'The Jesuits in Mughal India: The Ritual Use of Catholic Art in Imperial Mural Painting.' *Art Journal* 57, no. 1 (Spring 1998): 24–30.

– *The Jesuits and the Grand Mogul: Renaissance Art at the Imperial Court of India, 1580–1630.* Washington, 1998.

– 'The Jesuits and Painting in Italy, 1550–1690: The Art of Catholic Reform.' In *Saints and Sinners: Caravaggio and the Baroque Image.* Ed. Franco Mormando, S.J. Boston, 1999, pp. 105–28.

– 'Abandoning Taste? Jesuit Artists in China and Art for Jesuits in Paraguay.' In *Comparative Colonialisms.* Ed. Charles Burroughs. Minneapolis (forthcoming).

– '*Le style jésuite n'existe pas*: Jesuit Corporate Culture and the Visual Arts.' In O'Malley et al. Toronto (forthcoming).

– 'The Truth-Showing Mirror: Jesuit Catechism and the Arts in Mughal India.' In O'Malley et al. Toronto (forthcoming).

Bailey, Gauvin Alexander, Lisa Golombek, and Robert Mason. *Tamerlane's Tableware: A New Approach to the Chinoiserie Ceramics of Fifteenth- and Sixteenth-Century Iran.* Costa Mesa and Toronto, 1996.

Bailey, Gauvin Alexander, Stuart Cary Welch, Oleg Akimushkin et al. *The St. Petersburg Muraqqa': Album of Indian and Persian Manuscripts from the Sixteenth through the Eighteenth century.* Lugano, 1995.

Baird, Joseph Armstrong. *The Churches of Mexico 1530–1810.* Berkeley and Los Angeles, 1962.

Balestreri, Isabella. 'L'architettura negli scritti della Compagnia di Gesù.' In Luciano Patetta et al., *L'architettura della Compagnia di Gesù in Italia XVI-XVII secolo*. Brescia, 1990, pp. 19–26.

Banco de Credito del Perú en la Cultura. *Pintura Virreynal*. Lima, 1973.

Bargellini, Clara. 'Representations of Conversion: Sixteenth Century Architecture in New Spain.' In *The Word Made Image*. Boston, 1998, pp. 91–102.

– 'Jesuit Devotions and Retablos in New Spain.' In O'Malley et al. Toronto (forthcoming).

Barişta, H. Örcün. *Istanbul Çeşmeleri: Bereketzade Çeşmesi*. Istanbul, 1989.

– *Istanbul Çeşmeleri: Beyoğlu Cihetindeki Meyva Tabağı Motifleriyle Bezenmiş tek Cepheli Anit Çeşmeler*. Istanbul, 1989.

Barrett, D.C., S.J., 'A "Jesuit Style" in Art?' *Studies* 45 (1956): 335–41.

Barrio, Maximino de. 'Las colecciones de las Misiones jesuíticas del Paraguay existentes en el Museo de La Plata.' *Revista del Museo de La Plata* 33 (1932): 195–205.

Bartoli, Daniello. *Missione al Gran Mogor*. Rome, 1663 (rpt. Piacenza, 1819).

Bartolomé, Miguel Alberto. *Chamanismo y religion entre los Ava- Katu-Ete*. Mexico City, 1977.

Baumstark, Rheinhold, ed., *Rom in Bayern: Kunst und Spiritualität der ersten Jesuiten*. Munich, 1997.

Bayón, Damián, and Murillo Marx. *History of South American Colonial Art and Architecture*. New York, 1992.

Beach, Milo Cleveland. 'The Gulshan Album and Its European Sources.' *Museum of Fine Arts, Boston, Bulletin* 63 (1965): 63–91.

– 'The Mughal Painter Kesu Das.' *Archives of Asian Art* 30 (1976–7): 34–5.

– *The Grand Mogul*. Williamstown, 1978.

– *The Imperial Image*. Washington, 1980.

– 'The Mughal Painter Abu'l-Hasan and Some English Sources for His Style.' *Walters Art Gallery Journal* 38 (1980): 7–33.

– *Early Mughal Painting*. Cambridge MA, 1987.

– *Mughal and Rajput Painting*. Cambridge, 1992.

Begley, W.E., and Z.A. Desai, eds. *Taj Mahal: The Illumined Tomb*. Cambridge MA, 1989.

Benavente Velarde, Teofilo. *Pintores Cusqueños de la Colonia*. Rpt. Cuzco, 1995.

Benedetti, Sandro. *Fuori dal Classicismo*. Rome, 1984.

Bernard, Henri. 'L'art chrétien en Chine du temps du P. Matthieu Ricci.' *Revue d'histoire des missions* 12 (1935): 199–229.

– 'Valignani ou Valignano, l'auteur véritable de récit de la première ambassade japonaise en Europe, 1582–1590.' *Monumenta Nipponica* 1 (1938): 378–85.

Bernard, Henri, et al., eds. *La première ambassade du Japon en Europe*. Tokyo, 1942.

Bernardo Strozzi. Milan, 1995.

Bernier, François. *Travels in the Mongol Empire A.D. 1656–68*. Trans. Archibald Constable. Oxford, 1914.

Bettray, Johannes, S.V.D. *Die Akkomodationsmethode des P. Matteo Ricci S.I. in China*. Rome, 1955.

Beurdeley, Cécile, and Michel Beurdeley. *Giuseppe Castiglione: A Jesuit Painter at the Court of the Chinese Emperors*. Rutland VT and Tokyo, 1971.

Bhabha, Homi K. *The Location of Culture*. New York, 1994.

Biblia Sacra Hebraice, Graece & Latine. Antwerp, 1569–72.

Biker, Judice. *Coleção de Tratatos*. Vol. 14. Lisbon, 1887.

Binyon, Laurence, J.V.S. Wilkinson, and Basil Gray. *Persian Miniature Painting*. London, 1933.

Blochmann, H. 'Note on a Persian MS. Entitled "Mir-a't ul Quds," a Life of Christ Compiled at the Request of the Emperor Akbar by Jerome Xavier.' *Proceedings of the Asiatic Society* (May 1870): 140ff.

Block, David. *Mission Culture on the Upper Amazon*. Lincoln NE and London, 1994.

– 'Priests and Providers: The European Mission Experience in Moxos.' Paper presented at the conference 'The Jesuits: Culture, Learning, and the Arts,' Boston College, 29 May 1997.

Bloom, Jonathan M. 'The *Qubbat al-Khadra'* and the Iconography of Height in Early Islamic Architecture.' *Ars Orientalis* 23 (1993): 135–42.

Bolton, Hubert Eugene. 'The Mission as a Frontier Institution in the Spanish-American Colonies.' *American Historical Review* 23 (1917): 42–61.

Boone, Elizabeth. 'Pictorial Documents and Visual Thinking in Postconquest Mexico.' In Cummins and Boone (1998), pp. 149–200.

Boone, Elizabeth, and Walter Mignolo, eds. *Writing without Words: Alternative Literacies in Mesoamerica and the Andes*. Durham NC, 1994.

Borges, Charles, S.J. *The Economics of the Goa Jesuits: 1542– 1759*. Panjim, 1994.

Bösel, Richard. 'Die Nachfolgebauten von S. Fedele in Mailand.' *Wiener Jahrbuch für Kunstgeschichte* 37 (1984): 67–87.

– *Jesuitenarchitektur in Italien 1540–1773*. Vol. 1. Vienna, 1985.

– 'La chiesa di S. Lucia: L'invenzione spaziale nel contesto dell'architettura gesuitica.' In *Dall'isola alla città: I Gesuiti a Bologna*. Ed. Gian Paolo Brizzi and Anna Maria Matteucci. Bologna, 1988, pp. 85–93.

– 'Typus und Tradition in der Baukultur Gegenreformatorischer Orden.' *Römische Historische Mitteilungen* 31 (1989): 239–53.

Bösel, Richard, and J. Garms. 'Die Plansammlung des Collegium Germanicum-Hungaricum.' *Römische Historische Mitteilungen* 23 (1981): 225–75; 25 (1983): 335–84.

Bourdon, Léon. *La Compagnie de Jésus et le Japon, 1547–1570*. Paris, 1993.

Boxer, Captain C.R. 'Portuguese Influence in Japanese Screens from 1590 to 1614.' *The Connoisseur* 98 (1936): 79–85.

– 'Some Aspects of Portuguese Influence in Japan, 1542–1640.' *The Japan Society: Transactions and Proceedings* 33 (1935–6): 13–64.

– *The Christian Century in Japan*. Cambridge, 1951.

– 'A Note on Portuguese Missionary Methods in the East.' *Ceylon Historical Journal* 10 (1961): 77–90.

– *Portuguese India in the Mid-Seventeenth Century*. Delhi, 1980.

Boyer, Martha. *Japanese Export Lacquers*. Copenhagen, 1959.

Bragança Pereira, A.B. de. *Arquivo Portugues Oriental*. Bastora, 1940.

Brand, Michael, and Glenn D. Lowry. *Akbar's India*. New York, 1985.

– *Fatehpur Sikri: A Sourcebook*. Cambridge MA, 1985.

– eds. *Akbar and Fatehpur Sikri*. Bombay, 1987.

Braun, Joseph, S.J. *Die belgischen Jesuitenkirchen: Ein Beitrag zur Geschichte des Kampfes zwischen Gotik und Renaissance*. Freiburg im Breslau, 1907.

– *Die Kirchenbauten der Deutscher Jesuiten*. 2 vols. Freiburg im Breslau, 1908–10.

– *Spaniens alte Jesuitenkirchen*. Freiburg im Breslau, 1913.

Brosh, Na'ama, and Rachel Milstein. *Biblical Stories in Islamic Painting*. Jerusalem, 1991.
Brown, Jonathan. *Images and Ideas in Seventeenth-Century Spanish Painting*. Princeton, 1978.
Brown, Patricia Fortini. 'Painting and History in Renaissance Venice.' *Art History* 7 (1984): 263–94.
– *Venetian Narrative Painting in the Time of Carpaccio*. New Haven and London, 1988.
Bruxel, Arnaldo, S.J. *Los treinta pueblos guaraníes*. Posadas, 1984.
Bulgheroni, Raúl. *Summa Chaqueña-Argentina: Imagen de un pais*. Buenos Aires, 1996.
Burgaleta, Claudio, S.J. 'The Jesuit Theological Humanism of José de Acosta (1540–1600): A Study in the History of Theology.' PhD diss., Boston College, 1996.
Burkhart, Louise. *The Slippery Earth: Nahua-Christian Moral Dialogue in Sixteenth-Century Mexico*. Tucson, 1989.
– 'Pious Performances: Christian Pageantry and Native Identity in Early Colonial Mexico.' In Boone and Cummins (1998), pp. 361–82.
Busaniche, Hernán. *La arquitectura en las misiones jesuíticas guaraníes*. Santa Fé, 1955.
Buschiazzo, M.J. *La arquitectura de las misiones de Mojos y Chiquitos*. Buenos Aires, 1953.
– 'La arquitectura en madera de las misiones del Paraguay.' In *Latin American Art and the Baroque Period in Europe*. Princeton, 1963.
– *Estancias jesuíticas de Córdoba*. Buenos Aires, 1969.
Buser, Thomas. 'Jerome Nadal and Early Jesuit Art in Rome.' *The Art Bulletin* 58 (1976): 424–33.
Butler, John F. *Christianity in Asia and America*. Leiden, 1979.
Cadogan, León. *Ayvu Rapyta: Textos míticos de los Mbyá-Guaraní del Guairá*. Asunción, 1953.
– 'Some Plants and Animals in Guaraní and Guayakí Mythology.' In *Paraguay: Ecological Essays*. Ed. J. Richard Gorham. Miami, 1973.
Cahill, James. *The Compelling Image*. Cambridge MA, 1982.
– 'Late Ming Landscape Albums and European Printed Books,' in Sandra Hindman, ed., *The Early Illustrated Book: Essays in Honor of Lessing J. Rosenwald*. Washington, 1982, pp. 150–71.
Camps, Arnulf. *An Unpublished Letter of Father Cristoval de Vega, S.J.: Its Importance for the Second Mission to the Mughal Court and for the Knowledge of the Religion of the Emperor Akbar*. Cairo, 1956.
– *Jerome Xavier S.J. and the Muslims of the Mogul Empire*. Schoeneck-Beckenried, 1957.
Caraman, Philip. *The Lost Paradise: An Account of the Jesuits in Paraguay*. London, 1975.
Carbonell de Masy, Rafael. *Estrategias de desarrollo rural en los pueblos guaraníes (1609–1767)*. Barcelona, 1992.
Carswell, John. *New Julfa*. Oxford, 1968.
Cartas anuas de la Provincia del Paraguay, Chile y Tucumán de la Compañía de Jesús (1615–1637). Buenos Aires, 1929.
Carvalho, José Antonio. *O colegio e as residencias dos jesuitas no Espirito Santo*. Rio de Janeiro, 1982.
Castedo, Leopoldo. *The Cuzco Circle*. New York, 1976.
Cellini, P. *La madonna di San Luca in Santa Maria Maggiore*. Rome, 1943.
Chaghatai, M. Abdullah. 'Mirat Al-Quds: An Illustrated Manuscript of Akbar's Period about Christ's Life.' *Lahore Museum Bulletin* 1, no. 2 (1988): 93–100.
Charpentrat, P. 'Jésuite (Art).' *Encyclopaedia Universalis* (1971), vol. 9, pp. 421–6.
Chateaubriand, François-Auguste-René de. *Génie du christianisme*. Paris, 1802.

Chaves, Jonathan. *Singing of the Source: Nature and God in the Poetry of the Chinese Painter Wu Li*. Honolulu, 1993.

Chen, Min-sun. 'Li Chih-tsao and the *T'ien-hsüeh ch'u-han*.' In *Actes du VIIè colloque international de sinologie, Chantilly 1992*. Taipei and Paris, 1995, pp. 35–44.

Chicó, Mario T. 'Algumas observações acerca da arquitectura da Companhia de Jesus no distrito de Goa.' *Garcia de Orta: Numero Especial*. Lisbon, 1956, pp. 257–72.

The Chinese Rites Controversy: Its History and Meaning. Nettetal, 1994.

Clastres, Hélène. *The Land-without-Evil: Tupí-Guaraní Prophetism*, Trans. Jacqueline Grenez Brovender. Urbana, 1995.

Clendinnen, Inga. *Ambivalent Conquests: Maya and Spaniard in Yucatan, 1517–1570*. Cambridge, 1987.

Clifford, James. *The Predicament of Culture*. Cambridge MA, 1988.

Clooney, Francis X., S.J. 'Christ as the Divine Guru in the Theology of Roberto de Nobili.' In *One Faith, Many Cultures*. Boston, 1988, pp. 25–40.

– 'Roberto de Nobili: Adaptation and the Reasonable Interpretation of Religion.' *Missiology* 18, no. 1 (1990): 25–36.

– 'Translating the Good: Roberto de Nobili's Moral Argument and Jesuit Education Today.' In *The Jesuit Tradition: Education and Missions*. Ed. C. Chapple. Scranton, 1993, pp. 268–80.

– 'Religious Memory and the Pluralism of Readings: Reflections on Roberto de Nobili and the Taittirīya Upanisad.' *Sophia* 34, no. 1 (1995): 204–25.

– 'Roberto de Nobili's Dialogue on Eternal Life and an Early Jesuit Evaluation of Religion in South India.' In O'Malley et al. Toronto (forthcoming).

Clunas, Craig. *Art in China*. Oxford, 1997.

– *Pictures and Visuality in Early Modern China*. Princeton, 1997.

Cohen, Monique, and Natalie Monnet. *Impressions de Chine*. Paris, 1992.

Collier, G., ed. *The Inca and Aztec States: 1400–1800*. New York and London, 1982.

Comentale, Christophe. 'Les recueils de gravures sous la dynastie des Ch'ing: La série des eaux-fortes du *pi-shu shan-chuang*, analyse et comparaisons avec d'autres sources contemporaines, chinoises et occidentales.' In *Actes du VIIè colloque international de sinologie, Chantilly 1992*. Taipei and Paris, 1995, pp. 81–114.

Compendium catholicae veritatis. 3 vols. Tokyo, 1997.

The Constitutions of the Society of Jesus. Trans. George E. Ganss. St Louis, 1970.

Consuelo Maquívar, María del. *Los retablos de Tepotzotlán*. Mexico City, 1976.

Cooper, Ilay. 'Sikhs, Saints and Shadows of Angels: Some Mughal Murals in Buildings along the North Wall of Lahore Fort.' *South Asian Studies* 9 (1993): 11–28.

Cooper, Michael, S.J., ed. *The Southern Barbarians*. Tokyo, 1971.

– *Rodrigues the Interpreter*. New York and Tokyo, 1974.

Correia-Afonso, John. *Jesuit Letters and Indian History*. Bombay, 1955.

– 'More about Akbar and the Jesuits.' *Indica* 14, no. 1 (1977): 57–62.

– 'Christian Art in India.' *Art and Artists* 14, no. 2 (1979): 28–33.

– *Letters from the Mughal Court*. Bombay, 1980.

– 'Mission to the Great Moghul; An Historical Attempt to Convert Akbar, Ruler of Northern India.' *Worldmission* 31 (1980): 54–8.

– 'Indo-American Contacts through the Jesuit Missionaries.' In *Asia and Colonial Latin America*. Ed. Ernesto de la Torre. Mexico City, 1981, pp. 45–60.

– 'A History of the Society of Jesus in India.' In *Jesuit Presence in Indian History*. Ed. Anand Amaladass. Anand, 1988, pp. 3–11.

– 'The Second Jesuit Mission to Akbar (1591).' *Indica* 28, no. 2 (1991): 73–93.

Costa, Lucio. 'Arquitetura dos Jesuitas no Brasil.' *Revista do Serviço do Patrimonio historico et artistico nacional* 4 (Rio de Janeiro, 1941).

Costelloe, Joseph, S.J., ed. *The Letters and Instructions of Francis Xavier*. St Louis, 1992.

Couseiro, Gonçalo. 'L'Eglise de Notre-Dame de l'Assomption (ou de St. Paul) à Macao et l'art de la Compagnie de Jésus en Chine – art et adaptation.' PhD diss., Sorbonne, 1992.

– 'Pintores jesuítas na China.' *Oceanos* 12 (Nov. 1992): 92–101.

– *A igreja de S. Paulo de Macau*. Lisbon, 1997.

Coutinho, Maria Inês. 'Arte de las misiones jesuíticas.' Paper delivered at the symposium entitled 'Misiones Jesuíticas, Una Herencia en Común Argentina y Brasil,' Buenos Aires, 4 September 1996.

Coverte, Robert. *A True and Almost Incredible Report*. Ed. Boies Penrose. Philadelphia, 1931.

Cracraft, James. *The Petrine Revolution in Russian Architecture*. Chicago and London, 1988.

Cragg, Kenneth. *Jesus and the Muslim*. London, 1985.

Creswell, K.A.C. *Early Muslim Architecture*. Oxford, 1932–40.

Cummins, Tom. 'Abstraction to Narration: Kero Imagery of Peru and the Alteration of Native Identity.' PhD diss., University of California at Los Angeles, 1988.

– 'Representation in the Sixteenth Century and the Colonial Image of the Inca.' In *Writing without Words*. Ed. Elizabeth Hill Boone and Walter D. Mignolo. Durham and London, 1994, pp. 189–219.

– 'Let Me See! Reading Is for Them: Colonial Images and Objects 'como es costumbre tener los caciques Señores.' In Cummins and Boone (1998), pp. 91–148.

Cummins, Tom, and Elizabeth Hill Boone, eds. *Native Traditions in the Postconquest World*. Washington, 1998.

Cummins, Tom, and Joanne Rappaport. 'Between Images and Writing: The Ritual of the King's Quilca.' Paper delivered at the symposium 'Early Modern Trans-Atlantic Encounters,' City University of New York, 6–7 March 1997.

Cunninghame Graham, R.B. *A Vanished Arcadia*. Rpt. London, 1988.

Dainville, François de. 'La légende du style jésuite.' *Etudes* 257 (1955): 5–16.

Damian, Carol. *The Virgin of the Andes*. Miami Beach, 1995.

Das, Asok Kumar. *Mughal Painting during Jahangir's Time*. Calcutta, 1978.

Dawson, Christopher. *Mission to Asia*. Toronto, 1980.

Dean, Carolyn. 'The Renewal of Old World Images and the Creation of Colonial Peruvian Visual Culture.' In *Converging Cultures*, 171–82.

Decorme, Gerard. *La obra de los jesuitas mexicanos durante la época colonial*. Mexico City, 1940–1.

De Dieu, Ludovico. *Historia Christi*. Leiden, 1639.

– *Narratio brevis rerum* ... Leiden, 1639.

d'Elia, Pasquale M., S.J. *Le origini dell'arte cristiana cinese*. Rome, 1939.

– 'La Madonna di S. Maria Maggiore in Cina.' *Ecclesia* 1, no. 9 (1950): 30–2.

– ed. *Fonte Ricciane*. 2 vols. Rome, 1942, 1949.

De Kesel, W. *Japanese Export Lacquers (16th–17th Century) from the Castle of Beloeil*. Drongen, 1994.

De Laet, Johannes. *The Empire of the Great Mogol*. Trans. J.S. Hoyland and S.N. Banerjee. Bombay, 1924.

The Delights of Harmony: The European Palaces of the Yuanmingyuan and the Jesuits at the Eighteenth Century Court of Beijing. Worcester MA, 1994.

Desideri, Ippolito. *Viaggi*. Ed. Luciano Petech. Rome, 1954.

De Sousa, Teotónio R. 'A Arte Cristã de Goa: Uma introdução histórica para a dialéctica da sua evolução.' *Oceanos* 19/20 (1994): 8–14.

de Vitray-Meyerovitch, Eva, and Faouzi Skali. *Jésus dans la tradition soufie*. Marseilles, 1985.

Devrapriam, Emma. 'Le ripercussioni della Controriforma sulle opere dei pittori moghul e fiorentini: Il realismo del tardo XVI e primo XVII secolo.' In *Lo Speccio del Principe*. Ed. Dalu Jones. Rome, 1991, pp. 120–9.

Díaz, Marco. *La Arquitectura de los Jesuitas en Nueva España*. Mexico City, 1982.

Dibble, Charles E. 'The Nahuatlization of Christianity.' In *Sixteenth-Century Mexico: the Work of Sahagún*. Ed. M.S. Edmunson. Albuquerque, 1974, pp. 225–33.

Drucker, Philip. *The Native Brotherhoods*. New York, 1958.

D'Souza, Augustus L. 'The Jesuits at the Court of the Grand Mughal.' *The Examiner* 132, 11 (14 March 1981).

Dudink, Adrian. 'Christianity in China: Five Studies.' PhD diss., Rijksuniversiteit Leiden, 1995.

Du Jarric, Pierre. *Akbar and the Jesuits*. Trans. C.H. Payne. London, 1926.

Dunne, George H., S.J. *Generation of Giants*. Notre Dame, 1962.

Dunne, Peter Masten, S.J. *Pioneer Jesuits in Northern Mexico*. Berkeley and Los Angeles, 1944.

Durand, Antoine, and Regine Thiriez. 'Engraving the Emperor of China's European Palaces.' *Biblion: The New York Public Library Bulletin* 1 (1993): 81–107.

Duviols, Jean-Paul, and Rubén Bareiro Saguier. *Tentación de la Utopia*. Barcelona, 1991.

Duviols, Pierre. *La lutte contre les religions autochtones dans le Pérou colonial: L'extirpation de l'idolâtrie entre 1532 et 1660*. Lima, 1971.

Edgerton, Samuel. *The Renaissance Rediscovery of Linear Perspective*. New York, 1975.

– *The Heritage of Giotto's Geometry: Art and Science on the Eve of the Scientific Revolution*. Ithaca NY and London, 1991.

– 'Leon Battista Alberti vs. Quetzalcóatl: The Role of Italian Renaissance Art Theory in the Sixteenth-Century "Conversion" of Mexico.' Paper delivered at the symposium 'Cultural Transmission and Transformation in the Ibero-American World, 1200–1800,' Virginia Polytechnic Institute and State University, 21 October 1995.

– 'Missionaries and Indians in Sixteenth-Century Mexico: The Art of the Art of Christian Conversion.' Paper delivered at the annual meeting of the Renaissance Society of America, College Park MD, 26–9 March 1998.

Egaña, Antonio de. *Historia de la Iglesia en la América española*. 1955–60.

Elison, George. *Deus Destroyed*. Cambridge MA, 1973.

Elliot, H.M. *Bibliographical Index to the Historians of Muhammadan India*. Calcutta, 1849.

Endo, Shusaku. 'The Final Martyrs.' In his *The Final Martyrs*. Trans. Van C. Gessel. New York, 1994, pp. 9–27.

Entenmann, Robert. 'The Establishment of Chinese Catholic Communities in Early Ch'ing Szechwan.' In *Actes du VIIè colloque international de sinologie, Chantilly 1992*. Taipei and Paris, 1995, pp. 147–61.

Escobar, Ticio. *Una interpretación de las artes visuales en el Paraguay*. 2 vols. Asunción, 1980.
– *La belleza de los otros: Arte indígena del Paraguay*. Asunción, 1993.
Escudero de Terán, Ximena. *América y España en la escultura colonial quiteña*. Quito, 1992.
El espejo salvaje: Imaginería franciscana en la mirada indígena. Asunción, 1992.
Esplendor e Devoção: Os relicários de S. Roque. Lisbon, 1998.
Estrada de Gerlero, Elena. *Nueva España*. 4 vols. Mexico City, 1994.
Ettinghausen, Richard. *Paintings of the Sultans and Emperors of India in American Collections*. Delhi, 1961.
– 'The Emperor's Choice.' In *De Artibus Opuscula*. Ed. Millard Meiss. New York, 1961, pp. 98–120.
– 'New Pictorial Evidence of Catholic Missionary Activity in Mughal India (Early XVIIth Century),' In *Perennitas. P. Thomas Michels O.S.B. zum 70 Geburtstag*. Ed. H. Rahner, S.J. Munster, 1963, pp. 385–96.
Examen et Constitutiones Decreta Congregationum Generatium Formulae Congregationum. Florence, 1893.
Exposição de Arte Sacra Missionaria. Lisbon, 1952.
Fabrici, Susana. 'Un antiguo libro en Guaraní: De la Diferencia Entre lo Temporal y Eterno de Juan Eusebio Nieremberg (impreso en las doctrinas, 1705).' *Incipit* 3 (1983): 173–83.
Fani, Muhsin. *The Dabistan, or School of Manners*. Ed. and trans. David Shea and Anthony Troyer. London, 1843.
Farago, Claire, ed. *Reframing the Renaissance*. New Haven and London, 1995.
Felix, Father, O.C. 'On the Persian Farmans Granted to the Jesuits by the Moghul Emperors, and Tibetan and Newari Farmans Granted to the Capuchin Missionaries in Tibet.' *Journal of the Asiatic Society of Bengal* (Sept. 1912): 325–32.
– 'Mughal Farmans, Parwanahs and Sanads Issued in Favour of the Jesuit Missionaries.' *Journal of the Punjab Historical Society* 5 (1916): 1–53.
Ferrão de Taveres e Távora, B. *Imaginária Luso-Oriental*. Lisbon, 1983.
Ferrari Peña, Claudio. 'La influencia de los jesuitas bávaros en la arquitectura y el arte chileños del siglo XVIII.' In *Symposium Internazionale sul Barocco Latino Americano*. Rome, 1980.
Ferreira Santos, Paulo. *O barroco e o jesuítico na arquitetura no Brasil*. Rio de Janeiro, 1951.
Fischer, Rainald P. *P. Martin Schmid, S.J., 1694–1772: Seine Briefe und seine Werken*. Zug, 1988.
Flores Ochea, Jorge A. *El Cuzco: Resistencia y continuidad*. Cuzco, 1990.
Fonseca, Ignatius. 'Jahangir and the Jesuits.' *Journal of the University of Bombay* 1 (1932): 204–8.
A forma e a imagem: Arte e arquitetura jesuítica no Rio de Janeiro colonial. Rio de Janeiro, n.d.
Foster, George M. *Culture and Conquest*. Chicago, 1960.
Foster, William. *Early Travels to India*. London, 1921.
Fraser, Valerie. *The Architecture of Conquest*. Cambridge, 1990.
Freedberg, David. *The Power of Images*. Chicago and London, 1989.
Freedberg, S.J. *Painting in Italy, 1500–1600*. New Haven and London, 1971.
Frings, Paul, and Josef Übelmesser. *Paracuaria: Die Kunstschätze des Jesuitenstaats in Paraguay*. Mainz, 1982.
Frois, Luis, S.J. *Die Geschichte Japans*. Ed. and trans. G. Schurhammer and E.A. Voretzsch. Leipzig, 1926.

Fuehrer, A. *The Monumental Antiquities and Inscriptions in the North-Western Provinces and Oudh*. Allahabad, 1891.

Fujita, Neils. *Japan's Encounter with Christianity: The Catholic Mission in Pre-Modern Japan*. New York, 1991.

Furlong, Guillermo Cardiff, S.J. *Los jesuitas y la cultura rioplatense*. Montevideo, 1933.

– 'La arquitectura en las misiones jesuíticas.' In *Estudio 64*. Buenos Aires, 1940.

– *Arquitectos argentinos durante la dominación hispanica*. Buenos Aires, 1946.

– *Historia y bibliografia de las primeras imprentas rioplatenses 1700–1850*. Buenos Aires, 1953.

– *José Cardiel, S.J., y su Carta-Relación*. Buenos Aires, 1953.

– *Historia del Colegio de la Inmaculada*. Santa Fé, 1962.

– *Misiones y sus pueblos de guaraníes*. Buenos Aires, 1962.

– *Artesanos argentinos*. Buenos Aires, 1966.

Furst, Jill Leslie McKeever. 'The Nahualli of Christ: The Trinity and the Nature of the Soul in Ancient Mexico.' *Res* 33 (Spring 1998): 209–24.

Gagliano, Joseph A., and Charles E. Ronan, S.J. *Jesuit Encounters in the New World: Jesuit Chroniclers, Geographers, Educators and Missionaries in the Americas, 1549–1767*. Rome, 1997.

Gahlin, Sven. *Indian Miniatures from the Collection of the Fondation Custodia, Paris*. Paris, 1991.

Galassi Paluzzi, Carlo. *Storia segreta dello stile dei Gesuiti*. Rome, 1951.

Gallagher, L., trans. *China in the Sixteenth Century: The Journal of Matthew Ricci 1583–1610*. New York, 1953.

Gálvez, Lucía. *Guaraníes y jesuitas: De la Tierra Sin Mal al Paraíso*. Buenos Aires, 1995.

Gardner, Victoria C. '*Homines non nascuntur, sed figuntur:* Benvenuto Cellini's *Vita* and Self-Presentation of the Renaissance Artist.' *Sixteenth Century Journal* 28, no. 2 (1997): 447–65.

Gasparini, Graziano. 'Análisis crítico de las definiciones de "arquitectura popular" y "arquitectura mestiza."' *Boletín* 3 (1965): 51–66.

Geagea, Rev. Nilo. *Mary of the Koran*. Trans. Rev. Laurence T. Fares. New York, 1984.

Gernet, Jacques. *China and the Christian Impact*. Trans. Janet Lloyd. Cambridge, 1985.

Gibson, Charles. *The Aztecs under Spanish Rule*. Stanford, 1964.

Gisbert, Teresa. *Iconografía y mitos indígenas en el arte*. La Paz, 1980.

Gispert-Sauch, G., S.J. 'Document: Another Letter of the Pope to Akbar the Great.' *Indian Missiological Review* (July 1987): 187–92.

Giuría, Juan. *La arquitectura del Paraguay*. Buenos Aires, 1950.

Glick, Thomas F., and Oriol Pi-Sunyer. 'Acculturation as an Explanatory Concept in Spanish History.' *Comparative Studies in Society and History* 11 (1969): 136–54.

Godard, Yedda A. 'Les marges du Murakka Gulshan.' *Athar-e Iran* 1, no. 1 (1936): 11–33.

– 'Un album des princes timourides de l'Inde.' *Athar-e Iran* 2, no. 2 (1937): 179–281.

Goetz, Hermann. 'The Early Muraqqas of the Mughal Emperor Jahangir.' *East and West* 8 (1957): 157–8.

Goldie, Francis. *The First Christian Mission to the Great Mogul*. Dublin, 1897.

Goldstein, Carl. *Visual Fact over Verbal Fiction*. Cambridge, 1988.

Gombrich, Ernst. 'In Search of Cultural History.' In *Ideals and Idols: Essays on Values in History and in Art*. Oxford, 1979, pp. 24–59.

Gómez, B. Hernán. 'Polémica en torno a los orígines de la arquitectura de las Jesuítas y la posible aceptación de un estílo.' PhD diss., Universidad de Oviedo, 1978.

González Echenique, Javier. *Arte colonial en Chile*. Santiago, 1978.

González Galván, Manuel. 'Influencia por selección de América en su arte colonial.' *Anales del Instituto de Investigaciones Estéticas* 13, no. 50 (1982): 43–54.
Goodman, Howard L., and Anthony Grafton. 'Ricci, the Chinese and the Toolkits of the Textualists.' *Asia Major* 3rd ser., 11, no. 2 (1990–1): 95–148.
Gossen, Gary H. 'Mesoamerican Ideas as a Foundation for Regional Synthesis.' In *Symbol and Meaning beyond the Closed Community*. Ed. Gary H. Gossen. Albany NY, 1986, pp. 1–8.
El grabado en la ciudad de Puebla de los Angeles. Mexico City, 1933.
Grimaldi, Floriano. *Il santuario di Loreto: Sette secoli di storia arte devozionale*. Rome, 1994.
Grizzard, Mary. *Spanish Colonial Art and Architecture of Mexico and the U.S. Southwest*. Lanham MD, 1986.
Gruzinski, Serge. 'Délires et visions chez les Indiens du Mexique.' *Mélanges de l'Ecole Française de Rome* 86, no. 2 (1974): 445–80.
– *Painting the Conquest*. Paris, 1992.
– *The Conquest of Mexico*. Trans. Eileen Corrigan. Cambridge, 1993.
Guarino, Carmen. 'The Interpretation of Images in Matteo Ricci's Picture for Chengshi Moyuan.' In *Ming Qing Yanjiu*. Naples and Rome, 1997, pp. 21–43.
Guerreiro, Fernão. *Relaçam Annual das cousas que fezerem os padres da Companhia de Jesus na India, & Japão, 1600–01*. Evora, 1603.
– *Relaçam Annual das cousas que fezerem os padres da Companhia de Jesus nas partes da India Oriental*. Lisbon, 1605.
– *Relaçam Annual das cousas que fezerem os padres da Companhia de Jesus nas partes da India Oriental, 604, 605*. Lisbon, 1607.
– *Relaçam annual das cousas que fezeram os padres da companhia de Iesus nas partes da India Oriental*. Lisbon, 1609.
– *Jahangir and the Jesuits*. Trans. C.H. Payne. London, 1930.
Guido, Angel. *Fusión hispano-indígena en la arquitectura colonial*. Rosario, 1925.
– *Redescubrimiento de América en el arte*. Rosario, 1940.
Guillen-Nuñez, César. *Macau*. Hong Kong, 1984.
Gutiérrez, Ramón. *Evolución urbanística y arquitectónica del Paraguay 1537–1911*. Resistencia, 1978.
– *The Jesuit Guaraní Missions*. Rio de Janeiro, 1987.
– 'The Jesuit Missions: City Planning, Architecture and Art.' In *Paradise Lost*. New York, 1988.
– 'La planificación alternativa en la Colonia: Tipologías urbanas de las misiones jesuíticas.' In *Un camino hacia la Arcadia*. Madrid, 1995, pp. 61–80.
– ed. *Pintura, escultura y artes útiles en Iberoamérica, 1500–1825*. Madrid, 1995.
Haar, B.J. ter. *The White Lotus Teachings in Chinese Religious History*. Leiden, 1992.
Hakhnazarian, Armen. *Nor Djulfa*. Milan, 1991.
Hanisch Espindola, Walter, S.J., *Historia de la Compañía de Jesús en Chile*. Buenos Aires, 1974.
Hanke, Lewis. *Aristotle and the American Indians*. Chicago, 1959.
Hargreaves, Cecil, and K.G. Mathew. *Twenty-five Indian Churches*. Calcutta, 1975.
Harle, J.C. *The Art and Architecture of the Indian Subcontinent*. Harmondsworth, 1990.
Harris, George, S.J. 'The Mission of Matteo Ricci, S.J.: A Case Study of an Effort at Guided Cultural Change in the Sixteenth Century.' *Monumentica Serica* 25 (1966): 1–168.
Haskell, Francis. *Patrons and Painters*. New York, 1963.
– 'The Role of Patrons: Baroque Style Changes.' In Wittkower and Jaffe (1972), pp. 51–62.

Havell, E.B., 'European Art at the Moghul Court.' *Journal of Indian History* 2, no. 1 (1922): 117–18.

Held, Julius. 'Rubens and the *Vita Beati P. Ignatii Loiolae* of 1609.' In *Rubens before 1620*. Ed. John R. Martin. Princeton, 1972, pp. 93–104.

Heras, Henry, S.J. 'The Jesuit Dwelling at Fatehpur-Sikri.' *The Examiner* [Bombay] 74 (1923): 297–8.

– 'Jahangir and the Portuguese.' *In Proceedings of the IX Meeting of the Indian Historical Records Commission, Lucknow, 1926*. Calcutta, 1927, pp. 1–11.

– 'Three Mughal Paintings on Akbar's Religious Discussions.' *Journal of the Bombay Branch of the Royal Asiatic Society* 3 (1927), pp. 191–202.

– 'A Treaty between Aurangzeb and the Portuguese.' *In Proceedings of the X Meeting of the Indian Historical Records Commission*. Calcutta, 1928.

– 'A Quotation from the Words of Jesus Christ in One of Emperor Akbar's Inscriptions.' *Islamic Research Association Miscellany* [Bombay] 1 (1949): 61–71.

– 'La casa de la Señora María: La mas antigua capilla catolica en el norte de India fue dedicada a Nuestra Señora.' *El Siglo de los Misiones* (1954): 422–25.

Hernández, Pablo. *Organización social de las doctrinas guaraníes de la Compañía de Jesús*. 2 vols. Barcelona, 1913.

Herskovits, Melville. *Man and His Works*. New York, 1941.

Herz, Alexandra. 'Imitators of Christ: The Martyr-Cycles of Late Sixteenth Century Rome Seen in Context.' *Storia dell'arte* 62 (1988): 53–70.

Hibbard, Howard. '*Ut picturae sermones:* The First Painted Decorations of the Gesù.' In Wittkower and Jaffe (1972), pp. 29–50.

– *Caravaggio*. New York, 1983.

Hickman, Money L. *Japan's Golden Age: Momoyama*. New Haven and London, 1996.

Hillar Puxeddu, Leo W. 'El jesuita santafesino Suárez, una honra de la ciencia americana.' *El litoral*, 25 August 1985.

Historia general de arte en la Argentina II. Buenos Aires, 1983.

Hodgson, Marshall. *The Venture of Islam*. Chicago and London, 1974.

Hollstein, F.W.H. *Dutch and Flemish Etchings, Engravings and Woodcuts*. Multiple vols. (1949–).

Hosten, Henry, S.J. 'List of Jesuit Missionaries in "Mogor."' *Journal of the Asiatic Society of Bengal*, n.s. 6 (1910): 527–42.

– 'Fr. Jerome Xavier's Persian Lives of the Apostles.' *Journal of the Asiatic Society of Bengal* (Feb. 1914): 65–84.

– 'Mirza zu-l-Qarnain, a Christian Grandee of Three Great Mughals, with Notes on Akbar's Christian Wife and the Indian Bourbons.' *Memoirs of the Asiatic Society of Bengal* 5, no. 4 (1916): 115–94.

– *The Annual Relation of Father Fernão Guerreiro, S.J. for 1607–1608*. Calcutta, 1918 [HIL, 275.4 Hos A-10974].

– 'European Art at the Moghul Court.' *Journal of the United Provinces Historical Society* 3, no. 1 (1922): 110–84.

– 'Jesuit Annual Letter from Mogor.' *Journal of Indian History* 1, no. 2 (Feb. 1922): 226–48.

– 'Fr. N. Pimenta's Annual Letter on Mogor'; 'Fr. N. Pimenta, S.J., on Mogor'; 'Fr. N. Pimenta's Annual of Margao, Dec. 1, 1601'; 'Eulogy of Father Jerome Xavier, S.J., a Missionary in Mogor'; 'Some Letters of Fr. Jerome Xavier, S.J., to His Family (1593–1612)'; 'Some Notes on Bro. Bento de Goes, S.J.'; 'Three Letters of Fr. Joseph de Castro, S.J., and the Last Year of Jahangir.' *Journal of the Asiatic Society of Bengal* 23 (1927): 57–65; 68–82; 83–107; 109–30; 131–6; 137–9; 140–66.

– 'The Jesuits at Agra in 1635–37.' *Journal of the Royal Asiatic Society of Bengal* 4 (1938).

– 'The Earliest Printing in India and Bibliographical Notes on Early Works – Mostly in the Vernacular.' n.d. [Typed manuscript, HIL, 275.4 Hos A-10975].

– *Jesuit Missionaries in Northern India and Inscriptions on Their Tombs, Agra 1580–1803*. Calcutta, 1907 [HIL, 275.4 Hos A-10974].

Hou Renzhi. 'Yuanmingyuan.' In *Yuanming cangsang*. Beijing, 1991.

Hsiang Ta. 'European Influences on Chinese Art in the Later Ming and Early Ch'ing Period.' Trans. Wang Teh-chao. In *The Translation of Art: Essays on Chinese Painting and Poetry*. Ed. James C.Y. Watt. Hong Kong, 1976, pp. 152–78.

Ibn al-'Arabi. *The Bezels of Wisdom*. Trans. R.W.J. Austin. London, 1980.

Idemitsu Museum of Arts. *The Beauty of Momoyama: Elaborate Shapes and Designs*. Osaka, 1998.

'Ilm al-Akhlāq. Trans. M.S.H. Ma'sumi. Islamabad, 1969.

Inden, Ronald. 'Ritual, Authority, and Cyclic Time in Hindu Kingship.' In *Kingship and Authority in South Asia*. Ed. D.S. Richards. Madison, 1978, pp. 252–85.

Inventário fotográfico de objetos de arte sacra existentes nas igrejas de Macau: Escultura e pintura. Macau, 1981.

Irepoglu, Gül. 'Topkapı Sarayı Müzesi Hazine Kütüphanesindeki batılı Kaynaklar Üzerine Düşünceler,' in *Topkapı Sarayı Müzesi, Yıllık* I (1986), 62–9.

Irez, Feryal. 'Topkapı Sarayı Harem Bölümündeki Rokoko Süslemenin Batılı Kaynakları,' *Topkapı Sarayı Müzesi, Yıllık* 4 (1990), 21–54.

Islamic Art. Vol. 1. London, 1981.

Jackson, Paul. 'Jesuits at the Mughal Court.' *Vidyajyoti* 44 (1980): 108–13.

Javellana, René. *Wood and Stone for God's Greater Glory: Jesuit Art and Architecture in the Philippines*. Manila, 1991.

Jennes, Jozef. *Invloed der Vlaamsche Prentkunst in Indie, China en Japan*. Leuven, 1943.

– *History of the Catholic Church in Japan*. Tokyo, 1959.

Jones, Pamela. *Federico Borromeo and the Ambrosiana: Art Patronage and Reform in Seventeenth-Century Milan*. Cambridge, 1993.

José, Regalado Trota. *Images of Faith: Religious Ivory Carvings from the Philippines*. Pasadena, 1990.

Kalbfleisch, Fleur. 'Invloed van de europese prentkunst op de Mogol-schilderkunst.' *Aziatische Kunst* 28, no. 1 (March 1998): 3–17.

Kapola, Mimumu. *The Zairian Mass: On the Way to Liturgical Inculturation*. Licentiate in Sacred Theology, Weston Jesuit School of Theology, 1995.

Kaufmann, Thomas da Costa. 'Italian Sculptors and Sculpture outside of Italy (Chiefly in Central Europe): Problems of Approach, Possibilities of Reception.' In Farago (1995), pp. 47–66.

Kawamura, Shinzo. 'Jesuit Confraternities in Japan before 1587: A Brief Case Study on the Japanese Confraternities.' In O'Malley et al. Toronto (forthcoming).

Keen, Benjamin. *The Aztec Image in Western Thought*. Rutgers, 1971.

Keil, Luis. *Alguns exemplos da influênçia portuguesa em obras de arte indianas do seculo XVI*. Lisbon, 1938.

Kelemen, Pál. *Baroque and Rococo in Latin America*. 2 vols. New York, 1951.

Keller, Francisco, S.J., ed. *Allerhand so Lehr als Geistreiche Brief, Schriften und Reise Beschreibung Welche von denen Missionariis der Gesellschaft Jesu*. Vienna, 1755.

Kennedy, T. Frank, '*Candide* and a Boat.' In O'Malley et al. Toronto (forthcoming).

Ketelaar, J.J. *Journaal*. 'sGravenhage, 1937.

Kimura, Saburo, 'Saint François-Xavier prêchant aux Indiens: Quelques aspects iconographiques.' In *Georges de la Tour ou la nuit traversée*. Ed. Anne Reinbold. Metz, 1994, pp. 133–43.

King of the World: The Padshahnama. London, 1997.

Kiracofe, James B. 'Architectural Fusion and Indigenous Ideology in Early Colonial Teposcolula: The Casa de la Cacica: A Building at the Edge of Oblivion.' *Anales del Instituto de Investigaciones Estéticas* 66 (1995): 45–84.

Kirschbaum, E. 'La Compagnia di Gesù e l'arte.' In *Il quarto centenario della costituzione della Compagnia di Gesù*. Milan, 1941, pp. 211–26.

Kitagawa, J.M. *Religion in Japanese History*. New York, 1966.

Klein, Cecilia. 'Editor's Statement: Depictions of the Dispossessed.' *Art Journal* 49, no. 2 (1990): 108–9.

Klor de Alva, J. Jorge. 'Christianity and the Aztecs.' *San José Studies* 5, no. 3 (1979): 6–2.

– 'Spiritual Conflict and Accommodation in New Spain: Toward a Typology of Aztec Responses to Christianity.' In *The Inca and Aztec States 1400–1800: History and Anthropology*. Ed. G. Collier. New York and London, 1982, pp. 345–66.

Kobayashi, Hiromitsu. 'Chinese Painting versus the Western Style of Painting.' Paper delivered at the symposium 'The Encounter between Europe and Asia during the Time of the Great Navigations.' Sophia University, Tokyo, 6 December 1998.

Kobayashi, Hiromitsu, et al. *Exhibition of Western-Style Paintings of China: Paintings, Prints, and Illustrations from the Ming to Qing Dynasties* [in Japanese]. Tokyo, 1995.

Kobe City Museum. *Pictorial Record of Kobe City Museum of Namban Art* [in Japanese]. Kobe, 1968.

Kobe City Museum. *Special Exhibition: A Record of Encounters with Namban Culture* [in Japanese]. Kobe, 1992.

– *Namban Arts Selection*. Kobe, 1998.

Koch, Ebba. 'The Influence of the Jesuit Mission on Symbolic Representations of the Mughal Emperors.' In *Islam in India*. Ed. Christian Troll. New Delhi, 1982, pp. 14–32.

– 'Notes on the Painted and Sculptured Decoration of Nur Jahan's Pavilions at Ram Bagh (Bagh-i Nur Afshan) at Agra.' In *Facets of Indian Art*. Ed. Robert Skelton. Leiden, 1982, pp. 51–65.

– 'Jahangir and the Angels: Recently Discovered Wall Paintings under European Influence in the Fort of Lahore.' In *India and the West*. Ed. Joachim Deppert. New Delhi, 1983, pp. 173–95.

– *Shah Jahan and Orpheus*. Graz, 1988.

– *Mughal Architecture*. Munich, 1991.

König-Nordhoff, Ursula. *Ignatius von Loyola: Studien zur Entwicklung einer neuen Heiligen-Ikonographie im Rahmen einer Kanonisationskampagne um 1600*. Berlin, 1982.

Konrad, Herman W. *A Jesuit Hacienda in Colonial Mexico: Santa Lucía 1576–1767*. Stanford, 1980.

The Koran. Trans. and ed. N.J. Dawood. Harmondsworth, 1983.

Kowal, David. 'The Evolution of Ecclesiastical Architecture in Portuguese Goa.' *Carl Justi Vereinigung* 5 (1993): 1–22.

– 'Innovation and Assimilation: The Jesuit Contribution to Architectural Development in the Portuguese Indies.' In O'Malley et al. Toronto (forthcoming).

Koyabashi, José María. *La educación como conquista: Empresa franciscana en México*. Mexico City, 1974.

Krautheimer, Richard. 'Introduction to an Iconography of Medieval Architecture.' *Journal of the Warburg and Courtauld Institutes* 5 (1942): 1–33.

Kris, Ernst, and Otto Kurz. *Legend, Myth, and Magic in the Image of the Artist*. New Haven and London, 1979.

Kroeber, A.L. *Anthropology*. New York, 1948.

Kuban, Doğan. *Türk Barok Mimarisi Hakkında bir Deneme*. Istanbul, 1954.

– 'Influences de l'art européen sur l'architecture Ottomane au XVIIIème siècle.' *Palladio* 5 (1955): 149–57.

Kubler, George. *Mexican Architecture of the Sixteenth Century*. 2 vols. New Haven, 1948.

– 'Introduction.' In *Acts of the XX International Congress on the History of Art*. Vol. 3. Princeton, 1963, pp. 145–7.

– 'Non-Iberian European Contributions to Latin American Colonial Architecture.' In *Studies in Ancient American and European Art*. Ed. Thomas F. Reese. New Haven and London, 1985, pp. 81–7.

– 'On the Colonial Extinction of the Motifs of Pre-Columbian Art.' In *Studies in Ancient American and European Art*. Ed. Thomas F. Reese. New Haven and London, 1985, pp. 66–80.

– *The Art and Architecture of Ancient America*. 3rd ed. Harmondsworth, 1986.

Kubler, George, and Martin Soria. *Art and Architecture in Spain and Portugal and Their American Dominions*. Baltimore, 1959.

Kühnel, Ernst, and Hermann Goetz. *Indian Book Painting from Jahangir's Album in the State Library, Berlin*. London, 1926.

Kuran, Aptullah. 'Eighteenth Century Ottoman Architecture.' In *Studies in Eighteenth Century Islamic History*. Eds. Thomas Naff and Roger Owens. Carbondale IL and Edwardsville, 1977, pp. 303–27.

Lach, Donald F. *Asia in the Making of Europe*. Chicago and London, 1970.

Lacouture, Jean. *Jésuites: Une multibiographie*. Paris, 1992.

Lafaye, Jacques. *Quetzalcóatl and Guadalupe*. Trans. Benjamin Keen. Chicago and London, 1976.

Langer, Erick, and Robert H. Jackson, eds. *The New Latin American Mission History*. Lincoln NE and London, 1995.

Lara, Jaime. 'God's Good Taste: The Jesuit Aesthetics of Juan Bautista Villalpando in the Sixth and Tenth Centuries BCE.' In O'Malley et al. Toronto (forthcoming).

Larson, Gerald James, Pratapaditya Pal, and Rebecca P. Gowen. *In Her Image: The Great Goddess in Indian Asia and the Madonna in Christian Culture*. Santa Barbara, 1980.

Laufer, Berthold. 'Christian Art in China.' *Mitteilungen des Seminars für Orientalischen Sprachen an der Königlichen Friedrich-Wilhelms-Universität zu Berlin* 13 (1910): 100–18.

– 'A Chinese Madonna.' *The Open Court* (Jan. 1912).

Lécrivain, Philippe. *Pour une plus grande gloire de Dieu: Les missions jésuites*. Paris, 1991.

Ledderose, L. 'Chinese Influence of European Art.' In *China and Europe: Images and Influences in Sixteenth to Eighteenth Centuries*. Ed. T.H.C. Lee. Hong Kong, 1991, pp. 221–37.

Lederle, Matthew, S.J. *Christian Painting in India through the Centuries*. Anand and Bombay, 1988.

Lee Yuk Tin. *Olhar as ruínas*. Macao, 1990.

Lehmann, Arno. 'A Brief History of Indian Christian Art.' *Indian Church History Review*, 2, no. 2 (1968): 147–58.

Lehnertz, Jay F. 'Lands of the Infidels: The Franciscans in the Central Montaña of Peru, 1709–1824.' PhD diss., University of Wisconsin, 1974.

Lentz, Thomas W., and Glenn D. Lowry. *Timur and the Princely Vision*. Washington, 1989.

Lettres edifiantes et curieuses. Multiple volumes. Toulouse, 1810.

Levenson, Jay, ed. *Circa 1492*. Washington, 1992.

Levinton, Norberto. 'Recursos de información para la restauración de las obras de arquitectura de las misiones jesuíticas: El regreso a las fuentes.' In *La salvaguarda del patrimonio jesuítico*. Posadas, 1994, pp. 187–95.

– 'Pervivencias mudéjares en la arquitectura del Colegio de San Cosmé y San Damian.' Paper delivered at the 49 Congreso internacional de Americanistas. Quito, 1997.

– 'Vivienda y vida privada: La transformación de los conceptos por la acción evangelizadora de la Compañía de Jesús (Provincia Jesuítica de Paraguay, 1604–1767).' *Hispania Sacra* 49, no. 99 (1997): 171–88.

Levy, Evonne. 'A Noble Medley and Concert of Materials and Artifice: Jesuit Church Interiors in Rome, 1567–1700.' In *Saint, Site and Sacred Strategy*. Ed. Thomas Lucas, S.J. Rome, 1990, pp. 46–62.

Lippiello, Tiziana, and Roman Malek, eds. *Scholar from the West: Giulio Aleni S.J. (1582–1649) and the Dialogue between Christianity and China*. Brescia, 1997.

Lippy, Charles H., Robert Choquette, and Stafford Poole. *Christianity Comes to the Americas*. New York, 1992.

Lockhart, James. 'Some Nahua Concepts in Postconquest Guise.' *History of European Ideas* 9 (1985): 465–82.

– *Nahuas and Spaniards*. Stanford, 1991.

– *The Nahuas after the Conquest*. Stanford, 1992.

– 'Three Experiences of Culture Contact: Nahua, Maya, and Quechua,' in Tom Cummins and Elizabeth Hill Boone, eds., *Native Traditions in the Postconquest World*. Washington, 1998, pp. 31–53.

Lockhart, James, and Stuart B. Schwartz. *Early Latin America*. Cambridge and London, 1983.

Loehr, George Robert. *Giuseppe Castiglione*. Rome, 1940.

– 'Missionary-Artists at the Manchu Court.' *Transactions of the Oriental Ceramic Society* 34 (1962–3): 51–67.

Lopetegui, León, S.J. *El Padre José de Acosta S.I. y las misiones*. Madrid, 1942.

Losty, Jeremiah. *The Art of the Book in India*. London, 1982.

Lotti, L., and P.L. Lotti. *La Comunità Cattolica Inglese di Roma: La Sua Chiesa e il suo Collegio*. Rome, 1978.

Löwenstein, Felix zu. 'Saint Magdalene – or Bibi Rabi'a Basri in Mogul Painting?' *Islamic Culture* 13 (1939): 465–69.

– *Christiche Bilder in Altindischer Malerei*. Münster, 1958.

Loyola, Ignatius of. *The Spiritual Exercises* Trans. W.H. Longridge. London, 1950.
Lucas, Thomas M. *Saint, Site and Sacred Strategy*. Rome, 1990.
Lundberg, Mabel. *Jesuitische Anthropologie und Erziehungslehre in der Frühzeit des Ordens, ca. 1450–1650*. Upsala, 1966.
Macaulay, Lord Thomas Babington. 'Ranke's History of the Popes.' (From the *Edinburgh Review*, October 1840.) In his *Critical and Historical Essays*. Boston and New York, 1900, vol. 6, pp. 1–25.
MacCormack, Sabine. 'From the Sun of the Incas to the Virgin of Copacabana.' *Representations* 8 (1984): 30–60.
– 'The Heart Has Its Reasons: Predicaments of Missionary Christianity in Colonial Peru.' *Hispanic American Historical Review* 65, no. 3 (Aug. 1985): 443–6.
– 'Pachacuti: Miracles, Punishments, and Last Judgment.' *American Historical Review* 93 (Dec. 1988): 960–1006.
– *Religion in the Andes*. Princeton, 1991.
– 'Art in a Missionary Context: Images from Europe and the Andes in the Church of Andahuaylillas near Cuzco.' In *The Word Made Image*. Boston, 1998, pp. 103–26.
Macioce, Stefania. *Undique Splendent: Aspetti della pittura sacra nella Roma di Clemente VIII Aldobrandini (1592–1605)*. Rome, 1990.
Maclagan, Sir Edward. 'Jesuit Missions to the Emperor Akbar.' *Journal of the Asiatic Society of Bengal* 65 (1896): 38–112.
– *The Jesuits and the Great Mogul*. London, 1932.
Maeder, Ernesto J.A. *Cartas anuas de la Provincia Jesuítica del Paraguay, 1632 a 1634*. Buenos Aires, 1990.
– 'Talleres artesanales en los pueblos de indios y en las misiones jesuíticas de Paraguay.' In *Formación profesional y artes decorativas en Andalucía y América*. Seville, 1990, pp. 31–45.
– *Misiones del Paraguay: Conflicto y disolución de la sociedad Guaraní*. Madrid, 1992.
– 'Historia de las misiones jesuíticas.' Paper delivered at the symposium 'Una Herencia en Común: Argentina y Brasil' Brazilian Embassy, Buenos Aires, 4 September 1996.
Maeder, Ernesto J.A., and Ramón Gutiérrez. 'La Imaginería jesuítica en las misiones del Paraguay.' *Anales* 23 (1970): 90–114.
Malatesta, Edward J., S.J., and Gao Zhiyu, eds. *Departed, Yet Present: Zhalan, the Oldest Christian Cemetery in Beijing*. Macau, 1995.
Maldavsky, Aliocha. 'Langues indigènes et mission: Recherches sur la crise de l'apostolat chez les jésuites de la province péruvienne au tournant des XVIe et XVIIe siècles' (forthcoming).
Mâle, Emile. *L'art religieux après le Concile de Trente*. Paris, 1932.
Mamboury, E. 'L'art Turc du XVIIIème siècle.' *La Turquie Kemaliste* 19 (1937): 2–11.
Mancini, Giulio. *Considerazioni sulla pittura*. Rome, 1956.
Manrique, F.S. *Itinerario*. Lisbon, 1946.
Manrique, Jorge Alberto. 'La estampa como fuente del arte en la Nueva España.' *Anales del Instituto de Investigaciones Estéticas* 13, no. 50 (1982): 55–60.
Manucci, Niccolò. *Storia del Mogol*. Trans. William Irvine. London, 1907.
Maravall, José Antonio. 'La Utopia politico-religiosa de los Franciscanos en Nueva España.' *Estudios Americanos* 1, no. 2 (1949): 199–207.
Markman, Sidney David. *Architecture and Urbanization of Colonial Central America*. Tempe, 1993.

Marreiros, Carlos. 'Traces of Chinese and Portuguese Architecture.' In *Macau: City of Commerce and Culture*. Ed. R.D. Cremer. Hong Kong, 1991, pp. 101–16.

Martin, F.R. *Miniature Painting and Painters in Persia, India and Turkey*. London, 1912.

Martin, Gregory. *Roma Sancta*. Ed. G. Bruner Parks. Rome, 1969.

Martín, Luis. *The Intellectual Conquest of Peru*. New York, 1968.

Martin Schmid 1694–1772: Missionär, Musiker, Architekt. Zürich, 1994.

Marx, José. *Las misiones jesuíticas*. Posadas, n.d.

Masini, Federico, ed. *Western Humanistic Culture Presented to China by Jesuit Missionaries*. Rome, 1996.

Mason, Penelope. *History of Japanese Art*. New York, 1993.

Mauquoy-Hendrick, Marie. 'Les Wierix illustrateurs de la Bible de Natalis.' *Quarendo* 6 (1976): 28–63.

– *Les Estampes des Wierix conservées au Cabinet des Estampes de la Bibliothèque Royale Albert 1er*. 3 vols. Brussels, 1978–83.

Maza, Francisco de la. *El Pintor Martín de Vos en México*. Mexico City, 1971.

McAndrew, John. *The Open-Air Churches of Sixteenth-Century Mexico*. Cambridge MA, 1965.

McCall, John. 'Early Jesuit Art in the Far East: (I) The Pioneers; (II) Nobukata and Yamada Emosaku; (III) The Japanese Christian Painters; (IV) In China and Macao before 1635; (V) More Discoveries.' *Artibus Asiae* 10 (1947): 121–37, 216–33, 283–301; 11 (1948): 45–69; 17 (1954): 39–54.

McInerney, Terence. 'Manohar.' In *Master Artists of the Imperial Mughal Courts*. Ed. Pratapaditya Pal. Bombay, 1991.

McNaspy, Clement, S.J. 'Notes on Jesuits in the Fine Arts.' *Jesuit Educational Quarterly* 31 (1969–70): 143–7.

– 'Art in Jesuit Life.' *Studies in the Spirituality of Jesuits* 5, no. 3 (April 1973): 93–111.

– *Conquest or Inculturation: Ways of Ministry in the Early Jesuit Missions*. Regina, 1986.

McNaspy, Clement, S.J., and J.M. Blanch. *Lost Cities of Paraguay*. Chicago, 1982.

Meersman, A. 'A Dutch Translation of an Unknown Letter of Francisco Corsi S.J. Missionary to the Great Mogul.' *Karnataka Historical Review* 5 (1940): 1–4.

Melià, Bartolomeu. *El Guaraní: Experiencia religiosa*. Asunción, 1992.

Melià, Bartolomeu, and Olga Blinder. 'Aquellos Paï-Tavyterä que por primera vez dibujaron.' *Humboldt* 58 (1975).

Melià, Bartolomeu, and Liane Maria Nagel. *Guaraníes y jesuitas*. Santo Angelo and Asunción, 1995.

Mendes Pinto, Maria Helena. *Lacas Namban em Portugal*. Lisbon, 1990.

Mesa, José de, and Teresa Gisbert. *Bernardo Bitti*. La Paz, 1961.

– 'Renacimiento y manierismo en la arquitectura "mestiza."' *Boletín* 3 (1965): 9–44.

– 'Determinantes del llamado estilo mestizo: Breves consideraciones sobre el término.' *Boletín* 10 (1968): 93–119.

– *Bitti, un pintor manierista en Sudamérica*. La Paz, 1974.

– *Historia de la pintura cuzqueña*. Lima, 1982.

– *La tradición bíblica en el arte virreynal*. La Paz, 1986.

Miller, Jean, and Ernst Roth. *Aussereuropäische Druckereien im 16. Jahrhundert: Bibliographie der Drücke*. Baden-Baden, 1969.

Milward, Peter, ed. *The Mutual Encounter of East and West, 1492–1992*. Tokyo, 1992.

Las misiones jesuíticas del Guayrá. Verona and Buenos Aires, 1995.

Moffitt Watts, Pauline. 'Languages of Gesture in Sixteenth-Century Mexico: Some Antecedents and Transmutations.' In Farago (1995), pp. 140–51.

Moisy, Pierre. *Les églises des Jésuites de l'ancienne Assistance de France*. Rome, 1958.

Moltedo, Alida. *La Sistina Reprodotta*. Rome, 1991.

Monserrate, Antonio, S.J. *The Commentary of Father Monserrate, S.J.* Trans. and ed. J.S. Hoyland and S.N. Banerjee. London, 1922.

Monssen, Leif Holm. 'Rex Gloriose Martyrum: A Contribution to Jesuit Iconography.' *Art Bulletin* 63, no. 1 (March 1981): 130–7.

Moore, Derek. 'Pellegrino Tibaldi's Church of S. Fidele in Milan: The Jesuits, Carlo Borromeo and Religious Architecture in the Late Sixteenth Century.' PhD diss., New York University, 1988.

Morales, Martín M., S.J. 'New Directions in Research on the Paraguay Reductions, 1610–1767.' Paper delivered at the symposium 'The Jesuits: Culture, Learning and the Arts,' Boston College, 29 May 1997.

Moran, J.F. *The Japanese and the Jesuits*. London and New York, 1993.

Moreno Villa, José. *La escultura colonial mexicana*. Mexico City, 1942.

Mörner, Magnus. *La Corona Española y los foráneos en los pueblos de indios de América*. Estecolmo, 1970.

– 'The Role of the Jesuits in the Transfer of Secular Baroque Culture to the River Plate Region.' In O'Malley et al. Toronto (forthcoming).

Moura Sobral, Luis de. 'L'estampe anversoise et la peinture portugaise au début du XVIIe siècle.' In *Portugal et Flandre*. Lisbon, 1991, pp. 57–67.

Muhammed, K.K. 'Excavation of a Catholic Chapel at Fatehpur Sikri.' *Indica* 28, no. 1 (March 1991): 1–12.

– 'Excavations at Fatehpur Sikri: Ibadat Khana (Hall of Interreligious Discussions) Discovered' (forthcoming).

Mujia Pinilla, Ramón. *Angeles apócrifos en la América virreinal*. Lima, 1992.

Mungello, David E. *Curious Land: Jesuit Accommodation and the Origins of Sinology*. Stuttgart, 1985.

– *The Forgotten Christians of Hangzhou*. Honolulu, 1994.

Münsterberg, Oscar. 'Die Darstellung von Europäern in der japanischen Kunst.' *Orientalisches Archiv* 1 (1911): 196–214.

Museo Nacional del Virreino, Tepotzotlán. *Pintura Novohispana*. 2 vols. Mexico City, 1992.

Nadal Mora, Vicente. *San Ignacio Miní*. Buenos Aires, 1955.

Nagayama, Tokihide. *Collection of Historical Materials Connected with the Roman Catholic Religion in Japan* [in Japanese]. Nagasaki, 1924.

The Namban Art of Japan. Osaka, 1986.

Namban Arts and Western Style Paintings [in Japanese]. Tokyo, 1980.

Narayan, J. Stephen. *Aquaviva and the Great Mogul*. Patna, 1945.

Nath, Ram. 'Important Christian Tombs at Agra.' *Indica* 4, no. 1 (March 1967): 19–34.

– *A History of Mughal Architecture*. Vol. 3. Jaipur, 1993.

Necker, Louis. *Indios Guaraníes y chamanes Franciscanos*. Asunción, 1990.

Neill, Stephen. *A History of Christianity in India*. Cambridge, 1984.

Neumeyer, Alfred. 'The Indian Contribution to Architectural Decoration in Spanish Colonial America.' *Art Bulletin* 30, no. 2 (June 1948): 104–21.

Nishimura, Tei. 'Study on the Fifteen Mysteries of St. Mary in Japan.' *Bijutsu Kenkyu* 81 (Sept. 1938).

– 'Paintings of the Society of Jesus in Japan and Those of Western Style at the End of the Ming Dynasty.' *Bijutsu Kenkyu* 97 (Jan. 1940).

– *Study of Early Western Style Paintings in Japan* [in Japanese]. Kyoto, 1946.

– *Namban Art, Christian Art in Japan, 1549–1639*. Tokyo, 1958.

No caminho do Japão. Lisbon, 1993.

Nunes, Judilia, *The Monuments in Old Goa*. Delhi, 1979.

Nurbakhsh, Javad, *Jesus in the Eyes of the Sufis*. London, 1983.

Objects Relating to Early Christian Faith in Japan [in Japanese]. Tokyo, 1972

O'Gorman, Edmundo. *The Invention of America*. Rpt. Westport CT, 1972.

Okada, Amina. 'Les Baigneuses du musée Guimet: une miniature moghole inspirée d'une gravure européene.' *La Revue du Louvre et des Musées de France*, 2 (1986), pp. 107–110.

– 'Cinq dessins de Basawan au Musée Guimet.' *Arts Asiatiques* 41 (1986): 82–8.

– 'Les peintres moghols et le theme de Tobie et l'Ange.' *Arts Asiatiques* 43 (1988): 5–12.

– *Miniatures de l'Inde Impériale*. Paris, 1989.

– *Indian Miniatures of the Mughal Court*. New York, 1992.

Okamoto, Yoshitomo. *The Namban Art of Japan*. New York and Tokyo, 1972.

O'Malley, John. *The First Jesuits*. Cambridge MA, 1993.

O'Malley, John, Gauvin Alexander Bailey, T. Frank Kennedy, and Steven J. Harris, eds. *The Jesuits: Cultures, Sciences, and the Arts*. Toronto (forthcoming).

Ortiz, Fernando. *Contrapunteo del tabaco y el azúcar*. Havana, 1940.

Ovalle, Alonso de, S.J. *Historia relatione del regno di Cile, e delle missioni, e ministerii che esercita in quelle*. Rome, 1646.

Pacheco, Diego (Yuuki Ryogo), S.J. 'Iglesias de Nagasake durante el "Siglo Cristiano," 1568–1620.' *Boletín de la Asociación Española de Orientalistas* 13 (1977): 49–70.

Padberg, John W., S.J., Martin D. O'Keefe, S.J., and John L. McCarthy, S.J. *For Matters of Greater Moment: The First Thirty Jesuit General Congregations*. St Louis, 1994.

Páez Rios, Elena, ed. *Repertorio de grabados españoles en la Biblioteca Nacional*. Madrid, 1982.

Pagani, Catherine. 'One Continuous Symphony: Automata and the Jesuit Mission in Qing China.' In *Contacts Between Cultures*. Vol. 4. Ed. Bernard Luk. Lewiston NY, 1992, pp. 279–84.

– 'The Clocks of James Cox: Chinoiserie and the Clock Trade to China in the Late Eighteenth Century.' *Apollo* n.s. 140, no. 395 (Jan. 1995): 15–22.

– 'Clockmaking in China under the Kangxi and Qianlong Emperors.' *Arts Asiatiques* 50 (1995): 76–84.

– 'Most Magnificent Pieces of Mechanism and Art: Elaborate Clockwork and Sino-European Contact in the Eighteenth Century.' *SECAC Review* 15 (forthcoming).

– *Eastern Magnificence and European Ingenuity: The Clocks of Late Imperial China* (forthcoming).

Pagden, Anthony. *The Fall of Natural Man*. Cambridge, 1982.

Pagés, Léon. *Histoire de la religion crétienne au Japon*. Paris, 1869.

Pal, Pratapaditya. *Master Artists in the Imperial Mughal Court*. Bombay, 1991.

– *Indian Painting*. Los Angeles, 1993.

Pallestrini, Luciana, and José A. Perasso. *Jeguakáva: Arte plumario indígena del Paraguay*. Asunción, 1988.

Palmer, Gabrielle, and Donna Pierce. *Cambios: The Spirit of Transformation in Spanish Colonial Art*. Santa Barbara, 1992.

Panikkar, K.M. *Asia and Western Dominance: A Survey of the Vasco da Gama Period of Asian History 1448–1945*. New York, 1954.
Paoletti, John T., and Gary M. Radke. *Art in Renaissance Italy*. Upper Saddle River, 1997.
Papi, Gianni. 'Le tele della cappellina di Odoardo Farnese della Casa Professa dei gesuiti a Roma.' *Storia dell'arte* 62 (1988): 71–80.
Parrinder, Geoffrey. *Jesus in the Qur'an*. London, 1965.
Parry, J.H. *The Spanish Seaborne Empire*. Berkeley, Los Angeles, and Oxford, 1990.
Pastells, Pablo, S.J. *Historia de la Compañía de Jesús en la Provincia del Paraguay*. 2 vols. Madrid, 1912.
Pastor, Ludvig von. *The History of the Popes*. London, 1924–53.
Patron Saint of the New World: Spanish American Colonial Images of St. Joseph. Philadelphia, 1992.
Pei-t'ang Library. *Catalogue de la Bibliothèque du Pé-t'ang*. Beijing, 1949.
Pelliot, Paul. 'La peinture et la gravure europées en Chine au temps de Mathieu Ricci.' *T'oung Pao* 20, series 2 (1921): 1–18.
– *Les Mongols et la Papauté*. 3 vols. Paris, 1923.
Pereira, José. 'The Art Historiography of Baroque India.' *Indica* 44 (1986): 159–170.
Pereira Salas, Eugenio. *Historia del arte en el reino de Chile*. Santiago, 1965.
Pérez, Lorenzo, O.F.M. 'Cartas y relaciones del Japón.' *Archivo Ibero-Americano* 3, ser. 6, nos. 16–17 (1926).
Peterson, Jeanette Favrot. 'The Virgin of Guadalupe: Symbol of Conquest or Liberation?' *Art Journal* (Winter 1992): 39–47.
– *The Paradise Garden Murals of Malinalco*. Austin, 1993.
Picard, René. *Les peintres jésuites à la cour de Chine*. Grenoble, 1973.
Pilar, Santiago. 'Philippine Painting: The Early Chinese Heritage.' *Arts of Asia* (Nov.–Dec. 1994): 62–70.
Pirazzoli-t'Serstevens, Michèle. 'The Emperor Qianlong's European Palaces.' *Orientations* 19, no. 11 (1988): 61.
– 'A Pluridisciplinary Research on Castiglione and the Emperor Ch'ien-lung's European Palaces.' *National Palace Museum Bulletin* [Taipei] 24, no. 4 (1989): 1–12; 24, no. 5 (1989): 1–16.
Pirri, Pietro, S.J. 'Sultan Yahya e il P. Acquaviva' *Archivum Historicum Societatis Iesu* 13 (1944): 62–76.
– *Giovanni Tristano e i primordi della architettura Gesuitica*. Rome, 1955.
– *Giuseppe Valeriano, S.I., Architetto e pittore 1542–1596*. Rome, 1970.
Plá, Josefina. *El barroco hispano Guaraní*. Asunción, 1975.
– 'Rasgos generales de un barroco desconocido.' Unknown source and date: 305–15.
– 'The Missionary Workshops (1609–1767): Organization and Operation; Labor and Achievements.' In *Paradise Lost*. New York, 1988, unpaginated.
– 'Los talleres misioneros.' In *Un camino hacia la Arcadia*. Madrid, 1995, pp. 81–106.
Plattner, Felix. *Deutsche Meister des Barock in Südamerika im 17. und 18. Jahrhundert*. Basel, 1960.
Polzer, Charles W., S.J. *Rules and Precepts of the Jesuit Missions of Northwest New Spain*. Tucson, 1976.
– *Kino: A Legacy*. Tucson, 1998.

Poncelet, Alfred, S.J. *Histoire de la Compagnie de Jésus dans les Anciens Pays-Bas*. Vol. 21, Part 1. Brussels, 1926.

Porteman, Karel. *Emblematic Exhibitions at the Brussels Jesuit College (1630–1685)*. Brussels, 1996.

Prunier, Maurice. 'Des peintures à fouler aux pieds.' *Bulletin de la Maison Franco-Japonaise* 11 (1939): 162–7.

Querejazu, Pedro, ed. *Las misiones Jesuíticas de Chiquitos*. La Paz, 1995.

Raby, Julian. 'El Gran Turco: Mehmed the Conqueror as a Patron of the Arts of Christendom.' PhD diss., Oxford University, 1980.

Raffino, Rodolfo. *Expresiones artísticas indígenas del Museo de Ciencias Naturales de La Plata*. La Plata, 1994.

Ramon, Francis, ed. *Bolton and the Spanish Borderlands*. Norman OK, 1964.

Rawson, Jessica. *Chinese Ornament: The Lotus and the Dragon*. London, 1984.

Reflexos: Símbolos e Imagens do Cristianismo na Porcelana Chinesa. Lisbon, 1997.

Reiter, Fred J. *They Built Utopia: The Jesuit Missions in Paraguay 1610–1768*. Potomac, 1995.

Renick, M.S. 'Akbar's First Embassy to Goa: Its Diplomatic and Religious Aspects.' *Indica* 7 (1970): 33–47.

Reyes-Valerio, Constantino. *Arte indocristiano*. Mexico City, 1978.

Rheinbay, P. *Biblische Bilder für der inneren Weg. Das Betrachtungsbuch des Ignatius-Gefährten Hieronymus Nadal (1507–1580)*. Engelsbach, 1995.

Ribera, Adolfo Luis, 'La pintura en las misiones jesuíticas de guaraníes.' *Boletín del Instituto de Historia Argentina y Americana 'Dr. Emilio Ravignani'* 26 (1980): 500–34.

Ribera, Adolfo Luis, and Hector Schenone. *El arte de la imaginería en el Río de la Plata*. Buenos Aires, 1948.

Ricard, Robert. *La conquista espiritual de México*. Rpt. Mexico City, 1986.

Rice, Louise. 'College Art: Prints, Poetry, and Music for the Academic Defense at the Collegio Romano.' In O'Malley et al. Toronto (forthcoming).

Rice, Tamara Talbot. 'The Conflux of Influences in Eighteenth-Century Russian Art and Architecture: A Journey from the Spiritual to the Realistic.' In *The Eighteenth Century in Russia*. Ed. J.G. Garrard. Oxford, 1973, pp. 267–99.

Richards, J.F. 'The Formulation of Imperial Authority under Akbar and Jahangir.' In *Kingship and Authority in South Asia*. Ed. J.F. Richards. Madison, 1978, pp. 252–85.

Rizvi, S.A.A. *The Wonder That Was India*. London, 1987.

Rizvi, S.A.A., and Vincent Flynn. *Fathpur-Sikri*. Bombay, 1975.

Robertson, Clare. *'Il Gran Cardinale': Alessandro Farnese, Patron of the Arts*. New Haven and London, 1992.

– 'Two Farnese Cardinals and the Question of Jesuit Taste.' In O'Malley et al. Toronto (forthcoming).

Robson, James. *Christ in Islam*. London, 1929.

Roca, Paul M. *Spanish Jesuit Churches in Mexico's Tarahumara*. Tucson, 1979.

Rodriguez Gutiérrez de Ceballos, Alfonso, S.J. *Bartolomé de Bustamente y los Origines de la Arquitectura Jesuitica en España*. Madrid, 1961.

– *Bartolomé de Bustamente y los Orígines de la arquitectura Jesuítica en España*. Rome, 1967.

Roe, Sir Thomas. *The Embassy of Sir Thomas Roe to India*. Ed. William Foster. London, 1926.

Ross, Andrew. *A Vision Betrayed: The Jesuits in Japan and China 1542–1742*. Maryknoll NY, 1994.

Röttgen, Herwarth. 'Zeitgeschichtliche Bildprogramme der katholischen Restauration unter Gregor XIII. 1572–1585.' *Münchner Jahrbuch der bildenden Kunst* 26 (1975): 89–122.

Rubin, Pamela Lee. *Giorgio Vasari.* New Haven and London, 1995.

As ruinas de S. Paulo. Lisbon and Macao, 1994.

Ruiz de Montoya, Antonio, S.J. *The Spiritual Conquest ... of Paraguay* Trans. and ed. C.J. McNaspy. St Louis, 1993.

Ruiz Moreno, A. 'El urbanismo en las misiones jesuíticas.' In *Estudio 64.* Buenos Aires, 1940.

Sahlins, Marshall. *The Islands of History.* Chicago, 1985.

Sainsbury, Noel. *Calendar of State Papers, Colonial Series, East Indies, China and Japan 1513–1616.* London, 1870.

Sakamoto, Mitsura, Ide Yoichiro, Yūjirō Ōchi, and Hidaka Kaori. *An Essay of Catalogue Raisonné of Namban Art I: Japanese Early European-Style Painting.* Tokyo, 1997.

– 'Christian Art and the Birth of Western Painting, with Special Reference to the Sixteenth Century.' Paper delivered at the symposium 'The Encounter between Europe and Asia during the Time of the Great Navigations.' Sophia University, Tokyo, 6 December 1998.

Sakamoto, Mitsura, and Yūjirō Ōchi. 'Classification of Folding Screens according to Christian Motifs.' Paper delivered the conference 'The Encounter between Europe and Asia during the Period of the Great Navigations.' Sophia University, Tokyo, 6 December 1998.

Sansom, G.B. *A History of Japan.* Stanford, 1961.

Santos de Oliveira, Beatriz. *Espacio e estrategia: Consideraçoes sobre a arquitetura dos jesuítas no Brasil.* Rio de Janeiro, 1988.

Saunders, J.J. *The History of the Mongol Conquest.* London, 1971.

Schenone, Hector H. *Historia general de arte en la Argentina.* 2 vols. Buenos Aires, 1983.

– *Iconografía del arte colonial.* 2 vols. Buenos Aires, 1992.

Schurhammer, Georg, S.J. 'Die Jesuitenmissionare des 16. und 17. Jahrhunderts und ihr Einfluss auf die Japanische Malerei.' In his *Orientalia.* Rome, 1963, pp. 769–79.

Schütte, Josef Franz, S.J. 'Christliche Japanische Literatur, Bilder und Drückblätter in Einem Unbekannten Vatikanischen Codex Aus dem Jahre 1591.' *Archivum Historicum Societatis Iesu* 9 (1940): 226–80.

– *Valignano's Mission Principles for Japan.* Trans. John J. Coyne, S.J., St Louis, 1980.

Sebes, Joseph. 'A Comparative Study of Religious Missions in Three Civilizations: India, China and Japan.' In *Colloque Internationale de Sinologie III.* Paris, 1983, pp. 271–90.

Selected Masterpieces of Asian Art: Museum of Fine Arts, Boston. Boston, 1992.

Sepp, Anton, S.J. *Relación de viaje a las misiones jesuíticas.* Buenos Aires, 1971.

– *Continuación de las labores apostólicas.* Buenos Aires, 1973.

– *Jardín de flores paracuaria.* Buenos Aries, 1973.

Serbat, Louis. 'L'architecture Gothique des Jésuites au XVIIe siècle.' *Bulletin Monumental* 66 (1902): 315–70.

Serrão, Vitor. *O Manierismo e o Estatuto Social dos Pintores Portugueses.* Lisbon, 1983.

– 'Quadros de Vida de S. Francisco Xavier.' *Oceanos* 12 (Nov. 1992): 56–69.

– 'A pintura na antiga Índia Portuguesa nos séculos XVI e XVII.' *Oceanos* 19/20 (1994): 102–13.

Seyller, John. 'Recycled Images: Overpainting in Early Mughal Art.' *Marg* 46, no. 2 (1995): 64.

Shatzman Steinhardt, Nancy. 'Zhu Haogu Reconsidered: A New Date for the ROM Painting and the Southern Shanxi Buddhist-Daoist Style,' in *Artibus Asiae* XLVIII 1, 2 (1987): 5–19.

Shimmura, Idzuru. 'Christian Relics Found at Mr. Higashi's House, North of Takatsuki, Settsu.' *Report upon Archaeological Research, Department of Literature, Kyoto Imperial University* 7 (1923).

– 'A Pair of Folding Screens Painted by a Japanese Artist in the European Style at the Beginning of the 17th Century.' *Bukkyo bijutsu* 3 (June 1925).

– 'L'Introduction de la peinture occidentale au Japon.' *Revue des arts asiatiques* 4 (1927): 195–203.

Sickman, Laurence, and Alexander Soper. *The Art and Architecture of China*. 3rd ed. Harmondsworth, 1987.

Sierra, Vicente D. *Los Jesuitas germanos en la conquista espiritual de Hispano-America*. Buenos Aires, 1944.

Simson, Otto von. *Peter Paul Rubens (1577–1640)*. Mainz, 1996.

Singh, Chandramani. 'European Themes in Early Mughal Miniatures.' In *Chhavi Golden Jubilee Issue*. Banares, 1971.

Skelton, Robert. 'Europe and India.' *In Europa und die Kunst des Islam 15. bis 18. Jahrhundert (XXV Internationaler Kongress für Kunstgeschichte CIHA)*. Vienna, 1983.

– 'Imperial Symbolism in Mughal Painting.' In *Content and Context of Visual Arts in the Islamic World*. Ed. Priscilla P. Soucek. University Park and London, 1988, pp. 177–87.

Smith, Edmund W. *The Moghul Architecture of Fathpur-Sikri*. Allahabad, 1894–7.

Smith, Jeffrey Chipps. 'The Art of Salvation in Bavaria.' In O'Malley et al. Toronto (forthcoming).

Smith, Robert Chester. *Arquitectura jesuítica no Brasil*. São Paulo, 1962.

Sobrón, Dalmacio, S.J. 'Acerca de la arquitectura del hermano Andrés Blanqui, S.J.' In *La salvaguarda del patrimonio jesuítico*. Posadas, 1994, pp. 19–33.

Solá, Miguel. *Las Misiones Guaraníes*. Buenos Aires, 1946.

Soliers, Philippe, et al. *Baroque du Paraguay*. Paris, 1996.

Soria, Martín S. *La Pintura del siglo XVI en Sud America*. Buenos Aires, 1956.

Soucek, Priscilla. 'Nizami on Painters and Painting.' In *Islamic Art in the Metropolitan Museum of Art*. Ed. Richard Ettinghausen. New York, 1972, pp. 9–21.

Soustiel, Jean, and David Soustiel, *Miniatures orientales de l'Inde*. Paris, 1986.

Souza, Teotonio de. 'Spiritual Conquest of the East: A Critique of the Church History of Portuguese Asia.' *Indian Church History Review* 19 (1985): 10–24.

– 'Re-Writing the History of the Society of Jesus in India: Questions of Facts and Relevance.' *Indian Missiological Review* (Oct. 1987): 269–277.

– ed. *Discoveries, Missionary Expansion and Asian Cultures*. Panjim, 1994.

Spence, Jonathan D. *The Memory Palace of Matteo Ricci*. New York, 1985.

– *The Search for Modern China*. New York and London, 1990.

Spicer, Edward. *Cycles of Conquest*. Tucson, 1962.

Standaert, Nicolas, S.J. 'The Jesuit Presence in China (1580– 1773): A Statistical Approach.' *Sino-Western Cultural Relations Journal* 13 (1991): 4–17.

– 'Chinese Christian Visits to the Underworld.' In *Conflict and Accommodation in Early Modern East Asia: Essays in Honor of Erik Zürcher*. Ed. L. Blussé and H. Zurndorfer. Leiden, 1993, pp. 54–70.

– 'New Trends in the Historiography of Christianity in China.' *Catholic Historical Review* 83, no. 4 (Oct. 1997): 573–613.
– 'Jesuit Corporate Culture as Shaped by the Chinese.' In O'Malley et al. Toronto (forthcoming).
Storni, Hugo, S.J. *Catálogo de los Jesuitas de la Provincia del Paraguay 1585–1768*. Rome, 1980.
Struve, Lynn A., ed. and trans. *Voices from the Ming-Qing Cataclysm: China in Tigers' Jaws*. New Haven, 1993.
Subrahmanyam, Sanjay. 'Sixteenth-Century Millenarianism from the Tagus to the Ganges.' In *Working Papers in Early Modern History*. Minneapolis (forthcoming).
Sullivan, Michael. 'Some Possible Sources of European Influence on Late Ming and Early Qing Painting.' In *Proceedings of the International Symposium on Chinese Painting, National Palace Museum*. Taipei, 1970.
– *The Arts of China*. Rpt. Berkeley, Los Angeles, London, 1984.
– *The Meeting of Eastern and Western Art*. Berkeley and Los Angeles, 1989.
Sullivan, Michael. 'The Chinese Response to Western Art.' In *Studies in the Art of China and South-East Asia*. London, 1991, vol. 1, pp. 311–34.
Summa Artis [Madrid]. Vol. 31.
Suntory Museum of Art. *Date Masamune and His Mission to Rome* [in Japanese]. Tokyo, 1990.
– *Suntory Museum of Art Collection*. Tokyo, 1991.
Surviving Early Christian Art in Japan [in Japanese]. Tokyo, Tokyo National Museum, 1973.
Susnik, Branislava. 'El rol de la Iglesia en la educación indígena colonial.' *Estudios Paraguayos* 3, no. 2 (1975).
– *Los aborigines del Paraguay*. Asunción, 1979–80.
– *Artesanía indígena: Ensayo analítico*. Asunción, 1986.
– *El indio colonial del Paraguay II*. Asunción, 1986.
Sustersic, Bozidar Darko 'Presencia de una imagen hispano- bizantina en America.' *Academia Nacional de Bellas Artes, Anuario* 18 (1991): 14–20.
– 'José Brasanelli: Escultor, pintor y arquitecto de las misiones jesuíticas guaraníes.' *Organización de Universidades Católicas de América Latina, Jornadas* 2 (1992): 267–77.
– 'La iglesia barroca de Trinidad y su friso de ángeles músicos.' *Jornadas de Teoría e Historia de las Artes* 5 (1993): 380–9.
– 'La fachada de San Ignacio Miní entre hallazgos y nuevos enigmas.' In *La salvaguarda del patrimonio jesuítico*. Posadas, 1994, pp. 196–213.
– 'Una antigua devoción misionera que perdura en el tiempo: El señor yacente de Corrientes.' In *El arte entre lo publico y lo privado VI*. Buenos Aires, 1995, pp. 51–62.
– 'Imaginería y patrimonio mueble.' In *Las misiones jesuíticas del Guayrá*. Verona and Buenos Aires, 1995, pp. 155–86.
– 'La escultura en el Río de la Plata durante el periodo colonial.' In *Pintura, escultura y artes útiles en iberoamerica, 1500–1825*. Ed. Ramón Gutiérrez. Madrid, 1995, pp. 271–82.
– 'El hermano José Brasanelli y las posibilidades de la reconstrucción de su trayectoria biográfica y artística.' Paper delivered at the Simposio Nacional de Estudios Missioneiros, Brazil, 1996.
Sweet, David. 'The Ibero-American Frontier Mission in Native American History.' In *The New Latin American Mission History*. Ed. Erick Langer and Robert H. Jackson. Lincoln NE and London, 1995.

Swietochowski, Marie Lukens, and Sussan Babaie. *Persian Drawings in the Metropolitan Museum of Art*. New York, 1989.

Tacchi Venturi, Pietro ed., *Opere storiche del P. Matteo Ricci*. 3 vols. Macerata, 1911–13.

Tavernier, Jean-Baptiste. *Travels in India*. Trans. V. Ball. 2 vols. Rpt. New Delhi, 1977.

Taylor, Richard W. *Jesus in Indian Paintings*. Madras, 1975.

Tedlock, Dennis. *The Spoken Word and the Work of Interpretation*. Philadelphia, 1983.

Texeira, Manoel. *A fachada de S. Paulo*. Macao, 1940.

– *O Culto de Maria em Macau*. Macao, 1969.

Thekkedath, Joseph. *History of Christianity in India II: From the Middle of the Sixteenth to the End of the Seventeenth Century (1542–1700)*. Bangalore, 1982.

Thomas, K.A. 'Christian Themes in Moghal Art.' *German News* [New Delhi] 20, no. 6 (1979): 8–9.

– 'Christian Paintings on a Mughal Monument.' *The Illustrated Weekly of India*, 10 May 1981, p. 30.

Thomas, P., *Churches in India*. New Delhi, 1964.

Three Thousand Years of Chinese Painting. New Haven and London, 1997.

Tirmizi, S.A.I. *Mughal Documents, 1526–1627*. New Delhi, 1989.

Torre Revello, José. 'Los navios de registro en el Río de la Plata.' *Boletín de la Academia nacional de la historia* 34, no. 2 (1937): 529–59.

– 'Un envio de imágenes con destino a las misiones jesuíticas.' *Boletin de la comisión nacional de museos y de monumentos y lugares históricos* 1, no. 1 (1939): 25–32.

Toussaint, Manuel. *Colonial Art in Mexico*. Trans. Elizabeth Wilder Weismann. Austin, 1967.

Trevisan, Armindo. *A escultura dos sete povos*. Porto Alegre, 1978.

Trexler, Richard C. 'Aztec Priests for Christian Altars. The Theory and Practice of Reverence in New Spain.' In *Scienze, Credenze, Occulte: Livelli di Cultura*. Florence, 1962, pp. 175–96.

Troll, Christian W. 'Christian-Muslim Relations in India, a Critical Survey.' *Islamochristiana* 5 (1979): 119–45.

Trota José, Regalado. *Simbahan: Church Art in Colonial Philippines, 1565–1898*. Manila, 1991.

Tūzuk-i Jahangīrī. Trans. Alexander Rogers. Ed. Henry Beveridge. Calcutta, 1909–14.

Twelve Centuries of Japanese Art from the Imperial Collections. Washington, 1997.

Üçerler, Antoni. 'Jesuit Humanist Education in Sixteenth-Century Japan: The Latin and Japanese MSS of Pedro Gómez's "Compendia" on Astronomy, Philosophy, and Theology (1593–95).' In *Compendium catholicae veritatis*. Tokyo, 1997, pp. 11–60.

Umberger, Emily. 'The Monarchía Indiana in Seventeenth-Century New Spain.' In *Converging Cultures*. Ed. Diane Fane. New York, 1996, pp. 46–58.

University Museum Faculty of Letters, Kyoto University. Kyoto, 1987.

Valente, Maria Regina. *Igrejas de Macau*. Macao, 1993.

Valignano, Alessandro. *Il ceremoniale per i missionari del Giappone*. Ed. Franz Josef Schütte. Rome, 1946.

Valle, Pietro della. *The Travels of Pietro della Valle in India*. Trans. Edward Grey. 2 vols. London, 1892.

Vallery Radot, Jean. *Le recueil de plans d'édifices de la compagnie de Jésus conservé a la Bibliothèque Nationale de Paris*. Rome, 1960.

Vanaya, Marta, ed. *Mitos y leyendas guaraníes*. Madrid, 1986.

Vanderstappen, Harrie, S.V.D. 'Chinese Art and the Jesuits in Peking.' In *East Meets West: The Jesuits in China, 1582–1773*. Ed. Charles E. Ronan, S.J., and Bonnie B.C. Oh. Chicago, 1988.
Van Goa naar Lisboa. Brussels, 1991.
Vargas Lugo, Elisa. 'Sobre el concepto tequitqui.' *Historia del arte mexicano* 35 (1982): 102–3.
Vargas Ugarte, Ruben, S.J. *Ensayo de un diccionario de artifices coloniales de la América Meridional*. Lima, 1947.
– *Los jesuítas del Perú y el arte*. Lima, 1963.
Velinkar, J. 'Francisco Aranha, Builder of Salsete Churches.' *Indica* 33 (1980): 139–52.
Vetter, Ewald M. *Die Kupferstiche zur Psalmodia Eucharistica des Melchior Prieto von 1622*. Münster, 1977.
Via Orientalis. Tokyo, 1993.
Videira Pires, Benjamim, S.J. *A Embaixada Martir*. Macau, 1988.
Vieira, Mabel Leal, and María Inês Coutinho. *Inventário da imaginária missioneira*. Porta Alegre, 1993.
Virdis, Caterina Limentani, et al. *Una dinastia di incisori: I Sadeler*. Padua, 1992.
Vlam, G.A.H. 'The Portrait of St. Francis Xavier in Kobe.' *Zeitschrift für Kunstgeschichte* 2, no. 1 (1979): 48–60.
Vogel, J. Ph. *Tile-Mosaics of the Lahore Fort*. Calcutta, 1920.
Voltaire, François Marie Arouet. *Essai sur les moeurs*. Paris, 1756.
Wadell, Maj Brit. 'The *Evangelicae Historiae Imagines*: The Designs and Their Artists.' *Quaerendo* 10 (1980): 279–91.
– *Evangelicae Historiae Imagines: Entstehungsgeschichte und Vorlagen*. Göteborg, 1985.
Wakakuwa, Midori. 'The Image of Saint Francis Xavier within the Renowned "Fifteen Mysteries of the Virgin Mary" Painting, Located at Kyoto University.' Paper delivered at the symposium 'The Encounter between Europe and Asia during the Time of the Great Navigations.' Sophia University, Tokyo, 6 December 1998.
Walker, James Bernard, O.P. *The 'Chronicles' of Saint Antoninus: A Study in Historiography*. Washington, 1933.
Walravens, Hartmut. *China Illustrata: Das europäische Chinaverständis im Spiegel des 16. bis 18. Jahrhunderts*. Wolfenbüttel, 1987.
Watt, William Montgomery. *Muslim-Christian Encounters*. London and New York, 1991.
Welch, Evelyn. *Art and Society in Italy 1350–1500*. Oxford and New York, 1997.
Welch, Stuart Cary. *Indian Drawings and Painted Sketches*. New York, 1976.
– *Imperial Mughal Painting*. New York, 1978.
– *India!* New York, 1985.
Wessels, C. *Early Jesuit Travellers in Central Asia 1603–1721*. The Hague, 1924.
Wethey, Harold. *Colonial Architecture and Sculpture in Peru*. Westport, 1949.
Wicki, Joseph, ed. *Documenta Indica (Monumenta Historica S.I.)*. Multiple volumes. Rome, 1948–88.
– *O Livro do 'Pai dos Cristaos.'* Lisbon, 1969.
Wilberg, Peter Vignau. 'Le finte cupole e la loro recezione nella Germania meridionale.' In *Andrea Pozzo*. Ed. Alberta Battisti. Milan, 1996, pp. 215–24.
Wilder Weismann, Elizabeth. *Art and Time in Mexico*. New York, 1985.

Wilkinson, J.V.S., and Basil Gray. 'Indian Paintings in a Persian Museum.' *Burlington Magazine* 66 (1935): 168–77.

Wittkower, Rudolf, and Irma Jaffe, eds. *Baroque Art: The Jesuit Contribution*. New York, 1972.

Wright, A.D. *The Counter-Reformation: Catholic Europe and the Non-Christian World*. New York, 1982.

Wu Hsiang-hsiang, ed. *Literature of Catholicism to the East* [in Chinese]. First series. Taipei, 1965.

– *Literature of Catholicism to the East* [in Chinese]. Second series. 3 vols. Taipei, 1966.

Wu Tung. *Tales from the Land of Dragons: One Thousand Years of Chinese Painting*. Boston, 1997.

Wyngaert, A. van der. *Sinica Franciscana*. Florence, 1929.

Xarque, Francisco. *Insignes misioneros de la Compañía de Jesús en la Provincia del Paraguay*. Pamplona, 1687.

Yang Boda. 'Castiglione at the Qing Court: An Important Artistic Contribution.' *Orientations* 19, no. 11 (1988): 44–51.

Ybot León, Antonio. *La Iglesia y los eclesiásticos en la empresa de indias*. 2 vols. Barcelona, 1954–63.

Yee, Cordell D.K. 'Chinese Cartography among the Arts: Objectivity, Subjectivity, Representation.' In *The History of Cartography*. Ed. J.B. Harley and D. Woodward. Vol. 5, book 2. Chicago, 1994, pp. 128–69, 170–202.

– 'Traditional Chinese Cartography and the Myth of Westernization,' in J.B. Harley and D. Woodward, eds., *The History of Cartography* V, 2. Chicago, 1994, pp. 170–202.

Yoshiho, Yonezawa. *Painting of the Ming Dynasty*. Tokyo, 1956.

Le Yuanmingyuan, jeux d'eau et palais européens du XVIIIème siècle à la cour du Chine. Paris, 1987.

Zeri, Federico. *Pittura e contrariforma: L''arte senza tempo' di Scipione da Gaeta*. Torino, 1957.

Zhang, Qiong. 'Cultural Accommodation or Intellectual Colonization? A Reinterpretation of the Jesuit Approach to Confucianism.' PhD diss., Harvard University, 1996.

– 'Translation as Cultural Reform: Jesuit Scholastic Philosophy in the Transformation of the Confucian Discourse on Human Nature.' In O'Malley et al. Toronto (forthcoming).

Zoratto, Bruno. *Giuseppe Castiglione: Pittore italiano alla corte imperiale cinese*. Fasano di Puglia, 1994.

Zuccari, Alessandro. *Arte e committenza nella Roma di Caravaggio*. Torino, 1984.

Zürcher, Erik. 'Giulio Aleni et ses relations dans le milieu des lettrés chinois au XVIIème siècle.' In *Venezia e l'Oriente*. Ed. L. Lanciotti. Florence, 1987.

– 'The Jesuit Mission in Fujian in Late Ming Times: Levels of Response.' In *Development and Decline of Fukien Province in the Seventeenth and Eighteenth Centuries*. Ed. E.B. Vermeer. Leiden, 1990.

– 'Jesuit Accommodation and the Chinese Cultural Imperative.' In *The Chinese Rites Controversy: Its History and Meaning*. Ed. David E. Mungello. Nettetal, 1994, pp. 31–64.

Zweite, Armin. *Martin de Vos als Maler*. Berlin, 1980.

General Index

Note: Figure numbers are in **bold**.

Index of Artists

Note: This index includes only artists who worked for, or in response to, the Jesuit world missions (figure numbers are in **bold**).